Of Free Trade and Native Interests

The Brookes and the Economic Development of Sarawak, 1841–1941

Ooi Keat Gin

KUALA LUMPUR
OXFORD UNIVERSITY PRESS
OXFORD SINGAPORE NEW YORK
1997

Oxford University Press

Oxford New York
Athens Auckland Bangkok Bombay
Calcutta Cape Town Dar es Salaam Delhi
Florence Hong Kong Istanbul Karachi
Madras Madrid Melbourne Mexico City
Nairobi Paris Shah Alam Singapore
Taipei Tokyo Toronto

and associated companies in
Berlin Ibadan

Oxford is a trade mark of Oxford University Press

Published in the United States
by Oxford University Press, New York

First published 1997

British Library Cataloguing in Publication Data
Data available

Library of Congress Cataloging-in-Publication Data
Ooi, Keat Gin, 1959–
Of free trade and native interests: the Brookes and the economic development of Sarawak, 1841–1941/Ooi Keat Gin
p. cm.—(South-East Asian historical monographs)
Includes bibliographical references and index.
ISBN 983 56 0023 6
1. Sarawak—Economic conditions. 2. Sarawak—Economic policy. 3. Brooke Family. 4. Sarawak—History. I. Title. II. Series.
HC445.5.Z7S276 1997
330.9595'4—dc21
96–49828
CIP

Typeset by Indah Photosetting Centre Sdn. Bhd., Malaysia
Printed by Kyodo Printing Co. (S) Pte. Ltd., Singapore
Published by Penerbit Fajar Bakti Sdn. Bhd. (008974-T),
under licence from Oxford University Press,
4 Jalan Pemaju U1/15, Seksyen U1, 40150 Shah Alam,
Selangor Darul Ehsan, Malaysia

To the memory of my father,
the late Mr Ooi Ewe Boo (1913–1989),
and
to my mother, Madam Tan Ai Gek,
and my sisters, Saw Lian and Saw Ean

Sarawak belongs to the Malays, the Sea Dayaks, the Kayans and other tribes; not to us. It is for them that we labour; not ourselves.

James Brooke (1803–1868)

Preface

No detailed study has yet been undertaken of the economic development of Sarawak during the period of Brooke rule (1841–1946). Research on particular and specialized subjects pertaining to the economy of Brooke Sarawak has been done, but a comprehensive overview has yet to be attempted. The existing literature tends to gloss over the economic aspects of the country's development, or make it an appendage of the political, historical narrative.

This study, originally entitled 'An Economic History of Sarawak during the Period of Brooke Rule, 1841–1946' and presented as a doctoral dissertation to the Centre for South-East Asian Studies, University of Hull, England, intends to fill this gap in the modern historiography of Sarawak. It accounts for Sarawak's slow pace of economic development and its relative 'backwardness' in comparison with other Western-governed territories in the region, particularly the former British possessions. A clearer understanding of the Sarawak economy helps to explain the conditions and challenges that confronted the Colonial Office administrators when they assumed the reins of power in mid-1946. It also provides an explanation for the present-day imbalance of development between Sarawak and the other states in the Federation of Malaysia.

I intend to demonstrate that the reasons behind Sarawak's sluggish pace of economic development were as much to do with natural and geographical factors as to deliberate Brooke policies. I shall argue that there existed unfavourable physical and climatic conditions which worked against a faster pace of development. Moreover, the relative poverty of natural resources was a decisive drawback even if the political will had favoured an accelerated rate of exploitation. But the Brooke vision of economic development was not concerned primarily with profit and dividends. Instead, it was spurred by humanitarian and altruistic motives. The Brookes viewed themselves as the custodians of the interests and rights of the indigenous peoples of Sarawak whose welfare and well-being were foremost in their thoughts. This singular paternalistic approach resulted in the adoption of policies that might be regarded

as economically unsound, or even, detrimental to development; nevertheless, the Brookes would not have had it any other way.

The study is divided into three parts: policies, implementation, and effects. The ideas, subsequently translated into policies, of James, Charles, and Vyner in developing the country's economic resources are presented with discussion of the background, purposes, and motivations behind their formulations. The implementation and operation of these policies and plans comprise the second section. The execution of policies relating to trade and commerce, the extractive industries, agriculture and land utilization, and infrastructure development, is discussed and elaborated, and their consequences evaluated. The third section then presents the effects and impact of the various policies on the indigenous inhabitants, the Chinese community, and Western capitalist enterprises.

The main materials for this study are drawn from archival documents ranging from personal papers and private letters to official documents (memoranda, reports, dispatches, and correspondences), both published and unpublished. Research was conducted at several archives, repositories, and libraries in the United Kingdom, Singapore, and Malaysia (Penang, Kuala Lumpur, and Sarawak). There was little difficulty in acquiring source materials relating to the reigns of James and Charles, especially from Rhodes House Library (Oxford), the Public Record Office (Kew), and other archives in Britain; and for the thoughts and ideas of Charles, the Sarawak Museum Archives (Kuching) is essential. The published letters and journals of James and the memoirs of Charles are of particular importance. The difficulty is in the case of Vyner because he left little in the way of private written materials, or even official records (except his reports as an officer during Charles's reign). He was steadfast in his 'unbroken rule not to appear in print'; this presents a perplexing problem for the researcher in extracting the ideas behind his policies. The predicament is to determine to what extent the policies pertaining to economic development (or for that matter, to all other areas of government) derived from Vyner's own deliberations, or came from the handful of senior Brooke bureaucrats in Kuching. In this connection, the personal papers, memoirs, and recollections of some of these officials do furnish some knowledge of the background discussions prior to the formulation of policies, but even at their best, they do not reveal Vyner's own thoughts. Moreover, 'the tandem rule' alternating between Vyner and his younger brother, Bertram, further accentuates the problem. Under such circum-

stances, and unless new materials become available, the policies adopted during Vyner's reign will be seen as his own, or at the least, enjoying his approval.

The single most important source is the semi-official *Sarawak Gazette* (referred to as the *Gazette*), undoubtedly a mine of information relating to the socio-economic development of the Brooke Raj from the 1870s.* Although it carried official Proclamations and Orders, always had a serving Brooke officer as its editor, and was published at public expense by the Government Printing Office, the *Gazette* was more akin to a review, or even a critic, of the Brooke administration than a government mouthpiece. The editorials, commentaries, and 'Letters to the Editor', are particularly frank in criticism of the Raj. The publication of monthly and annual administrative reports from the Divisions and districts and the various departments in the Kuching bureaucracy are also revealing of the condition of the government and country. If there was any censorship, it was minimal.

No undertaking of this scale could be accomplished without the kind assistance from various quarters. The research and writing of this study was made possible by an Overseas Research Studentship (ORS) Award (Britain), and an Assisted Staff Higher Education Scheme (ASHES) of Universiti Sains Malaysia. A Sarawak Foundation Research Grant (London) and a travel grant from the Centre for South-East Asian Studies (CSEAS) of the University of Hull assisted my archival research. A Universiti Sains Malaysia Short-Term Research Grant contributed to my stay in Sarawak throughout the summer of 1992 and another brief residence in mid-1993.

I would like to extend my appreciation especially to the staff of the Rhodes House Library, Oxford, the Public Record Office,

*For a discussion of the *Gazette* as an invaluable source for Sarawak historiography, see Conrad Patrick Cotter, 'A Guide to the Sarawak Gazette, 1870–1965', Ph.D. thesis, Cornell University, 1966, pp. 1–17; and Robert Pringle, *Rajahs and Rebels: The Ibans of Sarawak under Brooke Rule, 1841–1941*, London: Macmillan, 1970, pp. 368–9.

The *Gazette* must not be confused with the official publication, the *Sarawak Government Gazette*, which was first issued in 1908. From 1908 the *Sarawak Government Gazette*, carried all government proclamations, Orders, Notices, reports of the various Divisions, departmental reviews, reports of the Supreme Council and those of the triennial General Council (Council Negri), the minutes of meetings of the Committee of Administration, and all other official pronouncements.

Kew, and the Sarawak Museum Library and Archives, Kuching, for their untiring assistance. My thanks also go to the archivists and librarians of the United Kingdom archives, libraries, institutions, and repositories: in London, House of Lords Record Office; Guildhall Library; Department of Western Manuscripts, British Library; Geological Society of London; Royal Institute of International Affairs; Royal Geographical Society; Foreign Office Library; Royal Commonwealth Society Library; Post Office Archives; and, outside London, Bodleian Library, Oxford; Brynmor Jones Library, Hull; Liverpool Record Office, Liverpool; Devon Record Office, Exeter; Churchill College Archives Centre, Cambridge; West Sussex Record Office, Chichester; and Scottish Record Office, Edinburgh. In Singapore, I would like to thank the staff of the National Library, National Archives, Centre for Oral History, the Library of the National University of Singapore, and the Library of the Institute of Southeast Asian Studies (ISEAS). In Malaysia, appreciation is due to the staff of the National Archives (Arkib Negara), Kuala Lumpur; and the Library of Universiti Sains Malaysia, Penang.

My foremost appreciation and gratitude are to my thesis supervisor, Professor Victor T. King, both professionally and personally. His encouraging comments throughout the various stages of my work were invaluable; and as a friend, his concern and assistance are gratefully acknowledged and not forgotten.

I would also like to thank the following for their assistance: Mr and Mrs J. Cook (Dundee, Scotland); Mr Michael Williams, Secretary of the Sarawak Association (High Wycombe, England); Dr Naimah Talib (Institute of Southeast Asian Studies (ISEAS), Singapore); Dr Daniel Chew (formerly of the Centre for Oral History, Singapore); Mr Ong Yen Jin (Murdoch, Australia); Mr M. G. Dickson, CMG (London, England); Professor Bob Reece (Murdoch University, Australia); Dr G. E. D. Lewis (London, England); and Dr A. V. M. Horton (Bordesley, England).

Many thanks to Mrs Stella Rhind and Mrs Gina Cunningham, the secretaries of the Centre for South-East Asian Studies (CSEAS), University of Hull, for their ever cheerful disposition and helpfulness. To Dr Michael J. G. Parnwell, the Director, thank you for your support and friendship. And, to Mr Lewis Hill, a special thank you.

Special appreciation is owed to the following individuals who in their own personal way gave me encouragement and moral support, past and present: Dr Paul H. Kratoska (National University of

Singapore); Associate Professor Badriyah Haji Salleh (Universiti Sains Malaysia); Professor Jan Wisseman Christie (University of Hull); and Dr Hong Lysa (National University of Singapore).

Grateful appreciation is also due to the following of Universiti Sains Malaysia, Penang, Malaysia, for their unique assistance: Puan Hamidah Bee Yaacob (formerly School of Humanities) and Encik Husin bin Yahaya (Personnel). I am indebted to Tan Sri Dato' Haji Musa Mohamad, the Vice-Chancellor, for his support. The help of Encik Nor Azam bin Ramli (Personnel) is gratefully acknowledged.

I wish to convey my gratitude to Liaw King Nyen and Jennifer Liaw for their hospitality during my residence in Sarawak. Likewise, I would like to thank Robert and Maggie Ooi for my stay in Singapore. I gratefully acknowledge the kind gesture of help from Madam Chew Chui Gek. Special thanks are reserved for my dear friend, Teoh Boon Hoe, for his characteristic unspoken support and unstinting assistance.

I wish to record my appreciation to the Sarawak Museum for assistance in making available several of the plates reproduced in this study. A debt of gratitude is owed to Lim Cheow Teik for his help relating to photographic matters.

The warmth and friendship accorded me during my sojourn in Hull meant a lot, particularly from the Longhorns—Brian and Ian, Uncle Alf and Aunt Rosa—and the Smiths—Marlene and Alyson; Pat Smith; and Martyn too. And, to Rose (Mrs Glew) of Chestnuts, Cottingham, a delightful thank you.

Professor Kim McQuaid of the Department of Social Science, Lake Erie College, Ohio, USA, and Visiting Fulbright Professor at the School of Humanities, Universiti Sains Malaysia, deserves a special acknowledgement of gratitude for his advice and comments, but most importantly, for being a friend.

To my mother, Tan Ai Gek, and my sisters, Saw Lian and Saw Ean, their love and support throughout the whole period of my study cannot be overstated.

School of Humanities
Universiti Sains Malaysia
Penang
January 1996

OOI KEAT GIN

Contents

Tables

Figures

Maps

Plates

Between pages 198 and 199

Appendices

Abbreviations

ASPC	Anglo-Saxon Petroleum Company
BCL	Borneo Company Limited
BL	British Library, London
BM	*British Malaya*
BMJ	*Brunei Museum Journal*
BRB	*Borneo Research Bulletin*
CO	Colonial Office
CR	*China Review*
CSSH	*Comparative Studies in Society and History*
DRO	Devon Record Office, Exeter
EHR	*Economic History Review*
FAO	Food and Agriculture Organization (of United Nations)
FO	Foreign Office
GHL	Guildhall Library, London
HMSO	His/Her Majesty's Stationery Office
JAS	*Journal of Asian Studies*
JIAEA	*Journal of the Indian Archipelago and Eastern Asia*
JMBRAS	*Journal of the Malayan/Malaysian Branch, Royal Asiatic Society*
JMHSSB	*Journal of the Malaysian Historical Society, Sarawak Branch*
JOS	*Journal of Oriental Studies*
JRGS	*Journal of the Royal Geographical Society*
JRSA	*Journal of the Royal Society of Arts*
JSBRAS	*Journal of the Straits Branch, Royal Asiatic Society*
JSEAS	*Journal of Southeast Asian Studies*
JTG	*Journal of Tropical Geography*
KCCC	Kuching Chinese Chamber of Commerce
KCGCC	Kuching Chinese General Chamber of Commerce
KMB	Kuching Municipal Board
KMC	Kuching Municipal Council
LRO	Liverpool Record Office, Liverpool
MAS	*Modern Asian Studies*

MBRAS	Malaysian Branch, Royal Asiatic Society
MCS	Malayan Civil Service
MF	*Malayan Forester*
MHSSB	Malaysian Historical Society, Sarawak Branch
MR	*Monthly Review*
NAM	Arkib Negara (National Archives) Malaysia, Kuala Lumpur
NC	*New Commonwealth*
PRO	Public Record Office, Kew
RHL	Rhodes House Library, Oxford
RTC	Rejang Timber Concession
SAR	*Sarawak Administration Report*
SG	*Sarawak Gazette*
SGG	*Sarawak Government Gazette*
SMA	Sarawak Museum and State Archives, Kuching
SMJ	*Sarawak Museum Journal*
SOL	Sarawak Oilfields Limited
SSCo	Sarawak Steamship Company
SSSCo	Singapore and Sarawak Steamship Company
ST	*Sarawak Tribune*
USPG	United Society for the Propagation of the Gospel Archives, London
WSRO	West Sussex Record Office, Chichester

Glossary

adat	custom
amah	female domestic servant
antu kubal	rubber tree spirit
antu padi	rice spirit
arrack/arak	Arabic for liquor, rice wine (see also p. 286, n. 112)
bagi dua	*lit.* divide into two; equal sharing
bebunoh babi bebaik	*lit.* killing-a-pig-for-friendship; peace offering
bejalai	Iban custom of venturing in search of one's fortune (see also p. 245, n. 29)
bilek	apartment in a longhouse
blachu	black cotton fabric of inferior quality
borak	Kelabit term for rice wine
cangkul/changkul	hoe fixed with a wooden handle
Chettiar	South Indian caste of moneylenders
daging darah	*lit.* flesh and blood; belongings
datu	non-aristocratic Sarawak Malay chieftain
herta pesaka	*lit.* property; heritage
hueh/hui	Chinese term for brotherhood, secret society
kampung	village (kampong)
kangchew	Chinese headman in charge of a gambier and pepper plantation
konfrontasi	Sukarno's military confrontation in opposing 'Malaysia'
kongsi	*lit.* sharing; Chinese mutual-help organization
kuo-yu	vernacular Mandarin
landas	wet or rainy season of the north-east monsoon (October–February)
lemanta/lemantak	Malay term for wet sago flour
mandor	Tamil term for supervisor, foreman
mudal	capital
mui tsai	a betrothed Chinese female who in practice is treated as a common domestic servant

nakhodah	*lit.* 'those who sail to the right'; captain of a ship; ship-master (see also p. 244, n. 1)
Nanyang	Chinese term meaning 'South Seas'; referring to South-East Asia
ondong-ondong	written laws
pajak	*lit.* to rent
pangeran	a Javanese title of a prince of the highest rank; honorific denoting blood relations to Brunei royalty
pangkalan	landing place on river bank
penghulu	Iban headman of a district; a Brooke-created appointment
ripoh	rasped pith of sago palm; refuse or rubbish
samsu/samshu	Chinese term for rice wine
serah dagang	*lit.* submission of trade goods; practice of forced trade
sherif/sherip	honorific for person of Arabic blood; signifies descent from the Prophet
sinkheh	*lit.* newcomer, arrival, guest; new immigrant
tongkang	Chinese term for barge
towkay	*lit.* head of a family, organization; Chinese term for a wealthy businessman, usually owner of a shop, mine, or plantation (see also p. 114, n. 30)
tua kampong	village headman

Weights, Measures, and Currencies

Weights

Local Units	Imperial Equivalent (Approximate)
1 *tahil*	1.33 ounces
1 *kati* = 16 *tahils*	1.33 pounds
1 *pikul* = 100 *katis*	133.30 pounds
1 *koyan* = 40 *pikuls*	5,333.30 pounds
1 *bunkal* (gold) = 1 gold *tahil*	1.33 ounces
1 *gantang* (dry weight) = 8 *katis*	10.64 pounds
1 *passu* = 8 *gantangs*	85.12 pounds

Measures

Local Units	Imperial Equivalent (Approximate)
1 *depas* = an arm's length	20.00 inches
1 *chhun*	1.48 inches
1 *cheek* = 10 chhuns	14.75 inches
1 *panchang*	108 stacked cubic feet
1 *gelong* = coil of rattan tied in bundles, approximately 100 vines	

Currencies

Unless stated otherwise, all currencies refer to the Sarawak dollar, which was tied to the Straits Settlements dollar and tended to fluctuate in value. From 1906 the Straits dollar was pegged to sterling at the rate of $1 to 2s. 4d., or $8.57 to £1, which was generally maintained until the outbreak of the Pacific War (1941–5).

Spelling and Usage of Terms

GENERALLY, the spelling and names of places and of people are retained as they appear in documents, and if there are discrepancies, for instance, Seribas/Saribas, Rejang/Rajang, Milano/Melanau, or Shak Lak Mun/Shak Luk Mun, the more common version has been applied consistently throughout. Similarly 'Rajah' is used rather than 'Raja'. The personal names—James, Charles, and Vyner—are used when referring to the individual Brooke ruler rather than the formal title. English orthography is adopted in preference to Dutch, even for terms and names in Dutch Borneo. References to river basins are generally preferred, like the Baram and the Limbang, although occasionally when the need arises, administrative units such as the 'Fourth Division' and the 'Fifth Division' are used. 'Dayak' is applied throughout to mean 'Sea Dayak' or 'Iban' in line with general Brooke usage and in the majority of source materials. Likewise, 'Land Dayak' is preferred to the term 'Bidayuh'. No attempt is made to differentiate Melanaus according to their religious faith (Muslim, Christian, or pagan); nor in the case of Land Dayaks in terms of their dialect groupings. However, where it is known, the different Chinese speech groups (Hokkien, Teochew, Foochow, Hakka, and others) are designated. The terms 'natives', 'indigenous peoples', and 'indigenes' refer to the communities defined as such in 'Order No. I–1 (Interpretation) 1933' and listed in the 'Schedule'.

1
The Setting

THE establishment of the Brooke Raj has been adequately covered in general histories of Sarawak and the various biographies of the founder, James Brooke.[1] Only an outline of the founding of the Raj and its expansion, and a brief account of its administrative machinery are presented here to provide a context for the main subject of this study.

On his second visit to Sarawak in 1840, in return for his successful intervention in ending the revolt of the Sarawak Malays against their Brunei overlords, James Brooke was publicly installed as 'Rajah' in Kuching on 24 September 1841, and granted the territory from Tanjong Datu to the Samarahan River by the Brunei ruler, Sultan Omar Ali Saifuddin II. Subsequently he devoted his time and energy in suppressing raiding along the north-western Bornean coast; on several occasions the Royal Navy provided valuable assistance. Head-hunting was outlawed and various forms of local oppression of the indigenous inhabitants, mainly the Land Dayaks, were curtailed. James's campaigns against raiding, or 'piracy' as it was popularly called, were debated in the British Parliament, culminating in a Commission of Inquiry held in Singapore in 1854. Both in the House of Commons and in Singapore he was successfully vindicated. Meanwhile in 1853, James obtained a new treaty from the recently installed Sultan Abdul Mumin of Brunei whereby the territory from the Sadong to Tanjong Sirik, including the Rejang but excluding the Igan, was transferred to the Raj. In February 1857, the Chinese gold-miners of Upper Sarawak launched an attack on Kuching and almost destroyed the Raj. The assistance rendered by the Malays, coupled with the timely arrival of Dayaks, defeated the Chinese, and by March the government was restored. Three years later, a Malay conspiracy to topple the Raj was uncovered. This so-called 'Malay plot' was interwoven with political feuds at Mukah; the issue was concluded in James's favour in 1861 and the territory from the Igan River to Tanjong Kidurong was ceded to the Raj by Brunei. James died in 1868 and his nephew, Charles, became the Second White Rajah.

Charles further expanded the boundaries of the Raj at the expense of Brunei, and by 1905 the territory of Sarawak resembled its present-day configuration (Map 1.1). In 1888 Sarawak became a protectorate of Britain which assumed responsibility for the Raj's foreign relations but had no jurisdiction over nor powers to intervene in the internal administration of the country.

Charles organized the administration of the Raj, encouraged trade and commerce, promoted the exploitation of mineral resources and commercial agriculture, and developed infrastructure facilities. Law and order and relative peace and prosperity reigned during this period. Slavery was gradually phased out but head-hunting occurred sporadically in the interior. By the time of Charles's death in 1917, there had been a noticeable increase in revenue; there was a budget surplus and the country had no public debt.

Vyner succeeded his father in 1917, and became the Third and last White Rajah. He continued with the policies of his predecessors. Improvements were made in the social services, for example in the provision of more medical and educational facilities. Progress in agriculture and advances in infrastructure development were recorded. The country braved the economic recession of the period between the two World Wars without severe problems. On the centenary of Brooke rule, Vyner granted a 'Constitution' to his country and people, thereby ending the absolute rule of the Raj.

For a century, the Brookes ruled Sarawak as absolute monarchs with the seat of government at Kuching. Nevertheless, the advice and opinions of native leaders were constantly sought. The Supreme Council, established in 1855, comprising the Malay leaders (the *datu*) and senior Brooke officers, advised the Rajah on major policy decisions. In 1867, the General Council (or Council Negri) was instituted whereby the chiefs and heads of the various indigenous communities met the Rajah once every three years. Although it comprised a larger and more representative native consultative body than the Supreme Council, its primary aim was not to permit the airing of native opinion but to cement cordial relations between the Rajah and the leaders of his subjects. In the absence of the Rajah, a Committee of Administration comprising senior Brooke officers, presided over by the Officer Administering the Government (normally, the Resident of the First Division), assumed the reins of government. Nevertheless, major decisions affecting policy matters had to await the Rajah's approval upon his return, when the Committee automatically ceased to function. In

MAP 1.1

Expansion of Brooke Sarawak, 1841–1941

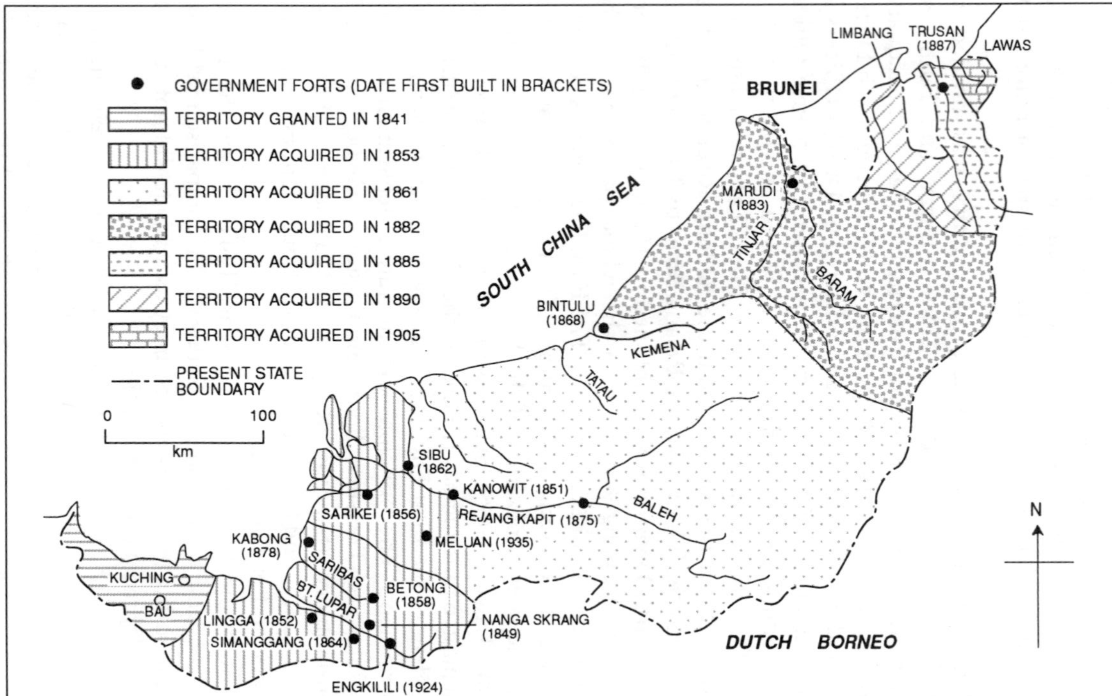

Sources: After Runciman, *The White Rajahs*, pp. 188–9; Jackson, *Sarawak*, p. 59; Maxwell and Gibson, *Treaties and Engagements Affecting the Malay States and Borneo*, pp. 188–9; and Pringle, *Rajahs and Rebels*, pp. 93–4.

accordance with the 'Political Will' of Charles, a tandem system of rajahship was instituted between Vyner, the Rajah Muda, and his brother, Bertram, the Tuan Muda; each alternating in administering the affairs of the Raj. The Sarawak State Advisory Council, constituted in 1912, based at Westminster and presided over by Bertram, acted as an intermediary between the Raj and the British government. The Council's members consisted of retired senior Brooke officers.

For administrative purposes, the country was divided into Divisions—the First, Second, Third, Fourth, and Fifth—each under the control of a Resident from their respective headquarters at Kuching, Simanggang, Sibu, Miri, and Limbang. Each Division was subdivided into Districts administered by District Officers and Assistant District Officers with the assistance of Native Officers. Three administrative Divisions were created in March 1873: the First Division comprised the area from Tanjong Datu to the Sadong River, the Second from the Sadong River to the Rejang River, and the Third from the Rejang River to Tanjong Kidurong. The Fourth Division was established in 1885, covering the territory from Tanjong Kidurong to the whole Baram basin, which came under Brooke rule in 1882. The Fifth Division was constituted in 1912 comprising the Trusan (1884) which was combined with the later annexation of the Limbang (1890) and the transfer of the Lawas (1905) river basins. In the central government at Kuching, a bureaucracy headed by the Chief Secretary (usually the Resident of the First Division) managed the day-to-day routine of government. The principal administrative departments included the following: Treasury, Trade and Customs, Medical and Health, Constabulary (Sarawak Rangers and Police), Public Works, Postal, Lands and Survey, Agriculture, Education, Forest, Chinese Affairs, and Native Affairs.

The outbreak of the Pacific War (1941–5) saw the Japanese invasion and occupation of Sarawak. In comparison with other neighbouring territories, the country as a whole did not suffer any severe depredations or atrocities.

In September 1945, Australian armed forces reoccupied the country, and a brief period of military rule ensued under the British Military Administration. Vyner returned to the country from Australia and decided that Sarawak should be transferred to the Crown. The instrument of cession was signed with His Majesty's Government and on 1 July 1946 Sarawak became a British Crown Colony.

From 1946 until 1963 Sarawak was administered by the Colonial Office from London. A programme of reconstruction was launched, and development plans were executed to improve the social and economic well-being of the country. Measures in preparing the country for eventual self-government were instituted, commencing with the establishment of Local Authorities throughout the country.

In 1963, Sarawak became one of the constituent states of the Federation of Malaysia and remains so to the present day.

The Land and People

Sarawak lies on the north-west coast of the island of Borneo, covering an area within its present political boundaries of some 124 485 square kilometres (48,250 square miles), and constituting about 38 per cent of the total area of the Federation of Malaysia. Its neighbours to the north-east are the Sultanate of Brunei Darussalam and Sabah (the latter formerly British North Borneo, and now a state within the Malaysian Federation), while Indonesian Kalimantan (formerly Dutch Borneo) flanks its southern and south-eastern borders.

Topographically Sarawak can be divided into three distinct units: an alluvial and swampy coastal plain, a broad belt of undulating hilly country, and a mountainous interior rising to above 1200 metres (4,000 feet) (Maps 1.2 and 1.3). The coastal plain is generally a few feet above sea-level, but in the south-west isolated mountains of 750 metres (2,500 feet) or more intrude into the coast. Mud beaches are the norm, with occasional pockets of sand. Coastal and deltaic swamps extend in some places as far inland as 80 kilometres (50 miles) while others are only 8 kilometres (5 miles) or less. This low-lying, poorly drained, swampy, alluvial plain comprises about one-fifth of the total land area. The rugged hilly country, most of which is less than 300 metres (1,000 feet) high, is dissected by steep limestone hills and numerous sandstone ridges. The mountainous interior forms part of the irregular mountain range that runs south-west through the middle of the island of Borneo. This seemingly impenetrable region consists of jumbled masses of dissected sandstone highlands with a few peaks exceeding 1800 metres (6,000 feet). The watershed along the mountain range where rivers flow north-westward to the South China Sea and south-eastward to the Sulawesi Sea serves as a natural boundary between Sarawak and Kalimantan.

MAP 1.2
Relief and Main Drainage Systems of Sarawak

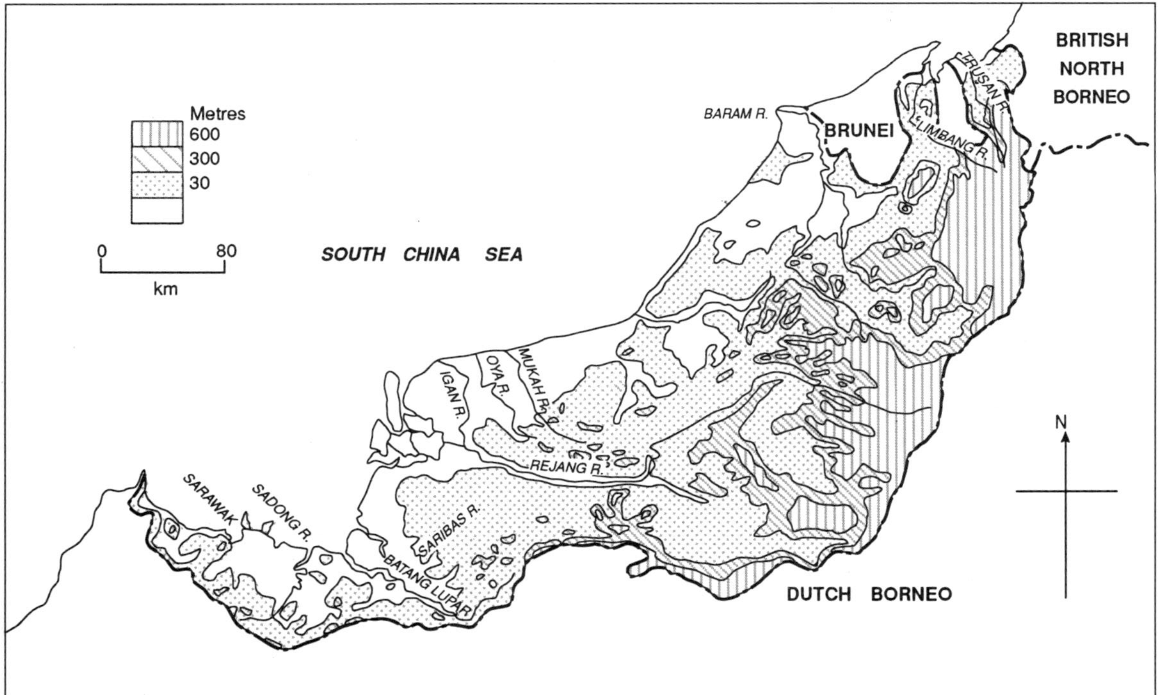

Source: After Jackson, *Sarawak*, p. 23.

MAP 1.3
The Three Main Topographical Units of Sarawak

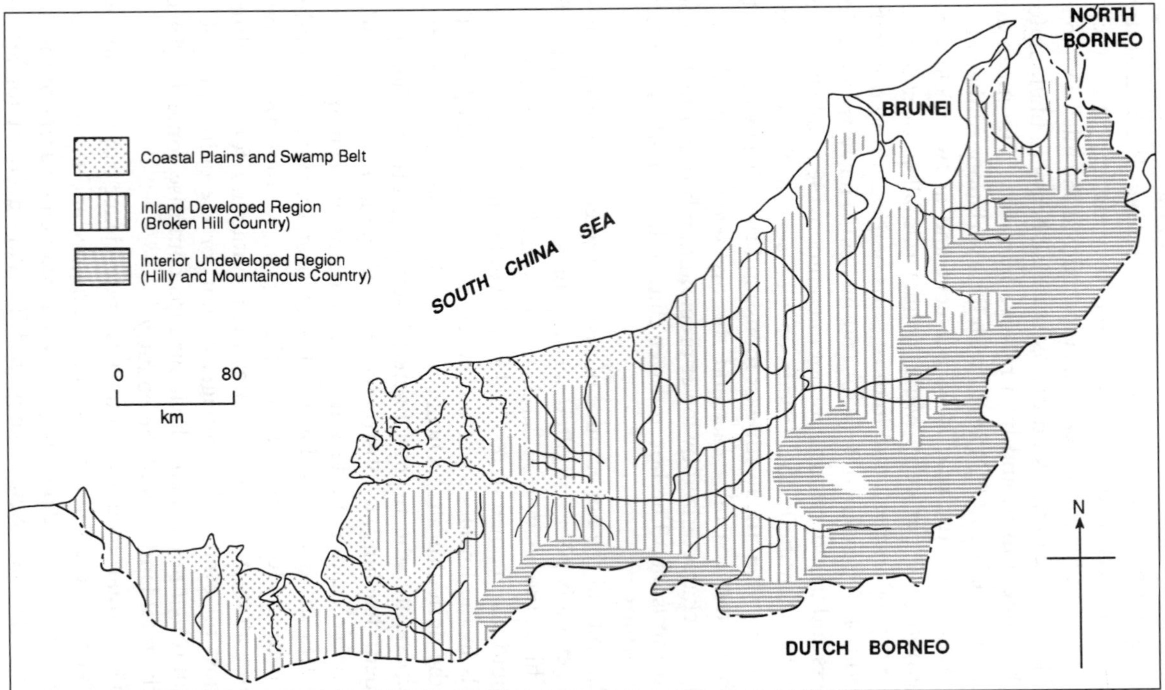

Source: After Lee, *Population and Settlement in Sarawak*, p. 4.

The rivers flowing into the South China Sea form a myriad drainage network criss-crossing the country. The principal river systems are the Sarawak, Samarahan, Sadong, Batang Lupar,[2] Saribas, Rejang, Bintulu, Baram, Limbang, and Trusan. Rivers and streams are the natural highways; even today they are important means of transport and communications, especially in the inland regions.

The climate of the country is equatorial: heavy rainfall, uniformly high temperatures, and high relative humidity. The mean annual temperature is 25.6°C (78°F) with little variation. At dawn relative humidity over the year is 98 per cent and at two o'clock in the afternoon, 70 per cent. Mean annual rainfall is over 250 centimetres (100 inches), and in most parts of the country precipitation is 300–400 centimetres (120–160 inches). Heavy tropical downpours and thunderstorms are not uncommon. Generally two seasons can be identified: the *landas* or wet season from October to February when the north-east monsoon brings heavy rain, particularly to the coastal areas; and the dry season, from April until August, characterized by lower precipitation brought by the south-west monsoon. The hot and wet climate has an adverse effect on soil fertility.

In spite of the appearance of lush evergreen vegetation, the soils are generally poor and often acidic. The highland areas suffer from leaching; the heavy tropical downpours leach the nutrients, leaving behind a thin cover of residual soil devoid of much natural fertility. Soils in the lowlands present an even more formidable challenge to the agriculturalist. Owing to poor drainage and constant high temperature, the normal bacterial action of organic decay is retarded; leaching is obstructed by the poor drainage, and the vegetable matter, undecomposed or partially decomposed, accumulates in increasing layers of acid peat reaching to depths of 12 metres (40 feet) or more. Deep peat swamps are commonly found along the coastal plain; their suitability for agriculture is almost nil even with drainage, except for the cultivation of sago palm (*Sagu metroxylon*). Peat swamps comprise some 12 per cent of the total land area of the country.[3]

Three-quarters of the country is under dense tropical rain forest, with large areas still inaccessible. Mangrove and *nipah* palm forests which occur on tidal swamps in sheltered deltaic areas of the larger rivers—the Sarawak, Rejang, and Trusan—account for less than 2 per cent of the total forest area. Peat swamp forest covers the coastal strip, extending in some places as much as 80 kilometres (50 miles) inland, and comprises about 16 per cent of the total forest area. Three distinct sub-types can be identified: mixed

swamp forest, *padang paya* forest, and *alan* forest. The swamp forest is more extensive and economically more important owing to the presence of trees of commercial value which are accessibile for exploitation. The remaining forest type, comprising an area of about 64 500 square kilometres (25,000 square miles), is the lofty and very dense lowland dipterocarp forest. Below the forest roof, which is 42–48 metres (140–160 feet) above ground level, there is scant undergrowth as little sunshine penetrates the thick sprawling canopy. However, climbing plants like lianas and rattans thrive in abundance.[4]

Sarawak was, and still is, a sparsely populated land. Although occupying more than one-third of the total land area of Malaysia, its present population is less than 7.5 per cent of the population of the Federation.

In the absence of any country-wide population census before 1939,[5] it is difficult to ascertain either the total population at certain times or its growth during the century of Brooke rule. 'It is important to remember', cautioned J. L. Noakes, Superintendent of the 1947 Population Census of Sarawak and Brunei, 'that the frontiers of Sarawak have been extended several times since James Brooke assumed the government in 1841, and territorially Sarawak is now over 20 times its original size.'[6] He went on to summarize the scattered references to population from the establishment of the Raj to 1947, the year the first modern census was undertaken.

> When in 1841 James Brooke assumed the Government of Sarawak the area under his administration extended from Tanjong Datu to Samarahan and was computed to contain about 10,500 inhabitants. Thirty years later in 1871 at the command of the Second Rajah a Census was made of the State, which then extended as far as Kedurong, and the population returned was 141,546: this Census was however confessedly inaccurate. Thirty-eight years after in 1909, when the State had attained its present extent, the population was estimated at 416,000. Thirty years after this in 1939 a count of population was made and the total resulting was 490,485. In 1947 the first scientific Census was made of the entire country and the population was found to be 546,385.[7]

Referring to the subject of population growth, Noakes confidently concluded that, 'the Chinese population has increased with startling rapidity', but 'as far as the native races are concerned, it is difficult to say whether the total population of the area now covered by Sarawak has increased or not during the last hundred years. It may well be that the increase in some races has been offset by the decline in others and that there has been little overall change.'[8]

Indigenous peoples as defined by 'Order No. I–1 (Interpretation) 1933' meant 'a subject of His Highness the Rajah of any race which is now considered to be indigenous to the State of Sarawak as set out in the Schedule: Bukitans, Bisayahs, Dusuns, Dayaks (Sea), Dayaks (Land), Kadayans, Kayans, Kenyahs (including Sabups and Sipengs), Kajangs (including Sekapans, Kejamans, Lahanans, Punans, Tanjongs and Kanowits), Lugats, Lisums, Malays, Melanos, Muruts, Penans, Sians, Tagals, Tabus, [and] Ukits. And any admixture of the above with each other.'[9] The definition of 'indigenous' adopted by the 1947 Census was 'those persons who recognize no allegiance to any foreign territory, who regard Sarawak as their homeland, who believe themselves to be a part of the territory and who are now regarded as native by their fellowmen'.[10]

Table 1.1 shows the population of Sarawak in 1939 and 1947. Table 1.2 lists the principal indigenous groups and their population in 1939 and 1947; Appendix 1 shows their spatial distribution, chief occupations, and major characteristics. The population figures of the other minor native communities in 1947 can be seen in Table 1.3, while Appendix 2 indicates their settlement patterns, livelihood, and characteristics. Table 1.4 shows the Chinese population in 1947; their dialect groupings, regional distribution, and major economic activities are in Appendix 3. The population of other immigrant communities (excluding Europeans) in 1939 and 1947 is shown in Table 1.5.

TABLE 1.1
Population of Sarawak, 1939 and 1947

Community	*1939*	*%*	*1947*	*%*
Dayak	167,700	34.2	190,326	34.8
Chinese	123,626	25.2	145,158	26.6
Malay	92,709	18.9	97,469	17.9
Land Dayak	36,963	7.5	42,195	7.7
Melanau	36,772	7.5	35,560	6.5
Other Indigenous	27,532	5.6	29,867	5.5
Others	4,579	0.9	5,119	0.9
European	704	0.2	691	0.1
Total	490,585	100.0	546,385	100.0

Source: L. W. Jones, *Sarawak: Census of Population, 1960*, p. 59.

TABLE 1.2
Population of the Principal Indigenous Groups, 1939 and 1947

Group	*1939*	*%*	*1947*	*%*
Sea Dayak	167,700	46	190,326	48
Malay	92,709	26	97,469	25
Land Dayak	36,963	10	42,195	11
Melanau	36,772	10	35,560	9
Others	27,532	8	29,867	7
Total	361,676	100	395,417	100

Source: L. W. Jones, *Sarawak: Census of Population, 1960*, p. 50.

TABLE 1.3
Population of Other Minor Indigenous Groups, 1947

Group	*Population*
Kayan	6,183
Kenyah	5,507
Kedayan	5,334
Murut	3,290
Bisayah	2,058
Punan and Others	5,883
Total	29,867

Source: L. W. Jones, *Sarawak: Census of Population, 1960*, p. 55.

TABLE 1.4
Population of Major Chinese Dialect Groups in Sarawak, 1947

Dialect Group	*Population*	*% of Chinese Population*
Hakka	45,409	31.2
Foochow	41,946	29.0
Hokkien	20,289	14.0
Cantonese	14,622	10.0
Teochew	12,892	9.0
Henghua	4,356	3.0
Hainanese (Hailam)	3,871	2.6
Others[a]	1,773	1.2
Total	145,158	100.0

Source: Noakes, *1947 Population Census*, p. 93.
[a]Include Chaoans, Liuchius, Shanghainese, and others.

TABLE 1.5
Population of Other Immigrant Communities
(Excluding Europeans), 1939 and 1947

Community	*1939*	*1947*
Javanese	1,885	2,397
Indian and Ceylonese	2,323	1,744
Bugis[a]	13	626
Filipino	64	43
Others[b]	294	309
Total	4,579	5,119

Source: Noakes, *1947 Population Census*, p. 40.
[a]The small number of Bugis in 1939 and their dramatic increase in 1947 was the mistaken inclusion of them with the Malays in the former enumeration.
[b]Include Arabs, Bataks, Banjorese, Siamese, etc.

The Local Economy on the Eve of the Establishment of the Brooke Raj

The territory of what is today Sarawak was under the suzerain rule of the Brunei Sultanate prior to the arrival of James Brooke in the late 1830s. The province of Sarawak then was roughly the area occupied by the river basin of the same name, extending eastwards as far as the Sadong River. The inhabitants were Malays and Land Dayaks under the rule of the Malay *datu*, and an independent Chinese mining community. Economic activities comprised the extractive industries of gold- and antimony-mining in Upper Sarawak, fishing on the coast, and subsistence shifting cultivation of hill-*padi* in the interior.

The chance find of antimony in Sarawak in the early 1820s attracted the interest of the Brunei authorities.[11] The ore was reportedly 'of a much richer nature than the antimony produced in Europe' which created a demand for it in the newly opened Singapore market.[12] The Brunei Sultanate obviously saw advantage in exploiting this ore. A settlement was founded at Kuching where Brunei officials and their followers took up residence.[13] Pangeran Mahkota, the Brunei official who was the nominal ruler of Sarawak, enlisted the Malays of Siniawan and the Land Dayaks of the neighbouring areas to work the antimony-mines. Ore was exported to Singapore during the 1820s and 1830s. Apparently,

this trade in antimony did not enrich the Brunei court for the 'proceeds seemed to melt away in transit between Sarawak and Brunei' for Pangeran Mahkota 'had very sticky fingers'.[14] Besides, he was also a hard taskmaster and exploited the mine workers. 'Makota did not choose to remember that workmen must eat to live, and the price he paid for the ore was so small that it was impossible for the people to obtain sufficient food. The natural consequence was that the mines were deserted, and force had to be employed to induce the people to return to their work.'[15]

Gold-mining was carried out by the Chinese in the auriferous district of Upper Sarawak. Hakka miners who had migrated across the frontier from the Sambas–Pontianak area created similar *kongsi*-style establishments in the Sarawak gold-fields.[16] Like their counterparts in Dutch Borneo, these *kongsi* were a power unto themselves, independent of the external control of the Malay *datu* or the Brunei authorities.[17] The gold was exported through Sambas to the ports of south-west Borneo. From these ports came their supplies of food and opium.[18]

The Land Dayaks practised subsistence shifting cultivation of hill-*padi*. Malay traders brought goods like cloth, iron, salt, and beads, in exchange for rice and some jungle products, like dammar, birds' nest, and rattan.

Beyond Mahkota's Sarawak, further eastwards from the Sadong, lay the Batang Lupar, Saribas, and Skrang rivers—the traditional lands of the Dayak head-hunters. The Dayaks owed allegiance to no authority but themselves.[19] The Brunei *pangeran*, who in theory had control over these river basins, had no power over them. Occasionally the *pangeran* would threaten the Land Dayaks that they would unleash the Saribas and Skrang head-hunters upon them but these were empty threats. Led by Arab *sherif*, but sometimes on their own, these Dayaks embarked on raiding expeditions along the north-western Bornean coast, preying on native craft for plunder and heads. They also sacked Malay settlements upstream.

Towards the north-east, in the swampy coastal districts, were the settlements of the sago-producing Melanaus. Brunei *pangeran* established their authority there even earlier than at Sarawak as the opening of Singapore in 1819 provided an attractive market for sago. Brunei Malay merchants conducted this profitable export trade with Singapore.[20]

Brunei Malay traders were also active in the Baram River exchanging cloth and salt for jungle products with indigenous inhabitants, like the Kayans and Kenyahs.[21]

Returning to Sarawak Proper, the disaffected Malays and the oppressed Land Dayaks staged a revolt against Mahkota in the mid-1830s. Despite the arrival in 1837 of Rajah Muda Hashim, the uncle of the Brunei sultan and heir apparent to the throne, the rebellion continued. Then, in 1839, the mast of the schooner *Royalist* appeared on the Sarawak River, with James Brooke, an English adventurer, on board.

1. For the general history of the Brooke Raj, see S. Baring-Gould and C. A. Bampfylde, *A History of Sarawak under Its Two White Rajahs, 1839–1908*, London: Henry Sotheran, 1909; and Steven Runciman, *The White Rajahs: A History of Sarawak from 1841 to 1946*, Cambridge: Cambridge University Press, 1960. For biographies of James Brooke, see Spenser St John, *The Life of Sir James Brooke: Rajah of Sarawak; from His Personal Papers and Correspondence*, Edinburgh and London: William Blackwood & Sons, 1879; Emily Hahn, *James Brooke of Sarawak: A Biography of Sir James Brooke*, London: Arthur Barker, 1953; and Nicholas Tarling, *The Burthen, the Risk, and the Glory: A Biography of Sir James Brooke*, Kuala Lumpur: Oxford University Press, 1982.

2. Although the word 'batang' means river and 'Batang Lupar', the Lupar River, the term 'Batang Lupar River' is used throughout this study, conforming to Brooke usage.

3. For instance, see J. A. R. Anderson, 'The Structure and Development of the Peat Swamps of Sarawak and Brunei', *JTG*, 18 (1964): 7–16; and J. R. D. Wall, 'Topography–Soil Relationships in Lowland Sarawak', *JTG*, 18 (1964): 192–9.

4. For vegetation and forest types, see F. W. Roe (comp.), *The Natural Resources of Sarawak*, 2nd rev. edn., Kuching: Government Printing Office, 1952, pp. 32–6; F. G. Browne, 'The Kerangas Land of Sarawak', *MF*, 15, 2 (1952): 61–73; F. G. Browne, *Forest Trees of Sarawak and Brunei and Their Products*, Kuching: Government Printing Office, 1955; and M. E. D. Poore, 'Vegetation and Flora', in Wang Gungwu (ed.), *Malaysia: A Survey*, New York: Frederick Praeger, 1964, pp. 44–54.

5. In 1939, for the purpose of wartime food rationing, an enumeration 'not amounting to a census' was undertaken in accordance with 'Order No. F–6 (Food Control) 1939' and 'Order No. C–12 (Census) 1938'. See J. L. Noakes, *Sarawak and Brunei: A Report on the 1947 Population Census*, Kuching: Government Printing Office, 1950, p. 9.

6. Ibid., p. 3.

7. Ibid.

8. Ibid., p. 8.

9. 'Order No. I–1 (Interpretation) 1933', *Sarawak Government Gazette* (*SGG*), 1 July 1933, pp. 160 and 164.

10. Noakes, *1947 Population Census*, p. 29. This definition was also applied to the 1960 Census. See L. W. Jones, *Sarawak: Report on the Census of Population Taken on 15th June 1960*, Kuching: Government Printing Office, 1962, p. 47.

11. See John Crawfurd, *A Descriptive Dictionary of the Indian Islands and Adjacent Countries*, London: Bradbury & Evans, 1856, p. 377; and George Windsor Earl, *The*

Eastern Seas; or Voyages and Adventures in the Indian Archipelago, in 1832–33–34, London: William Hallen, 1837, pp. 310–11.

12. Hugh Low, *Sarawak: Its Inhabitants and Productions, Being Notes during a Residence in that Country with His Excellency Mr Brooke*, London: Frank Cass, 1848; new impression, 1968, p. 17.

13. Pangeran Mahkota was credited as the founder of Kuching. The date of its establishment was reckoned to be some time between 1824 and 1830. See Craig Alan Lockard, *From Kampung to City: A Social History of Kuching, Malaysia, 1820–1970*, Ohio University Monographs in International Studies, Southeast Asia Series, No. 75, Athens, 1987, p. 11. See also Baring-Gould and Bampfylde, *A History of Sarawak*, p. 64.

14. Hahn, *James Brooke*, p. 41.

15. St John, *Life of Sir James Brooke*, p. 51.

16. A recent study maintains that early in the nineteenth century, Liew Shan Pang, apparently the leader of the Chinese in the anti-Brooke uprising of 1857, led Chinese miners from Sambas to Bau through Pangkalan Tebang, to look for gold. See Chang Pat Foh, 'The History of Gold Mining in Bau, Sarawak', *SG*, September 1992, pp. 32–44. See also G. E. Wilford, 'The Bau Gold Field', *SG*, 30 April 1962, p. 77.

17. For the functioning of Chinese *kongsi* in Sambas, Dutch Borneo, whence the Bau *kongsi* originated, see James C. Jackson, *Chinese in the West Borneo Goldfields: A Study in Cultural Geography*, University of Hull, Occasional Papers in Geography No. 15, Hull, 1970, pp. 46–70; Barbara E. Ward, 'A Hakka Kongsi in Borneo', *JOS*, 1, 2 (July 1954): 358–70; and Mary Somers Heidhues, 'Chinese Organizations in West Borneo and Bangka: Kongsis and Hui', in David Ownby and Mary Somers Heidhues (eds.), *'Secret Societies' Reconsidered*, New York and London: M. E. Shrape, 1993, pp. 68–88. For an elaboration of the word *kongsi*, see Wang Tai Peng, 'The Word Kongsi: A Note', *JMBRAS*, 3, 1 (1979): 102–5.

18. Jackson, *Chinese in the West Borneo Goldfields*, pp. 28–30 and 38–42; and John M. Chin, *The Sarawak Chinese*, Kuala Lumpur: Oxford University Press, 1981, p. 29.

19. See Robert Pringle, *Rajahs and Rebels: The Ibans of Sarawak under Brooke Rule, 1841–1941*, London: Macmillan, 1970, pp. 38–65.

20. See J. R. Logan, 'The Trade in Sago', *JIAEA*, 3 (1849): 307–11; Wong Lin Ken, 'The Trade of Singapore', *JMBRAS*, 33, 4 (December 1960): 220–1; and Rodney Mundy, *Narrative of Events in Borneo and Celebes, down to the Occupation of Labuan: From the Journals of James Brooke Esq.*, London: John Murray, 1848, Vol. I, p. 319.

21. See Robert Burns, 'The Kayans of North-west Borneo', *JIAEA*, 3, (1849): 140–52.

PART I
ECONOMIC POLICIES

2
The Economic Policies of the Brookes

THE three Brooke Rajahs expounded similar notions regarding the economic development of Sarawak. The essence of their shared ideas, subsequently translated into policies, was that development should be a gradual process, and most important, the protection of native interests and the improvement of their welfare should be adhered to without compromise. James, Charles, and Vyner steadfastly held to these principles in developing the resources of the country.

When James embarked on his 'great adventure' from Devonport on 16 December 1838, he had already a clear notion of what he planned to accomplish.[1] He envisaged making free trade the economic principle of the Eastern Archipelago,[2] believing fervently that this would improve the welfare of its inhabitants. The possession of territories, and not merely treaty relations with native rulers, he argued, was essential in ensuring that free trade was not obstructed. Circumstances presented James with the territory of Sarawak, ceded to him by the Brunei ruler. As Rajah, he instituted his concept of free trade, promoted British influence, and established a paternalistic form of governance for the 'development of the natives through their own exertions' under European guidance. James also formulated a grand design whereby the twin elements of Western capital investment and Chinese labour would promote the economic development of Sarawak.

Charles Johnson Brooke effectively took over the reins of power and the administration of Sarawak from his uncle, James, in 1863, when the latter left Kuching for England, never to return. Charles was proclaimed Rajah in 1868 on the demise of James, and continued his predecessor's policies. The safeguarding of the interests of the indigenous peoples and the improvement of their livelihood were the twin objectives of his government. The strategies for economic development focused on fostering trade, exploiting the country's mineral resources, and making settled agriculture the principal anchor of the economy.

Charles Vyner Brooke was proclaimed Rajah on 25 June 1917, exactly seven days after the death of his father, Charles. It was not

the most auspicious of times. The economic repercussions of the First World War were felt in far away Sarawak. The country that Vyner inherited existed in a world which was becoming more and more economically interdependent. His reign coincided with the years between the two World Wars which experienced trade fluctuations and faced economic problems culminating in the Depression (1929–31). During this period, Sarawak had to adjust to the ever-changing demands of the world economy. Notwithstanding these vicissitudes, Vyner adhered to the twin objectives of Brooke rule: the protection of native interest and the advancement of their welfare. Vyner, like his predecessors, advocated a gradual and steady development of Sarawak's resources with native interests in mind.

James, 1841–1868

James's Ideas of the Economic Development of the Eastern Archipelago

James was a staunch supporter of Sir Stamford Raffles's concept of the role of the British in the Eastern Archipelago and subscribed to Raffles's view that the occupation of territories was essential to British trade. The primary motivating force in advocating territorial possession was to loosen the 'intermediate clogs which tend to limit exports'.[3] These intermediary traders, the middlemen, were to be swept away so that both the buyer and the producer could derive maximum advantage from the transaction.

James warned that his advocacy of territorial possession should not be seen as the acquisition of territory *per se*; instead it was the duty of the government so installed *to advance native interests and develop native resources*.[4] What is more, the '*indefeasible rights of the Aborigines*' must be safeguarded, lest exploitation sets in.[5] The last point, in fact, became James's motto when he assumed the rajahship of Sarawak.

For James, the methods of trading must be in 'striking contrast to the commercial monopolies of the Dutch', by 'bringing the English merchant in contact with the original native dealer'.[6] Free trade was the cornerstone of James's 'commercial prosperity': 'I am convinced, however, that nothing but a free trade will benefit this country, and call its resources into existence; but it must be free trade which strikes at the monopolies of the interior—at Malay monopoly as well as others.'[7]

James Brooke was installed as Governor of Sarawak on 24 September 1841 and was accorded the title of 'Rajah'.[8] He was convinced of the deterioration and weakening authority of the native rulers and of their misgovernment. He attributed this weakened state not to the innate character of the rulers but to their intercourse with Western civilization.[9] Therefore, as Rajah of Sarawak, James embarked on his '*experiment of developing a country through the residence of a few Europeans, and by the assistance of its native rulers*'.[10] Notwithstanding his belief in the baneful influence of Western civilization, James was utterly convinced that 'no Asiatic is fitted to govern a country: under European guidance, yes—but alone, no'.[11] None the less, he condemned the practice of 'treating [the natives] as an inferior race'.[12] Instead, he maintained that 'utmost forbearance and liberality, guided by prudence' were the 'fundamental rules for managing men in so low a state of civilization'.[13] In later years he described his style of government thus: 'The principle upon which I have acted is—That a native government guided by superior intelligence, and acting in accordance with native pride and feeling, with European support when needed to maintain order, would promote the welfare of the people and largely increase commerce generally.'[14] It is clear that in his governance of Sarawak James was sincere in his exhortation. He established a paternalistic form of government that kept to the principle of maintaining the *status quo* as far as was possible; if there was need for changes to be made, they should be introduced gradually with the full consent of the natives. He restored his former adversaries of the recent 1836–40 Sarawak revolt, the Datu Patinggi, the Datu Bandar, and the Datu Temanggong, and enlisted them into his government as native advisers with whom he consulted informally.[15] In 1855, acting upon the advice given by his friend and supporter, Lord Grey, a council of state, called the Supreme Council, was established which institutionalized the practice of consulting native opinion.[16]

Economic Policies of James: Free Trade and Native Welfare

James had several economic objectives for Sarawak. His main concern was to facilitate the practice of free trade within his domain and with neighbouring countries, especially with the British settlement in Singapore. Free trade, according to James, meant the absence of any kind of monopolistic practices; instead profits were 'to be made by fair and honest dealing' which entitled producers to

'enjoy their gains' (see Appendix 4). Before unimpeded free trade could be established, however, several obstacles had to be removed, chief among which was 'piracy' or raiding along the Bornean coast and rivers, as well as some traditional indigenous economic practices. Several measures, which included the promulgation of a set of laws, were adopted in order to facilitate free trade and promote native commerce. James was not averse to territorial expansion if he thought that this was expedient in establishing peaceful conditions conducive to the promotion and sustenance of commercial intercourse.

Permanency, stability, and peace, he believed, were essential ingredients for Sarawak's prosperity and the elevation of the welfare of its native inhabitants. He argued that for Sarawak to survive beyond his lifetime it must come under the protection of a major imperial power. This conviction launched him on the unrelenting pursuit of support from the British government, his first choice for protection. Initially, he sought cession to the Crown; failing which, he attempted a 'Protectorate' and appealed for recognition; eventually he was only granted protectorate status.

European capital and Chinese labour were his twin strategies in developing the resources of Sarawak. However, the process of economic development had to be a gradual undertaking so that native interests were not compromised. He had a notion for the formation of a company to develop the economic potential of the country, but, at the same time, he opposed the influx of large capital investment which he believed would exploit the native inhabitants in the pursuit of profit.

Free Trade and Native Commerce

Borneo had long been famed for its trade in jungle products and sago.[17] But this trade with Borneo was a precarious venture due to coastal raiding which was rife throughout the Malay Archipelago during the eighteenth century and the first half of the nineteenth century.

'Piracy' was undoubtedly an active menace along the Bornean coast in the early 1840s when James first established himself at Sarawak. In addition to the Lanun (Illanun) and the Balagnini pirates of the Sulu Sea, the waters of the north-west coast of Borneo were frequented by Dayak head-hunters and raiders led by Malays and Arab *sherif*. The most active Dayaks were those of the Saribas and Skrang rivers. In the absence of trading vessels on the coast, they would plunder tribes along other rivers and even Malay settlements.[18]

Bona fide trading decreased in inverse proportion to active 'piracy'. Faced with such a situation, it was near impossible for James to open Sarawak to his concept of successful commerce. He was determined to eliminate this obstacle to trade, with or without outside support. However, assistance did come from the Royal Navy in 1843 and thus began James's campaign to wipe out coastal raiding. After deliberating on the problem with Captain (later Admiral) Henry Keppel, both men concluded that 'the only way to strike at the root of the evil would be to destroy the piratical strongholds in the interior'.[19] Between 1843 and 1849, with the support of the Royal Navy, James destroyed the raiders' strongholds in the Saribas and the Skrang and succeeded in breaking their power.[20] Yet his action in eliminating 'piracy' was severely criticized by a minority group in the British Parliament, resulting in the Commission of Inquiry of 1854.[21] His policy featured prominently in the proceedings. Although fully vindicated, James was deprived of the support of the Royal Navy to bring about the complete suppression of raiding.[22] Nevertheless, though not entirely eliminated, it no longer posed a serious threat to trade.

From James's perspective, commerce which was generally in the hands of the native chiefs was '*often ... the most fatal instrument of oppression*'.[23] Trade, instead of being beneficial to the native producers, was for James 'a curse' through the native custom of *serah dagang* or 'forced trade'. He described how this traditional custom was practised by the Brunei *pangeran* and the Sarawak Malay chiefs on their Land Dayak subjects.

> I may here mention the usual process demanded of the Dyaks.... One gantang of salt for three or four gantangs of rice, the value of the two articles being fourteen dollars for a royan of salt and fifty for a royan of rice!! When the chief has reduced the tribe to starvation, he returns the same rice and demands ten pekuls of antimony-ore for one rupee's worth of paddy or rice in the husk. Each pekul of antimony-ore may be sold for one and a half or two rupees on the spot. Half a catty of birds' nests are taken for one gantang of rice, being a moderate profit of 2,000 per cent.[24]

Furthermore, it was not uncommon for young Dayak women and children to be taken and sold into slavery.[25] The poorer Malays also suffered at the hands of their chiefs, and many became slave-debtors who were treated harshly and even sold abroad.[26] When antimony was discovered in Sarawak, the Land Dayaks and Malays of the poorer class were forced to mine the ore without wages or even the provision of food.[27]

James did away with such practices with the promulgation of his set of 'Laws', printed in the Malay language at Singapore in January 1842 (Appendix 4). All eight articles aimed at facilitating the practice of free trade by eliminating all obstacles and hindrances. Raiding and head-hunting were at once outlawed as grave offences punishable by heavy fines;[28] if unable to pay, the offender forfeited his life as punishment. All forms of slavery and forced labour were abolished, and those who laboured were paid a wage. Free passage ensured that goods from the producer reached the buyer without significant interference, while free trade allowed the producer a greater choice of customer, enabling him to realize better prices for his goods. The custom of *serah dagang* was abolished altogether, thereby ensuring that the interests of the Land Dayaks were safeguarded against their Malay chiefs.

James, as Rajah, held the monopoly of antimony, in lieu of taxation, to finance public expenditure.[29] He promised to introduce a fair system of taxation in place of the hitherto arbitrary practice exercised by the local Malay chiefs and Brunei *pangeran*.[30] Even when taxes were eventually imposed they were deliberately kept low 'to suit the feelings, and encourage the industry of [the] population', for James professed that 'a contented population is better than a full purse.'[31]

James adopted a forward policy that included the acquisition of territories when commercial intercourse was threatened and disrupted. His proceedings at Mukah, a dependency of Brunei consequently ceded to him in 1861, clearly showed his tenacity in maintaining the trade of this sago-rich port with Sarawak. This trade had been interrupted from the mid-1850s by the revival of raiding and internal strife.

A damaging result of the Commission of Inquiry of 1854 was the withdrawal of naval support against coastal raiders.[32] In a dispatch to the Foreign Office in July 1855, Spenser St John, then private secretary to James, blamed this resurgence of raiding on 'the results that have arisen from the want of the means of exercising a supervision over this coast and from the uncertainty that has characterized our [British] policy in these countries during the last three years'.[33] Even before the Commission sat, the Royal Navy was instructed to refrain from interfering with raiders 'unless they attack British ships'.[34] These instructions were reiterated after the conclusion of the Commission.[35] James was undoubtedly furious at such a policy which, he argued, contravened the Treaty of May 1847 with Brunei whereby the British government would 'use

every means in their power to suppress piracy within the seas, straits, and rivers subject to Bruni'.[36] Consequently, trade along the coast, including the valuable sago trade between Sarawak and Mukah, was severely threatened in the mid-1850s.

The sago trade was forced to be suspended altogether towards the end of the decade owing to internal dissensions. 'Another cause of the destruction of trade', according to St John, 'is the anarchy that prevails in most of the Sultan [of Brunei]'s dependencies to the north and south of the Capital.'[37] Mukah, a Melanau trading post at the mouth of the river of that name, was renowned for its trade in raw sago which was shipped to Kuching, processed into sago flour at the Chinese sago factories, and exported to Singapore thence to the world market. Oya, Matu, Igan, and Bruit in the delta of the Rejang and Bintulu to the north-east of Mukah prospered from this trade. These ports and their sago-rich hinterland were under the nominal sway of Brunei. It was obvious that in Sarawak's commercial interest peace and good administration should be fostered in these territories.

In mid-1855 a political feud between two local leaders disrupted the peace in Mukah.[38] Sarawak and Brunei took sides in the dispute. The situation deteriorated and trade came close to a standstill in 1860.[39] A showdown between the Sarawak forces under Captain John Brooke Brooke, James's nephew, and their local allies, and the opposing faction was inevitable. However, an imminent clash was aborted with the intervention of George Warren Edwardes, the British Governor of Labuan and Acting British Consul-General. Edwardes demanded that the Sarawak forces withdraw, and Captain Brooke Brooke complied under protest.[40] James together with St John, then British Consul-General,[41] hurried to the scene. Edwardes was reprimanded and relieved of his duties. James negotiated a peace settlement between the rival factions which received the approval and support of Brunei.[42]

In August 1861, Sultan Abdul Mumin of Brunei ceded to James the districts from the Rejang to Tanjong Kidurong, a 176-kilometre coast of sago forests, for an annual sum of $4,500.[43] The acquisition of these sago districts assured uninterrupted trade with Kuching, which contributed much to Sarawak's export earnings.[44] 'I look upon the present', James wrote in October 1861 to his younger nephew, Charles Johnson, 'as the turning-point of Sarawak affairs, which have received an impulse from recent events, to be sustained with gradual progress in well-marked prosperity ... [I]

impress upon you all the necessity of exertion to force progress in trade and revenue.'[45]

Cession, Protectorate, and Recognition

James was hopeful that his policy of the possession of territory which he had for the Eastern Archipelago would be adopted by the British government and accordingly offered Sarawak to the Crown. He desired to develop the 'resources of one of the richest and most extensive islands of the globe',[46] and 'to make Borneo a second Java'.[47] Support from the British Government was imperative, otherwise he 'might as well war against France individually, as to attempt all ... without any means'.[48]

However, in later years, he retracted from his original proposal of an 'immediate transfer' as it would affect adversely the native inhabitants by requiring an increase in taxation and undermine 'the popular character of the administration which is at the root of [its] success'.[49] As he elaborated, 'Sarawak is a native Government, and the natives administer it largely, and are always consulted before the imposition of new taxes. I have held it as a principle to keep the taxes as low as possible, and in this respect to suit the Government to the native mind.'[50]

Nevertheless, he still stressed the need for 'permanency' for he considered that 'it is not wise or safe to continue in our present anomalous position'.[51] Accordingly, in August 1858, he presented a memorandum to Sir E. B. Lytton, Secretary for Colonies in Lord Derby's Cabinet, which recommended 'that England should grant a Protectorate, and become the public creditor of Sarawak, with a stipulation that on *certain terms* she might take possession of the country whenever her interests required it'.[52] He added that this 'proposition appears to me to combine all the advantages of possession with none of its liabilities'.[53] However, the British government, then under Lord Derby, was unconvinced, and rejected the Deputation[54] which met him on 30 November 1858.[55]

It was, indeed, a great blow to James's hopes for the future of Sarawak. 'Progress', he was convinced, 'depends upon security, upon which it is dependent.'[56] 'The government of Sarawak was formed upon the support of England,' he wrote in 1861. This had 'failed, but I have nevertheless held by the principle on the knowledge that Sarawak *must have support*'.[57] So he persevered to obtain this support for Sarawak with the governments of the Netherlands, Belgium, France, and Italy, while, at the same time, pursuing the

issue with the British government.[58] All efforts, however, were in vain.[59] Finally, Britain granted recognition of Sarawak as an independent country in 1863.[60] 'Protection was not accorded till 1888, and then it was offered, not asked for, and was granted, not in the interests of Sarawak, but for the safeguarding of Imperial interests, lest some other foreign power should lay its hands on the little State.'[61]

In retrospect James regretted the attitude of his home government towards his policy of establishing British influence in the Eastern Archipelago. 'England', he lamented, 'had ceased to be enterprising, and could not look forward to obtaining great ends by small means perseveringly applied, and that the dependencies are not now regarded as a field of outlay, to yield abundant national returns, but as a source of wasteful expenditure to be wholly cut off.'[62]

Western Enterprise versus Native Welfare

James was not against capital investment to develop Sarawak's resources. His strategy for development was the introduction of 'European Capital, and Chinese labour'.[63] Nevertheless, his priority was that the welfare of the indigenous inhabitants must be safeguarded and not be sacrificed to Western-style economic exploitation.

> I do not desire an undue European development—it is a secondary object according to my views, though I fully recognize the aid which may be derived from foreign wisdom and foreign capital—but the great principle to be clearly kept in sight and expounded in season, is *native development by native advance, aided only by foreign elements so far as may be compatible with native government.*[64]

What he feared was a deluge of Western capitalists and speculators who envisaged instant returns for their investments. In this context he was troubled by the actions of his agent in London, Henry Wise.[65] Wise had successfully attracted the attention of the British government to Sarawak, but James hoped that he had not done so 'by garbling or high-colouring' James's statements concerning Sarawak.[66] Wise desired to float a big company with a large capital outlay for the development of Sarawak, and in the process to make James a rich man.[67] James thought that he had been sufficiently guarded against 'any rash commercial speculation' and cautioned John C. Templer, his friend and confidant, 'not to listen to foolish stories about making money in a hurry'.[68]

James favoured 'a gradual and natural development' which did not unduly disrupt or affect adversely native well-being.[69] He confessed that 'this development of the natives through their own exertions is a hobby of [mine]'.[70] 'I hold by one principle—that no prospect of personal advantage ought to induce me to risk the happiness of the many thousand people here—and risked it would be were a large capital thrown suddenly into this country, under the superintendence of a number of Europeans.'[71] He would lease out the monopoly of antimony, opium, and the diamond-mine for moderate terms to 'responsible parties'. 'The advantages are that the parties derive an immediate return for their money; a small capital is sufficient; it involves no difficulty of legislation; it precludes any mass of Europeans entering the country; it appeals to their pecuniary interest for their good conduct, and it is a project which may be indefinitely extended by slow degrees.'[72]

He considered Wise's 'measures as too rapid and his project too expensive', but admitted initially that their plans for developing Sarawak were not wholly incompatible; 'the difference is a short one, and refers more to time, than any real disagreement of principle'.[73] However, eventually James lost his patience with Wise who continued to pursue a plan incorporating investment on a grand scale. 'His projects are so extended', James complained to Templer, 'and his ambition so vaulting, that I am obliged to check his career, which must in the end fail.'[74]

Viewed from another perspective, James's opposition to Wise's plans displayed the insecurity of the former as to his position in Sarawak. The suggestion of establishing a company which would acquire all his rights in Sarawak and develop the resources of the country was a direct assault on his position as Rajah.[75] He was concerned about his own political ascendancy, based not on personal grounds but on his fear of the exploitation of the native inhabitants by a large commercial enterprise. It was a genuine anxiety on the part of James who foresaw the impending infringement of native well-being by powerful capitalists if the latter were allowed to establish themselves in Sarawak.

James himself refused to be party to any commercial venture for pecuniary aggrandizement was not his ambition. His 'rough and bitter experience' from his abortive *Findlay* venture to China in 1834[76] impressed upon him that 'trade has not only a direct influence, but exercises indirectly the worst drawbacks against success'.[77] The 'success' then was his nobler ambitions of exploration, adventure, and discovery. Consequently, he would not have any

commercial ambition on his part to interfere with his present far more magnanimous undertaking. He assured his mother that 'wealth will never be the upshot of [my] enterprise'[78] that 'so often disgrace[s] men in similar circumstances'.[79]

His paternal concern for the welfare of the natives dictated that very light taxes were imposed.[80] However, he hoped that the country through gradual development of its resources would pay its way. Meanwhile, he sacrificed his inheritance to subsidize the administrative costs in lieu of imposing higher taxes for he was 'deeply impressed with the conviction that the first projector of an enterprise is generally its victim, and that those who follow reap the benefit'.[81] His altruism was a means to attain his aim of ameliorating the conditions of the natives and gradually to raise them in the scale of civilization. Nevertheless, the pecuniary demands of governing a country were heavy and James could not rely indefinitely on his fortune, which was fast diminishing. He had to find other sources of income to sustain the government. Yet he was reluctant to involve himself in commerce even as a means to procure the necessary funds for the administration of government. Apart from his personal abhorrence of commercial dealings, he considered his position as ruler of the country incompatible with the role of a trader. 'You must, at the same time, bear in mind that had I acted on the *principle of a trader*, I should not have held my present position, and in grasping at my own advantage I should very likely lose the moral influence I possess over the people . . . and if I can govern with a moderate fortune, clear of trade, my influence would be very great.'[82] Notwithstanding his personal views of dissociating himself from commerce, he was pragmatic enough to hold the monopoly of antimony as a source of government revenue, though he confessed that it was 'wrong on principle'. Other sources of government revenue were income from the opium, gambling, and arrack farms derived from the Chinese community, and the nominal taxes collected from the natives. The revenue was adequate, although 'not enough to develop the country, but enough to sustain it'.[83]

James's experience with Wise and the dispute with the latter's Eastern Archipelago Company made him reluctant and ever suspicious of capitalist ventures and speculators, and none was allowed access to Sarawak or, even, to the neighbouring territories under nominal Brunei suzerainty.[84] He undoubtedly realized that Sarawak needed Western capital and enterprise to develop its resources.[85] But at the same time he laid out his conditions whereby

capital investment must be introduced gradually and any commercial undertakings should not disrupt or affect native welfare adversely. These prerequisites, in addition to the remoteness of the country and its physical and environmental obstacles, alienated many would-be investors.

Nevertheless, through Templer's influence, the mercantile firm of Messrs R. and J. Henderson established the Borneo Company Limited (BCL) in May 1856 with royalty rights 'to take over and work Mines, Ores, Veins or Seams of all descriptions of Minerals in the Island of Borneo, and to barter or sell the produce of such workings' as well as 'to organise the sago and gutta-percha trade, and finance further governmental commercial schemes'.[86] James viewed the extraction of mineral deposits as a commercial enterprise that would not unduly affect native welfare,[87] and the BCL's involvement in sago and gutta-percha would boost trade in terms of improving shipping services and opening up markets, thereby benefiting native producers and collectors. The mining royalties paid by the BCL were also a welcome addition to the state Treasury.

The Chinese Factor in Economic Development

James believed that the Chinese were invaluable in the development of Sarawak, a belief impressed upon him by the assiduous nature of the Chinese during his initial visit to Raffles's Chinese city-state of Singapore in 1830. Though he made rather uncomplimentary comments on their physical appearance and uncouth habits, he asserted that 'they are industrious and good tempered, cheerful and obliging'.[88] He extolled the future advantages to be gained from the hard-working Chinese. 'The Chinese are so industrious a people that the aspect of a country soon changes wherein they settle; and as they are most desirous to gain a footing here [Sarawak], there can be no doubt of success ultimately in developing the resources of the soil and working the minerals to great advantage.'[89]

James planned to encourage the immigration of the Chinese. Consequently, when the Pemangkat Chinese refugees, fleeing the Sambas wars, sought asylum in Sarawak in 1850, they were well treated.[90] The majority settled in the country as farmers while others joined the Bau Chinese gold workers.[91] Despite the Bau Chinese attack on Kuching in 1857[92] from which James barely escaped with his life, he was sanguine in his faith in the Chinese to

develop the country, and laid out plans for an immigration scheme.

I have some details of the Chinese Immegration [*sic*] scheme—Our funds are not large enough to enter into it upon a large scale and common prudence dictates that we should not throw a mass of Chinese, whose antecedants are far from inspiring confidence, into a peaceful country. I propose therefore making a trial by locating from 500 to 2000 and allowing the plan to grow gradually to its full proportions.[93]

Again, he wrote optimistically of possible Chinese immigration. 'I am going to Singapore in *Rainbow* for change and I hope profitable business, as there are bodies of Chinese Cultivators of Gambier and Pepper wishing to come to Sarawak from Johore where they are oppressed by the native government.'[94] Apparently nothing materialized from his efforts as there was no recorded exodus of Chinese to Sarawak under government auspices during this period. A plausible reason for James's failure to attract Chinese immigrants was that Sarawak then was *terra incognita vis-à-vis* the Straits Settlements and the Malay States.

Aside from their role as miners, farmers, and traders, the Chinese were valuable contributors to government revenue through the opium, *arrack*, and gambling farms. James relied on the counsel of the three Chinese community leaders, Ong Ewe Hai the Hokkien, Chan Ah Kho the Chaoan, and Law Kian Huat the Teochew, in dealing with Chinese matters.[95]

Review of James's Policies

Notwithstanding James's determination and energetic pursuit of his objectives, at the close of his 27-year reign, 'no great progress commercially and financially had been effected, and it was left to his successor to promote the commercial and industrial advancement of the State'.[96] On the other hand, James must be credited with providing a sense of political stability for Sarawak. His poor record in developing the state's economy may be due as much to his belief that it was incompatible for a ruler to be involved in commercial matters as to his personal incompetence and naivety in business affairs.[97] Nevertheless it must be borne in mind that James's turbulent reign was beset with problems and obstacles both on the Bornean coast and at Westminster. Furthermore, the physical obstacles posed by the country's difficult terrain, unfavourable climate, and poor soil which impeded

commercial agriculture, and the paucity of minerals worked against its economic development.

The main economic development of Sarawak was, therefore, left to James's nephew and successor, Charles Johnson Brooke.[98]

Charles, 1868–1917

Charles's Ideas of Governing Native Races

A decade spent as a young cadet in the forested interior of the Dayak homeland influenced Charles's ideas of governing native races. He fervently believed that 'the rules of government are framed with greater care for the interests of the majority who are not Europeans',[99] and that 'slow and gradual development'[100] should be the principles adopted in governing an Eastern land. But, most important of all, the main concern of a government should be 'peace, happiness, and contentment to all and *especially to the natives of the soil*',[101] a principle which he steadfastly upheld throughout his reign.

The essence of Charles's political philosophy was that a government should 'start from things as we find them, putting its veto on what is dangerous or unjust, and letting system and legislation wait upon occasion'.[102] The art of compromise, he believed, was the basic ingredient of his government's success.

On the governance of native races, in particular the turbulent and restive Dayaks, Charles prescribed a balanced dosage of 'kindness and severity'.[103] He displayed an undisguised admiration for the Dayaks' 'vitality, energy and activity', no doubt fostered by his prolonged sojourn among them; he believed them to possess the potential for great achievements in the future.

The Malays continued to enjoy Charles's favour and the *datu* were repeatedly consulted in the formulation of government policies. Charles utilized the Supreme Council and the General Council to tap native opinions and their feelings towards government intentions and, at the same time, to garner their support.[104] Both these institutions, though advisory in capacity, provided useful native reactions to official policies and feedback on the effects of implementing them.[105] A case in point was the issue of the abolition of slavery when Charles continually sought the advice and guidance of the two Councils in his quest to do away with this established native custom; he succeeded in doing so without any undue repercussions.[106]

Charles's Attitude towards the Chinese

Charles shared his uncle's admiration for the Chinese as well as his belief in the practical role they would play in the economic development of Sarawak, notwithstanding the uprising of 1857.[107] Writing in the mid-1860s, Charles displayed an unconventional appreciation of the Chinese which would seem outrageous in Victorian political circles. '[The] Chinese ... are second to no other in importance in the Eastern seas ... [and] as a race, are an excellent set of fellows, and a poor show would these Eastern countries make without their energetic presence.'[108] He confessed that he would 'as soon deal with a Chinese merchant in the East as an European one'.[109] He reminded his English brethren that 'intellectually, the Chinese are our equals, are physically as strong, and I believe, as brave; with surprising industry, energy, and activity in commercial enterprises',[110] and he claimed 'the respectable class of Chinese to be equal in honesty and integrity to the white men'.[111]

In their management, Charles considered the Chinese 'nearly as troublesome a people to govern as Europeans, certainly not more so', but who 'are a people specially amenable to justice, and are happier under a stringent than a lenient system'.[112] He warned that any 'bullying or harshness' would be reciprocated by rebellion.[113] An abstract from a letter of reprimand addressed to his Superintendent of Police in 1896 following a complaint from a senior Chinese community leader revealed Charles's views of the importance of the Chinese and in handling them correctly.

> They are the capitalists that we have most to depend on, and a certain amount of consideration and respect should always be paid to them. They may be sometimes a little difficult to manage, but they are generally ready to show respect and willingness to abide by orders, and assist whatever may be going in works of charity and liberality when treated well. They are always peculiarly sensitive to justice.[114]

Charles accomplished his uncle's plan of inducing Chinese immigrants to open the vast uncultivated land of the country and to create settled farming communities. His faith in the Chinese as the archetype peasant agriculturalist motivated him to invite them to Sarawak for agricultural pursuits with generous terms. He was rewarded for his foresight when gambier and pepper cultivated by the Chinese featured among Sarawak's export earnings during the 1880s and 1890s. However, Charles's vision of the Lower Rejang inhabited by a Chinese farming population producing rice was only partially realized at the turn of the century.

Charles as Rajah

As Rajah of Sarawak, Charles was even more paternalistic than his uncle. The interests of the indigenous people were protected from exploitation and oppression by foreigners, particularly by European speculators. Accessibility to Charles himself and to his European officers was a safeguard afforded the natives from oppression by their own chiefs. Laws were enacted to shield the natives from swindling by the more worldly Chinese merchants and traders. Bona fide European entrepreneurs were readily encouraged with liberal and generous terms to invest in the country. However, European capitalists of the speculative breed were barred from the country. Charles was deeply concerned that the natives should not, in any circumstances, part with their land, which he described as their '*Daging Darah*, flesh and blood ... the source of their self existence, their *herta pesaka* [heritage] which if once lost no amount of money could ever recover'.[115] At the height of the rubber boom in 1910, Charles forbade by law his subjects from selling their rubber lands to European firms or even to individuals.

Trade and agriculture, especially the latter, were to be the means of improving the livelihood of the native peoples. The promotion and expansion of commerce, especially the trade in jungle produce, directly benefited the Dayaks and other native collectors. Besides the contributions of trade to native well-being, Charles had a more permanent and long-term solution for improving the livelihood and material comforts of his native subjects. He sought to transform Sarawak's native swidden subsistence cultivators into settled farmers producing a mixture of food and cash crops. Permanent agriculture which ensured self-sufficiency in food crops, namely rice, and also produced marketable crops for cash, was to Charles the ideal solution for a prosperous livelihood for the native peoples. However, the improvement of the welfare of the indigenous peoples was to be realized not by sudden and radical means from without but through a gradual process by which slow osmosis-like changes were introduced from within.[116]

Charles was the quintessential autocrat who perfected the art of personalized rule. He literally had his hand in every aspect of government, even the routine of daily administration: from the formulation of basic policy to requisitioning stationery for his government offices. Charles obviously understood the native psyche for the need of a personalized ruler rather than an impersonal bureaucratic system. 'Personal rule is what the Asiatic respects and understands. He is not attuned to bureaucracy or government by a

machine, that, however efficient, cannot be sympathetic to circumstances. He wants government from a man who is human like himself and can understand his frailties. Personal rule means that ruler and ruled can meet on equal terms.'[117]

Charles did not possess either the charisma or the dashing personality of his uncle, James, but what he lacked in personal charm was compensated for by his insatiably energetic presence in every corner of his realm. His fatherly concern and invariable presence endeared him to his multiethnic subjects.

With the protection of native interest and the improvement of their welfare as his ultimate objectives, Charles placed Sarawak on a gradual but steady road of economic development. Invariably, as in all other aspects, Charles was personally and directly involved at every stage of this process and took setbacks and failures as personal failings. His programme of economic development centred on the promotion and expansion of trade and commerce, the exploitation of the various mineral resources, his persevering efforts in making agriculture the mainstay of the economy, a liberal though paternalistic land policy, and the rudimentary beginnings of a basic infrastructure.

Economic Policies of Charles: Continuity and Expansion

Promotion and Expansion of Trade

Charles Brooke continued his uncle's policy of promoting and expanding the practice of free trade. During the relatively more peaceful time of his reign, trade flourished and its benefits were felt not only on the coast but also in the interior.

The invaluable sago trade brought prosperity to the Melanau sago producers, and to the Chinese merchants of Kuching who undertook the processing of raw sago and its export to Singapore and the world market. The trade in jungle produce, a long-established and important component of Sarawak's trade, experienced a boom in the last quarter of the nineteenth century. The Dayaks, industrious and expert collectors of these jungle products, and other natives of the interior, like the Kayans and Kenyahs, reaped the benefits of their labour.

By the 1870s, coastal raiding, which had been an obstacle to trade during James's days, had waned and no longer posed a threat to commerce. However, the unsettling conditions in the interior of the country remained an obstacle to trade. Dayak head-hunting was a deterrent to both traders and travellers. Charles, though sympathetic to its practitioners,[118] was determined that this age-old

custom of decapitation had to be completely eradicated in order to afford safety and security to trading activities throughout the country. He was convinced that 'the only way of doing this effectually was by a strong hand and steady perseverance. An olive branch held in one hand, and broomstick in the other, was the method of rhyme and reason with such simple-minded beings.'[119]

The 'broomstick' that he wielded was indeed a formidable one. In his practical tone he explained that

> there is no cure but burning them out of house and home—dreadful as this may appear ... the burning down of a village, loss of goods, old relics,—such as heads, arms, and jars,—and putting the inhabitants, male and female, to excessive inconvenience—all this fills them with fear, and makes them think of the consequences of taking the heads of strangers.[120]

Following the gradual success of this policy from the 1880s onwards, Chinese traders began to venture into the outlying and interior districts in the pursuit of commercial opportunities.

There were, to be sure, certain restraints on Chinese merchants and traders lest their more sophisticated business skills tempt them to take advantage of the natives. Charles instituted safeguards like the non-residence rule in native longhouses for Chinese boat traders (which was a finable offence for both trader and native headman) and the monthly renewal of trading licences. A vigilant watch was also kept on unscrupulous bazaar Chinese shopkeepers who not uncommonly swindled the unsuspecting native with fraudulent weights and measures and other forms of trickery.[121]

The flourishing trade of Sarawak impressed upon Charles the need to consider the formation of a mercantile committee to oversee its development. As a result the Sarawak Chamber of Commerce was instituted in early 1873.[122] Charles entrusted the Chamber with the task of forming a shipping company to facilitate the carrying trade between Sarawak and Singapore. This was successfully accomplished in 1875.

Charles adopted James's forward policy in promoting and expanding trade. Circumstances presented Charles with the opportunities to annex territories under nominal Brunei suzerainty, consequently extending considerably the borders of the Raj (see Map 1.1). By the close of the first decade of the twentieth century, the Baram, the Trusan, the Limbang, and the Lawas came under Charles's rule at the expense of a weakened Brunei Sultanate.[123] These territorial acquisitions afforded new sources of jungle produce, which increased the trade in these products and improved the lot of native collectors.

Unlike James, who was convinced that Sarawak's survival was crucially dependent on a protective power, Charles happily embarked on an independent road with commendable success. Towards the last decade of the nineteenth century Charles confidently pronounced that Sarawak stood 'upon a surer and more solid basis than ever before' despite 'being left to work out the problem of government and development of commerce for ourselves ... to paddle our own canoe, with but scant assistance from without'.[124] Protectorate status, however, was accorded Sarawak by Britain in 1888, not so much for the country's sake but more in line with imperial purposes.[125]

Exploitation of Mineral Resources

Charles, like James, had hoped that the mineral resources of Sarawak would be the country's fame and fortune, or, at the least, its salvation. Antimony ore had attracted James to Sarawak in the first place. The rich auriferous district of Upper Sarawak centring around Bau seemed to promise greater wealth than had hitherto been realized by the rather primitive methods of the Chinese gold workers. The discovery of other minerals like cinnabar, diamonds, silver, and coal gave further evidence of the potential mineral richness of the country. None of these discoveries ever lived up to its promise; nevertheless Charles was undaunted and persevered in the hope that in the not-too-distant future minerals would contribute substantially to the state coffers. The prospecting and exploitation of minerals, with the exception of gold, had been entrusted to the BCL by James. Charles maintained this arrangement and at the same time allowed the Chinese to continue their gold workings.

In the case of coal, the BCL abandoned its efforts at Simunjan in the Middle Sadong so that from 1873 onwards the government undertook its exploitation. Despite the numerous favourable and encouraging reports from experienced prospectors of the promise of high-grade coal, the Silantek fields in the Batang Lupar was a great disappointment to Charles.[126] Several efforts to encourage the opening of Silantek, including grants with generous terms, were in vain.[127] An attempt by Charles himself to float a company for this purpose proved abortive for want of investors.[128] Nevertheless, in 1888 Charles purchased the coal-mines at Muara Damit in Brunei Bay.[129] Brooketon, as it was then named, turned out to be a financial nightmare. It is curious to note that despite his parsimonious nature Charles maintained both the Simunjan and

Brooketon mines at great financial loss. Apparently Charles's pragmatism was overruled by his optimism when it came to coal. However, it may not be as surprising as it appeared. Charles believed in the strategic importance of coal, viewing Sarawak as a possible coaling station for the Royal Navy.[130] He also shared James's optimism that minerals, like coal and gold, would be the answer to the country's prosperity. The financial setbacks of the collieries were tolerated while he patiently waited for their long-term returns. It was, however, neither coal nor gold but petroleum that fulfilled Charles's hopes of prosperity.

Mineral oil was reported as early as 1874 but apparently no serious exploration was undertaken until Charles Hose, a retired Brooke officer, convinced Charles of the potential of this 'earth oil'. The Anglo-Saxon Petroleum Company (ASPC), a subsidiary of Royal Dutch Shell, was granted a prospecting licence, and was rewarded for its efforts when it successfully spudded the first oil well in Miri in 1910.

Agriculture as the Mainstay of the Economy

Charles mapped out strategies to make agriculture the economic mainstay of the country, including the encouragement of settled farming, the introduction of new crops, a liberal land policy and other incentives to cultivators and investors, the promotion of the immigration of Chinese peasant farmers, and invitations with generous investment terms to European entrepreneurs and planters.

Charles continually reminded native leaders, and through them the general population, that 'the produce of the soil was what really made a country and people rich and prosperous'[131] and that 'cultivated products ... more so than jungle produce which, after a few years might become exhausted ... [were] the *mudal* [capital] of the country'.[132] 'We want population to turn our waste land into shape and create bustle and industry. I never saw the country as still as it is now, and this does not agree with me. I want to see ... the jungle falling right and left and people scattered over what are now lonely wastes and turning them into cultivated lands.'[133] Notwithstanding his encouragement of trade and commercial activities, Charles declared that he would 'rather see many small holdings, consisting of moderate sized plantations of sago and cocoanut trees, from which they [the native peoples] could obtain a regular livelihood, as well as from paddy farms, around neatly kept and well-built houses'.[134]

Brooke officers were instructed to report on the state of agricultural progress in their respective districts.[135] Furthermore, specific assignments pertaining to agricultural matters were carried out and, like all other official business, these were reported directly to Charles himself.[136] If encouragement and persuasion were deemed inadequate, other forms of inducement, such as competitions with cash prizes, were introduced to ensure the cultivation of certain desired crops.[137] More advanced farming techniques, particularly of settled agriculture, were also promoted. Charles personally attempted to introduce ploughing to the Dayaks of Skrang, but apparently with little success.[138]

In his plan to introduce new crops, Charles introduced a number of experimental farms to test the suitability and viability of these crops and the attendant problems encountered. He had no qualms in investing quite substantially in these gardens which in some cases ended in disappointment. His sincerity and altruism were clearly evident for 'his rule had been to suffer moderate losses himself rather than that strangers should come and embark their limited and valuable capital on untried and unsafe schemes'.[139] These experimental plantations were, in fact, to be 'an inducement to many to follow this example ... [and] people would gain experience from the experiments now being undertaken by the Government'.[140] Charles, in fact, brought to maturity a concept of James and his friend and benefactor, Miss (later Baroness) Angela Burdett Coutts, the concept of the experimental farm as a means of introducing new cultures to the native population.[141]

Several government experimental gardens were maintained throughout the country; the most celebrated example was that on Gunong Matang, about 16 kilometres from Kuching. Charles himself undertook the supervision of the clearing of the slopes of Matang for coffee planting. Brooke officers in the outstations were expected to maintain plots of land for botanical trials, not unlike the major government experimental gardens but smaller in scale and scope.

A multitude of crops, both foreign and indigenous to the country, were at one time or another grown in the government farms with varying success: coffee, tea, gambier, pepper, cocoa, tobacco, cotton, oil palm, sisal, Brazilian Para rubber, and the rearing of silkworms. Various native products of the jungle, like gutta, *jelutong*, resins, and plantain, were also nurtured in experimental gardens.

The rearing of silkworms to weave silk was initiated upon the suggestion of Odoardo Beccari, the renowned Italian botanist who visited Sarawak for scientific study in the mid-1860s. It was undertaken at Simanggang, Sibu, and Quop Estate.[142] Charles had a particular interest in its progress as portrayed in his journal entries.[143] However, this experiment proved abortive.[144] Although no figures are available, it is unlikely that the silkworm project was as great a financial loss as the tobacco failure at Lundu which suffered a $60,000 deficit,[145] or the disappointing coffee plantations at Matang and Satap which had cost Charles $176,000 by 1901.[146]

To compensate for these failures successes were fortunately evident in gambier and pepper, and the much celebrated species of Para rubber (*Hevea braziliensis*). In response to Charles's repeated invitation,[147] Chinese entrepreneurs successfully planted gambier and pepper; by the late 1870s gambier was being exported and the next decade witnessed the beginnings of Sarawak's profitable pepper industry. Para rubber seeds were nurtured in government nurseries for the first time in 1908. Charles then commissioned the Chinese merchants who, with their commercial network of contacts throughout the country, undertook the sale of these young rubber saplings to the indigenous people. Later Brooke officers in the outstations also sold rubber plants in their respective districts.

Wet-rice cultivation was continually promoted among the Dayaks in the hope that they would give up their swidden methods and convert to settled farming. High quality *padi* seedlings were entrusted to the Chinese for nurturing in nurseries and then sold to the native farmers.[148] However, unlike rubber, *padi* was not very successful despite all the efforts and encouragement of the government. Rice remained a major import item throughout the Brooke period.

Chinese Immigration into the Rejang

The lack of success in promoting wet-rice cultivation among the natives prompted Charles to propose the immigration of Chinese peasant families who would undertake to cultivate rice fields in the Lower Rejang area.[149] The organization of the immigration of Chinese from Singapore had been tried by James but apparently the scheme did not materialize. Events in China at the turn of the century afforded Charles the opportunity to contract an agreement with a Foochow Methodist, Wong Nai Siong, from Fukien Province.[150] The political upheaval in China after the collapse of the 'Hundred Days' reform movement (1898), followed by the Boxer Uprising (1899–1900), which was particularly anti-foreign

and anti-Christian in tone, was unsettling if not precarious for Chinese converts. Wong and his fellow Foochow Methodists decided to emigrate to Sarawak; 'New Foochow' was thus created around present-day Sibu. The initial years were hard on the pioneers but their perseverance saw them through the difficult period. Charles, who had envisaged an ample rice supply from the Foochow farms, was decidedly disappointed when, after repeated abortive attempts at *padi* cultivation, the Foochows turned to rubber for their salvation. Besides the Foochows, Charles also had arrangements with a Cantonese company which successfully settled a group of Cantonese peasant farmers at Sungei Lanang, several kilometres upstream from Sibu.[151] Hakka and Henghua farmers came on their own without Brooke government support.[152] These industrious Chinese immigrants converted the Lower Rejang from Sibu to as far upriver as Kanowit into an area of settled farming communities where food and cash crops, mainly smallholder Para rubber plantations, dotted the landscape.

A Liberal Land Policy

In his plans to promote agriculture, Charles offered a rather liberal land policy whereby European planters were given the freedom 'to choose their own land, in any portion of the territory not already occupied by Chinese gambier plantations, or by Dyak fruit gardens'.[153] However, his generosity was limited; outright unconditional alienation was prohibited. 'All lands granted whether upon lease or in Fee simple, are liable to revert to the State, in the event of one-fourth not being cleared and brought under cultivation, or otherwise made use of for pasturage, or building purposes within 10 years of the period of possession.'[154] Charles's aversion to speculators who might take advantage of his land grants was primarily the reason for the insertion of the above clause to James's original Land Law of 1863. Bona fide planters who could contribute to the agricultural development of the country were most welcome, *but not* those with 'soft and smiling countenances ... who carry the products out of the country to enrich shareholders'.[155] A land policy of lease and conditional ownership was designed to safeguard native interest against 'speculators who will become the masters and owners while they themselves, the people of the soil, will be thrown aside and become coolies and outcasts'.[156] Charles's cautious land policy was perhaps the reason so few European planters, either individuals or corporations, took up the offer to invest in Sarawak.

European Capitalist Investment

Like James before him, Charles believed that European capital investment was needed to develop Sarawak, but even more so than his uncle, he was particularly mistrustful of big commercial companies.[157] In fact Charles exhibited downright contempt of large capitalist enterprises. 'If a new and moderately-prosperous possession is to be ruined, the quickest way to do it is to grant concessions to City [of London] companies, which are often guilty of the most glaring irregularities, and, under the cloak of civilisation and religion, will prove black to be white whenever it suits their purpose.'[158]

To Charles's thinking, large capitalist and chartered companies stood against all the principles that he himself upheld. To ensure native well-being Charles forbade his subjects from parting with their land, instituted a land policy calculated to ban bogus planters and investors, and introduced a vigilant screening of would-be concessionaires.[159] He also constituted a London-based advisory committee to act as a watchdog against predatory incursions from without.

The Sarawak State Advisory Council was established in November 1912 comprising prominent retired Brooke officers residing in Britain, 'to stand as trustees, to handle any question that might turn up, and also be the responsible parties to manage any money that might be invested in the funds for the benefit of this country and Government'.[160] In addition to being financial adviser and trustee, the Council 'would ensure stability in negotiating with European parties and concerns' as well as act as 'a referee to the Eastern Raj in all affairs taking place outside of Sarawak'.[161] Bertram, the second son of Charles, presided at the Council's office in Westminster.

Charles was confident that there 'was not much fear of aspiring capitalists doing harm so long as he was alive', but he was convinced that 'such harm might arise in the future after his death'.[162] Therefore, in his 'Political Will', made in 1913, he elevated Bertram 'to hold a position of authority in the Raj second only to that of my eldest Son Vyner'.

> [I]t is my firm belief that it will require both of them working hand and heart together to keep the edifice on a firm base more especially in these times when eager speculators are always seeking for some new place to exploit in a money making sense when the white man comes to the fore and the dark coloured is thrust to the wall and when capital rules and justice ceases, whereas the main consideration should be an honest and upright

protection afforded to all races alike and particularly to the weaker ones.[163]

Charles was not against capitalist investors per se but those of the speculative and mercenary kind who exploited natives indiscriminately for their own financial gain. Several examples could be cited of Charles welcoming genuine capitalist investments. He was partial to the BCL which, according to him, 'has shown a solid and stolid example to other traders, and formed a basis for mercantile operations' as well as to its mining exploits which were undoubtedly invaluable to the country.[164] Another celebrated example was his relations with the ASPC which was afforded ample assistance in its operations. Both these large European capitalist concerns undoubtedly played according to Charles's rules: their activities neither exploited nor disrupted the indigenous inhabitants of the country and they largely relied on immigrant indentured Chinese labour and expatriate European specialists. In the case of the BCL, its trading and commercial business was mainly transacted with the large Chinese merchant houses and not with native producers.

The Beginnings of Infrastructure Development

There was hardly any infrastructural development during the reign of James. The only means of inland communication in the country when Charles became Rajah was by river. Slow as the rivers might be, and even dangerous occasionally, these natural waterways had been the sole means of transport and communication for centuries past, and still are in the remote interior.

Charles initiated road construction in and around Kuching. Metalled roads were built and an all-weather road linked the capital to Bau in the mineral-rich district of Upper Sarawak.

A singular achievement of Charles in the development of land transport was a railway that ran 16 kilometres southward from Kuching. Ironically, Charles, who was a keen horseman and dreaded motor cars, was enthusiastic for a railroad. As in all other matters, he took personal charge at every step of its development. By 1916 the tracks had reached the tenth-mile. He would have wished that this rail-line would someday connect Kuching to his favourite outstation of Simanggang, about 160 kilometres away, but it was not to be the case.[165]

The provision of a clean and regular water supply to Kuching was an important project initiated by Charles who 'considered a good water supply of greater value than a gold mine'.[166] The result was the Matang Waterworks that supplied Kuching in the early

1900s with fresh piped water from a mountain range 16 kilometres away.

Several public buildings were also constructed in Kuching under his watchful eye, if not under his direct personal supervision.[167] Numerous government offices, a fort and barracks for the Rangers,[168] police quarters, houses for European Brooke officers, two large hospitals, a dry dock, bathhouses, recreation grounds, and a museum. The museum, completed in 1891, was a showcase of the exotic fauna and flora of the country as well as the material cultures of its multiethnic inhabitants.[169] A government lay school at Kuching provided schooling for all ethnic groups, while several kampong (village) schools catered for Malay children.[170]

Government buildings in the outstations resembled to a certain extent their counterparts in the capital, though of a smaller scale and of less sophistication. The major outstations boasted a fort which was the symbol of Brooke authority and served as a focal point around which the entire district revolved. It was invariably built on a strategic location possessing a commanding position of the river traffic. The bazaar, where Chinese shophouses congregated, was either located adjacent to the fort itself or a stone's throw away.

Coastal and internal shipping was facilitated by six government steamers and supplemented by several smaller Chinese and native craft. The Singapore and Sarawak Steamship Company provided cargo and passengers for the Sarawak–Singapore traffic. At the turn of the century, telephone and telegraphic communications were established throughout the major government stations in the country. In 1916, just a year before Charles's death, wireless telegraphy connected the various outstations with Kuching, which in turn was linked to Singapore and to the world. A contemporary remarked that it 'gave a tremendous sense of security'.[171]

Review of Charles's Policies

Charles, who believed that Sarawak could survive on its own without any protective power from without, proved his uncle's apprehensions and anxieties about the country's future to be unfounded. The country's flourishing trade and its increasing revenue were testimonies of the healthy state of its economy. But far more important than economic achievements to Charles and his uncle was the satisfactory state of well-being and happiness of their native subjects.[172] This aspect of the native condition was alluded to by an impartial observer who had spent two months in the country in 1905. 'The impression of the country which I carry away

with me is that of *a land full of contentment and prosperity*', undoubtedly a fitting tribute to Charles's accomplishments.[173]

This state of 'contentment and prosperity' was to be continually fostered; accordingly Charles instructed both Vyner and Bertram, the heirs to the Raj, 'to continue the regular development of the material resources of the State and to promote to the utmost of their power the prosperity and happiness and the moral and material welfare of the inhabitants'.[174]

Vyner, 1917–1941

Vyner and His Government

Vyner was very different from his father in his style and management of government. In comparison to Rajah Charles, Vyner may appear to have been a lightweight in his attention, and even dedication, to the responsibilities of high office. He was by nature shy, unpretentious, with an aversion to pomp and ceremony. His wife, the Ranee Sylvia, referred to him as a 'shy recluse' who was extremely uncomfortable on formal occasions.[175] He was also straightforward in manners, good-natured, and unflamboyant, despite his status and position.[176]

In contrast to Charles, Vyner was neither conscientious nor concerned about the day-to-day conduct of government. He particularly disliked any form of paperwork. Illustrative of his informality in conducting the business of government, a story was told that

> over a drink at the [Sarawak] Club, he [Vyner] had agreed that a bridge should be built farther up across the river, [and] he had told his State Engineer to go ahead. The latter had asked for something in writing, so as to satisfy the Treasurer and Auditor, whereupon the Rajah had produced a crumpled envelope from his pocket and scribbled on it: 'Go ahead and build a bridge across the river. C. V. Brooke, Rajah'.[177]

The general policy of government was more important to him than the practical details of administration, much of which was left to his officers.

The joint rule of Vyner and his brother, Bertram, which was intended to strengthen the Brooke Raj, did not foster a vigorous and dynamic form of government. Instead, Vyner's prolonged absence from Sarawak of periods of up to six months in the year and Bertram's disinclination to upstage his brother when administering the government resulted in a pervading state of stagnation.[178] Initiative was obviously lacking at the top, where it was

most needed in an autocracy, and none, understandably, was forthcoming from the outstations. This absence of initiative was graphically depicted by A. J. N. Richards, who joined the Sarawak Civil Service as a cadet in 1938. 'No one seems bold enough to start anything. Things are discussed and somebody collects information, draws up a report & makes recommendations—and then its "read with interest", filed—and probably forgotten.'[179]

Vyner's European officers were grouped into two camps, divided geographically as well as ideologically. On the one hand, there were the old, experienced, and practical-minded District Officers and Divisional Residents based in the outstations who prided themselves as the protectors of native interests and the standard-bearers of the Brooke tradition. The decentralized nature of the administration, due to geographical factors as well as the lack of direction from central government, enabled these 'Sarawak' officers to wield substantial power over the native population. On the other hand, there were the bureaucrats in Kuching who were generally much younger and better educated; the majority of them, however, possessed either little or no practical outstation experience. These Kuching-based officers were the champions of the centralization and bureaucratization of the administration. A showdown was inevitable between the two factions.

Consistent with his nature of distancing himself from the daily work of government and because of the increasing workload of an expanding bureaucracy, Vyner, in 1923, created the office of Chief Secretary to whom he 'delegated many responsibilities previously discharged' by himself.[180] He was, however, ambivalent towards the Committee of Administration; he first abolished it in 1924, then reconstituted it as a permanent body in the following year, but rendered it dormant until 1934. From then onwards the Committee, dominated by senior officers, functioned as an executive decision-making body and generally assumed control of the day-to-day running of the government. And, for a brief period in the late 1920s, it was Vyner's enigmatic private secretary, G. T. M. MacBryan, who ruled the Raj.[181] Again, in the late 1930s, Anthony Brooke, Vyner's nephew and one-time heir apparent, held the reins of power.

The delegation of authority did not work well for Vyner. The opposition of the outstation administrators against the Kuching bureaucrats, personified in the Chief Secretary, nullified the latter's function in effecting greater efficiency in the government. MacBryan was not a popular figure, and neither was Anthony. The

Committee of Administration took advantage of Vyner's lack of interest in matters of daily administration and accumulated power to itself. This eventually led to a clash with Anthony who wanted to restore the *status quo* of the traditional Brooke brand of government. The inevitable clash between the Kuching bureaucrats and the outstation administrators came to a head in the so-called 'Sarawak Crisis' of 1939. The bureaucrats represented in the Committee of Administration were defeated in the showdown and consequently resigned *en bloc*.[182]

Vyner's Views on the Economic Development of Sarawak

In contrast to his predecessors who set down their ideas in writing, Vyner left very little on his philosophy of government. Perhaps his reluctance to commit his ideas to paper was influenced by his belief in 'the danger of assuming that any hard-and-fast rules can be laid down and followed',[183] instead of relying on pragmatism in attending to the affairs of government. Like Charles, he was partial towards natives; his views undoubtedly coloured by the two decades he had spent as an officer in his father's service. He emphasized the importance of possessing empathy—the ability to see issues from the viewpoint of the other party—in the governing of native races.

> The views of the other party alter according to conditions and circumstances, and these alterations must be followed with sympathy and understanding, if harmony is to be achieved. Similarly with the Native viewpoint. Trouble is bound to occur if the ruling power is lacking in adaptability, because it must be remembered that the demands of successive Asiatic generations alter mainly on account of changes brought about by the increasing Europeanization of their environment.[184]

Vyner was no radical, and happily continued his father's conservative approach to economic development: an unhurried and cautious pace of change primarily aimed at improving native welfare.[185] Any new proposal or programme was subjected to the litmus test of the effects it might have on native welfare, and, if deemed to be adverse, was discarded.

In fact, Vyner was more conservative than his father, particularly towards Western capitalist enterprise and the issue of Chinese immigration. He was not at all encouraging towards existing European companies, including the long-established BCL, and Chinese immigration was subjected to more vigilant control and stricter regulation. However, his seemingly cautious approach

towards the general economic development of Sarawak had to be seen, in part, in the light of the apparent uncertainties and instability of the world economic situation which had a direct impact on Sarawak's economic well-being. No longer was Sarawak isolated nor immune from these adverse international economic events.

Nevertheless, Vyner might have harboured doubts as to the rather slow rate of progress that he had imposed on the country, and perhaps realized that the world was changing too fast for Sarawak to keep pace. These anxieties were revealed in his speech to the General Council in April 1937.

> Owing to a natural process of events Sarawak is losing much of her former isolation, and it is necessary for us to face this fact, and to adjust our ideas accordingly.... If we are to improve our standards of living we must accept the fact of increasing material progress and do our best to adapt ourselves to the changed conditions which this progress brings about. This cannot be done by keeping our eyes shut to the developments that are taking place all around us.[186]

Economic Policies of Vyner: Consolidation and Improvement

Vyner continued to promote agriculture, both subsistence and commercial, in his belief that the future of the people and the country was dependent on the fruits of the land. Consequently the quality of agricultural exports and their competitiveness were improved in the increasingly discerning world market. Vyner's government had to face a food crisis (1919–21), the world-wide trade Depression (1929–31), and rubber restrictions (1934–41). It emerged relatively unscarred. Vyner attended to forest conservation to protect its exploitation by the general practice of native swidden farming. The land policy was improved and implemented. With the exception of the Miri oilfields, the mining industry entered its twilight years. Infrastructure development progressed steadily.

Agriculture as the Backbone of the Economy

Vyner promoted the cultivation of the land to ensure self-sufficiency in food production and to improve the livelihood of the people through the sale of their agricultural products.

Self-sufficiency in food production, in particular of rice, had been constantly stressed by the government from as early as the 1870s,[187] but had generally gone unheeded as rice imports were

relatively affordable. However, the food crisis of 1919–21 reduced drastically the amount of rice and other food imports.[188] The impact of shortages, notably of rice, was particularly grave among the Chinese agricultural communities in the Rejang who had neglected their rice fields for rubber gardens, but was less so on the indigenous population who had generally always been subsistence farmers, though some also cultivated cash crops. The lessons of the food crisis and another threatened rice shortage in the mid-1920s[189] strengthened Vyner's resolve that a concerted programme aimed at self-sufficiency in rice production was urgently needed.

A Department of Agriculture was set up in 1924[190] incorporating a mycology section, and an Agricultural Improvement Fund was established.[191] The Department's initial attention was focused on attaining the objective of self-sufficiency in rice. The idea of establishing rice-farming communities of experienced cultivators in order to capitalize on the demonstration effect was first suggested in the early 1870s.[192] This idea was incorporated in the establishment of *padi* reservations or colonies of Javanese, Bugis, and Japanese farmers.[193] The training of *padi* inspectors was initiated, and a *padi* demonstration farm was established.[194] Vyner at the same time discouraged people from being too dependent on rice and persuaded them 'that there are other foods which support existence besides rice and ... in many countries people depend upon other nutrients'.[195]

Vyner's general agricultural policy stressed the improvement of the quality of crops, the constant supervision of native farms by agricultural field officers, the establishment of agricultural stations as demonstration farms, the encouragement of the idea of school gardens where youngsters were instructed as part of the curriculum, and the improvement and maintenance of the government dairy farm.[196]

Vyner, like his predecessor, favoured smallholders rather than large estates. He maintained that 'preferential treatment' was accorded 'to the small holder in order to avoid the alienation of large areas of land and thus cause hardship to the natives of the State'.[197] The protection of native interest featured prominently in his rationalization of promoting smallholdings, as emphasized in a speech to the General Council in 1927.

It is not generally appreciated that the State [of Sarawak] is intersected with rivers and streams and the population is very widely diffused. These two factors render it difficult to find large and accessible areas, such as are required by concessionaires, without interference with the rights of the

natives and other occupiers of the land. Coupled with this is the fact that the many years' experience has proved that the division of available land among small holders, who are true colonists, yields a prosperous, contented and peaceful population which readily adapts itself to local conditions without friction and the consequent necessity of introducing special legislation; and those who cultivate the soil reap the full benefit of their labours and are not merely wage slaves. Thus, instead of large areas of land being withheld from development for a period of years, as is generally the case when it is leased to capitalists, it is developed as it is taken up.[198]

Throughout Vyner's reign there were no more than six large commercial estates operating in Sarawak.

Vyner shared his father's sentiments regarding rubber, possessing little faith in its future because of price fluctuations. He openly and persistently discouraged investment in rubber, and insisted repeatedly that the people should devote their energies to the cultivation of *padi*, sago, pepper, and coconut. Nevertheless, he realized the attraction rubber possessed during its boom years to both Chinese and native farmers alike. He, therefore, directed the Department of Agriculture to focus on the improvement of the planting of rubber and its production.[199]

The native method of swidden farming was also seriously questioned. A joint memorandum from the Departments of Land, Forests, and Agriculture 'suggesting that some definite steps should be taken to discourage this pernicious system of farming' was forwarded to Vyner in April 1931.[200] He agreed that steps should be taken to reduce such native forms of farming but, in characteristic Brooke manner, insisted that such measures should be gradually applied.

The Improvement of Sarawak's Exports

A Department of Trade was instituted in late 1923 with the aim of promoting and developing 'every branch of trade in the State, both Exports and Imports'.[201] In conjunction with this Department was a Board of Trade which was specifically commissioned to undertake the improvement of the quality of the country's exports. Vyner invited the representatives of the leading commercial and trading establishments of the country to serve on the Board.[202]

Notwithstanding his discouragement of rubber planting, Vyner adapted to the reality of its popularity by forming a Rubber Exports Improvement Board which came under the direction of the Board of Trade. The objective of this Board, set up in 1926, was to upgrade the quality of Sarawak's rubber exports and raise

their demand and price in the world market.[203] Pepper gardeners also enjoyed benefits from the assistance rendered by the Board of Trade through the Pepper Improvement Scheme.

Countering the Depression, 1929–1931

The world-wide Depression undoubtedly affected Sarawak when commodity prices, particularly that of rubber, fell drastically. The country's trade figures from 1930 onwards showed a downward trend when the effects of the Depression began to be felt.[204] During these lean years, Vyner appointed a Finance Committee to initiate appropriate measures to counter the Depression. The Committee, formed in 1931, recommended cut-backs in government expenditure. The closure of the Simunjan colliery and the railway were among the major economies that were carried out.[205]

The continual discouragement of large-scale rubber planting, the predominance of smallholdings, strict control of immigration, the channelling of the unemployed to public works, and the prudent reduction of public expenditure, combined to soften the effects of the Depression. 'I am glad to think', Vyner announced to the General Council of 1934, 'that the general impoverishment has been less felt in Sarawak than elsewhere and that now we are able to look forward with some confidence to renewed prosperity.'[206]

Rubber Restriction

The rubber slump of 1920–2 led to the implementation of rubber restriction known as the Stevenson Scheme (1922–8) in which Sarawak participated. This scheme was not effective as some rubber-producing countries refused to join, and instead flooded the market with their rubber. The Depression confirmed its failure.

Lessons learned from the Stevenson Scheme contributed to the formulation of a more stringent programme which managed to encompass all producer countries, namely, the International Rubber Regulation Agreement of 1934. Sarawak as a signatory, implemented restriction in June that year.[207] Vyner enacted legislation to ensure that the guidelines of the Agreement were faithfully adhered to. 'Order No. R–3 (Rubber Restriction) 1934', and 'Order No. R–4 (Rubber Dealers and Exporters) 1934', were enacted and immediately put into effect.[208]

But after two years of tapping holidays, the scheme had not been wholly effective and a far stricter method of regulation was eventually introduced.[209] Major W. F. N. Bridges from the Malayan Civil

Service was seconded to Sarawak for this purpose. His recommendation of a system of restriction by individual assessment was accepted and subsequently implemented in 1938, locally referred to as the 'coupon system', as rubber growers were each issued with a coupon.[210] Vyner made a plea to the people that only with their wholehearted commitment to this system of rubber restriction would they then reap its benefits.

> Although at first it may appear complicated and troublesome, I am sure that the coupon system will work satisfactorily when once it is understood by rubber growers.... I expect my people ... to co-operate loyally with my Government in this matter in the full realisation that it is only by scrupulously following these regulations that the desired object can be attained [that is] ... to assure the continuance of these high prices.[211]

Rubber restriction, in fact, played a large role in bringing Sarawak out of the Depression. The improved rubber prices as a result of restriction implemented after 1934 hastened the country's economic recovery.

Exploitation of Mineral Resources: The Twilight Years

Both the government-managed coal-mines at Simunjan and Brooketon, which had been costly ventures since the days of Charles, continued to be financial burdens during Vyner's reign. However, it was not until the exigencies of the Depression, which rendered cut-backs in public expenditure necessary, that the closure of the mines at Simunjan was effected in early 1932.[212]

As early as 1920, Vyner had in mind to dispose of the Brooketon mines. Negotiations were initiated with James Hatton Hall, an English entrepreneur, but these were unsuccessful.[213] Then Vyner decided to close the coal-mines in 1924, and, at the same time, arranged for their return, together with Muara, to Brunei when the newly enthroned young Sultan, Ahmed Tajuddin, came of age seven years later.[214] The return to Brunei of these properties was a friendly gesture on the part of Vyner. The transfer was made in 1931, appropriately coinciding with Vyner's austerity programme in reducing administrative costs.

The BCL decided to abandon their gold-mining operations at Bau in 1921 after several years of decreasing production. With the departure of the company, several small-scale Chinese miners moved in to work the remaining deposits without any spectacular success. However, a brief revival of gold-mining began in 1933, reached a peak in 1934/5,[215] and declined thereafter.

Likewise, oil production at Miri declined steadily after 1929, the year of peak output.[216] It was estimated that the Miri fields would be exhausted by the mid-1940s.[217] This forecast, made in 1935, proved to be partially true as post-war production figures until 1960 never attained the output of the 1920s and 1930s.[218]

Land Policy and Legislation

In 1920 Vyner enacted 'Order No. VIII', supplemented by 'Order No. IX', intended, according to its preamble, 'to consolidate and amend the regulations relating to land'.[219] Land for agricultural purposes was given an 'Occupation Ticket', and after its survey, a licence issued, which 'will run for twenty years, renewable at [the] occupant's option, for such term and at such rent as the Government may determine at the expiration of each term'.[220] Land was classified into 'Town and Suburban Lands', 'Country Lands', and 'Native holdings'. 'Native holdings' were for natives[221] to carry out the planting of *padi* and fruit 'in accordance with the customary laws', and they were encouraged to register their fruit groves and farm lands.[222] Under the 'Supplementary Order No. IX 1920', 'Native Land Reserves' were created and divided into 3-acre lots for free occupation by natives.[223]

Vyner considered land classification as necessary to facilitate future land grants. 'In formulating our combined land, forest and agricultural policy, it will be necessary to classify the land into forest and agricultural land; as far as possible to confine the grant of holdings for cultivation to uninhabited tracts of country; to separate different races; and to set aside areas for specific cultures.'[224] Equally important was the demarcation of land reserves. 'The policy for opening reserves for certain products and allocating each reserve to one particular race obviates inter-racial disputes.... It also renders control much more easy and does away with the endless boundary disputes and complaints of encroachment which complicate the ordinary system of land alienation.'[225] For these purposes the work of surveying was hastened, and a more precise survey system was introduced in 1930 resulting in the production of 'fairly accurate maps'.[226]

The need for a more comprehensive land law resulted in the enactment of a new land order which came into force on 1 January 1932.[227] The Land Order of 1931, 'Order No. L–2 (Land), 1931', repealed all previous orders[228] and clarified certain important but hitherto doubtful terms, notably, the distinction between

'grants' and 'leases', the definition of 'State Land', and the meaning of the term 'Native'. 'Native' referred to the indigenous races of Sarawak and excluded the various Chinese communities.[229]

A far more important legislation which guaranteed land titles and boundaries was the Land Settlement Order of 1933, 'Order No. L–7 (Land Settlement), 1933'.[230] It provided 'for the settlement of rights to land and the creation of a new Land Register based on an accurate and fully verified Cadastral survey'.[231] In order to facilitate its working, it was thought expedient once again to amalgamate the Departments of Land and Survey which was effected in 1933. Land settlement proceeded smoothly and Vyner reported on its progress. 'Settlement of rights in land has been completed in the coast districts of the Third Division, and land affairs there are for the first time on a sound basis as is proved by the remarkable falling off in litigation in these districts. Settlement is at present in progress in the Kuching and Sarikei districts.'[232]

The Land Rules of 1933 classified land into 'Mixed Zones' and 'Native Areas', the latter exclusively the preserve of natives.[233] Such a division of land together with the Land Settlement Order was a clear attempt to protect natives from the encroachment of non-natives, in practice generally the Chinese, on their land.

By 1938, matters relating to land were generally more defined than when Vyner became Rajah.[234] Of paramount importance to Vyner's land policy was the protection of native interests; for instance, natives had the exclusive right to farm and occupy lands in the inland regions administratively referred to as the 'Interior Area', and Native Reserves were solely for the use of indigenous peoples.

Forest Conservation

Forest conservation in Sarawak traced its beginnings to a decree by Charles Brooke in 1902 prohibiting the exportation of timber from Sarawak Proper, the then First Division.[235] In a speech to the Supreme Council in August that year, Charles lamented the destruction of the forest.[236] Although he wanted some kind of control over the exploitation of forest resources, namely timber, no other efforts, other than the embargo on timber exports, were made during his reign. Vyner was to consummate what his father initiated in the conservation of Sarawak's tropical rainforests.

A Forestry Department was established and a Conservator of Forests appointed in 1919.[237] A code of Forest Rules, based on that practised in the Federated Malay States, came into force on

1 January 1920, and the creation of forest reserves commenced with the passing of the Forest Reservation Order of 1920.[238] Work in designating suitable areas as forest reserves began in the First Division, and by mid-1921 the work had been extended to both the Second and Third Divisions.[239]

The implementation of the Forest Rules of 1921[240] and the continual creation of forest reserves caused a certain uneasiness among the general population who apparently feared the shortage of land for agricultural purposes. Vyner assured them that such was not the intention.[241]

The forest policy aimed primarily 'to insure the permanent maintenance of a sufficient area of forest to supply all needs of the inhabitants', and its secondary objective was 'to encourage the export of timber which is *surplus to internal requirements* and to maintain and increase the export of minor forest products'.[242] The rights of the natives to work jungle produce had been duly recognized for 'it is the intention of the Government to insure that a certain proportion of the forests shall be permanently maintained as such'.[243]

Similar to his land policy, Vyner's forestry policy, particularly the creation of forest reserves, was very much native oriented.

> Native claims in proposed reserves are inquired into by an impartial Officer and the Forest Department usually offers no opposition to claims being admitted that are recommended by that Officer. A claim to the practice of shifting cultivation which is quite incompatible with forestry is the only exception. If this claim were insisted on in particular cases the proposed reservation would usually be abandoned in part or in whole.[244]

The designation of forest reserves was deemed too restrictive and, in fact, was one of the major causes of disaffection among the Dayaks of the Kanowit district who rose in rebellion in 1929 under the leadership of Penghulu Asun.[245] Therefore, in 1934 legislation was enacted for the creation of 'Protected Forest'.[246] The main feature that differentiated a 'Protected Forest' from a 'Forest Reserve' was its greater accessibility whereby, 'general prohibitions are ... limited to a ban on farming and on commercial logging. Small quantities of produce may be taken for a person's own use, and trespass is not an offence.'[247] Nevertheless, the Senior Forest Officer was empowered to 'close up to one quarter of [its] area for sylvicultural purposes'.[248] Once again it can be seen that native welfare, in this case their greater convenience, influenced a shift in policy from the emphasis on Reserves to Protected Forests.[249]

After two decades of conservation efforts the percentage of demarcated forests accounted for just over 4 per cent of the total land area, equivalent to about 4806 square kilometres (1,863 square miles).[250]

The Provision of Infrastructure

Infrastructure development, initiated by Charles, continued during Vyner's reign. Transport and communications, waterworks and the provision of piped water, and banking were among the major developments in infrastructure. Vyner acknowledged the disadvantages of river transport and envisaged a network of roads linking the major urban centres to facilitate greater movement for purposes of trade and agriculture; he wished 'to see [a] definite policy of road making laid down for each Division and steadily worked to year by year'.[251] In 1928 a comprehensive road programme was launched; the most ambitious project was the proposed plan to link Kuching with Simanggang.[252] By 1930 this trunk road from Kuching had reached Serian, about 64 kilometres away.[253] Although Vyner was supportive of road construction and intended to invest further when funds were available, the Depression interrupted his programme. However, road construction was a controversial subject.[254] In 1937 there was apparently a shift in policy on road building with a re-consideration of the plans for arterial roads. Work on the Kuching–Simanggang Road was stopped at Serian.[255]

The railway continued running, and by 1925 the line had extended to the 13th Mile, which was the maximum it reached, although survey work had been completed to the 27th Mile in 1917.[256] As part of Vyner's austerity plan during the Depression, the railway service was discontinued altogether in March 1933.

A government air service was also inaugurated in late 1928 using seaplanes, but this was shelved the following year.[257] In 1935 preliminary plans were made for the construction of landing grounds at Kuching, Oya, Mukah, Bintulu, and Miri; three years later the Kuching airport at the 7th Mile was officially opened.[258]

Great strides were achieved in other areas: wireless telegraphy linked most of the major towns;[259] there was supply of piped-water in the outstations; and banking facilities were also improved.

Vyner, the Chinese, and the Depression

Vyner shared his father's belief that the Chinese were needed in the development of Sarawak's economy. In the mid-1920s, he initiated Foochow immigration into the Baram in the hope of pro-

moting agricultural development.[260] The relatively changed circumstances, particularly the turbulent situation in China from whence most of the Chinese emigrated, necessitated a more cautious immigration policy as well as a more vigilant watch over the Chinese who had settled in Sarawak. In 1929 a Protector of Labour and Chinese was appointed,[261] and a Secretariat for Chinese Affairs established to attend to matters relating to the various Chinese communities. Immigration and the protection of coolie labour from exploitation, including Chinese female domestic servants (*mui tsai*), were among the matters handled.[262] When the Depression set in and unemployment became more evident, immigration was subject to control and restriction.[263] With these measures there was a noticeable absence of labour unrest, and unemployment figures remained small and localized.[264] Even when the Depression receded immigration remained strictly controlled in order to facilitate the implementation of the rubber restriction scheme.[265] Strict regulation continued to be imposed on male immigration throughout Vyner's reign with some relaxation in 1937 to ease the labour shortage in the Third Division.[266]

Native Affairs

Throughout his reign, Vyner tried to keep the peace among the various indigenous people. Several *bebunoh babi bebaik* (literally, 'killing-a-pig-for-friendship') or peacemaking ceremonies were initiated to bring together traditionally antagonistic groups to end their feuds and establish amiable relations with one another.[267] Pacification was important for trade to progress and expand.

Vyner, like Charles, sought to prevail upon the natives the advantages of substituting the sword for the *cangkul* (hoe). Native migrations, particularly those of the Dayaks, and native swidden farming practices were discouraged.[268] Vyner shared his father's intention of gradually transforming shifting cultivators into permanent farmers. The *1935 Blue Report*[269] presented this objective in the following terms:

> It is generally agreed [among Brooke officers] that the ultimate Dayak problem must be sought in the gradual conversion of the Dayak into a permanent and independent cultivator of the land. *This policy will take generations to accomplish* (we must in fact move slowly in this matter) but it is necessary that we should begin now to plan for the future.[270]

A Secretariat for Native Affairs was established in December 1929 to attend to issues relating to native welfare. These included the Native Court and overseeing the work of Native officers and

headmen. The function of the Secretariat, headed by the Secretary for Native Affairs, was to protect native interest by countering any forms of abuse that might be perpetrated by their own chiefs or by Native officers, and from exploitation by Chinese.[271]

Vyner remained faithful to the Brooke tradition by placing the interests of the natives above all else. In doing so he earned the wrath of the business community in Singapore and London who saw him as a reactionary despot and an anti-capitalist.

In the past Sir James Brooke had been attacked by Mr Ware [*sic*, Wise?] with the backing of Joseph Hume and Richard Cobden and the Editor of a Singapore paper who later admitted he [had] done so for payment. Sir Charles Brooke had been attacked by certain capitalist interests and now questions were being asked by Labour Members about the present Rajah which were being reprinted in Singapore papers without comment. No doubt this sort of thing did no harm, but it certainly did no good. *The motive in every case had been the refusal of the Government to grant rights to commercial firms, as it was and still is the policy of the Government to grant no rights which might conflict with the interests of the natives.*[272]

Disinclination towards Western Capitalist Enterprises

Vyner, like his father, was against the influx of large foreign capital into the country, particularly that of a speculative kind. He reiterated his policy towards foreign capital, displaying a strong concern for native interest and welfare.

It is not my policy, and was never the policy of my predecessors, to increase the revenue of the State by inviting any influx of foreign capital. No doubt had such a policy been adopted the total wealth would inevitably have shown disparities that would have militated against the happiness of my people. *If their interests are to be safeguarded then development of the resources of the country must be gradual and so far as possible carried out by the people of Sarawak themselves.*[273]

It was evident that Vyner was not enthusiastic in promoting foreign investment, but bona fide investors whose enterprise did not conflict with native interests were allowed to operate.[274] Their numbers, however, were limited. There were less than ten foreign companies operating in Sarawak throughout the three decades of Vyner's rule. These foreign, largely European, companies were mostly involved in commercial agriculture, notably Para rubber, in oil production at Miri, and the few timber operations in the Rejang and Lawas.[275]

Review of Vyner's Policies

Vyner's views and his economic policies strongly adhered to the Brooke principles of native protection and welfare. The slow but steady progress, mainly relying on local resources with little foreign capital, was the hallmark of the economic development of Sarawak during the 1920s and 1930s. Undoubtedly there were advances made in various sectors of the economy during Vyner's reign, but on the whole the rate of progress was so slow that on the eve of the Pacific War Sarawak presented a picture of a tranquil, idyllic, tropical country of peasant smallholders of *padi* farms, sago and rubber gardens, and coconut groves, who transported their produce in boats utilizing the numerous rivers as the main means of transportation.

Conclusion

James, an adherent of Raffles's concept of territorial possession as against commercial outposts, succeeded in bringing the north-western coast of Borneo into the sphere of British free trade by his acquisition of Sarawak. Its occupation was consistent with James's policy of extending British influence in the Eastern Archipelago through territorial conquest. Once established, Sarawak offered a foothold, a starting-point for proceeding with his overall policy of commercial expansion. However, James's offer of Sarawak to Britain was rejected, much to his disappointment. Nevertheless, he persevered in his efforts to gain support from his home government; when cession was declined, he sought protection and recognition. He fervently believed that Sarawak could not stand alone as an 'Independent State' without the support of a 'Protective Power'. Support was essential for Sarawak's survival and he worked for this end. Rejected by Britain, James turned to other European powers, but with scant success. 'Recognition' was finally afforded him by the British government.

In Sarawak James pursued the following objectives: the amelioration of the conditions of the native population from oppression by their chiefs, the imposition of free trade, and the promotion of British commerce. These aims were interrelated: unfair dealings under the guise of customary obligations denied the native cultivator a just return for his produce, and obstructed the free flow of goods which was inimical to free trade. Free trade, James was convinced, would improve the well-being of the native inhabitants. He

made it the core of his economic policy. He successfully removed the two major hindrances to free trade—'piracy' and exploitative traditional trading practices; the former by force of arms with the assistance of the Royal Navy, and the latter through legislation accompanied by strict enforcement. When the obstacles were eliminated, native trade flourished and consequently benefited both the native producer and the Sarawak Exchequer. Native trade in jungle products and sago was the mainstay of Sarawak's revenue in its early days. James was also convinced that European capital together with Chinese labour could promote the development of Sarawak's resources. His eagerness for support from a protective power was to provide the confidence for Western investment in a hitherto unknown territory. But his insistence that native welfare should not be adversely affected by profit-seeking projects discouraged potential investors. Deterred by the unpleasant experience with Wise and his projects, James was suspicious of European capitalists in general. The BCL was the only Western enterprise operating in Sarawak; initially its operations were confined to the extraction of minerals utilizing imported Chinese indentured labour, a field far removed from the native inhabitants.

Chinese effort was deemed necessary in opening up the country, farming the land, working the mines, and engaging in trade. Chinese refugees from neighbouring Sambas in Dutch Borneo were welcomed and allowed to settle and work the land. The insurrection of the Bau gold-miners against the Brooke government did not adversely influence James's view of the Chinese role in the country's development. He encouraged, and in fact, initiated immigration of the Chinese to Sarawak, though on a limited scale, owing to financial constraints. Despite his efforts, his Chinese immigration scheme proved unsuccessful owing to Sarawak's relative obscurity.

Charles shared his uncle's ideas regarding the protection of native rights and interests; he opposed Western-type, large-scale commercial enterprise which might exploit the natives, held to the essential role of the Chinese, and emphasized the importance of gradual development. Charles presided over the steady growth and prosperity of the country, and in doing so, proved the fallacy of James's assumption that Sarawak could not progress independent of a protective power.

Charles achieved his objectives of gradual economic development while protecting native interests and improving their livelihood. The stability and security afforded by Charles's government enabled trade to reach into the interior and consequently it began

to benefit the native peoples. The expansion of internal trade and commerce was invariably the product of Chinese initiative. The extractive industries also made their mark during Charles's reign with several minerals, mainly gold, enjoying an upsurge in production towards the close of the nineteenth century. The remarkable exploitation of the Miri oilfields boosted the country's coffers and placed Sarawak on the world map. The agricultural landscape, personified in the native farmer enjoying the fruits of his labour from his own rice fields and fruit and rubber gardens was without doubt a fulfilment of Charles's vision. Peasant landlessness and absentee landlordism, facts of life in neighbouring colonial territories, were conspicuously absent, thanks to his land policy. Large, Malayan-style rubber plantations and European commercial and agricultural concerns were rarities. The birth and growth of Chinese peasant agricultural communities in the Rejang were a tribute to Charles's immigration policy. The Foochow and Cantonese diversion into commercial undertakings further contributed to the flourishing state of this branch of the economy, supplementing their Hokkien and Teochew counterparts in Kuching.

The inevitable but slow progress in infrastructure development reflected a conscious effort of Charles to maintain the *status quo* of Sarawak. As he admitted, nothing had been 'rushed or pushed' and everything was allowed to take its natural course. However, ultimately modern means of communications, like the telephone and wireless, were introduced, which undoubtedly benefited the country.

Considering that Charles inherited a country plagued with political uncertainty, with a public debt of about £15,000 incurred by his predecessor, and that he himself was without recourse to a personal fortune, he did remarkably well in the circumstances. At the time he penned his will in 1913, peace and stability were generally established and there was no public debt. A commentator remarked that he 'did a surprising amount for Sarawak on surprisingly little'.[276] Parsimony was a hallmark of Charles's character which undoubtedly extended to his government.[277] Aptly he reminded his heirs never 'to expect to be made rich at the expense of Sarawak' and, 'it must be clearly understood and recognized that the State of Sarawak is not private property' nor 'in any way belongs to a company of shareholders or speculators'.[278]

Vyner's policies relating to land and forestry, the preference for smallholdings, and the lack of enthusiasm for large foreign capitalist concerns were all designed to shelter the indigenous population

from exploitation. Even the expansion of the infrastructure progressed at a gradual rate, and by the late 1930s large areas of the country and much of the population were still untouched by modern facilities. The slow pace of development embodied a strategy to allow 'the more backward of the country's races to adapt themselves to higher standards of life, and fit themselves to share in the increased wealth which a steady, slow development will bring'.[279] This 'increased wealth' was the result of improving the quality of agricultural products for export, namely rubber and pepper, which benefited both native and Chinese producers.

The emphasis on the greater dependence on agricultural resources as against mineral exploitation proved to be a far-sighted and realistic policy. Sarawak's supposedly vast mineral resources did not live up to expectations and Vyner's reign witnessed the declining years of the mining industry. Even oil production at Miri did not offer much scope for optimism.

Although Sarawak was not immune from the Depression, its effects there were not as devastating as in neighbouring territories. This was mainly due to Vyner strongly discouraging his people from putting their faith in rubber and his policy of promoting smallholdings rather than large commercial estates employing wage labour. The fact that the people were independent producers, and the prompt attention to immigration control alleviated the problem of social unrest during the years of slump.

The political situation in China during the 1920s and 1930s coupled with the onset of the Depression witnessed a tighter grip by the Sarawak government over Chinese immigration and a more vigilant attitude towards the resident Chinese communities. Vyner's mistrust of the Chinese became more evident in the 1930s, and, in retrospect, appeared unfounded as the Sarawak Chinese apparently did not display much interest in political events in the motherland. The spectre of the 1857 Chinese uprising remained vivid in the minds of Vyner and his European officers and undoubtedly contributed to their collective paranoia.

The Chinese, even those born in Sarawak, continued to be classified as non-native, which barred them from privileges enjoyed by their native neighbours, particularly in the matter of land grants. Their status as aliens with the threat of deportation did not speak much for their future in Sarawak. An attempt by the Chinese to expand their agricultural holdings was met with a barrage of pro-native land legislation. Vyner's pro-native policies, in fact, tended to alienate the Chinese from contributing to and participating fully

in the economic development of the country.[280] Nevertheless, generally they prospered and on the eve of the Japanese invasion, Sarawak proved to be a land of contentment and serenity, unmarred by civil disturbance. It gave witness to

> the success he [Vyner] had in directing a mixed population into channels of peaceful trading, laying the foundations on which was built a standard of living unexcelled in the eastern tropics, establishing a nation of free men with their roots in their own soil, the soil of their coconut groves, their sago plantations and their rubber gardens, a people not to be unaffected by modern trade slumps but because of their position as independent producers never seriously embarrassed by them.[281]

1. He cautioned that there was bound to be some 'modification' to his original intentions, but he put forward his proposals in 'Expedition to Borneo' in the *Athenaeum* of 13 October 1838, and then in the form of an abstract in the *Journal of the Geographical Society* of 1838. This prospectus was reproduced in John C. Templer (ed.), *The Private Letters of Sir James Brooke, KCB, Rajah of Sarawak, Narrating the Events of His Life, from 1838 to the Present Time,* 3 vols., London: Bentley, 1853, Vol. I, pp. 2–33; and in Gertrude L. Jacob, *The Raja of Sarawak: An Account of Sir James Brooke, KCB, LLD, Given Chiefly through Letters and Journals,* 2 vols., London: Macmillan, 1876, Vol. I, pp. 70–89.

2. The term 'Eastern Archipelago', interchangeably used with 'Indian Archipelago', by nineteenth-century European writers, referred to the group of islands that today make up the countries of Malaysia and Indonesia.

3. 'Expedition to Borneo', in Jacob, *The Raja of Sarawak,* Vol. I, p. 75.

4. Emphasis added.

5. 'Expedition to Borneo', in Jacob, *The Raja of Sarawak,* Vol. I, p. 75. Emphasis added.

6. Ibid.

7. James Brooke, *A Letter from Borneo; with Notices of the Country and Its Inhabitants, Addressed to James Gardner, Esq.*, London: L. & G. Seeley, 1842, p. 38. This 'letter', ostensibly addressed to James Gardner, his agent in London at that time, but meant for the attention of government leaders, sets out his future intentions for Sarawak and argued that support and assistance from the British government was essential. His friend, John C. Templer, published this 'letter' and distributed it to key government leaders.

8. The territory of Sarawak then stretched from Tanjong (Cape) Datu to the mouth of the Sadong River and included also the Lundu, Sarawak, and Samarahan rivers, altogether an area of about 7740 square kilometres (3,000 square miles). The deed of cession was confirmed by the ruler of Brunei, Sultan Omar Ali Saifuddin II, on 1 August 1842, during James's visit to the kingdom.

9. See Templer, *Letters,* Vol. I, p. 19; and Rodney Mundy, *Narrative of Events in Borneo and Celebes, down to the Occupation of Labuan: From the Journals of James Brooke Esq.*, 2 vols., London: John Murray, 1848, Vol. I, p. 12.

10. J. Brooke, *A Letter from Borneo,* pp. 38–9. Emphasis added.

11. Spenser St John, *The Life of Sir James Brooke: Rajah of Sarawak; from His Personal Papers and Correspondence*, Edinburgh & London: William Blackwood & Sons, 1879, p. 7. See also Graham Saunders, 'James Brooke and Asian Government', *BMJ*, 3, 1 (1973): 105–17.

12. Brooke to Mother, 24 September 1843, in Jacob, *The Raja of Sarawak*, Vol. I, p. 256.

13. 'Expedition to Borneo', in Jacob, *The Raja of Sarawak*, Vol. I, p. 83.

14. Brooke to Burdett Coutts, 26 March 1861, in Owen Rutter (ed.), *Rajah Brooke and Baroness Burdett Coutts: Consisting of the Letters from Sir James Brooke, First White Rajah of Sarawak, to Miss Angela (afterwards Baroness) Burdett Coutts*, London: Hutchinson, 1935, p. 113. However, he envisaged that the perpetuation of this 'guidance' by Europeans based on their 'superior moral and intellectual character' is not necessarily indefinite, for, 'if ever the natives attain an equality in these respects, the European rule will cease, and deservedly so'. Abstract of a speech given at a public ball in honour of him, November 1861, as reported in the *Singapore Free Press*, quoted in Jacob, *The Raja of Sarawak*, Vol. II, p. 339.

15. The Datu Patinggi and the Datu Bandar controlled the tribes on the left and right branch of the Sarawak River respectively, while the Datu Temanggong held sway over the inhabitants on the coast. S. Baring-Gould and C. A. Bampfylde, *A History of Sarawak under Its Two White Rajahs, 1839–1908*, London: Henry Sotheran, 1909, p. 207. For their reinstatement, see ibid., pp. 77–8.

16. See Brooke to Templer, 22 October 1855, in Jacob, *The Raja of Sarawak*, Vol. II, p. 211. For an account of the Supreme Council, see T. Stirling Boyd, 'The Law and Constitution of Sarawak', Typescript, 1934, MSS Pac. s. 86, Box 4 Item II, pp. 29–32 RHL, Oxford; and R. J. Pole-Evans, 'The Supreme Council, Sarawak', *SMJ*, 7, 7 (June 1956): 98–108.

17. See D. E. Brown, *Brunei: The Structure and History of a Bornean Malay Sultanate*, Bandar Seri Begawan: Brunei Museum, 1970, pp. 63–6; Robert Nicholl, 'Brunei and Camphor', *BMJ*, 4, 3 (1979): 52–74; and James Francis Warren, *The Sulu Zone, 1768–1898: The Dynamics of External Trade, Slavery and Ethnicity in the Transformation of a Southeast Asian Maritime State*, Singapore: Singapore University Press, 1981, pp. 75–143.

18. For raids along the north-western Bornean coast in the mid-nineteenth century, regarded as 'piracy' by Western writers, see Spenser St John, 'Piracy in the Indian Archipelago', *JIAEA*, 3 (1849): 251–60; St John, *The Life of Sir James Brooke*, p. 63; Baring-Gould and Bampfylde, *A History of Sarawak*, pp. 52 and 92–7; and Owen Rutter, *The Pirate Wind: Tales of the Sea-Robbers of Malaya*, London: Hutchinson, 1930, pp. 31–42.

19. Henry Keppel, *A Sailor's Life under Four Sovereigns*, 3 vols., London: Macmillan, 1899, Vol. I, p. 290.

20. For a description of James's so-called 'pirate' campaigns, see Henry Keppel, *The Expedition to Borneo of HMS* Dido *for the Suppression of Piracy: With Extracts from the Journal of James Brooke Esq.*, 2 vols., London: Chapman & Hall, 1846, *passim*; Mundy, *Borneo and Celebes*, Vol. II, pp. 121–6; St John, *Life of Sir James Brooke*, pp. 138–58; Baring-Gould and Bampfylde, *A History of Sarawak*, pp. 97–102, 104–9, 116, 123–4, 132–9; and Robert Pringle, *Rajahs and Rebels: The Ibans of Sarawak under Brooke Rule, 1841–1941*, London: Macmillan, 1970, pp. 73–83.

21. For the case against James Brooke who was accused of being a 'butcher' annihilating 'innocent natives' and 'peaceable traders', see Henry Wise (comp.), *A Selection from Papers Relating to Borneo and the Proceedings of James Brooke, Esq., Now*

Agent for the British Government in Borneo, printed for the use of the government offices, London, 1844–6; Joseph Hume, *A Letter to the Right Honourable the Earl of Malmesbury, Secretary of State for Foreign Affairs, etc. etc., Relative to the Proceedings of Sir James Brooke, KCB, etc. etc. etc., in Borneo*, London: 1853; W. N., *Borneo*, London: Effingham Wilson, 1853; George Foggo, *Adventures of Sir James Brooke, KCB, Rajah of Sarawak 'Sovereign de facto of Borneo Proper'*, . . ., London: Effingham Wilson, 1853; *The Borneo Question, or the Evidence Produced at Singapore before the Commissioners Charged with the Enquiry into the Facts Relating to Sir James Brooke KCB Esq, Compiled from the Singapore Free Press and Other Sources*, Singapore: Alfred Simonides, 1854; L. A. Chamerovzow, *Borneo Facts versus Borneo Fallacies: An Inquiry into the Alleged Piracies of the Dyaks of Serebas and Sakarran*, London: Charles Gilpin, 1851; and Parliamentary Papers, Vol. XXIX, 1854–5, pp. 1–472. For Brooke's own views, see Jacob, *The Raja of Sarawak*, Vol. II, p. 65; and James Brooke, *A Vindication of His Character and Proceedings in Reply to the Statements Privately Printed and Circulated by Joseph Hume, Esq. MP, Addressed to Henry Drummond, Esq. MP*, London: Ridgway, 1853.

22. For instance, see Brooke to W. H. Read, 9 May 1855, in Jacob, *The Raja of Sarawak*, Vol. II, p. 192.

23. J. Brooke, *A Letter from Borneo*, pp. 9–10. Emphasis added.

24. Ibid., p. 11.

25. See Baring-Gould and Bampfylde, *A History of Sarawak*, p. 55.

26. See St John, *Life of Sir James Brooke*, p. 52.

27. This oppression was one of the causes of the rebellion of 1836–40 by the Sarawak Malays and the Land Dayaks against the rule of Pangeran Makota, the Governor of Sarawak. For the reasons for this anti-Brunei revolt, see R. H. W. Reece, 'Political Pioneers', in *Our Sarawak*, Kuching: Persatuan Kesusasteraan Sarawak, 1983, pp. 6–7.

28. The fines collected from offenders were distributed to loyal and law-abiding chiefs, both Malay and Dayak, 'and there was a clear understanding among all parties that the infliction did not mean that their English Raja wished to increase his finances, but it did mean that he had said piracy, whether by land or sea, should be abolished, and abolished therefore it must be'. Jacob, *The Raja of Sarawak*, Vol. II, p. 201.

29. He realized that the monopoly of antimony was against the principle of free trade but admitted it to be a necessary evil. See Brooke to Mother, 16 October 1842, in Jacob, *The Raja of Sarawak*, Vol. I, p. 223.

30. For the abuses in the system of taxation, see J. Brooke, *A Letter from Borneo*, pp. 21–4; and E. Parnell, 'The Tribute Paid in Former Days to the Sultan of Brunei by the Then Dependent Provinces of Sarawak', *SMJ*, 1, 1 (February 1911): 125.

31. Brooke to Burdett Coutts, 26 March 1861, in Rutter, *Rajah Brooke and Baroness Burdett Coutts*, p. 114.

32. For the revival of coastal raiding along the Bornean coast and plans to counter it, see John Brooke Brooke to Brooke, 26–28 April 1858, MSS Pac. s. 90, Basil Brooke Papers, Vol. 5, RHL, Oxford.

33. St John to Foreign Office, 16 July 1855, FO 12/22, PRO, Kew. See also St John, *Life of Sir James Brooke*, p. 326.

34. For the condemnation of these Admiralty instructions, see Lord Grey to John C. Templer, 24 January 1854, MSS Pac. s. 90, Basil Brooke Papers, Vol. 16, RHL, Oxford.

35. Baring-Gould and Bampfylde, *A History of Sarawak*, pp. 268–9.

36. Treaty with Brunei of 27 May 1847, Article III, FO 93/16(2), PRO, Kew. This clause of the suppression of piracy was, in fact, a restatement of the Treaty of 18 December 1846 whereby the British government undertook 'to use its best endeavours to suppress Piracy, and to protect lawful commerce, and the Sultan of Borneo, and his ministers, promise to afford every assistance to the British authorities'. Treaty of the Cession of Labuan of 18 December 1846, Article III, FO 93/16(1), PRO, Kew.

37. St John to Foreign Office, 16 July 1855, FO 12/22, PRO, Kew.

38. The political struggle in Mukah was between two rival *pangeran*, Ersat and Matusin, and involved anti-Brooke personalities like Sherif Masahor of Sarikei and the cashiered Datu Patinggi Abdul Gapur, who together hatched the supposedly 'Malay plot' and conspired the double murders of Charles Fox and Henry Steele at Kanowit in June 1859. For a detailed account of this political feud, see Charles Brooke, *Ten Years in Sarawak*, 2 vols., London: Tinsley, 1866; reprinted Singapore: Oxford University Press, 1990, Vol. I, pp. 325–63, Vol. II, pp. 6–71; Baring-Gould and Bampfylde, *A History of Sarawak*, pp. 213–16, 221–2, 246–65; Pringle, *Rajahs and Rebels*, pp. 110 ff., 118–20, and 152, for the conspiracies, pp. 113 ff., 125–8, 130–2. For the various interpretations of the double murders, see Robert Pringle, 'The Murder of Fox and Steele: Masahor's Version', *SMJ*, 12, 25–6 (July–December 1965): 215–27; and Tuton Kaboy, 'The Murder of Steele and Fox: Two Versions', *SMJ*, 12, 25–6 (July–December 1965): 207–14.

39. A reduction of as much as two-thirds of raw sago imports to Kuching, from 6,000 tons in 1859 to 2,000 tons in 1860, was recorded. St John to Foreign Office, 8 March 1861, FO 12/28, PRO, Kew.

40. For a detailed account of the so-called 'Mukah Incident' from Captain Brooke Brooke's perspective, see John Brooke Brooke to Brooke, 9 May 1860, MSS Pac. s. 90, Basil Brooke Papers, Vol. 5, RHL, Oxford.

41. Spenser St John, who had served as James's private secretary since 1848, succeeded to his position as British Consul-General in August 1855. See Clarendon to Brooke, 9 August 1855, in Jacob, *The Raja of Sarawak*, Vol. II, pp. 210–11; and Brooke to John Brooke Brooke, 12–24 August 1855, MSS Pac. s. 90, Basil Brooke Papers, Vol. 2A, RHL, Oxford.

42. For the translation of the firman of Sultan Abdul Mumin of Brunei to the *pangeran* and inhabitants of Mukah about the agreement reached with the Rajah of Sarawak following the 'Mukah Incident', and ordering them to submit to the latter, see Malay document dated 29 April 1861, MSS Pac. s. 90, Basil Brooke Papers, Vol. 16, RHL, Oxford.

43. St John to Foreign Office, 29 August 1861, FO 12/29, PRO, Kew. The Sultan was agreeable to the cession which assured him a yearly sum paid directly to him. Hitherto, he had, in fact, received scant revenue from these territories for the *pangeran* enriched themselves with the taxes collected.

44. When trade was restored in 1861, it was noted that processed sago amounted to more than 68 per cent of the total exports of Sarawak to Singapore. See Orfeur Cavenagh, *Report upon the Settlement of Sarawak*, Calcutta: J. Kingham, 1863, p. 46.; and Wong Lin Ken, 'The Trade of Singapore', *JMBRAS*, 33, 4 (December 1960): 90–1 and 220–1.

45. Brooke to Charles Johnson, 31 October 1861, in Jacob, *The Raja of Sarawak*, Vol. II, pp. 336–7.

46. J. Brooke, *A Letter from Borneo*, p. 6.

47. Brooke to Templer, 31 December 1844, in Jacob, *The Raja of Sarawak*, Vol. I, p. 272.

48. Ibid.

49. Brooke to Sir E. B. Lytton, August 1858, in Jacob, *The Raja of Sarawak*, Vol. II, p. 271.

50. Ibid.

51. Ibid.

52. Memorandum to Sir E. B. Lytton, August 1858, quoted in Jacob, *The Raja of Sarawak*, Vol. II, p. 270.

53. Speech by James Brooke at Manchester Dinner on 21 April 1858, *The Times*, 23 April 1858.

54. The Deputation, composing of prominent men from 'some three hundred firms, the most eminent and the most opulent' in Britain, including several members of Parliament, lobbied for 'retaining the State of Sarawak under the protection of the English Government'. See Jacob, *The Raja of Sarawak*, Vol. II, pp. 293–300.

55. See *The Times*, 1 December 1858. For James's response to Derby's remarks, see Brooke to Lord Derby, 4 December 1858, MSS Pac. s. 90, Basil Brooke Papers, Box 1/File 2, RHL, Oxford.

56. Brooke to Burdett Coutts, 4 February 1861, in Rutter, *Rajah Brooke and Baroness Burdett Coutts*, p. 104.

57. Brooke to Burdett Coutts, 26 March 1861, ibid., p. 113. Emphasis added.

58. For negotiations with these foreign governments, see MSS Pac. s. 90, Basil Brooke Papers, Vols. 2A, 2B, 3, and 16, RHL, Oxford.

59. On the issue of the cession of Sarawak to Britain or to another foreign power, James was opposed by his nephew and one-time heir, Captain John Brooke Brooke. Although the latter bowed to his uncle's wishes, Brooke Brooke personally felt that Sarawak should remain independent. See Brooke to Emma Johnson, 11–26 March 1859, MSS Pac. s. 90, Basil Brooke Papers, Vol. 1, RHL, Oxford; and Brooke to Charles Anthoni Johnson (later Brooke), 1 May 1859, MSS Pac. s. 90, Basil Brooke Papers, Vol. 1, RHL, Oxford. James's one-time secretary and confidant, Spenser St John, also disapproved of proposals to hand over the country to Britain, and was particularly opposed to approaches to foreign governments. See Spenser St John to Charles Johnson (Brooke), 10 November 1858 and 6 June 1859, MSS Pac. s. 90, Basil Brooke Papers, Vol. 15, RHL, Oxford.

60. It was thanks to John Abel Smith, later MP for Chichester, and an old friend of James's benefactor Miss Angela Burdett Coutts, who lobbied successfully for recognition by Palmerston's government. It is interesting to note that the United States of America had more than a decade ago (24 October 1850) recognized Sarawak as an independent state and had even dispatched an envoy to Kuching to establish friendly relations with the Rajah. See Baring-Gould and Bampfylde, *A History of Sarawak*, p. 144.

61. Ibid., p. 301.

62. Brooke to 'Ladies', 6 January 1866, 'Preface' to his nephew, Charles Johnson's [Brooke's] book *Ten Years in Sarawak*, in Rutter, *Rajah Brooke and Baroness Burdett Coutts*, p. 252. 'Ladies' refers to Miss Angela Burdett Coutts and her companion, Mrs Brown. See also C. Brooke, *Ten Years*, Vol. I, pp. xii–xiii.

63. 'Memorandum on Sarawak and the North-western Coast of Borneo' presented to Lord John Russell, then Foreign Secretary, by Mr John Abel Smith, in late April 1862, in Rutter, *Rajah Brooke and Baroness Burdett Coutts*, p. 140.

64. Brooke to Captain J. K. Jolly, 22 November 1856, MSS Pac. s. 90, Basil Brooke Papers, Vol. 1, RHL, Oxford. Emphasis added.

65. Henry Wise of Melville, Wise and Company, Broad Street, replaced James Gardner as Brooke's agent in London in late 1843. Wise was a capable and shrewd

businessman who never could understand Brooke's attitude towards the development of Sarawak.

66. Brooke to Templer, 13 April 1843, in Jacob, *The Raja of Sarawak*, Vol. I, p. 234.

67. Brooke to Templer, 12 February 1846, in ibid., Vol. I, p. 314.

68. Brooke to Templer, 13 April 1843, in ibid., Vol. I, pp. 234–5.

69. Brooke to Templer, 12 February 1846, in ibid., Vol. I, p. 314.

70. Journal entry 4 March 1845, in ibid., Vol. I, p. 285.

71. Brooke to Templer, 12 February 1846, in ibid., Vol. I, p. 314.

72. Brooke to Templer, 5 March 1846, in ibid., Vol. I, p. 315.

73. Brooke to Captain Brooke Brooke, 10 January 1846, in Templer, *Letters*, Vol. II, p. 111.

74. Brooke to Templer, 12 February 1846, in ibid., Vol. II, pp. 118–19. Brooke, indeed, checked Wise's career when he successfully brought a Chancery suit against the Eastern Archipelago Company, a brainchild of the latter. For the dispute between Brooke and Wise from various viewpoints, see Hugh H. Lindsay, *The Eastern Archipelago Company and Sir James Brooke*, London, 1853; St John, *The Life of Sir James Brooke*, pp. 234–6; J. Brooke, *A Vindication*, pp. 24–35; 'Dispute between Sir James Brooke and the Eastern Archipelago Company', Foreign Office and the Colonial Office versions, both dated 15 June 1852, 920 DER (14) 44/2, Papers of the 14th Earl of Derby, LRO, Liverpool.

75. Brooke to Templer, 5 March 1846, in Jacob, *The Raja of Sarawak*, Vol. I, p. 314.

76. For the *Findlay* venture, see ibid., Vol. I, pp. 54–7.

77. Brooke to Cruickshank, 30 May 1835, in ibid., Vol. I, p. 57.

78. Brooke to Mother, 19 July 1843, in ibid., Vol. I, p. 250.

79. Brooke to Mother, 16 October 1842, in ibid., Vol. I, p. 223.

80. The main taxes were 'head' and 'door' taxes levied on the Malay and indigenous, mainly Dayak, population, while the Chinese paid indirect taxes on liquor, opium, and gambling. The Dayak 'door' tax for a family was fixed at one dollar per annum throughout the Brooke period. However, the Dayaks were obliged to serve in government levies when called upon to do so. The majority of Malays paid an 'exemption tax' of two dollars per adult male, and then were exempted from participating in government expeditions as well as other unpaid public service. For a detailed account of these various taxes, see Pringle, *Rajahs and Rebels*, pp. 160–4.

81. Brooke to Templer, Spring 1842, in Jacob, *The Raja of Sarawak*, Vol. I, p. 201. See also pp. 228–9.

82. Brooke to Mother, 16 October 1842, in ibid., Vol. I, p. 223. Emphasis added.

83. Brooke to 'Ladies', 15 March 1863, in Rutter, *Rajah Brooke and Baroness Burdett Coutts*, p. 175.

84. An interesting example was the case of an individual named Robert Burns, trader, adventurer, and ethnologist, who in the late 1840s had dealings in the districts of Bintulu and Baram, then under the nominal rule of Brunei; this caused much anxiety to James. After his unsuccessful ventures which he blamed on Brooke, Burns settled in the British colony of Labuan and collaborated with others like James Motley, William Henry Miles, Meldrum, and Riley, who all bore grudges against James, and had connections with Wise and Hume. See Steven Runciman, *The White Rajahs: A History of Sarawak from 1841 to 1946*, Cambridge: Cambridge University Press, 1960, pp. 97–8 and 103–5; Nicholas Tarling, *The Burthen, the*

Risk, and the Glory: A Biography of Sir James Brooke, Kuala Lumpur: Oxford University Press, 1982, p. 116; J. Brooke, *A Vindication*, pp. 21–4; Graham Irwin, *Nineteenth-century Borneo: A Study in Diplomatic Rivalry*, The Hague: Martinus Nijhoff, 1955; reprinted Singapore: Donald Moore, 1965, pp. 130–3; and Tom Harrisson, 'Robert Burns—The First Ethnologist and Explorer of Interior Sarawak', *SMJ*, 5, 3 (November 1951): 463–94.

85. See Brooke to Cruikshank, 28 April 1843, in Jacob, *The Raja of Sarawak*, Vol. I, p. 235.

86. Henry Longhurst, *The Borneo Story: The History of the First 100 Years of Trading in the Far East by The Borneo Company Limited*, London: Newman Neame, 1956, p. 18; and Runciman, *The White Rajahs*, p. 123.

87. The BCL largely employed imported Chinese labourers and European technicians for its mining operations in Sarawak during the nineteenth century. See Daniel Chew, *Chinese Pioneers of the Sarawak Frontier, 1841–1941*, Singapore: Oxford University Press, 1990, pp. 181–202.

88. Brooke to Mother, 18 September 1930, in Jacob, *The Raja of Sarawak*, Vol. I, p. 21.

89. J. Brooke, *A Letter from Borneo*, p. 18.

90. See Brooke to John Grant, 20 November and 1 December 1850, MSS Pac. s. 90, Basil Brooke Papers, Vol. 4, RHL, Oxford.

91. St John, *Life of Sir James Brooke*, p. 225.

92. For a contemporary description of this Chinese uprising based on the Brooke letters and an account from his servant Penty, see Jacob, *The Raja of Sarawak*, Vol. II, pp. 237–44; the account of Brooke's secretary, Spenser St John, who recorded the incident five months later, see St John, *Life of Sir James Brooke*, pp. 294–315; from Ludvig Verner Helms, the BCL manager, see Ludvig Verner Helms, *Pioneering in the Far East, and Journeys to California in 1849 and to the White Sea in 1878*, London: W. H. Allen, 1882, pp. 164–92; from James's nephew and successor, Charles, see C. Brooke, *Ten Years*, Vol. I, pp. 214–25; and from Harriette McDougall's viewpoint and that of her husband, the Anglican Bishop Francis T. McDougall, see Harriette McDougall, *Sketches of Our Life at Sarawak*, London: Society for Promoting Christian Knowledge, 1882, pp. 120–56. See also Runciman, *The White Rajahs*, pp. 119–33. For a new assessment, see C. A. Lockard, 'The 1857 Chinese Rebellion in Sarawak: A Reappraisal', *JSEAS*, 9, 1 (March 1978): 85–98; Chang Pat Foh, 'Bau Chinese Rebellion 1857', *SG*, April 1986: 34–44; and Graham Saunders, 'The Bau Chinese Attack on Kuching, February 1857: A Different Perspective', *SMJ*, 62, 63 (December 1991): 375–96.

93. Brooke to 'Ladies', 29 April 1863, in Rutter, *Rajah Brooke and Baroness Burdett Coutts*, p. 189. For earlier discussions of this immigration scheme, see Spenser St John to J. Brooke Brooke, 26 September 1861, MSS Pac. s. 90, Basil Brooke Papers, Vol. 15, RHL, Oxford; and Charles Anthoni Johnson (Brooke) to J. Brooke Brooke, 30 November–3 December 1862, MSS Pac. S. 90, Basil Brooke Papers, Vol. 8, RHL, Oxford.

94. Brooke to Burdett Coutts, 12 June 1863, in Rutter, *Rajah Brooke and Baroness Burdett Coutts*, p. 201.

95. See Richard Outram, 'The Chinese', in Tom Harrisson (ed.), *The Peoples of Sarawak*, Kuching: Government Printing Office, 1959, p. 119; and Craig Alan Lockard, *From Kampung to City: A Social History of Kuching, Malaysia, 1820–1970*, Ohio University Monographs in International Studies, Southeast Asia Series, No. 75, Athens, 1987, pp. 52 and 68–70.

96. Baring-Gould and Bampfylde, *A History of Sarawak*, p. 304.

97. Henry Keppel writing to Wise on 2 September 1849, made the following unflattering remark as to Brooke's business acumen, 'My friend Brooke has as much idea of business as a cow has of a clean shirt.' CO 144/6, PRO, Kew. See also Runciman, *The White Rajahs*, p. 164, n. 2; and St John, *Life of Sir James Brooke*, pp. 64–5.

98. Acting upon his uncle's wishes, Charles Johnson, the Tuan Muda, adopted the name 'Brooke' in 1863. See Brooke to Emma Johnson, 27 and 31 December 1862, MSS Pac. s. 90, Basil Brooke Papers, Vol. 1, RHL, Oxford.

99. *Sarawak Gazette*, *SG*, 2 September 1872, n.p.

100. Quoted from the public address of Charles delivered on 15 August 1889 commemorating the fiftieth anniversary of the landing of James Brooke in Sarawak. The text of this speech was reproduced in the *Sarawak Gazette* of 2 September 1889 (pp. 126–7), and in Baring-Gould and Bampfylde, *A History of Sarawak* (pp. 408–9), with some variations in the wording between them. The quotation in this instance is from the latter version, hereinafter referred to as 'Charles's Speech 15 August 1889', Baring-Gould and Bampfylde, *A History of Sarawak*, pp. 408–9.

101. Charles Brooke, *Queries: Past, Present and Future*, London: The Planet, 1907, p. 14. Emphasis added.

102. *SG*, 2 September 1872, n.p.

103. C. Brooke, *Ten Years*, Vol. I, pp. 102 and 103.

104. A fervent believer that native opinion was all-important and should be consulted in the framing of government policies, Charles supplemented James's Supreme Council with his idea of a more general forum of native representation. His brainchild, the General Council, which had the encouragement and blessing of his uncle, held its inaugural meeting at Bintulu on 8 September 1867, fittingly presided over by Charles himself, who was then the Tuan Muda, acting as the representative of the Rajah. The General Council, the predecessor to the present-day Council Negri, which initially composed of European Brooke officers and prominent Malay leaders later included Dayak and other native chieftains in its triennial meetings. See Brooke to Charles Johnson [Brooke], 25 February 1865, quoted in 'Preamble' of *General Council*, 1867–1927, Kuching: Government Printing Office, 1927[?]. Critics might be sceptical of the usefulness of the Supreme Council and the General Council as showcases of formality, for, apparently, there was rarely any opposition to proposals from the Rajah. No doubt such was the case. However, the confidence and trust of members of the native élite in both Councils, coupled with the respect and awe for Charles as Rajah, resulted in his proposals and decisions being supported and upheld.

105. In his later life, Charles made scathing remarks on British colonial rule which, in comparison with his in Sarawak, he considered arbitrary in character, with a complete disregard for native opinion. 'Where can one point to a council of natives in the British dominions sitting and giving their opinions on matters which principally concern themselves, and about which they know, and naturally must know, better than any European? There may be such tribunals in name and appearance, but none in reality.' C. Brooke, *Queries*, pp. 4–5.

106. For discussion regarding the issue of the abolition of slavery in the Supreme Council, see *SG*, 1 August 1881, pp. 59–60 and *SG*, 1 February 1882, p. 1. With regard to the General Council, see 7th Meeting, 11 August 1883, in *General Council, 1867–1927*, p. 10; 8th Meeting, 15 September 1886, in ibid., p. 12; 9th Meeting, 27 August 1889 (Second Day), in ibid., p. 13; and 17th Meeting, 2 August 1912, in ibid., p. 24.

107. Characteristic of his pragmatic nature, Charles shrugged off this momentous event in Sarawak's early history; though admitting the severity of the incident, he defended the Chinese 'for we must make allowances for the frailties of human nature'. C. Brooke, *Ten Years*, Vol. I, p. 84.

108. Ibid., pp. 84–5.

109. Ibid., pp. 85–6.

110. C. Brooke, *Queries*, p. 12.

111. C. Brooke, *Ten Years*, Vol. I, p. 86.

112. Ibid.

113. Ibid.

114. Charles Brooke to [Charles William] Daubeny, 22 March 1896, Letters of C. Brooke, SMA, Kuching.

115. 18th Meeting, 17 August 1915, in *General Council, 1867–1927*, p. 27.

116. 'Charles's Speech 15 August 1889', in Baring-Gould and Bampfylde, *A History of Sarawak*, pp. 408–9.

117. A. B. Ward, *Rajah's Servant*, Cornell University Southeast Asia Program Data Paper No. 61, Ithaca: Cornell University Press, 1966, pp. 18–19.

118. He confessed that he 'could not very severely blame them for head-hunting. It was an old established custom of their forefathers, and they considered it their duty to maintain it.' C. Brooke, *Ten Years*, Vol. I, p. 144.

119. Ibid.

120. Ibid., pp. 160–1.

121. See Chapter 3.

122. See *SG*, 3 January, 1873, n.p.; and *SG*, 17 February 1873, n.p.

123. The Lawas river basin was transferred in 1905 from British North Borneo. For the events leading to these annexations and the Lawas transfer and their political ramifications, see Baring-Gould and Bampfylde, *A History of Sarawak*, pp. 341, 344, 352, 355, and 362; Runciman, *The White Rajahs*, pp. 186, 194, and 197; and Colin N. Crisswell, *Rajah Charles Brooke: Monarch of All He Surveyed*, Kuala Lumpur: Oxford University Press, 1978, pp. 182–5 and 193–5.

124. 'Charles's Speech 15 August 1889', in Baring-Gould and Bampfylde, *A History of Sarawak*, pp. 408–9.

125. See 'Agreement between Her Majesty's Government and Charles Brooke, Second Rajah of Sarawak, 5 September 1888', in Anthony Brooke, *The Facts about Sarawak: A Documented Account of the Cession to Britain in 1946*, Bombay, 1947; reprinted Singapore: Summer Times, 1983, Appendix B, pp. 19–20.

126. For instance, see *SG*, 1 October 1872, n.p.; *SG*, 17 June 1873, n.p.; *SG*, 16 May 1874, n.p.; *SG*, 16 September 1872, n.p.; James R. M. Robertson, *Report on the Coal Field of Silantik Borneo*, Sarawak: Government Press, 1877, p. 37; and *SG*, 30 April 1880, pp. 25–6.

127. For instance, see 'Indenture between HH The Rajah and Thomas Shaw Safe', 22 April 1889, Agreement Book, Vol. I, SMA, Kuching; 10 December 1877, HH The Rajah's Order Book, Vol. I, SMA, Kuching; *SG*, 16 September 1872, n.p.; and *SG*, 1 October 1872, n.p.

128. See *SG*, 17 February 1873, n.p.; and *SG*, 31 March 1873, n.p.

129. See Baring-Gould and Bampfylde, *A History of Sarawak*, p. 357.

130. For instance, see *SG*, 26 February 1876, n.p.

131. 6th Meeting, 14 September 1880, in *General Council, 1867–1927*, p. 8. For similar themes, see 8th Meeting, 15 September 1886, in ibid., p. 11; 11th Meeting, 20 September 1894, in ibid., p. 17; and 16th Meeting, 17 July 1909, in ibid., p. 23.

132. 9th Meeting, 27 August 1889 (Second Day), in ibid., p. 14.

133. 'The Journal of Charles Brooke, September 1866–July 1868', Appendix in C. Brooke, *Ten Years*, Vol. II, p. 354.

134. 7th Meeting, 11 August, in *General Council, 1867–1927*, p. 9.

135. These reports, or abstracts of them, addressed personally to the Rajah, were reproduced in the *Gazette*, providing an invaluable source of information on the development of agriculture in the individual locality.

136. For instance, Alfred R. Houghton was assigned in 1872 to undertake investigations of the Land Dayaks of the left branch of the Sarawak River as to their willingness to cultivate new crops. He reported favourably to Charles. See *SG*, 15 February 1872, n.p.

137. For instance, cash rewards were offered for the best and largest *padi* farm or coconut plantation. See *SG*, 1 December 1871, n.p.; and Leonard Edwards and Peter W. Stevens, *Short Histories of the Lawas and Kanowit Districts*, Kuching: Borneo Literature Bureau, 1971, p. 43.

138. See 'Journal', in C. Brooke, *Ten Years*, Vol. II, p. 359.

139. 'Charles's Speech 15 August 1889', in Baring-Gould and Bampfylde, *A History of Sarawak*, pp. 408–9.

140. 9th Meeting, 26 August 1889, in *General Council, 1867–1927*, p. 14. This aspect of the use of government experimental gardens was clearly pronounced by D. J. S. Bailey, Resident of the Second Division, at the failure of the government coffee estate near Simanggang in 1896: 'The garden has done what was required of it viz: assisted to introduce planting amongst the natives, and it does not matter much if it be now abandoned.' *SG*, 1 February 1897, p. 35.

141. See Chapter 7.

142. See Odoardo Beccari, *Wanderings in the Great Forests of Borneo*, London: Archibald Constable, 1904; reprinted Singapore: Oxford University Press, 1986, p. 369.

143. See 'Journal', in C. Brooke, *Ten Years*, Vol. II, pp. 350, 354, 357, 359, and 361.

144. See *SG*, 15 March 1873, n.p.

145. See *SG*, 2 February 1891, p. 19.

146. See *SG*, 1 April 1902, p. 59.

147. See Chapter 5.

148. See *SG*, 2 March 1874, n.p.

149. See 11 November 1880, HH The Rajah's Order Book, Vol. I, SMA, Kuching. This pronouncement was reproduced in *SG*, 29 November 1880, p. 59.

150. See 'Memorandum of Agreement between the Sarawak Government and Messrs [Wong] Nai Siong & Tek Chiong of Chop Sim Hock Chew Kang', 27 July 1900, Agreement Book, Vol. II, SMA, Kuching.

151. See 'C. Brooke to Messrs Chiang Cho Shiong & Tang Kung Shook', 5 March 1901, Agreement Book, Vol. II, SMA, Kuching.

152. See C. A. Lockard, 'Charles Brooke and the Foundations of the Modern Chinese Community in Sarawak, 1863–1917', *SMJ*, 19, 38–9 (1971): 98–9.

153. *Sarawak as a Field for Planters: Improved and Enlarged, 1879*, Sarawak: Sarawak Gazette Office, n.d., p. 5.

154. 'By Order of the Rajah in Council 11 June 1863 and 21 January 1871, Land Regulations', *Sarawak Government Orders 1860–1891*, Kuching, Government Printing Office, Vol. I, p. 61.

155. 18th Meeting, 17 August 1915, in *General Council, 1867–1927*, p. 27. Emphasis added.

156. Ibid. For an elaboration of Charles's land policy, see Baring-Gould and Bampfylde, *A History of Sarawak*, pp. 433–4.

157. See *SG*, 2 January 1915, p. 3.

158. C. Brooke, *Queries*, p. 10.

159. For the rejection of prospective investors, see, for instance, Charles Brooke to Harry Brooke, 5 March 1910, HH The Rajah's Letters, SMA, Kuching.

160. 17th Meeting, 2 August 1912, in *General Council, 1867–1927*, p. 24.

161. Ibid. The Council's functions were as follows:

1. To receive draft estimates from the Treasury, discuss and give advice on all questions of income and expenditure.
2. If there is an undue extravagance in the disposal of land to companies or other bodies or persons (other than natives) or of monies, Council to report to [the Rajah].
3. To purchase of government stores and machinery.
4. To keep in touch with HM's Secretaries of State for the Foreign and Colonial Offices.

'Growth of Sarawak—Chronology 1917–1924', Typescript, MSS Pac. s. 83, Brooke Family Papers, Box 7, File 8, Item 1, p. 26, RHL, Oxford. See also *SG*, 16 January 1913, pp. 17–18; *Sarawak Civil Service List, 1930*, Kuching: Government Printing Office, 1930, p. 47; and T. Stirling Boyd, 'The Law and Constitution of Sarawak', Typescript, 1934, MSS Pac. s. 90, Basil Brooke Papers, pp. 54–5, RHL, Oxford.

162. 17th Meeting, 2 August 1912, in *General Council, 1867–1927*, p. 25.

163. 'The Political Will of Sir Charles Brooke, Rajah of Sarawak, dated 16 December 1913', MSS Brit. Emp. s. 365, Fabian Colonial Bureau, Box 161/1, Item 12, pp. 7–8, RHL, Oxford. The formation of the Advisory Council and Bertram's appointment sparked a row between Charles and his eldest son, Vyner, the heir apparent, who was apprehensive of his inheritance. For this father–son dispute according to Vyner's wife, Sylvia, who was not herself on the best of terms with her father-in-law, see Sylvia Brooke, *The Three White Rajas*, London: Cassell, 1939, pp. 136–50.

164. *SG*, 16 January 1872, n.p.

165. See Charles Brooke to F. H. Dallas, Treasurer, 5 November 1915, HH The Rajah's Letters, SMA, Kuching.

166. 15th Meeting, 2 July 1906, in *General Council, 1867–1927*, p. 21.

167. Charles was reputed to have decided upon which type of marble slab was to be used in the Kuching fish market.

168. The Sarawak Rangers were the trained regular army of the Raj. Its members were mostly Dayaks under the charge of European officers.

169. Charles took pride in the museum 'which is considered one of the best in the East'. 'The Political Will of Sir Charles Brooke', MSS Brit. Emp. s. 365, p. 4.

170. See Ooi Keat Gin, 'Sarawak Malay Attitudes towards Education during the Brooke Period, 1841–1946', *JSEAS*, 21, 2 (September 1990): 340–59.

171. Ward, *Rajah's Servant*, p. 173.

172. Comparing Sarawak's native inhabitants with industrial England's working class population, Charles was convinced that the former 'presents a happier aspect than that of our countrymen. In point of creature comforts the Dyak certainly have the best of it.' C. Brooke, *Ten Years*, Vol. II, p. 214.

173. Alleyne Ireland, *The Far Eastern Tropics: Studies in the Administration of Tropical Dependencies*, London: Archibald Constable, 1905, p. 77. Emphasis added.

174. 'Political Will of Sir Charles Brooke', MSS Brit. Emp. s. 365, p. 4.

175. See S. Brooke, *Three White Rajas*, p. 160.

176. Ranee Sylvia related three anecdotes which revealed the 'utter simplicity and naturalness' of Vyner's character. See ibid., pp. 162–4.

177. 'From the Depths of My Memory', by R. N. Turner, MSS Brit. Emp. s. 454(2), Vol. II, p. 5, RHL, Oxford.

178. Bertram was so deferential to Vyner, the Rajah, that he would not even take up residence at the Astana, and was unobtrusive when administering the government. He undertook his duty, as willed by his father, as a matter of fact without harbouring any personal political ambitions of his own.

179. Anthony John N. Richards to L. Brian Walsh Atkins, 27 December 1938, MSS Ind. Ocn. s. 213/7, RHL, Oxford. Richards, an Oxford graduate, joined the Sarawak Civil Service as a cadet in September 1938. He was rather critical of his brother officers, in particular of those from the outstations.

180. 22nd Meeting, 17 October 1927, in *General Council, 1867–1927*, p. 36.

181. Upon the retirement of H. B. Crocker as Chief Secretary in 1928, MacBryan suggested that Vyner should personally assume Crocker's responsibilities, which, in practice, meant that MacBryan would rule the country, considering the enormous influence he had over Vyner. For MacBryan's character, his career, and relationship with Vyner, see R. H. W. Reece, *The Name of Brooke: The End of White Rajah Rule in Sarawak*, Kuala Lumpur: Oxford University Press, 1982, pp. 19–29 and 32–7.

182. From the viewpoint of participants, see T. Stirling Boyd, 'Government in Sarawak', Typescript, 1934, MSS Pac. s. 86, Box 3, File 5, pp. 2–12, RHL, Oxford; and Dr J. H. Bowyer 'A Note on the Administration of Sarawak under the Brooke Regime', MSS Ind. Ocn. s. 315, RHL, Oxford. See also R. H. W. Reece, *The Name of Brooke*, pp. 61–9; and K. H. Digby, *Lawyer in the Wilderness*, Cornell University Southeast Asia Program Data Paper No. 114, Ithaca: Cornell University Press, 1980, p. 36.

183. 'Foreword', S. Brooke, *Three White Rajas*, p. vii.

184. Ibid., p. viii.

185. See 'Notes on Policy, Administration and Trade issued by the Sarawak Government Commission in London—January 1945', MSS Brit. Emp. s. 365, Fabian Colonial Bureau, Box 161/1, Item 9, p. 3, RHL, Oxford. This statement of policy was issued by the Provisional Government of Sarawak in January 1945 which undoubtedly was applicable in the pre-war years.

186. 'The Rajah's Speech to Council Negri', 25th Meeting, 29 April 1937, *SG*, 1 May 1937, Supplement, p. viii.

187. For instance, see the editorials of the *Gazette* of 28 April 1871; 1 and 15 July, and 16 October 1871; 16 July 1872; 1 July 1874; and 16 April 1877. There was an ongoing struggle on the part of the government in trying to promote *padi* cultivation among the native population which preferred the working and collecting of jungle produce to their *padi* farms. Later, at the turn of the century, the government had to face the uphill task of dissuading the people from focusing on the more lucrative, less labour-demanding attraction of rubber at the expense of rice production.

188. For the food crisis (1919–21), see *SG*, 16 January 1919, pp. 17–18, and 1 May 1919, p. 105. See also Ooi Keat Gin, 'The Sarawak Rice Crisis of 1919–1921: Rajah Vyner and the Brooke Rice Self-sufficiency Policy', Paper presented at the First Conference of the European Association for South-East Asian Studies (EUROSEAS): 'Keys to South-East Asia', Leiden, The Netherlands, 29 June–1 July 1995. A Committee of Food and Supply Control was set up to regulate the

distribution of rice and other food essentials, and the promotion of the cultivation of *padi* and other food crops as rice substitutes was intensified.

189. See 22nd Meeting, 17 October 1927, in *General Council, 1867–1927*, p. 35.

190. A Department of Agriculture was first instituted in 1915 and entrusted primarily with the responsibility of land alienation and land survey. The former function had hitherto been carried out by officers acting in the name of the 'Land Office', while the latter had been undertaken by the Public Works Department. The Director of Agriculture, then, had no control over agricultural issues which were left to the outstation administrators. Then, in 1919 the Department of Agriculture was renamed the Land and Survey Department and the Director of Agriculture became Superintendent of Lands and Surveys. The Department of Agriculture was revived in 1924 and had direct responsibilities over agricultural matters. See A. F. Porter, *Land Administration in Sarawak*, Kuching: Government Printing Office, 1967, p. 46.

191. 21st Meeting, 16 October 1924, in *General Council, 1867–1927*, p. 32; and *SG*, 1 February 1924, pp. 56–7.

192. The idea of setting up rice-farming colonies was first mooted by P. E. Andresen in a letter to the *Gazette*, dated 26 June 1871, whereby he suggested the importation 'from Java or Madura, [of] say 200 families of rice cultivating people' whose skills and experience could be learned by the local people. This idea was debated in the columns of the *Gazette* but apparently there was no evidence that such a scheme was implemented by the government. See *SG*, 1 July 1871, n.p. For the debate, see *SG*, 15 July 1871, n.p.; *SG*, 31 August 1871, n.p.; *SG*, 16 October 1871, n.p.; and *SG*, 13 April 1872, n.p.

193. See *Sarawak Administration Report (SAR), 1929*, Kuching: Government Printing Office, p. 22; and, *SAR, 1931*, p. 8.

194. *SAR, 1929*, p. 22.

195. 22nd Meeting, 17 October 1927, in *General Council, 1867–1927*, p. 35.

196. *SAR, 1931*, pp. 12–13.

197. 22nd Meeting, 17 October 1927, in *General Council, 1867–1927*, p. 35.

198. Ibid.

199. For the improvement of rubber cultivation and in its production, see *SAR, 1929*, pp. 18–19.

200. *SAR, 1931*, p. 13.

201. *SG*, 3 December 1923, pp. 361–2. See also 21st Meeting, 16 October 1924, in *General Council, 1867–1927*, p. 32. The Department was also entrusted with the task of reviewing import and export duties.

202. See *SG*, 3 December 1923, p. 362.

203. See *SG*, 3 January 1927, pp. 5–6; and 22nd Meeting, 17 October 1927, in *General Council, 1867–1927*, p. 34.

204. For the statistics on trade for the years of the Depression, see *SAR*, 1929–33, inclusive; and *SG*, 1 February 1932, p. 23.

205. See *SAR*, 1931, pp. 1–2.

206. 'The Rajah's Speech to Council Negri, 24th Meeting, 21 April 1934', *SG*, 1 May 1934, p. 51.

207. Under the International Rubber Regulation Agreement each participating country was allocated a basic quota which represented its 'estimated potential production', and each producer country had to abide by a table of permissible exports with the allocated percentages for each two-monthly period commencing from June 1934. For the main points in the Agreement, and Sarawak's basic quota and the percentage of permissible exports for 1934, see *SG*, 1 June 1934, pp. 66–7. See also

Andrew McFadyean (ed.), *The History of Rubber Regulation 1934–1943*, London: George Allen and Unwin, 1944.

208. The former ensured that the main points of the International Agreement were followed by Sarawak's rubber community, while the latter insisted upon rubber dealers and exporters taking out annual licences by which the government sought to regulate and control their activities. Any violation of the agreed export quota would mean the cancellation of the dealer's export licence. See *SAR, 1934*, p. 11.

209. For the working of rubber restriction, see *Rubber Regulation during 1936*, Kuching: Government Printing Office, 1937.

210. See W. F. N. Bridges, *Rubber Regulation in Sarawak: Interim Report*, Kuching: Kuching Press, 1937; and *Rubber Regulation during 1937*, Kuching: Government Printing Office, 1938.

211. 'The Rajah's Speech to Council Negri, 25th Meeting, 29 April 1937', *SG*, 1 May 1937, Supplement, pp. iii–iv. For the functioning of rubber restriction under the coupon system, see *SAR, 1938*, pp. 8–9.

212. See *SAR, 1931*, p. 2; and, *SG*, 1 April 1932, pp. 71–2.

213. See *SG*, 1 April 1920, p. 87; *SG*, 1 June 1920, p. 132; and *SG*, 2 August 1920, p. 176.

214. See *SG*, 1 October 1924, pp. 309–10, and *SG*, 2 November 1931, p. 234.

215. Peak production exceeded 28,000 ounces for the years 1934 and 1935. See F. W. Roe (comp.), *The Natural Resources of Sarawak*, 2nd rev. edn., Kuching: Government Printing Office, 1952, p. 25.

216. See G. C. Harper, 'The Miri Field, 1910–1972', *SMJ*, 20, 40–1 (January–December 1972): 26 and 28.

217. C. D. Le Gros Clark, *1935 Blue Report*, Kuching: Government Printing Office, 1935, p. 4. For the background of this *Blue Report*, see n. 269 below.

218. See *Oil in Sarawak, 1910–1960*, Miri: Sarawak Shell Oilfields Ltd., n.d., p. 8.

219. 'Order No. VIII, 1920', *Sarawak Government Gazette* (*SGG*), 1 March 1920, pp. 54–60; and 'Order No. IX, 1920, Supplementary to Land Order No. VIII, 1920, Land Regulations', *SGG*, 1 March 1920, pp. 61–2. The Supplementary Order provided the necessary regulations for the implementation of the Order itself.

220. Porter, *Land Administration*, Appendix C (22).

221. The term 'Native' was defined as 'a natural born subject of his Highness the Rajah'. By this, it could mean all ethnic groups, including Sarawak-born Chinese; however, in practice the latter were excluded. See 'Order No. VIII, 1920', Section 2.

222. 'Order No. VIII, 1920', Section 22.

223. 'Order No. IX, 1920', Section 2(i).

224. 22nd Meeting, 17 October 1927, in *General Council, 1867–1927*, p. 35.

225. *SAR, 1929*, p. 13.

226. Porter, *Land Administration*, p. 48. The Land and Survey Department, established in 1919, was divided into two separate departments in 1925. A Superintendent of Lands and a Superintendent of Surveys were appointed to head their respective departments. See ibid., p. 46.

227. 'Order No. L-2 (Land), 1931', dated 13 December 1931, *The Laws of Sarawak*, rev. edn., Kuching: Government Printing Office, 1947, Vol. I, p. 179.

228. The exceptions were 'Order No. XXIX, 1921' and 'Order No. XXI, 1922' pertaining to the Miri oilfield concessions.

229. See Porter, *Land Administration*, p. 51, n. 9.

230. 'Order No. L-7 (Land Settlement), 1933', dated 22 June 1933, was largely based on the recommendations of V. L. O. Sheppard, an expert on land registration, who was commissioned in 1931 to look into the methods hitherto employed by the Department of Land, and accordingly devised 'a system of registration of titles based on the territorial unit'. *SAR, 1931*, p. 27.

231. Land and Survey Department File 6–1/8, Folio 140, quoted in Porter, *Land Administration*, p. 51.

232. 'The Rajah's Speech to Council Negri, 25th Meeting, 29 April 1937', *SG*, 1 May 1937, Supplement, p. v.

233. 'Natives' according to 'Order No. I–1 (Interpretation), 1933', excluded the Chinese. See 'Order No. I–1 (Interpretation), 1933', *SGG*, 1 July 1933, pp. 160 and 164.

234. See *SAR, 1938*, pp. 28–9.

235. See 'Order No. V 1902', *SG*, 1 October 1902, p. 190. See also 'Order No. IV, 1903', *SG*, 2 May 1903, p. 83.

236. *SG*, 1 September 1902, p. 177.

237. J. P. Mead, the designated Conservator of Forests, put forward his ideas and plans for the protection and conservation of forests and the management of forests for their economic resources. See J. P. Mead, 'Forest Reservation in Sarawak', *SG*, 1 December 1919, pp. 307–9.

238. See *SG*, 2 May 1921, p. 72.

239. See *SG*, 3 January 1922, p. 3. A Forest Office was opened in Sibu in late 1920 to oversee the work of reservation in the Third Division. See *SG*, 2 May 1921, p. 73.

240. The Forests Rules of 1921 revoked all previous forests regulations.

241. 20th Meeting, 17 October 1921, in *General Council, 1867–1927*, p. 30.

242. *SG*, 1 February 1924, p. 35. Emphasis in original.

243. Ibid.

244. Ibid., p. 36.

245. For this uprising, see Robert Pringle, 'Asun's "Rebellion": The Political Growing Pains of a Tribal Society in Brooke Sarawak, 1929–1940', *SMJ*, 16, 32–3 (July–December 1968): 346–76; and Ooi Keat Gin, 'Rentap, Bantin and Asun: Iban "Rebels" or Iban "Nationalists" of Sarawak, 1841–1941', Paper presented at 'Pergerakan Sosial Dalam Sejarah (Social Movements in History)' Seminar of the History Section, School of Humanities, Universiti Sains Malaysia, Malaysia, 23 March 1996.

246. 'Order No. F–1 (Forests) 1934' replaced all hitherto forest legislations. See *SAR, 1934*, p. 11. For Vyner's comments on the creation of 'Protected Forests', see 'The Rajah's Speech to Council Negri, 25th Meeting, 29 April 1937', *SG*, 1 May 1937, Supplement, p. iv.

247. *SAR, 1934*, p. 5. See also *SAR, 1935*, p. 5.

248. *SAR, 1934*, p. 5. The post of Conservator of Forests was abolished in February 1934, and the Forestry Department henceforth was directed by a Senior Forest Officer. Ibid.

249. Demarcated forests of whatever designation were also useful politically as buffers between two antagonistic native peoples, and as means of controlling incursions into disaffected areas. Such a utilitarian role was put into effect in 1937 as one of the measures to control Dayak unrest. A 'Protected Forest' was created encompassing a large area of the watershed between the Second and Third Divisions in order that the Dayaks of the former could not cross over to join the rebels in the latter. See *SAR, 1936*, p. 5; *SAR, 1937*, p. 6; and *SAR, 1938*, p. 6.

250. See *SAR, 1938*, p. 6.

251. 21st Meeting, 16 October 1924, in *General Council, 1867–1927*, p. 32. See also 20th Meeting, 17 October 1921, in ibid., p. 30.

252. See *SG*, 1 February 1929, p. 18.

253. *SG*, 1 October 1930, p. 253.

254. See Chapter 6.

255. See *SAR, 1937*, p. 16.

256. See *Sarawak Government Almanac*, Kuching: National Printing Department, 1993, pp. 3 and 4.

257. See *SG*, 1 February 1929, p. 17; *SG*, 1 February 1929, p. 20; and *SG*, 1 August 1928, p. 158.

258. See *SAR, 1935*, p. 21; and *Almanac*, p. 4.

259. See 21st Meeting, 16 October 1924, in *General Council, 1867–1927*, p. 32; 22nd Meeting, 17 October 1927, in ibid., p. 35; and *SAR, 1929*, p. 29.

260. See *SG*, 1 December 1925, p. 322. Nevertheless, in 1929, owing to the scarcity of land in the Foochow concession in the Baram and to avoid Chinese encroachment on native land, the Resident of the Fourth Division, H. D. Alpin, advised the cessation of Foochow immigration into the district. See *SG*, 1 July 1929, pp. 121 and 122.

261. Earlier in 1927, a Labour Department was established which Vyner described as 'necessary in order to give a guarantee to the Governments of countries [from] whence immigrants arrive, and to the immigrants themselves, that their interests are being safe-guarded'. 22nd Meeting, 17 October 1927, in *General Council, 1867–1927*, p. 35. Although the majority of immigrant labourers were of Chinese stock, arrangements were being made for the importation of Indian coolies. See *SG*, 3 January 1928, p. 2.

262. See *SAR, 1929*, pp. 55–6 and 58; and *SG*, 1 February 1929, p. 17. A *mui tsai* was usually a young girl who was brought over from China betrothed but in practice became a common domestic servant of the family. It appears that the Sarawak authorities were unaware of the differences between a *mui tsai* and a bona fide Chinese female domestic servant or *amah*. Nevertheless, 'Order No. M–3 (Mui Tsai), 1931' was to correct this abuse as it was designed 'to control and regulate the acquisition and employment of female domestic servants known as Mui Tsai'. *SAR, 1930*, p. 53. For details of *mui tsai*, see Victor Purcell, *The Chinese in Malaya*, Kuala Lumpur: Oxford University Press, 1967, pp. 179–84; and, for *amah*, see Ooi Keat Gin, 'Domestic Servants Par Excellence: The Black & White Amahs of Malaya and Singapore with Special Reference to Penang', *JMBRAS*, 65, 2 (December 1992): 69–84.

263. As a preventive measure against problems arising from unemployment, immigration into Miri was severely restricted from March 1930, and extended to the Third Division in July of the same year, together with a greater control of Chinese activities in all ports. In addition to the 'guarantee system', 'Order No. D–2 (Disembarkation), 1934' came into force by which newly arrived immigrants might be required to pay a deposit before being allowed to land. See *SAR, 1930*, p. 51 and *SAR, 1934*, pp. 11 and 17.

264. See *SAR, 1934*, p. 17.

265. See *SAR, 1935*, p. 28.

266. See *SAR, 1937*, p. 33. No restriction was put on female immigration except in the case of *mui tsai* who were strongly discouraged.

267. The peacemaking ceremonies were in 1920 at Simanggang, between the Dayaks of the Upper Batang Lupar and those of the Skrang, Lemanak, and Saribas

rivers; in 1924, there were two such ceremonies, one at Simanggang, between the Dayaks of the Upper Batang Lupar and those of the Lower Rejang, and the other at Kapit, between the Dayaks and their erstwhile enemies, the Kayans and Kenyahs. For details of these peacemaking ceremonies, see Pringle, *Rajahs and Rebels*, pp. 234, 235, 239, and 264; and Runciman, *The White Rajahs*, pp. 237–9. There were apparently some differences of opinion as to whether such ceremonies had indigenous origins or were a Brooke invention. See Pringle, *Rajahs and Rebels*, pp. 32, n. 1 and 239; and Reece, *The Name of Brooke*, p. 21.

268. For instance, see *SG*, 1 March 1921, p. 30.

269. The *1935 Blue Report* was commissioned by Vyner in 1934 to inquire into the results of the survey of the working of the administration; the report would act as a guide to the formulation of 'a definite policy for the future development of the State'. *SAR, 1935*, p. 34. The task was entrusted to a serving Brooke officer, Cyril Le Gros Clark, who was then the Secretary for Chinese Affairs and later became Chief Secretary in 1941. Although some of his recommendations were considered, the rest were shelved partly owing to financial constraints, but rather more because of the poor support it received from the Kuching bureaucrats.

270. Clark, *1935 Blue Report*, p. 49. Emphasis added. In fact, Le Gros Clark suggested the abolition of shifting cultivation and the longhouse system, both of which were incompatible with the ultimate objective of converting the Dayaks to being sedentary farmers. See ibid., p. 47. See also Chapter 7.

271. See *SAR, 1929*, p. 58; and *SAR, 1938*, p. 33.

272. 'Growth of Sarawak', MSS Pac. s. 83, p. 47. Emphasis added.

273. 'The Rajah's Speech to Council Negri, 24th Meeting, 21 April 1934, *SG*, 1 May 1934, p. 52. Emphasis added. See also 22nd Meeting, 17 October, 1927, in *General Council, 1867–1927*, p. 35; and 'The Rajah's Speech to Council Negri, 25th Meeting, Kuching, 29 April 1937, *SG*, 1 May 1937, Supplement, p. viii. It was clear that Vyner was not supportive of big foreign businesses investing in Sarawak nor the expansion of those already in the country. However, T. Charles Martine, the manager of BCL during the 1930s, blamed the Brooke officers and not Vyner himself for this anti-foreign capital stance of the government. See T. Charles Martine, 'The Borneo Company Ltd., in Sarawak (From "Notes written by me when in Singapore Changi Gaol, 1943–4")', Typescript, p. 4, SMA, Kuching; and Chapter 9.

274. See 22nd Meeting, 17 October 1927, in *General Council, 1867–1927*, p. 35.

275. Nissa Shokai, a Japanese-owned rubber estate in the Samarahan River, was the only non-European commercial plantation operating in the 1930s. See Chapter 9.

276. A. H. Moy-Thomas, 'Economic Development under the Second Rajah (1870–1917)', *SMJ*, 10, 17–18 (July–December 1961): 50.

277. Charles would not tolerate any form of extravagance whether by his family or his officers. For instance, see Runciman, *The White Rajahs*, p. 216, n.2.

278. 'Political Will of Sir Charles Brooke', MSS Brit. Emp. s. 365, pp. 3–4.

279. 'The Rajah's Speech to Council Negri, 24th Meeting, 21 April 1934', *SG*, 1 May 1934, p. 52.

280. The reasons behind Chinese susceptibility to subversive leftist propaganda during the 1950s could be traced to their alienation and treatment during the Brooke period. For a perspective of one of the main problems facing the Chinese community during the 1950s and early 1960s, namely the issue of education, see Ooi Keat Gin, 'Education in Sarawak during the Period of Colonial Administration, 1946–1963', *JMBRAS*, 63, 2 (December 1990): 35–68.

281. 'Notes on Policy–January 1945', MSS Brit. Emp. s. 365, p. 1.

PART II
IMPLEMENTATION

3
Trade and Commerce

THE concept of free trade was introduced by James with the promulgation of a set of laws particularly aimed at facilitating commercial intercourse, but, before free trade could be carried out several obstacles had to be removed. Traditional trade, namely in jungle produce and sago, was promoted, and this benefited the native participants. With the establishment of law and order and further territorial acquisitions during Charles's reign, domestic trade flourished, even in the interior, while foreign trade increased in volume and value. Jungle products and sago remained the mainstay of Sarawak's exports until the turn of the century when gold, pepper, mineral oil, and rubber succeeded as the chief foreign exchange earners. The country remained a rice importer throughout the period of Brooke rule.

The Brooke policies of native protection and the encouragement of small-scale peasant farmers created the problems of product adulteration and the generally low quality of the produce. Measures were undertaken to improve the quality of the country's exports. The Board of Trade, instituted during Vyner's rule, improved the quality and consequently the value of both rubber and pepper. The country's internal and external trade was mainly controlled by Chinese entrepreneurs working hand in hand with the BCL, which remained the main European commercial enterprise in Sarawak. Trade and commerce throughout the century of Brooke rule progressed steadily, and overall, Sarawak enjoyed a favourable trade balance. Economic downturns and trade depressions from without undoubtedly had repercussions on the country. Yet, with the cautious Brooke policies, recovery was effected without undue dislocation.

Free Trade and the Improvement of Native Livelihood

With the establishment of the Raj, James sought to ensure that free trade would improve native welfare. A commentator in the mid-1860s observed with pleasure that 'the trade of Sarawak, like that of Singapore, is absolutely free. No dues or customs whatever are

exacted from vessels entering the river, whether European or native, and the good results of this liberality will, no doubt, be shortly apparent.'[1] Although there were certain nominal duties on exports and imports, these were introduced as a device for controlling the trade in particular products rather than solely to enrich the state coffers. The concept and working of free trade were confidently assured by Charles in a speech to the General Council of 1915: 'So far as trade in this country was concerned ... [t]he Government fixed no rules and allowed it to take its own free course as much as possible. Parties knew best where and when to find what they wanted on the sea, or in the rivers, inland, or on the coast. *Trade ... should be left free in the broadest sense.*'[2]

Territorial acquisitions at the expense of Brunei expanded Sarawak's natural resources. The sago-rich coast was ceded in 1861, and sago featured as Sarawak's chief export for the next four decades. The Baram cession to Charles in 1882 proved a boon when mineral oil was struck at Miri in the early part of the twentieth century. Mineral oil remained the major foreign exchange earner up to the eve of the Japanese occupation. Charles's extension of Sarawak's borders further enlarged the sources of jungle produce. The trade in these together with that in sago was the mainstay of the country's economy before the advent of mineral oil and rubber, and, more than anything else, benefited the native participants—the Dayak, Kayan, and Kenyah collectors, and the Melanau sago producers.

Promotion of Native Commerce and Expansion of Trade

Prior to the establishment of Brooke rule, Sarawak's trade was carried out with the neighbouring islands and with China, the former mainly in sago and the latter in luxury jungle products. This trade, however, was intermittent and limited. Raffles's founding of Singapore introduced a new and relatively profitable market for Sarawak's products. When antimony ore was discovered in the early 1820s, this mineral found a ready market in Singapore. The Melanau sago producers of Sarawak also benefited considerably through Singapore which presented their sago to the world market. Some jungle products with medicinal properties, like bezoar stones and rhinoceros horns, and Chinese delicacies, such as birds' nests, found a ready and profitable outlet at Singapore. Imports during this pre-Brooke period were mostly salt, iron, steel, ceramics, brass gongs, cloth, beads, the much-prized Chinese earthen jars,[3] and other novelties.

The establishment of Brooke rule with its public order, law courts, and stability of government undoubtedly facilitated and promoted commerce. It increased the confidence of traders as to the safety of their person and properties, and this, in turn, led to the penetration of Chinese and Malay boat traders into the far interior. Native trade in jungle produce and sago increased in quantity and value. The increased demand for gutta, *jelutong*, and other jungle produce in the last quarter of the nineteenth century encouraged the working of these products by the energetic Dayaks and other indigenous peoples. In addition, the sago industry and trade along the coast flourished, particularly after 1870.

By the close of James's reign in the late 1860s, the main export products of Sarawak in order of importance were sago, gutta-percha, India rubber, antimony ore, and birds' nests. Sago remained an important export item for the next three decades. The trade in wild rubbers, rattans, and other jungle produce enjoyed a prosperous period towards the close of the nineteenth century. In fact, jungle products, particularly wild rubbers, together with sago not only sustained but also brought financial stability and some prosperity to the Brooke Raj in the first three decades of Charles's reign.

The Sago Trade and Industry

Sago had long been an important product and item of trade for the Melanau communities. The sago-producing rivers of Igan, Oya, and Mukah had been under the nominal jurisdiction of the Brunei Sultanate whose representatives positioned themselves strategically at the mouths of these rivers to control the valuable sago trade. Sago was exported in the form of baked biscuits which were consumed as a food substitute for rice by the poorer classes in the Eastern Archipelago. Besides the Melanau, other exporters included those in Cochin-China, Java, Sumatra, and other islands in the Netherlands East Indies.[4]

The opening of Singapore in 1819 revolutionized the sago industry and its trade. From the 1820s the European and American demand for sago as an industrial starch for their textile industry pushed up the price and made sago a very profitable trade item.[5] Raw sago was shipped to Singapore for processing into a form acceptable to the world market, either as sago flour or as pearl sago.[6] The trade was profitable to both manufacturers and cultivators alike. The Melanau sago districts of Borneo were the chief suppliers to the Chinese-owned sago mills of Singapore.[7]

The Malay traders of Sarawak competed with the Brunei merchants for the sago trade. The former as relative newcomers had to arrange for their agents to purchase sago direct from the upriver cultivators as they faced fierce competition from the more established Brunei buyers at the downriver districts.

When the Brooke Raj was constituted in 1841, its capital, Kuching, became a processing centre for Melanau sago. Factories were set up there by Chinese entrepreneurs who were supplied by the Malay sago traders. After being processed at Kuching, the sago was transhipped to Singapore and thence to the world market.

Dissatisfied with the running of the sago mills at Kuching whilst relying on their sago supplies from Malay traders, Chinese entrepreneurs and the BCL, after the 1861 cession, set up factories and retail shops in the sago districts, progressively replacing the Malay traders and their agents.[8] Chinese-owned shops cornered the retail trade in manufactured goods and imported rice which supplied the needs of the fast-prospering Melanau sago districts.

There was little interference on the part of the Brookes in the sago industry besides ensuring that peace and security were maintained.[9] The traditional social and political structures of the local Melanaus that governed sago production and its trade were left relatively intact.

By the mid-1870s Sarawak's sago trade was fast prospering. It was enthusiastically reported that:

> In 1865 the export of this article was only $67,207 since which time it has steadily advanced, and last year [1874] it reached $301,980 having increased nearly five fold in nine years; during the same period there has been a corresponding increase and improvement in the shipping employed in the carrying trade, and we have now a large fleet of European rigged native coasters.[10]

By the early part of the 1890s there were no less than ten sago factories operating in the country, located mainly at Kuching.[11] Mukah remained pre-eminent in the production and trade of sago, with Oya next in importance, followed by Bintulu, Matu, and Bruit.[12]

Sago flour remained the chief agricultural export of Sarawak throughout the nineteenth century, and tonnage increased yearly until it stabilized in the early 1890s, and from then remained constant throughout the Brooke period.[13] In the last three decades of the nineteenth century, 'the financial stability of Sarawak rested largely on the sago industry'.[14] Sarawak, in fact, supplied about half the world's sago needs during this period.

Trade in Jungle Produce

Prior to the advent of the Brooke Raj, a barter trade had long existed between the indigenous peoples and the Chinese. In exchange for such exotic items as kingfisher feathers, bezoar stones, birds' nests, rhinoceros horns, and casques of the helmeted hornbill (known as hornbill ivory or *ho-ting*), the natives received beads, iron, brassware, crockery, salt, and earthen jars from the Chinese traders.

However, this trade with China was limited.[15] It was only after the opening of Singapore that trade in Bornean products became more active, and then increased further in volume and value following the establishment of the Brooke Raj.[16] (Appendix 5 shows the individual products collectively referred to as jungle produce procured from Sarawak's rain forests and swampy marshes along the coast.)

Most of the jungle produce like rattan, and the varieties of dammar and gutta are to be found in the inland forest. Along the narrow strips of riverine alluvial soils in the upper reaches of fast-flowing streams, various species of *engkabang* are to be found, whereas along slow-flowing rivers, the hardwood *billian* predominates. The coastal mangrove swamps offer a valuable source of *nipah*, firewood, and charcoal.

As Mark C. Cleary[17] points out, the trade in jungle produce in Sarawak and the rest of Borneo conformed to the trading model devised by F. L. Dunn who identifies four groups in the trading network:

1. The collectors—usually the interior ethnic groups.
2. Primary traders—usually the interior ethnic groups who collect the product and in some cases sell or barter the goods to other ethnic groups in touch with secondary traders.
3. Secondary traders—Chinese/Malay usually located along the rivers or coasts at the junction of ecological, hence trading, zones.
4. Tertiary traders—usually Chinese located at port sites and engaged directly in the international trading of jungle products.[18]

The principal collectors and primary traders were the Dayaks, in particular those from the Batang Lupar, the Saribas, and the Rejang, who often ventured to other parts of the country and even to neighbouring territories. In the Baram and the Upper Rejang, the Kayans and Kenyahs competed with the Dayaks as collectors and primary traders. Traditionally the collection of jungle produce

by natives was a supplementary activity to subsistence rice farming. Jungle products were exchanged for salt, cloth, and other items that could not be found in the forest.[19] However, when demand for jungle products like gutta, *jelutong*, and rattan rose, the attraction of the high prices encouraged the natives to be collectors and primary traders, even to the extent of neglecting rice cultivation.[20]

Both Malays and Chinese functioned as secondary traders in jungle products. The Chinese gradually displaced their Malay counterparts and the Brunei traders in the Baram, and by the close of the last century had succeeded in excluding them altogether.[21]

While James had ensured that the coast was secure from raiders, it was then left to Charles to keep the peace and enforce law and order in the interior. Government stations, such as Kapit, Belaga, and Balleh in the Upper Rejang and Balleh rivers and Marudi in the Baram, were established to maintain the peace and function as collecting centres for jungle produce. The setting-up of such stations, garrisoned with Rangers, initially aroused the suspicions of the local inhabitants, but they were gradually won over as the economic benefits began to be realized.

It was the policy of the Brookes to promote trade in jungle produce which was seen as a means of improving native livelihood. James, writing in his *Journal*, stated that 'our intercourse with natives of the interior should be frequent and intimate ... a friendly intercourse would develop the resources of the interior, draw its produce to our markets, gradually tend to the enlightenment of the wild tribes and check their propensity for war'.[22] It was during Charles's reign that these 'resources of the interior', became significant trade items and export earners.

Charles's policy of expecting each division of the country to be financially self-reliant and at the same time contribute to the Kuching Treasury indirectly promoted the trade in jungle produce. Brooke administrators in the outstations encouraged the natives to collect jungle products for export thereby earning revenue for the district through export duties.[23] This policy was illustrated clearly in the early days of the Fourth and Fifth Divisions when local Brooke officers allowed Dayaks from other divisions to work jungle produce in their forests much to the displeasure of the local inhabitants, notably the Kayans and Kenyahs of the Baram.[24]

The collection of export duties on this trade enriched the Brooke government.[25] In fact, the revenue generated from jungle produce was second only to that from sago as the largest financial contributor to the Brooke Raj for the last three decades of the nineteenth-

TABLE 3.1

Exports of Jungle Products (Excluding Timber), 1870–1940

	Guttas																	
	Gutta-percha		India Rubber		Gutta-jangkar		Gutta-jelutong		Dammar		Rattans No. 1,2, & c.		Malacca Canes		Cutch (Mangrove)		Nipah Sugar	
Year	*Tons*	*£*	*Tons*	*£*	*Tons*	*£*	*Tons*	*£*	*Tons*	*£*	*Tons*	*£*	*Nos.*	*£*	*Tons*	*£*	*Tons*	*£*
1870	–	96,470	–	4,450	–	–	–	–	–	210	–	90	–	–	–	–	–	–
1900	476	91,970	208	41,040	–	–	24	270	298	1,950	2,458	32,670	–	–	–	–	292	1,690
1910	101	21,780	155	39,670	387	14,820	6,363	117,090	125	1,720	1,238	10,830	–	–	–	–	173	1,210
1920	24	16,320	–	130	71	5,310	5,227	233,820	679	42,490	1,054	12,080	271,300	2,460	3,640	56,300	577	13,540
1930	1	110	–	–	113	5,180	3,893	101,430	470	8,200	446	3,100	580,000	2,360	2,520	55,840	161	1,010
1940	12	3,770	2	10	173	13,240	1,429	90,440	1,292	3,700	190	1,420	200	–	2,510	55,510	–	–

Source: Smythies, 'History of Forestry in Sarawak', p. 174.

Note: Other produce included illipe nuts, beeswax, charcoal, *gaharu* wood, *laka* wood, mangrove bark, and *nipah* salt.

century.[26] The trade returns from the mid-1870s to the first decade of the twentieth century showed that the various jungle products overall accounted for one-third of the country's total exports annually.[27] (Table 3.1 shows the quantity and value of exports of the different jungle products.)

Important Exports and Main Imports

Jungle products and sago were the main export earners for the Brooke economy towards the close of the nineteenth century. These, more than mineral resources or the agricultural schemes of Charles's, generated the finances for the Raj and the consequent prosperity enjoyed by both government and people alike. However, the importance and contribution of jungle produce declined after the first decade of the twentieth century with the rise in the production of pepper and gold, and later Para rubber and mineral oil; these in turn became the main foreign exchange earners (Figure 3.1). Sago, however, remained an important export throughout Brooke rule.

Antimony ore, mined since the 1820s, reached its peak in the early 1870s and thereafter declined in importance. Gold, worked by the Chinese mainly in the district of Upper Sarawak in the 1840s and 1850s, did not contribute much to export earnings at that time. Production was small owing mainly to the primitive methods employed by the miners. The years following the Chinese uprising of 1857 were lean years for gold-mining, and it was another decade before the industry gradually started up again when the Chinese returned to Sarawak to resume their mining activities. The latter half of the 1890s witnessed a revitalization of the gold industry with the entry of the BCL and its introduction of modern extraction processes. Production rose dramatically when the celebrated cyanide method of extracting gold ore was applied to Sarawak's industry. By the turn of the century gold had displaced antimony as the most important mineral export, and was second only to pepper as the chief export in terms of value. Gold continued to be an important export item until the early 1920s when the BCL decided to abandon their gold works due to declining production.

Charles was convinced that the wealth of the country and its future well-being lay in its agricultural products. Accordingly, during the last quarter of the 1870s the cultivation of gambier and pepper was encouraged, with very generous offers to Chinese planters to establish this industry in Sarawak. Gambier was exported

FIGURE 3.1
Exports of Sarawak, 1840–1940

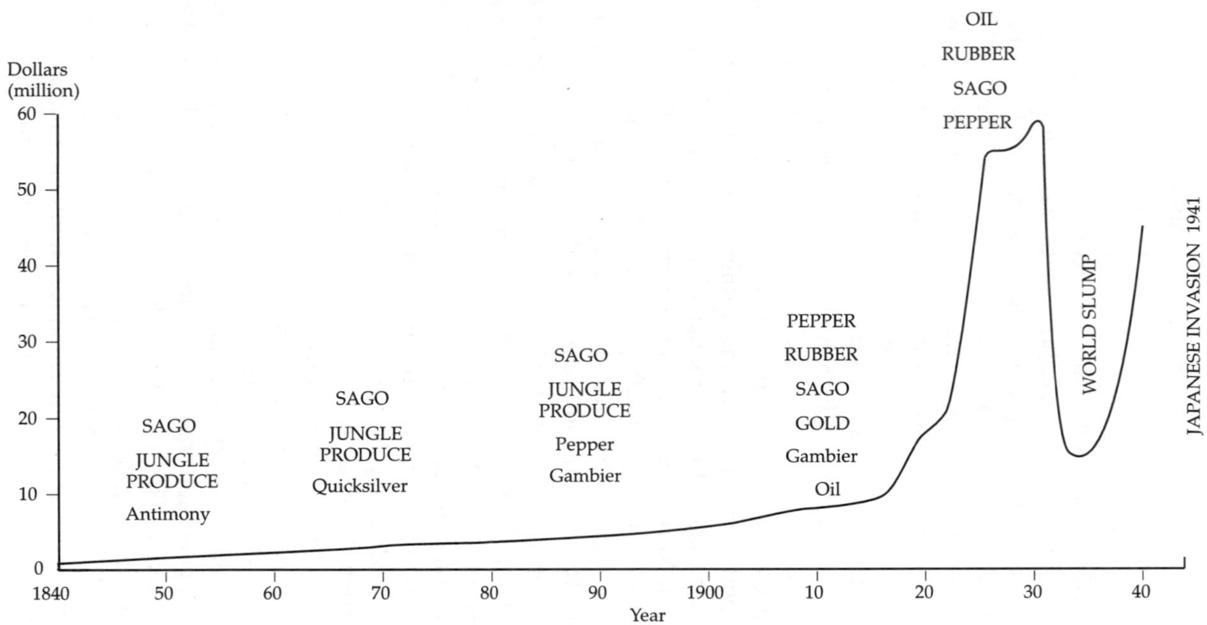

Source: After Rawlins, *Sarawak, 1839–1963*, p. 196.
Note: Capitalization denotes major exports.

in the late 1870s and continued thereafter but it never enjoyed the success of the more profitable pepper. Pepper had been cultivated in Borneo by Chinese settlers and featured as an important trade item of Brunei in the early nineteenth century.[28] The decline of the Sultanate saw the demise of the industry as well. Pepper was reintroduced in Sarawak initially as a secondary crop to gambier as the refuse from the boiled gambier leaves was utilized as manure for the pepper vines. Pepper was first exported in 1879 and the two decades that followed saw its fortunes flourish when world demand progressively increased. It was Sarawak's premier export at the turn of the century and continued to feature as an important trade item during the remaining period of Brooke rule despite problems of price fluctuations and disease.

Two new exports which were to dominate in the last twenty years of Brooke rule made their appearance towards the end of the first decade of the twentieth century. Rubber was first listed as an export item in 1910, and within a decade became the most important agricultural product of the country. Mineral oil was struck at Miri in 1910, and three years later saw the first shipment of Sarawak oil. By 1920 petroleum had outstripped all other exports and became the chief foreign exchange earner for the Brooke Raj until the outbreak of the Pacific War.

The Depression (1929–31) temporarily disrupted trade and saw a declining demand for Sarawak's products. Nevertheless, during this period of economic slow-down, the gold industry experienced a temporary revival, thereby softening the effects of the Depression and at the same time absorbing redundant, largely Chinese, labour. The abandoned gold-mines of the BCL were reworked by the industrious Chinese who then employed up-to-date mining methods and modern extraction processes. Gold once again re-entered the list of exports. Its production increased dramatically reaching a peak in 1935, and from then on declined again.

Sarawak's recovery from the Depression was relatively swift and by 1933 conditions had more or less returned to the pre-1929 level of prosperity. The mid-1930s also witnessed the expansion of the timber export trade with direct shipments to Europe and Britain. Timber had been exported to Hong Kong, Singapore, and China since the early 1870s but remained small, intermittent, and generally insignificant as a foreign exchange contributor.

Towards the close of Brooke rule the most important exports in order of value were petroleum, rubber, pepper, timber, sago flour, *jelutong*, and copra.

The main imports of Sarawak remained the same throughout

the Brooke period, namely rice and other foodstuffs and manufactured goods. Despite the efforts of the Brookes to promote self-sufficiency in rice production, particularly emphasized during Vyner's reign, rice remained the major and the most essential import.

Domestic Trade and Chinese Economic Domination

The internal trade of Sarawak during the pre-Brooke period was mainly in the hands of the local Malays and those from Brunei. It was carried out mostly through barter. During the early nineteenth century the Spanish dollar was gradually introduced as a mode of currency. But it was the Brookes who popularized the adoption of a cash economy with the minting of copper and silver coinage as a medium of exchange that gradually replaced barter. The greater participation of the Chinese in commercial activities during the decade following the 1857 uprising, and their preference for Brooke coinage in trade inevitably hastened the transformation of the traditional barter economy to one based on cash.

The Chinese involvement in Sarawak's domestic trade from the mid- and late 1860s gradually expanded. By the 1870s their domination and near-monopoly of internal trade was becoming apparent. Chinese entrepreneurs and traders increasingly displaced their Malay counterparts, not only in the coastal districts but also in the interior.[29] The following decades witnessed the consolidation of this hold on the country's commercial life. The Chinese entrepreneurs of Kuching, the big *towkay*,[30] and their lesser counterparts in the outstation towns controlled a network of business links that connected the various bazaars throughout the length and breadth of the country.

Brooke policy favoured a Chinese mercantile class. Chinese displacement of Malay traders was welcomed by the Brooke government which viewed trading as an inappropriate vocation for the Malays. The fact that the Brookes had incorporated the Malay aristocratic élite into their administrative system penalized them from participation in trade, for the Brookes were staunch advocates of the nineteenth-century British liberal ethic that those who governed should abstain from commercial activities lest their integrity be compromised. Even for the Malay peasantry, the Brookes advocated agricultural pursuits.[31]

The collection of all produce, from raw sago and jungle products, to pepper, gambier, and Para rubber sheets, was in the hands of the Chinese shopkeepers in the outstation bazaars, who in turn

had direct links with the Kuching *towkay*. The distribution and retail trade then flowed from the Kuching merchant houses to the bazaar shopkeepers, and thence to the downstream kampongs and upriver longhouses through the boat traders. This network of trade was based on clan and speech-group affiliation. This dialect-group affinity which pervaded all areas of Chinese life in Sarawak was particularly marked in commercial relationships from which 'outsiders' were completely excluded.

The dictum that 'trade follows the flag' was applicable to Brooke Sarawak. The erection of a Brooke fort would, in a short interval, inevitably witness the construction of Chinese shophouses.[32] The bazaars, some no more than a score of shophouses, served as the collection and distribution centres of trade goods.

Chinese Bazaar Shopkeepers and Boat Traders

Trade in the outstations rested in the hands of the Chinese bazaar shopkeeper, the sole economic link to the world beyond. The shopkeeper was the collector and purchaser of native agricultural and jungle products; these were forwarded to the shopkeeper's counterpart in Kuching, the *towkay* of the big Chinese firm. The latter in turn shipped them to his counterpart in Singapore. In reverse, the Kuching *towkay* received shipments of goods, like rice, ceramics, and manufactured articles, which he then passed on to the bazaar shopkeeper who sold them to the visiting native.

Another channel through which the native could purchase such imported goods was the boat trader who purchased his stock of goods from the bazaar shopkeeper and resold them to his native customers. Boat traders also acted as middlemen for the shopkeeper in the collection of native produce. Traditionally these boat traders were Malays, but they were gradually forced out of business by the Chinese.

The itinerant boat traders had a hard and precarious livelihood.

> [They] would get up at the crack of dawn and row until nightfall, for up to twelve hours at a stretch, under a hot sun, their journeys being interrupted by stops at longhouses along the way. If they rowed with the tide and current, their task was made much easier; if not, it could be a body-aching job, their arms having to move the oars continuously. Boat pedlars could be away from the bazaar for periods of a week to a month.[33]

They were in a more vulnerable position than the bazaar shopkeepers, and in many instances were literally at the mercy of the natives. They 'had to rely on their wits, bravery, and tenacity to survive, taking particular care over etiquette and the establishing of

goodwill'.[34] They could be robbed, and sometimes even murdered, by the natives, or drowned in the turbulent rivers.[35]

The majority of outstation shopkeepers and boat traders were Hokkiens and Teochews, the remainder being Hakkas, Chaoans, Hainanese, and Foochows. The domination of Hokkiens and Teochews was due to the fact that the Chinese wholesale trade in Kuching was also in the hands of these two dialect groups. The Chinese were notoriously exclusive in their business connections and, for that matter, all other relationships in general; these were guided by the principle of 'dealing with their own kind'.[36]

From Barter to Cash, Advances, and Credit

The establishment of Brooke rule and the introduction of coinage and its greater use by the Chinese transformed Sarawak's outstation trade into an economy based on cash rather than barter. Another innovation was the use of advances and credit in the trade with the natives, which the latter adopted with surprising acumen.

The credit chain stretched from the Singapore firms and banks to the Kuching *towkay*, the outstation shopkeepers, the upriver boat traders, and ultimately to the native producers/consumers. It was also not uncommon for natives who visited the bazaars with their goods to receive credit from the shopkeeper. However, the system of credit suffered several weaknesses. First, instability in any one of the links had repercussions along the whole chain. An illustration of this vulnerability was the collapse of a certain bank in Singapore that had dealings with Sarawak businesses; it affected far-away Simanggang shopkeepers.

> The failure of the Kong Aik Chinese bank in Singapore has indirectly affected some of the traders in this division. It appears that certain Kuching *towkays* have been obliged to find money to bolster up their affairs, and therefore summoned their debtors in the outstations.
>
> Traders here are dependent entirely on raw produce, and as trade has not been flourishing lately they are hard put to it to provide the necessary payments, and in any case the sudden call on their resources will be bound to affect trade especially as money is scarce in the bazaars and there will be probably insufficient [cash] to purchase the crop of illipe nuts (*engkabang*) which is now ripening.[37]

Secondly, the natives understood very well that the Brooke government favoured them in cases of indebtedness. Brooke policy decreed that natives could not be prosecuted in debt courts. 'Dayaks lived far away in the upper reaches of the river', Charles Brooke reminded a Sibu Court, 'and if they, the Chinese, gave

advances to such people they did so at their own risk.'[38] Thirdly, boat traders and bazaar shopkeepers alike, when deep in debt without much hope of settlement and unable to secure further credit, often absconded to escape prosecution. The favourite refuge for debtors was Brunei.[39]

Despite its apparent disadvantages and abuses, the system of credit was necessary as a means of expanding trade in the outstations. Although some shopkeepers and boat traders did suffer heavy losses from bad debts, their situation was not an entirely despondent one. In fact, the more sophisticated and knowledgeable Chinese shopkeepers and boat traders ultimately made their profits, for as middleman, 'they had the advantage of being able to buy jungle produce in one market and sell it in another ... capitalizing on [their] knowledge and market organization [they] made profits ... [they] were at home in both markets ... [taking] advantage of the gap between them'.[40] Naturally the bazaar shopkeepers with more capital and greater access to credit from their Kuching wholesalers were in a stronger position than the boat traders. The former could also afford to dabble in the futures market by retaining stocks of non-perishable products awaiting more favourable prices in Kuching before shipment.

Foreign and International Commerce

The Singapore Connection

Although there was an intermittent direct trade in timber with China and shipments of sago were sent direct to Britain, the bulk of Sarawak's trade throughout the Brooke period was carried out with Singapore. It remained the pre-eminent port for Sarawak's products to the world markets, and the major source of capital and credit for the Chinese trading houses of Kuching. By the early 1860s, 'it was evident that Kuching was the entrepôt port of the adjacent districts and was a feeder port of Singapore'.[41]

While Singapore handled Sarawak's exports to the world markets, it also acted as the importer of Sarawak's foodstuffs and manufactured goods.[42] Sarawak's rice supplies were wholly imported through Singapore. The dependence of Sarawak on Singapore was evident during the food crisis of 1919–20 when rice supplies and other foodstuffs suffered a serious shortage.[43] The vulnerability of this reliance on Singapore was apparently not addressed, for Sarawak continued its trade dependence.

The Chinese-owned banks in Singapore, in particular, played

prominent roles as financiers and creditors to Sarawak businesses. Banks incorporated in Sarawak, all owned by leading Chinese personalities, had close relationships with their Singapore counterparts.[44] For instance, in the late 1880s, 'recent failures of Chinese firms in Singapore have caused losses to their Chinese correspondents here [in Kuching]'.[45]

Direct Trading Links with China

There was some intermittent and limited trade direct with other countries. During the late 1860s sago and antimony ore were exported direct to Britain. There was an irregular trade in timber exports to Hong Kong and China which bypassed Singapore altogether. In fact, timber from the Rejang even bypassed Kuching and was exported direct to Hong Kong and China. In the mid-1930s timber shipments were contracted direct to Britain and Europe.[46]

Junks from South China also traded directly with Sarawak ports bringing cargoes of goods, usually salt, foodstuffs, and sometimes coolies. Apparently this trade had commenced in the early 1870s, but their visits were rather uncertain and irregular, undoubtedly dictated by political and economic conditions on the Chinese mainland.[47] These junks would be 'laden with salt and with deck cargoes of pigs, fowls, ducks and other live stock, seeking a favourable market'.[48] Although their arrival contributed in a small way to the foreign trade of Kuching, they nevertheless played an important and essential, if not vital, part to life in remote outposts, and in some instances, 'were about the only source of supplies to the upriver tribes'.[49] The case of Marudi in the Baram illustrates their importance when they arrived 'just at the end of that long period of weeks in February and March when the settlement had been cut off from any source of supplies by the heavy seas at Kuala Baram'.[50]

Chambers of Commerce

The Sarawak Chamber of Commerce

With increased trade, Rajah Charles proposed, in late 1872, the formation of a mercantile committee 'to bring before the Government any reforms, improvements or suggestions for facilitating trade in Sarawak'.[51] Charles laid down specifically the functions of this committee,[52] to be known as the Sarawak Chamber of Commerce. The Chamber held its inaugural meeting on 1 May 1873 in one of the rooms of the government offices, attended by a

multiracial membership of Europeans, Chinese, Indians, and Malays. Eligibility for membership was on the basis of wealth.[53] Meetings were to be held regularly; the Malay language was the medium used in discussions, but minutes were written in English by the secretary, a post invariably held by a staff member of the BCL.[54] In practice, however, the recommended three-monthly meetings were deemed unnecessary, and instead, meetings were held once every six months.

The first major challenge that faced the Chamber was Charles's suggestion that it should address the problem of the increasing volume of trade between Sarawak and Singapore, which hitherto had been carried by government vessels. According to Charles, the formation of a private shipping company to cope with this increased freight was long overdue; he 'offered to sell any persons interested [in this project] the Government steamer *Royalist*'.[55] In mid-1875 this task was accomplished, and the Singapore and Sarawak Steamship Company (SSSCo) was founded.[56]

Apart from the formation of the shipping company, the Chamber confined itself to the levying of export duties, initially on rattans, then on other export items like sago, gambier, pepper, and birds' nests.[57] No record exists as to the duration of this Chamber.

Apparently the formation of another Chamber was mentioned in the late 1890s to the effect that 'a Chamber of Commerce has been established in Kuching and Mr J. C. Ferrier of Messrs The Borneo Company, "Limited" is the first Secretary'.[58] According to one account, it was the efforts of the BCL which successfully persuaded Charles to approve the formation of this second Chamber.[59] Its first chairman was C. D. Harvey, the BCL's Sarawak manager, with Ong Tiang Swee, the prominent Kuching *towkay* and acknowledged paramount Chinese leader, as deputy chairman.[60]

Evidently the function of this second Chamber was 'to take some steps to, amongst other things, ensure the purity of the gambier placed on the market here, the adulteration of which has several times occupied the attention of the Singapore Chamber of Commerce'.[61] Accordingly, the Chamber formulated a six-point proposal, adopted by the government, in the drawing up of a regulation to counter gambier adulteration.[62] The Chamber apparently 'lasted only four years, finishing its short life on account of a tendency to dabble in political affairs'.[63]

It is rather curious as to why there were two Chambers of Commerce existing side by side in the last four years of the nine-

teenth century. W. J. Chater dramatically stated, 'Then, suddenly, without any given reason, it [the first Chamber] was closed in January, 1900.'[64] The closure of the second Chamber in 1900 apparently coincided with the closure of the first. A plausible explanation for this puzzle may lie in the fact that the first Chamber became ineffective due to being overburdened with multifarious responsibilities; the formation of the second was in effect a revival, perhaps with new blood, to carry out the multitude of duties entrusted to it. This explanation is supported by the action of Charles, who, in the mid-1890s, had requested the manager of the BCL to set up a Municipal Council 'with the object of relieving the Chamber of Commerce of some of its duties which were probably becoming increasingly heavy'.[65] This Municipal Council was accordingly formed sometime in 1895, but proved unsuccessful, and ceased to exist at the close of the century. In 1906 a municipal office, an adjunct of the Public Works Department, was established in Kuching which took over most of the municipal responsibilities hitherto entrusted to the Chamber of Commerce.[66] The departure of the Chambers of Commerce might also be due to the creation of a Chinese Chamber of Commerce which came about in the late 1890s.

The Kuching Chinese Chamber of Commerce (KCCC)

The Kuching Chinese Chamber of Commerce was established in 1897 which made it the first Chinese Chamber in the region.[67] The early existence of the KCCC may be attributed to the notable absence of Chinese secret societies in Sarawak.[68] The Chinese secret societies (*hui*) or triads were prominent in Chinese communities throughout South-East Asia; they provided leadership functions which the Chambers later assumed.[69]

A note must be made regarding another Chinese commercial organization, the Kongkek, which preceded the KCCC. The Kongkek was formed by leading Hokkien and Teochew *towkay* in 1876 to settle issues relating to the pepper and gambier industry. Later it also acted as an intermediary between the Chinese planters of these two crops and the Brooke administration.[70] This organization ceased to be mentioned after 1896; presumably its functions were taken over by the KCCC. If the Kongkek was managed by a Hokkien–Teochew clique of pepper and gambier export merchants, the KCCC possessed a wider membership made up of big wholesalers as well as smaller retail traders, transcending dialect

groups. Nevertheless, the Hokkien–Teochew domination persisted in the KCCC; its president for more than a decade was the Hokkien *towkay*, Ong Tiang Swee. He was succeeded by the Teochew, Lau Ngee Siang. The seven-man executive committee was also dominated by Hokkiens, Teochews, and Chaoans.

The formation of the KCCC was to promote and protect Chinese trading and commercial interests. In practice, it assumed the role of an intermediary between the Chinese business community and the Brooke government: it acted as negotiator of export duties, taxes, and postal rates; as an advisory body to the courts in Chinese commercial proceedings, particularly those involving property; and also encouraged its members to settle their debts and other business commitments.[71]

The KCCC operated until the end of the First World War; without any known reason, it was not referred to again until 1930 when the Kuching Chinese General Chamber of Commerce (KCGCC) came into being.[72] The KCGCC discharged similar functions as its predecessor, but increasingly took on other roles which were more political than commercial, for instance, in the nomination of candidates to various government boards, and even to the extent of representing the Sarawak Chinese community to the Kuomintang central government in China.[73] It served Chinese business interests until the eve of the Japanese occupation.

The Improvement of Sarawak's Exports

Inexperience, lack of information, and, in some cases, unscrupulous practices instigated by the profit motive resulted in the poor quality and consequently low prices of some of Sarawak's exports. The problem of coarse sago troubled the industry intermittently throughout the Brooke period. The dishonest act of adulterating products like guttas and gambier to increase their weight, and hence their price, also adversely affected the reputation of Sarawak's exports in the Singapore market. The poor quality of rubber sheets exported reduced their price as well as demand. Disease plagued the pepper vine and threatened the viability of the industry.

Measures were taken to address the problems, ranging from legislation to curb dishonest practices to the dissemination of information to improve the quality of export products, and specialist advice and assistance from experts engaged by the Brooke government.

The Problem of Coarse Sago

In the processing of sago by the natives at the village level, care had to be taken to ensure that the raw sago was of a fine texture and ready for milling into flour at the mills.[74] The use of a fine mat and a good quality, finely meshed straining cloth produced sago of fine texture. Ignorance or attempts to reduce the work resulted in these measures being dispensed with or neglected. As a result coarse sago was produced which fetched low prices in Singapore. Now and then local regulations were issued to ensure that only good quality sago was exported, and the producers of inferior sago fined.[75] But the problem of coarse sago persisted; only its rejection in the market prevented its further production. It was suggested that only through the collective efforts of all those involved in the sago trade 'to mutually bind themselves not to accept raw sago unless it reached a certain standard of purity' would good quality sago commanding attractive prices be ensured.[76]

Another problem affecting Sarawak's sago export was the addition of *ripoh* or rubbish to the sago to increase its weight.[77] Such practices were often brought to the notice of the authorities and those guilty were generally fined for their offences.

On the whole the problems of coarse sago and its adulteration were promptly dealt with by the authorities, and at no time did such incidents seriously affect the sago trade.

The Adulteration of Gutta and Gambier

The adulteration of gambier and gutta to increase their weight was more common than of sago. These products were sold according to their weight. Gambier had to be thoroughly dried, then weighed, before export. In order to improve profits it was not uncommon for gambier to be insufficiently cooked on purpose to allow it to retain water. Alternatively, large chunks of unprepared gambier adulterated with soil, stones, and other materials were exported. Not surprisingly complaints were received from purchasers in Singapore and Kuching. As early as the late 1870s the matter was discussed by the Brooke authorities.[78] In the mid-1890s, the Singapore Chamber of Commerce was infuriated at the 'serious falling off in quality of the gambier exported from Sarawak' and complained specifically of the 'heavy loss in weight frequently incurred in shipments of Gambier to Europe and America'.[79] The situation had developed to the extent that

Singapore purchasers were reluctant to accept consignments of Sarawak gambier. In response, the Brooke government imposed fines on and imprisonment for offenders.[80]

Enforcement of the regulation was apparently lacking, for two years later a similar complaint was again lodged by the Singapore purchasers. Sarawak gambier 'had greatly deteriorated in price, and had acquired such a bad name in the Singapore Market that, in some cases, exporters there had refused to buy it'.[81] By the close of the nineteenth century gambier had lost its economic attractiveness among the Chinese planters who were then more keen on pepper which enjoyed higher prices.

Gutta also suffered from adulteration, commonly performed by mixing bark dust and other materials to increase its weight. By the early twentieth century, the situation had become untenable; gutta exported from Sarawak had become 'almost unsaleable and when sold commands but a very poor price'.[82] 'Order No. III, 1902' decreed adulteration of *getah jelutong* as a criminal offence.[83] Despite fines, and even imprisonment, it appeared that 'Malays adulterate their gutta almost with impunity'.[84]

Convictions of transgressors were uncommonly few, owing to the reluctance of the Chinese purchasers to take legal action against native collectors. A Brooke officer explained the reason behind this.

> With regard to those cases in which summonses were not asked for, the Chinese [purchasers] stated, 'they preferred to settle them out of Court, if possible, as if settled by jurisdiction they would suffer in the long run, should defendants [native jungle collectors] be fined they would be sure to ask their [Chinese] Towkays to advance payment, which they [the Towkays] were not prepared to do, also they [the Towkays] could not afford to lose that time which defendants would spend in gaol in default of fines'. I am, however, inclined to think that in some cases the gutta when bought was known to be of an inferior quality and so a very low price was paid; the Chinese themselves trying to impose upon their Towkays in Kuching, thus hoping to make a substantial profit.[85]

Similarly such connivance by the outstation Chinese shopkeepers who purchased from native gutta collectors revealed the myopic attitude of both parties who sacrificed long-term benefits for short-term gains.[86] Even if the Chinese shopkeepers had wanted to assist the authorities in identifying the culprits, they faced much difficulty as the adulterated product had passed through so many persons before it reached the bazaar.[87]

Wet Pepper and Poor Grade Rubber

As with gambier, pepper also had to be thoroughly dried prior to export. A high moisture content adversely affected its quality and price. Sarawak's pepper had been highly regarded in the Singapore market since the late 1870s when it first made its appearance. However, in the early years of the 1900s there were complaints there about wet pepper from Sarawak. Such an occurrence undoubtedly threatened the product's reputation and price.[88]

Para rubber was first listed as an export item of Sarawak in 1912, and in less than a decade had become its most important agricultural export. Brooke policy ensured that rubber production was mainly in the hands of smallholders, who generally regarded it as a secondary cash crop to their subsistence farming. Consequently the rubber produced was of the lower grade owing to the lack of experience and to the absence of expert assistance and advice in improving its quality.

The establishment of specialist agencies by the Brooke government during the 1920s succeeded in upgrading the quality and hence the prices of both rubber and pepper in the world market.

The Department of Trade (1923): Efforts in Improving Rubber and Pepper Exports

By the early 1920s Sarawak's products had acquired a rather poor reputation due to the deterioration of quality and the too common occurrence of adulteration that affected gutta, *jelutong*, and Para rubber. Pepper, once an important item of export, had been hard hit by disease. It was, therefore, deemed necessary to take corrective measures.

A Department of Trade was established in 1923 with the aim of reviving the high quality once enjoyed by Sarawak's exports. Standards were to be set by the Department whereby all export products would be evaluated and approved as of good quality, thus making it 'possible for the exports of Sarawak to regain and even excel their reputation on all local as well as European markets'.[89] The Brooke policy of improving the livelihood of the people was evident in the objectives of the Department which sought '*the betterment of the inhabitants of the State through their own efforts, not by the introduction of outside capital*'.[90]

A Board of Trade, attached to the Department of Trade, was set up in 1924 as part of the strategy to improve Sarawak's exports.[91]

Representatives from the leading commercial firms were invited to serve on the Board and their participation offered the opportunity for both government officers and the trading community to work together to upgrade the quality of the country's exports.[92] In order to publicize its activities and objectives, the Board organized a 'show' at Kuching in October 1924 of agro-horticultural exhibits as well as native products and craftsmanship.[93]

The Rubber Exports Improvement Board was established in 1926 under the aegis of the Board of Trade to assist rubber smallholders in improving the quality of their rubber and its market value.[94] It was not an easy task convincing rubber cultivators that producing good quality rubber was to their long-term advantage as the situation had developed to such an extent that it was no longer profitable to produce rubber of high quality.

> While there is only a comparatively small quality [*sic*] of good rubber as opposed to a large proportion of bad rubber produced in a district, the good rubber suffers and does not receive its proper price. Therefore the producer complains of the uselessness of making good stuff or of trying to improve anything as he only gets the same as the producer of the inferior quality rubber.[95]

A fund drawn from 'a surtax of 2 ½ % *ad valorem* on all exports of adulterated or wet rubber in lieu of prosecution and fines', known as the Rubber Exports Improvement Fund, was established. It rendered free professional assistance to rubber producers and, to help improve the quality of their rubber, furnished them with materials at cost price, such as coagulants, timber for the construction of smoke houses, and equipment.[96]

Rubber inspectors were dispatched throughout the country to offer their assistance and expert advice to both Chinese and native rubber smallholders.[97] It was admitted that the Malays and the Dayaks were much more easy to teach, though slower to learn, than the Chinese. Because of their larger holdings Foochow Chinese rubber owners in most cases employed workers to work the rubber, and it was these coolies who often disregarded advice rendered by the rubber inspectors.[98]

The results within a year of the establishment of the Rubber Exports Improvement Fund were encouraging.[99] When 'Singapore Standard' was priced at $86 per *pikul*, Sarawak's Chinese producers presented theirs at $85 to the *pikul* while their native counterparts in the Saribas managed to produce grades No. 2 ($83 a *pikul*) and No. 3 ($78 a *pikul*).[100] Before the operation of the Fund, the Saribas producers sold their rubber between $10 and $13 below

the 'Singapore Standard'. Equally of importance was the progressive decline in the production of low quality rubber as demonstrated by the reduction in the amount of surtax collected.[101]

The work of rubber improvement continued during the late 1920s and throughout the following decade, notwithstanding the Depression and the introduction of rubber restriction during the latter half of the 1930s.[102]

The Sarawak pepper industry suffered from numerous problems. One of the most serious was pepper-vine disease, partly the result of ignorance and neglect on the part of the cultivators who were mostly Chinese.[103] A mycology section, attached to the Department of Agriculture, attended to the problems of plant disease, foremost of which were 'black fruit' (*Cephaleuros mycoidea*) and the so-called 'footrot' or 'sudden death' caused by the fungus *Phytophthora cinnamomi*.[104] Experiments were carried out to find ways and means of combating such diseases. Efforts in the 1920s and 1930s by the Board of Trade working closely with the Department of Agriculture succeeded in reviving the pepper industry.

In the early 1930s a Pepper Improvement Scheme was initiated to raise the quality of Sarawak's exported pepper. A part of this scheme involved the Sarawak government pledging a guarantee of quality on each shipment of pepper to the world market. The scheme enjoyed 'an unqualified success', as demonstrated by the fact that Sarawak pepper 'fetches the same price as the [Sumatra] Muntok product, hitherto regarded as the standard of high quality'.[105]

The Board of Trade also effected improvements in the production of sago and *jelutong*. In the case of sago the only assistance the Board could render to the producers was support relating to planting and other agricultural matters; processing was left to the factories which were more acquainted with consumer demands and levels of quality acceptable.[106] The stricter surveillance against *jelutong* adulteration and the changing attitude towards such unscrupulous practices gradually improved its quality. By 1927 Sarawak's *jelutong* had earned a respectable name in the world market and had surpassed its rival, Banjarmasin *jelutong*, in price.[107]

The Conservation and Protection of Jungle Produce

Jelutong was an important export and native collectors benefited from its trade. It was deemed necessary to preserve this natural resource from overexploitation as improved prices in the early

years of the twentieth century resulted in thousands of *jelutong* trees being 'so terribly mutilated by reckless and careless tapping and ... so infested with white ants that no amount of care or attention can now save them from a premature death'.[108]

Permits were issued to those who intended to work *jelutong*. The granting of permits was a means of limiting the number of workers, thereby indirectly the supply. It was also aimed at facilitating easier detection of those who mutilated or destroyed the trees. Guidance on methods of proper tapping was circulated among the local population.[109] The felling of *jelutong* trees was also forbidden by law. Fines were imposed for the violation of these regulations, and inspectors were appointed to ensure that proper tapping methods were implemented.

Notwithstanding these rules and surveillance, violations were reported occasionally and punished accordingly with a fine.[110] The worst offenders, as one Brooke officer noted, were 'subjects of neighbouring states who have come in to work and get as much as possible out of the trees in the shortest possible time'.[111] In some instances, when a fine lacked the deterrent effect, imprisonment was imposed on those culprits who persistently damaged or felled *jelutong* trees.[112] The granting of permits to work *jelutong* was also subject to abuse.[113] Nevertheless, on the whole the regulations helped to reduce transgressions and allowed the continued working of this valuable export product.

In the mid-1890s, a method was developed whereby pure gutta-percha could be extracted from the *gutta-rian* leaves.[114] Despite initial difficulties in persuading natives to collect the leaves, the project developed from the experimental stage to a profitable enterprise. As the price of *jelutong* rose during the second decade of the twentieth century, there was a corresponding demand for *gutta-rian* leaves. Eager to obtain fast profits, 'the Malays instead of climbing the trees had fixed ropes near the top and then pulled them over'.[115] In September 1918 regulations were enacted for the protection of *gutta-rian* trees.[116] Following the strategy employed for *jelutong*, collectors of *gutta-rian* leaves were issued with permits.

The illipe or *engkabang* tree, which fruited irregularly, was another important jungle product that was protected by legislation which forbade the felling of these trees, a not uncommon practice of the natives when burning the jungle for their *padi* clearings.[117]

Characteristics of Sarawak's Trade and Commerce

Steady Growth and Gradual Progress

The development of trade in Sarawak during the period of Brooke rule was steady and sustained despite the numerous trade depressions and economic dislocations from without. This review, though relating to the year 1889, is representative of the situation in Sarawak throughout the period of Brooke rule: 'The past year, 1889, shews as other years gone by have done, an ever increasing prosperity to the State of Sarawak. No rapid jump or stride ahead has been made but the Country thrives and forges along steadily, becoming day by day, month by month more firmly established and with an increasing trade and revenue.'[118] Table 3.2 illustrates this trend in Sarawak's trade showing the gradual increase in the value of exports and the corresponding revenue from the mid-1850s to the eve of the Japanese occupation.

TABLE 3.2
Value of Exports and Revenue of Sarawak, 1855–1940 (Straits $)

Year	*Exports*	*Revenue*
1855	304,764	n.a.
1860	400,226	n.a.
1870	1,494,241	122,842
1880	1,193,195	229,718
1890	1,700,142	413,123
1900	6,865,861	915,966
1910	8,152,293	1,407,360
1920	18,067,121	2,646,265
1930	23,020,456	5,562,035
1940	45,770,407	7,463,314

Source: Roe, *The Natural Resources of Sarawak*, p. 6.

Coping with Wars and Trade Depressions

The First World War (1914–18) affected Sarawak exports, which were generally consumed by the European and American markets. One report described the situation as: 'There is no sale for jungle produce, pepper or other trade commodities in the bazaar just now, the markets in Singapore being closed. A Chinese trader who

arrived from an Outstation a day or two ago with a cargo of raw sago and jelutong gutta had to take it back again as he could not dispose of it.'[119] Measures were accordingly instituted to alleviate the trade slow-down. A Food and Produce Advance Committee was established which was 'prepared to advance up to $400,000 against produce ... [that would] have enabled stocks to be held in anticipation of the recovery, and even improvement', but due to prior commitments in Singapore, this measure was only partially successful.[120] The authorities promptly took over the food supply and regulated food prices to prevent any undue hardship, particularly among the Chinese coolie population who were temporarily displaced by this economic slow-down.[121] By 1916 the situation had apparently returned to normal.[122]

In the early 1920s another trade depression, far more serious than that of the First World War, made its effects felt in Sarawak. Rubber suffered a severe slump owing to overproduction in the world market. Other commodities, like pepper, also experienced low prices. In Sarawak, many Chinese coolies, who were employed in rubber gardens, were made redundant.[123] The most hard hit were the Chinese Foochows of the Lower Rejang who 'trusted entirely to their rubber, and, though most of them have their [unharvested] padi, this brings them nothing for the time being'.[124] Relief work on public projects was instituted to alleviate the situation.[125] However, the unemployed pepper coolies of Upper Sarawak, despite government offers of employment in public projects in Kuching, preferred to cross the border to the Dutch territory of Sambas where apparently they could find work.[126]

On the whole Sarawak emerged from the depression of the early 1920s without much serious dislocation or suffering. Notwithstanding the difficult time experienced by certain groups in the country, this depression was salutary. Notably, it proved the ingenuity and far-sightedness of Charles's policy regarding rubber cultivation, which was faithfully adopted by his son Vyner.[127]

Similarly, when the Depression of 1929–31 set in, the sagacious Brooke policy of discouraging dependence on a single commodity, particularly rubber, softened its impact. The lessons of the early 1920s 'emphasized the need for a diversity of products as opposed to a blind dependence on one commodity to the exclusion of all else'.[128] Even in the midst of the world Depression, the year 1930 for Sarawak was 'one of steady progress', a remarkable achievement under the circumstances.[129]

By 1933, it was evident that the worst had already passed, and 'the good effect of this is reflected in the fact that not only is unem-

ployment now negligible, but that in some districts there is even a shortage of labour'.[130] The revival of gold-mining in the early 1930s practically absorbed the redundant labour from the pepper and rubber gardens.[131] Rumours of impending rubber restriction fuelled an appreciation of its price towards the close of 1933, prices rose even further when restriction was actually implemented the following year. Both pepper and gold experienced a minor boom in 1934, and, together with the upward trend of rubber prices over the following years, these spread prosperity throughout the country.[132] From 1935 onwards Sarawak's trade continued its steady progress until December 1941 when the dark war clouds broke.

Protecting Natives from Exploitation

Several rules and regulations were enacted to protect the non-Malay native peoples from exploitation by Malay and Chinese traders. Brooke administrators were especially vigilant over trading activities between the non-Malay indigenous inhabitants of the interior and the Chinese. One particularly common form of exploitation practised by Chinese merchants as well as Malay traders on their native clients was the use of false weights and measures.[133] In the sago trade at Mukah, it was 'well known that Chinese buyers of raw sago generally have what is locally known as *passu China*, but the native seller may, if he prefers it, elect to have his *lemanta* measured out by government *passu* in which case he receives a lower price'.[134]

Incidents of outright deception, particularly by Chinese shopkeepers and traders, were often brought to the notice of the authorities and the perpetrators punished with a fine.[135] Regular inspection of weights and measures was carried out and those found in possession of false equipment were summarily fined.[136] Registration of weights and measures was effected to ensure fair dealing in trading transactions.[137]

Furthermore, there was the unwritten rule that forbade Chinese and Malay boat traders from settling and trading among the native peoples in their longhouses. This was primarily aimed at Chinese traders as they were also barred from living in Malay kampongs. It was thought that traders in such proximity with natives would have ample opportunity to deceive them. Moreover, traders resident in native longhouses possessed a decided advantage over their travelling competitors.[138] This non-residence rule became a finable offence in the late 1870s as court records indicate.[139] Native headmen who allowed a trader to live in the longhouse were also

punished for connivance.[140] But the wily Chinese often circumvented this ruling. An example from the Melanau district of Oya in 1909 illustrates the resourcefulness of one Chinese boat trader who utilized 'large covered boats ... fitted up partly as house and partly as shop ... [and] moor[ed] at some landing stage in a *Kampong*, where they trade'.[141]

The 'proper manner' for conducting trade with the indigenous peoples was the establishment of bazaars located in close proximity to the government office or fort. A report of mid-1919 from the Baram typified official intentions: 'Informed all the Chinese towkays that after this year not one Chinese or Malay will be allowed to build a house or trade at a Kayan *pangkalan*, but they must make bazaars and from there they can visit different houses with trading goods, but will only be allowed a limited time at each place.'[142]

On the other hand, incidents of natives cheating Chinese shopkeepers, as in cases of the adulteration of gutta, were not unusual.[143] Moreover, certain prerogatives, like immunity from prosecution accorded to native peoples to protect them from exploitation by outsiders, were abused.[144] Nevertheless, the protection of natives from exploitation by traders, particularly the Chinese, remained the cornerstone of Brooke policy.

Conclusion

The development of trade and commerce during the period of Brooke rule presents several salient features of interest. A prominent one was the generally poor quality of Sarawak's exports, from coarse sago to adulterated *jelutong*, to low-grade rubber. Repeated complaints from Singapore buyers placed the Brooke government in an embarrassing position when it was trying to promote the country's trade.

The Brookes had high hopes for mineral exports like gold and mineral oil but these were not sustained. The production of the much celebrated mineral oil only lasted for close to two decades, from 1913 to 1929, 1929 being the peak output year for the Miri field, before a decline in production. Similarly gold exports enjoyed a prosperous period from about 1900 until 1923 when the BCL decided to cease operations because of unprofitable returns. The revival of mining by the Chinese during the mid-1930s was but a brief interlude. The prospects of coal deposits, particularly during Charles's reign, were embarrassingly disappointing, despite

all attempts to promote sales abroad. Small quantities of coal were exported from government-owned mines, but the main bulk of production was consumed locally, mainly by government steamers.

The Brookes, especially Charles, tried their best to encourage commercial agriculture, but with limited success. Attempts to promote tea, coffee, tobacco, and other crops did not even take off from the experimental stage, much less for export. Gambier enjoyed brief success as an export in the late 1870s, but petered out towards the close of the century. It was fortunate that pepper was more successful as an export but it faced innumerable difficulties from poor quality and disease to planter–exporter contract problems, to constant price fluctuations. Fluctuations in price made pepper an unreliable export earner. Rubber, like pepper, suffered from the problems of low quality, and during the 1920s and 1930s attempts at improvement were initiated with limited success. As the cultivation and production of the crop were mainly in the hands of small-scale peasant producers, it was difficult to introduce any major innovation to improve it. In fact, to the native peoples the growing of rubber was a secondary interest to subsistence rice farming. Large-scale Malayan-style rubber plantations were not widely established in Sarawak. Therefore, it was understandable that, although rubber was the main agricultural export product from the 1920s onwards, the quantity exported was comparatively small *vis-à-vis* other rubber-producing countries.[145]

Significant were the contributions of jungle produce and sago to the Brooke economy during the nineteenth century. Both these export items, more than anything else, sustained the Brooke Raj for almost half the period of its existence.

> In general, the new economic regimes in Sarawak ... continued to rely very heavily on those traditional products which had long characterized the indigenous economy. Products such as sago, birds' nests, camphor, rattans and precious timber provided upwards of one-third of all exports and, as a result, major government revenues. In some ways, it might be argued that the strength of the indigenous economy provided a lifeline for the governments of Sarawak.[146]

It was always a deliberate policy of the Brookes to promote the trade in jungle produce and sago, the dual pillars of the traditional indigenous economy, as it benefited the local inhabitants. Undoubtedly the hard-working Chinese boat pedlar, the itinerant Malay petty trader, the outstation Chinese bazaar shopkeeper, the affluent Kuching Chinese *towkay* exporter and wholesaler, profited as well in the trade in sago and jungle produce. The Chinese, in

particular, functioned as essential elements in the commercial chain, and in fact, fulfilled the role the Brookes had for them as catalysts in the promotion and expansion of trade and commerce.

It was also the deliberate policy of the Brookes to limit the operation of large-scale commercial agriculture in Sarawak's economy, in contrast to the neighbouring colonial territories, namely British Malaya and the Netherlands East Indies. However, it cannot be denied that Charles did attempt to promote commercial agriculture and new industries, but capitalist investors interested in these ventures had to abide by his rules, namely that taking advantage of the native inhabitants was forbidden.[147]

Capitalist entrepreneurs who acknowledged the Brooke rules were given official assistance and support; their enterprises prospered, the most heralded being the BCL and the oil companies, Anglo-Saxon Petroleum Company and Sarawak Oilfields Limited. The BCL's diversified operations performed vital commercial and trading functions, ranging from export and import to banking, shipping, and insurance. Its mining operations of gold, quicksilver, antimony, and other minerals produced important exports and contributed to the country's economy.

Notwithstanding the low output of rubber, the Brookes were satisfied that large-scale rubber plantations should not be encouraged. Charles was adamant that estates like those in the Malay States with a huge coolie work-force would never be the norm in Sarawak. Despite the booms in rubber prices, Charles and Vyner were unconvinced that rubber should be the main agricultural produce for the country. Both made frequent appeals to the people that they should not place too much faith in rubber, but instead grow crops like sago, coconut, pepper, and tobacco. Rubber, in spite of the Brookes, did become the main agricultural product of the country. But when the fall in rubber prices occurred in the early 1920s and during the Depression (1929–31), the wisdom of the Brooke policy in discouraging rubber cultivation proved its point. As rubber remained a smallholder's crop the periods of low rubber prices did not affect Sarawak too much, and the country was saved from major economic dislocation and large-scale unemployment.

Sarawak's dependence on the entrepôt of Singapore as the outlet for its products was the consequence of the country's geographical disadvantage. Kuching, Sarawak's capital and chief port, lay outside the shipping and trade routes of world commerce. Although there was some direct trade between some Sarawak ports and other countries, the bulk of the export and import trade was

dependent on Singapore. What was more, ignorance of Sarawak was commonplace throughout the period of Brooke rule, and, to a certain extent, this lack of knowledge about the country was injurious to its trade and commerce. The Brookes' anti-capitalist stance did not help either.

The fact that Sarawak's trade remained small relative to its size and was almost insignificant when compared to the flourishing economies of such territories as the British Protected Western Malay States was due as much to the deliberate economic policies of the Brookes as well as to the natural and geographical disadvantages of the country.

1. Frederick Boyle, *Adventures among the Dyaks of Borneo*, London: Hurst & Blackett, 1865, p. 317. For a similar comment, see Hugh Low, *Sarawak: Its Inhabitants and Productions, Being Notes during a Residence in that Country with His Excellency Mr Brooke*, London: Frank Cass, 1848; new impression, 1968, p. 133.

2. 18th Meeting, 17 August 1915, in *General Council, 1867–1927*, Kuching: Government Printing Office, 1927[?], p. 26. Emphasis added.

3. The Chinese jars were valuable articles and their possession bespoke the wealth of its owner. The Dayaks believed these jars to be endowed with supernatural powers as well as healing properties. Dayak households treasured them as family heirlooms. These jars were of different types with varying values. The most valued and venerated was the *Gusi*, standing at 45 centimetres (18 inches) in height; the *Rusa* was the least valued. For the market values of Chinese jars, see S. Baring-Gould and C. A. Bampfylde, *A History of Sarawak under Its Two White Rajahs, 1839–1908*, London: Henry Sotheran, 1909, pp. 26–7.

4. J. R. Logan, 'The Trade in Sago', *JIAEA*, 3 (1849): 308.

5. Ibid., p. 307.

6. For a detailed description of the manufacturing process, see J. R. Logan, 'Manufacture of Pearl Sago in Singapore by Chinese', *JIAEA*, 3 (1849): 303–7.

7. For the Singapore sago trade figures of the 1820s and 1840s, see Logan, 'Trade in Sago', pp. 307–10. For a description of the Singapore sago factories, see Song Ong Siang, *One Hundred Years History of the Chinese in Singapore*, London: John Murray, 1923; reprinted Singapore: University of Malaya Press, 1967, p. 34.

8. H. S. Morris, 'The Coastal Melanau', in Victor T. King (ed.), *Essays on Borneo Societies*, Hull Monographs on South-East Asia 7, Oxford: Oxford University Press for University of Hull, 1978, p. 40. For a descriptive account of the BCL's operations at Mukah in the mid-1860s, see Boyle, *Adventures*, pp. 122–3.

9. The Brooke government, particularly after the 1870s, introduced measures to improve the quality of exported sago, as well as regulations to prevent Chinese traders from exploiting the Melanaus.

10. *Sarawak Gazette (SG)*, 16 March 1875, n.p.

11. See *SG*, 2 January 1891, p. 2; and *SG*, 2 January 1892, p. 2. A sago factory was set up at Limbang in 1891, shortly after its annexation.

12. See Baring-Gould and Bampfylde, *A History of Sarawak*, p. 213.

13. See Judith Satem, 'The Changing Nature of Sarawak's Export Trade from 1841 to the Present', *SG*, 31 July 1970, p. 138.

14. Morris, 'The Coastal Melanau', p. 40.

15. See Wang Gungwu, 'The Nanhai Trade: A Study of the Early History of Chinese Trade in the South China Sea', *JMBRAS*, 31, 2 (June 1958): 113–17.

16. See Wong Lin Ken, 'The Trade of Singapore', *JMBRAS*, 33, 4 (December 1960): 220–1.

17. See Mark C. Cleary, 'Changing Patterns of Trade in North-West Borneo, *c.*1860–1930', MSS (Personal copy), n.d., p. 6.

18. See F. L. Dunn, *Rain-forest Collectors and Traders: A Study of Resource Utilization in Modern and Ancient Malaya*, Monographs of MBRAS No. 5 (1975), Kuala Lumpur: MBRAS, pp. 99–103.

19. It was not uncommon for Dayaks to work jungle produce in order to barter them for rice during bad harvests. For instance, see *SG*, 31 January 1872, n.p.

20. The task of collecting jungle products like rattan, gutta, dammar and *jelutong*, entailed less labour, therefore was much easier than the heavy work of *padi* farming. It was therefore not surprising that Dayaks preferred to be collectors and traded in jungle products, particularly evident when prices were high. The cash the Dayaks earned from the sale of jungle products allowed them not only to purchase rice but also to buy other articles in the bazaar. For instance, see *SG*, 1 April 1872, n.p.; and *SG*, 16 July 1872, n.p.

21. See Chapter 8.

22. Rodney Mundy, *A Narrative of Events in Borneo and Celebes, down to the Occupation of Labuan: From the Journals of James Brooke, Esq.*, 2 vols., London: John Murray, 1848, Vol. II, p. 30.

23. See Vinson H. Sutlive, 'From Longhouse to Pasar: Urbanization in Sarawak, East Malaysia', Ph.D. thesis, University of Pittsburgh, 1972, p. 25.

24. See Chapter 7.

25. For details of the imposition of export duties on rattans, gutta-percha, and India rubber, see *SG*, 1 December 1874, n.p.; *SG*, 1 May 1875, n.p.; *SG*, 16 January 1877, p. 1; *SG*, 14 October 1879, p. 64; and *SG*, 24 November 1879, p. 72.

26. See Cleary, 'Changing Patterns of Trade', pp. 16 and 19; and Satem, 'Sarawak's Export Trade', p. 138.

27. See Sarawak trade returns in *SG* from 1876 to 1908 inclusive, and in *Sarawak Government Gazette* (*SGG*), after 1908.

28. See Baring-Gould and Bampfylde, *A History of Sarawak*, pp. 430–1; James R. Hipkins, 'The History of the Chinese in Borneo', *SMJ*, 19, 38–9 (July–December 1971): 114; Horace St John, *The Indian Archipelago: Its History and Present State*, 2 vols., London: Longman, Brown, Green & Longmans, 1853, Vol. I, p. 199; J. H. Moor (ed.), *Notices of the Indian Archipelago, and Adjacent Countries*, London: Frank Cass, 1837; reprinted 1968, p. 94; and Thomas Forest, *A Voyage to New Guinea and the Moluccas from Balambangan Including an Account of Magindano, Soloo and Other Islands*, London: G. Scott, 1779; reprinted Kuala Lumpur: Oxford University Press, 1969, pp. 381–3.

29. See Chapter 8.

30. *Towkay*, a Chinese term in the Hokkien dialect, denoting a prosperous merchant, a big-time trader, or a wealthy businessman. Sometimes it is applied as an honorific showing respect and, perhaps, awe, for an individual.

31. See 7th Meeting, 11 August 1883, in *General Council, 1867–1927*, p. 9.

32. For the beginnings and growth of bazaars in the various outstations, see Daniel Chew, *Chinese Pioneers of the Sarawak Frontier, 1841–1941*, Singapore: Oxford University Press, 1990, pp. 65–79.

33. Chew, *Chinese Pioneers*, pp. 78–9.

34. Ibid., p. 79.

35. For a descriptive account of the life of such Chinese boat traders during the pioneering days, see ibid., pp. 79–96.

36. For an analysis of the role and preponderance of Chinese dialect-group affiliation in commercial relations in Sarawak, see T'ien Ju-K'ang, *The Chinese of Sarawak: A Study of Social Structure*, Monograph on Social Anthropology No. 12, London: Department of Anthropology, London School of Economics and Political Science, 1953, pp. 19–68. Though this study is based on the situation in Sarawak during the late 1940s, no major changes were effected during the initial period of Colonial Office Administration when the fieldwork was conducted from September 1948 to October 1949.

37. *SG*, 16 April 1914, p. 96.

38. *SG*, 16 September 1910, p. 199. See Chapter 7.

39. For instance, see *SG*, 1 June 1888, p. 77.

40. Richard H. Goldman, 'The Beginnings of Commercial Development in the Baram and Marudi Following the Cession of 1881', *SG*, 31 March 1968, p. 63.

41. Wong, 'The Trade of Singapore', p. 89.

42. The Sarawak Importers and Exporters Association at 5 Teo Hong Road, Singapore, exemplified the strong trading links between Singapore and Sarawak to the present day.

43. See *SG*, 16 January 1919, pp. 17–18; and *SG*, 1 May 1919, p. 105.

44. See Chapter 8.

45. *SG*, 1 January 1890, p. 2.

46. For the timber industry, see Chapter 8.

47. See *SG*, 15 March 1873, n.p. For instance, Hainanese junks visited Marudi throughout the 1880s but petered out in the 1890s and ceased altogether by the turn of the century. See Goldman, 'Baram and Marudi', p. 57.

48. Charles Hose, *The Field-Book of a Jungle Wallah: Being a Description of Shore, River and Forest Life in Sarawak*, London: H. F. & C. Witherby, 1929; reprinted Singapore: Oxford University Press, 1985, p. 51.

49. Ibid., p. 52.

50. Goldman, 'Baram and Marudi', p. 56.

51. *SG*, 3 January 1873, n.p. See also *SG*, 2 November 1872, n.p.

52. See Chapter 2.

53. For individual merchants, land and other properties 'amounting to $2,000' were required for membership, and in the case of a company, 'a capital of $10,000'. All members 'must reside within the territory of Sarawak'. Supreme Council, 10 February 1873, HH. The Rajah's Order Book, Vol. I, *SMA*, Kuching. See also *SG*, 17 February 1873, n.p.

54. None of these minutes is available; probably, they did not survive the Japanese occupation. Apart from an occasional mention in the *Gazette*, little record is left of the activities of the Chamber.

55. W. J. Chater, 'Pieces from the Brooke Past—III: The First Sarawak Chamber of Commerce', *SG*, 31 July 1964, p. 165.

56. See Chapter 6.

57. For instance, see *SG*, 1 December 1874, n.p.

58. *SG*, 4 January 1897, p. 2.

59. See Henry Longhurst, *The Borneo Story: The History of the First 100 Years of Trading in the Far East by The Borneo Company Limited*, London: Newman Neame, 1956, p. 66.

60. C. D. Harvey was the son of John Harvey who was one of the managing directors of the Borneo Company in London during its pioneer days. Ong Tiang Swee, the son of Ong Ewe Hai, was the Kapitan China General of Sarawak, President of the Chinese Court, as well as a close associate of Charles. For a biographical sketch and the career of Ong, see Craig Alan Lockard, *From Kampung to City: A Social History of Kuching, Malaysia, 1820–1970*, Ohio University Monographs in International Studies Southeast Asia Series, No. 75, Athens, 1987, pp. 52–3, 70–1, 103, 106–7, 114–17 and 128; and Ong Boon Lin, *Ong Tiang Swee of Sarawak*, Kuching: Lee Ming Press, 1990.

61. *SG*, 4 January 1897, p. 2.

62. See *SG*, 1 May 1897, p. 87.

63. Longhurst, *The Borneo Story*, p. 66. As to the nature of the 'political affairs' alluded to, nothing was mentioned.

64. Chater, 'Sarawak Chamber of Commerce', p. 165.

65. Ibid.

66. It was not until the early 1920s that a semblance of a Municipal Council was created, beginning with the Kuching Sanitary and Municipal Advisory Board in 1922 and its transformation from an advisory board to a full-fledged municipal authority in 1934 with its new name of Kuching Municipal Board (KMB), later changed to the Kuching Municipal Council (KMC). See Lockard, *Kampung to City*, pp. 108–10 and 160.

67. In was in the early years of the twentieth century that Chinese Chambers of Commerce were created in other South-East Asian lands. The one in Penang was formed in 1902, and there was another in Batavia (Jakarta). The Chinese in Bangkok established theirs in 1905 while those of Singapore and Manila were founded a year later. See Song, *One Hundred Years*, p. 387; Donald E. Willmott, *The Chinese of Semarang*, Ithaca: Cornell University Press, 1960, p. 27; G. William Skinner, *Chinese Society in Thailand: An Analytical History*, Ithaca: Cornell University Press, 1957, p. 170; and Edgar Wickberg, *The Chinese in Philippine Life, 1850–1898*, New Haven: Yale University Press, 1965, p. 205.

68. The lessons learnt from the Chinese uprising of 1857 made the Brookes mistrustful of the Chinese and ever vigilant of their activities. Such clandestine, and to the Brookes, subversive, organizations were banned; those involved faced long imprisonment or deportation, and even execution. For instance, see *SG*, 22 April 1879, p. 1; *SG*, 4 August 1903, p. 150; *SG*, 2 July 1906, p. 156; *SG*, 2 March 1914, p. 58; *SGG*, 16 February 1915, pp. 39–40; and *SG*, 1 September 1932, pp. 158 and 160.

69. See Lockard, *From Kampung to City*, p. 68.

70. See *SG*, 1 September 1888, pp. 109–10; *SG*, 1 August 1894, p. 118; and Charles Brooke to Messrs Donaldson and Burkinshaw, Solicitors, Singapore, June 2, 1896, HH The Rajah's Letters, SMA, Kuching.

71. See Sir Percy Cunynghame to Charles Brooke, 25 September 1905, HH The Rajah's Letters, SMA, Kuching; Charles Vyner Brooke to Resident, Matu, 9 March 1909 and 10 March 1909, HH The Rajah's Letters, SMA, Kuching; *SG*, 16 June 1911, p. 112; *SG*, 17 June 1912, p. 129; and Charles Brooke to C. C. Robison, Postmaster-General, 8 May 1913, HH The Rajah's Letters, SMA, Kuching.

72. *SG*, 1 March 1930, p. 66.

73. See *Sarawak Tribune (ST)*, 27 September 1950; and *SG*, 23 February 1958, p. 14.

74. For a description of native sago processing, see Ong Kee Hui, 'Sago Production in Sarawak', *SG*, 1 November 1948, p. 213.

75. For instance, see *SG*, 1 September 1892, p. 168.

76. *SG*, 3 September 1923, p. 288. See also, *SG*, 1 August 1924, p. 262.

77. For instance, see *SG*, 1 April 1884, p. 26.

78. See *SG*, 19 February 1879, p. 9.

79. *SG*, 2 January 1894, p. 4.

80. See 'Order No. 1, 1894', *SG*, 2 January 1894, p. 3; and 'Order No. V, 1897', *SG*, 2 May 1897, p. 84. See also *SG*, 1 May 1897, p. 87.

81. *SG*, 1 February 1899, p. 25.

82. *SG*, 3 May 1904, p. 82.

83. 'Order No. III, 1902', *SG*, 1 May 1902, p. 85.

84. *SG*, 1 November 1911, p. 215.

85. *SG*, 3 May 1907, p. 119.

86. For instance, see *SG*, 16 July 1909, p. 157; and *SG*, 1 November 1911, p. 215.

87. See *SG*, 1 May 1924, p. 165.

88. For instance, see *SG*, 1 October 1902, p. 189.

89. *SG*, 3 December 1923, p. 362.

90. Ibid. Emphasis added. The Department of Trade also undertook the task of revising import and export duties with the aim of improving, and at the same time, expanding this branch of the country's economy.

91. See 21st Meeting, 16 October 1924, in *General Council, 1867–1927*, p. 32.

92. See *SG*, 3 December 1923, p. 362.

93. See *SG*, 1 July 1924, p. 214; *SG*, 3 November 1924, pp. 343–4; and *SG*, 2 January 1925, p. 2.

94. See 22nd Meeting, 17 October 1927, in *General Council, 1867–1927*, p. 34.

95. *SG*, 3 January 1927, p. 5.

96. Ibid.

97. For instance, see *SG*, 1 February 1927, p. 43. For the progress and activities of the Rubber Exports Improvement Fund in the various districts, see *SG*, 2 May 1927, pp. 118–19; *SG*, 2 May 1927, pp. 119–20; and *SG*, 1 July 1927, pp. 169–70.

98. See *SG*, 2 May 1927, p. 124.

99. See *SG*, 1 July 1927, p. 170.

100. *SG*, 3 January 1927, p. 6.

101. For instance, the surtax receipts at Sibu, a major rubber export centre, declined 'from $23,000 a few months ago to $16,000, $11,000 and now $8,000 per mensem'. Ibid.

102. For instance, see *SG*, 1 December 1936, p. 312.

103. For other problems of the pepper industry, see Chapter 8.

104. See *SG*, 1 February 1924, pp. 55–6; *SG*, 2 January 1925, p. 2; and *Sarawak Administration Report (SAR), 1934*, Kuching: Government Printing Office, p. 3.

105. *SAR, 1930*, p. 5.

106. *SG*, 2 January 1927, p. 6.

107. Ibid.

108. *SG*, 2 May 1910, p. 96.

109. For instance, see *SG*, 17 May 1909, p. 113.

110. For examples of violations of the *jelutong* regulations, see *SG*, 16 June 1910, p. 133; *SG*, 1 August 1910, p. 170; *SG*, 16 January 1912, p. 27; and *SG*, 1 December 1913, p. 278.

111. *SG*, 16 June 1910, p. 133.

112. For instance, see *SG*, 16 September 1910, p. 200.

113. For instance, see *SG*, 2 January 1920, p. 9.

114. Such a method possessed certain advantages. First, it did away with the wasteful native method of felling the tree for its sap. Secondly, it became an inexhaustible source of gutta-percha, as plucking the leaves did not in any way injure the tree which would continue to put out new foliage as well as seed and thus reproduce its species. Thirdly, even the stumps of such felled trees that have sprouted out small shoots were useful for 'though these stems are too small to produce gutta, their leaves are as good as those of an adult tree'. *SG*, 1 April 1895, pp. 57–9.

115. *SG*, 16 February 1917, p. 48. See also *SG*, 17 November 1919, p. 300.

116. See *SG*, 16 January 1919, p. 14.

117. *SG*, 16 January 1913, p. 14.

118. *SG*, 1 January 1890, p. 1.

119. *SG*, 17 August 1914, p. 183.

120. *SG*, 17 May 1915, p. 112. See also *SG*, 16 January 1915, p. 16.

121. For instance, see *SG*, 16 March 1915, p. 65.

122. See *SG*, 1 February 1917, p. 27.

123. Initially, it was reported that thousands were unemployed owing to the rubber slump, 'but it was soon found that the distress was not so serious as was at first imagined'. *SG*, 1 February 1921, p. 1.

124. *SG*, 1 February 1921, p. 15.

125. For instance, see *SG*, 1 February 1921, p. 13; and *SG*, 2 May 1921, p. 73.

126. See *SG*, 16 December 1920, p. 272; and *SG*, 1 April 1921, p. 47.

127. An editorial of the *Gazette* paid a tribute to Charles's prudent policy on rubber. See *SG*, 3 January 1922, p. 1. For Vyner's views on rubber, see 20th Meeting, 17 October 1921, in *General Council, 1867–1927*, p. 30.

128. *SG*, 2 February 1931, p. 23.

129. Ibid., p. 24.

130. *SG*, 2 January 1934, p. 1.

131. Ibid.

132. For accounts of prosperity that was evident from the mid-1930s, see *SG*, 1 February 1935, p. 11; *SG*, 1 March 1937, p. 70; *SG*, 1 April 1937, p. 93; and *SG*, 2 January 1941, p. 8.

133. For instance, see *SG*, 16 April 1912, p. 88.

134. *SG*, 2 October 1916, p. 216.

135. For instance, see '*Government* v. *Ah Wan*, 10 August 1893', Simanggang Court Case Book, Vol. 6, p. 84, SMA, Kuching; *SG*, 1 September 1892, p. 167; *SG*, 3 May 1905, p. 128; *SG*, 1 October 1919, p. 260; and *SG*, 2 July 1923, p. 214.

136. For instance, see *SG*, 1 December 1904, p. 234; *SG*, 16 February 1920, p. 49; and *SG*, 2 May 1921, p. 84.

137. See *SG*, 1 April 1924, p. 131; *SG*, 1 May 1924, p. 165; and *SG*, 1 February 1927, p. 42.

138. The Brooke objection to Chinese or Malay traders settling among natives was not based on economic considerations alone; political and social factors were involved as well. The safety of the Chinese in the longhouse during times of trouble could not well be safeguarded. But, of much more importance, was the political aim of the Brookes to segregate the different communities in order to avoid interethnic

friction and strife. See Robert Pringle, *Rajahs and Rebels: The Ibans of Sarawak under Brooke Rule, 1841–1941*, London: Macmillan, 1970, pp. 297 and 299–301.

139. For instance, see '*Government* v. *Ah Toon*, 15 June 1878', Sibu Court Case Book, Vol. 3, p. 96, SMA, Kuching; '*Government* v. *Chau Soon*, 5 July 1882', Simanggang Court Case Book, Vol. 2, p. 1, SMA, Kuching; '*Government* v. *Cho Soon*, February–December 1914', ibid., Vol. 25, p. 75; '*Government* v. *Ah Fatt*, 23 April 1914', ibid., Vol. 25, p. 130; and '*Government* v. *Ah Kang*, 25 May 1920', Sibu Court Case Book, p. 212, SMA, Kuching.

140. For instance, in '*Government* v. *Cho Soon*', the Dayak headman was fined 15 *kati* of *padi*; whereas in the case of '*Government* v. *Banta, Tuai Rumah*', the accused was dismissed from his post for harbouring four Chinese traders overnight. '*Government* v. *Cho Soon*, February–December 1914', Simanggang Court Case Book, Vol. 25, pp. 70–1, SMA, Kuching; and '*Government* v. *Banta, Tuai Rumah*', December 1920–March 1922, ibid., p. 25, SMA, Kuching.

141. *SG*, 15 October 1909, p. 221.

142. *SG*, 16 September 1919, p. 247.

143. For instance, see '*Government* v. *Lawar, Munkong, Malisma and Rancha*, 11 January 1895', Simanggang Court Case Book, Vol. 4, p. 287, SMA, Kuching; *SG*, 4 April 1906, p. 92; and *SG*, 16 July 1909, p. 157.

144. See Chapter 7.

145. See Andrew McFadyean (ed.), *The History of Rubber Regulation 1934–1943*, London: George Allen & Unwin, 1944, pp. 226–9.

146. Cleary, 'Changing Patterns of Trade', p. 13.

147. See Chapter 9.

4
Exploitation of Mineral Resources

THE Brookes had high hopes for the mineral resources of Sarawak and accordingly promoted their exploitation. The mining of antimony, gold, and cinnabar was carried out mostly in Upper Sarawak, coal at Simunjan in the Sadong and at Brooketon, and mineral oil at Miri. Some successes were enjoyed by the gold industry at the turn of the century with the adoption of new techniques of ore extraction, and mineral oil was an important foreign exchange earner during the 1920s. Nevertheless, the expectations of rich mineral deposits were not realized despite untiring attempts at prospecting by the Borneo Company Limited (BCL). The truth of the matter was that Sarawak was generally poor in mineral resources. In addition, the country's relative remoteness hindered its coal production; it had neither a sustained demand nor a regular and wide market. Notwithstanding the continual efforts to open up the Silantek coalfields in the Lingga, they remained untapped throughout the Brooke period.

Sanguine Hopes of Mineral Exploitation

European optimism about the supposed mineral richness of Sarawak proved to be unwarranted. In a letter to his agent in London, dated 10 December 1841, the supposed mineral wealth of the country captured James's imagination. He was of the view that Sarawak was '*equal in vegetable and mineral productions to any [country] in the world*'.[1]

Despite the occurrence of a wide variety of minerals scattered throughout the country, the quantity and quality of such deposits were generally not of commercial importance.[2] Only antimony, gold, coal, cinnabar, and mineral oil were mined on a commercial basis. Even then, the results of their exploitation were, on the whole, disappointing.

Antimony as Government Monopoly

Antimony-ore is a staple commodity,
which is to be procured in any quantity.[3]

James declared antimony a government monopoly in 1841. He maintained that 'no person is forced to work [the ore]', and in the case of those who did, they 'will be paid for at a price when obtained' (Appendix 4). The revenue derived from the monopoly proved inadequate and James decided to lease it to a private company in England. The firm of Melville & Street agreed to an annual payment of £2,500 for both the antimony and opium monopolies.[4] It was to be a five-year lease commencing from 1846, but during 1847–8 the company went bankrupt and in 1849 the antimony and opium monopolies reverted to the government. In 1850, the antimony-mines were leased to a new syndicate, R. and J. Henderson & Company.[5] This arrangement remained intact until the formation of the BCL in 1856 which took over all mineral exploitation of the country, with the exception of gold.[6] Shortly after abortive attempts at coal-mining in the Sadong, the BCL relinquished its coal concession.

Chinese Gold Workings in Upper Sarawak

Gold of a good quality certainly is to be found in large quantities. The eagerness and perseverance of the Chinese to establish themselves is a convincing proof of the fact; and ten years since a body of about 3000 of them had great success in procuring gold by their ordinary mode of trenching the ground.... *The most intelligent Chinese are of the opinion, that the quantity here exceeds that at Sambas; and there is no good reason to suppose it would fall short of it were once a sufficient Chinese population settled in the country.*[7]

Before 1857

Gold was found 'in crevices of limestone rocks, in alluvial soil, and in the sand and gravel of rivers'.[8] In the 1820s and 1830s, the Chinese from Sambas and the Lower Kapuas in Dutch Borneo established themselves in the auriferous district of Upper Sarawak despite harassment from the local Malays.[9] The 'push factor' of stricter Dutch control and the 'pull factor' of the relative stability of Brooke Sarawak encouraged further Chinese migration from Sambas to Upper Sarawak in the 1840s. The Brooke Raj allowed the Chinese to pursue their mining activities undisturbed.

Originally gold, and also antimony, were worked by Malays on a piecemeal basis 'for the Malays do not think the profit of washing worth its labour and discomfort'; moreover, 'the average profits of gold-washing will scarcely reach the eighteen cents which form the usual daily wage in Sarawak'.[10] But the Chinese, accustomed to conscientious labour, 'worked on the alluvial at the foot of the hills; much harder work but probably more rewarding', while 'the Malays and the Land Dayaks preferred to work in the crevices of the limestone hills or from the beds of the rivers by panning' which was 'relatively simple but less rewarding'.[11]

In 1850 there was a flood of Chinese refugees, numbering about 3,000, from Pemangkat who had crossed over to Upper Sarawak as they fled the troubles in Sambas.[12] The majority of these Pemangkat Chinese were rice farmers but, because of their dire circumstances, they reluctantly accepted the assistance of the Chinese gold companies in Bau and many became gold workers.[13] At the same time, another group of about 300 refugees entered the Simanggang area. James was delighted with the arrival of these Chinese as this 'influx of a large body of Chinese promises well for the future, and the fact of these immigrants being agriculturalists and having wives ensures the quiet of the country'.[14] Those in the Simanggang area established a gold-mining community at Marup in the Upper Batang Lupar.[15] The Chinese communities were regarded as useful by James not only because they developed the land as miners and farmers but they also contributed to the state Treasury in the form of indirect taxation from opium, *arrack*, and gambling farms which were government monopolies.[16]

The Chinese in Upper Sarawak were proudly independent and, like their counterparts in Sambas, organized themselves into self-governing *kongsi*. The *kongsi* organization, jealously guarding its independence, eventually clashed with James's assertion of authority, culminating in the Chinese uprising of 1857 that almost obliterated the Raj.

From 1857 to 1898

Whatever the reasons that prompted the Chinese gold-miners of Bau to raise the flag of rebellion against James's government, the consequences of their action were disastrous for both parties in the conflict. Practically the whole of the Chinese mining and agricultural communities of Upper Sarawak were slaughtered by the Malays and by Charles's overzealous Dayak irregulars 'who thought that every man who "wore a tail" ought now to be put to death'.[17] The

Brooke Raj was financially devastated, but its prestige was strengthened and the loyalty of its Malay and Dayak subjects proved invaluable during the fateful days.[18] Convinced that the rebellion was instigated and carried out by subversive elements of the Chinese secret societies, the Brooke government henceforth decreed that such organizations were illegal and kept a vigilant eye on all Chinese activities.[19]

The Chinese uprising of 1857 literally destroyed the once flourishing gold industry of Upper Sarawak. As one account noted, it 'ruined the gold-mining industry, and, though some of the rebels returned and others came with them, the industry never fully recovered'.[20] Between 1857 and 1870 there was no evidence to indicate the activities of the Chinese in Upper Sarawak, but according to the government census of 1870, 1,145 Chinese were found in the gold, antimony, and cinnabar mines there.[21] The majority of the Chinese were directly employed or worked for contractors engaged by the BCL, which had started its mining operations in the 1860s.[22]

Those Chinese not connected with the BCL formed *kongsi* and carried out mining on their own.[23] There were more Chinese *kongsi* established during the post-1857 period than before, but membership in each was small.[24] In addition, there were also individuals who worked on their own. Apparently the Chinese working gold at Marup in the Upper Batang Lupar were performing well, and speculation of a gold-rush was even rumoured in the mid-1870s.[25] However, production began to decline in the late 1880s and the miners suffered heavy losses.[26]

In general, this period saw the end of the Chinese domination of mining activities in Upper Sarawak as they increasingly played a subordinate role to the ever-expanding BCL. Besides, Chinese involvement in mining began to wane in the 1870s and 1880s with the introduction of gambier and pepper cultivation. Charles's liberal land laws and attractive planting regulations made cash cropping a more profitable enterprise than mining.[27] Yet, the gold industry did continue, and entered its heyday with the application of modern technology by the BCL in the mid-1890s.

Diamonds at Suntah

It is said by Sir Stamford Raffles, that few 'courts of Europe could perhaps boast of a more brilliant display of diamonds than, in the prosperous days of the Dutch, was exhibited by the ladies of Batavia, the principal and only mart then opened for the Bornean diamond mines'.[28]

Statements such as the above fired the imagination of the Europeans with regard to the presence of diamonds in the region. In other parts of Borneo, namely in Sangow, Landak, and Banjarmasin, the occurrence of diamonds was noted with enthusiasm, convincing the Europeans that Sarawak too would yield similar finds. Moreover, the Malays of the other parts of Borneo were anxious to work diamonds in Sarawak, which fostered the belief that the country was indeed rich in such precious stones.[29] Not surprisingly, James also embraced this view. 'The diamonds' at Suntah, he reported, 'are stated to be found *in considerable numbers, and of a good water*'.[30] However, James's mine at Suntah, a tributary of the Penrissen branch of the Sarawak, was not a success as the individual in charge of it apparently abused his position.[31]

Malays of the poorer class were the main diamond prospectors in Sarawak, but their mining methods were rather crude[32] and their work was described as 'very desultory and imperfect'.[33] In early 1872, a Brooke officer reported to Charles 'that there would be a good prospect for a small company to work the diamond earth properly, *as there can be no doubt of the fact that the diamonds are in large quantities*, but the rude way in which they are worked can never be of any great benefit to the revenue of the country'.[34]

Yet, no systematic or scientific surveys were undertaken to verify the claims pertaining to diamonds in Sarawak. The only recorded prospecting by an 'expert' was in 1874 when a Mr Gray, 'a gentleman of considerable experience of Diamond working at the Cape [South Africa]', carried out work at Suntah 'with modern machinery and paraphernalia'.[35] But, after about ten days' work, he concluded that there was no prospect of diamond-mining paying, despite the application of the most modern equipment. The local Malay diamond washers claimed that Gray 'never reached the true gem-bearing stratum',[36] and A. Hart Everett, a Brooke officer knowledgeable in minerals, questioned the brief duration of 'an essay of ten days' or a fortnight's' which was deemed to be unsatisfactory.[37]

Notwithstanding the absence of scientific prospecting, the fact remained that diamonds did exist in Sarawak. However, the claim that 'they are found in *abundance in the soil*' should be regarded with caution.[38] The so-called 'Brooke Diamond' that James forwarded to England, when subjected to expert examination, appeared, embarrassingly, to be a white topaz.[39] Besides the abortive exploration by the expert from the Cape, there was no other reference to diamonds thereafter, and none whatsoever during Vyner's reign.

Sarawak Coal

[W]e will make our fortune with coal—like Lady Londonderry. I shall work myself and become a Great Collier! and you will work in white muslin, pink ribbon and diamonds.[40]

This exuberant spirit of James merely reflected his ever-optimistic outlook for Sarawak. In reality, despite the fact that thirty locations throughout the country had been identified as containing coal deposits, *only* at Simunjan in the Middle Sadong was mining carried out.[41]

The Simunjan Coal-mines in the Sadong

Coal was apparently discovered at Simunjan sometime during the 1850s.[42] The coal was formed on the western slope of Gunong Ngili, a hill located about 5 kilometres east of the small township of Simunjan in the Middle Sadong.[43] It was probable that some attempts at mining were initiated but came to nothing.[44] Neither did the operations carried out by the BCL in 1857–8 fare any better. In fact, a contemporary, in a condescending tone, pronounced it a financial fiasco.

On our way to Brunei we called in at Sadong to view the Borneo Company's coal-mines. The Rajah had a good look at them, but came back probably as wise as he went. This attempt to open a coal-mine in Borneo was a costly failure—rumour said £20,000—and all because, to save a few hundreds, the opinion had been taken of a practical miner who could have developed a real seam, instead of obtaining a report from a scientific engineer, who, by boring or other means, would have discovered if a workable seam existed. That is the way companies are too often managed.[45]

After this rather disastrous endeavour, it seemed that nothing was done for the next thirteen years.

The year 1870 marked a turning-point in the fate of Simunjan coal. Charles commissioned a Mr St John to 'carry out a thorough exploration of the area [Silantek and Simunjan]'. After two years of work and misadventure, he submitted his report 'which indicated that coal was, indeed, to be found in abundance at both Silantek and in the region of the Gunong Sadong [*sic*]'.[46] In early 1872 some Chinese labourers were 'engaged to work coal at Simunjan and to bring it to the landing place and deliver it to Government at 4 dollars a ton'.[47] Samples of coal were dispatched to Singapore to

determine its quality. The results were favourable, as indicated in a report from the Singapore Gas Company Limited: 'I consider the [Sarawak] coal superior to any of the Labuan [coal] that has come under my notice, and it is well adapted for Gas making purposes; I also consider that it is a good coal for steam as it has a tendency to coke, and does not burn away so rapidly as the Eastern coals in general.'[48]

Charles, confident of the high quality of Sarawak's coal, published this announcement in September 1872: 'The coal seams of Simunjan in the Sadong river and Silantek in the Batang Lupar ... may be worked by any individual or company on a payment of 10 cents per ton brought to grass.... Anyone desirous of examining the above seams, may have passage free by Government steamer "Royalist" from and back to Singapore.'[49] Meanwhile, more Chinese coolies were contracted to work in the mines 'while steps have been taken to promote a company to commence mining operations on a larger scale'.[50]

No European concern responded to Charles's offer. In 1874 it was reported that the government itself had assumed the management of the Simunjan coal mines.[51] Towards the end of the year, attempts were made to transfer the management of the Simunjan mines to other parties but these did not materialize as there was no reference to such a take-over.[52] They remained a state enterprise until their closure in the early 1930s.

The government-owned Simunjan colliery employed Chinese indentured labour for the skilled but highly precarious work below ground.[53] The key positions, that of mining engineer and manager which were usually held concurrently by the same individual, were invariably the domain of Europeans, often Englishmen recruited from Britain.[54] Capital investments included a railway with steam locomotives to haul the coal from the mines to the wharf, an onerous task when water buffaloes were initially used, as the distance was about 5 kilometres.[55] The brigantine *Black Diamond* and the steamers SS *Vyner* and SS *Breid* served as colliers.[56]

Throughout the almost sixty years of its working, the Simunjan colliery produced close to a million tons of coal, of which over 800,000 tons were sold; the remainder was utilized by mining operations and railways which generally consumed from 4,000 to 5,000 tons annually. Only a small proportion of the quantity sold was purchased abroad, mainly in Singapore, Manila, and Hong Kong; the bulk was consumed locally by government steamers and by the machinery of the gold-mining industry.[57] Production

TABLE 4.1
Annual Sale of Coal from Simunjan Colliery, 1874–1931 (long tons)

Year	*Coal Sold*	*Year*	*Coal Sold*	*Year*	*Coal Sold*
1874	500	1894	13,315	1913	21,589
1875	1,595	1895	14,029	1914	24,111
1876	400	1896	20,640	1915	28,514
1877	1,950	1897	29,080	1916	24,577
1878	1,225	1898	31,390	1917	27,288
1879	1,050	1899	30,483	1918	25,228
1880	2,492	1900	22,504	1919	23,175
1881	2,615	1901	15,113	1920	17,941
1882	1,318	1902	12,468	1921	21,454
1883	5,039	1903	15,547	1922	15,879
1884	5,866	1904	15,767	1923	14,459
1885	7,055	1905	19,958	1924	18,959
1886	7,481	1906	17,586	1925	19,678
1887	7,376	1907	23,292	1926	19,682
1888	6,377	1908	18,083	1927	16,445
1889	7,072	1909	21,170	1928	17,679
1890	8,510	1910	19,433	1929	13,610
1891	12,800	1911	21,458	1930	14,680
1892	12,480	1912	27,000	1931	18,213
1893	11,627				

Source: Haile, *Starp and Sadong Valleys*, p. 86.
Notes: Total coal sold 1874–1931 was 876,345 long tons.
The annual tonnage of coal generally represented annual production of the mines exclusive of the colliery consumption, which amounted to about 4,000 long tons a year when the mines were fully established.

peaked in 1898, and thereafter gradually declined, averaging about 20,000 tons annually (Table 4.1).[58] There was a total surplus of revenue over expenditure during the period from 1881 to 1899 (Table 4.2) but thereafter the reverse was the case. Towards the close of 1931, as part of Vyner's austerity policy, the coal mines at Simunjan were closed.[59]

The Untapped Silantek Coalfields in the Lingga

The earliest recorded investigation of the supposedly extensive coalfields of Silantek was by Hugh Low whose report was dated 19 July 1868, followed in December by the first of a series of

TABLE 4.2
Simunjan Colliery Account, 1881–1899 (dollars)

Year	*Excess of Expenditure over Revenue*	*Excess of Revenue over Expenditure*
1881	4,030.57	–
1882	8,059.38	–
1883	24.85	–
1884	–	909.89
1885	–	4,377.93
1886	–	5,147.51
1887	–	6,273.55
1888	11,805.98	–
1889	5,505.08	–
1890	–	4,049.05
1891	4,418.68	–
1892	–	5,527.55
1893	510.17	–
1894	–	8,217.66
1895	5,082.40	–
1896	–	4,760.35
1897	–	41,789.80
1898	–	44,337.19
1899	–	991.59
Total for 19 years	39,437.11	126,382.07
Surplus of Revenue	–	86,944.96

Source: *SG*, 2 July 1900, p. 132.

investigations undertaken by William Walters.[60] These investigations, together with similar work carried out in subsequent years, proved without doubt that coal existed 'in abundance' at Silantek (Table 4.3).

The rather extensive coalfields were situated about 13 kilometres from Pantu in the Lingga, a tributary of the Batang Lupar. The known coal outcrop 'extends west-southwest from Silantek for about 18 miles along the lower part of the north-facing scarp of the Klingkang Range'.[61] Like the deposits at Simunjan, the coal proved to be of high quality.[62] The successful trial runs of steamships to Singapore confirmed the quality of Silantek coal.[63]

TABLE 4.3
Estimates of Coal Reserves at Silantek, 1880–1931

Year	*Authority*	*Estimated Tonnage ('000 long tons)*	*Remarks*
1880	Sarawak Gazette, April 1880. Probably work by W. Walters or J. R. M. Robertson between 1868 and 1876.	Over 6,000	W. Walters examined outcrops and bored. The estimated tonnage is believed to underlie 980 acres.
1887	Sarawak Gazette, November 1887. Possibly work by A. J. Swinney.	6,298	Basis of estimate unknown.
1921	C. F. J. Galloway	4,500	Estimate based on outcrop examination: the coal is believed to underlie 960 acres.
1928	J. Oswald	5,184 in Main Seam 2,448 in Middle Seam	Based on outcrop examination.
1928–31	J. M. Kennedy (for Messrs. Osborne & Chappel, Malaya)	1,615 780 7,185	Estimate for Main Seam based on outcrop examination, headings, shallow bores, and one deep bore. Total proved tonnage 2,329,000. Total tonnage 3,235,000, assuming coal to continue ¼ mile down dip. Total tonnage 12,940,000, assuming coal to continue 1 mile down the dip.

Source: After Haile, *Starp and Sadong Valleys*, p. 77.

Charles was evidently delighted by reports of the quality and quantity of the Silantek coal. In 1872, as noted above, he invited investors to work the deposits. A year later, much encouraged by the very optimistic and glowing accounts, he proposed the formation of a company to exploit the 'extensive coal fields at Silantek'.

This company, the Lingga Coal Mining Company (Limited), was to be 'under the patronage of the Sarawak Government, and promoted by H.H. the Rajah of Sarawak'.[64] There was, however, no response. Likewise, Charles's offer of generous grants to any company to work the Silantek coal seam attracted no interest. He was disappointed but remained ever hopeful of the prospects for coal.[65]

Charles was not only hopeful about the potential returns from coal to the Treasury, but was equally if not more keen on the benefits that the industry would provide by way of employment opportunities for the people. In a speech to the General Council of 1886, he mentioned the probable formation of a company in London 'with an extensive capital to work the coal-fields [of Silantek] in the Lingga district'. Although 'he [Charles] could not say that this Company was yet a certainty ... if it did come into existence *it would be the means of giving work to thousands, both on land and sea.* No other mineral, however valuable, could employ the same amount of labour, and scatter the same amount of capital among different branches of work, as coal mining operations.'[66] Even though some interested parties did send their own experts to evaluate the deposits, none went beyond the stage of investigation.[67] Despite a series of favourable reports by experts during the 1920s and in the early 1930s, the Silantek coalfields remained untapped throughout Brooke rule.

Charles and the Financially Disastrous Brooketon Colliery

William Clark Cowie was granted the concession of the Muara district, which included the coalfields at Muara Damit, by Sultan Abdul Mumin of Brunei in 1883. Four years later, all rights over the Muara district were ceded in perpetuity to him. With the opening of the mine, a small township developed around Muara Damit. Cowie named the settlement as well as the coal-mines 'Brooketon' in honour of Charles. Because of a lack of capital, mining operations were carried out 'in a hand-to-mouth fashion by a few coolies under a manager with but little experience ... the output being confined to meeting the very limited local demand in Labuan'.[68] In 1887, in order to cut his own losses, Cowie offered the concession to Charles, but the latter declined. Then, in September 1888, Charles changed his mind and decided to acquire Brooketon.[69]

The Brooketon coal-mine was about 2.5 kilometres west–northwest of the little mining village which fronted a sheltered and deep-

water anchorage. Charles expended much capital investment on this project; 'expensive, though necessary, machinery, locomotives, a steam collier, lighters, etc., have been purchased, extensive and solid wharves built, and a new [rail] line laid down' that ran from the mine to the wharf.[70] Experienced managers and mine engineers were engaged at great expense. Improvements were continually made to improve the production and efficiency of the colliery.[71] Initially the coal was mined by opencast methods 'until the removal of overburden became prohibitively expensive and underground [mining] had to be introduced' at the turn of the century.[72] Annual exports from the Brooketon mines averaged between 10,000 tons and 25,000 tons; overall the estimated production totalled 650,000 tons, including coal consumed on the mine itself (Table 4.4).[73]

In spite of the large investment and the improvement in output over the years, the Brooketon colliery was a nightmare for the Sarawak Exchequer. The total loss for the period from 1888 to 1908 exceeded $800,000, excluding the purchase price of about $210,000, and the accumulated interest thereon.[74] 'In no one year', it was lamented, 'have the receipts exceeded the expenditure, and the chances of financial improvement appear to be vastly remote.'[75] During its thirty-three years of operation, the Brooketon colliery incurred a staggering $1.5 million loss, and the capital expenditure was never recovered.[76] In addition to the financial woes, Charles had to face a plethora of problems involving the Brunei Sultanate and the British government: the land and revenue farms, the coal monopoly, export duties on coal, and the question of jurisdiction.[77]

The Brooketon colliery continued to function until the early 1920s despite its losses. It enjoyed favourable years in 1918 and 1919. Its changing fortunes attracted the attention of an English entrepreneur, James Hatton Hall, who initiated several attempts to acquire the concession. Brunei once again raised the subject of the export duty on coal and gave notice that such a duty would commence in 1921.[78]

The recession of the early 1920s, the imposition of the export duty in 1921, the drop in the price of coal after the First World War, the increased cost of production especially in labour and materials, collectively contributed to Vyner's decision to give up the Brooketon concession in 1924, and the mine officially closed in November. The population removed to Sarawak and the jungle reclaimed both the mine and village. In September 1931, Vyner, in

TABLE 4.4
Sale and Export of Brunei Coal [Brooketon], 1883–1941

Year	*Coal Sales (long tons)*	*Coal Exports (long tons)*	*Export Value (Straits $)*	Year	*Coal Sales (long tons)*	*Coal Exports (long tons)*	*Exports Value (Straits $)*
1883	2,409	–	–	1913	22,841	23,743	145,686
1884	4,609	–	–	1914	22,938	25,378	161,585
1885	3,654	–	–	1915	20,971	22,633	148,730
1886	4,491	–	–	1916	17,810	17,810	206,077
1887	–	–	–	1917	19,420	12,594	295,800
1888	6,832	–	–	1918	21,008	21,008	413,910
1889	10,337	–	–	1919	19,798	17,363	296,621
1890	10,780	–	–	1920	20,839	17,000	296,003
1891	14,179	–	–	1921	18,446	16,210	275,570
1892	12,828	–	–	1922	10,592	7,440	104,160
1893	10,865[a]	–	–	1923	11,821	8,941	102,820
1894	12,982	–	–	1924	18,323	10,337	98,202
1895	14,214	–	–	1925	–	676	6,760
1896	9,882	–	–	1926	–	–	–
1897	9,499	–	–	1927	–	52	624
1898	10,718	–	–	1928	–	25	300
1899	10,774	–	–	1929	–	–	–
1900	7,068	–	–	1930	–	–	–

1901	20,839	–	–	1931	–	57	330
1902	20,810	–	–	1932	–	168	1,730
1903	15,412	–	–	1933	–	78	618
1904	29,213	–	–	1934	–	28	298
1905	22,836	–	–	1935	–	25	200
1906	20,352	14,533[b]	–	1936	–	49	392
1907	16,576	7,714[b]	51,230	1937	–	3	27
1908	14,415	20,925[b]	–	1938	–	54[c]	459
1909	12,000[d]	14,878[b]	–	1939	–	32	–
1910	12,472	17,311[b]	–	1940	–	–	–
1911	19,134	25,607[b]	–	1941	–	–	–
1912	12,588	12,724[b]	80,248				
				Total	597,575	315,396	2,688,400

Source: Wilford, *Seria and Miri Oilfields*, p. 161.

Notes: The above figures are quoted from Roe, 1949, Tables 4 and 13, and Posewitz, 1892, p. 486. The bulk of the coal came from Brooketon Colliery with small quantities from Buang Tawar, Bull Hill, and the Kianggeh Valley. Inconsistencies occur in some of the records, e.g. the exports figures cannot be correlated with the figures for sales, probably because different methods have been used at different times to record the coal obtained and exported. The figures for coal sales generally represent the annual production of the colliery exclusive of colliery consumption which, in some years was as much as 5,000 tons.

[a] In 1893 Brooketon sold 7,290 tons to Singapore at $6.24 per ton and 3,469 tons to Manila at $5.75 per ton.

[b] From Brooketon and Buang Tawar Collieries, the coal sold for an average of $7.00 per ton.

[c] 1938 coal produced totalled 464 tons.

[d] Approximate; records incomplete.

a diplomatic gesture on the occasion of the coming of age of Sultan Ahmed Tajuddin of Brunei, relinquished his land rights in the Muara district altogether.[79]

The Borneo Company Limited and Exploitation of Mineral Resources

Under the terms of the concession from the Sarawak government, the Borneo Company Limited (BCL) had 'the privilege of working each mineral discovered', with the exception of gold; in the event that it failed to mine the minerals, 'the government can resume the mineral and let it to others'.[80] In order to encourage the company's efforts, James even suspended temporarily the government's annual royalty of £1,000 after the BCL's abortive and expensive attempt at coal-mining at Simunjan in 1857–8.

During the 1860s the BCL placed its agent in Upper Sarawak as the main purchaser of antimony ore from native producers, which it then forwarded to Kuching for export. It also supplied equipment, like mining tools and gunpowder, to the local miners. The BCL was instrumental in transforming the rather rude paths to the mines into roads and tramways to facilitate transportation of the ore.[81] In the late 1860s, the BCL itself was involved in the mining of antimony. In 1871, for example, it employed some 750 men, mostly Chinese, for its antimony mines and works at Jambusan, Paku, and Busau.[82]

In the absence of experts like geologists or mineralogists on the spot, 'specimens of every "find"' were sent to Britain 'for analysis ... where recommendations for action were made, at a range of ten thousand miles and on a purely theoretical basis'.[83] In the 1860s, the BCL decided to erect a smelter at Busau to serve the antimony-producing areas.[84]

Meanwhile, prospecting work was carried out during the 1860s, mainly by the energetic Ludvig Verner Helms, the first manager of the BCL in Sarawak. In September 1867 Helms claimed the discovery of cinnabar at Tegora, reputed to be the only such mines in the region.[85] Mining commenced 'which made the jungle resound with the miner's blast and the engine's puff';[86] within a year of its discovery, mercury was exported. Further prospecting revealed traces of cinnabar and metallic mercury in the Samarahan and Sadong districts. Nevertheless, apart from the Tegora works, it was only at Gading, a few kilometres to the west, that the BCL embarked on mining operations.[87]

In the 1870s the BCL did not involve itself directly in the mining of gold. It did contribute to the development of the industry by introducing new technology and hiring out machinery to the Chinese mining companies. Then, from the 1880s, the BCL became actively involved in gold-mining operations with the opening of several large-scale gold works at Bau and Paku.[88] In 1882, it erected a mill at Bau for crushing and grinding the ore hitherto done by hand.[89] Two years later mechanical pumps were provided on loan, mostly to Chinese mining companies, which revolutionized the mining of deposits below the water-table.[90] Interest in gold-mining initially rose when the BCL's mining engineer, M. N. Grey, discovered an important deposit near Bau, later called 'Grey's Ridge' among the Europeans and 'Tai Parit' in official documents. However, as gold-mining was excluded in the terms of the mining concession made with the government, the BCL could not itself be involved in mining operations.[91] To overcome this, the 'tributer system' was applied and, through their Chinese tributer, exploitation commenced at Grey's Ridge; it proved profitable.[92] The indirect participation of the BCL understandably caused friction with the other Chinese mining concerns, notably the Shak Lak Mun which was the most prominent.[93] Under the circumstances and considering the potential of Tai Parit, the BCL decided on a take-over, and by 1894 had succeeded in buying out the Shak Lak Mun. With this purchase it had in effect secured a near-monopoly of all gold-mining in the country.[94] In the mid-1890s the BCL obtained further concessions from Charles, including the right to prospect for gold.[95]

By the early 1890s it was becoming evident that the methods of sluicing and panning were ineffective in extracting the finer gold particles and more efficient techniques had to be employed. In 1896 a series of experiments was carried out on ore samples from the BCL's mines by its experts in London using various new methods of extraction, including the recently discovered cyanidation process.[96]

Brief Successes

The Cyanidation Process of Gold Extraction

The cyanidation method of extracting gold was the brainchild of J. S. McArthur, a scientist from Glasgow. The process involved dissolving the ore 'by a solution of Cyanide of Sodium, precipitated or deposited on zinc wool,' then 'collected from that,

smelted, refined and cast into those massive [gold] bars which weigh half a cwt'.[97] This revolutionary process was to have an immense impact on the BCL's gold works in Sarawak. In fact, its Bau plant was reputed to be the 'first place in the world where the cyanide method to extract gold was used commercially and successfully'.[98]

In order to attain the maximum percentage of extraction as well as to overcome the various technical problems, innovations and modifications to the original cyanidation process were necessary.[99] The ore from the BCL's Tai Parit mine, the largest opencast working, was the first to undergo the cyanidation process at the Bau factory.[100] The success of the Bau plant led to the opening in 1900 of another factory at Bidi, which received its supply of ore from Bidi itself and from the Jagui Mountain mines.[101] By 1908 it was decided to convert the Bau factory to an all-sliming plant to attend to the refractory primary gold ore of Tai Parit.[102] The conversion was rewarded with a significant improvement in gold recovery, from 68 per cent to 85 per cent.[103] Two years later the rich eluvial gold ore from the BCL's Tai Ton Mine was brought by rail and treated at the Bau plant.[104]

The cyanidation process produced 'an extraction of 70 to 80 per cent ... obtained on charges of ore varying from 4 to 8 dwts. per ton'.[105] However, some types of ore proved difficult to extract, and, after treatment, only produced a rather unsatisfactory percentage of gold.[106] Generally, the introduction of the cyanidation method significantly increased production from a mere 984 ounces exported in 1898 to 24,192 ounces in the following year when the new process was implemented.[107] Thereafter, until 1921, gold was the main mineral export of Sarawak (Table 4.5).

The 'Celebrated Earth Oil' of Miri

Long before Brooke records noted the existence of mineral oil in the vicinity of the Baram and Miri rivers, local inhabitants had utilized 'earth oil' mixed with resin in caulking boats and for domestic purposes as a substitute for kerosene. This second use was not without some disastrous effects.[108] In mid-1878 A. Hart Everett mentioned briefly 'petroleum' as among other minerals that have 'been detected in other parts of the N. W. and W. Borneo beyond the limits of the Sarawak territory'.[109] But he did not specify its whereabouts.

In June 1882 the Baram was acquired from Brunei. Its administration was then incorporated with that of the Third Division

TABLE 4.5
Exports of Gold, 1899–1940

Year	*Ounces*	*Declared (Value $)*	*Value per Ounce*
1899	–	541,711	(13,984 Bongkals)
1900	–	843,709	(26,575 Bongkals)
1901	38,782.00	1,246,114	$32.13
1902	36,768.00	1,368,360	37.21
1903	61,198.50	1,819,200	29.72
1904	61,295.00	1,824,320	29.76
1905	61,285.00	1,839,956	30.02
1906	57,403.00	1,415,470	24.65
1907	68,108.25	1,513,800	22.22
1908	43,142.75	1,130,760	26.20
1909	45,085.00	1,139,440	25.27
1910	46,999.50	951,119	20.23
1911	40,650.25	992,915	24.42
1912	42,407.50	1,070,200	25.23
1913	41,874.90	1,077,400	25.72
1914	39,355.60	1,078,600	27.41
1915	47,138.40	1,256,500	26.65
1916	51,590.00	1,209,050	23.43
1917	29,236.00	675,600	23.10
1918	35,982.00	923,100	25.65
1919	31,008.00	808,100	26.06
1920	22,922.00	612,200	26.70
1921	19,403.00	559,190	28.82
1922	1,662.80	40,350	24.26
1923	2,173.00	37,200	17.12
1924	857.72	32,300	37.66
1925	709.76	24,808	34.95
1926	249.10	6,367	25.56
1927	–	–	–
1928	–	–	–
1929	972.00	35,200	36.21
1930	4,025.60	127,420	31.65
1931	10,450.92	326,962	31.29
1932	8,359.20	408,930	48.92
1933	17,397.66	865,640	49.75
1934	29,380.00	1,668,441	56.79
1935	28,120.00	1,630,466	57.98
1936	22,628.00	1,319,620	58.32
1937	19,643.00	1,161,006	59.10
1938	18,486.00	1,113,348	60.23
1939	17,925.00	1,141,155	63.66
1940	12,634.00	875,680	69.31

Source: Lucas, 'Production of Gold in Sarawak', p. 32.

under Claude Champion De Crespigny, the Resident, whose new headquarters in the Baram was at Claude Town (Marudi), named by Charles in his honour.[110] It was De Crespigny who first brought the attention of the Brooke government to the oil seepages. 'The celebrated earth oil at Mirih [*sic*]', he reported in September 1882, 'is found in about 18 wells which some people dug a few years ago in the hope of its being purchased by possible buyers.'[111] In his diary entry of May 1884, De Crespigny recommended that the 'oil district near the mouth of the Miri River should be thoroughly searched and reported on'.[112] Whether acting on De Crespigny's suggestion or otherwise, a geologist did conduct an investigation of the Miri area in the early 1880s. However, he 'appeared to be more interested in gold and cinnabar than in petroleum', and not surprisingly he was 'not favourably impressed' by the oil seepages.[113]

Charles Hose, who served as a cadet under De Crespigny and went on to become Officer-in-Charge of the Baram in 1888 and then Resident in 1891, spent much time in examining and recording the oil seepages. He then prepared a map of the location of the twenty-eight seepages that he was able to identify.[114] Hose was very much convinced that the Lower Baram was a petroliferous district and, like his predecessor, strongly recommended that geological investigations should be carried out.[115]

Early in 1896 it was reported that some attempts 'were made to prove the value of the mineral oil deposits at Miri, but these appear to have been dropped owing to difficulties met with at the outset'.[116] It was not improbable that these efforts were conducted by the BCL, presumably at Charles's behest.[117] Charles also gave his blessing to Hose, who, in 1905, undertook a rather amateurish attempt at ascertaining the 'quantity of oil by digging holes of some few feet in depth' with the assistance of an engineer named Macreath; this proved futile and was abandoned.[118]

Meanwhile, oil was discovered in the Brunei territory. Its exploitation was possible as Charles possessed the concession for oil from Brunei.[119] Similar findings were reported at Buang Tawar, on Berembang Island, in Brunei.[120]

Undaunted, and armed with his 'consistent faith that oil production was economically viable', Hose, while in England in 1907, shortly after his retirement from the Brooke government, successfully persuaded Charles[121] to authorize him to negotiate with the Anglo-Saxon Petroleum Company (ASPC) on behalf of the Sarawak government.[122] An agreement was signed on 9 March 1909 whereby the ASPC was granted the concession for the 'sole

and exclusive right and license' to prospect for petroleum within the territories of Sarawak for three to five years commencing from 30 June. In the event that oil was discovered, the ASPC would be offered a mining lease with exclusive rights for seventy-five years.[123] Charles, exhibiting patriotism and loyalty to his homeland, requested the incorporation in the concession of a clause whereby a permanent 'quantity of ten thousand tons of liquid fuel' be stored 'for the purpose of supplying the ships of the navy of Great Britain or any of her Colonies'.[124] Dr J. T. Erb, a geologist of ASPC, went to Sarawak to conduct a geological survey (August to December 1909) of the northern part of the country 'covering some 400–500 miles', and 'reported the existence at Miri of a dome-shaped, unsymmetrical anticline, with a steep Eastern flank and numerous oil shows'.[125] By February 1910, a location was fixed for boring work on the first well. Nine months later on 10 October oil was struck at a depth of 134.1 metres (447 feet) and 'Miri Well No. 1' produced 4 tons of water-free oil a day.[126] Charles was undoubtedly exhilarated, and so were the directors and shareholders of ASPC. Further capital was raised for the development of the Miri oilfield.[127]

The early days of Miri, hitherto a small fishing village, were extremely difficult. There were colossal problems in the transportation ashore of heavy drilling and other mining machinery. Bad weather conditions and rough seas exacerbated the difficulties. Logistical problems of supplies, almost all of which had to be brought in, and acute labour shortages tested to the limits the tenacity and determination of the pioneers.[128] Notwithstanding these difficulties, more wells were sunk and no less than eight were in operation when the first shipment of Sarawak oil was made on 18 April 1913. On this historic occasion, some 500 tons of crude oil was carried by two lighters which were towed out from the Miri River to tankers lying offshore.[129] The oil was then shipped to Shell's refineries in Sumatra.[130]

The interrelated issues of finding sites for a deep-sea port and a refinery and the transportation of the oil from the wells to these two locations remained throughout the 1910s.[131] In August 1914 it was decided that an undersea pipeline be laid 'through which oil could be pumped to a tanker lying at anchor in deep water'.[132] The initial submarine line, of 15-centimetre diameter and about 4.2 kilometres in length, was floated out to sea with its 'shore end about 500 yards south of the mouth of the Miri River'.[133] The first loading from this submarine line directly into a tanker was effectively

accomplished on 12 September.[134] It was, however, not a complete success.[135] In September 1916, a line with a 20-centimetre diameter was laid, this time not at Miri but about 11 kilometres northwards at Lutong where the flat terrain was more suitable for the new methods of launching which had been successfully adopted at Mexico.[136] This new line, 4.4 kilometres long, was in fact the longest submarine pipeline in the world then. In October 1916 the distillation of crude oil employing a topping plant on the Trumble system was started at Tanjong Lobang near Miri.[137] This plant successfully produced fuel oil for the Royal Navy and its allies (namely Japan) during the First World War.[138] The laying of the third pipeline, over 3 kilometres in length, was completed in April 1919.[139]

With the sea-loading line as well as storage tanks located at Lutong, it was inevitable that the refinery would also be situated at this site. Transfer of equipment from Miri to Lutong was only effected in late 1918, due to war conditions, and the refinery commenced operations in mid-1919 with a single unit affectionately known as 'Trumble 1'. Trumble 2 and 3 followed in 1921 and 1924 respectively.[140] Since then no other major distillation plants for crude oil was erected.[141]

Charles was supportive of the activities of the ASPC, but remained steadfast that the oil company did not exploit his native subjects. However, as the nature of the industry required technically skilled personnel, the Dayaks found themselves at a severe disadvantage except as common labourers; even so, they had to compete with imported Chinese coolies.[142]

In 1921 there was a corporate change whereby the ASPC was replaced by the Sarawak Oilfields Limited (SOL), also a subsidiary of the Royal Dutch Shell Group.[143] Whereas the ASPC was incorporated in London, SOL was locally registered and two Brooke government officials sat on its Board of Directors.[144]

The effects of the First World War and the years that followed retarded the development of the Miri oilfield. It was only from the early 1920s that expansion could be envisaged (Table 4.6 and Figure 4.1). However, this was dependent on the reserves in sight as well as the demands of the world market. From 1920 to 1930 production was maintained at an average of 2,000 tons per day.[145] Rotary drilling was introduced in 1925, replacing the rather slow and cumbersome cable tool method; from then to 1930, a further 250 wells were drilled with production improving appreciably.[146] Production peaked during 1929 when some 5.5 million barrels

TABLE 4.6
Sarawak Crude Oil Production, 1911–1941

	Crude Oil	
Year	*Barrels*	*Royalty (Malayan $)*
1911	1,275	5,346.43[a]
1912	41,539	
1913	194,160	7,068.86
1914	472,948	25,541.28
1915	497,770	26,957.28
1916	655,248	35,179.21
1917	565,930	28,518.68
1918	513,782	23,783.21
1919	612,998	28,429.07
1920	1,061,190	118,125.88
1921	1,498,938	190,063.52
1922	3,025,450	406,161.29
1923	4,187,205	578,007.93
1924	4,424,646	612,554.81
1925	4,520,296	618,685.28
1926	5,248,439	718,956.59
1927	5,236,602	710,045.66
1928	5,506,568	756,506.09
1929	5,552,117	791,148.48
1930	5,114,182	737,597.27
1931	3,891,027	557,565.82
1932	2,540,460	359,236.83
1933	2,441,677	344,249.94
1934	2,085,279	297,903.02
1935	1,902,853	271,836.09
1936	1,668,390	238,341.45
1937	1,574,204	224,886.34
1938	1,498,901	214,128.74
1939	1,223,917	174,845.20
1940	1,094,022	156,288.85
1941	707,772	101,110.31
Total	69,559,849	9,359,068.50

Source: Wilford, *Seria and Miri Oilfields*, p. 146.
Notes: One barrel contains 42 United States gallons.
[a]Royalty paid for 1911 and 1912 production, that is, oil output between 1911 and June 1913.

FIGURE 4.1
Crude Oil Production of the Miri Field, 1911–1940

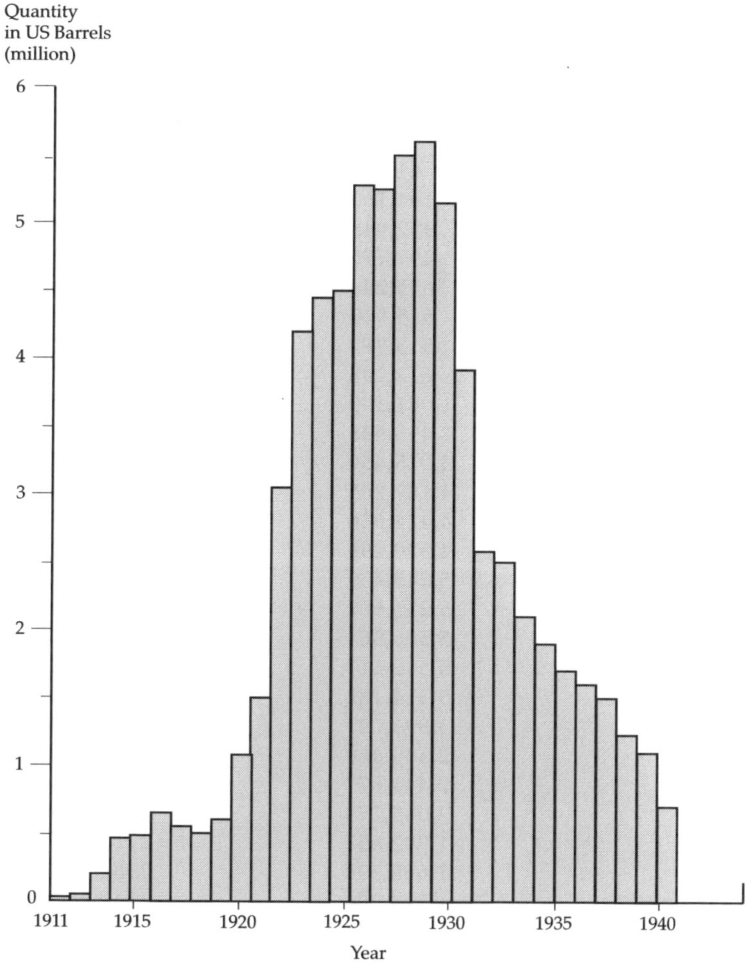

Source: After *Oil in Sarawak, 1910–1960*, p. 8.

were recorded, and thereafter steadily declined.[147] On the eve of the Pacific War, 'field production had fallen to 480 tons per day, 597 wells had been drilled of which 408 were still producing oil'.[148]

Oil, more than any other export item, was Sarawak's single major foreign exchange earner during the last twenty-five years of

Brooke rule. In 1915 exports were about $0.4 million; in 1925 they were valued at $24.0 million, and exceeded $45.0 million during 1929, the year of peak production.[149]

Blighted Hopes and Disappointments

The successes in gold and oil production were short-lived. By the first decade of the twentieth century the gold-mining areas in Upper Sarawak had been exhausted and, despite untiring prospecting, no major new finds were in sight. The Miri oilfield was not a rich field, and by the mid-1920s practically all the wells which had been discovered were in production and there was no prospect of new ones. The collieries, particularly Brooketon, were costly disappointments. Sarawak coal, despite the evidence of its quality, could never maintain a regular market. Minerals like antimony and cinnabar were almost exhausted by the late nineteenth century though they continued to be exported until the early part of the twentieth century.

Antimony and Mercury: Diminishing Output

Antimony, mined in Upper Sarawak since the 1820s, began to show signs of decline by the mid-1880s. Even as early as the mid-1860s, visitors at the Bidi mine already commented that it 'was almost exhausted'.[150] Although such an observation was premature it was not entirely unprophetic. In fact, out of a total of 83,000 tons of antimony ore produced in Sarawak since 1823, over four-fifths of this amount was mined before 1886.[151] In 1907 the BCL's smelting works at Busau was closed.[152] From 1885 to 1907 production continued in a fluctuating manner (Figure 4.2). At the turn of the century antimony was no longer mined on a large-scale and production was 'entirely kept up by numbers of independent workers'.[153] From then until the outbreak of the Pacific War small quantities were exported on an irregular basis. After 1916 antimony as an export item had become unimportant.

The mining of mercury, started at Tegora in 1867 and a little later at Gading, lasted for less than two decades. By 1877 the deposits at Tegora had already been exhausted and the mine closed in that year.[154] Mining proceeded in other areas for about another decade before production began to decline. Most of the high quality ore had already been extracted. From 1886 onwards

FIGURE 4.2
Antimony Ore Production in the Bau Mining District, 1864–1950

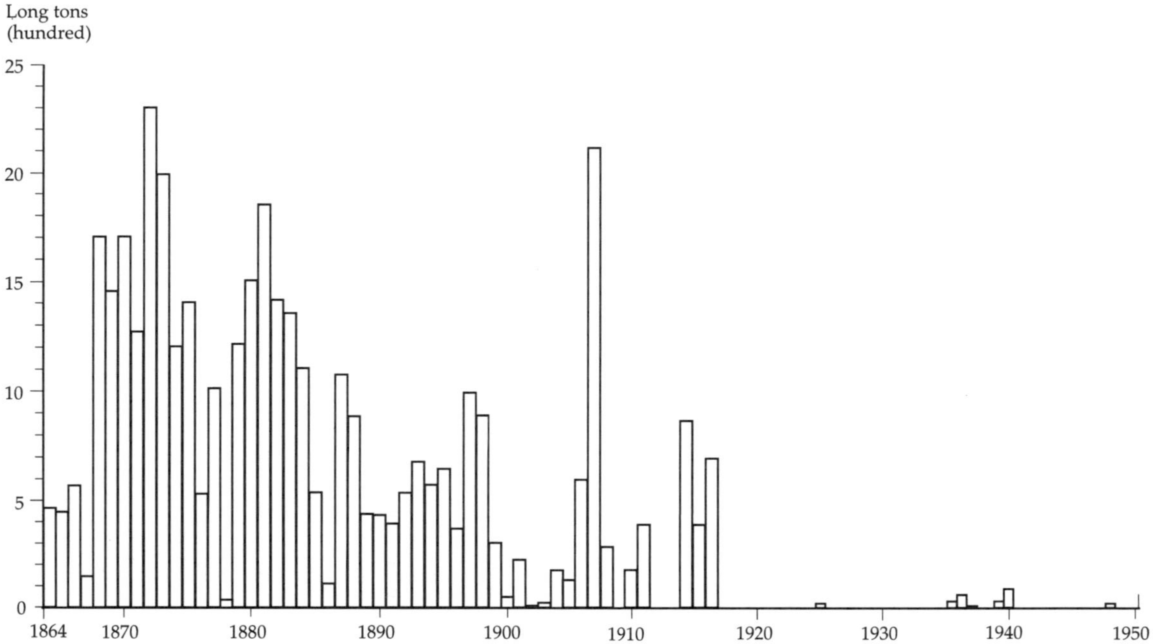

Source: After Wolfenden, *Bau Mining District*, p. 56.
Note: Antimony ore was first mined in 1823, and the estimated production between 1823 and 1863 was 42,400 long tons.

only sporadic mining operations were conducted. After 1898 production was negligible. Besides the small quantities exported in 1908–9, there was no further production of mercury in Brooke Sarawak.[155]

Gold: Exhaustion, Difficulties, Revival, and Decline

By the first decade of the twentieth century, the known eluvial ore deposits of gold in the Bau area were almost exhausted. Owing to declining production and the impracticality of re-treating the tailing dumps, it became uneconomical to continue at Bidi and the BCL decided to close it in 1911.[156] Meanwhile, Tai Parit had developed into a huge opencast mine by 1920. Close to 3 million tons of overburden had been removed and it became increasingly difficult and expensive for mining operations to be carried out.[157] Flooding during the wet season made the task of keeping the mine water-free increasingly expensive. There was also the ever-imminent danger of the walls of the mine collapsing. Then, in 1921, 'as a result of abnormal rainfall and the breaking through of subterranean watercourses and an adjacent stream, the mine became totally flooded ... the enormous pumps there installed being unable to cope with the inflow'.[158] It was then that the BCL, acting upon expert advice, decided to close Tai Parit in August 1921. At the same time it gave up its mineral rights held since 1857. 'The Company's geologists had made repeated surveys of the country, and the Directors now came to the conclusion, that, antimony and quicksilver being, as far as they were concerned, worked out, and gold no longer worth working, it was no longer profitable to make annual payments to keep the concession alive.'[159]

But with the BCL's departure, Upper Sarawak did not resemble a desolate mining district nor Bau a ghost town, like the abandoned gold sites in California or Australia. Former employees of the BCL and others saw the possibilities of utilizing the cyanidation process, albeit on a small-scale, on the huge 'mountains' of tailing dumps left behind. There was a flurry of activity during the 1920s with both Chinese and Malays scrambling for mining leases from the government.[160] Former miners returned and several Chinese companies were established. New deposits were discovered and mined in the vicinity of Bau. That new gold deposits were uncovered then, and not earlier, came as no surprise, given the problems of prospecting in a country like Sarawak. 'Like all tropical countries with a heavy rainfall, rocks have been subjected to extreme weathering action and most are buried under many feet of clay,

thus it is frequently only from stream beds or the steeper hills that any indication of the underlying formation can be gained.'[161] Both the Bau and Bidi tailings were reworked by the Chinese companies using the cyanidation method.[162] By 1930 gold exports were resumed, and steadily rose during the next five years.[163] The early 1930s witnessed a kind of gold-rush with a mushrooming of Chinese mining companies.[164] The revival of the gold industry could not have occurred at a more opportune time than during the Depression.[165] Peak production was attained during 1934–5 when almost 29,000 troy ounces were exported annually (Figure 4.3).[166] Thereafter a gradual decline in production set in.

FIGURE 4.3
Gold Production in the Bau Mining District, 1864–1950

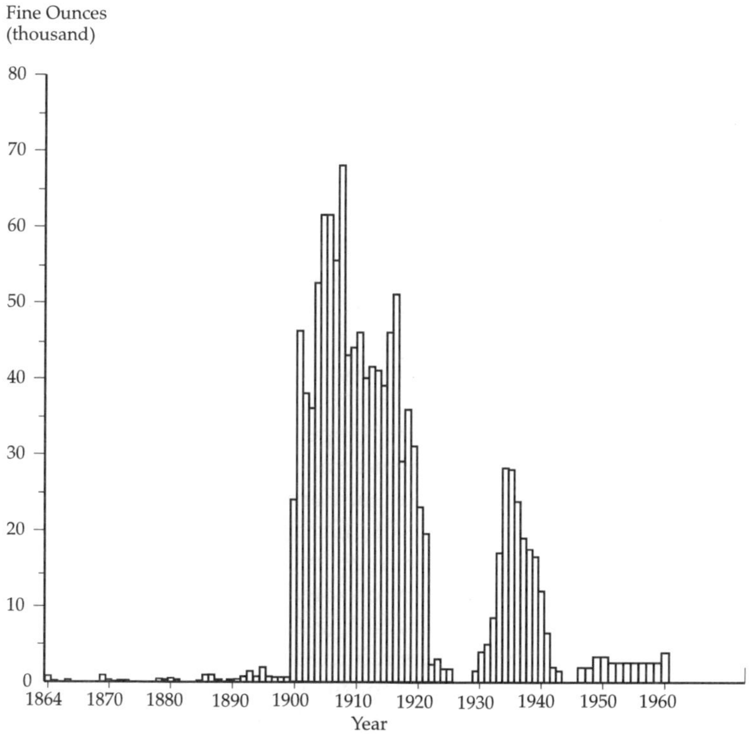

Source: After Wolfenden, *Bau Mining District*, p. 56.
Note: The graph is based on gold export from 1864 to 1927, and on total recorded production from 1929 to 1960. Gold was mined during the 1840s but no records are available, neither of export nor of production.

Decline of the Miri Oilfield

By 1926 it was apparent that 'most of the oil accumulation had been discovered'.[167] Notwithstanding the claim that wells in the Miri field generally have 'a long life' and decline at 'comparatively a very slow rate',[168] it was becoming clear that decline had begun from 1930 onwards (see Table 4.6). Furthermore, expert opinions within the industry predicted that 'the oil-fields at Miri will cease production about the year 1947', adding that 'there appears to be no immediate certainty that oil will be worked in other parts of the country'.[169] Untiring efforts at prospecting, employing up-to-date geophysical surveying techniques including the seismic method, revealed no potential reserves of any kind throughout the country.[170] Neither did the oil industry at Miri undergo any kind of renaissance as experienced by the gold industry of Upper Sarawak.

The Problems of Coal

The overriding problem of poor demand had plagued Sarawak coal since production commenced at the government-owned collieries of Simunjan and Brooketon. In the end it had to be satisfied with catering for local needs[171] and the occasional export abroad.[172] Even Charles's offer to the Royal Navy of a coaling station with '200 tons always ready at Pinding in the Quop river for the use of men of war' was apparently turned down.[173]

Consequently, with heavy capital investment and poor receipts, the collieries were financial embarrassments. Apart from a brief period as a profitable venture, the Simunjan mines were a financial burden on the Exchequer for the greater part of their three decades of existence.[174] The reasons for Brooketon's financial failure and the decision to terminate mining operations in 1924 ranged from the fall in coal prices, the imposition of the coal export duty in 1921, the increasing decline in demand for coal in ships as oil became more popular, to technical problems concerning the coal seams.[175] The mines were finally closed during Vyner's reign, and Brooketon was returned to Brunei.

Besides the occasional extraction for testing purposes,[176] the coalfields at Silantek were never exploited on a commercial basis during the Brooke period. Like Simunjan and Brooketon coal, there were no doubts whatsoever of both the quality and quantity of the coal deposits at Silantek. However, two formidable problems had to be solved before any viable mining operations could be undertaken.

James R. M. Robertson, in his report of 1877 on the Silantek coalfields,[177] succinctly presented the problems and their probable solutions. First, there was the issue of labour shortage, which for all practical reasons, had to rely on imported Chinese coolies, as at Simunjan.[178] The second problem, of equal or even more demanding proportions, was the question of transportation; the construction of a railtrack, conservatively estimated at £112,000 to £135,000, was the only solution.[179] These problems obviously discouraged would-be investors from developing the Silantek coalfield, despite all efforts on the part of the Brookes to promote it.[180]

Conclusion

The 'supposed mineral wealth of Sarawak' that 'first brought it into notice' among Europeans[181] was a myth. The country possessed a wide range of minerals, but apart from antimony, gold, cinnabar, coal, and petroleum, most of these did not occur in sufficient quantity nor quality to render them of much economic importance. Even those which were exploited on a commercial basis were neither substantial nor long-lasting. There was no equivalent of a Kinta Valley or a Witwaterstrand. Notwithstanding the difficulties of prospecting in a land like Sarawak, continual efforts were made throughout the Brooke period but were disappointing. The BCL, responsible for most of the mineral prospecting during the last quarter of the nineteenth century, experienced countless set-backs. By the late 1870s there was already indication that Sarawak 'cannot be looked upon as a mineral-producing country'.[182]

The most important mineral-producing district in the country, Upper Sarawak, was by the early 1920s declared exhausted of 'any workable deposit of any size' and it was 'very doubtful if Upper Sarawak will ever again become a centre of mining activity'.[183] This opinion was further confirmed by a thorough survey undertaken during the mid-1960s which concluded that 'there is little prospect of any resumption of large scale mining in the area'.[184] It should be pointed out that the brief revival of gold production in the Bau area during the early 1930s was *more from the reworking of the tailing dumps and old mine sites than from the discovery and extraction of new deposits.*

The Miri oilfield proved to be another blighted hope. Fifteen years after the first well was spudded, no new deposits had been

discovered. Untiring prospecting, employing the latest survey techniques and equipment, was all unfruitful. Even with the utilization of improved techniques during the post-Brooke period the result was equally disappointing. In fact, Sarawak Oilfields Limited, in December 1957, 'after a long, disappointing and unsuccessful campaign' of prospecting work, decided to surrender '77 % of the land area of their Sarawak holdings' ahead of the dates in the concession terms.[185] In comparison, the neighbouring Seria oilfield in Brunei, which was discovered in 1929, proved to be much bigger and substantially richer than that of Miri (Figure 4.4).

The Brookes, particularly Charles, were most supportive and even became directly involved in the promotion and development of the mining industry. Prospecting licences were granted to companies as well as individuals.[186] Liberal concession terms were

FIGURE 4.4
Oil Production of the Miri Oilfield of Sarawak and the Seria Oilfield of Brunei, 1910–1960

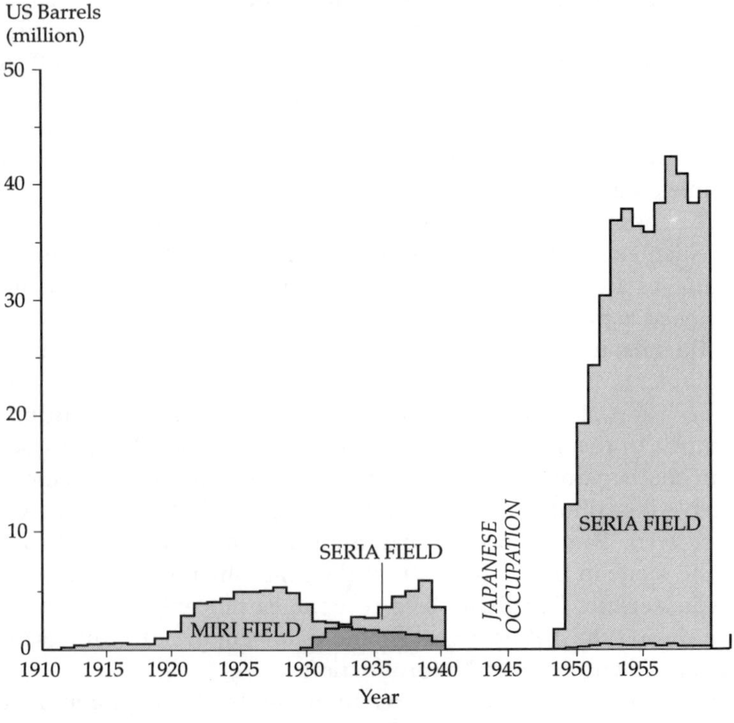

Source: Wilford, *Seria and Miri Oilfields*, p. 148.

granted for commercial exploitation.[187] Belief in and hope for richer finds of minerals were often echoed by the Brookes. Typically, in a speech to the General Council of 1889, Charles was sanguine about the future prospects of minerals: 'Minerals too ... showed a falling off [in production], though it was impossible to say when they might come across fresh veins of antimony and cinnabar which *doubtless existed some where underground.*'[188] In such ways the Brookes added further credibility to the eldorado myth of Sarawak.[189]

It was not for want of effort nor encouragement on the part of the Brookes that the mining sector did not flourish. A particular disappointment was the absence of a sustained market for Sarawak coal; this may be attributed to several factors. A possible contributing factor might be the doubts about its quality, as coal mined in the East tended in general 'to be so wretchedly bad, particularly for steaming purposes'.[190] Despite several successive trials that proved the high quality of Sarawak coal, the problem of a lack of buyers remained. Another cause might have been the competition from other coal-producing countries in the East, for example, Vietnam and Manchuria. But the most likely obstacle was the geographical marginality of Brooke Sarawak—an unknown land situated off the main trade and shipping routes. Ignorance of the availability of its coal more than anything else contributed to the poor demand for it. Even Charles's patriotic offer to the Royal Navy of coaling facilities was apparently declined.

The country's obscurity also contributed to the lack of success of the Silantek coalfields, despite repeated offers and the favourable results of numerous tests on the quality of its coal. Silantek remained a great disappointment to the Brookes.

Minerals, in fact, did not feature prominently as export earnings Table 4.7). Even the long-established antimony and gold from Upper Sarawak together with cinnabar and coal did not contribute as much to the state revenue as had been anticipated. It was only from the beginning of the twentieth century that gold became a notable contributor to export earnings. Even then its heyday was short-lived. Blessed was Brooke Sarawak when mineral oil came on the scene in the early 1910s at the time when the gold industry was in decline. Petroleum as a revenue earner only came into its own during the 1920s, but then the following decade witnessed a gradual downward trend in production.

Notwithstanding their efforts to promote the exploitation of Sarawak's mineral resources, there was a tacit recognition by the

TABLE 4.7
Mineral Production and Exports of Brooke Sarawak, 1868–1938 (Sarawak $)

Year	*Value of Sarawak Produce Exported*	*Value of Mineral Exports*	*Percentage of Mineral Exports to Exports of Sarawak Produce*	*Mineral Royalties Paid to Sarawak Government*	*Remarks (Mineral Exports in Their Order of Value; the Most Valuable Export is Shown First)*
1868	n.a.	38,001	–	n.a.	Antimony, quicksilver, gold, diamonds
1878	809,325	83,086	10	13,333	Antimony, quicksilver, gold, diamonds
1888	1,322,325	118,915	9	8,889	Antimony, coal, quicksilver, gold
1898	3,089,017	323,230	10	10,177	Coal, antimony, gold, quicksilver
1908	5,732,723	1,177,266	21	77,367	Gold, coal, antimony, quicksilver
1918	9,221,459	n.a.	–	98,109	Gold, oil, coal
1928	53,302,340	39,302,340	74	770,835	Oil
1938	23,244,666	12,482,134	54	387,636	Oil, gold, silver

Source: After Roe, *The Natural Resources of Sarawak*, p. 24.

Brookes that, though the extraction of minerals was financially important to both participants and the government, it was only a short-term benefit. Minerals, a wasting asset, eventually diminish and likewise their revenues, while for the Brookes the long-term prosperity of their country lay in the cultivation of the soil.[191]

1. James Brooke, *A Letter from Borneo with Notices of the Country and Its Inhabitants, Addressed to James Gardner, Esq.*, London: L. & G. Seeley, 1842, p. 17. Emphasis added.

2. See Hugh Low, *Sarawak: Its Inhabitants and Productions, Being Notes during a Residence in that Country with His Excellency Mr Brooke*, London: Frank Cass, 1848; new impression, 1968, pp. 17–19; A. Hart Everett, 'Notes on the Distribution of the Useful Minerals of Sarawak', *JSBRAS*, 1 (July 1878): 13–30; and J. S. Geikie, 'A List of Sarawak Minerals', *SMJ*, 1, 1 (February 1911): 194–201.

3. Brooke, *A Letter from Borneo*, p. 17.

4. J. Brooke to John C. Templer, 11 October 1850, John C. Templer (ed.), *The Private Letters of Sir James Brooke, KCB, Rajah of Sarawak, Narrating the Events of His Life, from 1838 to the Present Time*, 3 vols., London: Bentley, 1853, Vol. III, pp. 14–15; and J. Brooke to The Right Honourable Sidney Herbert, MP, 22 June 1852, in ibid., pp. 122–3.

5. The opium monopoly was taken over by one of the Brooke officers who managed it as a state enterprise. See J. Brooke to The Right Honourable Sidney Herbert, MP, 22 June 1852, in Templer, *Letters*, Vol. III, pp. 122–3.

6. After its abortive attempts at working the Simunjan coal deposits in the late 1850s, the company's coal concession lapsed and reverted to the Brooke government. See J. Brooke to 'Ladies', 29 April 1863, in Owen Rutter (ed.), *Rajah Brooke and Baroness Burdett Coutts: Consisting of the Letters from Sir James Brooke, First White Rajah of Sarawak, to Miss Angela (afterwards Barroness) Burdett Coutts*, London: Hutchinson, 1935, pp. 186–8.

7. Brooke, *A Letter from Borneo*, p.16. Emphasis added.

8. Low, *Sarawak*, pp. 19–20.

9. See S. Baring-Gould and C. A. Bampfylde, *A History of Sarawak under Its Two White Rajahs, 1839–1908*, London: Henry Sotheran, 1909, p. 5.

10. Frederick Boyle, *Adventures among the Dyaks of Borneo*, London: Hurst & Blackett, 1865, p. 70.

11. Chang Pat Foh, 'Major Events in the History of Bau', *SG*, April 1987, p. 29. For a description of Chinese gold workings, see Low, *Sarawak*, p. 22.

12. From 1850 onwards the Dutch began to assert their hegemony over the Chinese gold-mining communities in the Sambas region which led to clashes between them and the Chinese *kongsi*. See James C. Jackson, *Chinese in the West Borneo Goldfields: A Study in Cultural Geography*, University of Hull, Occasional Papers in Geography, No. 15, 1970, pp. 71–3; Spenser St John, *The Life of Sir James Brooke: Rajah of Sarawak; from His Personal Papers and Correspondence*, Edinburgh and London: William Blackwood & Sons, 1879, p. 225; and Barbara E. Ward, 'A Hakka Kongsi in Borneo', *JOS*, 1, 2 (July 1954): 369.

13. See Spenser St John, *Life in the Forests of the Far East*, 2 vols., London: Smith, Elder & Co., 1862; reprinted Kuala Lumpur: Oxford University Press, 1974, Vol. II, p. 328.

14. Henry Keppel, *A Visit to the Indian Archipelago in HM Ship* Maeander *with Portions of the Private Journal of Sir James Brooke, KCB*, 2 Vols., London: Bentley, 1853, Vol. II, p. 51. Later, in 1856, some 500 of these refugees were resettled as rice cultivators at Sungei Tengah, about 10 kilometres north of Bau. Ibid., pp. 329–30. See also Harriette McDougall, *Letters from Sarawak*, reprint edn., London: Wheldon & Wesley, 1924, pp. 117–18.

15. Charles noted in his memoirs, dated October 1856, the role he played in negotiating the settlement of the Chinese at Marup with the local Dayaks. However, according to Liew Peck Kwee, the establishment of the Marup community was effected in 1850 when the refugees crossed the border and settled there. It was probable that some of these Chinese were already working gold at Marup and were formally emplaced with the assistance of Charles. See Charles Brooke, *Ten Years in Sarawak*, 2 vols., London: Tinsley Brothers, 1866; reprinted Singapore: Oxford University Press, 1990, Vol. I, p. 199; and Liew Peck Kwee, *A History of the Hoppo Chinese with Special Reference to Sarawak* [text in Chinese], Singapore: Tung Yet Publishing House, 1978, pp. 46–7, quoted in Daniel Chew, *Chinese Pioneers on the Sarawak Frontier, 1841–1941*, Singapore: Oxford University Press, 1990, p. 34, n. 19.

16. See Chapter 8.

17. St John, *Life in the Forests*, Vol. II, p. 364.

18. The newly established BCL rendered valuable financial assistance during these dark days. See Chapter 9.

19. See Chapter 8.

20. Baring-Gould and Bampfylde, *A History of Sarawak*, p. 6.

21. Monthly Reports: Upper Sarawak, 1 October 1871, pp. 331–2, SMA, Kuching.

22. Ibid., p. 331.

23. In the late 1860s, a group of Hakkas from Simunjan moved to Upper Sarawak to revive the gold-mining industry. They initially arrived in the country from Sambas during the early 1840s, and, unlike the majority of their fellow countrymen who worked the gold deposits of Upper Sarawak, they proceeded east to the coalfields in the Middle Sadong. See Chang, 'Major Events of Bau', p. 30.

24. For instance, in 1876, at Piat, the biggest *kongsi* had forty-seven members, and five other smaller *kongsi* had a combined labour force of 113; whereas at Paku, the two major *kongsi* had forty and twenty-two members respectively. In comparison, the *kongsi* in Bau, known as the 'Twelve Company', in 1848 boasted a manpower of 400. See *Sarawak Gazette* (*SG*), 17 July 1876, p. 3; *SG*, 8 September 1876, p. 14; and St John, *Life in the Forests*, Vol. II, p. 323.

25. See *SG*, 1 July 1874, n.p.; and *SG*, 16 January 1877, p. 2.

26. See *SG*, 4 January 1886, p. 2; *SG*, 1 August 1887, p. 131; and *SG*, 2 January 1896, p. 2.

27. See Chapter 5.

28. Low, *Sarawak*, p. 27.

29. However, these Malays 'being very bad characters' were not allowed to work diamonds in Sarawak territory. See Low, *Sarawak*, p. 28.

30. J. Brooke, *A Letter from Borneo*, p. 16. Emphasis added.

31. 'I will say nothing of my works at Suntah', James recorded in his journal entry dated 27 April 1842, 'except that they run away with my money, are badly conducted by my Chinese hadji [Hadji Ibrahim], and, above all, that I have great reason to suspect the integrity and steadiness of this said hadji.' Henry Keppel, *The Expedition to Borneo of HMS* Dido, *for the Suppression of Pivacy: With Extracts from*

the Journal of James Brooke Esq., 2 vols., London: Chapman & Hall, 1846; reprinted Singapore: Oxford University Press, 1991, Vol. I, p. 293.

32. For a description of the methods used by the Malays in diamond-mining, see Low, *Sarawak*, p. 28.

33. Everett, 'Notes', p. 28.

34. *SG*, 15 February 1872, n.p. Emphasis added.

35. *SG*, 16 May 1874, n.p.

36. *SG*, 1 August 1874, n.p.

37. Everett, 'Notes', p. 28.

38. Low, *Sarawak*, p. 27. Emphasis added.

39. Brooke to Templer, 13 July 1840, in Templer, *Letters*, Vol. I, p. 88 n. *.

40. Brooke to 'Ladies', 6 May 1863, in Rutter, *Rajah Brooke and Baroness Burdett Coutts*, p. 188.

41. Theodor Posewitz, *Borneo: Its Geology and Mineral Resources*, London: Edward Stanford, 1892, p. 287. Emphasis added. See also Everett, 'Notes', p. 27.

42. N. S. Haile asserted that coal at Simunjan was 'discovered soon after the first Rajah arrived in Sarawak in 1841'; similarly James Lau and Victor Hon maintained that coal was 'known to occur in abundance as early as the 1840's', but these writers did not mention who made this discovery or how it was made. Neither Haile nor Lau and Hon cited any references. It seems unlikely that coal deposits at Simunjan were discovered in the 1840s for this would not have been overlooked by so keen an observer as Hugh Low who had chronicled, in some detail, the minerals found in the country without alluding to this deposit. Only coal on the island of Labuan featured in Low's narrative. It is more likely that the Simunjan deposits were discovered sometime in the mid-1850s. It was in 1855 that Alfred Russel Wallace, the naturalist, sojourned at Simunjan, staying with a Mr Coulson, apparently an engineer in charge of the mines. Wallace noted that the path from the mine to the landing place (the Sadong) consisted 'solely of tree-trunks laid end to end' which 'bare-footed natives walk and carry heavy burdens [coal?] with the greatest ease', whereas 'to a booted European [like himself] it is very slippery work'. He also mentioned that for several months 'from twenty to fifty Chinamen and Dyaks were employed almost exclusively in clearing a large space in the forest, and in making a wide opening for a railroad to the Sadong River, two miles distant'. This observation probably suggests that preparations were underway and that even some rudimentary mining operations were being carried out. See N. S. Haile, *The Geology and Mineral Resources of the Starp and Sadong Valleys, West Sarawak, 'Including the Klingkang Range Coal'*, Geological Survey Department, British Territories in Borneo, Memoir 1, Kuching: Government Printing Office, 1954, p. 84; James Lau and Victor Hon, 'History of Mining in Sarawak', *JMHSSB*, 2 (March 1976): 19 and 28; Low, *Sarawak*, pp. 12–16; and Alfred Russell Wallace, *The Malay Archipelago: The Land of the Orang-Utan, and the Bird of Paradise*, New York: Harper & Brothers, 1869; reprinted Singapore: Oxford University Press, 1986, pp. 46–8. See also James C. Jackson, *Sarawak: A Geographical Survey of a Developing State*, London: University of London Press, 1968, p. 141.

43. Contemporary writings prefer the usage 'Sadong coal/mines' to 'Simunjan coal/mines', understandably as the Brooke administrative centre near it was called Sadong. Nevertheless, 'Simunjan coal/mines', which is more precise and appropriate, is the preferred term in this study.

44. See Wallace, *Malay Archipelago*, pp. 46–8.

45. St John, *Life of Sir James Brooke*, p. 319. After this costly debacle, the BCL gave up its coal concession which reverted to the government. See J. Brooke to

'Ladies', 29 April 1863, in Rutter, *Rajah Brooke and Baroness Burdett Coutts*, pp. 186–8.

46. St John encountered opposition from local inhabitants who 'claimed that some fearful calamity would befall them if the coal were disturbed and many representations were made to the Resident calling for a halt to the operations'. A. H. Moy-Thomas, 'Economic Development under the Second Rajah (1870–1917)', *SMJ*, 10, 17–18 (July–December 1961): 50.

47. *SG*, 31 January 1872, n.p.

48. Quoted in *SG*, 30 July 1872, n.p.

49. *SG*, 16 September 1872, n.p.

50. *SG*, 15 March 1873, n.p.

51. *SG*, 16 May 1874, n.p.

52. See *SG*, 16 November, 1874, n.p.

53. For the procurement of Chinese coal workers for the Simunjan mines and a description of their working and living conditions, see Chapter 8.

54. William Walters was a typical case. Before his appointment in Sarawak, he was attached to the Clay Cross Coal and Iron Works, Derbyshire. Before leaving England, he was in charge of the Churnate Valley Company's Mines, North Staffordshire. In the late 1860s, he was engaged to examine the coal seams of Silantek and accordingly submitted his first report dated 24 December 1868. He continued a series of reports on Silantek throughout the 1870s. In 1875, he was appointed manager of the Simunjan colliery. See *SG*, 16 September 1872, n.p.; and *SG*, 16 March 1875, n.p. The BCL often acted as the go-between in the recruitment process, acting as agent on behalf of the Rajah and the Sarawak government. For a typical work contract, see 'Memorandum of Agreement between the Borneo Company Limited as Agent for and on behalf of HH The Rajah and John Robertson', 18 May 1886, Agreement Book, Vol. I, SMA, Kuching.

55. In September 1874, Robert Henderson of the BCL, during a visit, mentioned that the workmen 'brought the coal two and a half miles to the landing stage on a wooden tramway in heavy wagons which wore out the rails in a fortnight. Some of the wagons were pushed by Chinamen, two were drawn by buffaloes'. Henry Longhurst, *The Borneo Story: The History of the First 100 Years of Trading in the Far East by the Borneo Company Limited*, London: Newman Neame, 1956, p. 59. In mid-1876 it was reported that a tramway was being constructed, and by the time Charles visited the mines in September that year, it was already operational. In early 1877 it was reported that the 'tramway to the coal mine in Simunjan has been remade with permanent rails and a locomotive on which the Government has laid out £4,000'. *SG*, 16 January 1877, p. 1. See also *SG*, 20 May 1876, p. 3; *SG*, 10 October 1876, p. 3; and *SG*, 1 October 1881, p. 81. Then, in 1895, 'iron rails' replaced the wooden tracks, and the wharves were reconstructed. *SG*, 2 January 1896, p. 2; and Lau and Hon, 'Mining in Sarawak', p. 29. The locomotives were aptly named, *Sampson*, *Sadong*, and *Skipalong*. See Moy-Thomas, 'Economic Development', p. 52.

56. The *Black Diamond* and SS *Vyner* were government vessels. The latter was too small and the SS *Borneo* occasionally assisted. Later the Norwegian-owned SS *Breid* was chartered to replace the *Vyner*. The SS *Lorna Doone* was also responsible for coastal transfers of the coal, particularly from Brooketon. See *SG*, 1 January 1890, p. 3; *SG*, 2 January 1896, p. 2; and Moy-Thomas, 'Economic Development', p. 52.

57. See F. W. Roe (comp.), *The Natural Resources of Sarawak*, 2nd rev. edn., Kuching: Government Printing Office, 1952, p. 26.

58. Jackson, *Sarawak*, p. 142.

59. For the closure of the Simunjan colliery, see *Sarawak Administration Report (SAR), 1931*, Kuching: Government Printing Office, pp. 1–2; *SG*, 1 April 1932, pp. 71–2; and *SG*, 1 May 1932, p. 87.

60. See *SG*, 16 September 1872, n.p.; *SG*, 16 September 1872, n.p.; and *SG*, 1 October 1872, n.p. Walters continued his investigations until 1874, with regular reports of his work appearing in the *Gazette*. See *SG*, 31 May, 17 July, 1 August 1873, and 1 December 1873, and 1 January and 15 March 1874.

61. Haile, *Starp and Sadong Valleys*, p. 1.

62. The high quality of Silantek coal was vouched by three British ship engineers: W. P. Innes (Chief Engineer, Royal Navy), W. Hargreaves (Colonial Surveyor of Steam Vessels, Singapore), Wm. F. Call (Engineer, Royal Navy), and A. McAllan (Chief Engineer, SS *Royalist*). See *SG*, 17 June 1873, n.p.

63. According to the Chief Engineer of the SS *Royalist*, A. McAllan, 'the result of the trial trip to Singapore was *equal to that obtained by using the best English coal*'. *SG*, 16 May 1874, n.p. Emphasis added. Further tests were conducted, and all, without exception, confirmed the excellent quality of Silantek coal. For instance, see *SG*, 16 October 1874, n.p.; and Everett, 'Notes', pp. 27–8.

64. 'Advertisement: Lingga Coal Mining Company (Limited)', *SG*, 17 February 1873, n.p. See also 'Notification', *SG*, 31 March 1873, n.p.; and *SG*, 2 January 1900, pp. 7–8.

65. See 10 December 1877, HH The Rajah's Order Book, Vol. I, SMA, Kuching.

66. 8th Meeting, 15 September 1886, in *General Council, 1867–1927*, Kuching: Government Printing Office, 1927[?], p. 11. Emphasis added.

67. For instance, see *SG*, 2 January 1885, p. 2; *SG*, 4 January 1886, p. 2; *SG*, 1 August 1887, p. 130; *SG*, 1 January 1890, p. 3; *SG*, 1 July 1891, p. 100; and *SG*, 1 March 1892, p. 51.

68. Baring-Gould and Bampfylde, *A History of Sarawak*, p. 358.

69. The Sultan of Brunei displayed no interest in the transaction and the British Government approved this acquisition 'so long as the Rajah bought as a private individual and not as a ruler of Sarawak'. Steven Runciman, *The White Rajahs: A History of Sarawak from 1841 to 1946*, Cambridge: Cambridge University Press, 1960, p. 193.

70. Baring-Gould and Bampfylde, *A History of Sarawak*, p. 358.

71. For instance, see *SG*, 3 January 1898, p. 2.

72. G. E. Wilford, *The Geology and Mineral Resources of Brunei and Adjacent Parts of Sarawak with Descriptions of Seria and Miri Oilfields*, Geological Survey Department, British Territories in Borneo, Memoir 10, Brunei: Brunei Press Limited, 1961, p. 164.

73. F. W. Roe, *The Mineral Resources of Sarawak*, British Borneo Geological Survey Annual Report, London: HMSO, 1949, p. 37; and Wilford, *Seria and Miri Oilfields*, p. 164.

74. Wilford, *Seria and Miri Oilfields*, p. 160.

75. Baring-Gould and Bampfylde, *A History of Sarawak*, p. 368.

76. See *SG*, 1 May 1925, p. 95; and Runciman, *The White Rajahs*, p. 194.

77. Principal among the issues was that of the levying of an export duty on coal by the Brunei authorities, supported by the Colonial Office. This move in 1906 infuriated Charles who threatened to terminate mining operations altogether. Brunei relented on this occasion but the principle of its right to impose a duty on coal was not abandoned, and this issue resurfaced in the early 1920s. For the vari-

ous disputes, see Baring-Gould and Bampfylde, *A History of Sarawak*, pp. 368–70; Colin N. Crisswell, *Rajah Charles Brooke: Monarch of All He Surveyed*, Kuala Lumpur: Oxford University Press, 1978, pp. 204–5; K. G. Tregonning, *Under Chartered Company Rule (North Borneo 1881–1946)*, Singapore: University of Malaya Press, 1958, pp. 35–6, 368–70; and A. V. M. Horton, 'The Development of Brunei during the British Residential Era 1906–1959: A Sultanate Regenerated', Ph.D. thesis, University of Hull, 1985, pp. 85–98.

78. See Horton, 'The Development of Brunei', pp. 102–4. Vyner was initially keen on the offer made by Hall but in mid-1921 decided otherwise. Hall tried again in 1937 to acquire the rights from Brunei but was unsuccessful. For the negotiations on the fate of Brooketon, see ibid., Appendix 1.2; and for the role of Hall in Sarawak and Brunei affairs, see Appendix 1.4. See also A. V. M. Horton, 'James Hatton Hall (1866–1945): Planter, Merchant, Soldier', *JMBRAS*, 68, 1 (June 1995): 139–47.

79. See *SG*, 1 October 1924, pp. 309–10; and *SG*, 2 November 1931, p. 234.

80. J. Brooke to 'Ladies', 29 April 1863, in Rutter, *Rajah Brooke and Baroness Burdett Coutts*, p. 186.

81. See Lau and Hon, 'Mining in Sarawak', p. 24; Chang, 'Major Events of Bau', p. 30; and Jackson, *Sarawak*, p. 140.

82. Monthly Reports: Upper Sarawak, 1 October 1871, Vol. I, p. 331, SMA, Kuching.

83. Longhurst, *The Borneo Story*, p. 55. In the early 1870s mention was made of a Dr Groger, an Austrian geologist and mining engineer employed by the company. He was probably the first specialist in this kind to work in Sarawak. See ibid., pp. 57–8; and Everett, 'Notes', pp. 24–5.

84. See Longhurst, *The Borneo Story*, p. 55. See also Lau and Hon, 'Mining in Sarawak', p. 24. Busau was the obvious location for the smelter as it was an important interior port from where antimony ore was sent to Kuching by launches and native *tongkang*. See *Sarawak Mining Bulletin*, Vol. 1, Second Issue (December 1981), p. 29.

85. Ludvig Verner Helms, *Pioneering in the Far East, and Journeys to California in 1849 and to the White Sea in 1878*, London: W. H. Allen, 1882, pp. 243–4. Helms's claim, though widely credited in secondary works on Sarawak, was disputed by T. Charles Martine, the BCL's manager in Sarawak during the 1930s. Martine asserted that 'London correspondence towards the end of 1867, however, shows that Mr Russell was responsible, Mr Helms being out of the Country at the time of the discovery'. Curiously, Henry Longhurst, the historian of the BCL, who acknowledged Martine's assistance in his work, supported Helms's claim. See T. Charles Martine, 'The Borneo Company Ltd., in Sarawak (From "Notes written by me when in Singapore Changi Gaol, 1943–4")', Typescript, p. 17, SMA, Kuching; and 'Author's Foreword' in Longhurst, *The Borneo Story*, and p. 55.

86. Helms, *Pioneering*, p. 244.

87. The chance discovery of cinnabar was made at Gading in 1874. This was made by Robert Henderson and Professor James R. M. Robertson during a tour of inspection of the company's mining operations at Busau, Jambusan, and Tegora. The operations incorporated prospecting work for coal at Gombang and Gading. See Longhurst, *The Borneo Story*, p. 58.

88. See *SG*, 1 October 1881, p. 80.

89. See *SG*, 31 December 1881, p. 108.

90. See *SG*, 1 May 1884, pp. 36–7 and p. 39; and E. B. Wolfenden, *Bau Mining District, West Sarawak, Malaysia, Part 1: Bau*, Geological Survey Borneo

Region, Malaysia, Bulletin 7, Kuching: Government Printing Office, 1965, p. 55. See also *SG*, 1 December 1884, p. 119.

91. In a sense, Grey's discovery, undoubtedly involving prospecting work, should be disqualified as infringing on the original agreement with the Brooke government. It demonstrates the bias of Charles in favouring the BCL over Chinese mining interest.

92. Martine, 'The Borneo Company Ltd.', p. 21.

93. The Chinese gold-mining companies obviously resented the BCL's encroachment into an industry which hitherto had been exclusively their domain. Incidences of 'ore stealing' and 'labour crimping' became increasingly common, but more serious was the issue of water supply. See ibid.; and *SG*, 1 August 1887, p. 131.

94. Although Longhurst stated that 'in 1884 the Company bought out the biggest and almost the last of the kongsis, the Shak Lak [Lung] Mun' such an occurrence was improbable, as three years later it was reported that there were some problems between the BCL and this particular Chinese gold company over the matter of water supply which were eventually settled in court. The likely date of the suggested take-over would be '1894' as this was the year that the BCL was granted the exclusive right of prospecting for gold, the mineral hitherto excluded from the mineral concession originally obtained from James (see n. 95 below). See Longhurst, *The Borneo Story*, p. 67; and Martine, 'The Borneo Company Ltd.', pp. 6 and 21. For the BCL's dispute with the Shak Lak Mun, see *SG*, 1 August 1887, p. 131. However, it was not until 1898 that the BCL finally accomplished the complete monopolization of the gold industry in Sarawak. For the acquisition of Chinese gold-mining companies, see *SG*, 2 March 1896, p. 80; *SG*, 1 June 1896, p. 117; and *SG*, 1 April 1897, p. 70.

95. In 1894 the BCL was granted the monopoly of using a 'Quartz Crushing Machine and of prospecting for gold reefs in the Sarawak River District ... for fifteen years from 25 March 1894'. This prospecting licence was renewed thereafter. See 'Memorandum of grant by HH The Rajah to the Borneo Company Limited', 15 May 1894, Agreement Book, Vol. II, SMA, Kuching. For the renewal of the licence, see the entries dated 31 October 1895, 13 November 1900, 24 October 1905, Agreement Book, Vol. II, SMA, Kuching; and 14 February 1907, Agreement Book, Vol. III, SMA, Kuching.

96. See *SG*, 2 January 1896, p. 2.

97. A. C. Vivian, 'Autobiography of A. C. Vivian', MSS Brit. Emp. s. 345, p. 18, RHL, Oxford. Vivian served as the BCL's metallurgist at the Bau and Bidi gold works in the late 1900s.

98. Chang Pat Foh, 'The History of Gold Mining in Bau, Sarawak', *SG*, September 1992, p. 33. Benito Howe was credited with successfully implementing the cyanidation process at Bau. Martine, 'The Borneo Company Ltd.', p. 21.

99. Notable technical improvements perfected at the Bau plant included 'the oil flotation process' and the 'designing of a filter plant capable of separating and washing the pulp from the gold bearing cyanide solution'. The latter involved the creation of a completely different form of vacuum filter which was so successful that it was adopted elsewhere. N. A. Lucas, 'The Production of Gold in Sarawak', *SG*, 1 February 1949, p. 30; and *SG*, 1 April 1922, p. 92.

100. The Tai Parit Mine, situated a stone's throw from Bau town, commenced operation in 1899.

101. See *SG*, 1 May 1900, pp. 83–4; and *SG*, 1 April 1922, p. 92.

102. See *SG*, 1 April 1922, p. 92; and Lau and Hon, 'Mining in Sarawak', p. 27.

103. Chang, 'Gold Mining in Bau', p. 33.

104. Lau and Hon, 'Mining in Sarawak', p. 27.

105. J. Somerville Geikie, 'The Occurrence of Gold in Upper Sarawak', Part III, *SG*, 16 January 1909, p. 22.

106. Lucas, 'Production of Gold in Sarawak', p. 30.

107. Jackson, *Sarawak*, p. 144.

108. Such a 'primitive lamp' had a serious drawback; it 'spluttered a good deal, and as it occasionally set light to their [native] leaf-built dwellings, this practice was discontinued'. Charles Hose, 'The Metamorphosis of Miri', *BM*, 2, 2 (June 1927): 41. See also *SG*, 3 January 1949, p. 8.

109. Everett, 'Notes', pp. 15–16.

110. The Baram and the area south to Kidurong Point were administered as part of the Third Division from 27 June 1882 until 28 July 1885. On 28 July 1885 the Fourth Division was constituted which covered the Baram and the newly acquired Trusan which had been ceded in January that same year.

111. *SG*, 1 September 1882, p. 72.

112. Quoted in *Oil in Sarawak, 1910–1960*, Miri: Sarawak Shell Oilfields Ltd., n.d., p. 4.

113. Charles Hose referred to this unenthusiastic expert as a 'Government geologist' whereas Brian Durrans stated 'consultant geologist'. Neither gave his name. Hose, 'Miri', p. 41; and Brian Durrans, 'Introduction', in Charles Hose, *Natural Man: A Record from Borneo*, London: Macmillan, 1926; reprinted Singapore: Oxford University Press, 1988, p. x.

114. *Oil in Sarawak*, p. 4.

115. See Hose, 'Miri', p. 41. Emphasis added.

116. *SG*, 4 January 1897, p. 2.

117. It was most likely that Charles commissioned the BCL, apparently avoiding publicity, to undertake the investigations, as revealed in a brief letter of 11 April 1903 from him addressed to E. Llewelyn, the BCL's manager. 'You may charge to oil A/C [account] any clothes spoiled or damaged by the oil superintendence. In case of any people, native or Europeans, asking to see the oil spring, I wish to prevent their doing so.' Quoted in *Oil in Sarawak*, p. 4. This seemingly low-key approach was perhaps an indication of Charles's characteristic caution to avoid attracting undue attention from Western oil interests; but also, after so many past disappointments, he preferred a less publicized profile lest this oil issue proved to be abortive and another embarrassment to the Raj.

118. Hose, 'Miri', p. 41.

119. See *SG*, 2 May 1903, p. 87; and *SG*, 4 August 1903, p. 156.

120. See *SG*, 1 June 1909, p. 122.

121. Hose must have been incredibly persuasive to have won over Charles to the economic potential of oil. One writer admiringly noted this point: 'Hose must have had strong powers of persuasion to have convinced the Rajah of the potential benefit of oil. Sir Charles was then approaching 80 years of age, and was strongly opposed to anything "new-fangled", as he called it. He even refused to have electric light installed in his Astana.' G. C. Harper, 'The Miri Field 1910–1972', *SMJ*, 20, 40–1 (January–December 1972): 22, n. 2.

122. Durrans, 'Introduction', in Hose, *Natural Man*, p. x; and Hose, 'Miri', pp. 41–2. The BCL, which carried out some preliminary exploration in the late 1890s and the early 1900s, was initially approached and offered the oil concession

but had refused for it was considered too large a commitment. See 'Growth of Sarawak—Chronology 1917–1924', Typescript, MSS Pac. s. 83, Brooke Family Papers, Box 7, File 8, Item 1, p. 17, RHL, Oxford. The Anglo-Saxon Petroleum Company was registered in London on 29 June 1907, and the following April, became a private company and a subsidiary of the Royal Dutch Shell Group. As a British concern, it came under the direct control of the Shell Transport and Trading Company. See A. V. M. Horton, '"A Pauper with a Valuable Property for Sale": The British-Borneo Petroleum Syndicate and the Search for Oil in Brunei, 1906–1932', MSS (Personal copy), n.p.; and *SG*, 1 August 1910, p. 167.

123. See 'Indenture between C. Brooke and the Anglo-Saxon Petroleum Company Limited', 9 March 1909, Agreement Book, Vol. III, SMA, Kuching.

124. 'Article 14', quoted in T. G. Cochrane, 'Empire Oil: The Progress of Sarawak', *JRSA*, 72, 3723 (28 March 1924): 309. The only exceptions to this clause was that fuel oil was stored at Singapore, instead of at Miri, during and immediately after the First World War, and also Britain's naval ally, Japan, was given access to the reserved supply during the same period. Ibid. The actual amount supplied to the British and Japanese navies during the course of the war varied from a figure of 150,000 tons to 287,000 tons. Ward, a senior Brooke officer, in his recollections, stated the former amount but publications from the oil companies recorded the higher figure. See A. B. Ward, *Rajah's Servant*, Cornell University Southeast Asia Program Data Paper No. 61, Ithaca: Cornell University Press, 1966, p. 192; *Oil in Sarawak*, p. 7; Harper, 'Miri Field', p. 26; and Sarawak Shell Berhad, *The Miri Story: The Founding Years of the Malaysian Oil Industry in Sarawak*, Lutong, 1978, p. 16. This pre-emption clause was not unique as it was purported to be, and was in line with the Trinidad 'model' concession of 1904 where it originated, and thereafter was imitated throughout the British Empire. See Harper, 'Miri Field', p. 24; and Charles Hose, *Fifty Years of Romance and Research; or a Jungle Wallah at Large*, London: Hutchinson, 1927, p. 235. For details of the Trinidad 'model', see Geoffrey Jones, *The State and the Emergence of the British Oil Industry*, London: Macmillan, 1986, pp. 9–28 and 105–13.

125. Cochrane, 'Empire Oil: Sarawak', p. 309. See also *SG*, 5 January 1910, p. 2; and *SG*, 17 January 1910, p. 26.

126. Cochrane, 'Empire Oil: Sarawak', p. 310; *SG*, 1 November 1910, p. 226; *SG*, 16 January 1911, p. 2; and 'New Borneo Oil Field', reprinted from *Daily Telegraph*, 17 January 1911, *SG*, 1 March 1911, p. 38.

127. Sir Marcus Samuel, the chairman of the Shell Transport and Trading Company, which directly owned and controlled ASPC, reminded shareholders that 'it is quite useless and fallacious to hope to develop petroleum fields on small capital, and it is merely courting disaster to attempt it.' Furthermore, he recounted that Charles thought 'that it was better to give the concessions to a company like this [ASPC], who would develop them satisfactorily and spend upon them any amount that might be required, rather than give them to the ordinary company promoter'. 'Sarawak Oil Fields [Annual General Meeting of the Shell Transport and Trading Company, Limited, 22 June 1910]', *SG*, 1 August 1910, p. 167. See also 'The Sarawak Oil Fields [Meeting of the Preference Shareholders of the Shell Transport and Trading Co. Ltd., 2 February 1911]', *SG*, 16 March 1911, p. 47.

128. For a detailed description of the various problems and their solutions during the pioneering days of Miri, see Cochrane, 'Empire Oil: Sarawak', pp. 309–10; Moy-Thomas, 'Economic Development', p. 54; and Harper, 'Miri Field', pp. 24–6.

129. See *SG*, 1 June 1914, p. 125; *Oil in Sarawak*, p. 9; and Cochrane, 'Empire Oil: Sarawak', p. 311.

130. See *SG*, 1 November 1913, p. 247.

131. Choices of a deep-water anchorage and site for a refinery included the island of Muara and Kidurong Point; for the transportation of the oil, a pipeline across Brunei territory from Miri to Brooketon was considered. However, none of these proposals proved viable. For the pipeline proposals, see *SG*, 17 April 1911, pp. 67–8. For the posssible use of the island of Muara as a port, see *SG*, 1 June 1911, pp. 97–8; and *SG*, 17 April 1911, p. 68; Kidurong Point, see *SG*, 1 June 1911, p. 98. For the search of other possible sites for the port and refinery, see *SG*, 1 August 1912, p. 168; and *SG*, 1 July 1913, p. 140.

132. Cochrane, 'Empire Oil: Sarawak', p. 311.

133. Ibid.

134. The MV *Vulcanus* had the honour of being the first vessel to be loaded via the submarine pipeline which injected 2,500 tons of crude oil. *SG*, 16 February 1915, p. 43.

135. The rough sea conditions during the *landas* season along the entire coast of Sarawak made it extremely difficult for loading operations to be carried out. On three occasions loading had to be aborted and the tankers sent away empty. *SG*, 1 May 1916, p. 80.

136. See *SG*, 16 November 1916, p. 251; and *SG*, 16 March 1917, p. 74. For a detailed description of the launching method employed, see Cochrane, 'Empire Oil: Sarawak', pp. 314–15.

137. See *SG*, 16 March 1917, p. 74; and Lau and Hon, 'Mining in Sarawak', p. 29.

138. Cochrane, 'Empire Oil: Sarawak', p. 311.

139. See *SG*, 2 June 1919, p. 147. In 1928, another pipeline measuring 4560 metres was successfully launched. See *SG*, 1 February 1929, p. 17.

140. See *SG*, 1 April 1919, p. 77; Sarawak Shell Berhad, *The Miri Story*, p. 12; and Lau and Hon, 'Mining in Sarawak', pp. 29–30.

141. However, smaller works like 'a lubricating oil recovery unit, an asphalt plant for the production of bitumen, and a kerosene refining plant' were added prior to the outbreak of the Pacific War. *Oil in Sarawak*, p. 12.

142. The majority of the labour force in the Miri oilfields were imported Chinese coolies from south-eastern China. Malay artisans and Dayak labourers were also represented on the payroll but their numbers together with others like Indians and Javanese collectively did not exceed the Chinese. The managerial and technical staff were invariably Europeans while the clerical personnel were denoted as 'Asiatics', often Chinese or Sinhalese (Ceylonese) and Indians. For the statistics of the workforce, see *SG*, 16 January 1912, p. 17; *Sarawak Government Gazette* (*SGG*), 1 March 1913, p. 21; *SG*, 1 July 1913, p. 139; *SGG*, 16 February 1915, p. 43; *SGG*, 3 April 1916, p. 74; *SGG*, 16 March 1917, pp. 59–60; and *SGG*, 17 May 1920, p. 173. For the imported Chinese labour force in the oilfields, see Chapter 8. There were undoubtedly conflicting opinions as to the suitability of Dayaks as workers at the oil installations. One report described them as 'most satisfactory and easy to control', but another, commenting on their work under contract with Sarawak Oilfields Limited in British North Borneo, complained that 'a large proportion of the men ceased work without notice and demanded to be returned to Simanggang [in Sarawak]'. *SG*, 1 October 1914, p. 226; and *SG*, 1 September 1938, p. 140.

143. See 'Indenture between C. V. Brooke and the Anglo-Saxon Petroleum

Company Limited', 27 April 1921, Agreement Book, Vol. IV, SMA, Kuching; *SG*, 1 October 1921, p. 202; and *Oil in Sarawak*, p. 2.

144. See Cochrane, 'Empire Oil: Sarawak', p. 315.

145. *SG*, 3 January 1949, p. 9.

146. Wilford, *Seria and Miri Oilfields*, p. 155.

147. Harper, 'Miri Field', p. 28.

148. *SG*, 3 January 1949, p. 9.

149. Mark C. Cleary, 'Changing Patterns of Trade in North-west Borneo, *c.*1860–1930', MSS (Personal copy), n.d., p. 18.

150. Boyle, *Adventures*, p. 68.

151. Jackson, *Sarawak*, p. 140.

152. Longhurst, *The Borneo Story*, p. 66.

153. *SG*, 1 February 1901, p. 31. See also *SG*, 16 October 1908, p. 262.

154. For the closure of the BCL's antimony and cinnabar mines, see Chapter 9.

155. Jackson, *Sarawak*, p. 141.

156. See *SG*, 16 January 1912, p. 17; and *SG*, 16 February 1912, p. 45. For other reasons, see Chapter 9.

157. G. E. Wilford, 'The Bau Gold Field', *SG*, 30 April 1962, p. 78; and Chang, 'Gold Mining in Bau', p. 33.

158. Lucas, 'Production of Gold in Sarawak', p. 30.

159. Ibid. However, according to the recollections of Martine, it was 1923, and not 1921, that these developments occurred. '[O]wing to unprecedented rains and flooding in May 1923, it was decided to abandon the Mine which had reached a depth of 250 ft.— the Company relinquished all its Mining Rights and at the same time, all their dumps of lower grade ore and tailings which were numerous.' Martine, 'The Borneo Company Ltd', p. 23. See also Longhurst, *The Borneo Story*, p. 69.

160. For instance, see *SG*, 2 November 1922, p. 282.

161. *SG*, 1 April 1922, p. 92.

162. For instance, see *SG*, 3 January 1933, p. 7.

163. For some remarkable successes during this period of revival, for instance, see *SG*, 1 April 1935, p. 51; and *SG*, 2 March 1936, p. 54.

164. An expanding list of Chinese gold-mining companies working in Upper Sarawak became evident particularly from early 1933. For the list, see under the headings 'First Division News—First Divisional Reports, Upper Sarawak District', or similar, in the *Gazette* commencing from February 1933.

165. See *SG*, 1 August 1932, p. 142; *SG*, 1 April 1933, p. 47; *SG*, 2 January 1934, p. 1; and *SG*, 1 February 1935, p. 12. It was also noted that there was a migration of Chinese labourers from the pepper gardens of the Engkilili district in the Second Division to the gold-fields of Upper Sarawak. See *SG*, 1 December 1933, p. 159.

166. Wolfenden, *Bau Mining District*, p. 55; and Chang, 'Gold Mining in Bau', p. 34.

167. Wilford, *Seria and Miri Oilfields*, p. 155.

168. Cochrane, 'Empire Oil: Sarawak', p. 313.

169. C. D. Le Gros Clark, *1935 Blue Report*, Kuching: Government Printing Office, 1935, p. 4. Le Gros Clark cited the general manager of SOL as the source of this authoritative forecast. See also *SG*, 3 January 1949, p. 9.

170. See *Oil in Sarawak*, pp. 13–14.

171. For instance, see *SG*, 2 January 1895, p. 3; 'J. Hardie, Acting Manager of the Borneo Company Limited as Agent for the Sarawak Steamship Company

Limited, to Charles Samuel Pearse, Treasurer, Sarawak Government', 20 October 1877, Agreement Book, Vol. I, SMA, Kuching; and Moy-Thomas, 'Economic Development', p. 51.

172. There appeared to be a ray of hope in the late 1880s of overcoming the problem of securing 'a steady and certain market' when Chinese merchants in Singapore contracted for a regular monthly supply. However, it seemed that whatever agreement had been negotiated had not been very successful as, during the early 1890s, the problem of poor demand again resurfaced. See *SG*, 4 January 1886, p. 2; *SG*, 3 January 1887, p. 2; and *SG*, 1 August 1892, p. 142.

173. There was only one Royal Navy visit recorded. In February 1876, Admiral Ryder in HMS *Vigilant* accompanied by a small flotilla, the *Egeria*, *Thistle*, and *Lily* anchored at Pinding. All the ships were supplied with coal from the Simunjan mines. *SG*, 26 February 1876, n.p.; and *SG*, 16 January 1877, p. 2. Mention of this offer was again made in 1881. See *SG*, 1 February 1881, p. 10.

174. For the yearly reports of revenue and expenditure from 1900 to 1907, see the *Gazette*, and thereafter, until their closure in 1931, see *Sarawak Government Gazette*.

175. See Wilford, *Seria and Miri Oilfields*, p. 164. At first sight it seemed rather strange that Charles, whose thriftiness was legendary, would, after more than a decade's experience of the difficulties attending Simunjan, decide on the purchase of Brooketon. However, as events unfolded during the 1890s and 1900s, it became apparent that Charles's acquisition of Brooketon was not entirely driven by economic objectives but was also a shrewd political manoeuvre to establish a 'beachhead' for the intended future annexation of Brunei. See 9th Meeting, 27th August 1889 (Second Day), in *General Council, 1867–1927*, p. 14. However, Baring-Gould and Bampfylde stated that Brooketon, though a financial burden, was maintained for humanitarian reasons: 'The greatest possible benefits have been conferred upon the people by the establishment of a large and growing [coal] industry among them'. Baring-Gould and Bampfylde, *A History of Sarawak*, p. 358. For Charles's political designs on Brunei, see Crisswell, *Rajah Charles Brooke*, pp. 152–203; Horton, 'The Development of Brunei', pp. 97–8; and Runciman, *The White Rajahs*, pp. 174–201.

176. For instance, see *SG*, 15 March 1873, n.p.; *SG*, 1 January 1874, n.p.; ibid; 1 August 1874, n.p.; *SG*, 1 March 1887, p. 37; *SG*, 1 August 1887, p. 130; and Moy-Thomas, 'Economic Development', p. 51.

177. Robertson, an English geologist, was commissioned by the BCL to conduct a thorough investigation of the coalfields of Silantek. He carried out his work in 1876 and submitted his report the following year. See James R. M. Robertson, *Report on the Coal Field of Silantik Borneo*, Sarawak: Government Press, 1877.

178. Robertson, commenting on the subject of the suitability of workers for the coal mines, regarded the Dayaks as inexperienced and their lifestyle inappropriate for such skilled and regular work, whereas the Malays were considered unreliable. Based on his observations of the ability and adaptability of Chinese in the antimony, cinnabar, and gold works of Upper Sarawak, he was convinced that they offered the best choice as workers for the coal-mines. He also believed that the problem of the shortage of Chinese labour was 'more imaginary than real'. Robertson, *Report on Silantik*, pp. 14 and 22. See also *SG*, 30 April 1880, p. 25.

179. Robertson, *Report on Silantik*, pp. 25–35. A. J. G. Swinney, who investigated the Silantek coalfields during the mid-1880s, concurred with Robertson regarding the provision of a railway system as the 'only feasible plan'. He was also of the opinion that the construction of the railtrack was neither 'an arduous under-

taking' nor 'an expensive one' if the work was properly carried out and supervised. *SG*, 2 February 1885, pp. 16–17. In 1896 Charles inquired of the estimated costs of this railtrack—from Silantek to Lingga—and the amount quoted was not dissimilar to that proposed by Robertson. See Moy-Thomas, 'Economic Development', p. 51.

180. Immediately after the Pacific War, two brief investigations were conducted (October 1947 and March 1948) by a British firm, Powell Duffryn Technical Services Limited. Nothing developed thereafter. During the late 1950s and early 1960s, a Japanese company, the Nippon Coal Mining Company, showed interest in developing the Silantek coalfields. The troubles with Indonesia during Sukarno's *Konfrontasi* in the 1960s disrupted plans for commencing operations owing to the fact that the field lay 3 kilometres from the international border. In a joint-venture with Ataka Company, further investigations proceeded in 1969–70 but no definite plans to develop the coalfield materialized thereafter. In the 1970s the Utah Development Company acquired the prospecting lease and began its own investigations. See Haile, *Starp and Sadong Valleys*, pp. 51 and Table 10; Lau and Hon, 'Mining in Sarawak', pp. 25–6; and Jackson, *Sarawak*, pp. 143–4.

181. Baring-Gould and Bampfylde, *A History of Sarawak*, p. 435.

182. Everett, 'Notes', p. 29.

183. *SG*, 1 April 1922, p. 92.

184. Wolfenden, *Bau Mining District*, p. 59. For the evidence supporting this conclusion, see ibid., pp. 59–60.

185. *Oil in Sarawak*, p. 14. See also Lau and Hon, 'Mining in Sarawak', p. 31.

186. Apart from the BCL and the ASPC and its successor the SOL, other companies were also given grants to search for minerals. For instance, see 'Memorandum of Agreement between HH The Rajah and the Central Borneo Company Limited', 22 January 1890, Agreement Book, Vol. I, SMA, Kuching. For mineral concession to individuals, for instance, see 'Indenture between HH The Rajah and Thomas Shaw Safe', 22 April 1889, Agreement Book, Vol. I, SMA, Kuching; and, 'Deed between Charles Vyner Brooke The Rajah and Henry Edwin Coley', 31 May 1923, Agreement Book, Vol. V, SMA, Kuching.

187. For the oil concession, for instance, see *SG*, 1 August 1910, p. 167.

188. 9th Meeting, 27 August 1889 (Second Day), in *General Council, 1867–1927*, p. 14. Emphasis added.

189. Contemporary visitors to the country also held similar aspirations for Sarawak. For instance, Frederick Boyle, a visitor during the mid-1860s, predicted a gold-rush by Europeans to Sarawak similar to that of 'California, Australia and Vancouver's Island'. See Boyle, *Adventures*, p. 70.

190. *SG*, 1 March 1887, p. 37.

191. For instance, see *SG*, 1 May 1896, p. 85.

5
Promotion of Agriculture

THE Brookes had repeatedly emphasized that the future prosperity of Sarawak lay in the cultivation of its soil. The promotion of agriculture was a Brooke preoccupation, particularly with Charles and Vyner who expended both time and energy to ensure that farming remained the main activity of the population. Their ideal was the promotion and protection of the independent smallholder farmer. Cash crops, rather than minerals or jungle produce, were to be the mainstay of the economy. Several strategies, including the introduction of new crops and new farming methods, government-sponsored Chinese immigration, and liberal land laws to attract European investment, were implemented to encourage commercial agriculture. At the same time, traditional subsistence rice production (hill-*padi* and wet-*padi*) and sago cultivation were developed and expanded. Indeed, some successes were achieved in commercial agriculture and in rice and sago cultivation. But, overall, the Brooke policy in agriculture remained an unfulfilled ambition. The majority of the new crops did not develop beyond the experimental stage, there were few European investors, Chinese immigrants as a whole did not become rice farmers, and in general the country's agricultural exports were of poor quality. The geographical disadvantages of difficult terrain and poor soils, and Sarawak's remote location worked against Brooke agricultural objectives. The protectionist land policy designed to deter the exploitation of natives in turn precluded would-be European investors.

Brooke Emphasis on the Importance of the Cultivation of Land

James, writing in 1842, boasted of the incomparable agricultural wealth of the country where the 'moist and rich' soil and the terrain are well suited to a variety of cultivation.[1] The plains, according to him, were 'calculated for the growth of rice' which he envisaged 'would become an article of extensive export'. They were also 'well adapted for the growth of sago', whereas the 'undulating

ground' and the 'slopes of the higher mountains, are admirably calculated for the growth of nutmegs, coffee, pepper, or the more valuable vegetable productions of the tropics'.[2]

Although agriculture was a priority, James was too preoccupied with a multitude of political and military issue to give reasonable attention to it. It was Charles who embarked on a programme to develop agriculture, particularly commercial crops. Charles emphasized the benefits of agriculture as a worthwhile occupation that would not only profit the people but also contribute to the country's economy.[3] It was farming and not trade that was 'a far more regular way of getting a livelihood'.[4] The symbiotic relationship between land and agriculture was highlighted by Charles in a speech to the General Council of 1909: 'We might look on land as our principal friend and helpmate and man is given bone and sinew to work the land as from it springs almost every source of wealth and prosperity.'[5] Charles envisaged the ideal of the native population of swidden Dayak cultivators as settled farmers with permanent habitations.[6]

Vyner inherited his father's objectives and consolidated and further developed established schemes. A Department of Agriculture was founded in 1924. He upheld Charles's smallholding policy and discouraged rubber monoculture, persuading the people to cultivate crops like sago and pepper. Throughout the 1920s and 1930s, he sought to improve the quality and price of Sarawak's agricultural exports.

The Brooke emphasis on the importance of agriculture did have some influence on the country's inhabitants. By the mid-1890s there was a general realization among the Malays of the benefits of agriculture over trade.[7] Similarly, Chinese mining communities, faced with declining mineral production, turned to agricultural pursuits, particularly pepper planting, as an alternative livelihood.[8] But the dramatic price increases and booms of Para rubber, more than any other factor, convinced the general population, including Dayaks and other indigenous peoples, that prosperity lay in the cultivation of the land: *padi* cultivation with rubber as the chief cash crop.

Strategies for the Promotion of Agriculture

The Concept of the Experimental Farm

The idea of an experimental farm can be traced back to the early days of the 1840s when James himself experimented with the cultivation of nutmeg, while a fellow Englishman, a Mr Hentig who had settled in Kuching, planted his garden with cinnamon, nutmeg, and cloves.[9] During the mid-1860s, Burdett Coutts showed interest in establishing a farm as a means of displaying by experimental planting the agricultural possibilities of the country; also it was intended to instruct the natives in Western methods of tilling the soil.[10] There was also mention of 'paddy-working mills at Lundu' owned by her.[11]

The Quop Estate, as it was known, situated in the vicinity of the confluence of the Quop and Sarawak rivers, was established in late 1864. A variety of crops was cultivated, including wet-*padi*, areca, coconut, coffee, pepper, oil palm, indigo, and sugar cane. Farming methods, like buffalo ploughing, were likely to have been employed.[12] But after less than a decade, it was decided to sell the estate.[13] The project was unsuccessful, partly as a consequence of mismanagement,[14] but more significantly, because the 'land was very poor' and attempts to cultivate new crops 'proved to be a complete failure'.[15]

Despite the failure of the Quop Estate, its concept was incorporated in Charles's agricultural programme, *inter alia* the establishment of government-managed experimental gardens. Several farms were set up in and around Kuching and the neighbouring districts. The most important during Charles's reign were the coffee estates at Matang Mountain and Satap, and the tobacco plantation at Lundu.[16] Brooke officers in the outstations were expected to establish similar undertakings. In fact, the outstation experimental gardens were influential carriers of new agricultural information to the native peoples.[17]

Vyner shared Charles's philosophy. A 'Nursery for Imported Economic Plants' was established at the 12th Mile Penrissen Road, near Semonggok, in 1926 'to provide a trial station for plants of economic importance introduced from abroad and to conduct experiments on pepper'.[18] Two years later an agronomist specializing in rice cultivation was appointed, and an agricultural

chemist headed a government analytical laboratory which was to serve all departments but which in practice largely undertook agricultural work.[19] Special attention was also accorded to *padi* cultivation in the late 1930s with the setting up of two agricultural stations, one at Kanowit (1937) and another at Rantau Panjang (1939).[20]

Introduction of New Crops and Promotion of New Industries

The introduction of new crops, undertaken at the experimental gardens, was an important feature during Charles's rule, although some crops, like sugar cane, gambier, and coffee, had been introduced during James's reign. In general, only a handful of these crops, namely, pepper, gambier, and Para rubber, enjoyed a measure of success beyond the experimental stage. The rest were embarrassing failures, some incurring heavy financial losses. Likewise, the promotion of new industries, such as the rearing of silkworms and the manufacture of plantain fibres and ramie, did not succeed.

The cultivation of sugar cane and sugar manufacture were undertaken by the Sarawak Sugar Company Limited in the early 1860s. But within a short period it faced insolvency and had to be liquidated.[21] Throughout the 1870s several attempts were made, mainly by Chinese, to make a success of sugar cane,[22] but when more profitable crops like gambier and pepper came on the scene, sugar cane cultivation was abandoned. No European entrepreneurs showed any interest in this crop.

Gambier, a tanning and dyeing substance procured from the leaves of a shrub (*Uncaria gambir*) through a simple process of boiling,[23] and pepper (*Piper nigrum*), were initially cultivated at the foot of Matang Mountain by a group of Chinese invited from Singapore at the expense of the Brooke government. They opened up twelve gambier and pepper gardens, cultivating the two crops together.[24] This initial attempt at commercial planting was a failure owing to the 'wayward character' of the Chinese planters who absconded with the advances from the government, and 'either ran away or took wages at the mines'.[25] Nevertheless, faith in the Chinese persisted.[26] In May 1872 Charles again invited Chinese planters who were eventually successful in the commercial cultivation of the two crops.[27]

As early as the 1840s coffee was reported to have thrived 'remarkably well'.[28] A government experimental coffee garden, established on the slopes of Matang Mountain, commenced

operation with Arabian coffee (*Coffea arabica*) seed in 1867.[29] The following year at Peninjauh, 'Dyaks were ordered by Government to make coffee gardens, and it was arranged that each door should plant 200 trees, under the inspection of a Government agent'.[30]

In the late 1870s, Charles started experimenting with Liberian coffee (*Coffea liberica*) on the Astana grounds and at Matang.[31] Progress was favourable and attracted much interest from the European coffee and tea planters of Ceylon and India.[32] There was a growing interest among the local population in Liberian coffee during the 1880s and 1890s owing largely to rising prices. A government coffee garden was established at Simanggang in the late 1880s which undoubtedly gave impetus to coffee planting among the Dayaks.[33] An experimental garden was also established at Lubok Antu and attracted local Chinese and Malay participation.[34] The slump in coffee prices during the early twentieth century and the introduction of the more profitable Para rubber contributed to the loss of interest in coffee growing. During the 1930s there was a brief revival in coffee cultivation but none to match the enthusiasm of the last two decades of the nineteenth century.[35]

Tea cultivation was also attempted at Matang and was favourably reported on. Apart from some difficulties encountered in its manufacture during the initial years due to the lack of experience and technical knowledge, Matang tea catered for local consumption; a small quantity was exported to Britain and was reportedly well-received.[36]

Tobacco had long been grown by Dayaks for their own consumption.[37] The Dayaks in the Upper Rejang, near the government station at Balleh, had successfully planted Java tobacco from seeds given to them in 1871 by a manager of Quop Estate.[38] It was not until the late 1880s that interest in commercial tobacco cultivation began to attract the attention of European planters. Alexander MacDonald Gibson was appointed by Charles to manage the government experimental tobacco estate at Lundu which commenced planting in late 1887.[39] Leaf samples from the 1889 crop sent to London and Amsterdam were favourably received.[40] 'Sarawak cigars', it was noted, 'were on sale in London with a picture of main bazaar on the box.'[41] During the Depression years of the early 1930s, tobacco was promoted as an alternative to Para rubber, and many Chinese took up this culture with assistance from the Agriculture Department.[42] Local demand for tobacco afforded 'employment and small profit to a large number of Chinese' throughout this decade.[43]

As early as the mid-1880s some South American Para rubber trees (*Hevea braziliensis*) had been planted by Dayaks at Kapit.[44] The first rubber trees to be cultivated in Kuching at the turn of the century were by the Anglican Bishop, G. F. Hose, who planted 'one in the Rest House grounds and two in the garden of the Bishop's house'.[45] Charles established an experimental rubber plantation at the Matang Estate,[46] growing the local variety *getah rian* (*Isonandra gutta*), Ceara rubber (*Manihot glaziovii*), and later, Para rubber.[47] Similar projects were also started by the government at Satap and Sigu.[48] The BCL experimented with Para rubber by setting up estates on a portion of its Poak Concession (Dahan Rubber Estate) and at Bidi (Sungei Tengah Rubber Estate) in Upper Sarawak in 1902 and 1907 respectively.[49]

Para rubber seedlings from these experimental estates were distributed to government stations throughout the country for planting. Charles enlisted the assistance of the leading Kuching Chinese merchants to sell rubber seedlings through their network of trading links.[50] Later, Brooke officers in the outstations sold rubber stumps to local inhabitants at nominal prices. As a result, when rubber prices rose appreciably during the first decade of the twentieth century, there appeared no obstacles to its widespread cultivation. Charles favoured a policy of promoting rubber smallholdings rather than large, Malayan-style estates.[51]

Several other non-indigenous crops including indigo, cinchona, oil palm, and pineapple were introduced, while some local plants like tapioca, coconut, and cotton were actively promoted among the people with varying success. Notwithstanding Brooke efforts, only coconut planting enjoyed some degree of success while the others, for one reason or another, were disappointing.

The earliest new industry to be promoted was the rearing of silkworms, with the cultivation of mulberry trees at Marup, Simanggang, and Sibu in the late 1860s. Charles took a personal interest in this.

Then, in the mid-1870s there was the idea of manufacturing paper from wild fibre. The Rejang basin, where there was unlimited supply of wild plantain, was ideal for the promotion of this industry.[52] In the mid-1880s, it was reported that a European firm had applied for a concession for the monopoly of manufacturing plantain fibres, but there were no further details.[53] During the early 1890s, there was a suggestion of manufacturing fibre from wild banana trees in the Rejang, which could then be utilized for paper

making; samples sent to London and India received favourable reports.[54] Sisal fibre from Kapit also received good reviews from London, and was even 'said to be able to compete with Manila hemp'.[55] Charles also sought to promote the cultivation and manufacture of ramie (*Boehmeria nivea*) fibre which had been worked successfully in France.[56] A European concern, the Malayan Ramie Company, commenced the planting and manufacture of ramie at Lawas in 1908.[57]

In the mid-1870s there was a suggestion to farm dairy and beef cattle on a large-scale.[58] On the Astana grounds a small stock of dairy cattle was maintained by the government, and there were smaller versions of the Astana farm in the outstations.[59] Later, a Government Dairy Farm was established on the Pending Road, Kuching. In 1932, a New Government Dairy Farm was built on the Simanggang Road, next to the Semonggok Agricultural Station.[60]

Finally, an experimental *jelutong* plantation at Bukit Lan, near Sibu, was tried in the mid-1930s by the American Methodist Mission.[61]

Encouragement of Sago Cultivation

By the turn of the century, sago had been overshadowed, first by pepper, then Para rubber. Nevertheless, the Brookes still had hopes for this traditional crop and continually fostered its cultivation and the development of the industry.

Since the 1860s Chinese merchants and the BCL had been encouraging the Melanaus to expand their sago cultivation by providing them with financial assistance.[62] Charles persistently stressed the importance of sago as a valuable export product, vital to the country's economy.[63] During the 1920s, Vyner attempted to promote sago growing among the people to avoid the increasing over-dependence on Para rubber. He also considered sago as a food substitute for rice for the native people, and his encouragement of its cultivation was an attempt to increase food production.[64] Early in 1924, Reverend James Hoover,[65] the enterprising Methodist missionary, submitted a proposal for a Chinese sago scheme in the Rejang which received official sanction.[66] The success of Hoover's scheme was reflected in the numerous Chinese-owned sago plantations in the districts of Sibu, Oya, Dalat, and Bintulu.[67]

Efforts at Increasing Rice Production

'From the known industry of the Dyaks, and their partiality to rice-cultivation,' James was confident that 'there can be little doubt that it would become an article of extensive export.'[68] This was not to be the case. Undoubtedly he misjudged the Dayaks' capacity to produce rice. On occasion they produced surplus hill-rice which they traded with the coastal Malays, but the excess rice hardly constituted an amount for export that was comparable with either Javanese or Siamese production. Subsistence hill-rice farming was the Dayaks' main occupation whereas the Malays in the coastal districts relied more on trade than rice farming for their livelihood. When the population increased during the early 1850s, notably in the Chinese mining community of Upper Sarawak, rice was increasingly imported from Singapore.

In 1861 the boundaries of the Raj were extended to the Bintulu River. It was then that there was a growing concern to increase local rice output to cater for the additional population. Charles, then the Tuan Muda, was actively involved in agricultural promotion, including wet-*padi* cultivation among the Dayaks.

By the early 1870s there was already mention of problems of rice shortage and over-dependence on foreign imports.[69] Charles encouraged local rice production among the natives by awarding prizes for the best crops and well-maintained farms,[70] and promoted *padi* growing among the Chinese of Upper Sarawak.[71] In the columns of the *Gazette* a lively debate was conducted as to the best means of increasing local rice output and overcoming the dependence on imports. Suggestions ranged from the proposal to import experienced rice planters, like the Javanese and the Madurese, to establish *padi* farming communities in the country, to 'forcing' the 'indolent' local Malays to grow more *padi*.[72]

The labour shortage in the gambier and pepper plantations of Upper Sarawak in the late 1870s was blamed on the high price of imported rice which made recruitment of Chinese coolies difficult.[73] This adversely affected Charles's programme of promoting commercial agriculture. When gambier and pepper growing became more established from the 1880s onwards and the number of Chinese coolies working on the plantations increased, it became apparent that more positive steps had to be taken to increase local rice output.

Charles then decided to establish Chinese agricultural settlements in the Rejang by sponsoring the immigration of Chinese rice farmers and their families. An invitation was made in 1880

TABLE 5.1
Comparison of Rice Imports and Rubber Exports, 1931–1940

Year	*Rice Equivalent Imports (tons)*	*Rubber Exports (piculs)*
1931	16,436	174,747
1932	14,472	118,507
1933	16,505	187,270
1934	26,241	297,323
1935	31,443	333,190
1936	36,864	360,456
1937	33,105	445,532
1938	34,222	302,192
1939	34,043	403,725
1940	37,490	590,470

Source: F. W. South, 'Report on Agriculture in Sarawak, September 8 to October 30 1946', 12 November 1946, Typescript, MU 6136/47 (Malayan Union 9301/1946), NAM, Kuala Lumpur, p. 3.

(Appendix 6) and agreements were contracted at the turn of the century. By the first decade of the twentieth century there were permanent Chinese agricultural communities in the Rejang around Sibu. However, this plan of using Chinese to boost rice production to meet local consumption and even for export was unsuccessful as these settlers, faced with the difficulties of *padi* cultivation[74] turned their attention to other more profitable crops like pepper and Para rubber and relied on imported rice (see Tables 5.1 and 5.2). Rice imports, therefore, instead of decreasing, further increased to cater for these newly established Chinese communities.

TABLE 5.2
Increase in Rice Imports, 1922–1926

Year	*Weight (piculs)*	*Value ($)*
1922	132,291	903,899
1923	224,247	1,523,710
1924	273,003	2,179,827
1925	323,220	2,620,852
1926	373,220	3,060,852

Source: *SG*, 1 October 1926, p. 251.

Government encouragement of *padi* cultivation continued during Vyner's reign. Calls were made on the Chinese colonists in the Rejang to fulfil their original obligation as rice farmers.[75] Some attempts were made by the Foochows and Henghuas to cultivate *padi*,[76] but such efforts were insufficient to address the issue of rice deficits which came to the fore during the food crisis of 1919–21.

A Department of Agriculture report of 1929 on *padi* cultivation in the First Division revealed that farming methods were 'everywhere very primitive', double-cropping in general was non-existent, 'true wet-*padi* cultivation is hardly ever undertaken', there was an indifference to weeding, '[i]rrigation, drainage and systematic tillage are hardly attempted', and the 'use of any form of plough, or . . . changkol for tillage, seems to be unknown'.[77] It called for the need to make *padi* growing profitable, 'at least as attractive as the production of crops for export, however profitable these other crops may be'.[78] This was never to be the case as, from the last quarter of the nineteenth century, *padi* growing had to compete with other more lucrative activities, like the collection of jungle produce, and later, the cultivation of Para rubber. The report argued against imposing regulations and legislation as a means of improving the rice output 'because of the difficulty of their enforcement'. Instead, it recommended a programme of instruction in agricultural methods and gave its full support to the proposed scheme of establishing *padi* settlements.[79]

The concept of designating areas of *padi* reserves and establishing *padi*-farming communities of Chinese, Javanese, Japanese, and Bugis was implemented during the 1930s.[80] Agricultural stations specializing in *padi* culture were set up in the late 1930s to conduct research into the adaptability of *padi* strains for local planting. Personnel from the Agriculture Department were sent to Malaya to undergo courses in wet-*padi* cultivation.[81] The Agricultural Improvement Fund, set up in the 1920s, assisted the Roman Catholic Mission in its efforts to introduce buffalo ploughing among the Dayaks.[82]

Innovations in Farming among Dayaks and Malays

In order to discourage the migratory lifestyle of the Dayaks in search of new land for their swidden farming, Charles sought to introduce to them new farming methods that he hoped would encourage them to settle permanently.

I wish now to show them a specimen of farming and ploughing and if they can be persuaded to take it so much the better. *If we could get them to purchase buffaloes and cattle ... to use them for cultivating purposes whereby they might consider their own habitations to last for generations. This would be a step in advance and a proper step.*[83]

'But so long as Dyaks live in one longhouse,' he lamented, 'this is next to impossible.'[84] He even contemplated the dismantling of the longhouse system to achieve this end of settled agriculture and permanent living for the Dayaks.[85]

The Roman Catholic Mission at Ranan, near Kanowit in the Rejang, established a kind of model farm which introduced new crops like coffee, cocoa, and wet- and swamp-*padi*, as well as new agricultural expertise including ploughing by draught animals.[86] Dusuns from British North Borneo were engaged to instruct Dayaks in the ways of buffalo ploughing.[87] During the 1930s a Government Padi Farm was established near the Mission's operation at Ranan, and an Agriculture Inspector was permanently stationed at Kanowit.

Innovations in the processing of *padi* were introduced with a *padi*-husking mill operating at the experimental farm of Burdett Coutts at Lundu. The energetic and inventive Reverend Hoover had his own version of a *padi*-husking machine run by oil that 'works up about a hundred *pasus*, or 33 bags of paddy a day', producing 'beautifully clean [rice] fit to be put on the table'.[88]

Double-cropping of wet-*padi* cultivation was also encouraged. A fast-growing *padi* variety known as *agit*, which ripened within four months and was used by the Kayans, was introduced to the natives in the Baram and in the Upper Sadong.[89]

Encouragement of the Immigration of Chinese and Other Farmers

The Brookes were great admirers of the Chinese who fitted their vision of the archetypal peasant farmer. There were, in fact, already resident in the country Chinese, mostly Hakka, miners during the period of James's rule. But in the Brooke view, a more permanent, agriculturally based Chinese settlement, rather than a transient mining population, was needed to develop the country.[90] It was to this end that Brooke policy was directed from the 1860s onwards, beginning with James's efforts to encourage small groups of Chinese gambier planters from Singapore and Johore. It was

under Charles that Chinese planters from the Straits Settlements and the Malay States were invited successfully to open up gambier and pepper gardens in the country. The initial attempt was a financial disaster. But undeterred, in May 1872 Charles invited Chinese farmers to Sarawak with very generous terms including grants of land 'free of all payments and up to six years' exemption from export duty on gambier and pepper (see Appendix 7). A slightly modified version of this invitation was published in 1876 (see Appendix 8). By early 1876, an agreement was reached between Charles and Law Kian Huat (Ken Wat) of the firm Ghee Soon, a prominent Chinese merchant house in Kuching, whereby both parties agreed to furnish $30,000 each as an advance to three Chinese gambier and pepper companies to develop commercial cultivation in Sarawak.[91] From the early gardens in Upper Sarawak, gambier and pepper plantations spread to other parts of the country.

Charles was keen on the idea of encouraging the immigration and permanent settlement of Chinese rice planters. In 1898 a group of Hakka Christians of the Basel Mission entered Sarawak and was granted 60 hectares (150 acres) of good land, situated south of Kuching in the present-day Sungei Maong and Batu Kawa areas, for *padi* cultivation. An indenture was made between Charles and these Hakkas whereby they would devote their energies to *padi* planting in exchange for land and initial financial assistance including the provision of free house-building materials.[92] When *padi* planting was found to be unsuitable, the Hakkas turned to vegetable gardening with favourable results.[93] At the turn of the century, more of their countrymen came on their own account and contributed to the expansion of this Hakka agricultural community along Penrissen Road on the outskirts of Kuching.[94]

Charles had been impressed with the huge expanse of the Rejang basin; he had a grand vision for its development including the establishment of immigrant Chinese agricultural communities there.[95] In November 1880, Charles announced the terms of government support for the immigration into the Rejang of 'Chinese settlers with wives and families numbering not less than three hundred souls, who will employ themselves in gardening and farming *padi* or in other cultivations' (see Appendix 6). It was not until the early 1900s that Chinese immigration to the Lower Rejang became a reality. Government-sponsored immigration of batches of Foochow and Cantonese farmers arrived at Sibu direct from their home provinces in South China. The Hakkas and the Henghuas

came on their own without government support.[96] Initial hardships were undoubtedly the lot of the pioneer Chinese immigrants.[97] Beset with the enormous problems of *padi* cultivation, the Chinese immigrants in the Rejang turned to commercial crops for their survival.[98]

The encouragement of the immigration of Malayan-Muslim peoples was undertaken during pre-Brooke times. Rajah Muda Hashim was known to have settled some Boyanese in Kuching, and migrants from Sumatra came during the mid-nineteenth century.[99] Early in 1868, Charles, the then Tuan Muda, issued a regulation outlining the conditions required of 'Boyans, Javanese, Bugis, Banjarmasins or any other of such people' who wished to take up residence 'between the mouth of Sadong & Sirik point in Sarawak territory' as farmers growing food and cash crops (see Appendix 9). Small pockets of agricultural settlements were established by these migrants; some assimilated with the local Malay population while others, like the Javanese and the Boyanese, maintained a distinct cultural identity.

Liberal Land Laws Accorded Bona Fide Planters

In general, most indigenous groups in Sarawak during the pre-Brooke period adhered to a system of customary land tenure and *adat* law which acknowledged no permanent ownership but only rights to occupy and work the land. The act of clearing and farming an area of virgin jungle, in accordance with native *adat*, gave rights to land use which could be passed on to heirs and descendants. However, if the cultivator abandoned the land, the rights reverted to the community so that the land would then be free for felling by others.[100]

The first Brooke land legislation to oversee the utilization of land was made in 1863 by James, whereby 'all unoccupied land & waste lands, the property of Government, required for agricultural purposes ... shall be granted at the pleasure of the Government to applicants on lease of 900 years at the rate of 50 cents per acre, with an annual quit rent of 10 cents p[e]r acre exclusive of a survey fee of 25 cents p[e]r acre', with the option that 'at the expiration of 3 years of purchasing the land in fee simple upon the payment of the additional sum of $1 per acre.'[101] Incorporating traditional native customary land tenure practice, Clause 3 insisted that 'all lands granted whether upon lease or in fee simple to be liable to resumption by the [S]tate in the event of one fourth not being

cleared and brought under cultivation within 10 years of possession.'[102]

James's Land Order of 1863 made land a government property. It restricted native rights of access within their existing domain while any rights to land outside came under State jurisdiction. Natives wanting to open new land had to seek government permission. Private land ownership in the form of leases from the government was made possible by this legislation.

Charles adhered to the basic principles of the 1863 Land Order when he issued a revised version in 1871.[103] However, to promote commercial agriculture and Chinese immigration, Charles made some modifications in the granting of land. Article One of his Proclamation of 1876, regarding the terms and conditions offered to prospective gambier and pepper planters (see Appendix 8), declared the government's intention

> to make grants of lands suitable for planting gambier and pepper for *ninety nine years* at a nominal rent, each lot will be 1000 fathoms square or thereabouts & the grants will be subject to a condition that *not less than 300 fathoms square to be opened & planted.... On the breach of either condition or in the event of the grantees abandoning the land or any part of it by permitting it to return to jungle the grant will become null and void, and the Government be entitled to execute upon the land and take possession there of again.*[104]

The substitution of the 900-year lease for a 99-year term became the norm thereafter. The reversion to government as a penalty for abandonment or non-cultivation was a clear indication that Charles wanted bona fide cultivators and was determined to eliminate land speculation. The Land Regulations of 1882 discontinued the practice of issuing titles in fee simple as well as the option of lessees to obtain a fee simple title after the three-year leasehold term had lapsed.[105]

This land legislation, apart from a few minor regulations regarding sago cultivators[106] and some revisions pertaining to gambier and pepper planters,[107] dictated overall Brooke land policy up to 1941. The following summarizes the Brooke stance on the issue of land speculation.

> *Bona fide* planters receive every encouragement, though none is held out to speculators in land. The indiscriminate alienation of large tracts of land for unlimited periods and for indefinite purposes is an unsound policy, which does not find favour in Sarawak. It leads to land being locked up, sometimes for a long period, and to placing ultimately in the hands of a foreign speculator profits which the State should reap, and to the natives it causes many hardships.[108]

The policy of offering land to *genuine* planters was both generous and encouraging, and, as already shown, the Chinese took up the offer with favourable results. Even more generous was the immigration proposals of 1880 (see Appendix 6) for permanent Chinese settlement in the Rejang whereby '*the Government will provide land sufficient for their requirements free of charge*'.[109] As for prospective European planters, a pamphlet entitled *Sarawak as a Field for Planters*, issued in 1879, contained the following proclamation: 'Intending settlers would be allowed to choose their own land, in any portion of the territory not already occupied by Chinese gambier plantations, or by Dyak fruit gardens.'[110] Furthermore, the government would 'be prepared to make special arrangement in the case of settlers wishing to take up large tracts' of land for agricultural pursuits.[111] The success of this liberal land policy is evident in the numerous land grants and leases given to both private individuals and public companies recorded in the Agreement Books.[112] During the 1890s when the Chinese were actively involved in gambier and pepper cultivation, the government hastened the process of issuing land permits to these planters.[113]

The implementation of Charles's Chinese immigration policy during the first decade of the twentieth century, the continual influx of Chinese thereafter, and the promotion of commercial agriculture created an increased demand for land and inflated its value. Further revisions and amendments were therefore necessary and were effected during Vyner's reign. The primary objective of Vyner's land legislation was to safeguard native rights against foreign and non-native, which included Chinese, encroachments.

Amidst the 'planting craze' for plantation rubber, Charles stood alone as a pessimistic prophet predicting the inevitable slump in prices, the dangers of speculation, and the imminent disinheritance of natives from their land if precautionary steps were not adopted. As early as 1909, Charles advised caution and denounced speculation.[114] A landmark legislation was issued in November 1910 (see Appendix 10) aimed at *prohibiting the alienation of rubber gardens 'to any European or Europeans or any individual, firm, or company of white nationality'*.[115] Such a policy was intended

> *to develop the cultivation of the land for the good of the inhabitants in order that they may have the profits and benefit in the possession of such gardens as an inheritance or pesaka to their descendants—and this object would not be achieved or realised unless the plantations were protected and strictly prohibited from falling into the hands of the richer and more speculative class of the white races.*[116]

This rather strong pro-native policy also intended to demonstrate

> what the absolute and bona-fide value [of rubber] may be reduced to when planted by the native races, the real workers of the soil, without the extraneous and surrounding influences connected with [European] companies floated by promoters and supported by shareholders ... *and the European in all countries will derive the benefit of obtaining the Rubber at a tenth of the price more or less that has to be paid for it at the present time.*[117]

In a speech to the General Council of 1912, Charles assured native leaders that the Exchequer would never be increased by the sale of land to European capitalist companies.[118]

The lands of the indigenous peoples also had to be protected from Chinese encroachments which became increasingly common from the 1910s when Chinese immigration and competition for land accelerated, particularly in the Rejang. The Upper Sarawak district and the Simanggang area also had their share of cases of land disputes between the Chinese and the natives.[119]

Some Achievements

Brooke attempts to promote commercial agriculture achieved some notable successes. New crops like gambier, pepper, and Para rubber enjoyed a measure of prosperity during boom periods. As more people took up these cultures, undoubtedly motivated by high prices, the acreage under these crops expanded, particularly in the case of Para rubber, which, by the last decade of Brooke rule, was the major commercial crop of the country.

Gambier and pepper were among the first of the new crops introduced in the country to attain some measure of success.[120] From the 1880s onwards there was a marked increase in gambier and pepper cultivation.[121] Gambier became an important export item during the 1880s and 1890s, but thereafter its significance waned. Pepper, on the other hand, continued as a successful export product throughout the Brooke period despite price fluctuations, disease, and contractual problems between planters and sponsors.[122] Between 1935 and 1939, Sarawak was the second largest producer of pepper in the world, after the Dutch East Indies.[123]

Pepper cultivation spread from Upper Sarawak to other parts of the country. Foochow and Cantonese immigrants to the Rejang in the early 1900s took to pepper planting. The pepper-producing areas were Simanggang, Engkilili, Lingga, the Simanggang Road, Sarikei, Binatang, Kanowit, Kapit, and Limbang. There were also

pockets of cultivation in other areas like Trusan, Lawas, Kalaka, Sibu, and Sadong.[124] Pepper growing remained a smallholders' concern and was almost exclusively Chinese; the Hakkas dominated the Kuching–Serian area while the Foochows and the Cantonese were prominent in the Sarikei–Binatang enclave.[125]

Brooke efforts to foster the cultivation and manufacture of sago also enjoyed some success. Official promotion of sago growing proved encouraging, illustrated by the fact that besides the Melanaus, others, especially the Chinese in the Rejang, took up sago planting with reasonable success.[126]

It was the introduction of Para rubber that had an enormous impact on Sarawak. Its commercial cultivation intensified from 1910 onwards. From Lundu in the west to Lawas in the east, Malays, Chinese, Dayaks, Kayans, and other indigenous peoples enthusiastically grew plantation rubber.[127] Unlike pepper cultivation which remained largely a Chinese preserve and sago a Melanau speciality, the planting of Para rubber transcended ethnic lines. None the less, the Chinese maintained a pre-eminent position in its cultivation, processing, and trade. Furthermore, Brooke policy dictated that Para rubber growing should be a smallholder's crop. A report of 1938 states that

> Out of a total of approximately 93,000 rubber holdings, covering an area of 230,000 acres, only 17,302 acres, or approximately 7.5 %, represent holdings of 100 acres and over. Of these latter holdings 10,066.6 acres represent large estates assessed on standard production, with reliable statistics of production. It may be said, therefore, that large estates form only 4.4 % of the total area under rubber in the State.[128]

In some areas, like the Rejang, rubber monoculture among the Chinese was not uncommon, though it was greatly discouraged by the authorities. There were some Chinese-owned medium-sized holdings, and a small number of large Malayan-style operations owned and managed by Europeans employing a largely imported coolie labour force.[129] The widespread attraction of Para rubber was not shared by Charles and Vyner. None the less, the Brookes could not deny the fact that the crop was a success and brought a measure of prosperity to those involved in the industry.

Overall Failure

> I do not flatter myself when I say that I have tried my best to advance this branch [that is, agriculture], but *have most signally failed*, and am in consequence much disappointed; but I still entertain hopes that a time for its

development is not far too distant, and I am prepared to take any pains, to receive any amount of advice, or undergo any trouble, could I see my way to successfully spreading gardens and plantations in the place of our vast jungles.[130]

This admission of failure by Charles in a public speech in early 1872 revealed the realities faced in the promotion of agriculture. In spite of the success in some areas, the general picture was one of disappointment. Most of the new crops that were tried in the government experimental gardens failed for one reason or another. European planters stayed away despite favourable land offers. The attempt to increase rice output (with even hopes of export) by the introduction of Chinese peasant farmers was unsuccessful.

Failure in the Introduction of New Crops

By the early 1870s there was already the realization that many new crops had no future in the country. Sugar cane, coffee, tobacco, indigo, cinchona, oil palm, and pineapple all failed. In particular, coffee and tobacco were expensive failures.

Sugar cane failed because the land which the Sarawak Sugar Company utilized was unsuitable due to the 'poverty of the soil'; it was claimed that 'even weeds will only sparingly grow'![131] It is inconceivable that there could have been such ignorance and folly in matters relating to cultivation or processing considering that Arthur Crookshank, who initially managed the concern, had observed the operation of the plantations at Province Wellesley in Malaya. It is also unlikely that 'neglect and mismanagement', as alleged by James, was 'the root of the mischief,'[132] for the manager of the plantation, Mr Pasley, was formerly 'manager, for fully ten years, of one of the largest of Mr Horsman's Sugar Estates in Province Wellesley'.[133] Also, it is improbable that insufficient capital, as contended by W. H. Read, one of the shareholders, was to blame.[134] In addition to the poor soil, the failure of sugar cane might have been due to the absence in Sarawak of a long dry season, found in Java or the West Indies, which was necessary for the canes to flourish.[135]

Hopes for sugar cane remained.[136] It was claimed that with the suitability of Sarawak conditions the crop would undoubtedly enjoy 'as great success as it [does] in Demerara [British Guiana]'.[137] Convinced that sugar cane possessed commercial potential in Sarawak, Charles, in mid-1894, offered to 'grant, free of charge or rent, two thousand, (or in an approved case even more) acres of selected land in the Rejang River ... to whosoever will first estab-

lish a Company to plant Sugar in that district'.[138] Disappointing as it was, it was perhaps fortunate that this rather generous offer was not taken up.

In the case of coffee cultivation, high hopes were held for both the government experimental garden at Matang Mountain and the Dayak plots at Peninjauh. The Arabian coffee trees were reported to be looking 'exceedingly well', and it was believed that if success was attained, 'it will be a great boon to the Dyaks and the cultivation would then spread throughout the Dyak community'.[139] This promise was not fulfilled. The failure of coffee was initially a puzzle as illustrated by the following comment:

> In 1867 a coffee estate was commenced on Matang mountain at an elevation of from 210 to 300 metres. The soil was pronounced good, and it was generally thought that coffee would fruit with less trouble than pepper. The estate has now been 6 years in hand and has over 100,000 plants upon it, for the most part looking healthy, but the yield has as yet been next to nothing. A manager from Ceylon has of late years superintended, and *last year the plants should have brought in a return, but from one cause or another the blossoms never properly set*.[140]

It was not lack of supervision that caused the failure, for, as pointed out, Charles had engaged experienced and knowledgeable European planters from Ceylon. Upon closer examination, the reason for failure was again the poor soil. 'The soil on Matang,' the *Gazette* reported, '*although at first looking suitable, has been found to be poor, of light sandy formation, and not the chocolate colour so sought after in Ceylon.*'[141] Furthermore, 'the downfall of rain and want of [a] more defined season' were 'the great drawbacks'.[142] The government coffee plantations on Matang Mountain and Satap had, by 1901, cost an estimated $176,000, a grave financial loss and disappointment to Charles.[143] By the turn of the century, when coffee prices suffered a serious slump, interest and planting correspondingly waned. Charles decided to close the Matang coffee plantations in 1912.

Tobacco grown at the government experimental plantation at Lundu under the supervision of an experienced Deli planter also showed promise initially. Charles even drew up 'a tentative prospectus for a tobacco company' with the BCL in mind, and had plans for 'the sale of small acreages' of 'guaranteed tobacco land'.[144] But the second crop, harvested and shipped to Europe during mid-1890, received unfavourable reviews by experts in Amsterdam.[145] It was then decided to cease operations altogether in the hope that the plantation would be taken over by private

enterprise, presumably the BCL. The company, however, decided against the idea,[146] and the Lundu plantations proved another failure. Altogether, the trial planting of tobacco at Lundu incurred a total deficit of $60,000, no small investment then.[147]

The failure of tobacco was attributed once again to the 'rainy' condition of the country. The *Gazette* 'described tobacco planting as a "doubtful industry"' but, without totally dismissing this culture, it went on to comment that 'although we proved that tobacco can be grown at Lundu, we really do not know yet if it can be grown at a profit'.[148]

Another 'victim' of Sarawak's heavy rainfall was ramie cultivation, attempted at Lawas. The planting of ramie carried out by the French-owned Malayan Ramie Company Limited failed.[149]

Indigo and tapioca were cultivated by the Chinese in the 1870s but a lack of interest set in with the appearance of far more lucrative crops like gambier, pepper, and Para rubber.[150] Despite encouraging reports from London of cinchona bark samples produced at the government experimental plantation at Matang, this native South American tree (*Rubiaceae*) was never exploited as a commercial crop.[151]

The cultivation of the West African oil palm (*Elaeis guineensis*) was first attempted in the 1860s on Burdett Coutts's Quop Estate without much success. Thirty years on, trial planting was again instituted.[152] Initial reports from London of Sarawak palm oil samples were favourable, but, of more importance, the feedback from a potential purchaser of the oil in Britain was discouraging.[153] Undeterred, Charles proceeded with the promotion of the oil 'which in his opinion cannot fail, in the future, to be a source of great wealth'.[154] Oil palm was also grown in the government experimental garden at Simanggang,[155] but, Charles's hopes were not shared by others and no commercial cultivation of this crop was undertaken.

For some reason or other, commercial pineapple cultivation was never attempted at all. Despite evidence that Sarawak pineapple 'can be canned successfully' although 'they require very much care in handling and processing than the Malayan pines',[156] no investor came forward.

Cotton was traditionally grown by the Dayaks for cloth weaving.[157] In the late 1880s, an attempt was made to grow cotton at Kanowit but the experiment was unsuccessful because of the poor soil.[158] Cotton cultivation as a commercial enterprise was never tried.

Tea, although it thrived fairly well at Matang, was never grown by others. Neither the Chinese nor the native peoples took to tea planting and its manufacture, and no European entrepreneur expressed interest.

In short, these crops—indigo, tapioca, cinchona, oil palm, pineapple, cotton, and tea—neither went beyond the stage of the experimental garden nor captured the interest of the people or European investors. They were all failures.

Poor Response to New Farming Methods by Dayaks and Malays

The introduction of new methods of working the land, like ploughing the fields using water-buffaloes, had limited influence on the Dayaks despite the untiring efforts at promotion. Charles's attempts during the late 1860s were without apparent result. Equally disappointing was the work of the Roman Catholic Mission in their Ranan demonstration farm. In spite of almost four decades of encouragement and demonstration they had little to show.[159]

The plausible explanation might be that the terrain in the Dayak areas was more suited to shifting cultivation of hill-rice than to this type of farming. It must be pointed out that among other indigenous communities, like the Muruts, Kelabits, Kedayans, and Bisayas, wet-rice cultivation with irrigated fields and the use of buffaloes for ploughing had been traditional practices. But with the little contact the Brookes had with these minorities, except the Muruts, these practices might perhaps have escaped official notice.

The paucity of information regarding the attempts at promoting the double-cropping of *padi* makes it difficult to ascertain their outcome. Efforts by their *penghulu* to persuade the Bintulu Dayaks to practise double-cropping were unsuccessful; only the very desperate who were short of food showed 'any inclination to break through their custom' and plant a second crop.[160] If the Bintulu example is anything to go by, it is doubtful that double-cropping of *padi* was attempted by other indigenous communities. The statement from an official report of 1929, based on an investigation into *padi* cultivation in the First Division, summarizes the native attitude towards double-cropping which also prevailed in other parts of the country: '[A]lmost nowhere is the same field cultivated in two successive seasons. Among both Malays and Dyaks there is *a general belief that it is impossible to grow two successive crops*

on the same area, however good the soil may be: their methods of agriculture being what they are, this is no doubt their experience.'[161]

In general, the great majority of the indigenous inhabitants maintained their traditional modes of subsistence farming. They were unconvinced and mistrustful of innovations in farming technology.

Unsuccessful Introduction of New Industries

The introduction of new industries, like the rearing of silkworms and silk weaving, the manufacture of paper from wild fibre, the cultivation of *jelutong* trees, and dairy and beef cattle farming, all failed.

After three years of 'consequent trials and failures' the silkworm and silk manufacture project was abandoned. 'The successes', Charles pronounced, 'are reserved for those who take to the work afterwards and have learnt by our experience that changes and modifications are required to adapt patterns to our country and soil and climate.'[162] The *Gazette* concluded that 'only Chinese would make it remunerative'.[163] However, the Chinese were not keen to embark on this industry; perhaps they were aware that Simanggang was no Soochow which is famed for its silk.

In August 1875, it was reported that a Chinese entrepreneur was about to embark on the manufacture of fibre from wild plantain, but nothing else was heard thereafter.[164] Curiously enough, two years later, the government announced that it was not prepared 'to grant any monopoly for the working of fibres in the Rejang river', and, in addition, it imposed an export duty 'from 50 cents to one dollar' on each ton of 40 cubic feet of fibre, with a minimum duty 'charged on those fibres intended for making, and the maximum on more valuable fibres which may be used for rope'.[165] The imposition of this duty was perhaps in anticipation of the flourishing of this new industry, but it was sadly miscalculated as no investors came forward.

In the mid-1880s interest in fibre was again revived, and it was reported that a European firm had applied for a concession for the monopoly of manufacturing plantain fibre but no details were forthcoming.[166] The economic utilization of wild plantain in the Rejang never became a reality.

Because of crop failure and huge overhead costs, the Malayan Ramie Company abandoned the cultivation of ramie after less than one and a half years of operations.[167] The scheme to plant *jelutong* trees during the mid-1930s also appeared to be a failure. Apart

from the mention of a possible expansion of 20 or more acres, an encouraging effort by all counts, nothing was heard thereafter of this project.[168] The attempt to encourage the rearing of dairy and beef cattle as a large-scale commercial venture met with little interest among the local inhabitants. The lack of wide stretches of grazing pasture apparently deterred would-be investors.

Absence of European Planting Interest

The BCL's reluctance to work the government tobacco plantations at Lundu as a private enterprise typified the general non-involvement of European companies in Sarawak. The reasons might have differed among them but the fact remained that only a handful of European firms set up agricultural ventures in the country.

There was, apparently, some interest shown by European planters during the late 1870s that led Charles to issue the pamphlet, *Sarawak as a Field for Planters*, to provide more detailed information regarding the conditions of the country.[169] But on the whole no major European agricultural investments was undertaken during the last quarter of the nineteenth century.

In the late 1880s Charles, who had high hopes for Liberian coffee, proposed the floating of a company, the Matang Planting Company 'Limited', and accordingly a prospectus was published in 1886. The grants of land for this proposed company were generous.[170] The prospectus furnished details of expenditure corresponding to the yearly expansion of acreage, and the expected receipts were all calculated and presented in an attractive and factual manner.[171] In spite of such liberal land grants and such detailed information on operations, no investor took up the offer, much to Charles's disappointment.

Para rubber at least attracted some European planting interest. None the less, towards the closing years of Brooke rule, there were no more than five foreign commercial plantations in Sarawak, and the number of individual European planters was negligible.[172]

The impression that the Brookes, particularly Charles, were against foreign capitalist investment, in large measure dissuaded would-be investors from the country. Charles's insistence on a land policy especially designed to exclude speculation and to ensure the permanent settlement of genuine cultivators was in general unappealing to European planters. This policy was based on lease or rental rather than outright alienation, with a clause that allowed the government to reclaim the land in the event of non-cultivation or abandonment.

Even more damaging because it confirmed Charles's anti-European stance, was the highly protectionist policy of the prohibition of the sale of rubber plantations, owned by Sarawak's indigenous people and other Asian inhabitants, *'to any European or Europeans or any individual, firm, or Company of white nationality'* (Appendix 10).[173] Furthermore, Charles offered scarcely any inducement to European rubber planters, unlike the practice in the British Protected Western Malay States or neighbouring British North Borneo where favourable terms, including the exemption of export duties, were given. Equally discouraging was the Brooke policy of favouring smallholdings, which in practice translated into a general reluctance to grant huge tracts of land to concessionaires.[174]

The shortage of labour, which necessitated its importation, was another discouragement.[175] For instance, the BCL's Para rubber estates employed imported Javanese labour while the Malayan Ramie Company at Lawas relied on imported Chinese coolies.[176] Apart from the unsuitable climatic conditions for ramie cultivation, the French manager, Emil F. Pumpin, attributed the lack of success of the latter company to the high wages of its Chinese labour force which made the continuation of operations uneconomical.[177] The Chinese gambier and pepper plantations also suffered chronic labour shortages.[178]

Conclusion

The overall failure of the Brooke efforts in agricultural development, particularly in promoting the cultivation of commercial crops, was due to a combination of geographical and physical factors, such as poor soils, unsuitable terrain, unfavourable climate, and geographical isolation, and the government policy of emphasizing native interest and welfare. In other words the unfavourable natural environment and deliberate Brooke policy worked against the successful commercialization of agriculture.

Sarawak, as a whole, is not blessed with favourable conditions for agriculture. As early as 1873, it was admitted that the soil of the country, apart from a few select localities, was generally poor, 'far inferior to that of either Java or Manila, and is about equal to Rhio, Johore and Malacca'.[179] James's claims that the soils were of the 'richest description' and 'admirably calculated for the growth' of numerous crops proved to be far from accurate.[180] His favourable comments were certainly not out of step with the general belief of

the time, that the luxuriant growth of plant life in the humid tropics was an indication of the richness of its soil. Yet, as we now know, the soil in the tropics is generally poor due to the action of leaching and erosion brought about by heavy rainfall in 'intense localized showers'.[181] It was therefore not surprising that many of the newly introduced crops did not flourish. Coupled with infertile soil is the physical nature of the country which is not conducive to agricultural pursuits such as those practised in other South-East Asian lands. The flat deltaic plain is covered by deep peat swamp which is unsuitable for agriculture. Other than small areas on the riverbanks in this deltaic area which could be utilized for wet-*padi* cultivation, the area of hilly country and the mountainous interior with thin and poor soils are inappropriate for agriculture apart from native swidden farming.[182]

The significant absence of European agricultural investment was mainly due to the Brookes' highly protectionist land policy designed to prevent speculation and alienation of native land. The Brooke preference for smallholdings to large estates and the difficulty of acquiring huge tracts of suitable agricultural land worked against the establishment of large-scale, Malayan-style plantations. The perennial shortage of labour and the high expense and problems of securing and managing imported coolies were other drawbacks that dissuaded European agricultural investment. In comparison with neighbouring lands, like the western Malay States, Dutch Java, British Lower Burma, and French Cochin-China, Sarawak was at a severe disadvantage as a field of agricultural investment.

Another contributing factor may have been the fact that Sarawak was an unknown land among the circle of European entrepreneurs and planters. James might have made an impression among a generation of British people with his adventurous and romantic exploits, but his successors, Charles and Vyner, were, at their best, uncharismatic personalities who carried out the mainly mundane administrative tasks of ruling over a multiethnic, mainly rural, and subsistence-based population, located off the major trade routes and cut off from the outside world. Brooke Sarawak was indeed a backwater.

Agriculture in Sarawak remained, in general, a smallholding subsistence concern owned and managed by families. Commercial crops, particularly Para rubber, were grown as a secondary cash crop providing supplmentary income for the subsistence rice farmer. James's dream of making Sarawak 'a second Java'

remained unfulfilled in spite of the determined and untiring efforts of Charles to promote the agricultural development of the country. The physical constraints of poor soil, unsuitable terrain, and unfavourable climatic conditions coupled with a protectionist Brooke policy worked against commercial-scale agricultural development in Sarawak.

1. James Brooke, *A Letter from Borneo; with Notices of the Country and Its Inhabitants, Addressed to James Gardner, Esq.*, London: L. & G. Seeley, 1842, p. 14.

2. Ibid., pp. 14–15.

3. Brooke officers also expressed similar viewpoints as can be seen in their reports to Charles. For instance, see *Sarawak Gazette* (*SG*), 1 October 1881, p. 81; and *SG*, 20 May 1876, pp. 2 and 5.

4. 7th Meeting, Kuching, 11 August 1883, in *General Council, 1867–1927*, Kuching: Government Printing Office, 1927[?], p. 9.

5. 16th Meeting, 17 July 1909, in *General Council,* 1867–1927, p. 23.

6. See 'The Journal of Charles Brooke, September 1866–July 1868', in Charles Brooke, *Ten Years in Sarawak*, 2 vols., London: Tinsley Brothers, 1866; reprinted Singapore: Oxford University Press, 1990, Vol. II, p. 359. As one writer pointed out, the 'ideal type was less the semi-nomadic shifting cultivator than it was the yeoman freeholder, a tropical variation on the familiar sturdy English peasant theme'. Robert Pringle, 'The Brookes of Sarawak: Reformers In Spite of Themselves' *SMJ*, 19, 38–9 (1971): 69.

7. For instance, see *SG*, 1 February 1894, p. 22.

8. For instance, see *SG*, 2 January, 1896, p. 2; *SG*, 1 May 1896, p. 85; and S. Baring-Gould and C. A. Bampfylde, *A History of Sarawak under Its Two White Rajahs, 1839–1908*, London: Henry Sotheran, 1909, p. 436.

9. Hugh Low, *Sarawak: Its Inhabitants and Productions; Being Notes during a Residence in that Country with His Excellency Mr Brooke*, London: Frank Cass, 1848; new impression, 1968, p. 33.

10. Although Baring-Gould and Bampfylde stated that James 'induced' Burdett Coutts to start this experimental farm, it is unlikely to have been the case as evidenced by a letter from James regarding his willingness to grant her a piece of land for her proposed farm. See Baring-Gould and Bampfylde, *A History of Sarawak*, p. 319; and J. Brooke to 'Ladies', 8 June, 1864, in Owen Rutter (ed.), *Rajah Brooke and Baroness Burdett Coutts: Consisting of the Letters from Sir James Brooke, the First White Rajah of Sarawak, to Miss Angela (afterwards Baroness) Burdett Coutts*, London: Hutchinson, 1935, p. 227.

11. See Baring-Gould and Bampfylde, *A History of Sarawak*, pp. 319–20; and *SG*, 29 September 1870, n.p.

12. See 'Memorandum for the Tuan Muda and the Resident', by James Brooke, n.d., in Rutter, *Rajah Brooke and Baroness Burdett Coutts*, p. 228; J. Brooke to Burdett Coutts, 4 January 1865, in ibid., p. 246; and J. Brooke to Burdett Coutts, 30 April 1865, in ibid., p. 238; *SG*, 1 June 1891, p. 83; and Henry Longhurst, *The Borneo Story: The History of the First 100 Years of Trading in the Far East by The Borneo Company Limited*, London: Newman Neame, 1956, p. 57.

13. See *SG*, 18 March 1872, n.p.; *SG*, 16 September 1872, n.p.; and *SG*, 1 June 1891, p. 83.

14. See J. Brooke to Burdett Coutts, 4 January 1865, in Rutter, *Rajah Brooke and Baroness Burdett Coutts*, p. 238; and J. Brooke to Burdett Coutts, 14 June 1865, in ibid., p. 247.

15. *SG*, 1 June 1891, p. 83.

16. Typical of Charles, he personally undertook the task, side by side with his Dayaks, in clearing the slope of Matang Mountain for coffee growing. 'Journal', in C. Brooke, *Ten Years*, Vol. II, p. 347.

17. See 9th Meeting, 27 August 1889 (Second Day), in *General Council, 1867–1927*, p. 14.

18. J. R. Dunsmore, 'A Review of Agricultural Research in Sarawak', *SMJ*, 16, 32–3 (July–December 1968): 309.

19. Vyner appeared to be committed to this project for it was said of this laboratory that 'nothing apears [*sic*] to have been spared in its equipment' and it cost the Treasury nearly $10,000. Although both appointments of agronomist and chemist were vacated during the Depression (1929–31), some research was carried out at the Semonggok Central Agricultural Station during the 1930s. See J. S. W. Bean, *Annual Report Department of Agriculture, Sarawak, for 1928*, Kuching: Government Printing Office, 1929, quoted in Dunsmore, 'Agricultural Research', p. 309; *Sarawak Administration Report (SAR), 1934*, Kuching: Government Printing Office, p. 4; and *SAR, 1935*, p. 4.

20. The Kanowit station undertook laboratory testing of Malayan *padi* varieties best adapted to local conditions, while at Rantau Panjang, an area in the Igan River below Sibu, experimental cultivation of various strains of wet-*padi* was conducted. According to J. Cook, Sarawak Director of Agriculture (1956–63), the 'first significant move towards scientific development in agriculture occurred in 1939 when a senior officer from the Malayan Department of Agriculture was seconded to Sarawak with a brief to concentrate on improving rice production'. Selected *padi* strains from Malaya were introduced and a series of trial cultivations was conducted throughout the country. Cook himself, then State Agricultural Officer, Brunei, assisted in implementing the project in districts in Limbang. J. Cook to A. H. M. Kirk-Greene, Oxford University Development Records Project, 3 September 1983 (Personal copy); and Interview with J. Cook, Dundee, Scotland, May 1993.

21. See Chapter 9.

22. For instance, see *SG*, 13 March 1871, n.p.

23. For gambier as a tanning agent, see *SG*, 17 May 1915, pp. 113–14.

24. The use of discarded gambier leaves to fertilize the pepper vines was considered a more agreeable alternative than 'prawn refuse, which the Chinese did not trouble to dig in and which could therefore be detected by more sensitive nostrils a mile away'. Longhurst, *The Borneo Story*, p. 65.

25. *SG*, 15 March 1873, n.p.

26. See ibid.

27. See p. 180 below.

28. See Low, *Sarawak*, p. 56.

29. See Odoardo Beccari, *Wanderings in the Great Forests of Borneo*, London: Archibald Constable, 1904; reprinted Singapore: Oxford University Press, 1986, pp. 98 and 108; and C. Brooke, *Ten Years*, Vol. I, p. 201.

30. See *SG*, 13 March 1871, n.p.

31. *SG*, 31 August 1879, p. 58.

32. See *SG*, 13 November 1878, p. 75; and *SG*, 16 January 1879, pp. 2 and 6.

33. For Dayak enthusiasm towards coffee planting, see *SG*, 1 August 1885,

p. 73; *SG*, 1 February 1894, p. 22; *SG*, 1 May 1894, p. 67; Robert Pringle, *Rajahs and Rebels: The Ibans of Sarawak under Brooke Rule, 1841–1941*, London: Macmillan, 1970, pp. 202–3; and R. A. Cramb, 'The Commercialization of Iban Agriculture', in R. A. Cramb and R. H. W. Reece (eds.), *Development in Sarawak: Historical and Contemporary Perspectives*, Monash Paper on Southeast Asia No. 17, Centre of Southeast Asia Studies, Melbourne: Monash University, 1988, pp. 110–11.

34. For Chinese and Malay interests, see *SG*, 4 January 1886, p. 6; *SG*, 3 January 1887, p. 2; *SG*, 1 December 1887, p. 189; *SG*, 1 January 1890, p. 3; and *SG*, 1 April 1890, p. 51.

35. For instance, see *SG*, 1 November 1930, p. 279; *SG*, 1 March 1932, p. 57; and *SG*, 4 January 1937, p. 21.

36. For tea growing, see *SG*, 16 January 1879, p. 2; *SG*, 1 July 1881, p. 51; and *SG*, 1 December 1890, p. 152. For the problems of processing, see *SG*, 1 January 1890, p. 3. For its consumption in the local market and good reports from London, see *SG*, 2 January 1892, p. 2.

37. See Beccari, *Wanderings*, p. 174.

38. See *SG*, 10 October 1876, p. 4.

39. See *SG*, 1 December 1887, pp. 189–90.

40. See *SG*, 1 January 1890, p. 3.

41. A. H. Moy-Thomas, 'Economic Development under the Second Rajah (1870–1917)', *SMJ*, 10, 17–18 (July–December 1961): 58.

42. See *SG*, 1 June 1931, p. 131; *SG*, 1 September, p. 196; and *SG*, 1 November 1932, p. 186.

43. For instance, see *SG*, 2 January 1934, p. 1.

44. The Para rubber trees were 'well grown and looking very healthy', but no details about extraction of latex was noted. See *SG*, 1 August 1885, p. 73.

45. W. J. Chater, 'Chinese Labourers and How They Came to Sarawak', *ST*, 21 February 1964. See also R. E. Tremeer, 'The Early History of Rubber Planting in Sarawak, 1880–1910', *SG*, 31 March 1964, p. 51.

46. It was said that Charles sought the assistance of Penghulu Dalam Munan, a Dayak chieftain, in the establishment of the government experimental rubber plantation at Matang in 1903. Munan was a pioneer in Para rubber cultivation in his home district of Sibu in the Lower Rejang. See Pringle, *Rajahs and Rebels*, p. 186.

47. See Tremeer, 'Early History of Rubber Planting', p. 51.

48. See *SG*, 4 January 1907, p. 2; *SG*, 1 October 1908, p. 247; and *SG*, 1 December 1908, p. 297.

49. See Chapter 9.

50. See Pringle, 'The Brookes of Sarawak', pp. 63 and 70.

51. Apart from the large estates (over 400 hectares (1,000 acres) each) of the BCL, the Lawas Planting Company, the Japanese-owned Nissa Shokai Company, and Rejang Estates Limited, and several medium-sized Chinese plantations (40–120 hectares (100–300 acres) each), rubber smallholdings averaging from 0.6 to 2.4 hectares (1.5 to 6 acres) dominated Sarawak's rubber industry. See James C. Jackson, *Sarawak: A Geographical Survey of a Developing State*, London: University of London Press, 1968, pp. 89–90; and R. H. W. Reece, *The Name of Brooke: The End of White Rajah Rule in Sarawak*, Kuala Lumpur: Oxford University Press, 1982, pp. 53–4.

52. See *SG*, 16 July 1875, n.p.

53. See *SG*, 1 August 1885, p. 73; and *SG*, 1 January 1890, p. 3.

54. See *SG*, 1 April 1893, p. 54.

55. *SG*, 1 March 1894, p. 38.

56. China grass is a shrub indigenous to India. China grass or *Chu-ma* (ramie) is considered a textile substance of the first rank. A fabric known as Swatow-grass cloth, woven from *Chu-ma* and a famous product of China, has a higher durability and outwears linen by many years. See Victor Purcell, *The Chinese in South-East Asia*, London: Oxford University Press, 1965, p. 524, n. 1.

57. See Chapter 9.

58. See *SG*, 1 September 1875, n.p.

59. See *SG*, 1 June 1891, p. 84.

60. See *SG*, 1 February 1932, p. 24; and *SAR, 1931*, pp. 11–12.

61. See *SG*, 2 December 1935, p. 231.

62. For instance, see *SG*, 1 March 1882, p. 15; and Longhurst, *The Borneo Story*, p. 60.

63. For instance, see 7th Meeting, 11 August 1883, in *General Council 1867–1927*, p. 9.

64. The drastic decline in rice imports during the food crisis (1919–21) and rumours of another shortage in the late 1920s undoubtedly had a bearing on Vyner's plans in promoting sago. See 11th Meeting, 20 September 1894, in *General Council, 1867–1927*, p. 17. For Vyner's efforts, see 20th Meeting, 17 October 1921, in ibid., p. 30; 21st Meeting, 16 October 1924, in ibid., p. 32; and 22nd Meeting, 17 October 1927, in ibid., p. 35.

65. Hoover arrived in Sibu in 1904 as the Methodist minister in charge of the Foochow Methodist community. When the Chinese proprietor of this Foochow colony faced deep financial difficulties and consequently gave up his post, Charles appointed Hoover as the 'Kapitan China of the Rejang Foochows'. Later, he also acquired the title of 'Protector of the Foochows'. See Frank T. Cartwright, *Tuan Hoover of Borneo*, New York: Abingdon Press, 1938, pp. 62–8.

66. For Hoover's Chinese sago scheme, see 'Plans for Planting Sago on the Rejang'; J. C. Moulton, Chief Secretary, to D. A. Owen, Resident, Third Division, 3 January 1924; Owen to Moulton, 7 January 1924; Moulton to Owen, 11 January 1924; '"Notice in Chinese", issued by D. A. Owen, Resident, Sibu, 3rd Division, 25 September 1924, regarding conditions of sago cultivation', MSS Ind. Ocn. s. 143(2), Walter Francis de Vere Skrine, RHL, Oxford.

67. For instance, see *SG*, 2 January 1924, p. 21; *SG*, 1 April 1924, p. 127; *SG*, 1 May 1924, pp. 157, 159, and 166; and *SG*, 2 January 1926, p. 15.

68. Brooke, *A Letter from Borneo*, p. 14.

69. For instance, see *SG*, 16 October 1871, n.p.; and *SG*, 1 January 1872, n.p.

70. For instance, see *SG*, 1 December 1871, n.p.

71. See *SG*, 28 April 1871, n.p.

72. For instance, see *SG*, 1 July 1871, n.p.; *SG*, 15 July 1871, n.p.; *SG*, 31 August 1871, n.p.; *SG*, 16 November 1871, n.p.; *SG*, 13 April 1872, n.p.; *SG*, 16 April 1877, p. 26; and *SG*, 26 March 1878, p. 19.

73. For instance, see *SG*, 16 April 1877, p. 25.

74. See J. M. Hoover, 'Cultivation of Rice in the Rejang', *SG*, 2 June 1919, p. 140.

75. For instance, see *SG*, 2 January 1918, p. 4; and *SG*, 1 July 1918, p. 160.

76. For instance, see *SG*, 16 October 1918, p. 272.

77. G. M. Goodall, *Report on Swamp* Padi *and Other Foodstuff in First Division of the Department of Agriculture for the Years 1928–29*, Kuching: Government Printing Office, 1929, p. 2.

78. Ibid., p. 8. On a hopeful note, the report concluded that 'in view of the great unused areas of fertile land, given an adequate agricultural population, Sarawak could probably become not only self-supporting but an exporter of rice'. Ibid.

79. Ibid.

80. See *SAR, 1929*, p. 22; *SG*, 1 November 1930, p. 279; *SG*, 2 January 1931, p. 11; *SG*, 1 April 1931, p. 83; *SAR, 1931*, p. 8; *SG*, 1 January 1932, p. 8; *SG*, 1 July 1932, p. 126; *SG*, 1 November 1933, p. 144; *SG*, 2 January 1936, p. 16; and *SG*, 1 April 1936, p. 87. However, a report of 1938 on *padi* growing considered it unnecessary to continue the policy of fostering *padi* settlements of foreign rice growers as a long-term measure in achieving rice self-sufficiency. Instead it recommended a greater reliance on the local inhabitants, such as the Dayaks, and the setting up of demonstration farms in effective rice-farming methods staffed by trained personnel. See C. L. Newman, *Report on* Padi *in Sarawak 1938*, Kuching: Government Printing Office, 1938, pp. 21 and 23.

81. See *SAR, 1936*, p. 3.

82. The Agricultural Improvement Fund provided for transportation of nineteen head of buffalo from Limbang to the Roman Catholic Mission farm at Ranan, and undertook to pay the wages of two Dusun drovers engaged by the Mission for instructional purposes in ploughing by buffaloes. See ibid.

83. 'Journal', in C. Brooke, *Ten Years*, Vol. II, p. 359. Emphasis added.

84. Ibid.

85. Apparently, this notion of Charles's of seeing a permanently settled Dayak farming community reveals an internal contradiction: on the one hand, Charles, like James, preferred the *status quo* rather than change, and he even contemplated having a longhouse of his own. On the other hand, he intended the Dayaks to give up their swidden farming lifestyle to become sedentary farmers. This objective was also expressed during Vyner's reign. Nevertheless, the process of transformation was a gradual one.

86. See Leonard Edwards and Peter W. Stevens, *Short Histories of the Lawas and Kanowit Districts*, Kuching: Borneo Literature Bureau, 1971, p. 137; and Father Bruggemann, 'The History of the Catholic Church in the Rejang 1882–1966', *Sarawak Teacher*, Special History Issue, 2 (1966): 19.

87. This was the 'buffalo scheme' initiated by Father Dunn that attempted to introduce wet-*padi* cultivation among the Dayaks in the Rejang. See John Rooney, *Khabar Gembira (The Good News): A History of the Catholic Church in East Malaysia and Brunei (1880–1976)*, London: Burns & Oates, 1981, pp. 162–3; *SG*, 1 June 1892, p. 100; *SG*, 2 January 1920, p. 2; and Bruggemann, 'Catholic Church in the Rejang', p. 19.

88. *SG*, 17 August 1908, p. 209.

89. See *SG*, 16 April 1918, p. 92; and *SG*, 16 July 1918, pp. 176–7.

90. Generally, Malays and Dayaks showed little interest in commercial agriculture. It could be said that only the Melanaus exhibited an inclination for this kind of livelihood with the cultivation and manufacture of sago. For instance, see 'Journal', in C. Brooke, *Ten Years*, Vol. II, pp. 354 and 356. However, it has been argued that deliberate Brooke policy assigned specific roles to the principal ethnic groups: the Malays for political and administrative posts, the Dayaks as the military arm of the Raj, and the Chinese in the economic sector. See Pringle, *Rajahs and Rebels*, pp. 323–5.

91. 'Agreement between HH The Rajah and Ken Wat of the firm of Ghee Soon', 11 February 1876, Agreement Book, Vol. I, SMA, Kuching.

92. See *SG*, 1 November 1899, p. 316; C. A. Lockard, 'Charles Brooke and the Foundations of the Modern Chinese Community in Sarawak, 1863–1917', *SMJ*, 19, 38–9 (1971): 93; and John M. Chin, *The Sarawak Chinese*, Kuala Lumpur: Oxford University Press, 1981, pp. 59–60. See also *SG*, 1 February 1900, p. 22.

93. See *SG*, 2 June 1902, p. 122.

94. Ibid.

95. See C. Brooke, *Ten Years*, Vol. II, p. 252.

96. For Hakka immigration to the Rejang, see *SG*, 2 January 1902, p. 1. For Henghuas, see *SG*, 17 July 1911, p. 136; *SG*, 16 July 1913, p. 165; and Lockard, 'Charles Brooke and Modern Chinese Community', pp. 98–9. It is interesting that, unlike the contracts made between the Brooke government and the Foochows and Cantonese, there was no similar arrangements with the Henghuas. The reason might be that the initial batch of 300 Henghua Methodists who arrived in 1911 from Fukien Province, China, was led by the Reverend Dr William Brewster, an American Methodist minister. Charles, perhaps, felt that it was unnecessary to have written contracts when dealing with a fellow European and a Methodist missionary. See Chin, *The Sarawak Chinese*, pp. 66–7 and 70, n. 13.

97. For the difficulties encountered by the Chinese Rejang pioneers, see Chiang Liu, 'Chinese Pioneers, AD 1900: The New Foochow Settlement', *SMJ*, 6, 6 (December 1955): 537–40; Lin Wen Tsung, 'The First Decade of New Foochow Colony in Sarawak', *Sarawak Teacher*, Special History Edition, 2, 2 (1966), p. 14; and Daniel Chew, *Chinese Pioneers on the Sarawak Frontier, 1841–1941*, Singapore: Oxford University Press, 1990, pp. 145–9.

98. *Padi* cultivation, however, was not abandoned altogether despite initial difficulties, and by the end of 1912 there were encouraging reports of Foochows and Henghuas resuming this activity. For instance, see *SG*, 1 November 1912, p. 245; *SG*, 1 March 1913, p. 51; and *SG*, 1 October 1914, p. 228.

99. See Craig Alan Lockard, *From Kampung to City: A Social History of Kuching, Malaysia, 1820–1970*, Ohio University Monographs in International Studies Southeast Asia Series, No. 75, Athens, 1987, p. 16.

100. For detailed accounts of the system of native customary land tenure, see A. J. N. Richards (comp.), *Sarawak Land Law and Adat*, 1961; A. J. N. Richards (comp.), *Dayak Adat Law in the Second Division*, 1963; A. J. N. Richards (comp.), *Dayak Adat Law in the First Division, Adat Bidayuh*, 1964; and *Report of the Land Committee, 1962*, 1963, all published by Government Printing Office, Kuching.

101. *Sarawak Government Orders, 1860–1891*, Kuching: Government Printing Office, Vol. I, p. 3.

102. Ibid.

103. Ibid., pp. 61 and 63; 21 January 1871, HH The Rajah's Order Book, Vol. I, SMA, Kuching; and *SG*, 24 January 1871, n.p.

104. *SG*, 3 January 1876, n.p. Emphasis added.

105. *Sarawak Government Orders, 1860–1891*, Vol. I, p. 343.

106. See 'Grants', 28 March 1876, ibid., p. 175; and 'Sago Land Regulations', April 1876, ibid., p. 177. See also 5 September 1871, HH The Rajah's Order Book, Vol. I, SMA, Kuching.

107. See 'Gambier and Pepper Order No. I', 1 September 1896, *Orders Which Have Not Since Been Cancelled, Issued by HH The Rajah of Sarawak or with His Sanction, from 1896 to 1898 Inclusive*, Kuching: Government Printing Office, 1900, Vol. IV, p. 14.

108. Baring-Gould and Bampfylde, *A History of Sarawak*, pp. 432–3.

109. *SG*, 29 November 1880, p. 59. Emphasis added.

110. *Sarawak as a Field for Planters, Improved and Enlarged, 1879*, Kuching: Sarawak Gazette Office, n.d., p. 5. The phrase 'Improved and Enlarged' meant that there was an earlier version, but to the extent of the writer's knowledge, none has been found. The 1879 version contains nine pages and was found wanting, prompting the publication of another in 1886, that was twice the length and gave 'an enlarged and more general account' of Sarawak and its resources. See *Sarawak as a Field for Planters, Improved and Enlarged, 1886*, Kuching: Sarawak Gazette Office, n.d.

111. *Sarawak as a Field for Planters, 1879*, p. 7.

112. The Agreement Books, in five large volumes, covering the years 1872 to 1922, presently kept at the Sarawak Museum Archives, Kuching, contain records of contracts, indentures, and agreements between the Brooke government and commercial companies as well as private individuals. See Bibliography, p. 366.

113. See 'Order No. VIII, 1894', *SG*, 1 August 1894, p. 116; and ibid., p. 119.

114. See *SG*, 16 April 1909, p. 85.

115. Emphasis added.

116. *SG*, 1 November 1910, p. 227. Emphasis added.

117. Ibid. Emphasis added.

118. See 17th Meeting, 2 August 1912, in *General Council 1867–1927*, p. 24.

119. See Chapter 7.

120. Pepper, strictly speaking, could not be classified as a 'new' crop in Borneo as it had been cultivated by Chinese in areas of present-day Brunei and Sabah and exported during pre-Brooke times. Nevertheless, during the Brooke period, pepper was being introduced in Sarawak as a commercial crop and promoted in conjunction with gambier cultivation. See G. Dalton, 'Pepper Growing in Upper Sarawak', *SMJ*, 1, 2 (February 1912): 53–4; and Chapter 3.

121. See *SG*, 4 January 1886, p. 2; *SG*, 3 January 1887, p. 2; *SG*, 2 January 1902, p. 1; *SG*, 4 January 1904, p. 1; and *SG*, 2 January 1913, p. 4.

122. For planter–sponsor contractual problems in the pepper industry, see Chapter 8.

123. See Jackson, *Sarawak*, p. 39.

124. For instance, see *SG*, 1 April 1891, p. 58; *SG*, 16 February 1914, p. 46; *SG*, 1 May 1916, p. 84; *SG*, 17 August 1908, p. 209; *SG*, 1 May 1924, p. 157; and *SG*, 1 December 1932, p. 205.

125. See Jackson, *Sarawak*, p. 99.

126. For instance, see *SG*, 4 January 1886, p. 6; *SG*, 1 February 1894, p. 22; *SG*, 16 January 1911, p. 2; and *SG*, 16 September 1913, p. 219.

127. Apparently only the Melanaus exhibited indifference to Para rubber, preferring to rely on their traditional sago palms. For instance, see *SG*, 1 July 1912, p. 147. But for a description of the 'planting craze' among other groups, see A. B. Ward, *Rajah's Servant*, Cornell University Southeast Asia Program Data Paper No. 61, Ithaca: Cornell University Press, 1966, p. 145.

128. *SAR, 1938*, p. 8.

129. See Chapter 9.

130. *SG*, 16 January 1972. Emphasis added.

131. *SG*, 15 March 1873, n.p.; and *SG*, 19 July 1879, p. 47. See also Baring-Gould and Bampfylde, *A History of Sarawak*, p. 432.

132. J. Brooke to Burdett Coutts, 7 February 1866, in Rutter, *Rajah Brooke and Baroness Burdett Coutts*, p. 258.

133. C. H. H. Wilsone to Sir James Brooke, 17 September 1864, Add MSS 22,427/41, WSRO, Chichester.

134. See J. Brooke to W. H. Read, 6 October 1865, Add MSS 22,427/49 WSRO, Chichester.

135. In Sarawak, rain falls on an average of 226 days in a year, and rainless months rarely occur. Such wet conditions are undoubtedly detrimental to sugar cane cultivation. For Sarawak's rainfall regime for the last quarter of the nineteenth century, see John Hewitt, 'Notes on Kuching Rainfall', *SG*, 2 February 1906, pp. 27–31; and *Rainfall Statistics of the British Borneo Territories (Sarawak–Brunei–North Borneo), 1896–1957*, compiled by the Department of Civil Aviation and Metereological Services, British Borneo Territories, September 1961, pp. 6–23. I would like to thank Dr G. E. D. Lewis for drawing my attention to the adverse climatic conditions in Sarawak for sugar cane cultivation.

136. For instance, during the late 1870s, an ambitious attempt was initiated by a Chinese entrepreneur who brought in 150 coolies to open up an estate in the Quop district for the cultivation of sugar cane and tapioca; but, without any apparent reason, his plans were aborted. See *SG*, 31 August 1878, p. 59; and *SG*, 16 January 1879, pp. 2 and 6.

137. *SG*, 19 February 1879, p. 14.

138. 'Notification No. VI, 1894', *SG*, 1 June 1894, p. 82.

139. *SG*, 13 March 1871, n.p.

140. *SG*, 15 March 1873, n.p. Emphasis added. See also *SG*, 7 January 1881, p. 1.

141. *SG*, 15 March 1873, n.p. Emphasis added.

142. *SG*, 7 January 1881, p. 1.

143. See *SG*, 1 April 1902, p. 59. See also Loh Chee Yin, 'Pieces from the Brooke Past—XVII: Matang Coffee Estate', *SG*, 30 September 1965, pp. 279–83. An attempt was made in early 1897 to sell the Matang Estate, obviously to cut losses, but there were no bidders, and it reverted to government. See *SG*, 1 April 1897, p. 64.

144. *SG*, 2 June 1890, p. 73. The sale of small parcels of suitable tobacco land was deemed 'advantageous to purchasers [rather] than that they should buy an immense tract of country, en bloc, a large part of which would naturally be unsuitable for tobacco'. Ibid., p. 74.

145. See *SG*, 10 October 1890, p. 126.

146. Much to the BCL's 'general relief', it was Charles himself, who decided to close the Lundu tobacco plantations, and did not insist strongly that the company assume control of them. See Longhurst, *The Borneo Story*, p. 61.

147. *SG*, 2 February 1891, p. 19.

148. Ibid.

149. See Chapter 9.

150. For indigo cultivation, see *SG*, 10 September 1870, n.p.; *SG*, 13 March 1871, n.p.; and *SG*, 17 May 1872, n.p. For tapioca, see *SG*, 31 August 1878, p. 59; *SG*, 16 January 1879, pp. 1 and 6; and *SG*, 16 January 1913, p. 23.

151. See *SG*, 1 July 1881, p. 51; *SG*, 1 December 1881, p. 108; *SG*, 1 September 1883, p. 82; and *SG*, 1 April 1887, pp. 53–4 and 55–6. Extracts from the bark of the cinchona tree is used in the manufacture of the drug known as quinine, a remedy for malaria.

152. See *SG*, 1 June 1891, p. 83.

153. See *SG*, 2 November 1891, p. 162; *SG*, 2 January 1892, p. 2; and *SG*, 1 November 1892, p. 197.

154. *SG*, 1 June 1894, p. 81.

155. See *SG*, 16 September 1908, p. 235.

156. *SG*, 1 December 1936, p. 302.

157. For instance, see Low, *Sarawak*, p. 55; and Beccari, *Wanderings*, p. 174.

158. See Edwards and Stevens, *Short Histories*, p. 117.

159. In fact, a government-commissioned investigation in 1938 on *padi* cultivation in the country concluded that the use of buffaloes in *padi* growing was in general unnecessary, as 'no advantage accrues from buffalo cultivation except on hard clay where water supply is deficient.' Newman, *Report on Padi*, p. 25.

160. *SG*, 17 June 1918, p. 143.

161. Goodall, *Report on Swamp Padi*, p. 2. Emphasis added. A notable exception was the case of Tanjong Purun at Lundu where Malay and Sebuyau Dayaks reaped the benefits of double-cropping. See ibid., p. 10.

162. 'Journal', C. Brooke, *Ten Years*, Vol. II, pp. 359–60.

163. *SG*, 30 March 1871, n.p.

164. See *SG*, 2 August 1875, n.p.

165. *SG*, 20 July 1877, p. 51.

166. See *SG*, 1 August 1885, p. 73; and *SG*, 1 January 1890, p. 3.

167. See Chapter 9.

168. See *SG*, 2 December 1935, p. 231.

169. For the interest displayed by European planters, especially those from Ceylon and India, for instance, see *SG*, 13 November 1878, p. 75; and *SG*, 16 January 1879, p. 6.

170. See 'Proposed Matang Planting Company "Limited"—Prospectus', *c.*1886, 916. 18. s. 2 Borneo Collections, Item 12, p. 1, RHL, Oxford.

171. Ibid., pp. 1–11.

172. These were Dahan Rubber Estates, Sarawak Rubber Estates, Nissa Shokai, Lawas (Sarawak) Rubber Estates Limited, and Rejang Estates Limited. See Reece, *The Name of Brooke*, pp. 53–4.

173. Emphasis added.

174. In the early 1890s, the *Gazette*, in supporting Charles's smallholding policy, deplored the granting of large land concessions as in the case of the action of the Sultan of Sambas. See *SG*, 1 November 1890, pp. 140–1; and *SG*, 2 February 1891, pp. 18–19.

175. It was argued that the high price of rice, owing to the fact that the bulk of it was imported, discouraged the influx of cheap Chinese labour to the country, consequently creating a labour shortage. See *SG*, 16 April 1877, p. 25. See also *SG*, 1 July 1881, p. 51.

176. For Javanese contract labourers employed in the BCL's estates, see *SG*, 16 February 1912, p. 45; *SG*, 17 August 1914, p. 182; P. Eaton, 'A History of Bau District', *SG*, 31 May 1967, p. 128; and Lockard, *From Kampung to City*, p. 86.

177. He suggested that the answer to any continuation of ramie planting had to be the introduction of 'suitable machinery' in order 'to save labour, money and time'. However, the proprietors considered the project a failure and withdrew altogether. See *SG*, 17 January 1910, p. 19.

178. For instance, see *SG*, 15 August 1876, p. 1; *SG*, 26 February 1878, p. 8; *SG*, 19 July 1879, p. 46; and *SG*, 1 February 1890, p. 18.

179. *SG*, 15 March 1873, n.p.

180. J. Brooke, *A Letter from Borneo*, pp. 14 and 15.

181. Jackson, *Sarawak*, pp. 25 and 29.

182. F. W. Roe (comp.), *The Natural Resources of Sarawak*, 2nd rev. edn., Kuching: Government Printing Office, 1952, p. 8. See also Jackson, *Sarawak*, p. 30.

1 Rajah Sir James Brooke (r. 1841–68). (Courtesy Sarawak Museum)

2 Rajah Sir Charles Antoni (Johnson) Brooke (r. 1868–1917). (Courtesy Sarawak Museum)

3 Rajah Sir Charles Vyner Brooke (r. 1917–41). (Courtesy Sarawak Museum)

4 Kuching in 1840. (Courtesy Sarawak Museum)

5 The Upper Baram in the early 1910s. (From Hose and McDougall, *The Pagan Tribes of Borneo*, 1912)

6 Mangrove swamps along the coast. (Courtesy Sarawak Museum)

7 A Kayan of the Balui lifting dammar on to his boat. (Courtesy Sarawak Museum)

8 Kayans working gutta-percha in the Baram, *c.*1912. (From Hose and McDougall, *The Pagan Tribes of Borneo*, 1912)

9 Penans collecting camphor crystals. (From Hose and McDougall, *The Pagan Tribes of Borneo*, 1912)

10 Ibans haggling over the price of old Chinese jars, *c.*1902. (From Furness, *The Home Life of Borneo Headhunters, Its Festivals and Folklore,* 1902)

11 Ong Tiang Swee (1864–1950), the most prominent and influential Hokkien during the reigns of Rajah Charles and Rajah Vyner. (Courtesy Sarawak Museum)

12 A row of Chinese shophouses in Kuching, *c.*1904. (From Beccari, *Wanderings in the Great Forests of Borneo*, 1904)

13 The Kuching Chinese General Chamber of Commerce (KCGCC). (Courtesy Sarawak Museum)

14 A Chinese bazaar at Claude Town (Marudi), *c*.1902. (Furness, *The Home Life of Borneo Headhunters, Its Festivals and Folklore*, 1902)

15 A Foochow shopkeeper dealing with Meluan Dayak customers. (Courtesy Sarawak Museum)

16 The courtroom in Baram Fort, *c.*1912. (From Hose and McDougall, *The Pagan Tribes of Borneo*, 1912)

17 A Chinese boat trader on the Bawan River near Kanowit. (Courtesy Sarawak Museum)

18 Shifting cultivation of hill *padi* by Dayak farmers near Kanowit. (Courtesy Sarawak Museum)

19 Transporting antimony ore by pony carts, *c.*1870s. (Courtesy Sarawak Museum)

20 Mining activities of the BCL in Upper Sarawak, *c.*1880s. (Courtesy Sarawak Museum)

21 A gold working in Bau, *c.*1890s. (Courtesy Sarawak Museum)

22 The BCL's Tai Parit gold-mine at Bau. (From Mullen, *The Story of Sarawak*, 1967)

23 Miri Oil Well No. 1. (Courtesy Sarawak Museum)

24 A Chinese smallholder harvesting pepper. (Courtesy Sarawak Museum)

25 A Foochow mother and her young daughter working a rubber roller. (Courtesy Sarawak Museum)

26 A Hakka woman market gardener on the outskirts of Lawas. (Courtesy Sarawak Museum)

27 Malay fishermen and their catch. (Courtesy Sarawak Museum)

28 Iban longboats at Nanga Pais, Skrang River. (Courtesy Sarawak Museum)

29 Transportation of logs in the roadless interior of Sarawak's jungle. (Courtesy Sarawak Museum)

30 *Bulan*, one of the railway engines of the Sarawak Government Railway. (From Mullen, *The Story of Sarawak*, 1967)

31 Ludvig Verner Helms (1825–1918), the first manager of the BCL in Sarawak (From Helms, *Pioneering in the Far East*, 1882)

32 Wong Nai Siong (1849–1924), the founder of 'New Foochow'. (From Cooper, *Men of Sarawak*, 1968)

6
Infrastructure Development

THE development of infrastructure in transport and communication only began to take shape during Charles's reign in order to facilitate trade and commerce. Particular attention was given to the improvement of the carrying trade between Sarawak and Singapore as well as coastal shipping, and to a lesser extent, internal riverine traffic. Focus was also directed on road and rail transport, with greater emphasis accorded to road building during Vyner's rule. Although civil aviation was a post-Brooke accomplishment, landing grounds were constructed for strategic purposes. The expansion of telecommunications and the growth of banking facilities were effected. Development was slow and inadequate, particularly in the construction of roads and the provision of port facilities because geographical factors led to high costs. In addition, the road-building programme suffered from the ongoing debate about its utility over river transport which had hitherto served the majority of the population.

The Provision of Transport

Water-borne Transport

Rivers and Streams: The Arteries of Internal Trade

Settlements grew on the banks of rivers and streams while communities were established and flourished on the estuaries and along the coastal strip. Kuching and Sibu are typical inland river ports. Transportation using rivers was the traditional mode of intercourse but it was often slow and difficult. Sandbars at river mouths, mud banks, the shallowness in the lower courses of rivers, and swift currents, tested to the utmost the skills of the boatmen. None the less, the notable absence of roads throughout the country, apart from localized urban networks, made rivers the indispensable mode of transport and the essential means of communication.

The Carrying Trade

The carrying trade along the north-western Bornean coast and upriver commerce had long been the province of Malay *nakhodah* until the establishment of the Brooke Raj and the eventual domination by Chinese merchants and traders. Initially, James ran his own schooner, the *Royalist*, to Singapore, more as a mail-boat than for commercial cargo, and later, when the *Swift* was purchased in early 1841, it served in a similar capacity. The Kuching–Singapore run was irregular, for the *Royalist*, in particular, was often dispatched to Brunei on political errands or to Sambas, in both instances as a 'reminder to their inhabitants that Sarawak had become a power in the land'.[1] James's main priority was the acquisition of a man-of-war to eliminate coastal raiding. The BCL's steamer, *Sir James Brooke*, which arrived at the height of the Chinese uprising of 1857 and helped quell the troubles, was a commercial carrier of the country's exports as well as its supply ship, representing a lifeline to the outside world.

Initially Brooke government ships possessed dual functions, primarily to carry out administrative work in linking the various outstations with Kuching, and to Singapore as a mail run, and, to a lesser extent, as cargo carriers for trade goods and supplies. The government maintained a small but expanding fleet of steamers and launches of varying sizes for such purposes, including colliers for the coal-mines.[2] Charles proudly noted in 1913 that 'there are six steam Vessels belonging to Government of from 50 to 300 tons employed in Government service'.[3]

As trade increasingly flourished during the more peaceful reign of Charles and with the greater participation of Chinese merchants in commerce, more private, mostly Chinese-owned, vessels assumed the responsibilities of the carrying trade both along the coast and the main river systems.[4] Government steamers, then, devoted more attention to carrying out administrative work, a greater part of which was conveying officers from one outpost to another in the course of their duties.

In the upriver regions non-motorized, small, hand-paddled native craft were the main carriers of trade goods and people. Malay and Chinese boat hawkers travelled for considerable distances to inland settlements to conduct their trade. The sound of outboard motors on the interior waterways was barely heard until the late 1930s,[5] and the impact of such motors became significant only during the post-Brooke years when they 'revolutionize[d] travel in interior Sarawak'.[6]

The Singapore and Sarawak Steamship Company, 1875

Up to 1875 Brooke government steamers maintained communication along the coast and a few inland river ports, whereas Chinese and native boats covered the internal trade. The conveyance of the country's export products to Singapore and the handling of imports were left entirely in the hands of the BCL. By the mid-1870s, with flourishing trade creating a pressing demand for cargo space, Charles entrusted the newly constituted Sarawak Chamber of Commerce to set up a private shipping line. Thus, in July 1875 the Singapore and Sarawak Steamship Company (SSSCo) was born.[7]

The majority of its financiers were the prominent Kuching Chinese merchants, particularly the sago flour exporters. The BCL was also a shareholder and provided its management. The *Royalist*, purchased from the Sarawak government, became the first vessel of the SSSCo, later to be joined by the *Rajah Brooke*, *Ranee*, and others. The main sector of operation was the Kuching–Singapore cargo run. When Charles embarked on his programme to encourage the opening of gambier and pepper plantations by Chinese entrepreneurs, arrangements were made with the SSSCo for the conveyance of *kangchew* and coolies between Singapore and Kuching.[8]

The domination by the SSSCo of the carrying trade between Kuching and Singapore, particularly in the sago trade, made it a very profitable concern 'with shareholders securing between 40–50 per cent. dividends each year'.[9] This monopoly made the SSSCo a power unto itself; it made trips whenever it suited its purpose without maintaining a regular timetable of operations. The BCL capitalized on its management of the SSSCo's day-to-day operations by giving priority to its own cargoes and those of its associates, much to the vexation of other merchants. The situation became more pressing after the loss in July 1896 of the *Rajah Brooke*. Instead of replacing it,[10] the SSSCo chartered a steamer, *Vorwarts*, a larger vessel with a carrying capacity of over 1,000 tons which necessitated the reduction in the number of voyages. The highly unsatisfactory practice of sailing only when all cargo space was utilized, no doubt profitable to the SSSCo itself, was the cause of frustration among the mercantile community.

Charles was strongly opposed to such a situation and, during a meeting in September 1896, proposed the establishment of another shipping line running two smaller vessels, each undertaking 'two trips a month to the very great advantage of traders' as well as to

the mail service.[11] However, this proposition attracted no investors. Meanwhile, a barrage of complaints and expressions of dissatisfaction appeared in the columns of the *Gazette*.[12]

Towards the end of 1901, the SSSCo's new steamer, *Rajah of Sarawak*, commenced operation. The following year, an alternative shipping line, launched by a group of Chinese entrepreneurs, offered competition with the running of two steamers to Singapore.[13] But unhappily, after only a year of intense rivalry, this smaller Chinese company was forced to close for want of funds.[14] This brave venture 'effected one purpose', which was 'to prove that two steamers were required for the [Kuching–Singapore] trade'.[15] Consequently, the SSSCo acquired another steamer, *Kuching*, and to a certain extent improved its services, thereby diffusing adverse public criticism.

The arrival in Kuching of the steamer *Dr Hans Jurg Kiaer* from Hong Kong in mid-1901 raised prospects of the possibility of opening a trade route with the British Colony.[16] However, all hopes were dashed for, apart from this one appearance, the Hong Kong ship never made a return visit as 'probably it was not thought good business'.[17]

Attempts were also made by local Chinese shipping companies in the Rejang ports to sail direct to Singapore, bypassing Kuching altogether. In 1911 it was reported that a Chinese-owned steamer, *Flevo*, operated 'with great regularity' between Sibu and Singapore.[18] Several followed this example.[19] Cantonese logging companies in the Rejang shipped their timber from Sibu direct to Hong Kong and to the Chinese mainland.[20]

Coastal and Internal Shipping

At the turn of the century when the BCL's extractive industries in Upper Sarawak were flourishing, it invested in another steamer to supplement its existing vessel, *Nyamok*.[21] Complementing this move, a group of Chinese entrepreneurs purchased a stern-wheel steamer for upriver use to cater for the ever prosperous and increasing Chinese mining and agricultural communities of this district.[22]

Meanwhile, Charles was striving to develop coastal and upriver trade by running steamers to link the river ports with Kuching. Purchases of new vessels for this domestic traffic were frequently made. In 1908, as a means of improving and expanding internal trade, Charles insisted that the SSSCo serve the coast stations as well in order to lift the burden from the government vessels.[23] The government, however, did not leave coastal and internal shipping

entirely in the hands of the SSSCo, but maintained steamer services of its own. In 1916 the government decided to reassume responsibility for coastal shipping as the performance of the SSSCo proved to be wanting.[24] Accordingly, arrangements were made whereby the *Adeh*[25] and the *L'Aubaine* covered the northern coast stations while the SSSCo's *Gladys* and *Sarawak* served the Rejang ports and Miri.[26] This move undoubtedly improved and further developed the coastal and interior trade of the country.

The Sarawak Steamship Company, 1919

In 1919 a consortium of leading Kuching Chinese *towkay* led by the Hokkien, Ong Tiang Swee, launched a take-over bid of the SSSCo. It bought out the BCL's shares, acquired all the assets of this shipping company, and liquidated it. In its place a new shipping line, the Sarawak Steamship Company (SSCo), was inaugurated with its head office in Kuching.[27] In less than three years of operation a satisfactory state of affairs was noted, with vessels making regular runs to Singapore while others serviced the coastal and inland river ports.[28]

This gave some concern to the Singapore-based Straits Steamship Company, which since 1914 had entered the coastal shipping business of the territory of British North Borneo.[29] In order to secure its own position, the company decided that a takeover was necessary. The opportunity came during the Depression when it bought out the debentures held by the Brooke government in the SSCo. The acquisition was effected in July 1931, and the SSCo became a subsidiary of the Straits Steamship Company.[30] With greater co-ordination of operations between the company and its subsidiaries—the SSCo and the Sabah Steamship Company—a more efficient and reliable system of coastal and upriver communication was effected on the north-western Bornean coast (see Map 6.1).

Port Facilities

The main anchorage in Sarawak throughout the Brooke period was the inland port town and administrative centre of Kuching. Like the second most important port town of Sibu, it was accessible only to medium-sized ocean vessels with a maximum draught of 4.8 metres (16 feet).[31] Apart from Miri, an open sea port, all the other anchorages of the country were inland river ports with the furthest from the river mouth being Kapit, 224 kilometres (140 miles) up the Rejang.

MAP 6.1
Coastal and Inland Shipping in Sarawak by the Sarawak Steamship Company and Its Parent Concern, the Straits Steamship Company, *c.*1930s

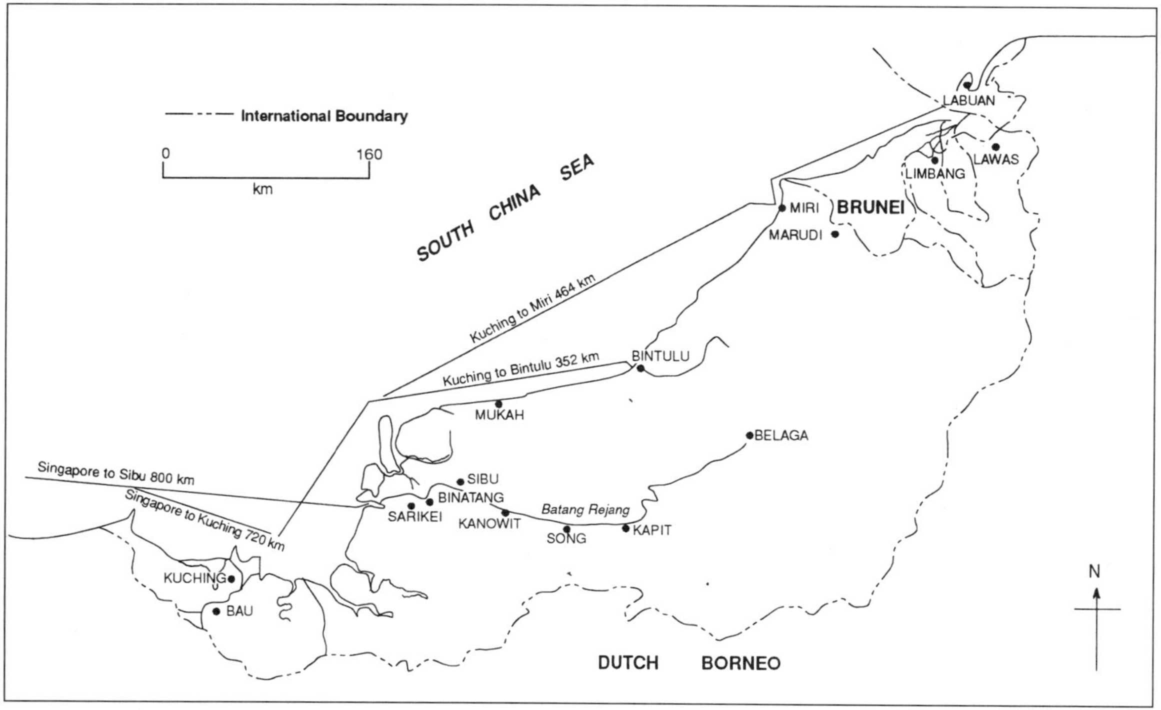

Source: After Tregonning, *Home Port Singapore*, p. 122.

Kuching boasted four good wharves ranging from 39 metres (130 feet) to over 240 metres (800 feet). Warehouses and godowns, cranes for loading and unloading, workshops, and a dry dock were the facilities available. Plans for the construction of a dry dockyard were mooted by Charles in 1901, and excavation work commenced in late 1908; in May 1912 the Kuching Dry Dock (later renamed Brooke Dockyard) was officially opened.[32] Located adjacent to it were other related facilities, including a slipway for vessels of 12 metres (40 feet) in length and 3.9 metres (13 feet) beam, and a machine workshop for general engineering, repairs, and maintenance work.

At Kuching along the river front, where the Main Bazaar is now located, an embankment was constructed in the mid-1890s which enabled small native craft to land their cargoes rapidly and efficiently.[33] A retaining wall was added, stretching from Pengkalan Batu to the end of Gambier Road.[34]

Lighthouses were built along the coast at strategic points; the prominent ones being Tanjong (Cape) Datu at the extreme west, Tanjong (Cape) Sirik in the delta of the Rejang, and Tanjong Baram (or Baram Point) at the eastern tip, close to the Brunei border. Markers were also emplaced at the entrance of the major rivers and bar crossings to indicate the depth of the channels.[35]

The Development of Land Transport

On the High Road

A significant feature of the infrastructure of Brooke Sarawak was the absence of a permanent, all-weather road system between the major population centres. Road networks were localized, radiating from the main townships, namely the capital Kuching, the mining town of Bau, the river port of Sibu, and the oil-rich town of Miri. Only a limited number of main roads within these urban centres were all-weather, metalled roads suitable for motorized traffic.

Unsurfaced earth roads, which transformed into rivers of mud during the rainy season, linked Kuching to Lundu, Bau to Serian, Sarikei to Saratok, Oya to Mukah, and Lawas to Trusan. A path through the jungle connected the Baram valley to the Limbang.[36] There were numerous footpaths and rough jungle tracks used by the indigenous peoples for overland travel.[37]

The district of Upper Sarawak was the only area, apart from the major urban centres, to have a system of roads, although not all were metalled. Roads connected Paku to Buan, Bau to Buan, Paku to Jambusan, and Bau to Tundong. The so-called ‘Poak Road’

linked the BCL's Poak Concession of gambier, pepper, and rubber plantations near the Staat River to Bau. Bau was also connected to Lidah Tanah, and a road ran from Siniawan to Batu Kitang (the crossing place, via a bridge, of the left branch of the Sarawak River).[38] It was, therefore, possible to travel by road from Kuching to Bau, and from there to proceed and tour the main mining centres and agricultural plantations of the district.

In the mid-1890s, a Chinese entrepreneur had introduced the man-powered jinrickshaw as a mode of public transportation, and when the number of these vehicles increased, regulations were issued for their operation.[39] The motor car and motor cycle both made their début in 1907.[40] A motor lorry service, the forerunner of the present-day bus service, was operated by an enterprising Chinese in 1912. It ran along Rock Road to the outskirts of Kuching town, thereby providing a means of transport to the Chinese agricultural community.[41]

The most important road-building project was the proposed construction of a trunk road to connect Kuching with Simanggang, a distance of over 160 kilometres (100 miles).[42] Apart from improving land communications, it was also aimed at making more land available to the increasing Chinese population.[43] However, the work which commenced in the late 1920s suffered from a multitude of problems.[44] A decade later, on the eve of the outbreak of the Pacific War, only 64 kilometres (40 miles), extending to Serian, had been completed.

In fact, by 1938, a mere 1094.4 kilometres (684 miles) of roads existed in the whole country, with less than 10 per cent of these of the Macadamized all-weather variety.[45] It was clear that road building was not high on the Brooke agenda.

Charles's Railway

In the mid-1890s, Charles decided that Sarawak should have a railway. He believed that a railroad running from Kuching to the south into the hinterland where there were no inland waterways would serve to open the interior to economic prosperity.[46] However, it was another decade before his plans came to fruition. Equipment and materials, including locomotives, were ordered and imported from abroad.[47] Work began on the railroad, and by 1913 tracks were laid to the 6th Mile while survey work had been completed to the 10th Mile.[48] By early 1915 passenger traffic was

opened to the 7th Mile, charging 2 cents per mile, and proved to be a delightful spectacle.[49] By 1916, service was extended to the 10th Mile (see Map 6.2). Fares were minimal, 'being as little as 3 cents between stations and 20 cents for the full journey to 10th mile'.[50]

The bulk of the traffic, apart from joy rides, was from the Chinese market gardening community living on the outskirts who used the railway to transport their produce of fresh vegetables and poultry for sale in Kuching town. It was also, in part, for these farmers that the decision was taken to extend the railhead to the 20th Mile instead of halting at the 10th Mile, as had been originally proposed.[51] Accordingly, survey work was conducted and went beyond the 20th Mile, reaching the 27th Mile by early 1918.[52] In fact, Charles hoped that his railway would someday extend to Simanggang, 160 kilometres to the east, but the furthest it reached was only to the 13th Mile in 1925.[53]

Vyner continued the running of this railway and expanded its operations by adding a night service in mid-1920.[54] The railway continued to operate throughout the 1920s and the early 1930s despite the construction of a road running parallel to it. 'The building of [this] road killed the Railway,' it was argued, 'as a host of ramshackle buses appeared on the scene' and undercut the rail fares.[55] As part of Vyner's austerity plan during the Depression, the railway service was discontinued altogether in March 1933, thereby closing a chapter in the country's history of land transport.[56] Altogether, in 'its lifetime as a fully fledged railway it lost $1,063,760—a not inconsiderable figure for those days'.[57]

Airstrips and Landing Grounds

The development of civil aviation was a post-Brooke accomplishment. Some work was nevertheless carried out during the period as interest within military circles in the strategic importance of Sarawak was heightened during the mid-1930s, and plans were laid for the construction of airstrips in the country.[58] In 1935 preliminary work began in the selection of sites, namely at Kuching, Oya, Mukah, Bintulu, and Miri.[59] Work began on the construction of the Kuching, Miri, and Bintulu landing strips, but was discontinued at Bintulu in October 1938.[60] In September 1938, the Kuching Landing Ground situated at Bukit Stabar (7th Mile) was completed.[61]

MAP 6.2
Sarawak Government Railway, 1916

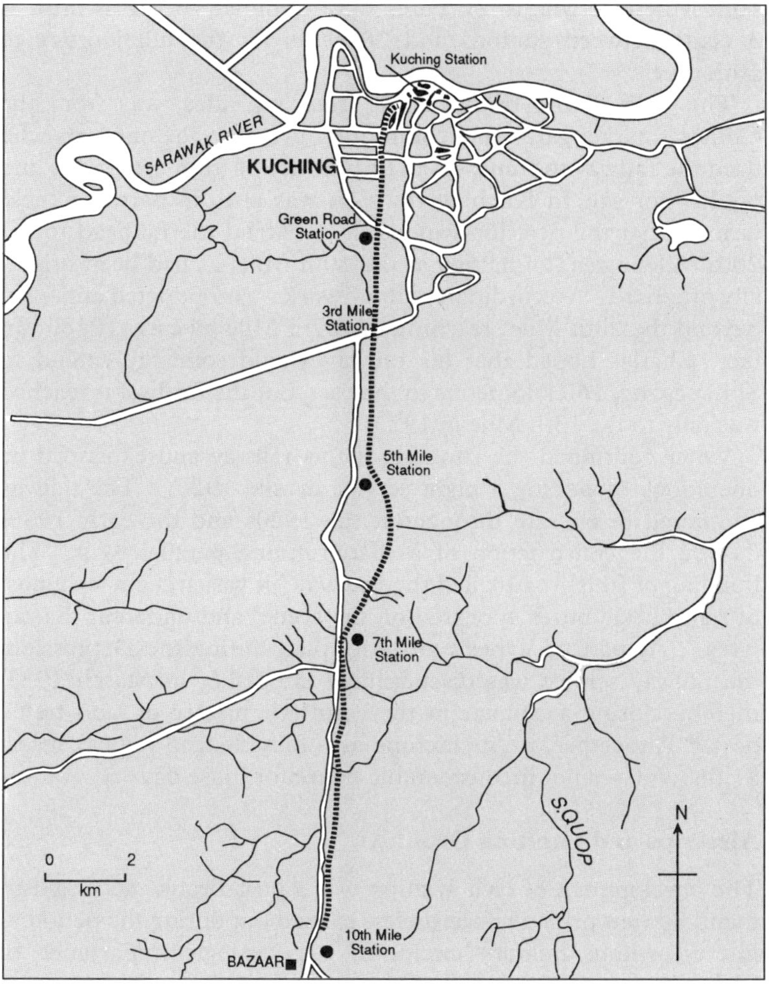

Source: After Pollard, *Kuching: Past and Present*, p. 48.

Problems Faced in the Development of Transport

Obstacles to the Development of a Country-wide Road Network

The notable absence of a system of roads linking the major population centres owed as much to geographical and natural causes as to Brooke policy. The terrain of Sarawak posed an almost insurmountable challenge to road builders.[62] The swampy coastal plain required considerable drainage and reclamation work before any road construction could be undertaken (see Map 1.3). Such work required both time and expertise to accomplish, but what was more crucial, it involved substantial expenditure. The numerous river systems which dissected the country in an east to west and south-east to north-west direction meant the construction of many bridges as essential linkages in a nation-wide road network.[63] The high rainfall with torrential downpours not only disrupted road building in the short-run, but more importantly, roads had to be well-built with an all-weather surface to withstand the ravages of the heavy precipitation. Furthermore, the acute shortage of good roadstone impeded road construction programmes.[64] In short, the physical obstacles to road building made it a highly expensive undertaking, not to mention the heavy maintenance costs.

In addition to the expense, there was ambivalence on the part of the Brooke administrators regarding the provision of land transport *vis-à-vis* the utilization of the existing waterways. One school of thought in this controversy objected to further road development on the grounds that

> Malays will never leave the river sides and it is difficult to see how Dyaks can be induced to leave their homes to live along a high road in the pursuit of agriculture.
>
> Sarawak is a very sparsely populated country, and high roads, unless an incentive to agriculture, are useless. We have no Agricultural or Industrial centres which need high roads or communications. The many rivers will always be the natural highways of Sarawak as they always have been.[65]

Refuting such claims, is this *Gazette* editorial of February 1873 which advocated the beneficial effects of roads to the native inhabitants.

> With regard to roadmaking, there is no necessity to bring forward arguments in support of its importance in many districts, where all are satisfied of its utility.... It also occurs to us, hearing as we do continually of the abject poverty and destitution which prevail in large sections of the native

population, that it would be no great hardship to these people to be set to work for moderate wages, in which food might be included, on roads which they would afterwards have to keep in repair. A tribe might often be so saved from semi-starvation, and the roads would afford favourable lines both for bringing them within reach of the principal Government stations, and for making their own farms, or inducing others, more industrious than themselves, to settle for agricultural and trading purposes among them, or their labour might be accepted partly in lieu of revenue.[66]

Charles, apparently deterred by the high cost involved, preferred to concentrate on urban networks, particularly in Kuching. But Vyner pronounced his commitment to 'the construction of roads not only round Kuching but at Outstations as well' which would contribute to the development of agriculture and trade.[67] Furthermore, he envisaged a 'definite policy of road making laid down for each Division and steadily worked to year by year', while at the same time he reiterated the benefits of job opportunities for the people, especially the Dayaks, that road construction would afford.[68] However, neither Dayaks nor unemployed Chinese coolies were keen to work on public road-building projects.[69]

A start was made in 1929 for an arterial road system linking Kuching with Simanggang. This major road building project had to be temporarily suspended during the years of the Depression. However, work, it seemed, did not resume when the economy recovered in the mid-1930s. It appears that the anti-road lobby had successfully persuaded Vyner to adopt their viewpoint for it is inconceivable that the programme was shelved owing to inadequate funds as the country had by then recovered fully from the Depression.[70]

The Problems of Coastal and Inland Shipping

The 720-kilometre Sarawak coast is devoid of good, sheltered, natural harbours. Accessibility to the two main ports of Kuching and Sibu was restricted to medium-sized ocean-going vessels (Table 6.1). Such restrictions undoubtedly limited their potential.

What was more, a major obstacle to shipping was the occurrence of sand bars at the entrance of most rivers, which, in some cases, extended for several kilometres.[71] A bar lies at the Muara Tebas entrance to the Sarawak River where the port of Kuching lies 28.8 kilometres (18 miles) upriver. This bar crossing has a minimum depth of 5.1 metres (17 feet). The Rejang also has a bar with a minimum depth of 4.8 metres (16 feet) whereas the one at Lawas permits navigation only at half this depth. However, the

TABLE 6.1
Ports of Sarawak, *c.*late 1940s (feet)

	Vessels			
Port	*Draft*	*Length*	*Wharf*	*Depth L. W.*
Kuching	16	300	191	12
"			222	8
"			127	6
"			809	4
"			40	3
At Pending	20	450	–	–
Binatang	16	280	144	16
Sarikei	16	280	100	15
Sibu	16	280	140	16
"			100	8
"			140	5
Miri	Open sea anchorage		–	–
Lundu	8	100	–	–
Simunjan	12	220	–	–
Lingga	12	220	–	–
Simanggang	6	80	–	–
Betong	6	50	–	–
Kabong	6	50	–	–
Mukah	8	120	–	–
Oya	8	100	–	–
Balingian	6	60	–	–
Tatau	7	100	–	–
Bintulu	8.5	150	100	5
Niah	5	40	–	–
Sibuti	5	40	–	–
Baram	7.5	200	–	–
Limbang	8	200	150	16
Lawas	8	200	20	6

Source: Hepburn, *Handbook of Sarawak*, p. 171.

worst obstacle belongs to the 3-kilometre long bar at the mouth of the Baram which affords a maximum depth at high water of 2.4 metres (8 feet); coupled often with a rough sea, it made this river entrance the most difficult crossing. The flat-bottomed, paddle-wheel steamer, *Adeh*, was commissioned specifically to tackle this problem bar but failed to overcome it.[72] There are no records to indicate any attempt at dredging the river's entrance. The high cost of such a measure, no doubt, dissuaded its implementation.

The mouth of the Batang Lupar, which is the approach to the inland river port of Simanggang, suffers from shallow water of a mere 2.1 metres (7 feet) depth at low water. In addition, it possesses a dangerous tidal bore that 'runs up river on Spring tides starting some miles above Lingga which is five miles from the mouth'.[73]

Rapids in the upper reaches of rivers test to the utmost the skill and experience of the boat captain. Disastrous encounters with protruding rocks were not uncommon, particularly in the Upper Rejang.

The absence of good, sheltered harbours meant that coastal travel, especially in small native craft, was inadvisable during the six-month season of the north-east monsoon from October to March when heavy rains, strong winds, and high seas were the rule. Shipping was restricted to large vessels that could withstand the stormy weather and rough seas. Such weather conditions, which in effect almost paralysed coastal shipping for the greater part of the year, adversely affected trade and communication.

These physical and climatic drawbacks not only limited trade but also raised tariffs on goods in transit because of the high risks involved. The development of trade at Marudi in the Baram typified the difficulties encountered in coastal and inland shipping during the Brooke period.[74]

Development of Communications

Telegraph, Telephone, and Wireless

In early 1893 negotiations were underway for the laying of a telegraph cable from Hong Kong to Singapore via Labuan, and by the following year work by the Eastern Extension Telegraph Company had begun.[75] Sarawak was able to tap this facility through Labuan, although it proved most cumbersome.[76] Within the country, telegraphic communication was only possible by the late 1890s,

between Kuching and the district of Upper Sarawak.[77] Apart from this link there was no telegraphic service until wireless telegraphy was introduced in 1916.

Meanwhile, in 1899 a telephone line, was installed, linking Kuching with Upper Sarawak.[78] By the 1920s most of the main outstations had their own local telephone networks as well as connections with neighbouring outposts and Kuching.[79] Undoubtedly this was a boost to business and trade and facilitated administration.

Charles engaged a French firm, the Anglo French Wireless Company, for the installation of a wireless network.[80] Wireless stations were established at Simunjan, Sibu, and Miri, and all three were in turn connected with Kuching.[81] By late 1916, installation work had been completed, and on 5 January 1917 the first message was transmitted. Three months later, the service was opened to the public and was well-received, especially in the Chinese business circles.[82] Towards the end of 1919, wireless communication was effected with British North Borneo and Labuan via Miri.[83] Vyner was determined that the whole country should be connected by wireless communication.[84] During the 1920s wireless telegraphy was extended to more outposts; by 1928, twenty-one wireless stations were dotted throughout the country.[85]

Experiments in wireless telephony were conducted in the early and mid-1920s, and by 1932 the inhabitants of Kuching could listen to the news on the British Broadcasting Corporation (BBC) services from London.[86] The Sarawak Broadcasting Service was inaugurated in September 1939 with broadcasts in three languages—English, Chinese, and Malay.[87]

Banking Facilities

Although James informed Burdett Coutts in a letter of 1863 of his plans for the 'establishment of a Sarawak Bank', no mention was made of it thereafter.[88] Banking facilities were afforded by the BCL which acted as the Brooke government's unofficial banker.[89] Chinese businesses relied on their own system of finance and credit that extended from the banking district of downtown Singapore to bazaar shophouses in Sarawak's remote upriver districts. This Chinese 'banking' system was a wholly Chinese preserve, and generally operated along dialect and clan lines.

No similar credit or banking facilities existed for the indigenous people; the little trading in which they were involved tended to be

by barter transactions. As the cash economy gradually penetrated native communities and the demand for jungle products increased from the late 1860s, a notable change was evident among the indigenous population.

While the coastal Melanaus and Malays tended to fall into debt with Chinese bazaar shopkeepers, the reverse was the case with the Dayaks. The proximity of the Malays and Melanaus to towns and bazaars with their attractive array of consumer goods made them more prone to resort to credit and more willing to incur large debts to meet social obligations. Indebtedness to Chinese shopkeepers was not an uncommon phenomenon among them.[90] On the other hand, the Dayaks' induction to the cash economy assumed a different mode. The Dayaks, accomplished collectors of jungle produce, took advantage of the boom prices and accumulated a reasonable amount of cash, which they in turn loaned out, with interest after the fashion of bankers, to Chinese traders, or even to bazaar *towkay* who faced insolvency.[91] Chinese indebtedness to their Dayak 'bankers', though a refreshing change from the typical native indebtedness to Chinese in other South-East Asian lands, was of some concern to the Brooke authorities. It must have been a common occurrence to have prompted Charles to insist, with the intention of safeguarding Dayak interest, that all such loan transactions should be registered with the government by creditor as well as debtor, failing which, both parties 'will be liable to [a] term of imprisonment or heavy penalty'.[92]

Private banking institutions only made their appearance during the first two decades of the twentieth century.[93] The first locally established private bank was the Cantonese-managed Kwong Lee Bank which started operations in 1909 at Kuching and had an office in Sibu.[94] This was followed by the Hokkien- and Chaoan-controlled Sarawak Overseas Chinese Banking Corporation.[95] The third to open was the Bian Chiang Bank, a Hokkien concern.[96] Another Hokkien establishment was the Wah Tat Bank, a small, privately owned, family-managed organization with a single office in Sibu. Apparently it functioned more like a moneylender than a full-fledged banking institution.[97] Then in 1924, responding to Vyner's request, the British-owned Chartered Bank of India, Australia and China established a branch in Kuching; it was described as 'a very welcome increase in trading facilities generally'.[98] It was not surprising that Chinese banking institutions outnumbered Western concerns as the bulk of commerce and trade was in the hands of the Chinese. None the less, the Chartered Bank,

despite its late entry and competition from local Chinese rivals, performed reasonably well.[99]

As a measure to encourage savings among the people, Vyner instituted the Post Office Savings Bank in 1924.[100] Gradually over the years this facility extended to the interior districts. However, this government-sponsored bank faced stiff competition from the customary 'banking' the Dayaks had with the local Chinese traders. An official report of 1926 voiced this unfavourable state of affairs: 'The temptation to Dayaks to "invest" their savings at a high rate of interest is at present too great to allow them to take the safer course of investing at 3 per cent [with the Post Office Savings Bank].'[101] By 1938 the amount credited to depositors' accounts was close to $650,000. This represented the savings of its more than 2,000 depositors.[102] Evidently it had made an impact only on a mere fraction of the total population which then stood at nearly half a million.

Conclusion

In typical Brooke fashion, the development of infrastructure in Sarawak was cautiously slow. There was nothing significant in this development during the time of James apart from the establishment of a regular shipping link with Singapore, which undoubtedly boosted the country's commerce. The development of infrastructure largely occurred during the rajahship of Charles, who characteristically monitored its every progress: from initiating the creation of a shipping line and the construction of a railroad to the introduction of wireless communication.

It was a surprising departure for Charles to initiate and personally oversee the introduction of such 'new-fangled' contraptions like the telephone, telegraph, and wireless.[103] He was known to have refused a drive in an automobile,[104] yet he endeavoured to have metalled roads around the capital specifically suited for such vehicles. Far from being a contradiction to his conservative outlook, the acceptance of such modern developments was a clear manifestation of Charles's practical-mindedness. His pragmatism dictated that Sarawak should be abreast of current developments in infrastructure facilities, thereby ensuring that the country would not be in any way handicapped, in particular with regard to its trade and commercial intercourse.

Fittingly Vyner improved and expanded on his father's work, and on his part introduced facilities like electricity and an air service

(though abortive) further to integrate Sarawak in the fast-changing modern world of the 1920s and 1930s.

In spite of efforts by the Brookes to improve sea and land communications, formidable physical obstacles and natural disadvantages impeded their progress. The lack of deep-water, sheltered anchorages along the coast made it necessary to rely on inland river ports. However, bars and tidal bores at river mouths and rapids in the upper reaches made inland shipping a hazardous enterprise. The swampy coastal plain, the existence of numerous rivers criss-crossing the entire country, and the acute shortage of roadstones, made the construction of a country-wide road network a difficult and expensive undertaking. Furthermore, the conflicting arguments between the road lobby and the apologists of water-borne communication worked against a positive land transport policy.

1. Gertrude L. Jacob, *The Raja of Sarawak: An Account of Sir James Brooke, KCB, LL D, Given Chiefly through Letters and Journals*, 2 vols., London: Macmillan, 1876, Vol. I, p. 197.

2. Coal from the government Simunjan mines was conveyed by two colliers, the brigantine, *Black Diamond*, and the steamer, *Vyner*. Another steamer, the *Lorna Doone* also assisted in coastal coal transfers. In addition, arrangements were contracted with Chinese boatmen and Malay *nakhodah* for transporting Simunjan coal to Kuching. See A. H. Moy-Thomas, 'Economic Development under the Second Rajah (1870–1917)', *SMJ*, 10, 17–18 (July–December 1961): 52. For examples of agreements with local boat owners, see 'Agreement between Kuek Ah Jee and the Sarawak Government', 29 December 1915, Agreement Book, Vol. IV, SMA, Kuching; and, 'Agreement between Haji Hassim bin Haji Mohamad Arip and the Kuching Municipal Department', 12 September 1923, Agreement Book, Vol. V, SMA, Kuching.

3. 'The Political Will of Sir Charles Brooke, Rajah of Sarawak, dated 16 December 1913', MSS Brit. Emp. s. 365 Fabian Colonial Bureau, Box 161/1, Item 12, p. 4, RHL, Oxford.

4. For instance, see *Sarawak Gazette (SG)*, 1 November 1900, p. 199; *SG*, 2 January 1901, p. 2; *SG*, 2 June 1913, p. 118; and *SG*, 2 January 1915, p. 4.

5. In the *Gazette* of September 1937, under the heading 'Third Division News', is related an historical event of interior Sarawak. 'Penghulu Sibat has purchased a small outboard engine, and after several days' training in Kapit, returned with it to the Melinau. He is the first local Dayak to purchase an outboard, and his venture has aroused some interest amongst the people.' *SG*, 1 September 1937, p. 204.

6. Robert Pringle, 'The Brookes of Sarawak: Reformers In Spite of Themselves', *SMJ*, 19, 38–9 (1971): 71.

7. *SG*, 1 September 1885, p. 81. There were discrepancies as to the date of establishment. The *Gazette*, and W. J. Chater, who wrote about the Sarawak Chamber of Commerce, maintained 'July 1875' as the date of inauguration, whereas K. G. Tregonning placed it a month later. However, A. H. Moy-Thomas

claimed that the formation of this shipping line was in 1877. It is unlikely that the Chamber of Commerce, constituted in mid-1873, could have taken almost four years to establish this private shipping company. See W. J. Chater, 'Pieces from the Brooke Past—III: The First Sarawak Chamber of Commerce', *SG*, 31 July 1964, p. 165; K. G. Tregonning, *Home Port Singapore: A History of Straits Steamship Company Limited*, Singapore: Oxford University Press for Straits Steamship Company Limited, 1967, p. 124; and Moy-Thomas, 'Economic Development', p. 53.

8. For instance, see 'W. G. Brodie, Manager Borneo Company Agent for Sarawak Steamship Company, and HH The Rajah', 24 April 1876, Agreement Book, Vol. I, SMA, Kuching.

9. Tregonning, *Home Port Singapore*, p. 125.

10. The non-replacement of the *Rajah Brooke* might have been due to financial difficulties as it was largely uninsured, and to the fact that, for the shipping company's own purposes, a single vessel was deemed adequate for the time being. See *SG*, 1 September 1896, p. 170.

11. *SG*, 4 January 1897, p. 3.

12. In an attempt to move public opinion against the monopoly of the SSSCo and to effect improvements, the *Gazette* invited the public to protest in writing 'with a view to moving the Government, to bring about a more enlightened state of affairs', thereby upholding the principle of 'free competition [that] is always the best means of securing the greatest good and welfare to the people'. Ibid. From 1897 to the turn of the century, the *Gazette* published a continual flow of correspondence condemning the monopolistic position of the SSSCo, interspersed with the occasional response from the management of the BCL which argued against the allegation that it enjoyed special privileges.

13. See *SG*, 4 January 1904, p. 1.

14. This failure undoubtedly vindicated the poor response from investors to Charles's proposal of 1897. See *SG*, 4 January 1897, p. 3.

15. *SG*, 4 January 1904, p. 1. It was said that the SSSCo 'at considerable loss have succeeded in beating the new one off the run' and caused the latter's consequent liquidation. Ibid.

16. See *SG*, 1 July 1901, p. 139; and *SG*, 2 January 1902, p. 2.

17. 'Growth of Sarawak—Chronology, 1917–1924', Typescript, MSS Pac. s. 83, Brooke Family Papers, Box 7, File 8, Item 1, p. 8, RHL, Oxford.

18. Ibid., p. 21.

19. For instance, see *SG*, 2 January 1915, p. 4.

20. See Chapter 8.

21. See *SG*, 1 November 1900, p. 199; and *SG*, 2 January 1902, p. 2.

22. See *SG*, 2 January 1902, p. 2; and P. Eaton, 'A History of Bau District', *SG*, 31 May 1967, p. 128.

23. To effect this measure, the government in 1908 transferred two of its steamers, the *Adeh* and the *Kaka*, to the SSSCo, with the understanding that the coast stations of the Melanau districts of Bintulu, Tatau, and Mukah were to be added to their original coverage of the Rejang as far as Kapit. See 'Memorandum of Agreement between HH The Rajah and the Borneo Company Limited on behalf of the Sarawak & Singapore Steamship Company Limited', 27 December 1907, Agreement Book, Vol. III, SMA, Kuching; and *SG*, 5 February 1908, p. 27.

24. Complaints were also voiced regarding the irregular service rendered by the SSSCo in these local sectors. For instance, see *SG*, 1 May 1911, p. 82.

25. This paddle-wheel steamer was repurchased by the government from the SSSCo.

26. See *SG*, 1 February 1917, p. 28.

27. See *SG*, 16 April 1919, p. 100; and *SG*, 16 January 1920, p. 18.

28. For instance, see *SG*, 2 July 1923, p. 207.

29. Tregonning, *Home Port Singapore*, p. 128.

30. For details of this take-over, see ibid., pp. 128–30.

31. See B. A. St J. Hepburn (comp.), *The Handbook of Sarawak: Comprising Historical, Statistical and General Information Obtained from Official and Other Reliable Records*, Singapore: Malaya Publishing House for the Government of Sarawak, 1949, p. 170; and James C. Jackson, *Sarawak: A Geographical Survey of a Developing State*, London: University of London Press, 1968, p. 162.

32. See *SG*, 1 February 1901, p. 19; *SG*, 5 January 1910, p. 2; *SG*, 1 June 1912, pp. 117–18; *SG*, 16 July 1912, p. 157; 'Growth of Sarawak', MSS Pac. s. 83, p. 25; and Sylvia Brooke, *Sylvia of Sarawak: An Autobiography*, London: Hutchinson & Co., 1936, pp. 174–5. For its layout and dimensions, see *SG*, 16 January 1912, p. 17.

33. See 'Future of Sarawak: II—Economic Development', *Morning Post*, 20 July 1914.

34. This single public construction work which was begun in 1902 took eleven years to complete! See Elizabeth Pollard, *Kuching: Past and Present*, Kuching: Borneo Literature Bureau, 1972, p. 61.

35. For instance, see *Sarawak Administration Report (SAR)*, Kuching: Government Printing Office, 1938, p. 15.

36. This path was opened by Charles Hose, Resident of Baram, in the early 1890s. See *SG*, 2 February 1891, pp. 23–4.

37. A typical example of a footpath system was that in the interior that linked village to village, to Lawas and Trusan bazaars. See Leonard Edwards and Peter W. Stevens, *Short Histories of the Lawas and Kanowit Districts*, Kuching: Borneo Literature Bureau, 1971, p. 47.

38. See Eaton, 'Bau District', p. 128.

39. Four jinrickshaws were first introduced in mid-1895 and by early 1896 there were more than fifty such vehicles plying for hire in Kuching town. This prompted the proclamation of 'Order No. I of 1896' that laid out the rules and regulations, including licence fees, fares, and safety measures, pertaining to the running of these vehicles. See *SG*, 1 February 1896, p. 21; and 'Order No. I, 1896', *SG*, 2 March 1896, p. 40. For a description of the conditions of work of a Kuching jinrickshaw-puller in the 1930s, see *SG*, 1 October 1933, pp. 142–3.

40. The first motor car, a 10–12 hp Coventry Humber, belonged to J. M. Bryan, the BCL's manager, while Vyner, then Rajah Muda, introduced the motor cycle to the roads of Kuching. See Pollard, *Kuching*, p. 64.

41. See *SG*, 16 January 1913, p. 14; and Pollard, *Kuching*, p. 65. For further development of this motor bus service, see *SG*, 2 November 1925, pp. 286–7.

42. See *SAR, 1929*, p. 7; *SAR, 1930*, p. 9; and *SAR, 1931*, p. 56.

43. See K. H. Digby, *Lawyer in the Wilderness*, Cornell University Southeast Asia Program Data Paper No. 114, Ithaca: Cornell University Press, 1980, p. 13. For a study of these Chinese settlers along the Kuching–Simanggang Road, see T'ien Ju-K'ang, *The Chinese of Sarawak: A Study of Social Structure*, Monograph on Social Anthropology No. 12, London: Department of Anthropology, London School of Economics and Political Science, 1953.

44. The Depression (1929–31) forced cut-backs in public spending and several public projects, including road building and railway expansion, were shelved, the latter permanently. However, during the post-Depression years, the controversy of the need for roads once again emerged. See pp. 209–10 below.

45. *SAR, 1938*, p. 16.

46. 'Rajah Charles, letter dated 21 November 1894', quoted in Steven Runciman, *The White Rajahs: A History of Sarawak from 1841 to 1946*, Cambridge: Cambridge University Press, 1960, p. 219. See also Sylvia Brooke, *The Three White Rajas*, London: Cassell, 1939, p. 77; Moy-Thomas, 'Economic Development', p. 55; and Colin N. Crisswell, *Rajah Charles Brooke: Monarch of All He Surveyed*, Kuala Lumpur: Oxford University Press, 1978, p. 215.

47. Locomotive engines were ordered from Britain while passenger and goods rolling-stock were bought from Burma Railways and Federated Malay States Railways respectively. All these materials were transported to Sarawak by the SSSCo's steamer, *Natuna*, which made a special round voyage for the purpose. See Moy-Thomas, 'Economic Development', p. 55.

48. See 'Growth of Sarawak', MSS Pac. s. 83, p. 30. It was thought expedient that the railroad should extend to the 10th Mile as the mode of transport by bullock-drawn carts for goods and passengers was unsatisfactory. The rather clumsy bullock carts, besides being notoriously slow, were seriously damaging the roads 'by their wheels not running true'. *SG*, 1 August 1912, p. 211.

49. See 'Growth of Sarawak', MSS Pac. s. 83, p. 38. For a descriptive account of travel on this railway, see S. Brooke, *Three White Rajas*, p. 77.

50. Moy-Thomas, 'Economic Development', p. 56. Later, in mid-1917, fares were increased by 1 cent which accounted for the increased receipts though recording a decrease in passenger volume which was attributed 'to the novelty of the railway having worn off, therefore less joy riding'. *SG*, 16 January 1918, p. 15.

51. See *SG*, 17 May 1915, p. 112.

52. The 27th Mile mark was 'Mungo Babi situated on the Bukar River—a tributary of the Samarahan and within a few miles of the divide between the Samarahan and Sadong valleys'. *SG*, 16 January 1918, p. 15.

53. See *Sarawak Government Almanac*, Kuching: National Printing Department, 1993, p. 4.

54. The train left Kuching Station at nine o'clock in the evening and this night service was well-received. See 'Growth of Sarawak', MSS Pac. s. 83, p. 45. But, according to the *Gazette*, this service which commenced on 1 July 1920 was 'not well patronized' and subsequently provision reverted to '3 trains per day'. *SG*, 1 February 1921, p. 3. Pollard dated this night service as commencing operation two years later than the *Gazette*'s report, but Runciman mentioned that 'it was possible after 1920 to travel along its ten miles after dark'. Both authors did not cite their sources. See Pollard, *Kuching*, pp. 75–6; and Runciman, *The White Rajahs*, p. 233.

55. Moy-Thomas, 'Economic Development', p. 56.

56. See *SAR, 1931*, p. 2; and *Almanac*, p. 4.

57. Moy-Thomas, 'Economic Development', p. 56.

58. See 'Report Upon Defence Measures Adopted in Sarawak from June 1941 to the Occupation in December 1941 by Imperial Japanese Forces; also, an account of the movement of British and Sarawak Military Forces during the Japanese invasion of Sarawak', by J. L. Noakes, Formerly Secretary for Defence, Director of Air Raid Precautions and Security Officer, Sarawak, 15 February 1946, MSS Pac.s.62

Sir Charles Vyner Brooke, RHL, Oxford; and Ooi Keat Gin, *The Japanese Period in Sarawak, 1941–1945*, University of Hull, Centre for South-East Asian Studies, Monograph Series (forthcoming).

59. See *SAR, 1935*, p. 21.

60. See ibid.; and *SAR, 1938*, p. 23.

61. *SAR, 1938*, p. 1.

62. For instance, see Jackson, *Sarawak*, pp. 164–5; and Y. L. Lee, 'The Development of Resources in Bitish Borneo and Its Impact on Settlement', *SMJ*, 11, 19–20 (July–December 1962): 565.

63. The construction of stout bridges required both technical expertise and good quality materials which in practical terms required finance. Proper and continual maintenance thereafter involved high recurrent overheads. Flimsy bridges, like those found in Upper Sarawak at the turn of the century, obviously did not last long. For instance, see Eaton, 'Bau District', p. 128.

64. A study in the early 1960s described this stone shortage as 'almost unbelievable'. 'Good stone', it remarked, 'occurs only in west Sarawak, and then there is nearly 100 miles of coast before further occurrences of good quality rock are reached in the south-east of North Borneo.' Lee, 'Development of Resources', p. 565.

65. *SG*, 1 December 1921, p. 245. For a similar view, see *SG*, 1 February 1922, pp. 31–2.

66. *SG*, 1 February 1873, n.p.

67. 20th Meeting, 17 October 1921, in *General Council, 1867–1927*, Kuching: Government Printing Office, 1927 [?] p. 30.

68. 21st Meeting, 16 October 1924, in *General Council, 1867–1927*, p. 32.

69. For instance, during the periods of economic recession, Vyner's attempt to channel out-of-work Chinese coolies to public road building projects generally failed, for few took up his offer, while the rest turned to the gold industry of Upper Sarawak or crossed the border to Dutch Borneo for employment opportunities. See *SG*, 1 April 1920, p. 47; *SG*, 1 August 1932, p. 142; and *SG*, 1 April 1933, p. 47.

70. For the economic recovery, see 'The Rajah's Speech to Council Negri, 25th Meeting, 29 April 1937', *SG*, 1 May 1937, Supplement, pp. ii–iii.

71. See Hepburn, *Handbook of Sarawak*, p. 170.

72. See *SG*, 2 June 1884, p. 49. On one occasion, the notorious rough seas at the entrance to the Baram, 'completely washed [the *Adeh*] forward, sweeping a man off the forecastle and smashing the bulkhead of the captain's cabin'. Richard H. Goldman, 'The Beginnings of Commercial Development in the Baram and Marudi Following the Cession of 1881', *SG*, 31 March 1968, p. 56.

73. Hepburn, *Handbook of Sarawak*, p. 170. Somerset Maugham described his personal encounter with this horrific tidal bore during his visit to Simanggang in 1921. See W. Somerset Maugham, 'The Yellow Streak', in *The Complete Short Stories of W. Somerset Maugham*, London: Heinemann, 1951,Vol. I, pp. 456–80.

74. See Goldman, 'Baram and Marudi', p. 56.

75. See *SG*, 1 February 1893, pp. 17–18; and *SG*, 2 January 1894, p. 7.

76. The connection was from Labuan to Brooketon, a distance of some 32 kilometres by sea, and from Brooketon to Kuching, another 640 kilometres by steamer, which ran twice a month. See *SG*, 16 September 1910, p. 196.

77. Arrangements were made between the Sarawak government and the BCL whereby the latter agreed to undertake the construction and maintenance of a telegraph line between the major mining and agricultural centres in Upper Sarawak and Kuching. See 'Memo of Agreement between the Sarawak Government and the

Borneo Company Limited', 21 April 1898, Agreement Book, Vol. II, SMA, Kuching.

78. See *SG*, 2 January 1900, p. 2.

79. See *SG*, 2 January 1909, p. 2; *SG*, 16 January 1912, p. 18; *SG*, 1 August 1912, p. 168; *SG*, 16 January 1913, p. 24; *SG*, 17 August 1914, p. 189; and *SAR, 1929*, pp. 29–30.

80. See *SG*, 2 March 1914, p. 50.

81. For the development of the wireless in the outstations, see *SG*, 17 July 1916, p. 148; *SG*, 2 October 1916, p. 214; *SG*, 16 October 1916, p. 226; *SG*, 1 November 1916, p. 238; *SG*, 16 November 1916, pp. 249 and 251; *SG*, 1 February 1917, pp. 28, 29, and 30; *SG*, 16 March 1917, pp. 73–4; and *SG*, 16 July 1917, p. 179.

82. See *SG*, 16 January 1918, p. 14.

83. *SG*, 2 January 1920, p. 10.

84. See 21st Meeting, 16 October 1924, in *General Council, 1867–1927*, p. 32; and 22nd Meeting, 17 October 1927, in *General Council, 1867–1927*, p. 35. For a persuasive argument for the extension of this facility to the more remote parts of the country, see 'Views on a Wireless Telegraph Station in the Lawas and Trusan District of Sarawak', Walter Francis de Vere Skrine, Assistant Secretary to the Government, 2 January 1924, Typescript, MSS Ind. Ocn. s. 143(2), RHL, Oxford.

85. See *SG*, 3 August 1925, p. 185; *SG*, 2 January 1926, p. 2; *SG*, 1 September 1926, pp. 224–5; *SG*, 1 October 1926, p. 256; *SG*, 3 January 1927, p. 2; and *SAR, 1929*, p. 29.

86. See *SG*, 3 March 1924, p. 72.

87. See *SG*, 2 October 1939, p. 161. The Dayak language was originally proposed, but it was not implemented, probably for want of capable broadcasters. It is uncertain what was meant by the term 'Chinese language'; it was unlikely to have been the official Chinese language, Mandarin, or its vernacular version, *Kuo-yu*, as the Chinese in Sarawak then were strongly dialect-based. If a dialect was adopted, the likely choice would have been Hokkien considering the socio-economic position of the Hokkiens, particularly in Kuching, although it would be a dialect wholly unintelligible to 86 per cent of the Chinese populace in the country. Alternatively, a multi-dialect broadcast might have been adopted, viz., in Hokkien, Hakka, Foochow, and perhaps also in Cantonese.

88. See 'J. Brooke to "Ladies", 18 April 1863 (entry 19 April 1863)', in Owen Rutter (ed.), *Rajah Brooke and Baroness Burdett Coutts: Consisting of the Letters from Sir James Brooke, First White Rajah of Sarawak, to Miss Angela (afterwards Baroness) Burdett Coutts*, London: Hutchinson, 1935, pp. 182–3.

89. James relied on his agents in London and Singapore for financial and monetary transactions. From the 1860s, the BCL assumed these banking functions and acted on behalf of the Brooke government in financial matters. In 1912 when the Sarawak State Advisory Council was constituted at Westminster, it took over most of these banking functions from the BCL. For the BCL's role as 'banker', see Chapter 9.

90. See Chapter 7.

91. For instance, see *SG*, 1 April 1872, n.p.; and S. Baring-Gould and C. A. Bampfylde, *A History of Sarawak under Its Two White Rajahs, 1839–1908*, London: Henry Sotheran, 1909, pp. 376–7.

92. 'Order dated 27 June 1885', *Orders Which Have Not Since Been Cancelled, Issued by HH The Rajah of Sarawak or with His Sanction from 1863 to 1890, Inclusive*, Kuching: Govenment Printing Office, 1891, Vol. I, pp. 21–2. The amount involved

was quite substantial as a report of the Rejang district of 1902 indicates, whereby, 'about sixty registered documents were issued to Dyaks at Kapit in regard to sums of money deposited by them with Chinese and others amounting in the aggregate to over ten thousand dollars'. *SG*, 3 March 1903, p. 52. It was also not uncommon for a Dayak to invest in the purchase of bazaar shophouses. Such a shophouse would be rented out to a Chinese who would run a business on its premises. In a sense, this arrangement was no more than another variation of the Dayak as a 'banker' to a Chinese: the shophouse resembling a cash loan, the rental as the interest, and the business as security in case of default. See Robert Pringle, *Rajahs and Rebels: The Ibans of Sarawak under Brooke Rule, 1841–1941*, London: Macmillan, 1970, pp. 294–5.

93. There has yet to be an in-depth study of the development of banking in Sarawak during the Brooke period to provide more information on business operations, particularly those of the Chinese.

94. See *SG*, 17 April 1949, p. 94; and Craig Alan Lockard, *From Kampung to City: A Social History of Kuching, Malaysia, 1820–1970*, Ohio University Monographs in International Studies, Southeast Asia Series, No. 75, Athens, 1987, pp. 114 and 124–5.

95. Ibid., p. 114.

96. Ibid.

97. I owe this information to Mr Ong Yen Jin, late manager of Hock Hua Bank, and the first Asian manager of the Hongkong and Shanghai Banking Corporation. Ong Yen Jin, correspondence, 25 October 1994.

98. *SG*, 2 January 1925, p. 2. Before 1914, there had been a suggestion that an agency be opened at Kuching 'but the prospects then had not seemed favourable enough to justify such a step'. Compton MacKenzie, *Realms of Silver: One Hundred Years of Banking in the East*, London: Routledge & Kegan Paul, 1954, p. 267.

99. Information of its general meetings including current reports of performance during the late 1930s are published in the *Gazette* under the heading 'The Chartered Bank of India, Australia and China'. For instance, see *SG*, 1 June 1937, pp. 132–4 and 142; *SG*, 2 May 1938, pp. 67–72; *SG*, 1 May 1939, pp. 64–7; *SG*, 2 October 1939, p. 171; *SG*, 1 April 1940, p. 110; *SG*, 1 May 1940, pp. 123–6; *SG*, 1 October 1940, p. 282; and *SG*, 2 June 1941, pp. 104–6. See also *SG*, 30 January 1954, p. 10.

100. See *SG*, 2 January 1925, p. 1.

101. 'Third Division Annual Report for 1926', *Sarawak Government Gazette (SGG)*, 1 September 1926, quoted in Pringle, *Rajahs and Rebels*, p. 294.

102. *SAR, 1938*, p. 17.

103. Charles was opposed to change and viewed with suspicion any, to borrow his expression, 'new-fangled', idea or device. This expression is quoted in G. C. Harper, 'The Miri Field 1910–1972', *SMJ*, 20, 40–1 (January–December 1972): 22, n. 2.

104. See A. B. Ward, *Rajah's Servant*, Cornell University Southeast Asia Program Data Paper No. 61, Ithaca: Cornell University Press, 1966, p. 173. He was noted to have been 'disgusted' when Vyner introduced the first motor cycle into the country. See Pollard, *Kuching*, p. 64.

PART III
EFFECTS AND IMPACT

7
On Malays, Dayaks, and Other Indigenous Peoples

BROOKE economic policies affected to a certain extent the lives of the native inhabitants of Sarawak. The Brooke period witnessed the gradual demise of Malay trading activities. The Melanaus attained a certain degree of prosperity from the sago trade; likewise, the Dayaks, and to a lesser extent the Kayans and Kenyahs, in the trade in jungle produce. The cultivation of commercial crops had a limited effect on the indigenous people, although, Para rubber had a singular impact. Undoubtedly Brooke land policy was responsible for the absence of landlessness among the indigenous people, the 'sons of the soil'. Developments in the extractive industries and the provision of infrastructure facilities hardly had any bearing on the natives. In general, the effects of economic development were confined to certain native communities, and within those communities, only certain sections were affected.

Trade and Commerce

Eclipse of Malay Trading Activities

A significant image in the commercial scene in the second half of the century of Brooke rule was the predominance of Chinese trading activities, apart from the Borneo Company Limited and a few Indian-Muslim trading firms in Kuching. Chinese commercial supremacy was well established by the early twentieth century and continued throughout the rest of the period of Brooke rule. However, this was hardly the situation at the beginning of the Brooke Raj in the early 1840s when Malay *nakhodah* and Brunei Malay traders were active along the coast and in the interior.

During the 1840s and 1850s, Sarawak Malay *nakhodah*, mostly from Kuching, were keen traders. Contrary to the tradition implied in their name,[1] it was not unusual for them to embark occasionally on trading expeditions to Singapore, Java, Bali, and the south-west coast of Borneo. During the 1840s they competed

with Indian-Muslim merchants in the trade of European manufactured goods imported from Singapore. By the mid-1840s the Malays had lost ground to the Indian-Muslims in the schooner carrying trade between Kuching and Singapore. The Kuching Malay traders left this branch of the import trade to the Indian-Muslim merchants with their sophisticated network of agents in Singapore.[2] Besides this carrying trade with Singapore, the Sarawak Malay traders also competed with Brunei merchants for the lucrative trade in sago.

Prior to the establishment of the Brooke Raj, Sarawak Malay traders were already active participants in the sago trade. Like Sarawak itself, the Melanau sago-producing coastal districts were under the nominal overlordship of the Brunei Sultanate. Brunei Malay traders, acting as the representatives of the Sultanate, settled at the mouths of the main rivers in these districts to control the sago trade. Unable to compete with the Brunei Malay merchants at the river mouths, the Sarawak Malay traders placed agents at upriver positions beyond Brunei control to buy sago direct from the Melanau producers and ship straight to Singapore, and later to Kuching, for processing.[3] From the late 1840s and early 1850s, when raiding along the north-west coast had been curtailed, the sago trade flourished and the Sarawak traders enjoyed comfortable profits.[4] In fact, the Mukah Incident of 1860 that led to the cession of the sago districts to the Sarawak Raj a year later, was an expression of Brooke support for the Sarawak Malay sago traders against their Brunei rivals for the lucrative Mukah trade.

Besides their involvement in the coastal sago trade, the Sarawak Malay traders also ventured upriver from settlements like Bintulu and Sarikei to trade in jungle products like camphor and beeswax, procured from the interior by native collectors, mostly Kayans, in exchange for salt, cloth, beads, brassware, and Chinese jars.[5]

The commercial hegemony of the Sarawak Malays began to decline in the late 1850s. Even by the late 1840s, in all branches of commerce, the Malay trader faced competition from other ethnic groups. In the Kuching–Singapore trade they had to compete with the richer and the relatively well-connected Chinese and Indian-Muslim schooner owners. In the trade with natives of the interior, Chinese boat traders had penetrated the Land Dayak areas in Kuching's hinterland. Kuching Chinese trading firms had also established shops at Skrang in the Batang Lupar and Sarikei in the Rejang as early as 1850 to take advantage of the trade in jungle products.[6]

But it was the sago trade that ushered in the decline of the Sarawak Malay traders. Ironically, the 'beginning of the end' became more evident after the transfer of the sago districts in 1861. In 1856 a Kuching Chinese firm set up a sago mill to process raw sago into flour. It was then no longer necessary to ship the sago direct to Singapore, but to Kuching instead. Subsequently similar factories were established, resulting in the Kuching Chinese monopoly of the sago-milling industry.[7] The BCL also interested itself in the sago trade, and when the cession of the sago districts was effected, it erected a sago-milling factory at Mukah, the centre of the source of supply.[8] The Chinese traders, as agents of Kuching trading houses, began to move into the sago districts to purchase sago direct from the Melanau producers. In less than two decades, the Chinese effectively cornered the sago trade.

Complaints were often made by Malay traders against their Chinese counterparts in the sago districts; this report of 1877 from Oya by a Brooke official is typical.

> At Oya also, a few Malay traders, some of that place, others from Kuching desired me to interfere with the Chinese traders up river, some of whom have opened shops in the different villages, and restrict them to trading in boats, upon the ground that they, the Malay traders, *could not compete with the Chinese* and were consequently unable to earn a livelihood. I replied that such a step would be an unusual one and I thought the Melanaus would deal with those who should sell goods the cheaper whether Chinese or Malays, and it being desirable to encourage the extension of trade I could not comply with the request preferred by them.[9]

Before the Brooke acquisition of the Melanau districts, Malay traders had exploited their monopolistic position in the sago trade with unfair demands on the Melanau producers. After the cession of 1861, the Melanaus then became 'too alive to their own interests to be oppressed' by the Malays.[10] The Malays lost out to the Chinese newcomers 'in consequence of not trading fairly nor being content with small profits'.[11]

By the late 1870s it was evident that the Malays were being eclipsed by the Chinese. The *Gazette* in its editorial of August 1876 remarked on the demise of Malay trading.

> Trade with the coast was in the hands of the few who made large profits, the Malay with his schooner made sufficient in one, or at the outside, two trips, in the fine season, to keep himself and family in comparative affluence for the rest of the year—*But times are now changed.* Open competition has brought John Chinamen to the field, and the result is the price

of the staple article of trade—sago, has increased during the last five years over fifty per cent, thereby leaving such a small margin for profit that *the Malays are unable to compete* with such shrewd traders who so thoroughly understand the principle of small profits and quick returns.[12]

The following decade witnessed the almost total eclipse of Malay trading activities.[13]

The decline of Malay commercial activities was welcomed by the Brooke government which viewed trading as an inappropriate vocation for them. The Brookes assigned the Malay aristocratic élite an administrative role, and for the rest agricultural pursuits should be their livelihood. Or to borrow the words of the *Gazette*, for the Malays 'planting sago will be more to their ultimate advantage' than participation in its trade.[14] Nevertheless, persuasion and encouragement should be the key strategy in achieving these ends for the Malays.[15] The following record of Charles's speech to the General Council of 1883 outlined his aspirations for the Malays which clearly excluded involvement in trade.

[Charles] *begged them* [the Malay *datu* and chiefs] *again to continue this encouragement [of agriculture]*, as there was plenty of waste ground for extension; that the planting of paddy should also be kept up, *as it was a far more regular way of getting a livelihood than the petty trade* that was in many instances sought after by those who were eager to have the name of Nakodah attached to their names. For [Charles's] part he would rather see many small holdings, consisting of moderate sized plantations of sago and cocoanut trees, from which they could obtain a regular livelihood, as well as from paddy farms around neatly-kept and well-built houses, which he considered to be the height of comfort for the majority of the population. There were others of course employed in carrying cargoes of productions during the fine monsoon, and there were fishermen; but *what was to be sought after principally, was bringing the bulk of the inhabitants to follow steady and industrious pursuits; this is what would bring prosperity most among them, and he felt it was gradually taking root, and people were living more on shore than in boats.*[16]

Melanaus, Sago, Prosperity, and Indebtedness

The pacification of the north-western Bornean coast in the late 1860s and the Brooke promotion of sago exports brought prosperity to the Melanau producers.

The organization of the sago industry from the Melanau end was based on the partnership of the sexes in the initial processing of the sago palm, and the patron–client relationship between the aristocrats and the peasantry. The specialization of labour between the sexes was conducted in the following way.

It was the men's job to fell the palms, to strip the bark from the trunk, and to chop the pith and to shred it into small pieces. The women then washed and trampled it on a very fine mat so that the starch went through the mat, mixed up with water, leaving the woody waste matter on the surface of the mat. When the starch and the water had settled the women drained the water off and dug the solid sago out, either to turn it into biscuit or sell it to a dealer.

The women who tramped the sago and the men who brought the pith worked together as interdependent partners. If the sago was sold for cash they divided the proceeds equally.[17]

As the ordinary Melanau did not have enough land for growing his own palms to sustain a living, he had to rely on procuring them from a noble as a patron who possessed large tracts of sago plantations. Both client and patron were dependent on each other.[18] The arrangement was usually a three-way division of the profits, that is to say, one-third for the aristocrat who owned the palms, one-third for the man, and one-third for the woman.

This patron–client relationship was strong and rooted in the socio-political structure of the community. It was then not a surprise that the BCL, which felt that it could partake more profitably of the sago trade by establishing a processing plant at Mukah, failed for want of the supply of palms.[19] No patron was willing to jeopardize his relationship with his peasant clients by selling his palms to the interloper with its modern machinery.

By the late 1870s, it was clear that prosperity was smiling upon the sago-producing Melanau communities. 'Melanau tribes alone', it was observed, 'can be said to be substantially well off, as they not only possess extensive sago plantations but have of late years added to them by new plantings.'[20]

During the 1910s, other sago producers, especially the Chinese, and to a lesser extent Malays, offered some competition, but Melanau predominance remained.[21] Sago prices undoubtedly determined the level of Melanau prosperity as this report of 1920 remarked.

Raw sago and jelutong still command very high prices. Money has never been so plentiful amongst the Melanaus as at present and they boast of the exorbitant prices which the Chinese compel them to pay for very inferior goods. They will pay any price for something which takes their fancy and at times Three Castles Tobacco has changed hands at $5.50 a tin.[22]

However, their extravagant spending sprees coupled with the convenience of their proximity to the bazaar made them susceptible to indebtedness. A rather exasperated Brooke officer complained

of this problem of Melanau debt that complicated their recruitment to the Sarawak Rangers.

> A Penat Milano was enlisted for the Rangers on the 15th [January 1904] but on the 17th I received orders from the Honourable the Administrator to enlist no more. All the Milano recruits whom I have enlisted are in debt, and it is impossible to secure any that are not, *as every Milano, in the Muka and Oya district is almost without exception more or less heavily in debt.*[23]

Similarly, in mid-1916 when the Island Trading Company's cutch factory at Selalang launched a recruitment drive in the Oya district, indebtedness was again an obstacle. Although many Melanaus were willing to work, they were 'unable to, owing to their debts; and their creditors will not trust them out of their sight'.[24]

Melanau indebtedness persisted throughout the Brooke period with no attempt to alleviate this problem. What was more, the advent of new players in the sago industry after 1861 gradually undermined the socio-economic relations in Melanau society, although the adverse effects only became apparent during the post-Brooke years.[25]

Dayaks and the Trade in Jungle Produce

Jungle products had become significant exports by the 1870s, and the Dayaks, more than any other natives, benefited as collectors and primary traders. Apparently there was a belief among Brooke officers that the Dayaks alone were the most knowledgeable and capable collectors, dismissing altogether the other native groups as incompetent or too indolent. For instance, a correspondent of the *Gazette* speaking of the Trusan made the following remarks.

> Riches are spoken of in the interior, but it is a question if the inhabitants of the river have the energy to unearth them for the market. However, if this be wanting ... the Dyaks will find their way there and awaken the residents of those regions, as they seem to have done pretty well all along the Saba (north) coast.... In fact these young fellows, for those who go are nearly all under eighteen years of age, are the working pioneers of jungle produce wherever it exists.[26]

It was for these reasons that encouragement was given to the Dayaks to work the jungle produce in the newly acquired territories of the Baram, Trusan, and Limbang. In fact, after the transfer of the Baram in 1882, Charles sanctioned Dayak migration into this new territory to work jungle produce.[27] In this manner, foraging expeditions by Dayaks received official blessing.[28]

The economic necessity of procuring jungle products as well as the instinctive Dayak craving for adventure and the cultural demands of *bejalai*[29] provided excellent reasons for Dayak men to venture far from their home districts. Even when the Dayaks were enjoying success with rubber, the 'sport and interest in life incites them to search for jungle products'.[30]

This trade allowed the Dayaks to attain a certain degree of prosperity. Their sense of thrift ensured a proper investment of their gains, either in valuable old jars and brassware, or in savings with interest entrusted to Chinese bazaar shopkeepers, or in acquiring shophouses which were then let to Chinese. For instance, a *Gazette* report of 1872 commented on the Dayak as 'banker' to the Chinese: 'Trade is very good ... the harvest promises to be above the average, and the Dayaks without doubt are amassing riches, money fast taking the place of jars, gongs &c. Some of them who possess their 500 or 600 dollars have even put it out at interest among the Chinese.'[31] It can be seen, from this observation, that the Dayaks were conscious of the advantages of hard cash over such traditional assets like jars and gongs, a clear indication of their move from barter to a cash economy. Safeguards were also in place to ensure that the Dayaks were not cheated of their savings. 'There is no man', it was pronounced, 'keener on the dollar than the Dayak, or keener upon retaining it when gained', which typified the Dayak attitude towards their accumulated wealth.[32]

Participation in the trade in jungle products and the benefits thereof were limited to certain communities of Dayaks, mainly from the Second Division, and especially from the Saribas. It was no more than three decades ago, that the Saribas Dayaks had been raiding along the coast, but in the 1870s these same people were contributing to the development of the country's economy and the Treasury while at the same time amassing riches for themselves. Charles discerned a continuum in their behaviour:

> Saribas was the most troublesome and toughest in holding out, although its inhabitants were from the first the most energetic traders, and as a rule, I shall not make an exaggereated [*sic*] assertion when I say that among the Dayaks the best headtakers are in nearly all cases the best traders; possessing energy for the one work, they are always ready to turn it to account in the other.[33]

Trade and Other Indigenous Peoples

Kayans and Kenyahs

The Kayans and Kenyahs in the Baram proved themselves neither indolent nor unknowledgeable as procurers of jungle produce as Brooke officials had initially labelled them. They were as capable as the Dayaks and, considering that this territory was their home country, undoubtedly more familiar with the terrain than the outsiders. It was no surprise then that these natives objected strongly to the intrusion of the Dayak collectors.[34] Clashes were inevitable between them. By early 1888 Kayan and Kenyah protests were acknowledged by the government. The fact that they proved to be quite adept at working jungle produce and were dependent on this activity to pay their taxes resulted in restrictions being placed on Dayak collectors. From April 1888 restriction on Dayak collectors permitted them 'to collect produce only in those streams where there are no people living'.[35]

Thus, the Kayans and Kenyahs were brought into the cash economy of the bazaar at Claude Town (Marudi). In less than a decade of their exposure to this new system of cash, credit, advances of goods, and contact with upriver boat traders, the Kayans and Kenyahs had seized these new opportunities to their advantage. They were given credit by upriver Malay and Chinese traders for bazaar goods in return for jungle products. The Kayans, it was reported in the early 1890s, took advantage of this credit system whereby they 'will not work except in debt, and if they can't get credit they won't work at all'.[36] Furthermore, they abused their immunity from summonses from the Court of Requests (dealing with debts)[37] by refusing to 'pay their old debts if the [upriver boat] trader will not give them fresh credit'.[38] While condemning these Kayans for taking advantage of their exemption from summonses and advocating the end to such leniency, the *Gazette*, pondered upon the practical difficulties of attending legal procedures 'owing to their want of a written language'. It argued that 'such cases might be heard on the spot by the officer who makes an occasional visit to the outlying districts'.[39] On the other hand, it questioned the fairness of the dealing of the Malay boat trader with his Kayan clientele: 'It is also highly probable that the transactions between a travelling [M]alay trader and Kyans would hardly bear investigation in court. The Malay after the manner of his race would charge at exhorbitant rates and the Kyan with his sense of immunity from prosecution would feel safe in making any extra-

vagant promise and bargains.'[40] But there were other occasions when the Kayans also committed 'a down right fraud ... to obtain goods with no intention whatever of paying for them'; this was particularly a common practice 'amongst small chiefs'.[41] For such fraudulent acts, it was suggested that criminal law should apply, and those found guilty punished accordingly.[42] Charles, however, did not adopt such stern measures, but continued to rely on the merits of the situation on a case-by-case basis, and on the discretion and judgement of his officers on the spot.

Land Dayaks

While Melanaus, Dayaks, Kayans, and Kenyahs had a taste of some prosperity as a result of the development of trade under the Brooke Raj, the economic conditions of the Land Dayaks were not as fortunate. Oppression by their former masters, the Sarawak Malays, had continued. As late as the 1890s Malay traders from Kuching, under the respectable cloak of trade, were in fact swindling the Land Dayaks. One irate contributor to the *Gazette* related the following account:

> The present Malay system of trading with the Land Dyaks is rotten to the core. Dyak bintings or villages are perpetually being visited and the commonest articles of trade thrust upon the Dyaks at exhorbitant rates which they could purchase ever so much cheaper at any of the numerous Chinese shops scattered throughout the river and which are easily accessible in a days' [*sic*] journey even from the remotest Dyak habitation; such commodities as waistcloths (chawats) and petticoats (jamoo) trimmed with a little common Turkey red cloth are sold previously to the rice harvest to be repaid in paddy at many times their respective values, nor does it end here, the purchaser being expected to deliver his payment to the house of the Malay merchant entailing perhaps a long journey on foot or miles of boat travelling and again is expected to fully provide for those traders stopping in his house such necessities as rice, firewood, provisions and the like which he does without the slightest grumbling.[43]

Happily, such goings-on did not escape official attention. A senior Brooke official, in a letter to Charles, reported what he considered 'a systematic cheating of the [Land] Dyaks being carried on by Malays under the name of trading'.[44] The remedy then was to extend the unwritten law regarding immunity from debt summonses to the Land Dayaks. They were in this way, protected from Malay transgressions; but, unlike the Kayans and Kenyahs, there were no indications that they abused this privilege of immunity.

Commercialization of Agriculture

The Cultivation of Cash Crops

Charles was disappointed with his efforts in the late 1860s to get the Dayaks to cultivate cash crops and adopt new farming methods. However, two decades later, the demonstration effect from Chinese efforts and the work carried out at government experimental farms influenced, to a certain extent, some of the indigenous inhabitants to adopt such commercial crops as pepper and Liberian coffee.[45]

Amongst the native communities, the Malays and certain groups of Dayaks, namely, those from Saribas, Paku, Kanowit, Bawang Assan near Sibu, and Kapit were the most open to commercial agriculture. From the 1880s, these Malays and Dayaks began growing pepper and coffee, apart from their subsistence rice crops.[46] Initiative on their part was not lacking as this example of a Saratok Malay indicates.

> One of the best pepper plantations belongs to a Malay Nacoda Ganti who formerly was a great trader but has now given up sailing[,] trading and devoted his whole time to his plantation which he finds a much more remunerative investment than his former avocation.
>
> His example is being followed by other Malays and some Dayaks, as well as by the Chinese who have gardens of considerable extent.[47]

By the mid-1890s, coffee exports from Dayak gardens were reported.[48] Coffee and pepper growing were obviously profitable ventures, and Dayak ingenuity for marketing the produce proved that they were as keen on making a profit as their shrewd Chinese counterpart. This example from the Batang Lupar shows the business finesse of the Dayak.

> One of the Dyak chiefs in this stream [Spouh] says he has made some $200 on pepper in two years (he does not reckon his own labour). He is still holding some ten pikuls until the price touches $10 a picul. Of late this man has let his pepper garden 'slide' and is diligently attending to a fine large coffee garden about two years old and he hopes for better profits from this than from the pepper.[49]

The enthusiasm of the Dayaks and Malays for coffee persisted throughout the decade until the price slump at the turn of the century, which led to the abandonment of this once profitable crop. Pepper continued to be cultivated but its fluctuating prices and competition from Chinese growers dampened native interest.

None the less, the momentum was already there for native adoption of cash crops so that when Para rubber came on the scene during the second half of the 1900s, these same communities proceeded with its cultivation without undue hesitation.

Some Dayaks and Kadayans grew coconut commercially for copra but this crop neither enjoyed the popularity nor attained the success of coffee and Para rubber.[50] When coffee experienced a revival during the mid-1930s, there was a high demand from Dayaks for seeds, which was supplied by the Agriculture Department.[51]

The Impact of Para Rubber Planting

The introduction of Para rubber as a commercial crop was the single most important phenomenon to influence agriculture in Sarawak during the period of Brooke rule. The majority of the indigenous population, including communities in the interior like the Kayans and Kenyahs,[52] took to its cultivation with much enthusiasm. As early as 1908 there were reports of Para rubber growing by Malays.[53] The so-called 'rubber fever' and 'planting craze' started in 1912, when practically everybody took to growing Para rubber trees.[54] Native enthusiasm continued throughout the decade, and despite a slump in prices during the early 1920s, interest was renewed when prices showed improvement in the mid-1920s.[55]

Unlike the Malayan plantations with their disciplined layout and well-kept, weed-free rows of trees, native rubber gardens in Sarawak resembled a chaotic array of trees interspersed with an assortment of undergrowth. Poor or improper tree maintenance, little or no use of fertilizers, and the absence of weeding were the hallmarks of native holdings. This report of 1912 from Mukah illustrates the typical native attitude towards Para rubber cultivation.

> Reports brought from Kuching of the success of rubber planting by natives seems to have created an impression that, *in order to make a fortune, it is only necessary to stick in some stumps and leave them until ready to tap.* There is at present a good deal of talk about planting, but I doubt whether any great results will follow. One garden belonging to a Chinese is doing fairly well, as is another the property of a native. The latter has, however, been rather neglected. *Another plantation also belonging to a native has been cleared once only during the last two years.*[56]

It was not uncommon for those who had no rubber gardens of their own to become tappers in other people's plantations. Two

popular arrangements were identified: the *bagi dua* (literally 'divide into two') system provided equal sharing of the yield between proprietor and tapper; while under *pajak* (literally 'rent'), the tapper would rent the entire garden for a fixed fee, work on it himself, and enjoy all the fruits of his labour.[57] Such arrangements were mutually beneficial to both owner and tapper and operated satisfactorily without undue problems. The success of the *bagi dua* system or profit-sharing arrangement worked exceedingly well, as shown in this report of 1915 from the Baram, even to the extent of creating labour shortages in other sectors. 'The price of para rubber here, 90 cents per katty, has made it very hard to obtain police, sailors or servants, as all the young men are employed in tapping. The prevailing Malay system, of dividing the daily proceeds between the owner and tapper make it a very lucrative employment for the latter.'[58] In the Lawas, the more prosperous natives rented out their rubber holdings under the *pajak* arrangement to the Chinese, 'granting Chinese the sole right to tap their rubber, and look after their plantations, for which they receive so much per tree per month'.[59]

Natives also worked as rubber-tapping coolies in the bigger and more prosperous holdings belonging to the Chinese or other natives, and also on Western, capitalist-owned rubber estates. Land Dayaks often tapped the trees on Chinese plantations, and their skill at this work was favourably commented on.[60] Dayaks also worked on the rubber gardens of other Dayaks; for instance, Saribas Dayaks employed Ulu Ai Dayaks as tappers.[61] The Lawas Planting Company's rubber estates in Lawas had Malays and Muruts as tappers on its payroll.[62]

The cultivation of Para rubber brought a certain degree of prosperity to native planters as this report of 1920 indicates: 'The Paku Dayaks are very wealthy and industrious. They nearly all have para [rubber] plantations which are tappable and with the proceeds intend to fell large stretches of jungle for planting sago.'[63] In addition to investment in other cash crops, instances of affluence were reflected in their stoutly constructed longhouses of *billian*.[64] However, there were negative effects. Flushed with cash, 'many of them [Dayaks] spend their money rapidly on cheap and useless articles from the bazaar'.[65] The rubber boom of the late 1930s effectively erased the lean years of the Depression (1929–31) as an air of extravagance pervaded the bazaar. 'It is feared', regretted a concerned Brooke official, 'that few persons are saving their

money. Many people, mainly Dayaks, are clamouring to plant rubber and it is obvious that the late slump has taught them nothing.'[66]

The Depression years no doubt brought some measure of hardship with plummeting rubber prices, but on the whole did not unduly inconvenience native rubber planters. Few, if any, natives practised rubber monoculture; in fact, earnings from the sale of rubber supplemented their income. Subsistence rice production remained the chief occupation of Dayaks and other indigenous people.

Native reaction to rubber restriction schemes implemented from the mid-1930s was generally positive. There was a general sense of awareness among the Dayaks that the government's action was necessary.[67] Nevertheless, there was some unease about the Rubber Census amongst indigenous planters, and cases of native contravention of the Rubber Restriction Order, which was a finable offence, were reported.[68]

Despite its attraction, Para rubber cultivation only affected a small group of indigenous people. The majority remained untouched; notably the Melanaus on the coastal districts, the Kelabits in the hilly interior uplands, and the nomadic Penans. It was perhaps the unsuitability of the soil and the swampy coastal terrain of the Melanau areas that dissuaded them from Para rubber growing. No doubt there were some attempts at cultivation, but the majority of the Melanaus exhibited indifference towards rubber, and continued to rely on sago.[69] In the case of the Kelabits, accessibility to markets from their isolated settlements in the upland interior regions presented a formidable obstacle.[70]

The more conservative indigenous communities were unmoved by the attractions of Para rubber growing and its profits. Many Dayak villages, like those of the Lower Batang Lupar and Banting, showed no interest. Conservatism and maintenance of the traditional way of life remained strong among many native communities. A notable example drawn from the mid-1920s illustrates the strong influence of conservative thinking in the native psyche. All of a sudden, many natives began to cut down their rubber trees lest the 'rubber spirit' offended the more important life-sustaining '*padi* spirit'. Such an occurrence was apparently a country-wide phenomenon for it was reported from among the Land Dayaks of the First Division as well as from the Balleh Dayaks in the remote interior of the Third Division.[71]

Protectionist Land Policy

From James's proclamation of 1863 to Vyner's land regulations of 1931 and 1933, Brooke policy on land was primarily aimed at safeguarding native interests. Charles's stern prohibition of 1910 of the sale of rubber plantations to Westerners effectively excluded investors. But if European capitalists and speculators were kept at bay, the ever-increasing number of land-hungry immigrant Chinese posed a serious threat to native land. Chinese encroachment became increasingly common, from Hakka pepper planters intruding on Land Dayak farmland in Upper Sarawak to Foochow rubber growers infringing on Dayak fruit gardens in the Lower Rejang. Native–Chinese land disputes filled the case books of the Brooke courts.[72]

On other occasions, the indigenous people adopted denial tactics to frustrate Chinese or other interlopers from acquiring land. The following is a typical illustration of such a strategy by the Land Dayaks of Upper Sarawak.

> Some months ago a Siniawan Chinese applied for a grant of swamp land which he proposed to irrigate and put under padi, but when he proposed to start operations the Serambo [Land] Dayaks stepped in and claimed the land saying they intended planting it up at once though they have never done so before. They then cleared a small corner and planted padi but did no more than prevent the Chinese from doing so. The resultant padi is excellent, but the procedure is typical of the Land Dayaks. *He cannot or will not plant himself and prevents anyone else from doing so.*[73]

Vyner's strategy in safeguarding native land was to create 'Native Holdings' and 'Native Land Reserves',[74] which came into effect in 1920. Further land legislation, like the Land Regulations of 1931 and 1933, maintained the principle of 'Native Land Reserves'. But, more importantly, the meaning of 'Native' was clarified in 1933 with the issue of Order No. I–1 (Interpretation) of 1933, which clearly specified the definition of 'Native' whereby Chinese were excluded.[75] Native landholdings and reserves were solely the preserve of the indigenous peoples, and no Chinese could claim otherwise. Non-natives were prohibited from acquiring land in the 'Native Area Land' whereas both natives as well as Chinese were allowed to buy and own land in the 'Mixed Zone Land'.[76]

On the whole, land disputes, whether involving natives and Chinese or among natives themselves, were handled adequately by the Brooke court system. The setting up of Native Land Reserves

reduced, to a certain extent, the 'endless boundary disputes and complaints of encroachment'.[77] Incidence of native landlessness was rare. The large majority of indigenous people farmed their own land and lived off it.

Limited Involvement in the Extractive Industries

Although it was known that Malays and Land Dayaks worked the antimony deposits during the decades prior to James's arrival, it was not from choice but out of coercion, a bending to the will of their Brunei overlords. During the Brooke period, panning for gold was an occupation of some of the poorer classes of Malays. Even then, such work was undertaken intermittently as a supplement to rice farming as, most of them felt it was not worth the effort and long hours. Some Land Dayaks also washed for alluvial gold, but they too attended to it in a piecemeal manner. Kayans in the interior were known to have mined iron and smelted the ore for making swords and other weapons.[78] The Miri Malays, employing primitive methods, managed to obtain oil for lighting purposes from the numerous seepages in their vicinity, and asphalt for caulking their boats.[79]

When coal-mining was instituted in the Sadong, the work-force was largely drawn from imported, indentured Chinese coolies, as was the case in the Miri oilfields.[80] The Brooketon collieries also had its fair share of imported Chinese workers which complemented its local native labour of largely Brunei Malays.[81]

The Dayaks, particularly from the Second Division, were keen to work in the oil industry at Miri, viewing it as a fulfilment of *bejalai*. 'There is much competition' among the Dayaks after the harvest, noted the Resident at Simanggang in 1913, 'to obtain work as labourers under the Anglo-Saxon Petroleum Co., at Miri, but naturally this source can only satisfy a limited number of workers.'[82] Those who succeeded were roundly praised for their satisfactory performance. The Dayaks were favoured by the company as they were 'easy to control' in comparison with the rather obstinate and at times rebellious Chinese workers.[83]

However, in later years (1930s) when the oil industry had developed and jobs had become more specialized, there was no place for the largely unskilled and illiterate Dayak labourer. Furthermore, the Dayaks' short-term aspiration of a *bejalai* adventure apparently did not coincide with the long-term commitment expected by the oil company of its employees. Many Dayaks then

were thought to be unsuitable and were denied employment in the oil industry.[84]

Overall, there was limited participation of indigenous people in the mining industries during the period of Brooke rule. This owed as much to their own lack of interest in the heavy work and long hours required as to their unsuitability for want of specialized skills and education. This minimal involvement was not viewed by the Brookes as a drawback. On the contrary, they were wholly satisfied that few natives worked as coolies in the mines as they were then not 'exploited' as labourers in the Chinese or BCL's gold works of Upper Sarawak, in the Simunjan collieries, or in the Miri oilfields.

The engagement of indentured Chinese coolies under poor working conditions in the government Simunjan coal-mines was not thought to be inconsistent with Brooke paternalistic policies that avowed to protect native rights and interests. For, as far as the Brookes were concerned, the Chinese were neither seen as indigenous inhabitants nor were they ever considered as such in practice.

Minimal Influence of Infrastructure Development

Improvements in shipping and the progress achieved in the carrying trade had a positive impact on the Dayak collectors of jungle produce, the Melanau sago producers, and the native Para rubber planters, for the fruits of their labours could reach the Singapore market more efficiently. Apart from this important effect, the development of other infrastructure facilities had minimal influence on the majority of indigenous inhabitants. These facilities and conveniences were largely confined to urban areas and designed to serve a literate community. Besides the Malay upper class and native civil servants (predominantly Malay) who resided in the capital Kuching and other major towns, the majority of the indigenous population were largely subsistence farming communities. The latter's access to such facilities as the telephone and piped water, was non-existent or, at the most, minimal. The government postal service, which linked the outstations with Kuching and the outside world, had little meaning for a largely illiterate native population. Radio broadcasting, which had the potential of bringing the scattered population of the country closer together, only made an appearance in the late 1930s and it is doubtful that receivers were readily available among remote native communities like those at Lio Matu in the Upper Baram, Bario in the Kelabit

highlands, or Ba Kelalan in the Upper Trusan. Even if receiver sets had been available, the broadcasts in English, Malay, and Chinese were wholly unintelligible to the majority of Dayaks and other non-Malay indigenous peoples.

Conclusion

In spite of all the encouragement to engage in agriculture, the end result was unimpressive as far as the indigenous population was concerned. There were native communities that participated in the economic changes introduced during the period of Brooke rule, but only certain groups were involved in such transformations, while the majority remained indifferent, or were too geographically remote and isolated to be affected.

The Melanaus of the sago-producing coastal districts obviously experienced the changes in the sago trade and industry. They witnessed the replacement of one group of intermediaries by another: Brunei Malays were displaced by Malays from Sarawak (Kuching) who, in turn, bowed out to Chinese merchants and the agents of the BCL. Throughout these changes, the Melanaus remained the dominant sago producers, although competition increasingly came from Malay and Chinese planters. The patron–client relationship in the Melanau socio-economic and political structure, revolving round the production and marketing of sago, was also beginning to display its vulnerability from the impact of such external forces as price fluctuations and the more aggressive techniques employed by Chinese middlemen. This structure remained intact during the Brooke period, but the harsh economic climate of slumps in sago prices during the mid-1950s saw its collapse.[85]

Dayak participation in the trade in jungle produce was confined to a small, though active, group of Dayaks from the Saribas, Rimbas and Paku (branches of the Saribas), and Krian rivers of the Second Division. They made expeditions as far away as the jungles of Sumatra, the Malay States, British North Borneo, and the southern Philippines (Mindanao). They, too, were the Dayak collectors who answered enthusiastically to Charles's call in the 1880s to enter the Baram, and subsequently, on their own initiative, ventured into the Trusan.[86]

When commercial crops like pepper, coffee, and Para rubber were introduced, it was again the Saribas and Paku Dayaks who led the way and reaped the benefits of their initiative and foresight.[87] In the late 1930s, when the Paku and Rimbas Dayaks

decided not to tolerate the exorbitant prices demanded by the local Chinese bazaar shopkeepers, they purchased their supplies direct from Kuching. Even plans for setting up a hawker's boat and acquiring a rubber dealer's licence were contemplated.[88] In the promotion of wet-*padi* cultivation and the utilization of buffaloes for ploughing, the Dayaks of Bawang Assan (Sibu), Kanowit, and Kapit were the most receptive.[89]

But inertia prevailed amongst the rest of the Dayak population, particularly those in the upriver districts, and even some downriver Dayaks; for example, those in the Lower Batang Lupar and the Balau Dayaks of Banting exhibited indifference.[90] Apart from the Kayans and Kenyahs who participated in the collection of and trade in jungle products, the other natives in the interior of the Rejang, Balleh, Baram, Tinjar, Limbang, and Trusan were generally left to their own devices. For instance, the Kelabits in their settlements in the highlands of the Baram headwaters barely had any effective contact with the Brooke administration.[91]

Surprisingly, the Land Dayaks with their settlements in the various branches of the Lundu, Sarawak, Samarahan, and Sadong rivers in the First Division, in close proximity to Kuching as well as to the numerous Chinese mining and agricultural communities of the district, were scarcely affected by economic change. An investigation, conducted in early 1872, reported their lack of initiative in introducing new crops, although they claimed that 'they were willing to do anything [regarding planting] *if ordered* by the Government, but they would wish to be taught before they attempted anything of the kind'.[92] At the closing years of Brooke rule, apparently nothing much had changed among the Land Dayaks who remained steadfastly conservative and withdrawn.[93]

Studies and observations during the immediate post-Brooke years of the late 1940s and the 1950s revealed that the traditional way of life of the indigenous communities remained relatively intact and unchanged, despite a century of Brooke rule.[94] For instance, subsistence swidden farming of hill-rice, the basic mode of production of the Dayaks, was still widespread.

There were attempts during the Brooke period to abolish this system of agriculture which was viewed as destructive. Charles, as early as the mid-1860s, intended to convert the Dayak from a shifting cultivator to a yeoman peasant farmer. The encouragement of wet-*padi* cultivation among the Dayaks, by far the best guarantee of settled agriculture, had little effect. In 1915, there was a call for government restriction against the Dayak practice of felling 'old

primitive jungle by which so much good and valuable wood is lost to the State',[95] and four years later a Forestry Department was created and a Conservator of Forests was appointed. During the mid-1930s, there was a consensus among Vyner's officers that some basic changes had to be effected to solve the Dayak problem. The *1935 Blue Report*, a critical review of Vyner's government, made the following recommendations concerning the future of the Dayaks.

> Opinion is unanimous that the long-house system must eventually be abolished.... It is emphasised that the future of the Dayaks undoubtedly lies in the individual ownership of land ... the solution of the Dayak problem must be sought in the *gradual conversion of the Dayak into a permanent cultivator of the land.* So long as the Dayak is confined to his long-house and the land is held on customary tenure by each household it is useless to expect any improvement.[96]

In 1937, the Acting Senior Forest Officer of Sarawak speaking at the Third Conference of Malayan Forest Officers in Kuala Lumpur, attacked the destructive effects of Dayak shifting cultivation on forests.[97] Notwithstanding all these attempts and intentions, little was accomplished. Dayak shifting agriculture and their longhouse system survived into the post-Brooke period.[98]

The minimal native participation in the country's economy was in part due to the natives themselves, their isolation, and the difficult environment as well as to Brooke design. The discouragement of Malay involvement in trading activities was in part dictated by James's rejection of the concept of the merchant-prince. What was more, according to the *Gazette*, the innate characteristics of the natives were such that it was thought inappropriate for them to work either in commercial agriculture or in the extractive industries.

> The Malays are too proud and too lazy to work.... The Land Dayaks are a quiet, docile people, content with agricultural pursuits sufficient to supply their daily wants.... [For] the Saribas ... [and] Batang Lupar [Dayaks] ... [the] great drawbacks to their labor is its uncertainty, as they invariably leave all work to assist their families at harvest time.[99]

It was then concluded that

> There is little doubt in our minds that the future development of Borneo can only be accomplished by Chinese; or a hybrid race between Chinese and the aborigines; and any private enterprise for opening up the resources of Sarawak by agriculture, or mining, must doubtless depend on imported labour, which, from our proximity to China, can be procured without difficulty.[100]

And so it was to the Chinese that the Brookes entrusted the economic development of their domain.

1. The honorific '*nakhodah*' as understood locally means 'people who sail to the right', that is to say, 'after leaving the entrances of the Sarawak rivers, all of which flow west, to sail right would take them to the north to trade with the territories' along the north-west Bornean coast. W. J. Chater, 'Pieces from the Brooke Past–III: The First Sarawak Chamber of Commerce', *SG*, 31 July 1964, p. 165.

2. A contemporary observer described the commercial rivalry between Kuching Malay–Indian rivalry in these terms:

'The klings [Indians] have a well-stocked bazaar in the town, and make expeditions from it to all the towns along the coast.... The Klings successfully compete with the native [Malay] merchants for goods of European manufacture, which they bring over, of a damaged description, they having been sold at Singapore at less than their original cost. This the Klings buy from their correspondents at Singapore cheaper than can the Malayan traders who visit that settlement; and as they are not at the expense of sailing ships of their own, but get their things on freight by the [Brooke government] schooner, the Malays generally leave this branch of the commerce to them, and confine themselves in the goods of Javanese and Chinese manufacture, the prices of which do not fluctuate.'

Hugh Low, *Sarawak: Its Inhabitants and Productions, Being Notes during a Residence in that Country with His Excellency Mr Brooke*, London: Frank Cass, 1848; new impression, 1968, pp. 134–5. See also Henry Keppel, *A Visit to the Indian Archipelago in HM Ship* Maeander, *with Portions of the Private Journal of Sir James Brooke, KCB.*, 2 vols., London: Bentley, 1853, Vol. II, p. 43; and Spenser St John, *Life in the Forests of the Far East*, 2 vols., London: Smith, Elder & Co., 1862; reprinted Kuala Lumpur: Oxford University Press, 1974, Vol. I, p. 149.

3. See H. S. Morris, 'The Coastal Melanau', in Victor T. King (ed.), *Essays on Borneo Societies*, Hull Monographs on South-East Asia 7, Oxford: Oxford University Press for University of Hull, 1978, pp. 39–40.

4. See Low, *Sarawak*, pp. 116–17, 339; St John, *Life in the Forests*, Vol. II, p. 314; and John C. Templer (ed.), *The Private Letters of Sir James Brooke, KCB, Rajah of Sarawak, Narrating the Events of His Life, from 1838 to the Present Time*, 3 vols., London: Bentley, 1853, Vol. II, p. 161.

5. See Low, *Sarawak*, pp. 323–4; and J. H. Moor (ed.), *Notices of the Indian Archipelago, and Adjacent Countries*, London: Frank Cass, 1837; reprinted 1968, pp. 9–10.

6. Craig Alan Lockard, *From Kampung to City: A Social History of Kuching, Malaysia, 1820–1970*, Ohio University Monographs in International Studies Southeast Asia Series, No. 75, Athens, 1987, p. 30.

7. By the last decade of the nineteenth century, there were ten sago factories in the country in operation. See *Sarawak Gazette* (*SG*), 2 January 1892, p. 2.

8. However, this sago mill was unsuccessful for want of palms. The failure was due to the rather delicate patron–client relationship between the aristocratic Melanau owners of sago plantations and the peasant sago workers. This relationship was not merely economic in nature but had socio-political ramifications in Melanau society. See H. S. Morris, 'How an Old Sarawak Society was Undermined', *SG*, March 1982, pp. 55–6.

9. *SG*, 24 June 1877, p. 45. Emphasis added.

10. SG, 22 January 1878, p. 3.

11. Ibid.

12. *SG*, 15 August 1876, p. 6. Emphasis added.

13. There were, however, a few Kuching Malays who continued as traders into the twentieth century. 'Although the position of nakoda almost disappeared, a few wealthier aristocrats and Sumatrans remained in the shipping business at least until the 1920s.... Occasionally a Malay went into partnership with a prominent Chinese. The last major Malay trader died in 1886, effectively marking the end of the Malay trading period in Kuching.' Lockard, *From Kampung to City*, p. 45.

14. *SG*, 15 August 1876, p. 6.

15. In the 1870s, there was a series of debates on dealing with the 'problem' of the disenfranchised Malays. A suggestion that Malays should be compelled to undertake agricultural pursuits faced firm objections. For instance, see *SG*, 16 April 1877, pp. 25–6; *SG*, 8 December 1877, pp. 84–6; *SG*, 22 January 1878, pp. 3–5; and *SG*, 26 March 1878, p. 19.

16. 7th Meeting, 11 August 1883, in *General Council, 1867–1927*, Kuching: Government Printing Office, 1927[?], p. 9. Emphasis added.

17. Morris, 'Old Sarawak Society', p. 55.

18. This patron–client relationship between the aristocrats and the peasantry extended beyond the working of sago and included other spheres of activity, from constructing a house to overseas trading expeditions. See ibid.

19. See ibid., p. 56.

20. *SG*, 8 December 1877, p. 85.

21. For instance, see *SG*, 1 July 1913, p. 148; *SG*, 16 September 1913, p. 219; and *SG*, 1 May 1916, p. 84.

22. *SG*, 16 March 1920, p. 75.

23. *SG*, 3 March 1904, p. 56. Emphasis added.

24. *SG*, 17 July 1916, p. 149.

25. See H. S. Morris, *Report on a Melanau Sago Producing Community in Sarawak*, London: HMSO, 1953, pp. 10 and 44–7.

26. *SG*, 1 December 1885, pp. 113–14.

27. Charles ordered Claude Champion De Crespigny to allow Dayaks 'to pass Kidurong Point in order that they may work jungle produce in Baram'. *SG*, 1 September 1882, p. 71. For the Trusan and Limbang, see *SG*, 4 January 1886, p. 2; and *SG*, 2 April 1894, p. 60.

28. Charles was ambivalent regarding Dayak migration: on the one hand, he felt that they should be permanent settlers of the land, but on the other hand, he believed that non-interference in their traditional way of life should be upheld. Nevertheless, in the new territories acquired during the 1880s, he was determined that the introduction of Dayaks as procurers of jungle produce would, within a short period, develop the trade of the territories. For Dayak migration into the Fourth and Fifth Divisions, see Robert Pringle, *Rajahs and Rebels: The Ibans of Sarawak under Brooke Rule, 1841–1941*, London: Macmillan, 1970, pp. 268–76.

29. According to J. D. Freeman, *bejalai* is described in the following terms: 'It is one of the most cherished customs of the Iban that men—and particularly young men—should periodically leave their long-houses and venture out into the world to seek their fortunes. These journeys, or bejalai, frequently last for several years on end, and often extend to the remotest corner of Borneo, and even to Malaya and the islands of Indonesia. They have two main aims: the acquisition of valuable property and of social prestige. For most young men these journeys are an

overruling passion.' J. D. Freeman, *Report on the Iban of Sarawak*, 2 vols., Kuching: Government Printing Office, 1955, Vol. I, p. 10. For a detailed study of *bejalai*, see Peter Mulok Kedit, 'Iban Bejalai', Ph.D. thesis, University of Sydney, 1987.

30. *SG*, 16 March 1917, p. 73.

31. *SG*, 1 April 1872, n.p. See also Pringle, *Rajahs and Rebels*, pp. 294–5.

32. S. Baring-Gould and C. A. Bampfylde, *A History of Sarawak under Its Two White Rajahs, 1839–1908*, London: Henry Sotheran, 1909, p. 377. See also pp. 376 and 387.

33. *SG*, 1 July 1871, n.p. See also *SG*, 1 December 1885, p. 114.

34. For Kayan opposition, see Richard H. Goldman, 'The Beginnings of Commercial Development in the Baram and Marudi Following the Cession of 1881', *SG*, 31 March 1968, p. 57.

35. *SG*, 1 June 1888, p. 77.

36. *SG*, 1 February 1892, p. 35.

37. In an attempt to discourage Chinese or Malay traders from giving advances to Dayaks or other natives of the interior, there was an unwritten rule in Brooke courts to refuse the serving of debt summons to the latter. Also, such a measure absolved the authorities from seeking out recalcitrant natives in the jungle. Charles explained as follows: 'About the Dayaks and other aborigines, we do not allow traders to give them credit, of if they do, they cannot take out summons to sue them in our courts—this [is] the rule but some exceptions are made.' Charles Brooke, Rajah, to Governor Creagh, British North Borneo, 10 September 1890, HH The Rajah's Letters, SMA, Kuching. This unwritten rule, however, did not apply to Malays or the Melanaus on the coast, neither was it enforced among the Dayaks of the Saribas. For implementation of this unwritten law, for instance, see *SG*, 1 July 1908, p. 173.

38. *SG*, 1 February 1892, p. 35.

39. *SG*, 1 February 1892, p. 24.

40. Ibid.

41. *SG*, 1 February 1892, p. 35.

42. For instance, see *SG*, 1 February 1892, p. 24.

43. *SG*, 2 July 1894, p. 98.

44. *SG*, 2 July 1894, p. 104.

45. See *SG*, 4 January 1886, p. 6; and *SG*, 1 April 1890, p. 51.

46. For instance, see SG, 3 January 1887, p. 2; *SG*, 1 October 1892, p. 187; *SG*, 1 December 1892, p. 217; and *SG*, 1 May 1894, p. 67.

47. *SG*, 1 January 1890, p. 12.

48. For instance, see *SG*, 1 May 1894, p. 67.

49. *SG*, 1 May 1894, pp. 67–8.

50. For instance, see *SG*, 16 April 1917, p. 97; and *SG*, 1 August 1927, p. 207.

51. For instance, see *SG*, 4 January 1937, p. 21.

52. For instance, see *SG*, 1 August, 1912, p. 174.

53. For instance, see *SG*, 17 August 1908, p. 212.

54. For instance, see *SG*, 16 January 1912, p. 18; *SG*, 1 August, 1912, p. 174; *SG*, 16 November 1912, p. 255; *SG*, 2 January 1913, p. 4; and *SG*, 17 March 1916, p. 50.

55. For instance, see *SG*, 1 August 1924, p. 257; and *SG*, 1 September 1925, p. 225.

56. *SG*, 1 July 1912, p. 147. Emphasis added. See also *SG*, 16 January 1912, p. 18; and *SG*, 17 March 1913, p. 62.

57. For a discussion of these tapping arrangements, see A. J. N. Richards (comp.), *Sarawak Land Law and Adat*, Kuching: Government Printing Office, 1961, pp. 52–4.

58. *SG*, 1 May 1916, p. 79.

59. *SG*, 1 September 1920, p. 199.

60. For instance, see *SG*, 16 September 1915, p. 218.

61. See *SG*, 2 April 1917, p. 87.

62. Initially the company recruited experienced tappers from Kuching, but after a few Muruts had signed up and proved their worth, many more were engaged. Murut women were employed in the tedious task of weeding and appeared to be competent workers. See *SG*, 2 January 1914, p. 7; and *SG*, 16 April 1917, p. 97.

63. *SG*, 1 March 1920, p. 62.

64. Such examples of longhouses constructed from *billian* could be seen in the Paku where earnings from rubber allowed such extravagance. For instance, see *SG*, 1 June 1927, p. 151.

65. *SG*, 1 March 1937, p. 70.

66. *SG*, 1 April 1937, p. 93.

67. For instance, see *SG*, 1 August 1935, p. 145.

68. Dayak reservation towards the Rubber Census was their suspicion that 'Government proposes to levy quit-rent on their rubber lands' in spite of propaganda efforts to allay such fears. See *SG*, 1 October 1935, p. 187. For examples of violations of the Rubber Restriction Order, see *SG*, 2 January 1936, p. 20; and *SG*, 2 August 1937, p. 167.

69. See *SG*, 1 July 1912, p. 147.

70. The Kelabit highland area had long been isolated from the rest of the country and the contact of this community with the world beyond the hills was minimal. Even as late as the second half of the 1950s, there was no outlet for their surplus rice except distilling *borak* (rice wine) with it. See Tom Harrisson, 'The Kelabits and Muruts', in Tom Harrisson (ed.), *The Peoples of Sarawak*, Kuching: Government Printing Press, 1959, p. 64.

71. A rumour was spread through the native grapevine of a belief, apparently originating from a dream, that the rubber tree spirit (*antu kubal*) was attacking the rice spirit (*antu padi*) and driving it away. It may appear to be a far-fetched tale, but to the indigenous people such a phenomenon was disastrous. Rice cultivation to these people was not merely a means of sustenance but a way of life. See J. D. Freeman, *Iban Agriculture: A Report on the Shifting Cultivation of Hill Rice by the Iban of Sarawak*, London: HMSO, 1955, p. 105; and W. R. Geddes, *The Land Dayaks of Sarawak: A Report on a Social Economic Survey of the Land Dayaks of Sarawak Presented to the Colonial Social Science Research Council*, London: HMSO, 1954, p. 97.

72. For Sino-Native land disputes in the Rejang, for instance, see *SG*, 1 September 1908, p. 225; *SG*, 16 October 1914, p. 239; *SG*, 2 January 1915, p. 3; *SG*, 2 August 1915, p. 179; *SG*, 2 April 1918, p. 79; *SG*, 1 November 1920, p. 241; and *SG*, 1 May 1924, p. 166. For disputes in other districts especially in Upper Sarawak and the Simanggang area, for instance, see *SG*, 2 January 1896, p. 11; *SG*, 1 August 1896, p. 160; *SG*, 2 January 1914, p. 3; *SG*, 16 September 1915, p. 218; and *SG*, 2 January 1932, p. 8. It was well-known that the natives, especially Dayaks, were exceptionally keen on litigation in the courts, not only in disputes involving land, but other disagreements over inheritance or matrimonial matters.

Nevertheless, some still had faith in traditional ways of resolving disagreements. For amusing accounts of land litigation by natives in the courts, for instance, see *SG*, 1 June 1938, p. 95; St John, *Life in the Forests*, Vol. I, p. 65; A. B. Ward, *Rajah's Servant*, Cornell University Southeast Asia Program Data Paper No. 61, Ithaca: Cornell University Press, 1966, p. 129; and Pringle, *Rajahs and Rebels*, pp. 190–2. For a typical illustration of a dispute being settled in the traditional native way, see *SG*, 1 June 1935, p. 99.

73. *SG*, 2 February 1920, p. 37. Emphasis added. In 1937, Siniawan Malays employed similar tactics in preventing a capitalist concern from acquiring land. See *SG*, 1 May 1937, p. 108.

74. This concept of a native land reserve was broached as early as 1896 by Reginald Awdry, Resident of Upper Sarawak, who felt that the extension of Chinese pepper gardens was fast encroaching on Land Dayak lands, and urged that 'there is a very pressing need of something in the nature of a land reserve for the Dayaks'. *SG*, 2 January 1896, p. 11. This was reiterated in 1915 by Donald A. Owen, Resident of Upper Sarawak, who feared that Chinese pepper planters were increasingly acquiring Land Dayak land on the sly.

'So I have suggested to His Highness the establishment of a Dyak Land Reserve properly surveyed and demarcated beyond which Chinese may on no account plant. This would obviate the constant bickering which now takes place between the parties as the Dyaks are perfectly willing to part with their rights over the land to Chinese for a consideration and cases are only reported by Dyaks when the Chinese are unable or unwilling to "square" them sufficiently.'

SG, 16 September 1915, p. 218.

75. 'Order No. I–1 (Interpretation), 1933', *Sarawak Government Gazette* (*SGG*), 1 July 1933, pp. 160 and 164.

76. See 'Order No. L–2 (Land) 1931', *SGG*, 2 January 1932, pp. 3–30 (especially Sections 90–93).

77. *Sarawak Administration Report (SAR), 1929*, Kuching: Government Printing Office, p. 13. For the constitution of the various Native Land Reserves, see *SGG* where details of each were published.

78. For instance, see Low, *Sarawak*, pp. 19 and 331; Rodney Mundy, *Narrative of Events in Borneo and Celebes, down to the Occupation of Labuan: From the Journals of James Brooke Esq.*, 2 vols., London: John Murray, 1848, Vol. II, pp. 387–8; Henry Keppel, *The Expedition to Borneo of HMS* Dido *for the Suppression of Piracy: With Extracts from the Journal of James Brooke Esq.*, 2 vols., London: Chapman & Hall, 1846; reprinted Singapore: Oxford University Press, 1991, Vol. I, p. 65; and John Crawfurd, *A Descriptive Dictionary of the Indian Islands and Adjacent Countries*, London: Bradbury & Evans, 1856, pp. 158–9.

79. In order to obtain the oil, pits of about a metre in depth were dug; 'Being in swampy ground these pits filled with water on the surface of which the oil floated' and was 'skimmed off by the natives using gourds or cocoanut shells.' T. G. Cochrane, 'Empire Oil: The Progress of Sarawak', *JRSA*, 52, 3723 (28 March 1924), pp. 308–9.

80. See Chapter 8.

81. For instance, see Baring-Gould and Bampfylde, *A History of Sarawak*, p. 368.

82. *SG*, 1 July 1913, p. 147.

83. See Chapter 8.

84. The District Officer of Simanggang commented on the poor attitude of Dayaks in his July 1938 report. 'I fear that it is correct to say that *the majority of these men have made little serious attempt to justify their employment but merely coveted the chance of a free holiday*. The Company [Sarawak Oilfields Limited] complained that a large proportion of the men ceased work without notice and demanded to be returned to Simanggang.' *SG*, 1 September 1938, p. 140. Emphasis added. In the 1950s and early 1960s, the Colonial government discouraged native peoples, especially Dayaks, from leaving their farms to seek temporary work in the oilfields. The government then made arrangements with the oil companies to reject Dayaks who seek such employment. See *Sarawak: Annual Report of the Labour Department, 1952*, Kuching: Government Printing Office, 1953, pp. 3 and 7.

85. See Morris, 'Old Sarawak Society', p. 56.

86. A party of these Saribas Dayaks were murdered by Trusan Muruts in 1885, and this incident subsequently led to the cession of that river from Brunei. See *SG*, 3 January 1885, p. 2; and W. H. Treacher, 'British Borneo: Sketches of Brunai, Sarawak, Labuan and North Borneo', *JSBRAS*, 21 (June 1890), pp. 20–1.

87. Incidentally, these Saribas Dayaks also accepted Christianity and welcomed mission schools and education. For instance, see Pringle, *Rajahs and Rebels*, pp. 199–202; and Ooi Keat Gin, 'Mission Education in Sarawak during the Period of Brooke Rule, 1841–1946', *SMJ*, 62, 63 (December 1991): 316–19.

88. See *SG*, 1 December 1939, p. 234.

89. For instance, see *SG*, 1 July 1931, p. 153; *SG*, 2 January 1936, p. 20; and *SG*, 4 January 1937, p. 21.

90. See *SG*, 1 October 1896, p. 204; and *SG*, 1 February 1897, pp. 34–5.

91. It was only during the Japanese occupation that contact was established with the Kelabits with the landing of a small party of Allied paratroopers. See Tom Harrisson, *World Within: A Borneo Story*, London: Cresset, 1959.

92. *SG*, 15 February 1872, n.p. Emphasis added. This attitude was shared by the various Land Dayak communities of the left branch of the Sarawak River.

93. For instance, in 1938, an experiment in introducing a kind of local government by the creation of village councils was attempted in Land Dayak kampongs, but met with little success for want of capable leadership. See *SAR, 1938*, pp. 33–4.

94. Several studies on the main indigenous groups in Sarawak, commissioned by the Colonial Social Science Research Council for the Colonial administration that governed the country from 1946, revealed few changes in these communities. Moreover, a series of radio broadcasts by European observers of the various ethnic groups in the country during the 1950s, and compiled in a single volume entitled *Peoples of Sarawak*, also confirmed that traditional livelihood was little affected by Brooke rule. See Morris, *Melanau Sago Producing Community*; Geddes, *Land Dayaks of Sarawak*; Freeman, *Iban Agriculture*; and Tom Harrisson (ed.), *The Peoples of Sarawak*, Kuching: Government Printing Press, 1959.

95. *SG*, 2 January 1915, p. 3.

96. C. D. Le Gros Clark, *1935 Blue Report*, Kuching: Government Printing Office, 1935, p. 47. Emphasis added. The Report cited the example of the Sebuyau Dayaks of Lundu who lived in permanent, individual, kampong-style houses under a *Tua Kampong* without undue problems. Ibid.

97. B. J. C. Spurway, 'Shifting Cultivation in Sarawak', *SG*, 1 April 1937, pp. 81–2.

98. In the late 1940s, the debate over Dayak shifting cultivation continued

among Colonial administrators. For instance, see *SG*, 7 May 1949, pp. 97–8; K. E. H. Kay, 'The Economy of the Peoples Living in the Basin of the Batang Sadong', *SG*, 7 September 1949, pp. 221–3; B. E. Smythies, '"To-morrow to Fresh Woods and Pastures New"—A Policy for Shifting Cultivation', *SG*, 7 October 1949, pp. 251–5; and *Agriculture Department Annual Report for 1948*, Kuching: Government Printing Office, 1949.

99. *SG*, 1 August 1874, n.p.

100. Ibid.

8
On the Chinese

JAMES'S and Charles's confidence in the Chinese for the economic development of Sarawak was handsomely rewarded. The Chinese controlled the trade in the chief agricultural exports, namely sago, jungle products, gambier, pepper, and rubber. Similarly, rice and other food imports and consumer necessities were handled by the Kuching Chinese merchant houses. The Chinese dominated the commercial life of the country by their elaborate financial network, credit systems, and banking institutions, and their monopoly of the shipping lines for internal and external trade. Success was also attained in commercial agriculture. The progress and achievements in commercial agriculture, which spurred further immigration, resulted in a Chinese thirst for land which subsequently led to conflict with the native population. The Chinese gold-mines of Upper Sarawak enjoyed fair returns, but the events of 1857 effectively nullified all their gains. The 1930s witnessed a brief revival of Chinese fortunes in the gold industry. Indentured Chinese coolie labour was engaged for the government Simunjan and Brooketon collieries and the Miri oilfields. During the 1920s and 1930s Chinese contract labourers, and Chinese immigration in general, were regulated and restricted for economic and political convenience.

Although the Chinese dominated the economy of the country and remained the largest contributor to the Brooke Treasury through indirect taxation, they were denied the rights and privileges accorded the indigenous peoples. Besides assigning them a non-native status, the Brookes viewed the Chinese with suspicion and caution, keeping constant vigilance over all their activities, lest the spectre of the 1857 uprising reappeared.

From Trusan to Singapore: Chinese Ascendancy in Trade and Commerce

The pacification of the coast and the interior coupled with the rudimentary Brooke legal system was a great impetus to Chinese trading and commercial enterprise. The Brooke court system,

based more on a practical and common sense approach rather than legal niceties, gave the Chinese merchants the assurance that commercial transactions, business agreements, and debts would generally be honoured. The Chinese with their array of entrepreneurial skills penetrated into the heartland of the country bringing consumer and other manufactured goods in exchange for native products and later for cash.

Displacement of Malay Trading

A notable consequence of Chinese trading activities was the gradual exclusion of Malay participation in this sector of the Brooke economy. A Brooke official in the Baram in the early 1880s proudly reported on the commercial expertise of 'our Chinese' that effectively eliminated Brunei Malay competition.

> Aban Nipa [Kayan Tua Kampong of Long Salai] who was formerly so averse to Chinese of Kuching going up to trade at his place, is now anxious they should do so, and he with the Kenniahs were surprised at the prices named by Ken Wat's [Law Kian Huat of Ghee Soon and Company of Kuching] man—who sold them superior blachu for $2 the Kayu, they have always been accustomed to pay $3 for blachu of an inferior description.[1]

Elsewhere, attempts were made by the Malays to regain some of the ground lost to Chinese rivals. Some of the tactics employed proved abortive and received official disapproval like this example of 1911 from Matu.

> The Towkays complained during the month that their trade in the upriver *kampongs* was being seriously interfered with by a number of small Malay traders who were buying up sago and jungle produce from the Milanoes, nearly all of which are under advances in the bazaar; these Malays have now been informed that if they wish to trade in sago and jelutong they must do so under the same conditions as the Chinese.[2]

By the late 1880s, it was apparent that Chinese hegemony was firmly entrenched with few rivals, Malay or otherwise, to contend their position.

Control of the Export Trade

The profitable trade in sago was effectively in Chinese hands by the 1870s. The Chinese dominated most of the country's coastal shipping. By successfully diverting the sago-processing industry to Kuching, instead of Singapore, the Kuching Chinese merchants

controlled both the processing and export of sago. Not content with this arrangement, Kuching Chinese firms established mills in the sago districts.[3]

The Chinese also had a hold on production by a system of advances to the Melanau cultivators. Typically, it operated as follows.

> An enterprising Chinaman is encouraging the natives to plant sago by advancing the money to buy the plants with, and after that more money to defray the expense of planting them out, on the condition that at the end of four years, he is to receive as his share one half the number of the palms originally planted out, and is to be repaid his advances in palms out of their share at the rate of a dollar a tree. Thirteen thousand trees are being planted out on these not illiberal terms.[4]

Besides advances to native planters, the possibility of embarking on large-scale sago cultivation was also explored.[5] During the 1920s Chinese agricultural communities in the Rejang embarked on sago planting which proved successful; but the more lucrative Para rubber, which the Chinese preferred, saved the Melanaus from a serious challenge.

In addition to dominating the sago trade, Chinese merchants also controlled the trade in jungle products. The outstation bazaar Chinese shopkeeper acted as the collecting point for jungle products from Dayaks and other native collectors. These products were then transported to Chinese merchant houses in Kuching for packing and grading before shipment to Singapore, and thence to the world market. As secondary and tertiary traders, the Chinese effectively controlled this important export item, which, together with sago, accounted for more than half the earnings of the Brooke Raj during the last quarter of the nineteenth century.

Unlike the trade in sago and jungle products where Chinese merchants had to rely on native producers and collectors, the direct entry to the market of new commercial crops like gambier, pepper, and Para rubber, further strengthened the Chinese grip on the export trade. In the case of these items, the Chinese not only controlled their trade and export, but were also involved actively in their cultivation. Although there were native pepper and Para rubber planters, the bulk of these two commodities was from Chinese producers.

The majority shares of the Singapore and Sarawak Steamship Company (SSSCo) were held by the main Chinese mercantile firms of Kuching for whose benefit this shipping line served.

Coastal and upriver shipping and the all-important Kuching–Singapore run were controlled by the SSSCo. Chinese domination in shipping was further strengthened in 1919 when the Sarawak Shipping Company (SSCo) replaced the SSSCo. This all-Chinese enterprise satisfactorily served the commercial shipping needs of the Raj, and together with the small fleet of government vessels, it provided adequate passenger facilities throughout the main river systems in the country.

Logging and Timber Exports

> The jungle between Sibu and the mouth of the river abounds in bilian wood; nothing is wanted except labour to make this a lucrative article of commerce. Last year an English Barque of 700 tons shipped a cargo of bilian from here for Hong Kong; and 40 Chinamen are now employed in preparing another; there is material enough to keep 500 at work, were any one to import them for the purpose.[6]

This report of 1871 relating to the Rejang River and Chinese logging activities points to Chinese initiative and industry in tapping this rich resource. But, for want of labour, logging operations were small and limited.[7] Labour shortage was a serious problem; in 1892, for example, logging work at Roban was paralysed for want of workers.[8]

The common mode of transportation of timber exports was by Chinese junks which undertook the journey south from Hong Kong, Macao, or China, to the Rejang ports like Binatang and Sibu.[9] The Chinese mainland, the British Colony of Hong Kong, and the Portuguese outpost of Macao were the chief importers of Sarawak timber.

Most commercial logging during the nineteenth century was in the peat-swamp forests of the Lower Rejang and the delta area, undertaken by Cantonese and Macao Chinese. In the mid-1890s, the Chinese also worked timber in the Baram district, with the first consignment exported in 1894.[10] During the early 1910s, some logging activities were also carried out in the forests above Kapit, and a proposal was put forward for a sawmill at this station.[11] The Chinese also made some attempts to tap the timber resources of the Second Division. Besides the abortive work at Roban, there was a plan by a Chinese Kuching firm to establish a sawmill in the Lower Saribas.[12]

The most sought after and valued timber was the *billian* (*Eusideroxylon zwageri*). It was primarily used by locals for the all-important house posts and for floors and shingles. The fame of this

'Borneo ironwood' even reached Europe. The *London and China Express* reported in the mid-1890s that *billian* from Baram, among various other hardwoods, was to be tested by the municipality of Paris to select the most suitable for paving blocks.[13] There were hopes that a new market would be opened for Sarawak timber but nothing appeared to develop thereafter. In 1908 enquiries were received by the headman of the Cantonese community in the Lower Rejang regarding the possibility of supplying railway sleepers to the Chinese Railway Company.[14] Likewise, there is nothing in the records to tell whether the Cantonese undertook this assignment. However, they did supply the timber requirements of the Public Works Department at Kuching and the long-established Hong Kong and Macao markets.[15]

The output of timber was small and largely consumed by the local market. During the 1920s and 1930s, a small amount of sawn timber was shipped direct to the United Kingdom and there was also a modest supply of logs to the Singapore market (Tables 8.1 and 8.2).

The bulk of timber production came from Chinese logging and sawmilling companies. There were fourteen sawmills in 1938, all Chinese-owned and concentrated mostly in the Rejang, except for one operated by the European-managed Vamco Timber Company in the Fourth Division. The Borneo Company Limited (BCL) had

TABLE 8.1
Production of Timber, 1929–1938

Year	*Volume (tons)*
1929	27,185.0
1930	24,827.0
1931	14,482.0
1932	n.a.
1933	n.a.
1934	13,041.0
1935	16,501.0
1936	15,044.0
1937	16,417.0
1938	20,116.5

Sources: *SAR, 1929*, p. 4; *SAR, 1930*, p. 6; *SAR, 1931*, p. 20; *SAR, 1934*, p. 5; *SAR, 1935*, p. 6; *SAR, 1936*, p. 9; *SAR, 1937*, p. 9; and *SAR, 1938*, p. 7.
Note: 1 ton of timber = 50 cubic feet.

TABLE 8.2
Timber Exports, 1934 and 1935

	Volume (tons)	
Destination	*1934*	*1935*
Borneo ports	1,085	1,638
Singapore	467	1,585
China	223	564
United Kingdom	399	905
South Africa	n.a.	74
Total	2,174	4,766

Source: *SAR, 1935*, p. 7.
Note: 1 ton of timber = 50 cubic feet.

over the years made several, albeit unsuccessful, attempts to enter the timber industry.[16] The Chinese, as can be seen, possessed a near-monopoly of the timber industry during the Brooke period. The scale of operation and amount exported, however, was extremely small compared to the large-scale industry of the post-Brooke years. (Table 8.3 shows the huge difference in the total amount of timber exported and their value between the Brooke period and 1950 and 1960.)

TABLE 8.3
Comparison of Timber Exports between Brooke and Post-Brooke Years

Year	*Logs (hoppus tons)*	*Sawn (cubic tons)*	*Total Timber (hoppus tons)*	*Value (£)*
Brooke				
1920	n.a.	3,910	7,820	3,140
1930	n.a.	n.a.	n.a.	12,170
1940	n.a.	2,500	5,000	3,960
Post-Brooke				
1950	26,500	19,000	64,400	348,440
1960	195,693	165,970	527,633	5,087,510

Source: After Smythies, 'History of Forestry in Sarawak', p. 174.
Note: 1 sawn cubic ton is approximately 2 hoppus tons.

Cornering the Fish Market

Although fishing was largely a Malay and Melanau occupation,[17] the Chinese dominated the sale of the catch in the local fish markets of Kuching and Sibu, acting as middlemen and stallholders. The fish trade at Kuching during the late nineteenth and early twentieth century was a near-monopoly in the hands of a small group of Chinese individuals, who 'buy at their own price from the fishermen, and with a market where the demand is far in excess of supply, they command their own prices, and secure large profits with little labour, and at no risks'.[18] How this came about was explained by a correspondent of the *Gazette*

> The fishermen receive advances, in goods or in money, from the stall-keepers at Kuching, and they are forced to bring their fish in payment of their debt. I go further and state that they are forced to sell the fish at whatever prices these middlemen choose to give. Remembering the fact that the holders of stalls in the fish market at Kuching are not very numerous, can we wonder at the result? These fish sellers combine among themselves as to what they will charge, and the buyer, who leaves one stall hoping to make a better bargain at the next, finds he has made a great mistake.[19]

But according to an editorial in the *Gazette*, the Chinese middlemen 'retain their influence over them [Malay fishermen] by insisting upon paying cash for fish supplied and refusing to credit the value of such fish in reduction of the supplier's debts'.[20] It went on to describe the dilemma faced by the Malay fishermen if they refused to bow to such an exploitative arrangement. 'Should a fisherman try to seek a better market for his fish, or decline to accept the middleman's sweating terms, he runs the risk of being summoned for a debt, which he is totally unable to pay, and consequently of being imprisoned for a long term.'[21]

Practically all the Malay fishermen supplying the Kuching fish market were indebted to the Chinese stallholders. Coupled with the interest charged on the debt, the amount owed was always increasing, thereby strengthening the grip of the middlemen. Such a situation had been in operation for at least a few decades.[22]

The lack of enterprise and the meagre resources of the Malay fishermen were seen as the twin causes of the domination by the Chinese. The Malay fisherman's want of capital to finance his fishing operations, like purchasing nets and food whilst setting up fish traps, forced him to rely on advances and credit given by the Chinese middleman. The middleman was always willing to offer his assistance knowing very well that the loan would ensure a favourable fish supply.

An investigation into the fish trade in the Rejang in 1941 revealed a similar situation of the domination by a few Chinese middlemen.[23] The Chinese operated fast launches which 'often intercept fishing boats at sea to corner the catch' and, storing the fish on board in ice chests or boxes, sped off to the main fish market at Sibu.[24] In this manner, the Chinese middlemen were able to corner the entire fish trade and determine prices to consumers. Besides the monopolistic control by Chinese fish traders, an adverse effect of such action was that coastal Malay and Melanau settlements frequently faced fish shortages; an ironic situation considering that the inhabitants were themselves fishermen.[25]

The report of the investigation recommended the setting up of a Fisheries Department, designating new fish markets, and the appointment of market inspectors as short-term measures for price regulation; and as long-term strategies, the constitution of a fishermen's co-operative and the provision of refrigeration facilities were suggested.[26] However, in less than two months after the report came out, the country was engulfed in the Pacific War.

The fish trade then, whether in Kuching or in Sibu, was clearly in the hands of Chinese middlemen, who were able to enjoy a profitable enterprise at the expense of native fishermen.[27]

Achievements in Commercial Agriculture

> Anyone who takes the trouble to study the difference of cultivation between Dyaks and Chinese *will easily arrive at the conclusion that one Chinese garden is of more value to the country than 50 Dyak holdings*, the former occupying permanently a plot of land of from 1 to 2 acres in extent on which the gardener and his family live and it is hoped will continue to do so for many generations.[28]

The immigrant Chinese gambier and pepper planters, mostly Hakka, made a success of these two crops in Upper Sarawak, which from the 1880s became export products of the country. Gambier cultivation petered out from the 1910s, but pepper continued to flourish. Foochow and Cantonese immigrants in the Rejang also had a hand in pepper cultivation in and around Sibu and in Binatang, Sarikei, and the Lower Rejang districts. The Chinese pepper industry, with its system of advances and contractual arrangements between plantation owners and planters, was plagued with problems, particularly during periods of price slumps when absconding by indebted planters was not uncommon.[29] The more lucrative Para rubber superseded pepper in the

Rejang districts from the 1910s, and from then pepper remained a minor cash crop.

From the 1910s the commercial crop that brought prosperity to the Chinese was undoubtedly Para rubber. The so-called 'rubber fever' and 'planting craze' spread contagiously throughout Chinese settlements in the country. Para rubber was especially popular among the Foochow, Cantonese, and Henghua immigrants in the Rejang districts around Sibu and in the Sarikei area. Foochow settlers in the Baram accounted for most of the district's rubber export.[30] By 1941, it was estimated that the total area under rubber amounted to 95 823 hectares (239,557 acres) of which more than half was Chinese-owned, medium-sized estates (40–120 hectares/100–300 acres) and smallholdings (about 2.4 hectares/ 6 acres).[31] Moreover, practically all the trade relating to rubber, including exports, was handled by Chinese firms in Kuching and Sibu. It was not surprising that the Chinese profited enormously during the boom years of this crop.

The highly profitable returns from rubber led some Chinese to practise monoculture at the expense of other crops, notably rice.[32] Such a move was officially discouraged because of the notorious price fluctuations of rubber.[33] Those who did not heed such warnings and relied wholly on the cultivation of Para rubber for their livelihood were given a harsh lesson during the recession years.[34]

When the Rubber Restriction Scheme was implemented in the mid-1930s, the Chinese on the whole gave their co-operation.[35] Still, there were isolated cases of poor response and outright contravention of the Rubber Restriction Order. In particular there was dissatisfaction with the patrols conducted by Rubber Restriction inspectors to check illegal tapping which resulted in incidents of violence.[36]

Market gardening was practised by the Hakka immigrants who had settled in the outskirts of Kuching. Like their Foochow counterparts in the Rejang, these Hakkas came in the late 1890s as rice farmers, but because of unsuitable conditions, became market gardeners supplying fresh vegetables, eggs, poultry, and pigs to the inhabitants of Kuching. The railway, which extended to the Kuching hinterland, served to transport the produce of these Chinese farms. Similarly on the outskirts of Sibu and Miri and other outstations, Chinese settlers kept poultry, engaged in vegetable gardening, and reared pigs for sale. It was noted that the Chinese 'is an admirable market-gardener and will get more out of half an acre of land than any man else'.[37]

Chinese agricultural enterprise was also evident in the introduction of new commercial crops. An ambitious coconut cultivation scheme 'to plant over 10,000 coconuts at Tanjong Sakol' in Lundu was proposed in 1907. The Chinese entrepreneur 'intends bringing over about 10 doors of Chinese for whose good behaviour he will be responsible' to serve as labour.[38] It was uncertain whether this project was successful. In 1912, at Kapit there were plans to set up a tapioca factory in conjunction with a sawmill, and a Chinese 'has been sent to Batavia and Penang to investigate the workings of such a plant and to ascertain if the project is feasible'.[39] Meanwhile, large areas of land at Kapit as well as at Sibu were cleared for tapioca cultivation employing imported Cantonese coolies.[40] However, the tapioca factory at Kapit was thought unpromising for want of competent workers.[41] In early 1915, the following was reported of Chinese initiative in the Rejang: 'An enterprising Chinese Company has erected steam machinery near Sibu by which they saw planks and work sago and tapioca, and they are said to have laid out $60,000 on this establishment.'[42]

Foochows who had migrated to Baram began Para rubber cultivation in that district. Likewise, when they moved to Sebauh, the Foochows planted coffee and coconut.[43] They also grew Chinese tobacco at Sibu.[44] In Sadong the Chinese farmers were also eager to plant tobacco which was cultivated around the colliery land from seeds supplied by the Agriculture Department.[45]

Chinese initiative and industry earned them success in cash cropping which in turn spurred the growth and expansion of agricultural communities. Charles's wish to convert jungle to 'cultivated lands' was to a large extent fulfilled, as the Lower Rejang exemplified.

Containing the Land-hungry Chinese

The beginnings of commercial agriculture and the arrival of Chinese farmers in the late 1870s created a Chinese demand for land. As already pointed out, cases of Chinese pepper planters encroaching on the farming lands of the Land Dayaks in the First Division were not uncommon. Complaints were aired during the 1890s of the slow process in the issue of land permits to Chinese gambier and pepper planters. In response, Charles ordered the Officer in Charge of the Land Office to hasten the procedure.[46]

Chinese agricultural settlers in the Rejang were growing in number, particularly during and following the years of the rubber

boom. This naturally exerted pressure on the original land granted to the pioneers. The expansion of Chinese settlements in the district became inevitable, and incidents of intrusion and encroachment on Dayak fruit gardens and farms were repeatedly reported, and featured in court proceedings.

Nevertheless native co-operation in allowing Chinese to cultivate their unused land demonstrated the cordial relations between the communities.[47] On occasion, there was resistance to Chinese acquisition of land, as in the case of the Land Dayaks. On the other hand, the Chinese also showed themselves to be difficult, seen here in this example from Sibu. 'The Foo Chow have been lent, for one farming season, sufficient farming land for their requirements. However, they are not satisfied and appear to consider they should be allowed to pick and choose at will and object to Malays and Dyaks farming land adjacent.'[48]

Charles and Vyner understood the Chinese need for land and arranged for such demands to be met over the years. Chinese agricultural settlements were established in the Lower Rejang at Binatang and Sarikei, and further upriver at Kapit, also at Bintulu, and in the Baram.[49] The creation of the Simanggang Land Reserve 'extending for half a mile on each side' of the trunk road was intended to accommodate, to a large extent, Chinese agricultural communities.[50]

There was, however, caution on the part of the government in granting land to the Chinese as they had a tendency to 'trade with and sell these lands to newcomers'.[51] Legislation was enacted to create 'Native Land Reserves' and constant vigilance was maintained to ensure that the shrewder Chinese did not beguile the indigenous people from parting with their land.[52]

Chinese Gold-mining: Prosperity, Setbacks, and Revival

The Chinese, mostly Hakkas, who had crossed from Sambas had worked the gold deposits in Upper Sarawak since the 1820s. By the 1840s gold production was estimated to be 'at least 7,000 ounces' per annum with a work-force of 'about 700'.[53] When the Sambas wars broke out later in the decade and during the 1850s, more Chinese fled across the border, giving a boost to the gold industry as many joined their fellow-countrymen in the mines, although some preferred farming. By the mid-1850s, the mining community, which occupied the area from Siniawan to the Dutch border, was estimated to be about 3,000, while another 500 farmers had

settled in Sungei Tengah and its vicinity.[54] On the whole it was a flourishing settlement under the control of a *kongsi* government with strong secret society influence, a replica of those in Sambas, which functioned and governed relatively independently of James's authority at Kuching.

It was a case of the proverbial 'two suns in the sky', to borrow the words of Mao Tse-tung, and 'one of these would have to be eclipsed'. It was the 'sun' of the Bau Hakka Chinese miners which marched on Kuching in 1857 to sack the town but was 'eclipsed' by the greater 'sun' of the Brooke government. The events of 1857 were a great setback to the gold-mining industry, but more importantly, the entire Chinese community in the country was tainted with this stigma that persisted throughout the period of Brooke rule. Apart from a few prominent Chinese community and business leaders, the entire Chinese population was treated with suspicion. As Chinese secret societies were blamed for the events of 1857, such clandestine organizations were proscribed, with the death penalty imposed on their leaders.[55]

Revival of gold-mining in Upper Sarawak was slow, but gradually the Chinese returned to the district during the 1860s. The BCL at this time also engaged Chinese labour for its antimony and cinnabar mines and its smelting plant at Busau. During the 1870s and 1880s, the BCL assisted Chinese gold-miners with equipment and set up a mill for crushing the ore. But the twilight years of Chinese gold-mining were clearly visible as their primitive methods of panning and sluicing had exhausted the more accessible ore, and were ineffective for the finer deposits. More sophisticated methods and greater capital investment in expertise and equipment were needed.

Under such circumstances, the BCL was poised for a take-over of gold-mining operations, and in the 1890s, bought out the Chinese gold workings and implemented the latest cyanide method of gold extraction. Many Chinese were employed by the BCL as mine coolies and workers in the plants.

It was only in the 1920s when the BCL decided to abandon its gold-mining operations that the Chinese once again, beginning with the BCL's employees, returned to mining gold on their own. Most of the Chinese concerns during this period were involved in reworking the tailings left behind by the BCL. The application of the cyanidation process on these and on the smaller deposits proved worthwhile. During the late 1920s there was a steady increase in the number of Chinese gold-mining companies. A

mini-boom during the first half of the 1930s seemed to indicate that Chinese fortunes in gold had returned, but it was short-lived, and production declined after 1935.

Chinese Coolie Labour and the Brooke Economy

The Brooke Raj had always been plagued with labour shortages, particularly in the extractive industries and in plantation agriculture. Therefore, any influx of immigrants from neighbouring countries was well-received. It was, then, not humanitarian reasons alone that prompted James's government to welcome the influx of Chinese refugees fleeing the Dutch–*kongsi* wars in Sambas in 1850. This influx was augmented by further waves in 1854 and 1856. The disastrous events of 1857 exacerbated the labour problem. The BCL which then had the monopoly of all mineral extraction (except gold) in the country faced an uphill task of acquiring sufficient manpower for its mining operations.

That the mining industry was dependent on Chinese coolie labour was obvious, not only because of their industrious capacity in such long, hard, and painstaking work, but also because 'Malays will not work upon land, proudly calling themselves "orang laut", men of the sea; Dyaks never dream of engaging themselves for any duties whatever except hunting.'[56] It was not surprising that within days of the suppression of the Hakka Chinese miners, James was already welcoming a party of Chinese refugees from Dutch Borneo.[57]

The dire need for Chinese labour motivated both James and Charles to embark on immigration schemes in the attempt to promote commercial agriculture. During the mid-1870s an arrangement was reached between Charles and Law Kian Huat of Messrs Ghee Soon and Company to introduce Chinese gambier and pepper planters into the country. Free passage from Singapore to Kuching was afforded to both plantation owners and their coolies.[58]

From the late 1870s there was a steady flow of Chinese coolies from Singapore, the hub of the coolie trade in the region, to Kuching.[59] Initially the BCL assisted in the recruitment of these coolies, both for its own needs and for the requirements of the Brooke government. The bulk of the coolies were engaged to serve in the government-managed collieries of Simunjan and Brooketon.[60] Later, Charles engaged agents in Singapore to handle the procurement of labourers.[61] Chinese entrepreneurs, whether in

the gambier and pepper industry, in gold-mining, or in the Kuching mercantile houses also recruited workers on their own.

There was, however, much undisguised dissatisfaction with the coolie labour from Singapore, and a paper war ensued between the Chinese Protectorate in Singapore and the Sarawak government. Each blamed the other for the ill health and poor condition of the coolies.[62]

Because of the problematic situation encountered in Singapore and inspired by the superior specimen of coolies landed by the occasional Chinese junks which came to Kuching during the 1870s, Charles turned his attention to the possibility of recruiting coolies direct from China.[63] The 1880s witnessed the closing of the doors to Chinese coolie immigration into countries like Australia, Peru, and the United States (California), which provided the opportunity for Sarawak to tap this supply of human resources. Natural disasters, for example the Hwang-ho River floods that swept the north China plains in the late 1880s, further forced many Chinese to seek a better life abroad. In spite of such 'push-factors', the high cost involved posed a serious obstacle. An editorial of the *Gazette* of 1885 spelled out the huge expenditure required of such an undertaking.

> To obtain coolies from China seems to be next to an impossibility without paying more than double the sum that used to be paid a few years ago. Advances from $25 to $30 are now required, and wages up to $8 and $10, so if any one wished to commence a plantation with one hundred coolies the advances he would have to pay would amount to some $3,000, an outlay which would take a long time to recover, and a good deal of this would be lost owing to absconding coolies and by death; probably it would be found that every tenth coolie suffered from some incurable complaint, so the loss on coolie outlay would be heavy at starting.[64]

Notwithstanding the large expenditure, Charles in 1885 made plans 'to import a large batch of colies [*sic*] direct from China'.[65] However, there was no indication that such measures were executed. Four years later, he suggested to the leading Kuching Chinese business leaders that the government and the Chinese commercial firms jointly fund a regular steamer to China, offering free passage and food on board. This proposal also proved abortive, probably because of the high cost involved.[66]

There was, however, a small traffic in coolies by junks sailing direct from China. The year 1873 saw the first of these junks drop anchor at Kuching 'bringing valuable cargoes and some coolies'.[67]

The visits were irregular and the number of coolies landed was not usually large during the 1870s. Owing to the troubled times in China, the following decades saw more coolies crowding the decks of these junks, with each man hoping for a better life in the *Nanyang*.

The coolies who made the month-long voyage either paid their own way as free emigrants, had their passage money paid by a broker to be repaid after employment, or were funded by a sponsor, often a clansman, whom they had to work for upon arrival as repayment. It was quite common for Chinese who had established themselves in Sarawak to return to their home village and recruit their fellow kinsmen.[68]

When the junks dropped anchor at Kuching, there was an air of pandemonium at the waterfront. 'Look-outs were posted at the mouth of the Sarawak River and as soon as the junks were sighted a mad scramble started to board them as soon as possible and press a half years advances of $30 into each man's hand thus buying him almost body and soul at the rate of 18 cents a day. Most of it went to the broker.'[69] Notwithstanding the long and precarious journey across the South China Sea under wretched conditions, these new arrivals or *sinkheh* were relatively fit and were much favoured for their physical robustness compared with the weak, and often diseased labourers from the Singapore coolie depots.

By the 1890s improvements were effected in the Singapore–Kuching coolie traffic. Outgoing coolies from Singapore and incoming ones to Kuching were subjected to medical checks; then in 1899, Charles issued a set of rules and guidelines 'for the management and regulation of Chinese immigration depots and the engagement of coolies'.[70] The number of indentured coolies for the period 1887 to 1914, where figures are available, was 7,533 males, some 48 women, and 21 children, making a grand total of 7,602.[71] Although there is no ethnic breakdown nor information as to the nature of employment, it can safely be assumed that the majority were Chinese and engaged by the Brooke government for the Simunjan and Brooketon collieries, while the non-Chinese, namely Tamil, served in Charles's Matang Estate.

After 1914, when the indenture system of recruitment was phased out in Singapore, the supply of labour was dependent on free immigrants, notably relatives and kinsmen who came over to join their brethren. But the far more attractive opportunities in the Malay States meant that fewer Chinese coolies were available for the Sarawak labour market. This was particularly felt in the collieries which faced perennial labour shortages.

Indentured Chinese Coolies and the Simunjan Collieries: Sickness and Labour Shortages

> The [Sadong] mine was run on the bad old system of 'indenture' which persisted down to the [19] twenties. Runaway miners were arrested and flogged, but it must not be thought that this treatment was reserved for the victims of 'indenture'. 'Absconding under advances' was a criminal offence, carrying severe penalties whether the erring employee was engaged on 'indenture' or not, and continued to be treated as a criminal offence by many magistrates even up to the last war [Pacific War], although no support for this view could be found in the law.[72]

Such was the plight of the Chinese coolies in the government collieries at Simunjan. Besides the harsh treatment, the work below ground was dangerous, and accidents, sometimes fatal, were not uncommon. There were few safety precautions and any mishaps were blamed on the carelessness of the coolies themselves.

The conditions in the mines were appalling as revealed by two European employees, M. Kendall and E. W. Taylor, reporting in 1904 to Percy Francis Cunynghame, Resident of the First Division.

> I [M. Kendall] am writing to you in regard of No:4 and No:5 Mines [at] Sadong in which I am in charge of, stateing [*sic*] *the bad condition* which I found them, both mines [i]ntake and return airways was as bad as they could be and both mines full of black damp, and scarcely a lamp would burn and here is the water in these mines up to my waist which I have to travel through everyday[;] between the black damp and the water is enough to kill any man.[73]

> Just a few lines to you about the way I [E. W. Taylor] found the 8 & 9 Mines and I was greatly disappointed in the *bad state* both with water and ventilation its too bad for any man in the state I get in everyday [.] I am like a man pulled out the Sadong river but I hope to improve the ventilation before long if I gets [*sic*] luck I have got half an hours [*sic*] walking to do in my wet clothes before I get to my bungalow and trust to a Chinese Dresser if we fall sick.[74]

Both Kendall and Taylor wished to renegotiate their appointments for higher wages, failing which they would terminate their services.

For the Chinese coolies, however, there was no bungalow to return to after work; instead they had to go back to the coolie lines, a row of wooden thatched houses which often flooded during the rainy season and posed potential fire hazards. The food was insufficient in quantity and quality; dietary deficiencies led to outbreaks of diseases, the most common being beriberi.[75]

Medical reports published in the *Gazette* were revealing about the poor conditions of the Chinese coolies. A report of 1891 illustrates the situation. 'Sadong coolies continue to arrive from the mines in a terribly broken-down state of health. Many, according to their own accounts, have been unable to do any work for 2 to 3 months before being sent to Kuching for treatment; one died in the hospital on the day he arrived in Kuching.'[76] Two years later a small ten-bed hospital was set up near the mines at Gunong Ngeli;[77] however, it proved inadequate owing to the high accident rate and level of sickness among the labourers.[78]

The Brooke government found it exceedingly difficult to procure coolies for the collieries, which was not particularly surprising considering the conditions prevailing in the mines. Production suffered for want of workers, and revenue proportionately decreased (see Table 4.2).[79] In 1927, five years before its official closure, the following was disclosed by a government report.

> The [Simunjan] colliery was unable to recruit any labourers, either at Singapore or Hong Kong, in place of those who had taken their discharge ... the labour force had been depleted so seriously by the end of the year that output had fallen short of the local demand, and the Sarawak Steamship vessels had been obliged to take in bunker coal at Singapore as a result.[80]

In 1922 there were 500 coolies employed, but a decade later, when the mine was closed, only 195 labourers were discharged.[81]

Chinese Workers in the Miri Oilfields: Labour Unrest and Militancy

Although the work-force of the oil industry at Miri was multiracial, the Chinese were the dominant ethnic group, particularly during the 1920s and 1930s. In 1920, for instance, Chinese labour accounted for 64 per cent of the total work-force: 47 per cent of the artisans employed, and nearly 70 per cent of the coolie population.[82] The recruitment of Chinese workers was similar to that adopted for the government collieries, namely through the Chinese Protectorate in Singapore. Although there was the problem of shortages, the alternative source of recruitment from Hong Kong during the 1920s, together with the Chinese network of sponsoring blood relatives and clansmen in the home counties, generally satisfied most of the oil company's requirements.[83]

Working conditions in the oil installations undoubtedly possessed an element of danger, but on the whole the situation was

not as precarious as the underground work performed by the colliery coolies of Simunjan.

In the work environment as well as after working hours, there was a distinct racial segregation of the work-force based primarily on the division of European and non-European.[84] Among the Chinese, a pyramidal social structure was evident, with the English-educated clerical staff at the apex while the coolies formed the base.[85] The former were obviously better off in terms of wages, housing facilities, and general standard of living. At the other end of the social scale, the coolies lived in comparatively indigent conditions. Their quarters were often insanitary, and the food provided was of low quality. Malaria and beriberi were common ailments among them, caused by unhygienic living conditions and poor nutrition.[86]

The Chinese coolies were more militant and more assertive of their rights and interests than the mine workers at Simunjan. Labour troubles and unrest, including secret society activities, now and then presented problems for the company management and the local authorities. For instance, in June 1911,

> sixty of the Anglo-Saxon Petroleum Company's coolies had arrived, armed, in front of the Miri Court House and attempted to rescue three prisoners from the Miri gaol; failing in this they proceeded to their *mandor*'s [overseer] and attempted to murder him but were driven off by the Assistant Resident and four others, one of their number sustaining a broken arm in the fight which took place.... The five ringleaders of the Chinese mob were arrested and sentenced in Court to seven years hard labour each.[87]

Three years later, an informant exposed the workings of a secret society among the Chinese coolies. The ingenious strategy employed by the management in publicly announcing during pay-day the penalty of involvement in such clandestine organizations, including the death sentence for the leaders, effectively succeeded in suppressing such activities.[88] In early 1922, a reoccurrence of the 1911 incident was reported. The coolies went on strike to demand 'justice for the supposed murder of their number', and when no action was taken, they 'tried to storm the Court House'. Local Chinese *towkay* interceded to diffuse further acts of violence and successfully 'persuaded the strikers to go home and, after conferring with the General Manager [of Sarawak Oilfields Limited] ... over various details, [the coolies] agreed to return to work the following day, which they did and there has been no further trouble'.[89] A year after this incident, an assault by a Javanese worker on a non-company Chinese was used as a pretext by the

Chinese coolies to voice their grievances to their employer by demonstrations, which subsequently got out of control, resulting in thirteen coolies dead and twenty-four wounded when the police were ordered to fire on the crowd.[90]

In general, the Chinese workers in the Miri oilfields fared better than their Simunjan counterparts. Their more forceful demonstration of disaffection, to a certain extent, allowed their complaints to be heard, though on certain occasions, with fatal consequences.

Restriction of Chinese Immigration: Economic Necessity and Political Expediency

Chinese immigration was encouraged throughout James's and Charles's reigns but some restrictions were enforced during Vyner's rule owing to the economic and political climate of the 1920s and 1930s. During these two decades there were no organized group immigration schemes; entry permits were only granted to relatives and dependants of those already resident in the country. In this instance, the Chinese extended family system enabled many more to enter the country. In addition, there was clan sponsorship for kinsmen in the home villages as, from a Chinese perspective, clansmen were considered 'family'. Owing to the need for labour, the government also allowed local contractors to travel to Hong Kong and China to recruit workers.

In order to control and streamline immigration and labour matters, both closely interrelated and largely Chinese affairs, Vyner created a Labour Protectorate in 1927, and two years later, amalgamated it with the newly established Secretariat for Chinese Affairs and appointed a Protector of Labour and Chinese.[91]

The recession of the early 1920s did not create any serious problems of unemployment among the coolie population, and few repatriations were carried out, although stricter screening of new immigrants was practised. But on the political front, as the situation in the Chinese mainland became increasingly unstable, the Brooke authorities became more vigilant of subversive elements and agitators entering the country, especially during the late 1920s.[92] The fact that, in addition to fresh immigrants, there was also a constant flow of Chinese from Sarawak returning to the homeland for brief periods and re-entering the country, made it a difficult task to monitor effectively this flow of new arrivals and returnees. In order to enforce greater surveillance, new immigrants were issued a kind of identity card with a photograph of the holder.

Arrangements have been made for all immigrants in future to produce their photographs in duplicate on arrival; their names will be registered and each man's name and number will be written on his photo for identification purposes. This photograph must be produced whenever he has any business with Government and all items of interest, including property acquired or disposed of, will be noted on his identification card filed with Government.[93]

Furthermore, as a preventive measure to stamp out troublemakers and political 'undesirables', an unwritten regulation, the so-called 'guarantee system' was imposed, whereby 'the community guarantees the immigrant, and is held for his well-being and behaviour for a period of twelve months after arrival in Sarawak'.[94] This had effective results. These measures were also particularly useful in deporting mischief-makers, like those involved in secret society activities.[95]

In 1933, when the situation in the Chinese mainland became more volatile, Vyner enforced stricter controls on immigration against 'undesirables'. This report from the Secretariat for Chinese Affairs described the measures undertaken.

During the month [March 1933], His Highness the Rajah authorized a stricter control of immigration, by land or sea, into the State. The effect of this authority will give the Protector [of Chinese] power to prevent the entrance into the country of undesirable persons, always providing that sanction is obtained from His Highness the Rajah. Order No. L–3 (Labour Protection), Section 9 (i), is thus given a clearer definition, and Residents have been informed by letter as to the class of immigrants who may reasonably be excluded under this authority, which will now extend the control of the Immigration Officer over all classes and nationalities.[96]

The success of the implementation of these measures was evidenced by the conspicuous absence of organized agitation by leftist elements.[97] The Administration Report for 1934 proudly attested to Sarawak's immunity from subversive activities that had plagued the Straits government, and boasted of the effectiveness of the strategies employed.

Sedition is non-existent, and there was nowhere any unrest or political disturbance, the Chinese throughout the State remaining everywhere peaceful and law-abiding. There is no doubt that the State's freedom from political agitators and other undesirable characters is in a large measure due to the present strict control of immigration, and particularly to the good effects of the 'guarantee system,' which has now been operating satisfactorily for several years. It is, however, a fact that the Chinese in Sarawak show a noticeable lack of interest in politics in China.[98]

The outbreak of the Second Sino-Japanese War in 1937 rattled the characteristic Chinese nonchalance regarding events in the motherland. But even this momentous happening did not stir the Chinese in Sarawak to a great display of patriotism and anti-Japanese behaviour. Their actions were limited to contributions to the China Relief Fund, the boycott of Japanese goods, and minor mischiefs that were 'hardly worth recording'.[99]

The Depression of 1929–31 was more severe than the trade recession of the early 1920s, and unemployment among the Chinese, especially in the First and Third Divisions, was considerable. Chinese coolies in pepper plantations accounted for most of the unemployed in the First and Second Divisions, while the majority of the unemployed in the Third Division comprised Chinese smallholders whose farms 'were not yet in bearing, and who rely on obtaining part-time employment from larger owners'.[100] The timely revival of Chinese gold-mining in Upper Sarawak was able to absorb most of the out-of-work coolies.[101] From March 1930 'immigration was rigorously restricted and control of the movements of Chinese was extended to all Sarawak ports'. As a result of these measures, unemployment was reduced and the situation 'returned to normal by the end of the year'.[102] In the Third Division, the government implemented special public works, like the construction of roads to link farming areas to the ports, to provide employment for the coolies who had been laid off.[103]

But the optimism aired during 1930 of the unemployment situation was dashed the following year, when conditions, instead of improving, became acute. Consequently more drastic measures were needed to alleviate unemployment. Towards the end of the year, it became inevitable that repatriation of 'all those Chinese whose age and physical condition made it improbable that they could find work' had to be carried out.[104] Although repatriation appeared to be an inhumane strategy, considering that such individuals undoubtedly would suffer considerable hardship upon their forced return to a war-torn and disastrous socio-economic situation in China, Brooke officials viewed the move as the 'most economical method' of dealing with the unemployment problem.[105] It was a situation in which economic expediency overrode humanitarian considerations. The Kuching Chinese Unemployment Relief Fund Committee, whose members were leading Chinese *towkay*, offered to assist the government in this difficult and expensive task by agreeing 'to pay one half of the expenses of repatriation' and 'to shoulder the responsibility of ascertaining that

the applicants were suitable subjects for Government assistance'.[106]

Although from 1934 the economic situation had begun gradually to recover, the Brooke government did not relax immigration control; in fact the contrary was the case.

> The immigration laws continued to be strictly enforced during the year, and were supplemented by the enactment of Order No. D–2 (Disembarkation) by which aliens may be required to pay a deposit before being permitted to land. No immigrant may now enter the State unless he is in possession of a Sarawak Certificate of Identity, Passport, or Landing Permit.[107]

Apart from political considerations, immigration control was strictly maintained after 1934 to the outbreak of the Pacific War as one of the strategies employed to regulate production under the Rubber Restriction Scheme. The effects of strict immigration control as a strategy in controlling rubber output were considered 'by no means negligible', as shown by the higher wages paid to tappers.[108] None the less, a note of warning was sounded that 'severe restriction of immigration is harmful to the interests of other industries in the State and cannot continue indefinitely to be employed as a method of rubber restriction'.[109] But, apart from the noticeable higher wages, W. F. N. Bridges in his government-commissioned report of 1937 on rubber regulation in the country, maintained that 'there is no satisfactory yardstick with which to measure their effect on rubber production'.[110]

The overall picture of Brooke legislation pertaining to Chinese immigration seemed at times extreme and overly cautious, but the end results were beneficial: low unemployment, minimal labour unrest, and a conspicuous absence of subversive communist activities and other political disturbances which troubled neighbouring countries in the region.

Contribution to the Brooke Treasury: 'Farms', Customs Duties, and State Revenue

> [A] Chinaman is willing to work on condition that he is well fed; he wants his four or five meals a-day, consisting mainly of rice, vegetables, and pork. He must have his tea, tobacco, opium, and samshu, a spirit distilled from rice, and, when he has ready money, he must gamble. He is, therefore, an excellent subject to tax, and from the opium, arrack, and gambling farms, the Sarawak treasury was largely replenished.[111]

The Chinese community was the single most important contributor to the State coffers in the form of 'farm' revenues which accounted for a large proportion of the total revenue collected. The government held monopolies for opium, arrack,[112] gambling, and pawn shops, which were commodities and activities almost exclusive to the Chinese community, and let or 'farmed' out the sale of these commodities and the running of these activities, either individually or collectively, to the highest bidder, usually to leading Kuching *towkay*. The acquisition of these farms was enormously profitable: it meant the possession of exclusive rights to the sale of opium and arrack, and control of the pawning and gambling activities of the entire Chinese population in the country.[113] The lucrative aspect of managing these farms can be ascertained from the following statistics: in 1859, contributions from government monopolies, namely opium, gambling, and spirits, amounted to $22,715, out of a total of $35,485 revenue collected, an astonishing 64 per cent.[114] On the average, revenue from the various farms contributed to about one-third of the total revenue.

During the reign of Charles, although farm revenues still remained a significant contributor to the Exchequer, there was a gradual decline in their share of the total revenue in the twentieth century. Offsetting this fall in farm revenues was a corresponding increase in export and import duties, to which the Chinese again were the largest contributors. Revenue from customs duties on the export trade from the 1870s were largely generated by Chinese participation, either directly, as in the cultivation of commercial crops, or indirectly, as in the trade in sago and jungle products. Moreover, the Chinese community, as the main consumers of imported rice and 'excisable and Manchester goods',[115] was responsible for most of the revenue from import duties.

Table 8.4 shows the revenue generated from the farms and customs duties during the Brooke period. The increase in the farm revenues between 1880 and 1890 was the result of the increase in the Chinese population when cash cropping of gambier and pepper became important.[116] The success of Charles's immigration scheme in the Rejang was not reflected in increases in farm revenues; instead, a decrease was recorded, from about 30 per cent in 1900 to 27 per cent in 1910. This was due to the fact that the Foochow community, by far the largest among the new immigrants, in compliance with Methodist tenets, did not allow the operation of farms in their settlements as stated in the agreement between their leaders and Charles.[117] The downward trend of farm revenue

TABLE 8.4
Farm Revenue and Customs Duties of Brooke Sarawak, 1870–1939

Year	*Farms*				*Total for Farms (& Percentage of Total Revenue)*	*Duties*		*Total for Duties (& Percentage of Total Revenue)*	*Total Revenue*
	Opium	*Gambling*	*Arrack*	*Pawn*		*Imports*	*Exports*		
1870	No Breakdown				47,420.00 (38.60)	7,449.40	3,835.08	11,284.48 (9.18)	122,841.79
1880	60,000.00	19,314.25	7,184.00	1,620.00	88,118.25 (38.35)	18,704.67	31,722.78	50,427.45 (21.95)	229,718.01
1890	144,240.00	34,096.00	20,780.00	3,196.50	202,312.50 (48.97)	28,153.47	34,332.25	62,485.72 (15.12)	413,112.69
1900	149,760.00	87,125.00	40,035.00	5,615.00	282,535.00 (30.84)	92,201.59	198,499.52	290,701.11 (31.74)	915,966.06
1910	No Breakdown				385,070.75 (27.36)	151,515.49	351,985.81	503,501.30 (35.78)	1,407,359.88
1920	No Breakdown				564,576.85 (21.33)	186,661.80	878,598.94	106,526.07 (40.25)	2,646,265.04
1930	Opium Only				493,457.02 (8.87)	946,091.00	323,864.00	1,269,955.00 (22.83)	5,562,034.59
1939	Opium Only				580,977.00 (12.20)	1,839,253.85	374,002.70	2,213,256.50 (46.45)	4,762,532.00

Sources: *SG*, 28 February 1871, n.p.; *SG*, 1 April 1881, p. 29; *SG*, 1 May 1891, p. 76; *SG*, 1 May 1901, p. 100; *SGG*, 1 May 1911, pp. 79–80; *SGG*, 1 June 1921, pp. 145 and 147; *SAR, 1930*, pp. 2, 4, and 36; *Sarawak Annual Report of the Government Monopolies for 1930*, p. 3; Hepburn, *Handbook of Sarawak*, p. 92; *Annual Report by the Sarawak Government Concerning Prepared Opium in the Sarawak Territory for the Calendar Year 1939*, p. 1; and 'Department of Trade and Customs: Annual Statistics and Accounts for the Year 1939', *Supplement to the SGG*, 15 June 1940, p. 34.

continued throughout the 1920s and 1930s. On the other hand, revenue from customs duties rose dramatically, from less than 10 per cent of the total revenue in 1870 to about 46 per cent in 1939. Particularly noteworthy was the significant 'jump' in export duties after the introduction in the late 1870s of gambier and pepper cultivation, a wholly Chinese enterprise from cultivation to marketing. A large amount of the revenue from export duties in 1910 was the result of the export of manufactured Para rubber, a sector also largely dominated by the Chinese. The drop in both revenues for 1930 was due to the effects of the economic slow-down during the Depression, felt in all branches of the economy.

In mid-June 1910, owing to financial problems faced by the tenderers of the farms, the government decided to release them from their contracts and created a syndicate to assume control. The Sarawak Farms Syndicate proved to be an unqualified financial success.[118] Encouraged by this achievement, Charles decided to 'privatize' the farm system and to relinquish altogether any government involvement. A new farms syndicate, wholly managed by the Chinese, was inaugurated on 1 July 1911.[119] But, apparently, when its tenure expired in mid-1914,[120] Charles decided that the government should once again actively involve itself by contributing $80,000 of the $200,000 capital outlay and appointing an European officer to the syndicate's board of directors.[121] The government's re-entry into the business of farms was probably a realization that this source of revenue was too important to leave entirely in the hands of a group of private Chinese individuals. It was also an attempt to eliminate any smuggling or illicit trading in these monopolies.

In 1924, conforming to the policies laid down by the League of Nations, Vyner's government reassumed full control of the opium monopoly that 'included the registration of opium smokers, the closing down of numerous retail shops and their replacement by a few Government divans' without undue opposition or difficulties.[122] A Chinese Advisory Committee was constituted to assist the authorities. The government undertook direct control of the importation, preparation, distribution, and sale of opium.

An investigation, headed by a committee with thirteen Chinese members and chaired by the government Controller of Monopolies, was conducted in 1928 to consider the practicalities of restricting public gambling in the country.[123] 'The object in view', stated in the Administration Report for 1929, 'being the gradual and final abolition of public gaming.'[124] Moral considerations were

undoubtedly behind this move, for any restriction would adversely affect the revenue from this gambling farm. On the other hand, greater and closer control could be effected to reduce illicit gaming. The restrictions introduced included a minimum age of 16, limitations in hours of play, a shortened period of the operation of public gambling booths to a fortnight during festive occasions like Chinese New Year, and the proscription of certain games altogether.[125]

A dwindling share in the revenue from farms *vis-à-vis* the greater proportion from customs duties during the closing years of Brooke rule was a clear indication that Sarawak was moving further into the world market economy and gradually shedding the image of its isolation.

Conclusion

There is but one people who can develop the islands of the Eastern Archipelago, and they are the Chinese. They are a most industrious and saving nation, and yet liberal in their households and free in their personal expenses. They are the only people to support an European government, as they are the only Asiatics who will pay good revenue.[126]

These words of Spenser St John, penned in the early 1860s, predicted the promise of the Chinese. Without any doubt, the Chinese, more than any other community in Brooke Sarawak, acted as a catalyst in economic development. Chinese shophouses close to the government fort was a typical scene in the outstation. From trading activities to cash cropping, the Chinese played a major role in their advancement. Chinese economic successes were shown by their domination of most branches of trade, in the cultivation of commercial crops, and as the bulk of the labour force in the extractive industries.

Furthermore, the free-spending qualities of the Chinese extended their contribution to the Brooke Treasury in the form of indirect taxation through government monopolies, namely in their consumption of opium and arrack, their recreational activities as compulsive gamblers, and their patronage of pawn shops. Moreover, the Chinese were also largely responsible directly for the increasing revenue from customs duties through their trading activities and agricultural pursuits and their enormous appetite for imported rice and Western-manufactured goods.

Notwithstanding their accomplishments and contributions, the Brookes were suspicious of Chinese intentions, and in general, mistrustful of the whole community. Chinese triad activities were

proscribed; those apprehended for involvement in such, from the Brooke perspective, subversive organizations, faced long terms of imprisonment, deportation, or even the death penalty. The Brookes also resorted to precautionary measures by enforcing stricter immigration control, particularly during the 1920s and 1930s, when the political situation in mainland China became increasingly unstable.[127] Tighter entry requirements and other arrangements like the 'guarantee system' were imposed to ensure that subversive elements, political agitators, and other malcontents fleeing China did not enter Sarawak to disturb the relatively peaceful existence of the resident Chinese community. These prudent measures were well-rewarded with the notable absence of political unrest, subversive propaganda, or leftist activities.

At the same time, immigration control was reinforced in the years of the Depression to alleviate the unemployment situation. Thereafter, during the post-Depression period, similar strict control was maintained as one of the strategies to ensure the success of the Rubber Restriction Scheme.

Nevertheless, during the early 1910s, Charles displayed his confidence and trust in Chinese communal leaders by endowing seven of them with magisterial powers to preside over a newly created Chinese Court. It was felt that the Chinese themselves would be in a far better position to handle matters relating to marriage and the division of properties where Chinese customary law and tradition applied.[128] At the same time, Charles handed over the running and management of the opium and other farms to a Chinese consortium of local Kuching *towkay*, thereby relinquishing government involvement in the day-to-day operations.

But apart from such concessionary overtures, the status of the Chinese in the country remained ambiguous until 1931. Vyner's land laws of 1920, which defined 'Native' as a 'natural born subject of His Highness the Rajah', legally included those Chinese born in the country as well as those who had successfully acquired a certificate of naturalization.[129] In practice, such was not generally the case even though 'Native', was a term denoting nationality, and not ethnic status. But from 1931, the Land Rules clearly excluded Chinese from the list of indigenes. Under the Land Rules of 1933, when land was classified into 'Native Area' and 'Mixed Zone', the Chinese as 'aliens' were prohibited from acquiring any rights to 'Native Area Land'. The growth in the Chinese population during the 1920s and 1930s increased their demand for land. By 1939, the Chinese, who accounted for a quarter of the total

population, had access to only one-tenth of the total land area in the country.[130]

Within Brooke official circles, the Chinese were seen as a mainly transient immigrant community. The fact that annually large numbers of Chinese voyaged back to the home country and after a brief period returned to Sarawak further reinforced their transient image. However, the notion of the Chinese coolie, who arrived penniless and after years of toil returned with a little savings to die in his native village, was unsubstantiated in reality. No doubt some Chinese regarded Sarawak only as a convenient place to seek their fortune, but few acquired such a fortune, and fewer still, for want of financial means and/or physical ability, retired to the homeland. But more significant was the fact that 'a considerable number of the wealthier and more powerful men in Kuching showed little inclination to leave their thriving businesses for retirement in China. The Hokkiens in particular developed a reputation among the Kuching Chinese for permanent settlement, which no doubt assisted them in achieving economic dominance.'[131]

Besides this general perception of their transient status, their non-payment of capitation taxes, like the 'head' and 'door' taxes that the Malays, Dayaks, and other indigenous peoples were obliged to pay, placed the Chinese community in a different category from the rest. The payment of such taxes by the natives, apart from its financial aspect, had socio-political connotations; it symbolized the close relationship between ruler and subjects, an expression of the loyalty of the latter to the former. The Chinese, then, were outside this close affinal relationship. To carry this point further, keeping in mind the significant exception of the Chinese Court, no Chinese was appointed to the administrative ranks of the Brooke government or allowed to hold magisterial powers.[132] Nevertheless, the Chinese graduates of the English mission school were welcome to join the civil service in clerical positions or the judiciary as court writers and interpreters.[133]

The Chinese status as non-natives was further emphasized by the fact that the Brookes had no qualms in allowing the exploitation of Chinese coolies in the generally disagreeable conditions prevailing in the Simunjan collieries or in the Miri oilfields. As *aliens*, Chinese labourers were not sheltered by the Brooke umbrella of paternalism.

Brooke–Chinese relations can be summarized in the following words.

There had been no real attempts to understand the Chinese. Because of indirect rule most contacts with the Chinese had always been through a small group of privileged Chinese leaders who traditionally belonged to the wealthy and influential merchant class, or were appointed area headmen and *kapitans*, and through European and Asian members of the Sarawak civil service. The Rajahs had respected the Chinese for their industry but had also been suspicious of their activities and intentions, which no doubt arose out of mutual ignorance and common disdain for each other's way of life.[134]

1. *Sarawak Gazette* (*SG*), 1 May 1883, p. 50.

2. *SG*, 16 June 1911, p. 113.

3. Chinese mills in the sago districts often preferred Chinese coolies who were assumed to be more efficient than natives, but were much more costly to maintain. For instance, see *SG*, 1 July 1913, p. 148.

4. *SG*, 1 March 1882, pp. 15–16.

5. For instance, in 1909 the Kuching firm of Messrs Ong Tiang Swee proposed a scheme to 'start a large sago working business either at Kaba or Pungkang, using Chinese labour, to supply which they will import 200 or 300 coolies'. *SG*, 2 August 1909, p. 171. Apparently this venture did not materialize as there was no mention of it thereafter.

6. *SG*, 24 January 1871, n.p.

7. For a typical Chinese sawmilling operation during the mid-1930s, see *SG*, 2 December 1935, p. 231.

8. See *SG*, 1 September 1892, p. 167. See also *SG*, 1 November 1911, p. 217.

9. For instance, see *SG*, 1 March 1882, p. 15; *SG*, 1 September 1884, p. 93; and *SG*, 3 January 1898, p. 16.

10. See *SG*, 2 January 1895, p. 2.

11. However, the outcome of this sawmill project, which was to combine with a tapioca factory that proved abortive and eventually abandoned, was unknown. See *SG*, 16 November 1912, p. 255; *SG*, 2 January 1915, p. 3; and *SG*, 1 February 1916, p. 36.

12. An official report of April 1923 mentioned that 'Mr Kon En Law, Manager Sarawak Steam Sawmills, Ltd., Kuching, made a tour of inspection of the lower Saribas with a view to obtaining permission to work timber there'. *SG*, 2 July 1923, p. 209. No further mention was made thereafter.

13. See *SG*, 1 February 1896, p. 22.

14. See *SG*, 16 November 1908, p. 288.

15. For instance, see *SG*, 1 February 1909, p. 32. In competition with the Cantonese in the Rejang, the Kuching firm of Messrs Yeo Ban Hock, working *billian* in the Sebuyau River near the Batang Lupar, also supplied the timber needs of the Kuching Public Works Department. See *SG*, 31 December 1910, p. 270.

16. See Chapter 9.

17. Chinese were also involved in fishing, notably the Henghua community at Sungai Apong on the outskirts of Kuching, but their numbers were small compared

to the natives. However, one striking difference between Chinese and native fishermen was that the former engaged in fishing as a full-time occupation while the latter combined fishing with other agricultural pursuits.

18. *SG*, 1 December 1900, p. 215. See also *SG*, 1 April 1889, pp. 47–8.

19. *SG*, 2 March 1900, pp. 46–7.

20. *SG*, 1 December 1900, p. 215.

21. Ibid.

22. An example was cited of an elderly Malay fisherman who had been kept in debt in this manner for a period of thirty years to the advantage of the Chinese middleman, while he eked out a bare subsistence. See ibid.

23. In February 1941, the Resident of the Third Division appointed a committee 'to enquire into, and make recommendations concerning, the fish trade generally, in the Rejang River'. The committee consisted of two European Brooke officers, a Malay Native officer, and a Chinese, presumably a court writer at Sibu. A report was submitted sometime in late October that year. See 'A Report on the Fish Trade in the Rejang Delta', *c.*October 1941, Typescript, MSS Ind. Ocn. s. 234(1), Anthony John N. Richards, p. 1, RHL, Oxford.

24. Ibid., p. 6. The operating costs of the launches appeared to be 'negligible': 'The boats are mostly run with a dead load of ice in the one direction to pick up one load of fish' on the return journey to Sibu. With low cost, it meant high profits for the Chinese middlemen. Ibid.

25. Ibid.

26. See ibid., pp. 6–8.

27. During the post-Brooke period, a Fisheries Survey Department, established in 1948, conducted a survey of the fishing industry. B. A. St J. Hepburn (comp.), *The Handbook of Sarawak: Comprising Historical, Statistical and General Information Obtained from Official and Other Reliable Records*, Singapore: Malaya Publishing House for the Government of Sarawak, 1949, pp. 64 and 122. A study in the 1960s revealed that Chinese control of the fish trade remained intact in both Kuching and Sibu. See James C. Jackson, *Sarawak: A Geographical Survey of a Developing State*, London: University of London Press, 1968, pp. 119–20.

28. *SG*, 2 January 1915, p. 3. Emphasis added.

29. The arrangement between planter and sponsor or owner, the latter usually the local Chinese bazaar shopkeeper or *towkay*, was that the planter would be given advances of money, materials, seeds, and provisions by the *towkay* to undertake the cultivation of the crop. The contractual understanding, which involved the signing of an agreement by both parties and the registration of this document with the local authority, was that the planter was contracted to sell his harvested crop to the *towkay*, often at a preferential price favourable to the latter. As long as the price was high, the planter would keep to his promise and sell to his *towkay*, for profits could still be made by both parties. However, when prices fell, the planter would be at a decided disadvantage. Therefore, in order to avert losses, the planter resorted to one of the following strategies: he sold his harvest to other *towkay* at a higher price, then ran away with the profits; after selling off his harvest to another *towkay*, he unscrupulously reported the 'theft' of his crop and continued to demand advances from his *towkay* for the next season's planting; he absconded altogether with the advances after some initial display of token planting. Absconders often crossed the border to Dutch Borneo, and to a lesser extent, to Brunei. The *towkay*, on their part, without the capability and manpower to manage their own gardens to ensure the guaranteed delivery of the harvest, had no alternative but to tolerate such an unsatisfactory contractual relationship. These problems were often referred to

arbitration bodies, like the Kongkek, to resolve. However, some *towkay* preferred the Brooke court system for justice. Safeguards against abuses of the system were incorporated in the 'terms and conditions' for encouraging gambier and pepper cultivation. See *SG*, 1 November 1895, pp. 193–4; *SG*, 2 March 1896, pp. 39–40; *SG*, 1 October 1896, pp. 190–1; *SG*, 1 November 1916, p. 239; *SG*, 7 March 1949, p. 54; and *SG*, 7 April 1949, p. 92.

30. See Richard H. Goldman, 'The Beginnings of Commercial Development in the Baram and Marudi Following the Cession of 1881', *SG*, 31 March 1968, p. 64.

31. See Jackson, *Sarawak*, pp. 90–1.

32. For instance, see *SG*, 1 February 1916, p. 36.

33. For instance, see *SG*, 16 May 1914, p. 119.

34. For instance, see *SG*, 1 February 1921, pp. 13 and 15.

35. For instance, see *SG*, 1 April 1936, p. 93; and, *SG*, 1 July 1936, p. 172.

36. For instance, see *SG*, 1 June 1937, p. 135; and *SG*, 2 August 1937, p. 178.

37. S. Baring-Gould and C. A. Bampfylde, *A History of Sarawak under Its Two White Rajahs, 1839–1908*, London: Henry Sotheran, 1909, p. 187.

38. *SG*, 2 November 1907, pp. 249–50.

39. *SG*, 16 November 1912, p. 255.

40. *SG*, 16 January 1913, p. 23.

41. *SG*, 1 February 1916, p. 36.

42. *SG*, 2 January 1915, p. 4.

43. See *SG*, 1 March 1932, p. 57.

44. *SG*, 1 June 1931, p. 131.

45. *SG*, 1 November 1932, p. 186.

46. See *SG*, 1 August 1894, p. 119; and 'Order No. VIII, 1894', *SG*, 1 August 1894, p. 116.

47. For instance, see *SG*, 2 January 1913, p. 4; and *SG*, 16 December 1915, p. 289.

48. *SG*, 1 July 1918, p. 160.

49. For instance, see Chiang Liu, 'Chinese Pioneers, AD 1900: The New Foochow Settlement', *SMJ*, 11, 6 (December 1955): 542–8; John M. Chin, *The Sarawak Chinese*, Kuala Lumpur: Oxford University Press, 1981, pp. 59–69; and Michael Leigh, 'The Spread of Foochow Commercial Power before the New Economic Policy', in R. A. Cramb and R. H. W. Reece (eds.), *Development in Sarawak: Historical and Contemporary Perspectives*, Monash Paper on Southeast Asia No.17, Centre of Southeast Asia Studies, Melbourne: Monash University, 1988, pp. 180–1.

50. See *Sarawak Administration Report (SAR), 1929*, Kuching: Government Printing Office, pp. 13–14; *SG*, 1 November 1930, p. 279; *SAR, 1930*, pp. 17–18; *SG*, 1 April 1931, p. 83; *SG*, 1 May 1931, p. 103; *SG*, 1 March 1933, p. 35; *SG*, 1 April 1933, p. 47; *SG*, 1 May 1933, p. 65; and *SG*, 1 June 1933, p. 77.

51. 'Father Halder, Roman Catholic Mission, to W. F. de V. Skrine, Resident, 3rd Division, 20 March 1925', MSS Ind. Ocn. s. 143(2), RHL, Oxford. See also 'J. M. Hoover, Protector of the Foochows, to W. F. de V. Skrine, Resident, 3rd Division, 3 March 1925', ibid.

52. During the post-Brooke years, similar caution was required. Sir Alexander Nicol A. Waddell, the last Colonial Governor of Sarawak, stated that 'if the natives are allowed to sell or rent their Customary Land to the Chinese, it would not be very long before the natives were driven further into the jungle'. 'A Glimpse of the Foochow-speaking Community in Sarawak', n.d. [*c*.1962], Typescript, MSS Pac. s. 105(6), Sir Alexander N. A. Waddell, p. 15, RHL, Oxford.

53. Hugh Low, *Sarawak: Its Inhabitants and Productions; Being Notes during a Residence in that Country with His Excellency Mr Brooke*, London: Frank Cass, 1848; new impression, 1968, p. 26.

54. Spenser St John, *Life in the Forests of the Far East*, 2 vols., London: Smith, Elder & Co., 1862; reprinted Kuala Lumpur: Oxford University Press, 1974, Vol. II, p. 335.

55. For the death penalty of the leader of a 'secret *hueh*', see Order dated 14 May 1870, '*Orders Which Have Not Since Been Cancelled, Issued by HH The Rajah of Sarawak or with His Sanction, from 1863 to 1890 Inclusive*', Kuching: Government Printing Office, 1891, Vol. II, p. 114; and *SG*, 24 January 1871, n.p. However, it has been pointed out that enforcement of such regulations was difficult, if not impossible.

'As the law now stands in Sarawak the simple fact of a man belonging to the Secret Society would entail his death, but this law is practically a dead letter, and would be almost impossible to carry out from the difficulty of procuring proof, and as very many of the Chinese have been affiliated before entering the country; and cannot leave the Hue after once entering it, the law of the Hue for such an offence being also death, they find themselves in an awkward predicament.'

N. Denison, 'Notes on the Land Dyaks of Sarawak Proper', *SG*, 16 January 1877, p. 7. Such draconian laws did not deter secret society activities which emerged now and then; for example, during the unfavourable economic environment of the early 1930s, the authorities uncovered such activities which were subsequently clamped down. See n. 95 below.

56. Frederick Boyle, *Adventures among the Dyaks of Borneo*, London: Hurst and Blackett, 1865, p. 69.

57. See St John, *Life in the Forests*, Vol. II, p. 364.

58. See 'Proclamation, 8 December 1875', *SG*, 3 January 1876, n.p. However, other Chinese with no connection with the gambier and pepper companies took advantage of this liberal offer of free steamer passage, prompting the government to issue a notice prohibiting such unethical practices. See *SG*, 1 June 1882, p. 39.

59. For a study of this Chinese coolie traffic, see Persia Crawford Campbell, *Chinese Coolie Emigration to Countries within the British Empire*, London: D. S. King, 1923; reprinted New York: Negro Universities Press, 1969, pp. 1–25. For the reasons for Chinese emigration to the *Nanyang* during the last quarter of the nineteenth century, see Wang Gungwu, *A Short History of the Nanyang Chinese*, Singapore: Donald Moore, 1959, pp. 23–7.

60. In addition, a smaller number of non-Chinese labourers, namely Tamil and Javanese, were also procured for Charles's experimental plantation at Matang. See Loh Chee Yin, 'Pieces from the Brooke Past–XVII: Matang Coffee Estate', *SG*, 30 September 1965, pp. 281–2.

61. A. L. Johnston and Company, and after 1889, Paterson, Simons and Company, acted as the agents of the Sarawak government in the recruitment of coolies. See *SG*, 1 October 1889, p. 136.

62. The Sarawak authorities accused the Chinese brokers of sending sickly and diseased labourers and at the same time blamed the officials of the Protectorate for failing to undertake proper supervision and checks on coolies before their departure for Kuching. In protest, the Sarawak government shipped back to Singapore some of the sickly and unfit coolies and demanded compensation from the brokers and recruiters. Rebutting such allegations, the Singapore Chinese brokers insisted that the poor conditions of the Sarawak collieries and overwork were to blame for the ill

health of the coolies. The Protectorate claimed that the coolies were in good physical condition when they left Singapore, and threatened to boycott Sarawak. See *SG*, 1 November 1888, pp. 133–5.

63. For instance, see *SG*, 1 February 1889, p. 18.

64. *SG*, 2 November 1885, p. 104.

65. *SG*, 4 January 1886, p. 2.

66. See *SG*, 1 February 1889, p. 18.

67. *SG*, 15 March 1873, n.p.

68. For example, the Teochew, Law Kian Huat, undertook trips to his native Swatow in 1880 and 1883 armed with letters of introduction from Charles to the British Consul seeking assistance for the recruitment of emigrants. See C. Brooke, Rajah, to British Consul, Swatow [China], 22 September 1880, and 10 August 1883, Second Rajah's Letters, SMA, Kuching.

69. W. J. Chater, 'Chinese Labourers and How They Came to Sarawak', *ST*, 21 February 1964, p. 9.

70. 'Order No. XX, 1899', *SG*, 1 December 1899, p. 340; and 'Order No. VI, 1898', *SG*, 1 February 1898, p. 25.

71. 'Annual Report of the Singapore Chinese Protectorate 1887–1914', in *Singapore Government Annual Report 1914*, Singapore: Government Printing Office, 1887–1914.

72. K. H. Digby, *Lawyer in the Wilderness*, Cornell University Southeast Asia Program Data Paper No. 114, Ithaca: Cornell University Press, 1980, p. 28.

73. M. Kendall, [Mine Engineer?], Sadong Mines, to The Hon'ble The Resident [of the First Division, Percy Francis Cunynghame], 23 November 1904, His Highness The Rajah Confidential, Vol. 1, SMA, Kuching. Emphasis added.

74. E. W. Taylor, [Mine Engineer?], Sadong Mines, to The Hon'ble The Resident [of the First Division, Percy Francis Cunynghame], 23 November 1904, His Highness The Rajah Confidential, Vol. I, SMA, Kuching. Emphasis added.

75. See *SG*, 3 October 1906, p. 237.

76. *SG*, 2 November 1891, p. 163.

77. *SG*, 1 March 1894, p. 42

78. For instance, during a visit in late 1898, A. J. G. Barker, the Principal Medical Officer, found that thirty patients were housed in the ten-bed hospital. See *SG*, 1 October 1898, p. 195. However, this hospital was given the maximum allocation of medical supplies during the 1890s. The number of patients dramatically increased owing to sickness and accidents in the decade of peak production. See *SG*, 1 April 1897, p. 69. For example, in 1898 a record 380 mine workers were treated at the hospital. See *SG*, 1 April 1899, p. 71.

79. During the last two decades of the nineteenth century, the Simunjan collieries registered an excess of revenue over expenditure, but its operations during the twentieth century showed a reversal of fortunes. For the yearly reports of the collieries from 1900 to 1907, see the *Gazette*, and from 1908, the *Sarawak Government Gazette* (*SGG*).

80. *SGG*, 16 May 1927, pp. 246–7.

81. See Haji Ahmad Zaidell bin Haji Tahir, 'Recollections of an Ex-Government Officer: Part I', *SG*, 31 January 1972, p. 7; and *SG*, 1 April 1932, p. 71.

82. *SGG*, 16 March 1921, p. 68.

83. See Daniel Chew, *Chinese Pioneers on the Sarawak Frontier, 1841–1941*, Singapore: Oxford University Press, 1990, p. 195.

84. The European management staff, engineers and technicians, formed the highest echelon in the social structure in the industry and in the oil-town of Miri.

The Europeans with their families kept to themselves with minimal social interaction with Asian employees. The Gymkhana Club and the Miri Rowing Club were exclusively European. These clubs offered recreation ranging from gambling and rowing to football, cricket, and tennis. Social functions like dances, parties, and picnics were also organized. See *SG*, 1 August 1914, p. 171; *SG*, 1 November 1930, p. 288; and Sarawak Shell Berhad, *The Miri Story: The Founding Years of the Malaysian Oil Industry in Sarawak*, Lutong, 1978, pp. 26–8.

85. The Asian clerical staff, largely English-educated Chinese and a few Sinhalese and Eurasians, aped the European élite in recreational activities. The Miri Recreation Club, and the Senior Asiatic Boat Club, for all intents and purposes, duplicated their European counterparts. For the coolies, however, the only entertainment was gambling, especially on pay day. See *SG*, 1 July 1925, pp. 161–2; Sarawak Shell Berhad, *The Miri Story*, p. 27; and Chew, *Chinese Pioneers*, pp. 196–7.

86. See Chew, *Chinese Pioneers*, p. 195.

87. *SG*, 1 August 1911, p. 153.

88. After the announcement, eleven Chinese, who were suspected of being connected with the secret society, absconded; among them were 'three of the ringleaders ... two of whom did not even wait to receive their pay'. They were all subsequently apprehended. *SG*, 2 March 1914, p. 58.

89. *SG*, 1 May 1922, p. 130. What transpired between the general manager and the *towkay* 'over various details' was not known, possibly some promise of financial compensation for the family of the deceased.

90. See *SG*, 1 August 1923, pp. 226 and 228 and *SG*, 3 September 1923, p. 277.

91. In 1927 a Labour Protectorate was established with the appointment of a Protector of Labour and Protector of Netherlands Indian Labourers. This department was created 'to give a guarantee to the Governments of countries whence labourers arrive and to labourers themselves that their interests are being safeguarded'. But since the number of non-Chinese labourers, namely Javanese and Netherland Indians, was small, and the bulk of the work of the Protectorate concerned mostly Chinese matters, including cases under the Women's and Children's Protection Order, it was thought expedient to amalgamate this department with the Secretariat for Chinese Affairs when the latter was set up in 1929. The work of the Secretariat for Chinese Affairs encompassed a wide range of matters, assuming the legal functions that were formerly held by the Chinese Court: namely as an arbitrating body in business and matrimonial disputes, and settling matters in relation to Chinese traditions and customary law (see n. 128); protecting women and children from abuses, the former from prostitution, forced marriages, and servitude (*mui-tsai*), and the latter from child labour; supervision of Chinese schools in respect of curriculum, textbooks, teachers, and board of management; keeping vigilance on Chinese political activities. The Secretary for Chinese Affairs also acted as Protector of Labour and Chinese, Registrar of Societies, and Protector of Women and Children, and functioned as the chief immigration officer. The Secretary himself and his officers, having undergone a course of training in China, were fluent in the language and familiar with the culture of the Chinese community. In the course of its work the department frequently sought the advice and assistance of Chinese community leaders, *towkay*, *Kapitan China*, and other influential individuals. See *SG*, 3 January 1928, p. 2; *SG*, 1 February 1929, p. 17; *SAR, 1929*, pp. 56–8; Hepburn, *Handbook of Sarawak*, p. 61; and Ooi Keat Gin, 'Chinese Vernacular Education in Sarawak during Brooke Rule, 1841–1946', *MAS*, 28, 3 (July 1994): 520–31.

92. The uneasy Kuomintang–Chinese communist alliance, forged in 1923, was beginning to show signs of strain, culminating in the massacre of the Chinese Left by Chiang Kai-shek in 1927. Those who escaped this 'White Terror', either went underground or fled the country, namely to Japan and countries in South-East Asia. For instance, the Chinese immigrants who landed at Sibu in April 1924 decided to join their relatives in Sarawak because they 'found China too hot [politically] for them'. *SG*, 2 June 1924, p. 198. For events in China, see Immanuel C. Y. Hsu, *The Rise of Modern China*, 4th edn., New York: Oxford University Press, 1990, pp. 518–34.

93. *SG*, 1 March 1928, p. 54. See also *SG*, 1 May 1928, p. 93.

94. *SAR, 1930*, p. 53.

95. During the early 1930s there was a spate of Chinese secret society activities which the Brooke authorities swiftly clamped down. See *SG*, 1 September 1932, pp. 158 and 160; *SAR, 1932*, p. 14; *SG*, 1 May 1933, p. 66; *SG*, 1 June 1933, p. 78; *SG*, 1 July 1933, p. 91; *SG*, 2 January 1934, p. 2; and *SG*, 1 October 1935, p. 186.

96. *SG*, 1 March 1933, p. 36. See also *SG*, 1 February 1935, p. 12. The Brooke authorities were afraid that some of the communists fleeing from China after 1927 might escape to Sarawak as they had done to Singapore, Penang, and the Malay States where they embarked on subversive activities.

97. Apart from 'a solitary communist pamphlet' that was 'found stuck to a tree in Sibu in August' of 1936, no other indication of leftist activities was uncovered in the country. See *SAR, 1936*, p. 27.

98. *SAR, 1934*, p. 18. Emphasis added.

99. *SAR, 1937*, pp. 34–5.

100. *SAR, 1930*, p. 54.

101. It was reported that there was an exodus of some 1,500 coolies from the Second Division, presumably from the pepper district of Engkilili, to the gold-mines of Upper Sarawak during 1933. See *SG*, 1 December 1933, p. 159.

102. *SAR, 1930*, p. 54.

103. Ibid.

104. *SAR, 1931*, p. 26. This policy of repatriation also applied to Tamil coolies. However, it was not considered expedient for the revival of trade to extend this policy to Foochows in the Third Division as their recruitment was direct from China and far more difficult to procure than those Chinese coolies who arrived from Singapore. See *SAR, 1930*, p. 51.

105. Ibid. China in the early 1930s was overtaken by a multitude of political and socio-economic problems. In addition to the civil war raging between the Kuomintang and the Chinese communists, runaway inflation and widespread economic dislocation, the consequences of decades of political instability plagued the entire country. See Hsu, *The Rise of Modern China*, pp. 540–73.

106. *SAR, 1930*, p. 51. In the years 1930 and 1931, a total of 5,619 aliens, mostly Chinese, were repatriated; another 358 in 1932, and only 31 in 1934. No figures are available for 1933. See *SAR, 1932*, p. 14; and *SAR, 1934*, p. 17.

107. *SAR, 1934*, p. 17.

108. *Rubber Regulation during 1936*, Kuching: Government Printing Office, 1937, p. 2.

109. Ibid.

110. W. F. N. Bridges, *Rubber Regulation in Sarawak: Interim Report 6 January 1937*, Kuching: Kuching Press, 1937, Appendix II, p. ii. See also *Rubber Regulation during 1937*, Kuching: Government Printing Office, 1938, p. 2.

111. Ludvig Verner Helms, *Pioneering in the Far East, and Journeys to California in 1849 and to the White Sea in 1878*, London: W. H. Allen, 1882, p. 159.

112. Arrack or the Malay term *arak* refers to the locally brewed wine from rice. The Chinese called this spirit *samsu* or *samshu*.

113. Initially the period of tenure was twelve months, later it was extended to three years. Also, the area of coverage was originally limited to the territory of the First Division, but as the borders of the Raj extended these exclusive rights held by the tenderer followed accordingly. However, in certain districts, like Limbang and Miri, a similar system of farm tenure was established with coverage limited to the respective district only. For instance, see 'Agreement between the Government of Sarawak and Messrs Ban Hock Tai', December 1897, Agreement Book, Vol. II, SMA, Kuching. Although the majority of the farms were held by Kuching *towkay*, tenderers from outside Sarawak were not unusual; for instance in 1899, the opium monopoly throughout the country was held by three Chinese businessmen from Penang. See 'Declaration [whereby] Khoo Han Yiang of Penang & Khoo Guat Cheng of Penang & Lim Tiang Hooi of Penang as Opium Farmers for the Territory of Sarawak from Tanjong Datu to the Baram inclusive, and the Gambling and Arrack Farmers for the Residency of Sarawak Proper', 25 April 1899, Agreement Book, Vol. II, SMA, Kuching. For details of the farms relating to the amount paid by the tenderers, period of contract, geographical coverage, rules and regulations of management, and other related matters, see the various entries in the Agreement Books, 5 vols., SMA, Kuching.

114. Sarawak Treasury Cash Book, 25 vols., SMA, Kuching. See also Spenser St John, 'Memorandum on Sarawak', 9 August 1860, FO 12/27, PRO, Kew. According to St John, ironically, instead of a reduction in farm revenue after the Chinese uprising of 1857, considering the drastic drop in the Chinese population, there was an increase in collection. He argued that it 'proves what an extensive system of smuggling had been carried on'. St John, *Life in the Forests*, Vol. II, p. 360. However, as St John did not provide any figures to support his contention and there are no statistics of revenue for the pre-1857 period, it is difficult to confirm if such was the case.

115. *SG*, 1 December 1874, n.p.

116. For instance, see *SG*, 1 September 1881, pp. 67–8; and *SG*, 31 December 1881, p. 107.

117. See 'Memo of Agreement between the Sarawak Government and Messrs [Wong] Nai Siong and Tek Chiong of Chop Sim Hock Chew Kang', 27 July 1900, Agreement Book, Vol. II, Article 13, SMA, Kuching. There were numerous comments by the *Gazette* on the decline in farm revenue from the 1910s. However, during the 1920s and 1930s, the gambling farm was allowed to operate in the Rejang ostensibly for other non-Christian communities like the Cantonese and Henghuas. See *SAR, 1930*, p. 35.

118. The arrangement was to allow the Syndicate a probationary one-year operation, commencing on 1 July 1910, to ascertain its viability. The paid-up capital was $150,000, with the government contributing $60,000 and the Kuching *towkay* the remainder. Its affairs were managed by seven directors comprising three government officers appointed by the Rajah, two Hokkien Chinese merchants elected by the Hokkien shareholders, and two other Chinese of any other dialect group elected by the other shareholders. Only persons residing in the country could become shareholders. After three months of operation, 'a dividend at the rate of 24 % per annum was paid to the shareholder and 25 % of their capital returned'. *SG*, 1 Nov-

ember 1910, p. 227. See also *SG*, 1 June 1910, p. 115; *SG*, 16 June 1910, pp. 129–30; and, *SG*, 1 May 1911, p. 78.

119. *SG*, 16 January 1912, p. 17.

120. A further two-year extension was granted after the expiration of its initial twelve-month tenure. See *SG*, 16 January 1913, p. 14.

121. *SG*, 1 May 1914, p. 104.

122. *SG*, 2 January 1926, p. 1.

123. See *SG*, 1 February 1929, p. 18.

124. *SAR, 1929*, p. 34.

125. See *SAR, 1929*, pp. 34–5; and *SAR, 1930*, pp. 34–5.

126. St John, *Life in the Forests*, Vol. II, p. 299.

127. 'Caution' was the keyword throughout Vyner's reign in dealing with the Chinese communities, whether in immigration matters, educational issues, secret societies, or other problems. An example of this extremely cautious attitude was the proscription of *Kuo-yu*, or vernacular Mandarin, in Chinese vernacular schools in Sarawak when it became widely adopted in Chinese schools in China after the May Fourth Movement (1919). Brooke officials believed that the use of this vernacular Chinese language in Chinese schools could spread subversive teachings among the schoolchildren. However, official circles in government overlooked the fact that, unlike the Straits Settlements or the Malay States, Chinese vernacular schools in Sarawak preferred dialects to *Kuo-yu* as their medium of instruction. The Order forbidding the use of *Kuo-yu* was sheepishly withdrawn within a year of its announcement. See Ooi, 'Chinese Vernacular Education in Sarawak', pp. 503–31.

128. The Chinese Court was inaugurated in 1911 with the Hokkien Ong Tiang Swee, then the most important Chinese leader, as the President or head magistrate. There were six deputies: three Hokkiens, representing their community as well as serving the Chaoann, Henghua, and Foochow speech groups, and three others representing the Teochews, Cantonese, and Hakkas. On their own insistence, all seven magistrates served on a voluntary basis. Although the magistrates were all Kuching *towkay* and there was no representation from the outstations, the Court had jurisdiction over the entire Chinese populace in the country. During its bi-weekly sitting, the Court, apart from marriage and property matters, also dealt with business disputes, conducted investigations into cases of bankruptcies, heard appeals from the Debtor's Court, and assisted the Superior Court whenever the need arose (the Brooke judicial system took into consideration the customary practices and traditions of the different ethnic communities and the differences among the Chinese dialect groups). A building was specifically built for this Chinese Court. In honour of the services of the Chinese magistrates, Charles ordered a seven-gun salute to be fired on Chinese New Year's day, a tradition which was carried out from 1912 until 1941. See *SG*, 17 April 1911, p. 67; *SG*, 16 June 1911, pp. 108–9 and 111–12; *SG*, 16 January 1912, p. 17; *SG*, 16 February 1912, p. 41; *SG*, 17 June 1912, p. 128; *SG*, 16 July 1912, p. 156; *SG*, 16 January 1913, p. 14; *SG*, 16 June 1913, p. 126; *SG*, 1 July 1914, p. 149; *SG*, 1 July 1916, p. 135; and *SG*, 2 July 1917, p. 162.

After the retirement of Ong as president, because he wanted to devote more time to his business affairs, the Court was dissolved in 1920. Robert Pringle stated that the Chinese Court 'ceased to function early in the reign of Vyner, soon after the death of its first and only president, Ong Tiang Swee'. This is incorrect because Ong did not die until 1950. According to Ong himself, the Court was discontinued after his resignation because Vyner could not find another suitable candidate. See Robert Pringle, *Rajahs and Rebels: The Ibans of Sarawak under Brooke Rule,*

1841–1941, London: Macmillan, 1970, p. 173 n. 2; *SG*, 20 October 1941, Centenary Number, p. xiv; and Craig Alan Lockard, *From Kampung to City: A Social History of Kuching, Malaysia, 1820–1970*, Ohio University Monographs in International Studies Southeast Asia Series, No. 75, Athens, 1987, p. 106.

129. For the regulation relating to naturalization, see 'Order No. XII, 1900', *SG*, 2 July 1900, pp. 128–9; 'Order N–2 (Nationality and Naturalization)', *SGG*, 16 July 1934, pp. 344–8; and *SAR, 1934*, p. 11.

130. The growth in the Chinese population was more a result of natural increase than immigration. See J. L. Noakes, *Sarawak and Brunei: A Report on the 1947 Population Census*, Kuching: Government Printing Office, 1950, pp. 33, 35, and 40; and Jackson, *Sarawak*, pp. 53 and 74.

131. Lockard, *From Kampung to City*, p. 67.

132. See Digby, *Lawyer in the Wilderness*, p. 85.

133. The few Chinese in such positions commanded respect, not only within the Chinese community, but also in the wider society, and even enjoyed a certain degree of influence and power. It was not unusual to find district reports being composed by Chinese court writers and clerks, particularly in the more remote stations where European officers were few and far between. For instance, the Hakka, Simon Than, who served as court writer at Kabong in the Krian from 1880 to 1887, wrote the monthly reports of that station which appeared in the *Gazette* alongside those of the European Residents. Cheyne Ah Fook, another Hakka, succeeded Than at Kabong and served for a quarter of a century; he enjoyed similar confidence of the Resident at Simanggang. In fact, both men wielded considerable power and for long periods were the sole government authority in the Krian. See *SG*, 1 May 1921, p. 71; and Pringle, *Rajahs and Rebels*, p. 156. The Kabong examples were undoubtedly exceptional cases; nevertheless, many Chinese aspired to a civil service post that provided a secure and comfortable living, besides respectability. It was, therefore, understandable to find a strong proclivity among the Chinese for mission school education in order to acquire the necessary paper qualifications for a clerical position in the Brooke administrative service. See Ooi Keat Gin, 'Mission Education in Sarawak during the Period of Brooke Rule, 1841–1946', *SMJ*, 62, 63 (December 1991): 307–10.

134. Chin, *The Sarawak Chinese*, p. 103.

9
On Western Capitalist Enterprise

THE conflict with Wise fostered James's scepticism of large Western capitalist investment. None the less as a pragmatist, he allowed the formation of the Borneo Company Limited (BCL), which in its infancy proved a stalwart supporter of the beleagured Raj. There was, however, an uneasy alliance between them. The BCL had a precarious beginning, but tenacity and perseverance carried the day. In the fashion of European agency houses in the East, the BCL possessed a diversified range of operations and had a stake in practically every sector of the economy, from mining operations and trading activities to shipping, banking, and cash cropping. James's suspicion of Western capitalists was nothing compared to Charles's outright hostility. Charles's objections were aimed primarily at 'speculators' and 'exploiters' who would beguile the natives and dispossess them of their land. He proved supportive of bona fide investors, and offered them encouragement and assistance. Those who attempted to exploit the local people were summarily denounced. Vyner was even more discouraging of European enterprises, and only a handful operated during his reign.

Sarawak's obscurity coupled with Brooke policy resulted in a mere trickle of Western investment to the country. With the conspicuous exception of the oil companies, European enterprises either failed after a brief period of operation or achieved success after long years of steadfast perseverance.

The Borneo Company Limited

Serious Teething Problems

The Borneo Company Limited (BCL) was registered in London in early June 1856 under the Joint Stock Companies Act of 1856 and guided by a Deed of Settlement dated 8 May 1856.[1] It started with an initial capital of £60,000, with Robert Henderson of R. & J. Henderson, Merchants of Glasgow and London, as the

chairman, John C. Templer, a friend and confidant of James, as vice-chairman, and four other directors.[2] Ludvig Verner Helms was appointed the first manager in Sarawak.[3]

The BCL acquired a steamer, diplomatically christened *Sir James Brooke*, which left Singapore for Sarawak in early 1857. It made its way up the Sarawak River and arrived at James's little settlement of Kuching under inauspicious circumstances: the Bau Chinese miners had just sacked the place. The steamer's arrival signalled the beginning of the end of the Chinese miners. But more important was the arrival of another BCL vessel, the *Water Lily*, with its cargo of arms and supplies, and a message to Helms from the company's representative in Singapore.

> By this schooner we ship arms, ammunition, and stores for the Sarawak Government, also specie for account of the Borneo Company. Out of this remittance you will furnish the Rajah [James] with such sum of money as he may require; and, generally, *you are authorised to place at the disposal of the Sarawak Government the whole resources of the Company in Borneo*, so far as they may be made available for the upholding of the government and the safety of the European and other residents in the Rajah's territory.[4]

The years following the Chinese troubles were a trying time for both the BCL and the Raj. The BCL was given the monopoly of prospecting and mining rights of all minerals (except gold). The defeat of the Chinese, their flight across the border into Dutch Borneo, and the general animosity towards them, made the situation increasingly untenable for the BCL in launching its mining operations, for Chinese labour was essential. James was aware of the predicament faced by the BCL, but resolved to carry on, with or without it.

From the BCL's perspective, circumstances seemed to point to a financial fiasco, and a collapse seemed imminent. Besides the labour supply problem, other factors came into play during this critical juncture: the serious sickness that James suffered in October 1858[5] coupled with the unfavourable response of Lord Derby to the deputation on Protectorate status undermined confidence in the fragile Raj. There was talk among the BCL's higher echelons of withdrawing from the Sarawak venture, to cut losses before the situation deteriorated further.[6] But opinion was not all for retreat; those who felt that some kind of rescue plan could be instituted brought forth the idea of a new company, the 'Sarawak Company', to work under the old one, acquire from James his '"rights under the Sultan [of Brunei]", put a steamer on the coast, and if, when, Sir James Brooke's health forced him to

retire, take the government into its own hands, and appoint its own governor'.[7] This scheme of a 'Sarawak Company' was rejected by James, who declared that 'whilst we [him and John Brooke Brooke] live we shall be independent'.[8]

Even before the BCL's fortunes had a chance to change for the better after the Chinese uprising, its plans to invest in the sago industry were threatened. Political intrigues had been brewing in the coastal sago districts since 1855. The news of the murders of Charles Fox and Henry Steele at Kanowit in June 1859, followed by rumours of a 'Malay plot' circulating among the European community and of their impending massacre, were most unsettling.[9] At the same time, across the border, news filtered through of the anti-Dutch revolt in Banjarmasin which had caused a considerable loss of European lives and property in southern Borneo. This was reminiscent of the horrors of the Indian Mutiny that had swept northern India just two years earlier and created alarm among the Europeans.[10] Helms, who had just returned to Sarawak from England, described the situation in April 1860.

> Still, these events [the double murders and the 'Malay plot'], following so soon upon the insurrection of the Chinese, when the Government had to rely upon the Malay and Dyak population, caused great uneasiness, and threw a gloom over the place, and which, of course, had also acted unfavourably upon all mercantile pursuits. In fact, when I accepted the offer of returning to Borneo, many of the Europeans had left, or were preparing to leave.[11]

Helms had much to be apprehensive about; he had drawn up ambitious plans for the BCL to invest in the sago industry, and had ordered sago-processing machinery from England at considerable expense, which was scheduled to arrive in mid-1860. Not surprisingly, he described the situation as 'a life and death matter for Sarawak [and the BCL] that Sharif Masahor is crushed and the sago trade restored'.[12] Happily the crisis at Mukah was resolved in Sarawak's favour with the cession of these districts. By the late 1860s, there was a glimmer of hope but there was still a long way to go.

Estrangement with James

The BCL had been generous in its financial support of the Raj when, as an aftermath of the Chinese uprising, the Brooke Treasury was at its lowest ebb. The financial status of the country had been precarious from the very beginning, with expenditure

exceeding revenue; only after the arrival of Chinese immigrants from Sambas in 1850 did the semblance of a healthy financial situation emerge.[13] Therefore, when the Chinese were driven out of the country following the insurrection, the Raj not only lost its work-force, but also an important source of revenue, namely the opium farm. It was a welcome relief when the BCL gave an advance of £5,000 for the immediate repair of the damage and other sundry expenditure. James was undoubtedly grateful for this timely financial hand-out.

However, as events unfolded during the next two years, relations between him and the BCL became increasingly strained. Two issues, the failure of the Testimonial and the demand by the BCL for the repayment of their £5,000 loan, marred their relationship.

At the time of James's convalescence towards the end of 1858, a few of his close friends headed by Thomas Fairbairn, John Templer, and Alexander Knox, decided to raise a Testimonial by public subscription,[14] 'as a simple, earnest, and affectionate testimony of friends to a noble character and disinterested services—services which instead of enriching, had left their author broken by illness and weariness of heart, with threatening poverty'.[15] The avowed intention was to afford James financial independence, unshackle him from dependence on Sarawak's revenue, and allow for his retirement.[16] It was hoped that £20,000 would be raised, but the actual amount totalled only £8,800, thereby making the Testimonial a failure.[17] 'Rightly or wrongly,' St John asserted, 'the Rajah always laid the blame of this failure on the shoulders of the Borneo Company, whose interest he thought it was to keep him dependent on them.'[18]

Further aggravating James's embittered attitude towards the BCL was its demand for the repayment of the £5,000 loan in 1859 which could not have been more untimely. The BCL could not be blamed for seeking repayment at this juncture, for, like James, it too was in poor financial circumstances. From the outset, the BCL had performed miserably. It suffered embarrassing losses in its coal-mining dèbut at Simunjan. The acute labour shortage, the revival of raiding, and the political feuds that disrupted the coastal sago trade, all acted against the BCL's operations. It was, therefore, understandable that it was anxious that the £5,000 loan be settled.

James, on the other hand, was infuriated, and described the BCL's conduct as 'discourteous and avaricious'.[19] 'The Company', Helms defended, 'was a commercial one, not a philanthropic

society; the directors had shareholders asking for dividends, and under all the circumstances, I cannot think the Rajah had any just cause for complaint.'[20] The matter, however, was settled by a 'friendly loan' from James's friend and benefactor, Angela Burdett Coutts.[21]

In spite of the strained relations, James was supportive of the operations of the BCL. A good example of this was the waiving of the annual royalty following the Simunjan failure.[22] The BCL, on its part, in the face of adversities, steadfastly maintained its primary objective of developing the resources of the country.

A Diversity of Operations

The BCL's original scope of operation was a royalty arrangement relating to Sarawak's mineral resources, but it later expanded into the sago industry, the coasting trade, Kuching–Singapore shipping, banking, insurance, infrastructure development, cash cropping, import and export, and as agents and brokers for a score of Western firms. The fortunes of the BCL became brighter from the late 1860s. By then more Chinese were coming to the country, thereby alleviating the labour problem.

The cession of the sago districts and peace on the coast allowed the development of the sago industry. The BCL, which already had a sago mill at Kuching, decided to establish an agency and erect a plant in the sago districts to improve production. Helms ordered steam machinery from England, and by May 1862 a sago mill was functioning at Mukah.[23] The BCL inaugurated a system whereby cash advances were made to native cultivators for planting purposes, and the latter promised to deliver the mature palms to the mill.[24] But it was difficult for the BCL to transgress the traditional relationships in Melanau society that revolved around sago production and trade. Consequently, the mills failed for want of palms.[25] There were other contributory factors, namely, competition from Chinese mills and the unsuitability of Mukah as a port.[26] During the 1890s experimental use of chemicals to improve the quality of sago flour was carried out by the BCL in alliance with a Chinese concern, but apparently, this research did not prove beneficial.[27]

On the mining front, it was decided that Bidi, where the BCL's first upcountry antimony mines were worked, was unsuitable as a collecting point for the ore owing to the shallowness of the Sarawak River. Busau, situated further downstream, became the BCL's depot for antimony where the work of 'Picking, Grading

and Payment for the ore were carried out'.[28] Busau also served as a collecting centre for pepper. From here, these commodities were transported by boat to Kuching for export.[29]

The two antimony mines at Bidi were constantly subject to flooding during the *landas*, and soon after 1873 it seemed that the BCL had abandoned its own mining operations and adopted the 'tributor system'.[30] At the same time, it was decided to stop the export of the 'raw' ore to England, and instead, to undertake the processing in Sarawak. Large reverbatory and calcining furnaces were erected at Busau. The molten ore was poured into uniform moulds to produce ingots bearing the BCL's insignia.[31] In this form, the antimony was exported.

By the first decade of the twentieth century, antimony-mining had become comparatively unattractive when other more lucrative activities like gold-mining enticed tributors away. Consequently, the furnaces at Busau were running at a loss for want of ore, and in 1907 the smelting works were shut down. Meanwhile, prospecting continued, and rewards were offered for reports of workable finds, but on the whole it was disappointing.[32]

An exciting find occurred in 1867 when cinnabar was discovered at Tegora. Shortly after this, in the early 1870s, cinnabar was also worked at Gading, near the border with Dutch Borneo. Ponies were employed to transport the ore from Gading to Tegora. Ores assaying 70 per cent and over were cased up and exported to London for sale.[33] When furnaces were set up at Tegora for processing the ore, the mercury was put into flasks and sent to the BCL's branch at Hong Kong, which was the distributing centre for this commodity throughout East Asia.[34] By the end of 1881 mining came to a halt and the mines were abandoned, presumably exhausted. Gading was closed around this time, while Tegora shut in 1894.[35] The BCL ceased payment of cinnabar royalty during the second half of 1881.[36]

Charles, in his efforts to promote the working of the extensive Silantek coalfields, contracted the BCL in 1874 to undertake delivery of 300–400 tons of coal for shipment to Singapore to supply the Peninsular and Oriental Steam Navigation Company.[37] The BCL's mining operations in Upper Sarawak relied on the supplies from the government collieries at Simunjan. In 1917 exploratory work was carried out to determine the possibility of a cheaper coal supply from Grogo, near Lundu, as an alternative to Simunjan. Transport of the coal 'by means of a rope-way' was put forward, but there is no further information of this scheme in the records.[38]

By the late 1870s, the activities of the BCL presented a picture of prosperity. The *Rangoon Daily News* paid tribute to its varied accomplishments.

To the Borneo Company Limited ... the foundation of the trade to Sarawak may be ascribed. They have large quicksilver mines at Tegora, which yield about 300 bottles of quicksilver, per day, each bottle weighing about 56 pounds.

Their antimony mines, at Busu [Busau], and Jambusan [,] yield them alone between 4 and 5 thousand tons annually. A large Sago Factory at Muka, about 320 kilometres up the coast also belonging to them, is their central trading depot. The mill can turn out 3,000 bags of Sago flour per day, and gives employment to 1,500 men and women. They have small stations at Bintulu, Sibu, Tatua [Tatau?] and Balleiuan from which they ship to Singapore large quantities of gutta percha [,] Indian rubber, vegetable tallow, and rattans. The success of the Company is mainly due to the energetic men in charge of the different stations.[39]

But better days lay ahead as the BCL entered its third decade of operations in Sarawak.

Meanwhile, in 1875, a new office building of brick replaced the old 'shack' used by Helms during the early days. This period too witnessed a serious threat to the very existence of the BCL when a lawsuit was filed by Helms against his former employer over the issue of his contract and the appropriation of profit-sharing. It seemed that this litigation might result in the collapse of the BCL, but a last minute out-of-court settlement saved the day.[40]

The decade of the 1880s witnessed the BCL's increasing involvement in the gold-mining industry of Upper Sarawak. It assisted the Chinese miners by loaning them more efficient mechanical equipment. During the 1880s, first through the 'tributor system', then by a take-over of Chinese gold companies, the BCL acquired a near-monopoly of gold-mining in the country. The early 1890s saw the slow-down of production owing to the exhaustion of accessible deposits. However, for the BCL, the later half of the decade proved to be auspicious. The cyanidation process of gold extraction had been developed; the necessary machinery and equipment were ordered, a plant was set up at Bau followed shortly by another at Bidi, and the new process was implemented with unqualified success. Owing to the shortage of ore supplies and their generally low quality, the plant at Bidi was underutilized, and in 1911 it was decided to cease operations altogether. Thereafter, all processing was carried out at Bau.[41]

By 1913 Tai Parit had become an opencast mine. Serious flooding during the early 1920s forced its closure, and shortly after this

the BCL withdrew from all mining operations in the country and surrendered its mineral lease held since 1857.

In conjunction with its mining operations in Upper Sarawak, the BCL developed the communication network of the district. Tramways, roads, pathways, and bridges were constructed to facilitate the conveyance of the ores from the mines to processing plants.[42] A wharf was erected at Busau, and launches and other vessels provided river transport to Kuching.[43] The BCL also established telephone and telegraph links between Bau and Kuching, and a telephone line connected Tegora with Gading.[44] A hospital was provided at Bau and another at Sejijak, a short distance from the BCL's rubber holdings at Sungei Tengah.

The BCL played a major role in the provision of shipping between Sarawak and Singapore, its steamers making regular runs. When the Singapore and Sarawak Steamship Company (SSSCo) was inaugurated in the mid-1870s, the BCL was not only a prominent shareholder but also handled its management. However, as pointed out, it was because of this direct BCL involvement in the conduct of the SSSCo's day-to-day operations that both it and the BCL were accused of unfair dealings and monopolistic practices. When a group of Kuching *towkay* launched a take-over of the SSSCo in 1919, the BCL sold it all its shares, effectively ceasing direct involvement in shipping. The BCL, however, maintained its role as agents to European shipping lines.

Ever since its inception, the BCL had acted as the 'banker' to the Sarawak government, arranging for the provision of Brooke coinage; its 'cheques' were 'legal tender' throughout the country.[45] The establishment of a branch of the Chartered Bank of India, Australia and China, at Kuching in the mid-1920s signalled the decline of the BCL's banking business. At the close of the Brooke period, it still retained a number of old accounts of Dayak customers, and 28 Fenchurch Street, its head office in London, continued to transact business relating to Sarawak.

The BCL also assisted Charles in his agricultural pursuits. A joint venture oversaw the experimental cultivation of tobacco at Lundu; however, it did not achieve much success, and was eventually abandoned. During the late 1890s, the BCL provided cash advances to Chinese pepper growers in Upper Sarawak, an arrangement not unlike the 'tributer system' practised in the mining industry.[46]

During the 1890s there was a good demand for gambier. The discovery whereby refuse from the boiled gambier leaves, after

being allowed to dry, could be applied as fertilizer to pepper vines, led the BCL to embark on the joint cultivation of gambier and pepper,[47] the ratio being about fifteen acres of gambier to sustain one and a half acres of pepper.[48] For this purpose the BCL acquired an 8000 hectare (20,000 acre) strip of land located to the south-east of Bau, referred to as the 'Poak Concession'. For a while the joint cultivation of the two crops produced good results. However, the different life span of pepper and gambier was overlooked: a pepper vine could last up to sixteen years whereas gambier is less than seven years, therefore, the former failed for want of the latter. The drop in demand for gambier during the early part of the 1900s also contributed to the decline of this crop. Nevertheless, as late as 1908 it was reported that 'there were still 30,000 acres under Gambier and 600 acres under Pepper'.[49]

Apart from pepper and gambier, *Gutta-rian* trees were also grown on the Poak Concession at the turn of the century. There was then a healthy demand for gutta in the electrical industry as material for insulation.

But the most important cash crop investment of the BCL was the cultivation of Para rubber, initiated in 1902 on a tract of land of about 1200 hectares (3,000 acres) situated on the western flank of the Poak Concession, near Sungei Dahan, from which it took its name, the Dahan Rubber Estate. By 1907 almost half the acreage was under cultivation.[50] Another rubber estate was opened at Sungei Tengah, near Matang (later it became Sarawak Rubber Estates Limited).[51] As at Dahan, it also relied on imported Javanese coolies.[52] It was a timely decision for the BCL to invest in Para rubber growing, for by the time the trees were ready for tapping in 1910, rubber was enjoying boom prices. A rubber-processing factory was erected at Sungei Tengah in 1912.[53] Both estates were relatively successful ventures.

The business of extracting gutta from the leaves of *gutta-rian* was revived after the First World War. Sarawak Rubber Estates Limited was involved in this trade, and like its main competitor, the British Malaysian Rubber Manufacturing Company (Goebilt), erected godowns at Simunjan, Gedong, Tebakang, and S'bangan for the storage of *gutta-rian* leaves before export.[54] However, the difficulties of procuring supplies, a result of the reluctance of Dayak collectors to take out permits for such activities in line with government policy of preventing the despoliation of the trees, eventually led to the discontinuation of this operation in the early 1920s.[55]

During the early 1860s the BCL in Sarawak conducted the export of rough-hewn logs, including *billian*, to its Hong Kong branch. The irregular arrivals of the ocean-going steamers at the mouth of the Rejang at Tanjong Mani to take delivery of the logs caused them, with the notable exception of *billian*, to be attacked by borer beetles known as 'teredos'.[56] It was undoubtedly a costly experience. Nevertheless, the exceptional qualities of the hardwood *billian* prompted the BCL to seek markets further afield. Samples of *billian* sleepers were sent through Messrs Forbes, Forbes, Campbell & Company of Bombay, for testing by the Bengal State Railways.[57] There was some export of logs from the Rejang to Hong Kong and Calcutta during the mid-1880s; the records show that this operation was brief, and had teredo trouble as well.[58]

At the turn of the century, when a proposal was submitted for the erection of a sawmill in the Rejang, the head office at London cautioned that this should not be a repetition of the previous fiasco.[59] Unfortunately, it was another fiasco, but this time, human folly was as much to blame as teredos. During the early part of the 1900s, there was a demand for timber in Hong Kong. The BCL, ever interested in tapping the rich timber resources of Sarawak, decided to purchase logs from Chinese logging companies working in the Rejang. The logs were floated downstream to the BCL's base at the delta where they were hauled ashore at high tide, presumably to avoid attack by teredos. Up-to-date milling machinery from Britain was brought out to the Rejang. But this apparently promising venture faced disaster from here on: an inexperienced manager caused the erection of the mill at an unsuitable site, inappropriate equipment for producing the log-squaring as required by the Hong Kong market, and teredos once again caused destruction to the logs that were not stacked clear of the mud.[60] By the late 1900s, when some of the problems had been rectified, there was a decline in demand resulting in a price slump, which made operations no longer cost-effective. The mill was dismantled and shipped to Surabaya in Dutch Java, where the BCL had interests in teak.

During the second half of the 1930s, the BCL's logging interest shifted to the Upper Rejang with the formation of the Rejang Timber Concession which undertook to exploit the hardwoods and semi-hardwoods of the interior of the country.[61] A base was established at the foot of the Pelagus Rapids and a sawmill at Salim. Working elephants were brought in from Siam. However, the formidable difficulties faced in tackling the Bornean forests,

the rapids which hindered logs from floating downstream, the damage done by ambrosia beetles, coupled with the poor demand in European markets for Sarawak timber, caused this project to be abandoned within a brief period. It was another considerable loss to the BCL.[62] The BCL had to be content with returning to the Rejang delta, where, through its subsidiary the Austral Timber Company, extraction of *ramin* (*Gonystylus bancanus*) timber for export was carried out.[63]

In the field of general merchandising and as agents for British, European, and American companies, the BCL was unsurpassed. The manager of the BCL in Sarawak[64] had, since the days of Helms, been appointed Lloyd's agent. Agencies held by the BCL covered a wide range of enterprises from shipping, airlines, and insurance to representing Western trading concerns. On the eve of the Pacific War, the BCL had its head office in Kuching with branch stations at Sibu, Sarikei, Binatang, and Miri.

European Capitalist Companies during Charles's Reign

In Praise of the BCL

> It [the BCL] has held fast and stuck to its work through the perils and dangers, the prosperity and adversity, which Sarawak has experienced and encountered. It has shown a solid and stolid example to other traders, and formed a basis for mercantile operations, and I do not attempt to deny or conceal the fact that the importance of the presence in a new state of such a large and influential body as the Borneo Company Limited cannot be over-rated.[65]

Charles paid this tribute to the BCL in 1872 at a public dinner held in its honour. His appreciation of the BCL was understandable; Charles was determined that the resources of the country should be developed, and realized that European expertise and capital were needed for such purposes. Besides the BCL, several other Western enterprises were encouraged; their operations ranged from the processing of sago, manufacture of cutch, treatment of *gutta-jelutong*, and cultivation of ramie, to oil exploration and exploitation, and Para rubber growing and production.

Short-lived Western Enterprises

Some European firms only survived briefly, while others, though in receipt of grants and concessions, carried out exploratory work but never commenced operations. Whatever the reasons for their

short-lived or abortive operations, the fact is that these companies *did* make an attempt.

The Oya Company Limited, established in the early 1870s, operated a sago-processing factory at Oya, using steam machinery. It also had a small steamer, *Bertha*, for the coasting trade between Kuching and Sibu.[66] But within a short period, its closure was announced.[67] No reason was given for the termination of its business; competition from Chinese mills might be the probable cause.

In the late 1880s, the Central Borneo Company was granted a mining lease for prospecting and working all minerals except coal in the newly acquired Baram district.[68] A decade later it was reported that analysis of samples of antimony from this concession was promising, but, it is uncertain whether this firm undertook mining, apart from prospecting work.[69] During this time, the Central Borneo Company was awarded the concession of the Silantek coalfields, but, apart from reports of its exploratory work, no mining work apparently was started.[70]

The antimony deposits in the Baram were worked in 1893 by another concern, the Borneo Minerals Company, which at the same time had also discovered cinnabar in the district.[71] In spite of reports of antimony-mining there, no exports were recorded. A possible explanation could be that the deposits, which initially seemed promising, proved to be too small to warrant further work when actual mining was undertaken, and were, therefore, abandoned.[72]

The French-owned Malayan Ramie Company acquired land in the Lawas district to cultivate ramie.[73] A ramie-decoticating machine, patented by Monsieur Emil F. Pumpin, the manager of the company, was to be used to manufacture ramie fibre.[74] Planting commenced in mid-1908, and from the report of the Resident of Lawas the following year, the venture appeared promising.[75] However, as already indicated, the crop failed as a result of the heavy Lawas rainfall, and with the high labour cost, this enterprise was abandoned in 1909.

Disappointments and Successes: A Tale of Two Companies

The processing of jungle produce utilizing Western technology was a branch of industry suited to European investors. Charles's enthusiasm in promoting such ventures is exhibited in this letter of November 1908 addressed to Vyner.

I am going to see an American tomorrow named Furness who was in Sarawak before collecting natural specimens and products—he is now employed by a rich firm of Americans and English—to collect products of the Eastern Archipelago for the purpose of purifying them before exporting to save the trouble and expense of doing it in Europe or America—he wishes to make Sarawak the head-quarters—and no doubt they will require land for their buildings. I look on this if it takes place the best thing I have heard of for some years. We want new blood to give the country and people fresh impulse and this Company should have the means of doing this.[76]

The reference here was likely to be the United British Malaysian Rubber Manufacturing Company Limited, popularly referred to as 'Goebilt'.[77]

Goebilt proposed to apply a certain scientific process which could extract rubber economically from *gutta-jelutong*. A great sense of optimism surrounded the launching of this venture in 1909 during the time of the rubber boom. At its statutory meeting in July 1910 in London, the chairman, Sir Percy Cunynghame, a former Brooke officer, confidently assured shareholders of the success of the operation, citing the 'practically unlimited extent' of the supply of both *jelutong* and native labour.[78] On this high note, the company erected a large factory at Tanjong Batu, near Muara Tebas, at the mouth of the Kuching River.[79]

However, within a brief period of commencing operations, this Anglo-American firm faced serious problems: the extraction of rubber from dry *gutta-jelutong* was never more than 3 per cent as against the 10 per cent claimed, and of acetone, a mere 15 per cent to the supposedly 90 per cent.[80] Then, there was the misunderstanding relating to its 'monopoly' of the export of *jelutong*; it accused Charles of going back on his agreement, but later withdrew its allegation.[81] Furthermore, it complained of the high prices demanded of the *jelutong* by Chinese middlemen.[82] In response to the company's complaints against the Chinese sellers, Charles remarked that 'it was not his wish for the government to mix up in trade concerns, but it was his desire to see fairplay, and a profit on both sides'; he would leave the matter to the parties involved to arrive at a satisfactory arrangement.[83] After several meetings between the parties at which three Brooke officers were present, an agreement was reached.[84]

In spite of this, the Chinese *towkay* presented Charles with a petition applying for official sanction to run a steamer to Singapore with their *jelutong*. Such a move would be in violation of the

company's monopoly, so, permission was denied.[85] However, the appearance of this petition 'evidently shows that prices offered by the Company do not sufficiently tempt them to sell at Goebilt, and that they prefer to pay duty and freight themselves and sell the gutta in Singapore'.[86]

At the same time, Charles was infuriated by the company which repeatedly exerted pressure on him, hoping that he would act in its favour. It was a grossly miscalculated strategy. 'Congo rule', Charles wrote to W. H. Galbraith, the company's manager in mid-1911, 'cannot be supported in Sarawak to please anyone or company.'[87] During a meeting in June 1912 relating to the *jelutong* issue, the following was reported: 'His Highness then informed the Manager of the Company that for the past two years he had suffered nothing but annoyance from the Company in England, threats and lawyers letters culminating in insults which would be impossible for him to forget and he held the three Directors responsible for these acts.'[88] Refusing to tolerate further the Company's overbearing behaviour and its attempt to ride roughshod over Chinese traders in the *jelutong* trade, Charles revoked its concession in mid-1915, while at the same time, lifted the prohibition on the export of *jelutong*, namely 'Order No. XVII, 1909'.[89]

The United British Malaysian Rubber Manufacturing Company, right from the very beginning was overambitious, with a large capital outlay and huge investments in buildings and equipment. Heavy losses were incurred over the years, and by the time it faced compulsory liquidation in 1921, a staggering £2.3 million deficit was recorded.[90]

This unhappy episode was perhaps compensated by the gradual successes achieved by the Island Trading Syndicate (later Company) Limited[91] which undertook the manufacture of cutch from mangrove bark.[92] This firm acquired a grant 'to collect and export Tengah Bruang Bahan & other barks in the manufacture of Cutch or tannin'.[93] A factory was built at Sungei Lalang (Selalang) in the Rejang delta where a steam engine with a huge flywheel operated the machinery.[94] Supplies of mangrove bark came from the swamp forest of the delta area worked by Dayaks, and some bark also came from the Lawas district.[95] The reliance on native collectors for its bark was a constant problem owing to the irregular and often insufficient supply.[96] Therefore, in 1915, the system of 'advance payments' was gradually replaced by cash-on-delivery.[97] Production steadily increased, and in less than a decade, this company was a flourishing concern. Continual capital investment in up-to-date equipment and improvements in transport facilities,

including the acquisition of a steamer, further enhanced its performance.[98] The Island Trading Company continued the production of cutch and survived into the post-Brooke years.[99]

Para Rubber Cultivation by European Companies

Following in the footsteps of the BCL, Western companies invested in Para rubber cultivation. The Lawas Planting Company under the management of J. H. Brodie, a former employee of the BCL, took over the land vacated by the failed Malayan Ramie Company and began the planting of Para rubber and coconut.[100] Progress was satisfactory; initial tapping commenced in late 1913 and early 1914.[101] Monthly output averaged from 675 kilograms to 900 kilograms (1,500 to 2,000 pounds).[102] By 1916, the company had nearly 280 hectares (700 acres) of Para rubber trees, an annual output of more than 27 450 kilograms (61,000 pounds), and a work-force of 170 (70 Chinese, 50 Muruts, and 50 Malays) of which 130 were tappers and the remainder worked in the factory and smoke house.[103] Progress continued into the 1920s with further expansion in acreage.[104]

The Kuching Trading Company, established in 1910, an affiliate of the Lawas Planting Company and also managed by Brodie, did not have its own plantations; instead it concentrated on rubber processing in its factory at Sungei Kuching.[105] In 1913, it acquired a two-year contract for tapping Para rubber trees belonging to the government.[106] The paucity of information relating to this company renders it difficult to provide a fuller sketch of its progress and development.

The Anglo-Saxon Petroleum Company (ASPC) and the Miri Oilfield

By far the most important achievement of European enterprise during Charles's reign belonged to the Anglo-Saxon Petroleum Company (ASPC).[107] Charles was naturally pleased with the accomplishments of the ASPC with its huge investments in buildings and equipment, the adoption of the latest technology, and infrastructure development in the Miri area. The ASPC was described as an *imperium in imperio*, and Charles very much left it to its own devices. The ASPC's progress, development, and successes have been dealt with in earlier sections; suffice it to add here that the company's operations placed Sarawak on the map of the British Empire and further enhanced the strategic importance of the Brooke Raj.

The Japanese Nissa Shokai

Nissa Shokai was the one and only major Japanese trading firm in Brooke Sarawak. It commenced business just after the turn of the century in the wholesale and retail trade of Japanese goods for the small Japanese community in Kuching and its outskirts.[108] It was also affiliated with a Japanese-owned Para rubber estate in Samarahan. Besides rubber, its other attempts in agriculture, like the growing of pineapple and the establishment of a rice-farming community, were abortive.[109]

Diminishing Presence of European Capitalist Enterprises under Vyner's Rule

The BCL and Vyner Brooke

> The Government Officers of to-day appear to consider it is duty to frown upon any material European-owned interests in the State and with the relinquishment of their extensive mining rights by the Company in 1923, it seems improbable that those who have since controlled the destinies of the Company [*sic*, Country?] for the 3rd Rajah will encourage any extensive commercial activity which entails the bringing in of Foreign (European) Capital or Control, or presents any possibilities of becoming a virtual monopoly.[110]

This was the opinion expressed by T. Charles Martine, manager of the BCL during the 1930s, when commenting on the future of his firm in Sarawak. In contrast to James and Charles, Vyner, it seemed, was not very supportive of the BCL. This sketch from a writer in the 1960s reveals Vyner's attitude towards the BCL: 'During the Depression of 1931–2 it was suggested to Rajah Vyner that he should advance some money to the Company. He replied that it had done its best to ruin his great-uncle, and he did not therefore see why he should help it now.'[111] The BCL too, after withdrawing from its mining operations, found that 'its importance to Sarawak has become less apparent and in the eyes of the more recent Government Officers must not again be granted any monopoly or rights that might enable it to regain its former position'.[112]

European Companies during the 1920s and 1930s

There were even fewer European capitalist establishments during Vyner's reign. There was a feeling prevalent during this period that

the government was not as encouraging of European enterprises as in the past. Nevertheless, some new European ventures were launched while existing firms continued and consolidated their operations.

In 1919, Charles Hose secured a grant 'to prosecute in Sarawak investigations and research into the possibilities of the cultivation, manufacture and utilisation in Sarawak for commercial and export purposes of Bamboo, Fibres, Timber, Guano, Shoklac, Acetic acid and Jungle produce generally', and these activities shall be confined 'within the limits of the fourth Administrative Division of the State of Sarawak'.[113] Armed with this concession, Hose and his colleagues went to the Baram district in mid-1920 to select a suitable site for the launching of the operations of their newly established company, Eastern Products Limited. A timber licence was also acquired during this time, so the party prospected for an appropriate area in the vicinity of the Suai River, as dictated by the terms of the grant (Article 1) for logging purposes.[114] Finally, the party settled for 1200 hectares of agricultural land and 258 square kilometres for logging operations, situated between the branch of Telavi Kechil and Sinyut in the Suai River.[115] However, apart from the signing of agreements and the identification of land, nothing apparently was started. It is unknown why both these ventures were abandoned.

Further east in the Lawas River, the VAMCO Timber Company Limited, established in 1922, was active in the timber export industry.[116] Originally a sawmill was set up at Merapok, but finding the location unsuitable, it was relocated to Sungai Kayengeran, and finally to Tagal. The company produced sawn timber for export. During the early 1930s, with the purchase of 'a special peeling machine', it manufactured plywood, becoming the first company to do so in Sarawak.[117] The company's operations at Tagal continued into the post-Brooke years.

Another successful venture during this period was the Rejang Estates Limited that began in 1926. This establishment, occupying the area of Sengayan on the north bank of the Rejang River, was reputed to be the largest rubber plantation in the country; in 1941 it boasted of 470 hectares (1,175 acres) under Para rubber.[118] Its experimentation with oil palm cultivation, however, proved unsuccessful. After the Pacific War, this property was sold to Chinese interests and became Lian Hup Estates.[119]

During the 1920s there was a spate of take-overs and changes in management within European company circles. In April 1921, the

ASPC signed over the transfer of its oil concession and prospecting licence to the newly established Sarawak Oilfields Limited (SOL), which assumed operations from July.[120] SOL continued operations into the post-war years.

The year 1923 witnessed a corporate take-over of the Lawas Planting Company by another concern, the Lawas (Sarawak) Rubber Estates Limited. At the time of the transfer, the property comprised a little over 400 hectares (1,000 acres), of which 298 hectares (745 acres), were planted with Para rubber.[121] Two years later, the Sarawak Rubber Estates Limited, a subsidiary company of the BCL, assumed the management of the rubber estates at Dahan and Sungei Tengah. Both these new companies continued the successful run of their predecessors, and survived through the vicissitudes of the slumps and booms of the late 1920s and the 1930s.

The Sarawak Trading Company Limited, an European agency house not unlike the BCL in the line of general merchandising, was taken over by Sime, Darby & Company Limited in 1928. Sime, Darby & Company Limited was established in 1910 in Malacca with wide-ranging business interests in the Straits Settlements and the Malay States, from proprietorship of rubber plantations, as tin-mine agents and valuers, to general trading, and as agents and brokers of European shipping and insurance companies. In Sarawak, its activities were confined to the trade in the import of Western-manufactured goods and as shipping and insurance agents.[122] It had a head office in Kuching (1928), and a branch in Sibu (1937). To all intents and purposes, it provided an alternative to the BCL. Like the BCL, Sime, Darby & Company Limited survived the Pacific War to continue its business during the post-Brooke years.

Conclusion

It strikes one as passing strange that Sarawak, with its fine soil, climate, and network of navigable rivers, has not, long ere this, attracted the attention of European planters, and been inundated with British capital, as was the case twenty years ago in Ceylon.

I am certain that, were the great advantages Sarawak possesses in soil, climate, transport, and, last but not least, in the very liberal terms which Government accord, better and more generally known, a speedy influx of planters would ensue.... That there will ere long be a rush of planters to this country and a *sudden* rush, as was the case in Ceylon, I feel confident. Jungle will then rise in value, while those who come at once can now get their land for nothing.[123]

This extract from a letter written in the middle of 1886 to the Editor of the *Gazette* by an European planter who 'had a good deal of experience of soil and planting in Coorg, and Wynaad in southern India' reflects the sad fact of the poverty of Western investment in Sarawak.[124] However, contrary to what he had predicted, there was no 'rush of planters'.

The conspicuous absence of European capitalist concerns in Sarawak can be attributed to a number of factors. Like the Chinese, who were largely ignorant of Sarawak and any information they had about the place was usually born of hearsay and rumours, the Europeans were equally unknowlegeable.[125]

The Brookes themselves, on their part, did not contribute to the promotion of the country as a land of opportunity for Western investment. The reputation of James, marred by the Parliamentary debates on his anti-piracy policy which culminated in the Commission of Inquiry in 1854 in Singapore, gave Sarawak 'bad publicity' which dissuaded British business interests both in the City of London and in the port-colony of Singapore to invest in the country. James's clashes with Wise, the lawsuit against the Eastern Archipelago Company, and the case of Burns, portrayed James as anti-capitalist and his Raj as 'off-limits' to Western entrepreneurs. Lord Derby's rejection of the Deputation of 1858 for Protectorate status did not help matters either. Charles was seen as even more opposed to European capitalist enterprise. His denunciation of and sarcastic remarks about Western companies undoubtedly made him few friends in British business circles in London as well as in Singapore. He seemed to be, to say the least, a 'hostile host' to would-be European investors with his pro-native land policy, his order of 1910 that forbade the sale of rubber gardens to those 'of white nationality', and his undisguised partisan protection of the interests and rights of the indigenous peoples. In direct contrast to the British administrators in the Malay States, Charles supported the Chinese merchants in their conflict with Goebilt to the extent that he revoked the latter's concession to work *jelutong*. The Goebilt–Chinese dispute further confirmed his poor opinion of Western companies and reinforced his mistrust of this breed of businessman. Charles at least gave encouragement to bona fide Western investors, but Vyner appeared to be less enthusiastic in such matters. There were fewer European companies operating during his rule, almost half the number than previously. It was also noted that his officers were unsupportive of Western enterprise, even of the long-established BCL. The attitudes and policies of the

Brookes undoubtedly accounted for the small presence of Western capitalist enterprises and investments in the country.

Those who managed to invest in Sarawak discovered that a huge dose of patience and perseverance was essential before success could be achieved. A clear case is the BCL which, for more than forty years, had 'no balance of profit'; instead 'there was a very considerable deficit' which had to be supported by its other operations in Dutch Java, the Western Malay States, and especially Siam.[126] In the end it was the new method of gold extraction—the cyanidation process—which was executed during the late 1890s that rewarded the BCL its long years of determination and hope.

But, unlike the BCL which could rely on its more profitable investments in neighbouring territories, other Western companies could not afford the luxury of perseverance. Because of unfavourable circumstances, several such ventures only managed a brief existence while others never even got off the ground. The failure of European planting enterprises, like the Sarawak Sugar Company and the Malayan Ramie Company, was the result of unsuitable soil and climatic conditions, whereas those in the mining sector, such as the Central Borneo Company and the Borneo Minerals Company, either found small, uneconomical deposits (antimony in the Baram district) or were faced with a high cost of operations (Silantek coalfields).

A significant exception to this catalogue of unpromising Western enterprises was the celebrated accomplishments of the oil companies—ASPC and SOL—which succeeded within a short period of the commencement of operations. Also, the companies that were involved in Para rubber cultivation enjoyed fair returns on their investments.

As the Brookes would have wanted it, there was no problem of native landlessness nor any large, labouring population nor troublesome unemployment difficulties during economic recession. Since the bulk of the work-force engaged by European companies were imported Chinese labour, whatever exploitation existed was tolerated or disregarded by the Brookes; after all the Chinese were aliens.

Nevertheless, it was doubtful if greater economic development could have been effected with more input of European capital. The trade in Western-manufactured merchandise, the forte of European agency houses and mercantile establishments, was limited in Sarawak owing to the small market, mainly confined to Chinese urban consumers. This branch of business did not offer much scope for expansion in a land where the majority of the population was rural-based and generally subsistence-oriented. The mineral

resources of Sarawak, including oil, were limited and increasingly diminishing, with little prospect of future rich finds. Large-scale commercial agriculture, especially of Para rubber in the fashion of Malayan-style estates, was made difficult because of the lack of suitable land available for such huge operations. Moreover, the problem of the shortage of labour presented a serious difficulty to plantation owners, and the solution in the form of an imported work-force with its high costs rendered the venture uneconomical. The British Protected Western Malay States with their comparatively cheaper labour costs, vast stretches of land for foreign alienation, and a more encouraging and sympathetic British administration, made them more attractive and profitable than the relatively 'restricted' situation encountered in Brooke Sarawak.

1. Henry Longhurst, *The Borneo Story: The History of the First 100 Years of Trading in the Far East by The Borneo Company Limited*, London: Newman Neame, 1956, pp. 17 and 64–5.

2. The other directors were James Dyce Nicol, John Smith, Francis Richardson, and John Harvey. There was a strong indication that the BCL had close connections with the firm of W. R. Paterson and Company, established in 1846, which had offices in Glasgow and Singapore. When Paterson retired in 1849, Robert MacEwen, the manager in Singapore, assumed control and the firm became MacEwen and Company. Harvey was appointed manager in Singapore, and apparently had an eye on James's Sarawak. It was uncertain how the two Glasgow firms of Hendersons and MacEwens came to establish the BCL; the presence of Richardson, a partner at MacEwens, and Harvey, was indicative of the MacEwens connection. Longhurst, who wrote the official history of the BCL, surmises that 'it would not be fair to say either that MacEwens found it on their own or that it was formed independently and then swallowed up MacEwens. Let us say that it was a case of six of one and half a dozen of the other'. Ibid., pp. 17–18.

3. Helms, of Danish extraction, arrived in Sarawak in 1851 initially 'as the agent of a commercial firm to buy up the antimonial ore, and generally to develop the trade of the country, which as yet was insignificant'. Ludvig Verner Helms, *Pioneering in the Far East, and Journeys to California in 1849 and to the White Sea in 1878*, London: W. H. Allen, 1882, p. 130. Although he did not mention his employer by name, there is a strong possibility that MacEwen and Company of Singapore could have been the firm that engaged him. If that was the case, it came as no surprise that he was the BCL's choice of manager at Sarawak. James, in fact, wanted his former secretary, Spenser St John, to be the candidate. See Spenser St John, *The Life of Sir James Brooke: Rajah of Sarawak; from His Personal Papers and Correspondence*, Edinburgh and London: William Blackwood & Sons, 1879, p. 282.

4. Helms, *Pioneering*, pp. 193–4. Emphasis added.

5. On 21 October 1858 after a speech to the mercantile community of Manchester, James succumbed to a stroke. 'I shall they say recover', he assured his nephew Brooke Brooke, 'but my active life is over.' J. Brooke to Brooke Brooke, 6 November 1858, MSS Pac. s. 90, Basil Brooke Papers, Vol. 2A, RHL, Oxford.

6. In the face of an imminent BCL withdrawal, James displayed his steadfast determination to succeed. 'Our revenue will not decrease', he told Templer, 'and will probably be increased. If we have no European development, we shall have a native one, and—"In native swords and native ranks, Our only hope of freedom dwells".' J. Brooke to Templer, 17 December 1858, in Gertrude L. Jacob, *The Raja of Sarawak: An Account of Sir James Brooke, KCB, LL D, Given Chiefly through Letters and Journals*, 2 vols., London: Macmillan, 1876, Vol. II, p. 303.

7. Jacob, *The Raja of Sarawak*, Vol. II, p. 303. Although the choice of Governor was not disclosed, the likely candidate might possibly have been James's eldest nephew, John Brooke Brooke. Ibid. See also Nicholas Tarling, *The Burthen, the Risk, and the Glory: A Biography of Sir James Brooke*, Kuala Lumpur: Oxford University Press, 1982, p. 241.

8. J. Brooke to Templer, 17 December 1858, in Jacob, *The Raja of Sarawak*, Vol. II, p. 303.

9. According to Harriette McDougall, the Anglican Bishop's wife, Christian Dayaks at Lundu and Banting had 'disclosed to their missionaries that Malays had visited them to say they had better turn Mahometans, for soon there would be no English left in the country', and 'trustworthy native friends ... advised the English to wear firearms, even the ladies'. Harriette McDougall, *Sketches of Our Life At Sarawak*, London: Society for Promoting Christian Knowledge, 1882; reprinted Singapore: Oxford University Press, 1992, p. 181.

10. For the so-called 'Bandjermasin War' (1859–67), see Graham Irwin, *Nineteenth-century Borneo: A Study in Diplomatic Rivalry*, The Hague: Martinus Nijhoff, 1955; reprinted Singapore: Donald Moore, 1965, pp. 175–6.

11. Helms, *Pioneering*, pp. 205–6. 'This did not seem a very good time', recalled Helms, 'at which to bring out a young wife, and to commence my labours.' Ibid. His remark was unfortunately true as John Brooke Brooke, then in charge of the government, had ordered the evacuation of women and children by the ship *Planet*, and the Fort and Government House at Kuching were manned and armed. Ibid., p. 206; and McDougall, *Sketches*, p. 183.

12. Helms to John Harvey, 23 August 1860, quoted in Estelle Gardner, 'Footnote to Sarawak, 1859', *SMJ*, 11, 21–2 (July–December 1963): 51. Brooke Brooke wrote to the Foreign Office in April 1860 relating the serious implication of the situation along the coast. 'The prosperity of this country mainly depends on this sago trade, and without it a heavy loss will accrue to the several [sago-processing] factories here [Kuching], *particularly to the Borneo Company, who have recently ordered out from England, expensive machinery for this manufacture.*' Brooke Brooke to Foreign Office, 6 June 1860, FO 12/27, PRO, Kew. Emphasis added.

13. During the first few years James relied on his own fortune to sustain the administrative expenses, and when this source became increasingly scarce, revenue was obtained from the antimony and opium monopolies. When these sources also proved to be inadequate, through the assistance of Henry Wise, James leased out the antimony and opium monopolies, initially to the firm of Melville & Street, and in 1850, to R. and J. Henderson & Company. Little came by way of taxation of the local inhabitants. See J. Brooke, Singapore, to John C. Templer, 11 October 1850, John C. Templer (ed.), *The Private Letters of Sir James Brooke. KCB, Rajah of Sarawak, Narrating the Events of His Life, from 1838 to the Present Time*, 3 vols., London: Bentley, 1853, Vol. III, pp. 14–15; J. Brooke to The Right Honourable Sidney Herbert, 22 June 1852, ibid., p. 123; Parliamentary Papers, Vol. X, 1850, pp. 1242–7; and St John, *The Life of Sir James Brooke*, p. 65.

14. The original plan was to solicit support from close friends and associates, but when these efforts failed to produce a respectable sum it was decided that a public appeal was needed. See Lord Ripon to Burdett Coutts, 17 May 1859, in Owen Rutter (ed.), *Rajah Brooke and Baroness Burdett Coutts: Consisting of the Letters from Sir James Brooke, First White Rajah of Sarawak, to Miss Angela (afterwards Baroness) Burdett Coutts*, London: Hutchinson, 1935, p. 61.

15. Quoted in S. Baring-Gould and C. A. Bampfylde, *A History of Sarawak under Its Two White Rajahs, 1839–1908*, London: Henry Sotheran, 1909, p. 244.

16. This Testimonial and the issue of James's resignation in favour of his eldest nephew, John Brooke Brooke, were among several matters which brought forth the unfortunate circumstances that ended with the disinheritance of the latter. See Jacob, *The Raja of Sarawak*, Vol. II, pp. 335–6, 344–52; Tarling, *The Burthen*, pp. 353–433; and Helms, *Pioneering*, pp. 213–39. See also Emily Hahn, *James Brooke of Sarawak: A Biography of Sir James Brooke*, London: Arthur Barker, 1953, pp. 223–30, 242, and 251–4.

17. Jacob, *The Raja of Sarawak*, Vol. II, p. 312. St John placed the figure at 'about £9000'. St John, *Life of Sir James Brooke*, p. 326. The bulk of the money went to the purchase of Burrator, 'an estate of about seventy acres, with a very small house, in the parish of Sheepstor, on the edge of Dartmoor'. Jacob, *The Raja of Sarawak*, Vol. II, pp. 313, 316–17. It was here that James spent his last days.

18. St John, *Life of Sir James Brooke*, p. 326. St John, ever the loyal supporter of James, hinted that success might be achieved 'had the project been carried out with equal zeal by all those who pretended to feel an interest in it'. Ibid. The failure of the Testimonial soured the more than twenty-year friendship between James and John Templer. See the series of correspondence between them quoted in Hahn, *James Brooke*, pp. 243–6.

19. St John, on his part, condemned this action of the BCL as a mistake and accused it of 'trying to snatch the fruit before it was ripe'. St John, *Life of Sir James Brooke*, p. 327.

20. Helms, *Pioneering*, p. 240.

21. See J. Brooke to Burdett Coutts, 3 June 1859, in Rutter, *Rajah Brooke and Baroness Burdett Coutts*, p. 62. The advance of £5,000 to clear the debt to the BCL, resembled more a friendly gesture, a 'gift', rather than a loan *per se*, as the arrangements relating to security, interest, and repayment, were flexible and 'unbusiness-like'. 'Still', her solicitor understood the matter perfectly, 'I imagine your object is rather to benefit Sir James Brooke than to be free from risk; and keeping that object in view you will accept the best security that circumstances allow.' The 'security' referred to were the antimony mines. William James Farrer, Lincoln's Inn Fields, London, to Burdett Coutts, 11 April 1859, ibid., p. 59.

22. 'I wish them [the BCL] to work, and not to abandon their undertaking,' James wrote to Burdett Coutts in May 1863, 'They are well established . . . and they have a staff, able to direct and accomplish a new undertaking, better than another party fresh to the country.' J. Brooke to 'Ladies', 29 April 1863 (entry 3 May 1863), in Rutter, *Rajah Brooke and Baroness Burdett Coutts*, p. 187. After the disastrous experience at Simunjan, the BCL gave up the coal lease. See J. Brooke to 'Ladies', 29 April 1863 (entry 6 May 1863), ibid., p. 188.

23. Helms, *Pioneering*, p. 212; and T. Charles Martine, 'The Borneo Company Ltd., in Sarawak (From "Notes written by me when in Singapore Changi Gaol, 1943–4")', Typescript, p. 6, SMA, Kuching.

24. Longhurst, *The Borneo Story*, p. 60.

25. See H. S. Morris, 'How an Old Sarawak Society was Undermined', *SG*, March 1982, pp. 55–6.

26. See Robert Pringle, *Rajahs and Rebels: The Ibans of Sarawak under Brooke Rule, 1841–1941*, London: Macmillan, 1970, p. 125; and Martine, 'The Borneo Company Ltd.', p. 6.

27. See 'HH The Rajah and Messrs The Borneo Company Ltd. and Tiong Been Ann Co.', 14 July 1893, Agreement Book, Vol. II, SMA, Kuching; and, 'E. J. Smith, Manager the Borneo Company Limited to Resident 1st Division', 3 May 1894, Agreement Book, Vol. II, SMA, Kuching.

28. Martine, 'The Borneo Company Ltd.', p. 13.

29. See N. Denison, 'Notes on the Land Dayaks of Sarawak Proper', *Sarawak Gazette* (*SG*), 16 January 1877, p. 7.

30. Ibid., p. 14. See also *SG*, 1 May 1884, p. 39.

31. Ibid. See also *SG*, 31 December 1881, p. 108; and *SG*, 4 January 1886, p. 2.

32. In order to assist in the work of prospecting, the BCL during the early 1890s offered substantial rewards for workable mineral finds. But, the *Gazette*, in an editorial of 1892, cast doubt on the employment of this strategy that 'has had the result of exciting natives to notice if not actually to search for signs of ore and several places have been opened up, only to end in disappointment the find proving to be only a small pocket or perhaps not even that'. *SG*, 1 August 1892, p. 142. For instance, the BCL commenced workings at Sarikei in the Lower Rejang in the late 1890s and at Buan Bidi in Upper Sarawak in the mid-1910s. But in both cases, the deposits were exhausted within a short period. See *SG*, 1 April 1893, p. 54; *SG*, 2 January 1896, p. 2; and, *SG*, 3 April 1916, p. 68.

33. Martine, 'The Borneo Company Ltd.', p. 20.

34. Longhurst, *The Borneo Story*, p. 35.

35. It seemed that the decision for the abandonment of Tegora was a hasty one, and not based on the recommendation or advice of a trained expert. Its closure came in 1894, a time when the BCL was distracted by the allure of its gold-mining operations. When investigations were carried out in 1940, there were indications that the decision of 1894 was premature. See Martine, 'The Borneo Company Ltd.', pp. 19–20. See also *SG*, 31 December 1881, p. 108.

36. *SG*, 1 October 1881, p. 80.

37. This mining and delivery of Silantek coal was a joint operation between the government and the BCL. See *SG*, 1 January 1874, n.p. See also Longhurst, *The Borneo Story*, p. 59.

38. See Martine, 'The Borneo Company Ltd.', pp. 29–30.

39. Quoted in *SG*, 26 March 1878, p. 20.

40. See Martine, 'The Borneo Company Ltd.', pp. 6 and 9–11; *SG*, 14 December 1876, p. 2; and *SG*, 26 February 1878, p. 8.

41. According to Martine, another contributing cause of Bidi's closure was the rivalry between Howe, the engineer in charge of Bidi, and Pawle, who, after effecting the closure of Tegora, was assigned to Tai Parit. After the dismissal of Howe over 'a comparatively unimportant matter', Pawle assumed control and 'centralised management and ore treatment of both Bedi and Bau Mines at Bau'. Although this move was in no doubt 'a more economical way of running things and it secured ample ore at Bau,' it was regretted that 'the Bedi Mining holes seem to have been abandoned before they were completely worked out'. Martine, 'The Borneo Company Ltd.', p. 22.

42. See James Lau and Victor Hon, 'History of Mining in Sarawak', *JMHSSB*, 2 (March 1976): 20–1.

43. For instance, see *SG*, 2 January 1902, p. 2.

44. See 'Memo of Agreement between the Sarawak Government and the Borneo Company Limited', 21 April 1898, Agreement Book, Vol. II, SMA, Kuching.

45. Martine, 'The Borneo Company Ltd.', p. 9. See also *SG*, 1 December 1892, p. 212.

46. Martine, 'The Borneo Company Ltd.', p. 38. See also *SG*, 1 February 1901, p. 31.

47. See 'License to plant pepper and gambier by the Borneo Company in Upper Sarawak', 8 July 1901, Agreement Book, Vol. III, SMA, Kuching.

48. See Longhurst, *The Borneo Story*, p. 65. Martine stated the ratio to be one and a half acres of pepper to 'about 50 acres of gambier to maintain such a Pepper Garden'. Martine, 'The Borneo Company Ltd.', p. 38. See also James C. Jackson, *Sarawak: A Geographical Survey of a Developing State*, London: University of London Press, 1968, p. 98.

49. Martine, 'The Borneo Company Ltd.', p. 39.

50. Ibid., p. 40.

51. See *SG*, 4 January 1907, p. 2; and *SG*, 4 January 1908, p. 2. Later, as planting expanded, more capital investment was needed, and the BCL decided that a new limited liability company be set up to oversee this operation. Thus, the Sarawak Rubber Estates Limited was created. This new concern functioned as a subsidiary of the BCL which retained a controlling interest in its management. See Martine, 'The Borneo Company Ltd.', pp. 41–2.

52. See *SG*, 16 February 1912, p. 45; and P. Eaton, 'A History of Bau District', *SG*, 31 May 1967, p. 128.

53. See *SG*, 16 September 1912, p. 210.

54. See *SG*, 17 March 1919, p. 67.

55. See *SG*, 16 December 1918, pp. 325–6; and *SG*, 1 March 1921, p. 30.

56. See Martine, 'The Borneo Company Ltd.', p. 2; and Longhurst, *The Borneo Story*, p. 54. See also A. H. Moy-Thomas, 'Economic Development under the Second Rajah (1870–1917)', *SMJ*, 10, 17–18 (July–December 1961): 53.

57. See Martine, 'The Borneo Company Ltd.', pp. 2 and 32.

58. See ibid., p. 32.

59. See 'Agreement between HH The Rajah and The Borneo Company Limited', 22 February 1902, Agreement Book, Vol. II, SMA, Kuching; Martine, 'The Borneo Company Ltd.', p. 2; and Longhurst, *The Borneo Story*, p. 54.

60. See Martine, 'The Borneo Company Ltd.', pp. 32–3. In fact, it was remarked unkindly that, 'the mill proved more up-to-date than the manager'. Longhurst, *The Borneo Story*, p. 65.

61. This venture was conceived, based on a report by an expert who had conducted a review of logging operations in the Philippines and British North Borneo, and had himself visited Sarawak. See Martine, 'The Borneo Company Ltd.', p. 34.

62. See ibid., p. 34; and 'RTC.–Facts that emerge and some Recommendations for future workings', ibid., pp. 34–6.

63. Longhurst, *The Borneo Story*, p. 93. *Ramin* is a light hardwood of rather fine texture and straight grain. It was the principal export timber of Sarawak during the 1950s. See F. W. Roe (comp.), *The Natural Resources of Sarawak*, 2nd rev. edn., Kuching: Government Printing Office, 1952, p. 21.

64. Until 1888, the BCL's manager at Kuching had held the post of Vice-Consul of Borneo. When Sarawak became a British Protectorate in that year, the Governor of the Straits Settlements acted as British Agent to the Sarawak government, thereby dispensing with the office of a Vice-Consul.

65. *SG*, 6 January 1872, n.p.

66. See *SG*, 31 January 1872, n.p.

67. See *SG*, 1 June 1874, n.p. See also *SG*, 16 June 1874, n.p.

68. See 'Memorandum of Agreement between HH The Rajah and the Central Borneo Company Limited', 22 January 1890, Agreement Book, Vol. I, SMA, Kuching. This grant was effective for five years from 25 June 1888.

69. See *SG*, 1 May 1891, p. 65.

70. See *SG*, 1 July 1891, p. 100; and *SG*, 1 March 1892, p. 51.

71. See *SG*, 2 January 1894, p. 2.

72. See *SG*, 2 January 1895, p. 3; and Richard H. Goldman, 'The Beginnings of Commercial Development in the Baram and Marudi Following the Cession of 1881', *SG*, 31 March 1968, p. 61.

73. See 'Agreement between C. Brooke and the Malayan Ramie Company Limited', 30 December 1907, Agreement Book, Vol. III, SMA, Kuching.

74. See *SG*, 16 June 1908, p. 152.

75. See *SG*, 1 March 1909, p. 59.

76. C. Brooke to Vyner Brooke, 22 November 1908, MSS Pac. s. 83, Brooke Family Papers, Vol. 3, RHL, Oxford.

77. This was the name given to its large plant at Tanjong Batu in honour of Robert Goelet and Cornelius Vanderbilt, two American magnates, who were its major investors.

78. *SG*, 16 September 1910, p. 196.

79. Another huge factory complex was built on land leased from the Dutch authorities on Kerinun Island. See Martine, 'The Borneo Company Ltd.', p. 36.

80. Ibid.

81. See 'Growth of Sarawak—Chronology 1917–1924', Typescript, MSS Pac. s. 83, Brooke Family Papers, Box 7, File 8, Item 1, pp. 21–2, RHL, Oxford.

82. Initially the company purchased direct from Dayak collectors, but its insistence that they bring the *jelutong* to a site near the factory was disagreeable to the latter, for 'if they [the Dayaks] refused the [price] offer [by the company] they would have to make the journey back to Kuching' which was undoubtedly troublesome. Ibid., p. 16a. Chinese middlemen then came on the scene, purchasing the *jelutong* from the Dayaks and selling it to the company. For instance, see *SG*, 16 June 1909, p. 134.

83. *SG*, 17 April 1911, p. 68.

84. 'Growth of Sarawak', MSS Pac. s. 83, p. 22. See also *SG*, 1 May 1911, pp. 77–8.

85. See *SG*, 1 May 1911, p. 77.

86. Ibid.

87. C. Brooke to W. H. Galbraith, Manager of the British Malaysian Rubber Manufacturing Company, 5 June 1911, HH The Rajah's Letters August 1906 to April 1913, SMA, Kuching.

88. *SG*, 17 June 1912, p. 130.

89. *SG*, 16 July 1915, p. 163; and *SG*, 17 January 1916, p. 13.

90. See 'Growth in Sarawak', MSS Pac. s. 83, p. 48. See also *SG*, 1 February 1913, pp. 29–30; *SG*, 16 January 1914, p. 13; *SG*, 16 February 1914, pp. 37–8; *SG*, 2 March 1914, p. 51; and *SG*, 1 May 1916, p. 80.

91. The name change was effected in 1911. See *SG*, 16 January 1912, p. 27.

92. Cutch, an Indian word, is a kind of wood oil extracted from mangrove bark used in the tanning and dyeing industries.

93. 'Deed between the Government of Sarawak and the Island Trading Syndicate Limited', 28 April 1910, Agreement Book, Vol. IV, SMA, Kuching.

94. See *SG*, 16 January 1911, p. 2; and Moy-Thomas, 'Economic Development', p. 58.

95. For instance, see *SG*, 1 April 1911, p. 61.

96. For instance, see *SG*, 16 August 1911, p. 163; *SG*, 1 November 1911, p. 217; *SG*, 17 July 1916, p. 149; *SG*, 2 January 1917, p. 6; and *SG*, 1 February 1926, p. 40.

97. See *SG*, 1 May 1916, p. 80.

98. For instance, see *SG*, 1 February 1917, p. 27; *SG*, 16 March 1917, p. 73; *SG*, 1 February 1921, p. 15; and, *SG*, 2 May 1921, p. 73.

99. It only ceased operation in 1957. See Moy-Thomas, 'Economic Development', p. 58.

100. See *SG*, 1 August 1910, p. 172; and *SG*, 16 January 1911, p. 2.

101. See *SG*, 1 June 1911, p. 98; *SG*, 2 January 1914, p. 7; and *SG*, 17 January 1916, p. 14.

102. See *SG*, 17 January 1916, p. 14.

103. *SG*, 16 April 1917, p. 97.

104. For instance, see *SG*, 1 April 1921, p. 48.

105. See *SG*, 16 January 1911, p. 2.

106. See 'Agreement between the Sarawak Government and J. H. Brodie, Manager Kuching Trading Co. Ltd.', 13 January 1913, Agreement Book, Vol. IV, SMA, Kuching.

107. The BCL was first approached to undertake prospecting and possible working of the oil deposits, but had declined 'as they thought it was too large a commitment'. 'Growth of Sarawak', MSS Pac. s. 83, p. 17. Nevertheless, when oil was first spudded at Miri in 1910, the BCL transferred its mineral rights to the ASPC in return for a marketing agreement as well as one stating that any mineral deposits discovered in the course of exploration would be disclosed to it. See Longhurst, *The Borneo Story*, p. 112.

108. Japanese immigrants first came to Kuching in the late 1880s as petty traders and hawkers; later arrivals during the early 1900s took up Para rubber cultivation and market gardening on the eastern fringes of the town, and as physicians, dentists, photographers, and prostitutes in the bazaar. See Craig Alan Lockard, *From Kampung to City: A Social History of Kuching, Malaysia, 1820–1970*, Ohio University Monographs in International Studies, Southeast Asia Series, No. 75, Athens, 1987, pp. 38, 44, 86, 90, 96, and 143.

109. Wet-*padi* cultivation undertaken by a small group of Japanese farming families on the Nissa Shokai property in the Upper Samarahan did not go beyond the experimental stage. See *Sarawak Administration Report (SAR), 1929*, Kuching: Government Printing Office, p. 22; *SG*, 2 January 1936, p. 16; *SG*, 1 April 1936, p. 87; and C. L. Newman, *Report on* Padi *in Sarawak 1938*, Kuching: Government Printing Office, 1938, pp. 8–9.

110. Martine, 'The Borneo Company Ltd.', p. 4.

111. Steven Runciman, *The White Rajahs: A History of Sarawak from 1841 to 1946*, Cambridge: Cambridge University Press, 1960, p. 284. Runciman did not cite his source but simply denotes 'personal information'.

112. Martine, 'The Borneo Company Ltd.', p. 4.

113. 'Agreement between HH Charles Vyner Brooke and Charles Hose', 1 November 1919, HCO 1986/1920, NAM, Kuala Lumpur.

114. See 'Agreement between HH Charles Vyner Brooke and Charles Hose', 5 July 1920, HCO 1986/1920, NAM, Kuala Lumpur. See also C. V. Brooke to Dr [Charles] Hose, 4 June 1920, HCO 1986/1920, NAM, Kuala Lumpur.

115. *SG*, 1 April 1921, p. 48. Initially, land around the foothills of Mount Lambier with the village of Bakam as a centre was selected and duly granted, but the discovery of oil seepages rendered it inadvisable to commence operations in the area. Ibid., p. 47.

116. VAMCO is the acronym of the five partners of the company: Vanscolina, Altman, Montgomery, Cook, and 'Orl of U.S.', the last named was apparently a silent partner. Leonard Edwards and Peter W. Stevens, *Short Histories of the Lawas and Kanowit Districts*, Kuching: Borneo Literature Bureau, 1971, p. 44.

117. Ibid. See also *SG*, 1 June 1932, p. 119.

118. Edwards and Stevens, *Short Histories*, p. 139.

119. Ibid., p. 169.

120. 'Indenture between C. V. Brooke and the Anglo-Saxon Petroleum Company Limited', 27 April 1921, Agreement Book, Vol. IV, SMA, Kuching; and *SG*, 1 October 1921, p. 202.

121. *SG*, 2 July 1923, p. 199; and *SG*, 1 August 1923, p. 231.

122. See B. A. St J. Hepburn (comp.), *The Handbook of Sarawak: Comprising Historical, Statistical and General Information Obtained from Official and Other Reliable Records*, Singapore: Malaya Publishing House for the Government of Sarawak, 1949, p. 104.

123. *SG*, 1 July 1886, pp. 114–15. Emphasis in original.

124. Ibid.

125. For instance, see *SG*, 1 July 1886, p. 104.

126. Baring-Gould and Bampfylde, *A History of Sarawak*, p. 428. For the BCL's other far more lucrative operations in the neighbouring lands, see Longhurst, *The Borneo Story*, pp. 31–52 and 72–93.

10
Epilogue

TOWARDS the end of 1941, on the eve of the outbreak of the Pacific War, Sarawak was a multiracial, sparsely populated country; it had a mainly rural-based subsistence economy with some cash cropping of rubber, sago, and pepper, and a declining oil industry. The trade and commerce of the country were largely in Chinese hands, with one or two European agency houses importing Western-manufactured goods and acting as agents and brokers for insurance and shipping. Apart from the mercantile concerns, other Western enterprises comprised an oil company, a cutch factory, two timber exporters of *ramin* and plywood, and less than half a dozen rubber plantations (collectively owning a little more than 4000 hectares (10,000 acres)). The country possessed basic telecommunication facilities; a telegraph and telephone network kept the capital in touch with the major outstations. Metalled roads existed only within the confines of the main urban centres of Kuching, Sibu, and Miri, in addition to a 64-kilometre (40-mile) trunk road extending from Kuching eastwards to a little slightly beyond Serian. Rivers and waterways remained the chief means of transport and communication; the Sarawak Steamship Company, a subsidiary of the Straits Steamship Company, provided shipping along the coast, up the Rejang, and connections with Singapore. Three local Chinese banks and a branch of the British Chartered Bank of India, Australia and China, handled most of the banking needs which were largely transacted with and through Singapore businesses. The Chinese mercantile community had their own exclusive system of 'banking and credit' for financing and promoting their business ventures.

Sarawak was relatively peaceful and fairly prosperous owing to its export of oil and rubber which were much needed as a result of the 1939–45 conflict in Europe. There was a significant absence of subversive political activities among the Chinese, the only political activities being efforts at contributing to the China Relief Fund and some mild expression of anti-Japanese feelings demonstrated

in the boycott of the products of that country. There was also fund-raising through the staging of plays, concerts, and funfairs for the British War Effort by the European community and local people.

On the internal political front, Vyner relinquished his power as an absolute monarch and presented a 'Constitution' to the country on the centenary of Brooke rule. But little had, in fact, changed, particularly from the perspective of the ordinary person; the basic symbols of the administration in the person of the Rajah and the General Council were still present (although under the new arrangement, the Rajah had to act as Rajah-in-Council).[1]

The Slow Pace of Economic Development

Brooke Sarawak was comparatively 'backward' *vis-à-vis* other neighbouring British-governed territories like the Protected Western Malay States, the Crown Colonies of the Straits Settlements, and Lower Burma. Sarawak's slow economic development was as much the consequence of the country's geographical and natural disadvantages as of deliberate Brooke policies.

The limitations of its natural resources—the relatively poor soil, difficult terrain, a climate unsuitable for most agricultural pursuits, a land dissected by numerous rivers presenting obstacles to the development of land transport, a coastline devoid of natural, deep, and sheltered harbours, and the general isolation of the country away from the main trade and shipping routes—were fundamental natural handicaps. Its isolation and remoteness rendered Sarawak a *terra incognita* to Europeans and Chinese alike; yet both European capital and Chinese labour were essential ingredients in the development of a country's economy, as shown by the examples in the British Protected Malay States of Perak, Selangor, and Negri Sembilan. Moreover, the lack of knowledge of the country was capitalized on by certain anti-Brooke elements in Singapore and Labuan who sought to create an unfavourable picture of Sarawak to the outside world, particularly to would-be investors. The problems of the shortage of labour and the reliance on imported Chinese workers adversely affected the development and expansion of agriculture, mining, and other economic activities. Furthermore, the country's physical disadvantages, compared with its neighbours in the region, coupled with Brooke pro-native policies discouraged the inflow of foreign investment.

The Problems of Resource Limitation

'Richness' of Soil and 'Abundance' of Minerals: Dispelling the Myth

James, in his *A Letter from Borneo*, written in 1841 shortly after securing the rajahship of Sarawak, boasted that 'the soil and productions of this country are of the richest description, and it is not too much to say, that within the same given space, there are not to be found the same mineral and vegetable riches in any land in the world'.[2] Hugh Low, who had spent 'a residence of about thirty months in Sarawak, and the west coast of Borneo' during the mid-1840s, further perpetuated the myth of the 'richness' of the country.[3] But more sober judgements appeared in 1848 in the *Journal of the Indian Archipelago and Eastern Asia*.

> That no very populous and powerful state ever grew up in Borneo is partly to be attributed to its comparative distance from the [Malay] Peninsula and Java, and its want of the commercial advantages of the ports on the [S]traits of Malacca, but chiefly to the *inferiority of the soil* and to the large and simple indigenous population, which from the first impressed a peculiar character on the Malay communities, by pampering their indolence and rapacity. If the soil had yielded luxuriant crops of rice instead of gold and diamonds, Borneo would have become populous and great like Java.[4]

Nevertheless, the last sentence in the above extract still presented the country as a mineral eldorado. This theme of Sarawak's potential mineral wealth, as well as its other natural resources, was again highlighted in Ludvig Verner Helms's memoirs published in 1882.

> This great island, inferior only to Australia, or perhaps to New Guinea, in extent, will doubtless, in time to come, be one of the most important countries of the Far East. Its vast resources only need development, and its numerous rivers, rising in the centre of the island, are ready to serve as natural highways for the transport of the mineral and vegetable products, which have as yet only been partially exploited.[5]

But a more realistic, and clearly more accurate, assessment of Sarawak's natural endowments was given by Odoardo Beccari, who went on a two-year sojourn in the mid-1860s investigating the botany of the country.

> Sarawak, up to the present [early 1900s], has derived its wealth more from nature's spontaneous products than from agriculture or human industries

of any kind. Agriculture has hitherto been less successful than might have been expected in a country whose soil has a reputation for great fertility.... In Borneo fertility is in a very great measure due to the humus accumulated in the forests, and when this is used up, or carried away by rain or floods, the soil which is left could scarcely be productive unless it were properly worked and manured. It is therefore doubtful if it would suffice to support a large and dense population, living exclusively or mostly on the produce of the land, and in a very limited degree on the results of its own industry.[6]

'But it would', Beccari postulated, 'be vain to expect in Borneo the grand agricultural results which are obtained in Java, where the soil is so different.'[7] Therefore, James's dream of Sarawak as 'a second Java' was unlikely to have been fulfilled because of the poverty of its soil. In the early 1870s, it was admitted that 'the soil of this country, except in some localities, is far inferior to that of either Java or Manila, and is about equal to Rhio, Johore, and Malacca.'[8]

It was mainly the poor soil and the unfavourable climatic conditions that frustrated Charles's efforts in promoting new crops. The disappointment encountered in his silk project during the 1860s is an example: 'But the want of well-defined seasons, rendered the results very uncertain, the silkworms being often and easily decimated by the various maladies to which they are liable.'[9] There were similar failures of other crops due to poor or unsuitable soil and/or climate, but Charles was reluctant to accept this conclusion, as shown in his response to the experimental work carried out at the Matang Estate. 'The Rajah had often attributed the failure of the estate to ill management. Perhaps after 46 years of trial and changes, he was finally convinced that *human factor was not the only cause of its failure*.'[10]

Expert opinion in the 1950s and 1960s confirmed the reality of Sarawak's poor soils. Drawn from results of a preliminary soil survey conducted during the late 1940s, F. W. Roe, the Director of Geological Surveys, presented the following evaluation.

Most of the soils are poor agriculturally, and there are few areas with the fertility of the volcanic districts of Java, or the rich alluvium of Burma or Indo-China.... The possibilities of intensifying tree and shrub crop production are however limited by the general poverty of the soils, severe transport difficulties, and the large quantities of fertilisers generally needed.[11]

The report by T. W. G. Dames, Soil Survey Expert of the Food and Agriculture Organization of the United Nations, which was submitted to the Sarawak government in 1962, further reinforced

the thesis of poor soil. 'The extremely wet climate', he maintained, 'has been largely decisive in producing highly leached very acid soils containing very low amounts of plant nutrients.'[12] Map 10.1 shows the various types of soils which overall are not conducive to agricultural pursuits.

Sarawak's supposed abundance of mineral wealth was equally untrue. Without dismissing the 'existence of gold and diamonds in Borneo ... in remote times', Beccari was disappointed that 'this fame of former days has helped considerably to maintain even to the present time an erroneous and highly exaggerated idea regarding the mineral wealth of the country'.[13] If the observations of a botanist were unconvincing, the views of specialists like A. Hart Everett (1878) and Theodor Posewitz (1892) could not be taken lightly.[14] The following statement from Posewitz is conclusive.

In nearly all writings which treat of Borneo, mention is made of the great mineral wealth of the island; and in the oldest works we find nothing else mentioned but the valuable minerals. From the day when the companions of the unfortunate Magellan cast anchor before Brunei, about three hundred years ago, to the beginning of this century, when [John] Hunt handed in to Sir S[tamford] Raffles his report 'On the Great and Rich Island of Borneo,' the wildest ideas have been in circulation with regard to its mineral wealth.

Time showed, however, that expectations had been raised to too high a pitch, and that, although useful minerals were widely distributed, they existed only too often in quantities that would not pay working.

In the earliest days it was only gold and diamonds which vouched for the richness of the island. Then the coal-beds became known; and antimony and quicksilver were worked (in Sarawak). Mining companies were floated, but their hopes were, in great part, doomed to disappointment.[15]

Moreover, investigations undertaken by specialist prospectors during the 1950s and 1960s confirmed the poor mineral prospects of Sarawak. Although gold deposits were known to be widespread, 'most occurrences' were 'too poor or too small to repay mining'.[16] Likewise, oil prospecting appeared to be unpromising.[17]

Unfavourable Physical Features of the Country

Besides the poverty of its soil, Sarawak's physical landscape is generally unfavourable for agriculture, especially large-scale commercial cultivation. There is a conspicuous absence of vast areas of flat plains, like those of British Lower Burma, the Menam delta, the Bangkok plain of Siam, and the Mekong delta of French Cochin-China. The Rejang delta area, although an alluvial plain, was

MAP 10.1
Schematic Soil Map of Sarawak, *c.*1960s

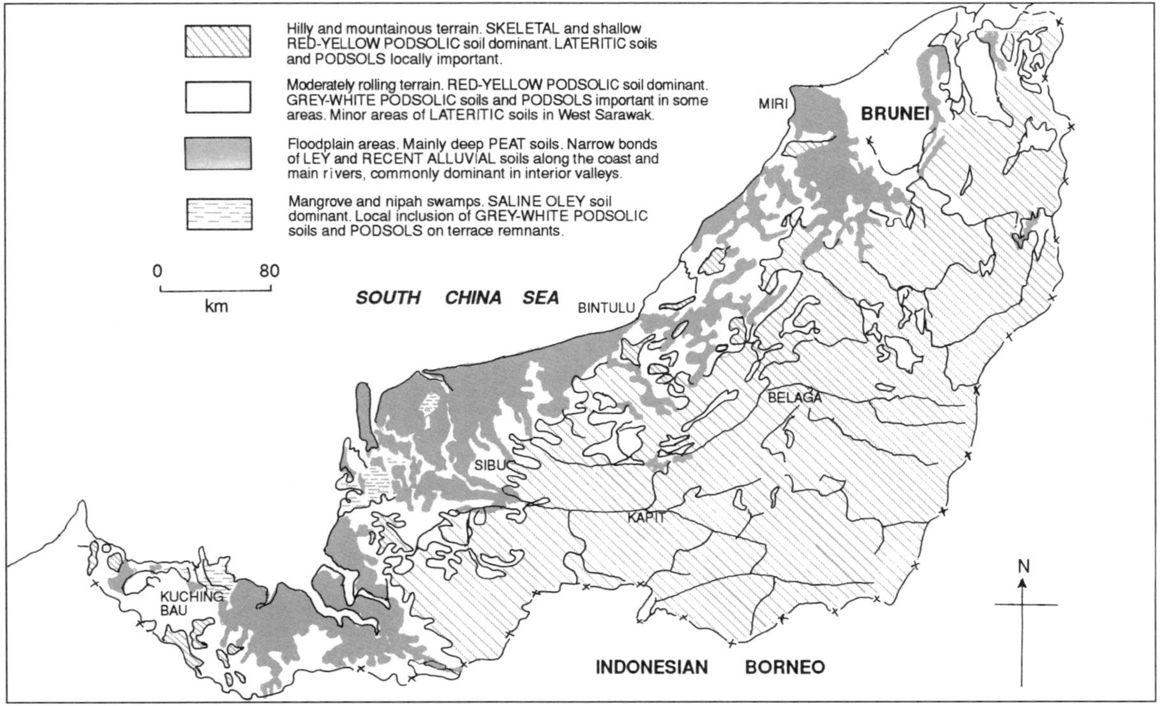

Source: After Dunsmore, 'A Review of Agricultural Research in Sarawak', between pp. 314 and 315.

covered with swampy mangrove forest. The three main topographical areas of Sarawak (see Map 1.3) are:

Firstly, an alluvial and swampy coastal plain in which isolated mountains and mountain groups rise to 2,000 feet or more, then rolling country of yellow sandy clay intersected by ranges of mountains and finally a mountainous area in the interior. The coast is generally flat and low-lying with heavy vegetation and flat sandy or mud beaches.[18]

Such a physical landscape is more suitable for the establishment of small farms rather than large plantations. The numerous rivers and streams posed difficulties in laying out large estates. Moreover, the huge expanse of tropical rain forest, covering more than three-quarters of the country, also limited settled agriculture. Even in the 1950s, the physical limitations remained formidable. (Map 10.2 shows land utilization and natural resources in 1952; Map 10.3 depicts the extent and predominance of forest and the types of land use in 1957.)

The zone of rugged hill country with its 'continuous sequence of ridges and valleys' is not only unsuitable for conventional sedentary agriculture but also 'severely inhibits road construction'.[19] The rivers, therefore, remain the highways of transport and communication as they have been for centuries. Inland river ports are indispensable owing to the significant absence of natural, sheltered, and deep harbours along the 720 kilometres (450 miles) of coastline. But, even then, obstacles, like rapids in the upper reaches, sandbars at the mouths, 'narrow and shifting channels, shallowness, [and] a complicated network of tides (twice a day along much of the coast)', make transport by river both difficult and dangerous.[20] The occurrence of tidal bores further adds to the hazards of river travel. Furthermore, the *landas* or rainy season, with its strong winds and choppy seas, from October until February when the north-east monsoon blows across the South China Sea, is perilous to shipping, especially to small craft.

The poor system of communications, relying primarily on a notoriously slow, and at times even hazardous, system of coastal and inland shipping, retarded commercial intercourse,

resulting in a disproportionate amount of the value of exports and imported consumer goods being eaten up by middlemen in moving them between consumer[s]–producers and the few ports of the country. The actual time-lapse caused by poor communications also tends to increase the number of times goods and services must be handled between producer and consumer, each single step being paid for at a comparatively high[er] rate.... The overhead resulting from poor communications must be enormous and no doubt has the effect of greatly reducing production.[21]

MAP 10.2
Land Utilization and Natural Resources, *c.*1952

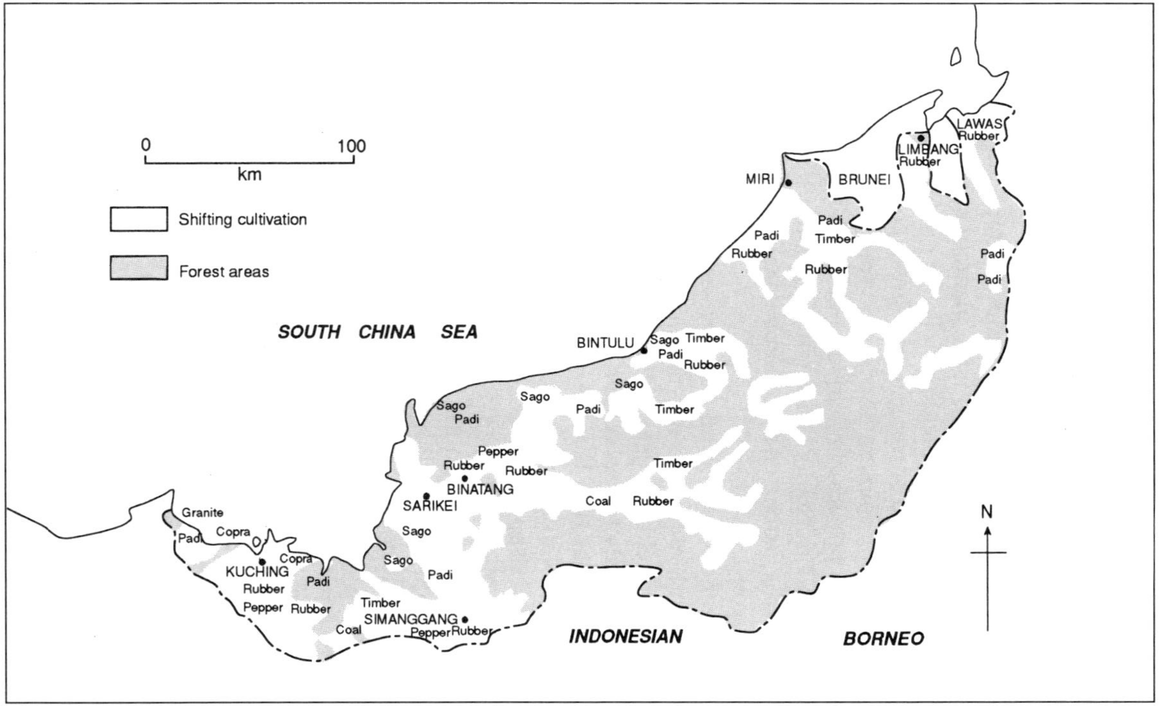

Source: After Roe, *Natural Resources of Sarawak*, n.p.

MAP 10.3
Land Use and Forest Type, 1957

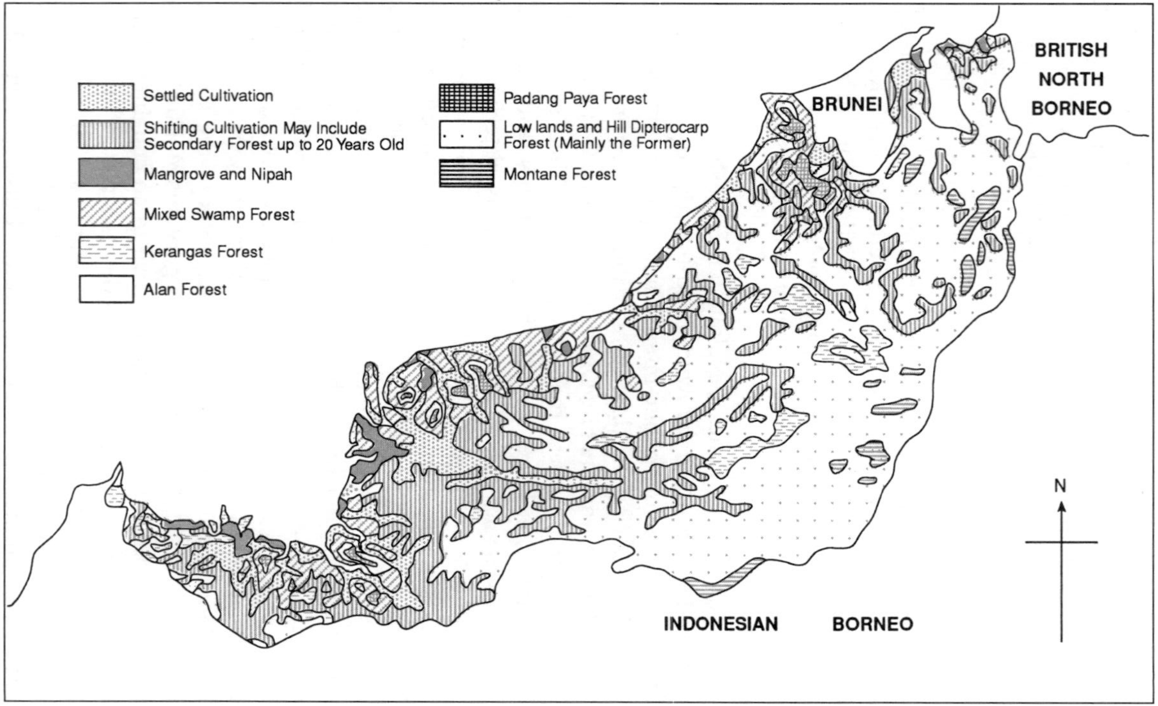

Source: Jackson, *Sarawak*, p. 33.

Sarawak's 'comparative distance from the [Malay] Peninsula and Java, and its want of the commercial advantages of the ports on the [S]traits of Malacca' further contributed to slow economic development. Situated away from the main trade routes, Sarawak existed in relative isolation. About 700 kilometres (440 miles) of the South China Sea separates Kuching from Singapore, the main outlet of the country's exports to the world market.

Terra Incognita

The remote location of Sarawak, far from the crossroads of trade and the major shipping routes, perpetuated the mystery of an unknown land, a *terra incognita*. Knowledge of it during the nineteenth and early twentieth century was largely drawn from hearsay and rumour. In general the majority of outsiders were ignorant of the country.

The romance of James's exploits, an Englishman as ruler of an eastern land peopled by wild head-hunting tribes, might have briefly excited some public interest among his fellow countrymen, particularly during the time of his triumphant return to Britain in 1847 when he was fêted by Queen and country. But, perhaps more accurately, the interest that was generated then and thereafter, focused more on James himself, his personality, and especially his swashbuckling adventures, rather than on his eastern kingdom.[22]

If his home-coming in the autumn of 1847 promoted positively Sarawak's name, then, his anti-piracy policy that led to exasperating parliamentary debates in the House of Commons and the establishment of a Commission of Inquiry in Singapore, created unfavourable publicity for the country despite James's exoneration in Parliament as well as in Singapore. The proceedings at Westminster and Singapore might have depicted Sarawak, from a distant and ill-informed vantage, as a land plagued by marauding pirates and bloodthirsty head-hunters.[23] Accounts of the Chinese insurrection of 1857 added further to this gory image. Furthermore, the country before 1888, 'though governed in an enlightened manner by European rulers, [was] not under the actual shadow of the British flag'.[24] It was James's argument that Sarawak needed a 'Protective Power', primarily for its survival, but also as a means of promoting public confidence to attract European capital investment. Notwithstanding British Protectorate status accorded in 1888, little was done to improve the marred image of Sarawak, thanks to the idiosyncrasies and policies of James's successors.

Compared with James's flamboyant personality, both Charles and Vyner were uncharismatic individuals. Neither of them presented anything comparable to the prolific writings of James; these gave an insight into his thoughts, personality, and his kingdom. Charles, at least, wrote about the period of his life spent as a cadet in the Dayak heartland in the service of his uncle (*Ten Years in Sarawak* (1866)), and in later years, vented in a pamphlet (*Queries: Past, Present and Future* (1907)) his anti-imperialist views, aimed particularly at the British colonial system. Vyner, apart from writing briefly about routine administrative matters, did not leave behind memoirs or journals that might have thrown light on his character and opinions.[25]

Charles's introvert personality and his distaste for socializing made him an unknown figure, a maverick outsider, in political and business circles, whether in London or Singapore. According to his wife, the Ranee Margaret, 'He stood alone, wanted no friends except in Sarawak.... He repelled any attempts at friendship made by people who were well disposed to him and refused invitations from those who could have been of great service to him.... Poor dear, he was not in any sense a man of the world.'[26] Such aloof behaviour coupled with his policies wholly estranged him from Whitehall, the City, and the European business establishment in Singapore, much to the disadvantage of Sarawak. In particular, his political ambitions towards Brunei ruffled the feathers of some Colonial Office officials.[27]

Vyner's shy and withdrawn manners made him few friends among the political and business élite. His continued advocacy of traditional Brooke policies also did little to improve Sarawak's image.

Examples of the ignorance of Sarawak may appear in retrospect to be amusing; but obviously those living at that time in Brooke Sarawak were not amused. This example gleaned from the *Gazette* of 1886 shows the outsider's persistent lack of awareness of the country: 'The fact is that so little is known of Sarawak or Borneo at home [in Britain], or of its climate, that no one ever takes the trouble to enquire. We know that two gentlemen with capital that only lately left Ceylon and went to Johore to plant, when asked why they did not try Sarawak remarked *they never heard of the place*.'[28] In 1910 an erroneous story was carried by the well-respected *Straits Times* of Singapore regarding the case of a man wanted by the Colony's police. The journalist *thrice repeated* in his article that the Sarawak authorities were alerted *via telegraph* by their

Singapore counterparts, unconscious of the fact that there was no telegraphic connection between Singapore and Sarawak.[29] This incident typically reflects the lack of awareness of Sarawak conditions at that time by those in Singapore.

This ignorance was still evident during the post-war period when Sarawak was a British Colony administered by the Colonial Office in London, as the following, rather humorous, story quoted from the *Gazette* illustrates.

'Sarawak, East Africa' 6 August 1949

It is *so common* for letters meant for Sarawak to be misdirected that we get little amusement out of such errors nowadays, but here is an outstanding example of ignorance which should shake the complacency of some of us.

The Director of Lands and Surveys has just received a letter addressed to him at Kuching, Sarawak, EAST AFRICA, which requests him to forward four types of maps of ZANZIBAR to London. That is not too bad, but the really amusing part of the request is that *it is made by a leading British firm of map publishers.* We sincerely hope that in their next world series they will not place little Sarawak somewhere in, or off the coast of Africa. Perhaps they have learnt that Sarawak is to be the next African colony.[30]

The Anti-Sarawak Lobby in Singapore and Labuan's Jealousy

The gradual development and steady success of Sarawak created some envious elements in Singapore and Labuan. These individuals or a group of them sought to present a poor image of the Raj in order to discourage would-be entrepreneurs from investing there.

The apparent anti-European capitalist stance of James, as perceived in the Burns's affair, and Charles's repeated denunciation of Western speculators and exploitative commercial concerns, culminating in his prohibition of the sale of rubber plantations to companies or persons 'of white nationality', gave rise to an anti-Brooke lobby within the European mercantile community of Singapore. The actions of this group in dissuading potential investors and visitors with unflattering and discouraging remarks were evident. The following *Gazette* editorial of June 1896 commented on this subject with regret and a degree of understandable anger.

We *frequently* hear from strangers who visit Sarawak a remark to the effect that, they are so glad that they came here 'after all'. On enquiry into the meaning of the 'after all' we *always* get the same story; that on the trav-

eller mentioning, in Singapore, his intention of going to Sarawak, he is at once cautioned against so doing, is told that the place is a swamp, that there is no town, nowhere to stop, etc. etc. He is recommended strongly to go in preference to Sandakan or Brunei. (!!!)

The kind folks of Singapore who give such disinterested advice to would-be visitors here speak either from the profundity of their ignorance or from some ill feeling towards this place. That they speak in ignorance of a port so close and so easy of access is difficult to believe. *Ill feeling does exist towards Sarawak in Singapore we know well and has existed since the days of Sir James Brooke....*

We would recommend intending visitors to Sarawak to pay no heed to evil accounts of Sarawak which the ignorance or malice of Singapore spreads with no niggard voice, but to come and see for themselves what manner of place we live in in preference to adopting an illfitting, ready made Singapore opinion.[31]

These false representations were not confined within the European enclave; they were also evident in the Chinese community. The rumour of Chinese coolies being pressed into slavery upon their disembarkation was but one example of libel against the Raj.

A group of Europeans casting aspersions on Sarawak might, in part, be a classic case of 'sour grapes'. Perhaps, they might have been rejected in their attempts to embark on speculative ventures in Sarawak, and in a vindictive manner sought to propagate an unfavourable picture of the country as a means of sabotaging its progress. Charles, for instance, had been notorious in declining applications from Western firms and individuals wishing to commence large-scale Para rubber cultivation in the country. But the cause of ill-feeling among the Chinese is harder to pinpoint; a plausible explanation might be the competition for coolies that made some individuals or parties resort to such rumour-mongering.

The Labuan authorities, from the assumption of the governorship of John Pope-Hennessy (later Sir) (1867–71), were also resentful of the Sarawak Raj.[32] It was a case of envious rivalry. The Colony of Labuan had not prospered as expected; trade was small-scale, and the coal-mines, although in operation, were running at a loss. Furthermore, Pope-Hennessy, as Governor of Labuan and also Consul-General of Borneo, viewed Charles as a rival for his power and influence in north-west Borneo, particularly in light of the latter's expansionist policy towards the Brunei Sultanate.

The *Gazette*, in early 1873, lamented this attitude of the Labuan authorities: 'It was apparently the policy of the Labuan authorities, at any rate until a year or two ago, to disparage the capabilities of

the Rajah's territories as far as they were able in England, and the advances made by Sarawak trading vessels northwards along the Brunei Coast have been occasionally viewed with considerable jealousy.'[33]

The Paternalistic Policies of the Brookes

The Brooke policy of the protection of the interests and rights of the indigenous peoples and the promotion of their well-being was unusually benevolent and philanthropic, in comparison with other contemporary colonial regimes in the region. Undoubtedly the Brookes were enlightened despots who had the welfare of the indigenous inhabitants of Sarawak foremost in their minds and actions. When James rejected the inflow of large European capitalist investment and the accompanying influx of Westerners on the scale suggested by Wise, his objection was based on the fear lest indigenous interests were compromised in favour of European, and native labour exploited for foreign gains. The unfortunate experience he had with his one-time agent, Wise, and the latter's Eastern Archipelago Company reinforced James's attitude towards the selfishness and insincerity of Western capitalist companies. The pressing demands from the BCL for the repayment of its loan at a time when James was still facing financial difficulties further added to his resentment of Western companies.

Charles was even more partisan of native interests. He was forthright in his contempt of Western speculators and exploiters. He shielded the native population by enacting land laws based on lease rather than outright alienation, rejecting large land concessions, and outlawing the sale of rubber holdings to all Europeans. His measures seemed harsh, unfair, and appeared to be prejudicial to European entrepreneurs. Consequently Charles earned the reputation of being anti-capitalist and anti-European and Sarawak was considered a 'no-go' area for Western investment. But this was a flawed view of Charles. His critics among the mercantile community of London and Singapore, resentful of his apparent 'closed-door policy', perpetuated this image of him as an insufferable despot who barred all European outsiders from his domain.

However, as a number of impartial observers have pointed out, Charles was not opposed to Western capitalist investors *per se* but to that breed of speculator and entrepreneur only interested in quick and handsome profits at the expense of the indigenous peoples. Beccari presented this clearer picture of Charles.

The Rajah considers himself the father of his people, who have all his thought and care, and he does his utmost to lead his subjects along the road of progress and civilisation, though without sudden or violent changes, to which he is absolutely opposed on principle. He has no wish that the country he rules should be taken advantage of by unscrupulous speculators of European nationalities for their own special benefit alone. He leases land on advantageous conditions to all persons who desire to cultivate it, and he is not opposed to investment of European capital in Sarawak, in undertakings of a rational kind, as has been wrongly asserted. But he has legitimate reason to decline to protect mere adventurers who swarm in new countries solely to fill their empty purses without the least consideration for the consequences which may accrue to others and to the country through the effects of their speculations. *Any honest trader, and better still any able agriculturist, who earnestly wishes to deal well with the natives, may always be sure of a hearty welcome in the dominions of Rajah Brooke.*[34]

His wife, the Ranee Margaret, although she cannot be said to be a disinterested observer, wrote that Charles's 'dearest wish' was 'to keep Sarawak for the benefit of its own people, and, in so doing, *from the devastating grasp of money-grabbing syndicates*'.[35]

Evidence of his welcoming bona fide European capitalist enterprises could be seen in his continual and unstinting support and assistance given to concerns like the BCL, the ASPC, and the Island Trading Company, to name but a few. The unfortunate affair with the ill-fated United British Malaysian Rubber Manufacturing Company (Goebilt) was exactly the nightmare that Charles tried so hard to avoid. The maverick Charles supported the local Chinese middlemen in their conflict with this Western firm which sought to apply pressure from its London office in an attempt to 'bully' him to favour its cause. His action was unconventional to say the least, in fact wholly radical, considering that British administrators in the Western Malay States were supportive of European establishments against Chinese competition.

Vyner was an equal if not more ardent a practitioner than Charles of the traditional Brooke policy. But he was no blind follower of tradition. 'Adaptability', he emphasized, should be adopted, for 'trouble is bound to occur if the ruling power is lacking in adaptability, because it must be remembered that the demands of successive Asiatic generations alter mainly on account of changes brought about by the increasing Europeanization of their environment'.[36] The measures that he undertook in meeting the vicissitudes and uncertainties of the 1920s and 1930s demonstrated his 'adaptability' and a great sense of practical-mindedness. Some of his policies might seem harsh, or even counter-productive,

as his restriction of Chinese immigration during the late 1920s and throughout the following decade, but such steps were deemed necessary under the then prevailing economic and political circumstances.[37] The gradual and cautious approach adopted in the development of the economy no doubt received strong criticisms during the boom years of the 1920s, but the quick recovery from the crushing Depression (1929–31) vindicated his prudent strategy. The editorial of the *Gazette* of January 1934, with undisguised smugness, made the following remarks.

> It may be stated that the slump, if it has nothing else, has triumphantly vindicated the policy of the Rajahs of Sarawak, which has been consistently adhered to since it was laid down by Sir James Brooke. This policy, which has before now been described by those not conversant with the true nature of traditions of the country as 'backward,' has now most signally proved its worth. *At the end of the three years of one of the worst depressions in history, Sarawak emerges with no unemployment, a balanced budget, and no debt.*[38]

The nature of Brooke traditions was succinctly described in 1928 by Vyner's cousin, Charles Hope Willes Johnson, who was the Secretary to the Sarawak Advisory Council at Westminster and Legal Adviser to the Raj.

> If we move away from the original and well-recognized Brooke policy, now of some 80 years' standing, the policy of working for the good of the inhabitants, if we countenance the extravagant ideas that have been so prevalent elsewhere since the war, so, surely as the sun rises, we shall fail in our trust. Simplicity has been the key-note to the success of Sarawak. Let us all ... keep it so, and help to see that the resources of the country are devoted to the best interests of gradual progress, not wasted in unremunerative undertakings or in producing a false standard of comfort which is unsuitable to the circumstances.... Let us not follow all western ideas and standards. We may and should base ourselves in principle upon British justice and British manners but let us adapt them to suit our surroundings and beware of importing quickly western methods which cannot be appreciated or even understood by eastern races. Do not let us think that only what happens in our own time matters. *The life of a country is a very long one, we who serve it may best do so by curbing our impetuosity and by building slowly and surely.*[39]

The Perennial Problem of the Shortage of Labour

The difficulty of procuring labour, whether for commercial agriculture, like gambier and pepper cultivation, or for mining operations, retarded the efficiency and expansion of these ventures.

Even the government experimental estate at Matang as well as the Public Works Department relied on imported indentured Tamil and Javanese coolies. The almost complete dependence on imported Chinese coolies for commercial agriculture and in the extractive industries made the high cost of labour a decided disadvantage. The labour shortage problem, in terms of quantity and quality, worked against any attempt at hastening the pace of economic development.

The recruitment of labour was not only an expensive exercise but also an uphill task. Ignorance of Sarawak presented a fertile ground for the breeding of ruinous rumours of the place; the relative high cost of living and the country's comparative unattractiveness *vis-à-vis* other neighbouring lands dissuaded many Chinese from coming. For example, even the offer of free steamer passage from Singapore to Kuching to gambier and pepper planters was met with lukewarm enthusiasm.

Comparative Unattractiveness of Sarawak

Sarawak versus British North Borneo

It was not that British North Borneo was endowed with richer natural resources than Sarawak that allowed it a more rapid pace of economic development, but, to use the analogy of two equally unattractive maidens, the former was better at presenting what few assets she possessed. British North Borneo enjoyed more positive publicity than its neighbour, and was quick to capitalize on whatever opportunities came its way. The Chartered Company's administrators maintained 'an informal and intimate relationship' with the Colonial Office, a relationship that Charles never had or aspired to. Besides, they also established close ties with the British authorities in the Western Malay States. In fact, the governors of British North Borneo and most of its officers were recruited from the prestigious Malayan Civil Service (MCS).[40]

But, more importantly, unlike Charles who was against large-scale European investments in Para rubber cultivation, William Clark Cowie, the managing director of the Chartered Company, was keen to attract such ventures. In December 1905, he announced two very attractive incentives: 'The government would guarantee a 4 per cent dividend for six years on all companies formed to plant rubber in North Borneo, and furthermore, that there would be no tax or levy on exported rubber for fifty years.'[41] Following this proclamation, 'twelve new concerns took advantage

of the offer', and, with the assistance of the Agriculture Department, 'planted large areas alongside the railway line [Jesselton to Beaufort] and elsewhere in North Borneo'.[42] The overall effect of Cowie's generous offer was impressive in comparison to Brooke Sarawak. On the eve of the outbreak of the Pacific War, large rubber holdings owned by Europeans accounted for almost half the total rubber acreage of British North Borneo, whereas the figure for Sarawak was less than 5 per cent.[43]

Sarawak Versus the Straits Settlements

In comparison with Brooke Sarawak, the British colonies of the Straits Settlements, situated along the all-important Straits of Malacca, possessed geographical advantages that prompted the faster pace of economic development. From the agricultural viewpoint, these settlements were not particularly well-endowed. Nevertheless, commercial cultivation of pepper, gambier, tapioca, and sugar cane enjoyed some degree of success during the nineteenth century. Although the hopes of making Penang 'a second Moluccas' were dashed, the achievements of sugar cane cultivation at Province Wellesley and Malacca more than offset the disappointments in the growing of spices on Penang island.

But what the Straits Settlements might have lacked in agricultural production, they more than made up for in their strategic location along the Straits of Malacca, one of the major sea-lanes of world trade. Penang, guarding the northern entrance to the Straits, Malacca, overseeing the shipping traffic midway at the narrowest section, and Singapore's prime location at the southern end, effectively dominated this important trade route between West and East.[44] The jewel among these British possessions was undoubtedly Raffles's Singapore.[45]

Singapore, which occupies the most enviable location in the Malay Archipelago, dominated the triangular trade system between South-East Asia, East Asia, and South Asia. Besides its strategic location, the island's natural and deep harbour, sheltered from the monsoons, was a major contributor to its success. Its free-port status, instituted from the very beginning, crowned its glory as the foremost entrepôt in South-East Asia.

Practically all the European mercantile firms dealing with the China trade established branch offices in Singapore and Penang. These Western agency houses were not only primarily involved in trading activities but they also had investments in a multitude of

enterprises, including mining and commercial agriculture, in the British Protected Malay States.[46]

Sarawak versus the British Protected Malay States of Perak, Selangor, and Negri Sembilan

The west coast Malay States of Perak, Selangor, and Negri Sembilan, possessed natural resources far exceeding those in Sarawak. The most striking of these were the rich tin deposits. The Malay nobles had invited Chinese miners to work these fields during the mid-nineteenth century. Exports of this mineral went through the ports of Penang and Singapore. When production was interrupted by political instability in these territories, the British authorities, urged strongly by the mercantile community of the Straits Settlements, adopted a forward policy that subsequently converted these three Malay States into British Protectorates. The advent of British political involvement set the stage for direct large-scale Western economic exploitation.

The Kinta Valley of Perak possessed the world's largest tin deposits, and together with other mining districts in Selangor and Negri Sembilan, collectively contributed half the world's output. Most of the tin produced during the nineteenth century was from Chinese mines employing simple and unmechanized methods relying largely on manual labour. Large-scale, capital intensive, and highly mechanized European mining operations became increasingly important during the twentieth century. The smelting industry was exclusively dominated by Western companies with plants located at the ports of Penang and Singapore.

To facilitate greater efficiency in tin exports, a railway system was constructed to link the mines to the ports. By 1910 a continuous rail link was established from Prai to Johor Bahru with the all-important feeder lines branching out to the ports on the coast, namely Taiping to Port Weld, Ipoh to Teluk Anson via Tapah Road, Kuala Lumpur to Port Swettenham (Klang), and Seremban to Port Dickson. A road network running almost parallel was also executed for similar reasons. The investments in an efficient transport system undoubtedly boosted the tin industry, and equally, or perhaps even of more importance, the rubber industry later on.[47]

The climate, soil, and terrain of the Western Malay States were conducive to large-scale cash cropping. Gambier, pepper, tapioca, and sugar cane were successfully grown on a commercial basis. As an export industry, sugar cane was the most important until the

introduction of coffee.[48] Liberian coffee was successfully planted by European planters from the 1880s. Unlike the disappointing results in Sarawak, this crop thrived well in Selangor; later, coffee planting spread to Perak and Negri Sembilan.[49] However, by the first decade of the twentieth century Para rubber had eclipsed both sugar cane and coffee as the main commercial crop.

It was the rubber industry, like tin in the last century, that put the Malay States on the map of the British Empire and the world. European capital rushed in to take a sizeable slice of this booming industry. The large European agency firms in Singapore, Penang, and Malacca, extended their trading business to commercial agriculture.

By 1913 it was clear that large-scale estates with trees planted in orderly rows, and the entire venture 'organised as a modern, highly capitalised industry' was the future prospect for Para rubber cultivation.[50] The Western Malay States, with their suitable terrain, soil, and climate, were ideal for the growth of this new industry. The efficient rail and road network, already well in place, played an essential role in the development of the rubber industry.

In contrast to the Brookes, the British authorities were partial towards Western capitalist enterprises and offered inducements to encourage the inflow of investment.[51] For instance, as a means of attracting commercial agriculture, the British administrators in Selangor waived all quit-rent on agricultural holdings from 1884.[52] Substantial loans, ranging from $2,000 to as much as $40,000, were granted by the Selangor government to would-be coffee planters with the condition that they invested a similar sum in establishing plantations.[53] For European rubber planters, a government loan fund was set up in the mid-1900s primarily 'to assist in maintaining existing cultivation on those plantations which had run out of funds'.[54] Advances of up to $500,000 were made at 6 per cent interest (as against the 9–12 per cent charged by private financiers) including another 0.5 per cent for administrative costs.[55] A smaller-scale version of this loan scheme was available to Malay rubber growers as well.[56]

In the tin-mining sector, government loans were given to Chinese tin-mining companies which were in need of capital; this financial assistance helped to avert the difficult years of the 1889–91 depression. The common practice of Chinese miners, who, when in need of funds resorted to the *Chettiar* who charged prohibitive interest rates, was seen as an unhealthy development: 'The Senior Warden of Mines declared in 1905 that mines de-

veloped and worked on borrowed capital from Chettiars meant an industry that was on sand and ready to collapse when the price of tin fell.'[57] It was a result of the government's intention to avert this situation that generous loans were granted on reasonable terms. Such assistance had been part of the policy of the British administrators since the establishment of the Residential system in 1874, designed to protect, nurture, and develop the tin industry of the Malay States. Infrastructure development in transport and communications, the institution of the Mining Code (1896) for the proper regulation of the industry, government control of all sources of water supply thereby eliminating disputes over this essential commodity, geological surveys for ascertaining new deposits, and official assistance in labour recruitment, were measures undertaken by the British authorities.[58] The active involvement of the government and its supportive stance gave ample confidence for the large-scale input of Western capital in tin mining during the early part of the twentieth century.

The land reform, instituted in Selangor during the early 1890s, which introduced the Torrens system of land registration allowed easier land acquisition by non-Malays.[59] This new system of land tenure was a great inducement to both planters and miners to invest in the state. It was not surprising therefore that the European coffee planters from Ceylon first started their operations in Selangor. The Torrens system was later adopted by Perak and Negri Sembilan when a uniform land policy was constituted.

While Brooke Sarawak had difficulty in attracting labour and consequently suffered a perennial shortage, the Protected Malay States had a continuous inflow of immigrants to serve their mines and plantations.[60] Although the bulk of the tin-mine labourers were recruited from China by the Chinese mining companies themselves through the notorious indentured system, the British authorities had, on a number of occasions, assisted this process.[61] The procurement of Tamil labourers, initially for the sugar plantations, then for the coffee holdings and the Public Works Department, and subsequently for the rubber estates, had official sanction.[62] The constant and ample supply of imported labour for agricultural and mining pursuits allowed these economic activities to develop and expand, while the availability of labourers for public works contributed to the task of providing essential infrastructure facilities.

The separate British administrations in Perak, Selangor, and Negri Sembilan, adopted policies that encouraged and boosted

economic development in their respective domains. When the Federated Malay States was constituted in 1896, the Federal government in Kuala Lumpur continued the policies of promoting the agricultural and mining industries. Commenting on the role of the government in 1894, Frank Swettenham (later Sir), then British Resident of Perak, later to become the first Resident-General of the Federation, declared that

> revenue and prosperity follow the liberal but prudently directed expenditure of public funds, especially when they are invested in high-class roads, in railways, telegraphs, waterworks and everything likely to encourage trade and private enterprise.... The Government cannot do the mining and the agriculture, but it can make it profitable for others to embark in such speculations by giving them every reasonable facility, and that we have tried to do.[63]

Insurmountable Geographical and Natural Obstacles to Development: The Experience of the Crown Colony Period, 1946–1963

It may be argued that the slow pace of economic development of Sarawak was the consequence of Brooke policy which was more geared to protecting the indigenous population rather than to exploiting the natural resources of the country. But the experience of Sarawak as a British Crown Colony[64] demonstrated that, despite the investment in capital, expertise and up-to-date technology, organized and co-ordinated development plans, and the political will for economic development, progress was slow and the achievements unimpressive.

The amount of investment ranged from the initial $38.6 million expended under the Colombo Plan for development programmes covering the period from 1951 to 1957, to the estimated $161 million allocated for the Second Sarawak Development Plan of 1959–63. In all the development plans, from the programme financed by Colombo Plan sources of 1951–7, the First Sarawak Development Plan of 1955–60, and the Second Sarawak Development Plan of 1959–63, more than half the expenditure was allocated for economic schemes.[65] (Table 10.1 shows the breakdown of expenditure for the Second Sarawak Development Plan (1959–63) which did not differ much from its predecessors.)

In order to execute the programmes proposed and designed under the various development schemes, the Colonial administration undertook a series of socio-economic and anthropological

TABLE 10.1
Allocation of Expenditure under the Second Sarawak Development Plan, 1959–1963

	Allocation (M$ 1,000)	*Percentage of Total Allocation*
Economic Schemes		
Agriculture	27,000	16.8
Forestry	732	0.5
Communications	60,961	37.8
Fuel and Power	4,100	2.6
	92,793	57.8
Social Services		
Education	17,732	11.0
Medical and Health	9,458	5.9
Water Supplies	8,202	5.1
	35,392	22.0
Miscellaneous	32,456	20.2
Total	160,641,000	100.0

Source: *Sarawak Annual Report 1962*, p. 24.

studies and geographical and geological surveys. A population census was conducted in 1947 and another in 1960, and together with the data collected from the studies and surveys, the Colonial government was in a better position to implement its development plans. The services of an array of technicians, specialists, experts, and professionals were engaged to supervise the implementation of the various development projects.

In response to the reality of a dwindling oil industry and the uncertainty of any new oil or other mineral finds in the near future, the main priority of development was focused on agriculture. Several projects were implemented during the second half of the 1950s. Results, however, were not encouraging. The attempt at achieving self-sufficiency in rice production proved abortive. As in the Brooke period, efforts at encouraging the Dayaks to practise wet-*padi* cultivation in the lowlands were unsuccessful. Similarly, the implementation of the Assistance to Padi Planters Scheme from 1958, whereby *padi* farmers were encouraged to open up new

lands for cultivation using improved farming techniques, and supported by the Agriculture Department in terms of advice, assistance, and even subsidies for materials, proved discouraging. On the eve of the formation of Malaysia in 1963, about 60 per cent of the country's rice requirement had still to be imported.[66]

Likewise, the implementation of other government agricultural subsidy schemes, like the Rubber Planting Scheme (1956) which aimed at replacing old and poor quality trees with high-yielding varieties; the Coconut Planting Scheme (1959) for encouraging new planting and replanting; and the Agriculture Diversification Scheme (1960) to encourage the development of a variety of cash crops, like pepper, coffee, and fruits, and promote animal husbandry, all produced limited results. The following observation from the Kanowit district typified the general situation.

> There is little doubt that these swamp padi schemes helped a number of farmers in the area. Unfortunately, however, the benefits could not be extended to people in the ulu rivers. It was also unfortunate that the work with such crops as cocoa, coffee, and hemp was never extended to other parts of the District. Today [early 1970s] there is no evidence of profitable cultivation of such crops.[67]

If the Brookes were guilty of not possessing the political will to develop the country's economy, there was no lack of commitment on the part of the Colonial government. If the Brookes had no development plans, the Colonial administrators had several to their credit. Notwithstanding all these, economic progress was slow and generally unimpressive.

The problem of economic development in Sarawak, according to T. H. Silcock, proved to be far more intractable than in Malaya.[68] Even during the Malaysia period (post-1963), despite an input of M$424 million (of which 90 per cent was from Federal funds) for the Sarawak Development Plan (1964–8) which was incorporated in the First Malaysia Plan (1966–70), the results were undramatic. The slow progress is illustrated by this example of the most developed part of the country, namely the area lying west of longitude 112 °East.

> Although this region comprises less than a quarter of the total land area, it contains about three-quarters of the total population, over two-thirds of the land devoted to settled cultivation and perhaps three-quarters of the acreage planted with wet-*padi* and rubber. The road network and the provision of public and social services have advanced furthest here; *nevertheless, even [it] is at a low level of development compared with western Malaya.*[69]

Defying the Theories of Imperialism and Colonialism

As a general first proposition it must be laid down that no dependency has ever been drawn within the scope of imperialist control in the interest of the dependent society itself. If there are exceptions to this proposition they are of the rarest.... Furthermore, it must be assumed as equally axiomatic that no colonial government has ever been established or maintained in order to bring an end or to hamper the 'legitimate' activities of the economic forces of the home entrepreneurs and investors.[70]

The above suppositions put forward by Rupert Emerson are not applicable to Brooke rule in Sarawak; it was evidently one of the 'exceptions', and indeed, 'of the rarest'. In direct contrast to Emerson's proposition, it was precisely 'in the interest of the dependent society itself' that Brooke rule was first established in 1841. The hallmark of the policy of the Brookes had, from the very beginning, been their dedication and steadfast adherence to the principle of native protection. 'Sarawak', in the words of James, 'belongs to the Malays, the Sea Dayaks, and Land Dayaks, the Kayans and other tribes; not to us. It is for them that we labour; not ourselves.'[71] In words as well as in deeds the Brookes fulfilled their promise to the people.

Charles reminded his successor that it was neither his predecessor's nor his intention of 'founding a family of Brookes to be European millionaires'. The Brookes could not be termed rich, but they were comfortable. The bulk of the revenue of Sarawak was either invested in development aimed at benefiting and improving the well-being of the population, or kept as reserves. In 1941, on the centenary of Brooke rule, Sarawak presented a picture of a healthy country with no public debt, adequate reserves, and a population enjoying a relatively comfortable standard of living.

The strict vetting of European capitalist investment in an attempt to prevent the entry of speculative and exploitative concerns, and allowing only bona fide investors into the country appeared 'to bring an end or to hamper the "legitimate" activities of the economic forces of the home entrepreneurs and investors'. The Brookes were dubbed anti-British and anti-Western, labels that they shrugged off without undue concern or acrimony.

If Emerson's suppositions of imperial rule are defied by the Brookes, equally untenable is the Marxian theory of imperialism as put forward by Lenin. Lenin maintained that 'under the old capitalism, under which free competition prevailed, the export of goods was typical. Under the newest capitalism, when monopolies prevail,

the export of capital has become typical.'[72] James's reign could be classified as belonging to the period of 'old capitalism',[73] but despite the fact that 'free competition prevailed' in Sarawak, there was no great inflow of goods into the country from the mother country, Britain. Similarly, during the period of Charles's rule, when 'the newest capitalism' prevailed, there was little of the so-called 'export of capital' from the home country, Britain, into Sarawak either. On the contrary, Charles was particularly opposed to the large influx of Western capital investment; one notable exception, however, was the oil company (ASPC). During Vyner's reign, even less foreign capital entered the country. Whatever capital had been invested in Sarawak was derived largely from the country's own sources of revenue, the bulk of which came from 'farms', excise duties, and royalties. The significant absence of foreign investment in the country made Brooke Sarawak an outsider among colonial territories in the region.

The Brookes were, perhaps, outside the circle of 'imperialist powers'; they were, in fact, a class of their own. The engine of their rule was fuelled, not by economic motives of gain and profit, but by humanitarian and philanthropic concerns.

The 'Genius' of the Brookes

The Brookes had achieved in principle and in practice what they professed to accomplish, namely the protection of native interests and rights, and the promotion of their welfare. The economic policies of James, Charles, and Vyner were singularly guided by this concern and the results were impressive.

The pro-native land policies ensured that the indigenous inhabitants of Sarawak owned the plot of land which they tilled; they were spared the ignominious situation of being landless in their own homeland, as in the case of the multitude of landless farmers in the Irrawaddy delta of British Lower Burma where absentee landlordism thrived. The native farmers of Sarawak were saved from uncaring landlords who demanded high land rents and avaricious moneylenders with exorbitant interest rates. There was no equivalent of the Indian *Chettiar* of British Burma in Brooke Sarawak.[74]

Exploitation of low-paid coolie labourers in the mining industries, or of oppressed farmers forced to plant and produce for the benefit of the state coffers, was largely absent.[75] The Brooke discouragement of Para rubber monoculture and a policy that favoured smallholdings to large estates averted widespread suffer-

ing and dislocation when prices fell, even during the major world-wide Depression (1929–31).[76]

The term 'native' was not derogatory in the Sarawak context, and unlike in other colonized lands in Africa or in the Caribbean, it did not carry the stigma of inferiority. On the contrary, being classified 'native' not only commanded respect but also gave certain privileges denied non-natives, as in matters relating to land.

Even the inflow of Chinese immigrants did not result in the indigenous peoples' interests and rights being compromised. There was no denying that land disputes between natives and Chinese did exist, but they were settled amicably through peaceful mediation by Brooke officers, in or outside the court, without undue difficulty. Although there was no substantial ethnic integration, there was generally mutual respect, interaction, and co-operation between Chinese traders and native producers. The presence of a large Chinese settler population, particularly in the Rejang, did not result in any trouble or racial antagonism of a serious nature, unlike the situation in Kenya where European settlers were greatly resented by the indigenes.[77] Neither was there indigenous landlessness as a consequence of the presence of a settler community, as in the case of Kenya during the colonial period.[78]

The Chinese presence was in fact lauded by the Brookes who viewed them as essential catalysts in most branches of the economy. Their entrepreneurial skills and financial prowess allowed the Chinese to develop the trade and commerce of the country, their immense capacity for mining work made them indispensable in the extractive industries, and as keen cultivators of cash crops they were unsurpassed. Moreover, the Chinese constituted the largest single contributor to the Brooke Treasury through revenue generated from the 'farms' and export and import duties. The economic expediency of the Chinese could not be overstated.

Nevertheless, the Chinese posed a political threat with their propensity for involvement in clandestine organizations, from secret societies to communist cells. A vigilant watch was kept over their activities, and suspicion and mistrust clouded Brooke–Chinese relations. However, apart from the unfortunate outburst of 1857, there were no serious threats. In retrospect, Brooke paranoia was uncalled for.

The Chinese, in Brooke perceptions, were seen as immigrants, sojourners, and accordingly classified as non-natives, 'aliens'. Their status as non-natives precluded them from the privileges afforded to the indigenes, most significant being their limited access to land. Existing beyond the fold of Brooke paternalism and

protection, the plight of the Chinese colliery labourers and oilfield workers was overlooked. They, however, numbered but a small fraction of the total Chinese population.[79]

Despite their non-native status, the Chinese as a whole performed very well and practically dominated most branches of the economy. The Chinese undoubtedly surpassed any indigenous community in terms of material comforts.

'"Backwardness" is Accepted in Backwaters'

It is quite true that for a full century the Brooke family ... did keep Sarawak 'back' in relation to the general surrounding economic and political pressures of the epoch.... But it would be a basic misunderstanding of the process to suppose ... that this general and positive slow-going (not *laissez-faire*) was something extraordinary or contradictory to the sense of the country. 'Backwardness' is accepted in backwaters.[80]

The *slow but steady* pace of economic development was nothing more than a reflection of the ideas of the Brookes's in practice. The preservation of the *status quo*, the rejection of sudden and radical change, and the disapproval of the mindless pursuit of gain regardless of native interests, were the hallmarks of Brooke policy. The view that the Brookes neglected social services like the provision of medical and educational facilities, areas that seemed to indicate a neglect of the well-being of the indigenous people, reflects a poor understanding of the administrative philosophy of the Brookes.[81] The Brookes respected native culture and tradition, intervening only when these practices were thought particularly baneful to the general good. The provision of Western medical facilities or Western-style schooling was low on the Brooke agenda simply because it was thought that such services would adversely affect the traditional native way of life.[82]

Therefore, if 'backwardness' was the price for such policies, it was a price that the Brookes were glad to pay. After all it was James, when explaining his dissociation from mercantile activities, who pronounced that he 'hope[d] that thousands will be benefited when I am mouldering in dust; and that my name will be remembered, whenever it is thought of, *as one whose actions showed him above the base and sordid motives* which so often disgrace men in similar circumstances'.[83]

The Brookes and their policies aside, Sarawak was indeed a 'backwater', poorly endowed with natural resources, yet richly endowed with physical and geographical disadvantages. Despite all

Brooke efforts in developing the country in mining and agriculture, it was its isolation and the physical constraints of limited mineral deposits, the poverty of the soil, difficult terrain, and unfavourable climate which worked *significantly* against the fruition of their labours.

1. For the details of the Constitution of 1941, see Anthony Brooke, *The Facts about Sarawak: A Documented Account of the Cession to Britain in 1946*, Bombay, 1947; reprinted Singapore: Summer Times, 1983, Appendices E and F. For a detailed analysis, see R. H. W. Reece, *The Name of Brooke: The End of White Rajah Rule in Sarawak*, Kuala Lumpur: Oxford University Press, 1982, pp. 72–93. See also Steven Runciman, *The White Rajahs: A History of Sarawak from 1841 to 1946*, Cambridge: Cambridge University Press, 1960, pp. 247–52.

2. James Brooke, *A Letter from Borneo; with Notices of the Country and Its Inhabitants, Addressed to James Gardner, Esq.*, London: L. & G. Seeley, 1842, p. 14.

3. See Hugh Low, *Sarawak: Its Inhabitants and Productions, Being Notes during a Residence in that Country with His Excellency Mr Brooke*, London: Frank Cass, 1848; new impression 1968, Chapters 1 and 2.

4. J. R. Logan, 'Traces of the Origin of the Malay Kingdom of Borneo, with Notices of Its Condition When First Discovered by Europeans, and at Later Periods', *JIAEA*, 2 (1848): 519. Emphasis added.

5. Ludvig Verner Helms, *Pioneering in the Far East, and Journeys to California in 1849 and to the White Sea in 1878*, London: W. H. Allen, 1882, p. 123.

6. Odoardo Beccari, *Wanderings in the Great Forests of Borneo*, London: Archibald Constable, 1904; reprinted Singapore: Oxford University Press, 1986, pp. 367–8.

7. Ibid., p. 368.

8. *Sarawak Gazette* (*SG*), 15 March 1873, n.p.

9. Beccari, *Wanderings*, p. 369.

10. Loh Chee Yin, 'Pieces from the Brooke Past—XVII: Matang Coffee Estate', *SG*, 30 September 1965, p. 283. Emphasis added.

11. F. W. Roe (comp.), *The Natural Resources of Sarawak*, 2nd rev. edn., Kuching: Government Printing Office, 1952, pp. 32–3.

12. T. W. G. Dames, *Report to the Government of Sarawak on Soil Research in the Economic Development of Sarawak*, FAO Report No. 1512, Rome, 1962, p. 81.

13. Beccari, *Wanderings*, p. 370.

14. See A. Hart Everett, 'Notes on the Distribution of the Useful Minerals of Sarawak', *JSBRAS*, 1 (July 1878): 13–30; and Theodor Posewitz, *Borneo: Its Geology and Mineral Resources*, London: Edward Stanford, 1892.

15. Posewitz, *Borneo*, p. 268. For the paper by Hunt, see John Hunt, 'Sketch of Borneo, or Pulo Kalamantan', *Malayan Miscellanies*, 1, 8 (1820). This paper is reproduced in Henry Keppel, *The Expedition to Borneo of HMS* Dido *for the Suppression of Piracy: With Extracts from the Journal of James Brooke Esq.*, 2 vols., London: Chapman & Hall, 1846; reprinted Singapore: Oxford University Press, 1991, Vol. II, Appendix II, pp. xvi–lxiii.

16. F. W. Roe, *British Territories in Borneo: Report of the Geological Survey Department, for the Year 1951*, Kuching: Government Printing Office, 1950, p. 5.

17. See *Oil in Sarawak 1910–1960*, Sarawak Shell Oilfields Ltd., n.d., pp. 13–14.

18. B. A. St J. Hepburn (comp.), *The Handbook of Sarawak: Comprising Historical, Statistical and General Information Obtained from Official and Other Reliable Records*, Singapore: Malaya Publishing House for the Government of Sarawak, 1949, p. 1.

19. James C. Jackson, *Sarawak: A Geographical Survey of a Developing State*, London: University of London Press, 1968, p. 24.

20. *Encyclopaedia Britannica*, 15th edn., 1990, Vol. 17, p. 765.

21. R. H. Morris, 'Our Economic Future', *SG*, 7 October 1949, p. 259.

22. The portrait of James by Francis Grant (later Sir), which today hangs in the National Portrait Gallery, London, depicts him as a youthful and handsome seafaring adventurer, an image that undoubtedly endeared him to the public of Victorian England. It was perhaps this image of a gallant James that initially attracted the attention of Angela Burdett Coutts who proved to be a loyal and trusted friend to him as well as a benefactor to Sarawak. The fact that shortly after his demise in 1868, she sold her property (Quop Estate) in Sarawak and ceased contact with the country altogether supported the thesis that her interest was more towards James than Sarawak. For instance, see Owen Rutter (ed.), *Rajah Brooke and Baroness Burdett Coutts: Consisting of the Letters from Sir James Brooke, First White Rajah of Sarawak, to Miss Angela (afterwards Baroness) Burdett Coutts*, London: Hutchinson, 1935, p. 310.

23. As an illustration, *The Times* article on the pirate exploits of the *Rainbow* in 1862 off the Bintulu coast and a fighting clergyman in the person of the Right Reverend Francis McDougall, Bishop of Labuan and Sarawak, caused an uproar within ecclesiastical circles in England. McDougall, who penned the account, was reprimanded by his superiors for such 'un-bishop-like' behaviour. This incident of 1862 was retold in later years: in the memoirs of Helms (1882), by McDougall's wife (1882), by Charles John Bunyon in his biography of McDougall (1889), and by Baring-Gould and Bampfylde in their 'official history' of the Raj (1909). When viewed from a distant England, it further reinforced the negative picture of Sarawak as a country rife with piracy. See Helms, *Pioneering*, pp. 212–13; Harriette McDougall, *Sketches of Our Life at Sarawak*, London: Society for Promoting Christian Knowledge, 1882; reprinted Singapore: Oxford University Press, 1992, pp. 204–14; Charles John Bunyon, *Memoirs of Francis Thomas McDougall, Sometime Bishop of Labuan and Sarawak, and of Harriette His Wife*, London: Longmans Green, 1889, pp. 227–40; and S. Baring-Gould and C. A. Bampfylde, *A History of Sarawak under Its Two White Rajahs, 1839–1908*, London: Henry Sotheran, 1909, pp. 269–74.

24. *SG*, 31 March 1873, n.p.

25. His only piece of writing was the brief 500-word 'Foreword' in his wife's book on the Brookes as rulers of Sarawak. His opening line was apologetic, more of an obligation than any intention to put forth his opinions. 'I regard my wife's invitation to write a foreword to her *Three White Rajas* as a graceful gesture that I feel it would be ungallant, in this instance, *to adhere to my hitherto unbroken rule not to appear in print*.' Sylvia Brooke, *The Three White Rajas*, London: Cassell, 1939, p. vii. Emphasis added.

26. Margaret Brooke, *Good Morning and Good Night*, London: Constable, 1934, pp. 242–3.

27. An official at the Colonial Office, Reginald Edward Stubbs, who championed Brunei's integrity, was particularly hostile towards Charles and Sarawak. See Stubbs's minute of 10 December 1906 (CO 144/81), reproduced in Robert Pringle,

Rajahs and Rebels: The Ibans of Sarawak under Brooke Rule, 1841–1941, London: Macmillan, 1970, pp. 358–60.

28. *SG*, 1 July 1886, p. 104. Emphasis added.

29. See *SG*, 16 September 1910, pp. 195–6. It was another six years before such a telegraphic connection was realized.

30. *SG*, 6 August 1949, p. 189. Emphasis added.

31. *SG*, 1 June 1896, pp. 105 and 106. Emphasis added.

32. Pope-Hennessy, for instance, in a speech to the Legislative Council of Labuan in June 1871, spoke disparagingly of James's policy. 'The policy promulgated thirty years ago by some enterprising and benelovent Englishman that the Dayaks could be civilised, and that Europeans could conduct the details of trade and administration in the rivers of Borneo has proved to be visionary.' Quoted in Baring-Gould and Bampfylde, *A History of Sarawak*, p. 331.

33. *SG*, 31 March 1873, n.p.

34. Beccari, *Wanderings*, pp. 376–7. Emphasis added. For similar views, see the 1899 report of the British Consul, A. L. Keyser, quoted in Baring-Gould and Bampfylde, *A History of Sarawak*, p. 433.

35. Margaret Brooke, *My Life in Sarawak*, London: Methuen, 1913, p. 313. Emphasis added.

36. 'Foreword', in S. Brooke, *Three White Rajas*, p. viii.

37. For a criticism of Vyner's labour policy, see T. Charles Martine, 'The Borneo Company Ltd., in Sarawak (From "Notes written by me when in Singapore Changi Gaol, 1943–4")', Typescript, pp. 5–6, SMA, Kuching.

38. *SG*, 2 January 1934, p. 2. Emphasis added.

39. Quoted in Reece, *The Name of Brooke*, pp. 11–12. Emphasis added.

40. See K. G. Tregonning, *Under Chartered Company Rule (North Borneo 1881–1946)*, Singapore: University of Malaya Press, 1958, pp. 73–4.

41. Ibid., p. 89. See also Ian Black, *A Gambling Style of Government: The Establishment of the Chartered Company's Rule in Sabah, 1878–1915*, Kuala Lumpur: Oxford University Press, 1983, pp. 184–5.

42. Tregonning, *Under Chartered Company Rule*, p. 89.

43. See ibid.; James C. Jackson, 'Smallholding Cultivation of Cash Crops', in Wang Gungwu (ed.), *Malaysia: A Survey*, New York: Frederick Praeger, 1964, pp. 265–70; and Jackson, *Sarawak*, pp. 90–1.

44. Penang and Singapore were the important ports while Malacca, although prominent during the fifteenth and sixteenth centuries, had by the nineteenth century been reduced to an outpost of Singapore. See L. A. Mills, *British Malaya, 1824–1867*, Kuala Lumpur: Oxford University Press, 1966, pp. 40–1, 59–60, and 192–5.

45. Ibid., pp. 198–200; and C. M. Turnbull, *The Straits Settlements, 1826–1867*, London: Athlone Press, 1972, pp. 160–88.

46. See G. C. Allen and Audrey G. Donnithorne, *Western Enterprise in Indonesia and Malaya: A Study in Economic Development*, London: George Allen & Unwin, 1962, pp. 49–66; Chai Hon-Chan, *The Development of British Malaya, 1896–1909*, Kuala Lumpur: Oxford University Press, 1964, pp. 159–60; and J. Kennedy, *A History of Malaya*, 2nd edn., London: Macmillan, 1970, pp. 217–18.

47. See Chai, *Development of British Malaya*, pp. 181–2 and 194–5; and Kennedy, *A History of Malaya*, pp. 197–201.

48. Chai, *Development of British Malaya*, p. 148.

49. Ibid., pp. 148–9.

50. Allen and Donnithorne, *Western Enterprise*, p. 117.

51. For the beginnings of European investment in the Western Malay States, see Khoo Kay Kim, *The Western Malaya States, 1850–1873: The Effects of Commercial Development on Malay Politics*, Kuala Lumpur: Oxford University Press, 1972, pp. 79–108.

52. Chai, *Development of British Malaya*, p. 149.

53. Ibid. See also James C. Jackson, *Planters and Speculators: Chinese and European Agricultural Enterprise in Malaya, 1786–1921*, Kuala Lumpur: University of Malaya Press, 1968, pp. 237–8.

54. Chai, *Development of British Malaya*, p. 160. See also Emily Sadka, *The Protected Malay States, 1874–1895*, Kuala Lumpur: University of Malaya Press, 1968, pp. 334, 336, and 337.

55. Chai, *Development of British Malaya*, pp. 160–1.

56. Sadka, *Protected Malay States*, pp. 361–2; and Chai, *Development of British Malaya*, pp. 161–2.

57. Ibid., p. 168.

58. See Wong Lin Ken, *The Malayan Tin Industry to 1914*, Association for Asian Studies Monograph No. XIV, Tucson, 1965, pp. 53–167. See also Chai, *Development of British Malaya*, pp. 20–2 and 171–5.

59. See ibid., pp. 24–6. For detailed studies of land legislation in the Western Malay States, see Jackson, *Planters and Speculators*; Lim Teck Ghee, *Peasants and their Agricultural Economy in Colonial Malaya, 1874–1941*, Kuala Lumpur: Oxford University Press, 1977; and Philip Loh Fook Seng, *The Malay States, 1877–1895: Political Change and Social Policy*, Kuala Lumpur: Oxford University Press, 1969.

60. See P. Loh, *The Malay States*, pp. 138–55.

61. See W. L. Blythe, 'Historical Sketch of Chinese Labour in Malaya', *JMBRAS*, 20, 1 (1947): 64–114; and Chai, *Development of British Malaya*, pp. 108–27 and 172–3.

62. See ibid., pp. 127–40. See also S. Arasaratnam, *Indians in Malaysia and Singapore*, Kuala Lumpur: Oxford University Press, 1970, pp. 10–27.

63. 'Annual Report Perak for 1894', quoted in Chai, *Development of British Malaya*, p. 22.

64. The history of the Crown Colony period (1946–63) has yet to receive a detailed study by historians. My study of the development of education during this period revealed the enormous problems faced by the Colonial Office administrators in approaching this most challenging task. See Ooi Keat Gin, 'Education in Sarawak during the Period of Colonial Administration, 1946–1963', *JMBRAS*, 63, 2 (December 1990): 35–68.

65. The sources of funding of these Sarawak development plans were largely provided by the Colonial Development and Welfare Scheme and the Colombo Plan. Later, during the 1950s, a Development, Welfare and Reconstruction Fund, known as the Capital Fund, was set up to finance development programmes. The Capital Fund was basically supported by three sources of funding: the Colonial Development and Welfare Scheme, loans, and surpluses from annual revenue and accumulated reserves.

66. For instance, see Hatta Solhee, 'The Rice Self-sufficiency Policy: Its Implementation in Sarawak', in R. A. Cramb and R. H. W. Reece (eds.), *Development in Sarawak: Historical and Contemporary Perspectives*, Monash Paper on Southeast Asia No. 17, Centre of Southeast Asia Studies, Melbourne: Monash University, 1988, pp. 72 and 89.

67. Leonard Edwards and Peter W. Stevens, *Short Histories of the Lawas and Kanowit Districts*, Kuching: Borneo Literature Bureau, 1971, p. 175.

68. T. H. Silcock, *The Commonwealth Economy in Southeast Asia*, London: Cambridge University Press, 1959, p. 29.

69. Jackson, *Sarawak*, pp. 203–4. Emphasis added.

70. Rupert Emerson, *Malaysia: A Study in Direct and Indirect Rule*, London: Macmillan, 1937; reprinted Kuala Lumpur: University of Malaya Press, 1964, pp. 467 and 468.

71. These words of James are enshrined in a plaque placed in the small village church of Sheepstor in Dartmoor, England. The cemetery in the church grounds is the final resting place of the Brookes—James, Charles, Vyner, and Bertram. A short distance from the church, a narrow lane leads to Burrator, the country house which James bought in August 1859 from funds of the Testimonial and where he spent his last days. Today, a plaque on the wall next to the doorway of the main building is the only reminder of its once illustrious owner and resident.

72. V. I. Lenin, *Imperialism: The Highest Stage of Capitalism*, rev. trans., London: Martin Lawrence, 1933, p. 57.

73. The year 1880 is used as the watershed between the period of 'old capitalism' and the 'new capitalism'. See Paul A. Baran and Paul M. Sweezy, 'Notes on the Theory of Imperialism', *Monthly Review*, 17 (1966): 17–18.

74. For instance, see Michael Adas, *The Burma Delta: Economic Development and Social Change on an Asian Rice Frontier, 1852–1941*, Madison: University of Wisconsin Press, 1974, pp. 66–7, 72–3, 78–9, 112–14, 118–19, 136–7, 142, 150, 173–4, 186–8, and 222–3; and Cheng Siok-Hwa, *The Rice Industry of Burma, 1852–1940*, Kuala Lumpur: University of Malaya Press, 1968, pp. 137–97.

75. Africa during the colonial period is a case in point. A classic example of forced native labour in the mines is the sad situation in the Union of South Africa; the Belgian Congo is a typical illustration of the exploitation of the indigenous peoples by the plantation system of agriculture. See A. T. Nzula, I. I. Potekhin, and A. Z. Zusmanovich, *Forced Labour in Colonial Africa*, London: Zed Press, 1979, pp. 59–91.

76. See Adas, *The Burma Delta*, pp. 7, 118, 127, 185–6, and 190; and Nzula, Potekhin, and Zusmanovich, *Forced Labour in Colonial Africa*, pp. 92–102.

77. For instance, see George Bennett, *Kenya: A Political History—The Colonial Period*, London: Oxford University Press, 1963, pp. 41–52; Marshall A. MacPhee, *Kenya*, London: Ernest Benn, 1968, pp. 71–4; and Dane Kennedy, *Islands of White: Settler Society and Culture in Kenya and Southern Rhodesia*, Durham: Duke University Press, 1987, pp. 128–47 and 148–66.

78. For instance, see Norman Leys, *A Last Chance in Kenya*, London: Hogarth, 1931, pp. 55–67; L. S. B. Leakey, *Kenya: Contrasts and Problems*, London: Methuen, 1936, pp. 63–84 and 102–16; and M. P. K. Sorrenson, 'Land Policy in Kenya, 1895–1945', in J. Harlow, E. M. Chilver, and A. Smith (eds.), *History of East Africa*, London: Oxford Unversity Press, 1965, Vol. II, Appendix I, pp. 672–89.

79. There were no more than 2,000 Chinese coolies serving at any one time in the Simunjan coal mines and the Miri oilfields. The average number of Chinese mine labourers at Simunjan was from 200 to 500 while the oil companies had a maximum of 1,500 on its payroll during the peak periods, but often this figure was much smaller in most years.

80. Tom Harrisson, *The Malays of South-west Sarawak before Malaysia*, London: Macmillan, 1970, p. 197.

81. For an example of such a viewpoint, see Amarjit Kaur, 'The Babbling Brookes: Economic Change in Sarawak 1841–1941', *MAS*, 29, 1 (January 1995): 65–109.

82. The Brookes questioned the benefits of Western education to the natives. James discouraged the provision of Western-style schooling on the basis that 'as the human mind more easily learns ill than good, they [the natives] pick up the vices of their [European] governors without their virtues, and their own good qualities disappear, the bad of both races remaining without the good of either'. Journal 20 January 1842, in Gertrude L. Jacob, *The Raja of Sarawak: An Account of Sir James Brooke, KCB, LL D, Given Chiefly through Letters and Journals*, 2 vols., London: Macmillan, 1876, Vol. I, p. 188. Charles was highly critical of British colonial educational practices. 'We stuff natives with a lot of subjects that they don't require to know, and try to teach them to become ourselves, treating them as if they had not an original idea in their possession.' Charles Brooke, *Ten Years in Sarawak*, 2 vols., London: Tinsley, 1866; reprinted Singapore: Oxford University Press, 1990, Vol. II, p. 327. But more importantly, he felt that Western education would lead to the disappearance of their cultural identity and alienate them from their community. For Brooke attitudes and policies towards educational development among the indigenous peoples and the Chinese in Sarawak, see Ooi Keat Gin, *World Beyond the Rivers: Education in Sarawak from Brooke Rule to Colonial Office Administration, 1841–1963*, University of Hull, Centre for South-East Asian Studies, Monograph Series (in press).

83. Brooke to Mother, 16 October, 1842, in Jacob, *The Raja of Sarawak*, Vol. I, p. 223. Emphasis added.

Appendices

APPENDIX 1
Major Indigenous Communities

Dayaks (Sea Dayaks or Ibans)

LARGELY rural-based with concentrations in the Batang Lupar, Saribas, and Rejang river systems.

Although some practise wet-rice cultivation in the lower reaches and deltaic flatlands of the rivers, the majority are shifting cultivators of hill-rice in the hilly inland areas. Their economy is basically subsistence, but some cash crops, like rubber, are cultivated to supplement their income.

They comprise the largest single indigenous group. Dayaks are a relatively homogeneous community, sharing a common language, certain characteristic cultural traits, and social organization. Typically they live in a longhouse, which consists of several 'doors' or *bilek*, each a wholly autonomous and economically self-sufficient unit occupied usually by a family. Dayak society is non-hierarchical, and basically, classless. Animism and pagan beliefs still command influence among the Dayaks, although Christianity is increasingly gaining ground especially among the younger generation. The traditionalist and non-Christian Dayaks regard rice growing, as not merely a means of sustenance, but an entire way of life with religious and spiritual significance. Ancient Chinese earthenware and ceramics are highly esteemed objects among them. Besides their practical functions as part of household utensils and for storage purposes, the earthen jars and ceramic bowls and plates also play important roles in ceremonial and religious observations. The possession of these highly prized articles expresses the material prosperity of their owner, and they are handed down through the generations as family heirlooms.

Malays

Their settlements are mainly in the coastal and riverine areas with almost half the population concentrated in the south-west and in the urban periphery of Kuching. Pockets of Malay communities are found in the delta areas of the Batang Lupar and Rejang, and in the districts bordering Brunei.

The rural Malays are chiefly engaged in wet-rice cultivation, mixed gardening, the growing of various tropical fruits, rubber and coconut cultivation, fishing, and boat building. A considerable number of urban Malays are civil servants.

Malay society is stratified with rather rigid hereditary ranking which precluded inter-class marriages; such attitudes, however, are gradually diminishing among the present-day community. Malays are Muslims. They live in individual houses, each comprising a family unit; it is, however, not uncommon to find two or three generations sharing a single house. A cluster of tens or hundreds of houses forms a *kampong* or village.

Melanaus

Melanau settlements are dotted along the low-lying coastal plain converging on the lower reaches of the Igan, Oya, Mukah, Balingian, Tatau, and Kemena rivers. The districts of Sarikei, Sibu, Bintulu, Binatang, and Mukah are their strongholds.

Although sago cultivation and production have remained dominant economic activities since the early nineteenth century, Melanaus are also involved in the timber industry, and many are fishermen.

A large number of Melanaus are Muslims. They are relatively indistinguishable from Malays as they adopt Malay-style attire and intermarry with them. Some Melanaus are Christians, while the remainder, referred to as *Likaus*, practise their traditional folk beliefs. Like the Dayaks, the Melanaus revere ancient Chinese ceramics and earthen jars; these articles form part of the household paraphernalia, are kept as prized heirlooms, serve as a form of gift in wedding ceremonies, and are used in burial rituals.

Land Dayaks (or Bidayuhs)

They are concentrated almost exclusively in the upper reaches of the Lundu, Sarawak, Kayan, Sadong, and Samarahan rivers.

The Land Dayaks are swidden farmers of hill-rice and longhouse dwellers like the Dayaks.

Unlike the aggressive and extrovert Dayaks, the Land Dayaks generally appear as submissive, docile, and inward-looking people. Although the Land Dayaks form a recognizable ethnic community, they, like the Chinese, are divided into numerous sub-groups marked by dialect differences and variations in certain customary practices. Some of them embraced Christianity, but the majority remain pagans, adhering to animistic and shamanistic beliefs.

Sources: Tom Harrisson (ed.), *The Peoples of Sarawak*, Kuching: Government Printing Office, 1959, pp. 13, 28, 35, 73–83, 85, 91–102, 104, and 107; James C. Jackson, *Sarawak: A Geographical Survey of a Developing State*, London: University of London Press, 1968, pp. 43–50; and Charles Hose, *Natural Man: A Record from Borneo*, London: Macmillan, 1926; reprinted Singapore: Oxford University Press, 1988, p. 6.

APPENDIX 2
Other Indigenous Communities

Kayans and Kenyahs

THEIR longhouse settlements are scattered in the valleys of the Upper Rejang and Balui, the Baram basin, and the branches of the Ulu Kemena river.

They are primarily shifting cultivators of hill-rice, although some also practise cash cropping of rubber, coffee, and groundnut.

The Kayans and Kenyahs share similar social and cultural traits, and spatial distribution. Both communities have a highly stratified social structure with an inherited aristocracy. Chinese jars, ceramics, and beads are regarded as material wealth, and also as articles used in religious ceremonies. Christianity has reached some Kayans and Kenyahs, but the majority adhere to old beliefs and their traditional religion.

Kedayans

They are Muslim, wet-rice farmers with settlements along the coastal regions around Miri and Limbang.

Muruts

The Muruts, who settle in the interior valleys of the Trusan and Lawas rivers, are excellent cultivators of wet-rice. They practise terracing and irrigation similar to that in the hilly areas of Java and Luzon. They are reputed to be among the most productive rice farmers in the country.

Kelabits

Existing almost in isolation in the mountainous uplands of the headwaters of the Baram and the Bario highlands, the Kelabits are equally as adept as the Muruts in wet-rice cultivation. Like the Muruts, the Kelabits are considered to be one of the most productive rice cultivators.

Bisayahs

The characteristic feature of the Bisayah people is their utilization of buffaloes in wet-rice farming, and their rearing of these draught animals. Bisayahs are generally found in the Middle and Upper Limbang valleys. Besides rice, sago and rubber are also cultivated. Bisayahs have a tendency to keep to themselves.

Kajangs (or Upriver Melanaus)

They comprise a constellation of diverse groups: 'Kanowit Dayaks', Tanjongs, Punan Bas, Skapans, Kajamans, and Lahanans. They inhabit the Upper Rejang valley, as far upstream as Belaga and beyond. Like the

Dayaks, they live in longhouses, but linguistically and culturally their affinity is to the coastal Melanaus. In terms of economic activities and general lifestyle, they are more akin to their immediate neighbours, the Kenyahs and Kayans.

Penans

The nomadic Penans are jungle dwellers, scattered thinly in the deep forests between the Upper Rejang and the Baram basin. They subsist as hunters and gatherers of forest produce.

Sources: As for Appendix 1.

APPENDIX 3
Major Chinese Dialect Groups in Sarawak

Hakka

RURAL areas of Upper Sarawak especially around Bau; outskirts of Kuching; area around Serian and along the Kuching–Simanggang Road; outskirts of Simanggang; Batu and Riam, and the area around Miri. Occupations: mining, especially gold; market gardening; tinsmithing.

Foochow

Dominant in the Rejang, within the triangle bounded by Igan, Kanowit, and Sarikei; Sebauh above Bintulu; Poyut in the Baram. Occupations: agriculturalists especially as rubber smallholders and pepper cultivators; retail traders of local produce; logging and timber industry; coastal and river transport business.

Hokkien

Largest group in Kuching; majority in Oya and Mukah; dominant in Limbang and Lawas. Occupations: major traders and merchants particularly in import and export business; shipping; banking.

Cantonese

Lower Rejang area; dominant group in Kanowit and its vicinity; some in the Miri area. Occupations: timber industry and trade; pepper cultivation; goldsmithing; clockmakers.

Teochew

Kuching and its suburbs; an important group in the Simanggang area; small numbers in Bintulu. Occupations: green grocers in urban areas; gambier and pepper cultivators.

Henghua

Major urban centres especially in Sibu. Occupations: fishing industry; coffee-shop business; bicycle retail trade; local transport like bus and taxi business.

Hainanese

Mainly in the major towns of Kuching, Sibu, and Miri. Occupations: catering and restaurant business.

Sources: T'ien Ju-K'ang, *The Chinese of Sarawak: A Study of Social Structure*, Monograph on Social Anthropology No. 12, London: Department of Anthropology, London School of Economics and Political Science, 1953, pp. 19–68; Richard Outram, 'Sarawak Chinese', in Tom Harrisson (ed.), *The Peoples of Sarawak*, Kuching: Government Printing Office, 1959, pp. 116–23; and James C. Jackson, *Sarawak: A Geographical Survey of a Developing State*, London: University of London Press, 1968, pp. 52–61.

APPENDIX 4
The Laws of James Brooke, 1842

JAMES BROOKE, ESQ., Governor (Raja) of the country of Sarawak, make known to all men the following regulations:-

1st. That murder, robbery and other heinous crimes will be punished according to the *ondong-ondong* (i.e. the written law of Borneo); and no person committing such offenses will escape if, after fair inquiry, he be proved guilty.

2nd. In order to ensure the good of the country, all men, whether Malays, Chinese, or Dyaks, are permitted to trade or labour according to their pleasure, and to enjoy their gains.

3rd. All roads will be open, that the inhabitants at large may seek profit both by sea and by land; and all boats coming from others are free to enter the river and depart, without let or hindrance.

4th. Trade, in all its branches will be free, with the exception of antimony ore, which the Governor holds in his own hands, but which no person is forced to work, and which will be paid for at a price when obtained. The people are encouraged to trade and labour, and to enjoy the profits which are to be made by fair and honest dealing.

5th. It is ordered that no person going amongst the Dyaks shall disturb them, or gain their goods under false pretenses. It must be clearly explained to the different Dyak tribes, that the revenue will be collected by the three Datus, bearing the seal of the Governor, and, except this yearly

demand from the Government, they are to give nothing to any other person; nor are they obliged to sell their goods except when they please, and at their own prices.

6th. The Governor will shortly inquire into the revenue, and fix it at a proper rate; so that everyone may know certainly how much he has to contribute yearly to support the Government.

7th. It will be necessary likewise to settle the weights, measures, and money current in the country, and to introduce doits that the poor may purchase food cheaply.

8th. The Governor issues these commands, and will enforce obedience to them: and whilst he gives all protection and assistance to the persons who act rightly, he will not fail to punish those who seek to disturb the public peace or commit crimes; and he warns all such persons to seek their safety, and find some other country where they may be permitted to break the laws of God and man.

Source: Quoted from Gertrude L. Jacob, *The Raja of Sarawak: An Account of Sir James Brooke, KCB, LLD, Given Chiefly through Letters and Journals*, 2 vols., London: Macmillan, 1876, Vol. I, pp. 186–7.

APPENDIX 5
Jungle Produce of Brooke Sarawak

Beeswax

WAX secreted by wild bees for honeycomb. It is found in the tall branches of the huge *tapang* trees and is used in polishes.

Bezoar stones

Bezoar stones or *geliga* are found in the gall-bladder of three species of monkeys from the genus *Semnopithecus*, namely the *wah-wahs*, *jelu-merahs*, and *jelu-jangkits*. The natives hunt these monkeys with blowpipes, and about seven out of every ten killed possess these exotic stones which are prized by the Chinese for their medicinal properties. Even more valuable owing to their rarity, are bezoar stones in porcupines.

Camphor (*Dryobalanops camphora*)

A type of scented wood from the Borneo camphor tree. It is referred to by the natives as well as in commerce as *Kapur Barus* or *Barus* camphor, after Barus which is a place in Sumatra whence it was originally exported. Apparently it can only be found in the northern part of the islands of Sumatra and Borneo. It is highly prized by the Chinese for medicinal purposes.

Canes or Rattans

They are stems of climbing trees, widely abundant in most of the forests, and are used as materials for tying and building, in the manufacture of furniture, as walking sticks, and cricket bats. A well-known and valuable species is the Malacca Cane.

Cutch

An extract from the bark of the cutch tree (*Acacia catechu*) and from other similar mangrove bark. It is used mainly in the tanning and dyeing industries, particularly for khaki cloth used for military uniforms.

Dammar

Resins of trees of the family *Dipterocarpaceae*. There are several kinds: the white type, known to the natives as dammar *mata kuching* or 'cat's eye dammar', is rare and much sought after for its high value as a trade item; and the dammar *daging* or 'flesh-like dammar' after its skin-like colour. Dammar is obtained either by tapping the trees or, more often, by collecting lumps of hard resin from the ground; also applied to the more valuable Manila Copal, which is the resin of the *bindang* (*Agathis alba*) tree. It is used in the manufacture of varnishes, for caulking boats, and as torches.

Edible Birds' Nests

Small semi-circular nests of swiftlets, derived from saliva built into the crevices of walls and roofs of limestone caves. The collection of these nests, which are perched high on the walls and ceiling of caves, is a skilled and highly dangerous occupation. For commercial purposes the nests have to be collected when freshly made, or containing fresh eggs, then thoroughly cleaned before being sold. Collection is made twice or three times in a year. Three species of swiftlets produce these edible nests, namely the *Collocalia fuciphaga* which make the top-quality white nest, the *Collocalia lowii* with its blackish nest, and *Collocalia linchii* with a nest of straw, moss, and gelatine. The nests are used in the preparation of a delicately flavoured soup which is a highly esteemed Chinese delicacy.

Wild Rubber

Jelutong or *Getah-Jelutong*. It is the latex of the *jelutong* trees of the genus *Dyera*. The latex is obtained by similar tapping methods used for Para rubber (*Hevea brasiliensis*). It is used as a principal ingredient in the manufacture of chewing gum.

Gutta Percha or *Getah-rian* (*Isonandra gutta*). It is the latex of *Palaquium gutta* usually found in most of the forest in the interior. The latex is collected by tapping in herring bone fashion all up the stem and along the main branches in a single day, after which the tree must be allowed to rest

for a minimum of a year. It is chiefly used as insulation for electric cables, for surgical purposes, in dentistry for temporary fillings, and as an outer covering for golf balls.

Getah Jangkar and *Getah Pelai. Getah Jangkar* is produced by various trees of the family *Sapotaceae*, and *Getah Pelai* by two species of *Alstonia*. They are mainly used as substitutes for Para rubber, and *Getah Pelai* may also be used in place of *jelutong*.

India Rubber (Ficus elastica). The India rubber tree is a huge tree with large and thick oblong shaped leaves of up to 30 centimetres (12 inches) long, and fig-like fruits appearing in pairs along the branches. The quality of its latex is inferior to that of Para rubber.

Rhinoceros Horns

Highly prized by the Chinese for medicinal purposes, reputed as a potent aphrodisiac.

Illipe Nuts or *Engkabang* (*Shorea*)

These are the oil-rich seeds of various species of *Shorea*, but principally *Shorea gysbertsiana*. The trees fruit irregularly, usually at rather long intervals of about once in four years. The seeds are extracted for the valuable vegetable fat known as Borneo tallow or illipe butter. It is used locally as cooking oil, and is exported chiefly for use as a substitute for cocoa butter in the manufacture of chocolates.

Incense Woods

Akar Laka (*Dalbergia parviflora*), a climber belonging to the family *Leguminosae*, is the principal incense wood; mostly exported to China and Japan.

Hornbill ivory or *Ho-ting*

Known to have been more valuable than Chinese jade, it is used mainly for ornamentation.

Timber

Only a small amount of timber, mostly *billian* and other heavy hardwoods, were exported mainly to Hong Kong and Singapore on an irregular basis.

Sources: Thomas Oxley, 'Gutta Percha', *JIAEA*, 1 (1847): 25–9; Charles Hose, *Natural Man: A Record from Borneo*, London: Macmillan, 1926; reprinted Singapore: Oxford University Press, 1988, p. 114; Charles Hose, *The Field-Book of a Jungle Wallah: Being a Description of Shore, River and Forest Life in Sarawak*, London: H. F. & C. Witherby, 1929; reprinted Singapore: Oxford University Press, 1985, pp. 171–9 and 182–3; Hugh Low, *Sarawak: Its Inhabitants and Pro-*

ductions, Being Notes during a Residence in that Country with His Excellency Mr Brooke, London: Frank Cass, 1848, new impression, 1968, pp. 44–5 and 154; B. E. Smythies, 'History of Forestry in Sarawak', *SG*, 30 September 1961, pp. 168–9; F. W. Roe (comp.), *The Natural Resources of Sarawak*, 2nd rev. edn., Kuching: Government Printing Office, July 1952, pp. 19–20; Issac Henry Burkill, *A Dictionary of the Economic Products of the Malay Peninsula*, 2 vols., London: Crown Agents for Colonies, 1935; reprinted Kuala Lumpur: Governments of Malaysia and Singapore by the Ministry of Agriculture and Co-operatives, 1966, Vol. I, pp. 15–17, 324–6, 549–55, 645–6, 768, 876–81, 889–97, Vol. II, pp. 1023–5, 1275–8, and 1651–2; *Encyclopaedia Britannica*, 15th edn., 1990, Vol. 6, p. 286; and Daniel Chew, *Chinese Pioneers in the Sarawak Frontier, 1841–1941*, Singapore: Oxford University Press, 1990, p. 100.

APPENDIX 6
Government Invitation of 1880 for the Settlement of Chinese Agriculturalists in the Rejang

GOVERNMENT announcement of 1880 regarding the terms of its support for Chinese who intend to settle permanently in the Rejang as agriculturalists, preferably as rice farmers.

I CHARLES BROOKE, Rajah[,] make known the following terms which the Government of Sarawak hereby agrees to fulfil with any Company of Chinese who will engage to bring into the Rejang River Chinese settlers with wives and families numbering not less than Three hundred souls, who will employ themselves in gardening and farming paddy or in other cultivations:-

1st. The Government will provide land sufficient for their requirements free of charge.

2nd. The Government on first starting will build them temporary houses, and make a good path to their landing place.

3rd. The Government will give them one pasu of rice per man or woman and a little salt and half the amount to every child for the first 12 months.

4th. The Government engages to keep up steam communication with Kuching and carry any necessaries for these settlers on the most reasonable terms.

5th. The Government will build a Police Station near them to protect them and assist in making themselves understood in the native language and generally look after them.

6th. In carrying out the above engagements the Government expect the said Chinese will permanently settle in the territory of Sarawak.

Kuching, 11th November, 1880.

Source: *SG*, 29 November 1880, p. 59.

APPENDIX 7

Concessions to Chinese Gambier and Pepper Planters, 1872

GOVERNMENT proclamation of 13 June 1872 regarding concessions granted to Chinese for the purpose of establishing gambier and pepper gardens.

Know all men by these presents that I[,] Charles Brooke, Rajah of Sarawak, do hereby engage and stipulate on the part of the Sarawak Government that the following points shall be enforced in good faith to all Chinamen who may come into the territory of Sarawak for the purpose of making gambier and pepper gardens.

1st. That they shall have land free of all payments and to any extent, if they engage to bring it under cultivation however gradually.

2nd. That coolies who stipulate to serve masters for certain periods will be obliged by the laws to do so, or incur punishment.

3rd. That the leading Chinamen of each river shall hold power from Government to exercise authority over coolies. The gardens will be visited periodically by a Government officer.

4th. That no tax shall be levied on exports of gambier and pepper for the first six years; and in the event of an export duty being levied after that time on pepper it shall not exceed 20 cents per pikul.

5th. That the Government engage to allow gambier and pepper gardens to have salt and tobacco free of duty on the spot for the terms of six years.

6th. That the Government engage to assist to recover runaway coolies, and in all other ways to assist the planters in accordance with rules of justice.

(Signed) C. BROOKE,
Rajah.

(Signed)
Signed, Sealed, and delivered
in the presence of &c.,&c.,&c.
May 1872.

Source: *SG*, 13 June 1872, n.p.

APPENDIX 8

Terms and Conditions to Gambier and Pepper Planters, 1876

GOVERNMENT proclamation of 8 December 1875 which was published on 3 January 1876 regarding terms and conditions offered to persons wishing to cultivate gambier and pepper in Sarawak.

The Government of His Highness the Rajah of Sarawak hereby make known the following terms and conditions to persons desirous of cultivating pepper and gambier in Sarawak.

1st. The Government are prepared to make grants of land suitable for planting gambier and pepper for ninety-nine years at a nominal rent, each

lot will be of 1,000 fathoms square or thereabouts and the grants will be subjected to a condition that not less than 300 fathoms square be opened and planted with gambier during the first year and a proportionate quantity for pepper in each successive year in a proper course of farming and that a proper and *bona fide* system of gambier and pepper cultivation be carried out. On breach of either condition or in the event of the grantee abandoning the land or any part of it by permitting it to return to jungle the grants will become null and void and the Government be entitled to execute upon the land and take possession thereof again. All minerals (except gold and diamonds) are reserved, the same being under lease to the Borneo Company Limited, should any land under gambier or pepper cultivation be required for mining purposes the Government reserve to themselves the right to take the same at a valuation to be made in the usual manner.

2nd. The Government will provide free passage from Singapore to Kuching for all Towkays and their coolies intending *bona fide* to cultivate gambier and pepper in Sarawak.

3rd. The Government will constitute the Kang Chews or heads of the different rivers as captains over the people of such rivers respectively and will hold them responsible for the maintenance of good order among their people giving them full power to deal with small cases subject to the Court at Kuching and the Government agent on the spot as to serious cases, and as to the decision of what cases come within the powers of the said Kang Chews. The Government will also be prepared to make arrangements that the Opium, Arrack, Gambling and Pawn farms at the different rivers shall be held by the said Kang Chews.

4th. The Towkays will be required to register all agreements with the planters in accordance with the laws of Sarawak and no agreement will be recognised unless so registered. The agreements may be for a term which may extend to fifteen years and during that time the planters will be compelled to deal both in selling produce and buying stores and other articles with the Towkays with whom they have made agreement. The Towkays must supply bags for packing pepper and gambier, and will receive gambier and pepper at the rate of ninety catties net for every one hundred catties gross weight, the Towkays will also be entitled to a commission of twenty cents in the dollar on all produce received and sold by them. The Towkays must supply provisions and other necessaries at fair market rates.

5th. The Government will provide a suitable penalty for any person who shall be found guilty of having bought pepper or gambier from any planter bound by any such agreement and also for any person receiving runaway coolies and the Government will also appoint a kong kek for the settlement of all disputes as to weight or quality of gambier and pepper between Towkays and Planters.

6th. For the term of four years from the present time there will be no export duty on gambier and pepper and after the expiration of that time the tax will not exceed twenty cents per picul on pepper and ten cents on

gambier. Persons coming to Sarawak and there opening gardens with their own capital (that is without advances from Government) will be allowed to export their produce free of duty per twelve years from the present time.

7th. All articles except opium and arrack required by the Planters and used by them will be admitted free of duty, and the planters will not be required to pay tax on salt and tobacco. This will remain in force for six years.

8th. Opium will be supplied to the planters at the rate of 1 tahil and 3 chees for the dollar for the next six years unless the price of opium at Singapore rises to $700 when another arrangement will be made.

9th. Should there be any sick on the gambier and pepper estates they will be taken care of and attended to at the Government Hospital.

10th. Any person found abusing the privileges hereby accorded to gambier and pepper planters by shipping or transferring articles otherwise subject to duty such as salt, tobacco and such like or by trading with them to others than those employed under them upon the plantation or by shipping coolies for other purposes under the pretence of being for the plantations or by otherwise attempting to defraud the Government of its Revenues or by underselling or attempting to undersell the farmer or farmers in Kuching with opium or other articles will be liable to a heavy penalty.

11th. Any person desirous of coming to Sarawak must apply to Messrs. A. L. Johnston & Co. of Singapore and obtain passes from them.

Source: *SG*, 3 January 1876, n.p.

APPENDIX 9
Terms and Conditions for the Settlement of Malayan–Muslim Agriculturalists in Sarawak Territory, 1868

GOVERNMENT Regulation regarding the terms and conditions of the settlement of Malayan-Muslim agriculturalists in Sarawak territory issued in 1868.

A regulation passed this day that all classes such as Boyans, Javanese, Bugis, Banjarmasins or any other such people who are brought up to cultivate the soil in their own countries. In future all such people wishing to reside between the mouth of Sadong + Sirik point in Sarawak territory are to bring 30 fathoms square or 900 square fathoms of soil under cultivation to be kept in proper order + planted with such cultures as Sugar-cane (+ to make sugar) Tapioca + Arrowroot (+ to make flour) chocolate for the market, Bribangs + vegetables, oranges, cocoanut + betelnut, coffee + pepper (such as sago palms, plantations + miscellaneous fruit trees will not be included).

The portion of land above named is to be fully brought under cultivation + the Government will periodically visit such plantations to ascertain

the state in which they are kept[.] [S]uch persons as may prefer leading a vagabon[d] life or occupying themselves in petty trade will incur a tax of $3. per annum viz. $1. every four months paid in advance. Such persons as through old age or chronic sickness may not come under the above regulation, must hold a certificate of exemption from Government.

N.B. All labourers employed in monthly wages on estates will not come under the above regulations.

The above regulations to be put in force a month after it be made known at which time the classes to whom it refers must report their intentions to the heads of the several kampongs.

C. Brooke Tuan Muda

Simanggang Feb[ruary] 22, 1868.

Source: 22 February 1868, HH The Rajah's Order Book, Vol. I, SMA, Kuching.

APPENDIX 10
Order No. XXV, 1910: Sale of Rubber Tree Plantations

GOVERNMENT Order prohibiting the sale or transfer of Para rubber tree plantations to Europeans issued in 1910 by Charles Brooke, Rajah.

Whereas I consider it is advisable to discourage the sale or transfer of plantations of rubber trees, I now notify the native inhabitants of Sarawak and settlers of Chinese, Indian, Eurasian, or any other Eastern nationality throughout the territory of Sarawak who are now or have been engaged in planting rubber trees that I do hereby prohibit the sale or transfer by them of any plantation of rubber trees unless permission for such sale and transfer has first been obtained from the Government, and anyone selling or transferring a plantation without such permission will be liable to a fine of Five hundred dollars or a penalty at the rate of Fifty dollars an acre for each acre thus sold or transferred as the Government may in each case decide, and the sale or transfer shall be null and void.

Further I direct that in the event of permission being granted by the Government for the sale or transfer of such a plantation a sum representing ten per cent of the purchase price shall be paid to the Government.

And I further direct that such permission will not in any case be granted to the native inhabitants and settlers to sell or transfer a plantation to any European or Europeans or any individual, firm, or Company of white nationality.

Given under my hand
and seal this 1st day of
November, 1910.

C. BROOKE,
Rajah.

Source: *SGG*, 1 November 1910, p. 168.

Bibliography

Manuscript Sources

Malaysia

Sarawak Museum and State Archives (SMA), Kuching

A. Letters of Rajah Charles Brooke, 10 vols., 1880–1912

The correspondence of Charles, on private and public matters, was copied into letter books, bound into volumes labelled as follows:

Second Rajah's Letters:	June to December 1880
	December 1882 to June 1885
HH The Rajah's Letters:	March 1887 to April 1890
	April 1890 to December 1892
	August 1896 to June 1898
	June 1898 to April 1901
	April 1901 to August 1906
	August 1906 to April 1913
	April 1913 to November 1915
	April 1907 to June 1912*
Letters of C. Brooke:	January 1893 to April 1896

B. Outstation Monthly Reports, 19 vols., 1870–1907

These reports were from the following outposts: Lundu, Sadong, Upper Sarawak, Simanggang, Kalaka (Krian), Oya, Mukah, Rejang, Bintulu, Baram, Limbang, and Trusan. Apart from the years 1870 to 1872, the majority of these reports were published in the *Gazette.*

C. Kabong Court Writer's Reports and Letters, 2 vols., 1892–3 and 1895–8

These are correspondence and reports from Cheyne Ah Fook, Court Writer of the Krain outpost, to D. J. S. Bailey, Resident of the Second Division, stationed at Simanggang.

*Should actually be classified as Rajah Vyner's letters as, from 1904, Charles often left the administration of the country to Vyner, the Rajah Muda (Heir Apparent).

D. Court Records

Simanggang Court Records, 33 vols., 1864–1930.
Betong Court Records, 12 vols., 1866–1930.
Sibu Court Records, 7 vols., 1874–1923.
Pusa Court Records, 7 vols., 1889–1941.
Second Division Police Court Book, 1920–3.
Third Division, Court of Requests (debt cases), 4 vols., 1914–22.
Fourth Division Civil Cases (debt cases), 4 vols., 1883–1916.
Fourth Division Police Court Books, 1919–23.

E. Other Manuscript Materials

Agreement Book, 5 vols.: Books I–IV (1872–1922), Book V (from 1922). Records of contracts and agreements between the Raj and other parties, both individuals and companies.

'Confidential to Government Officers', January–October 1938: A kind of in-house newsletter for internal circulation from Edward Parnell, Chief Secretary, to outstation officers.

HH The Rajah's Order Book, 4 vols., 1863–1920: Mostly administrative decisions by Charles prior to their enactment into law or 'Orders' which were then published in the *Gazette*, and from 1908, in the *Sarawak Government Gazette*; correspondence to and from Residents; also some reports of Supreme Council meetings.

His Highness The Rajah Confidential, 2 vols., 1904–6 and 1911–13: Reports submitted by the Resident of the First Division, the most senior officer, to Charles on the administration of the country.

Letter Book, 1918–22: Reports from A. B. Ward, Resident of the First Division, to Vyner. Similar to that of 'His Highness The Rajah Confidential' for Charles's reign.

Martine, T. Charles, 'The Borneo Company Ltd., in Sarawak (From "Notes Written by Me When in Singapore Changi Gaol, 1943–4")', Typescript.

Sarawak Government Orders, 1860–91: Orders and other related matters during the reign of Charles. From 1863, Charles, then Tuan Muda, effectively assumed the administration of the Raj, in the absence of James, who retired to England. These Orders were later compiled and published in a single volume (see 'Published Official Records').

Sarawak Treasury Cash Book, 25 vols., 1842–1900: Records of revenue and expenditure on a monthly basis, including some yearly accounts.

Sarawak Treasury Journal, 4 vols., 1884–92 and 1895–1900: Records of revenue and expenditure on a daily basis.

Sarawak Treasury Ledger, 7 vols., 1863–1900: Revenue and expenditure accounts with headings, 'Dayak Revenue', etc.

Sarawak Treasury Monthly Cash Account, 8 vols., 1871–4 and 1877–1900.

Arkib Negara (National Archives) Malaysia (NAM), Kuala Lumpur

HCO 1986/1920: Agreements and concessions from Rajah Vyner Brooke to Charles Hose relating to the 'Eastern Products Limited' and logging rights in the Baram.

MU 6136/47 9301/1946: 'Report on Agriculture in Sarawak, September 8 to October 3 1946', by F. W. South.

United Kingdom

Public Record Office (PRO), Kew

A. Colonial Office Documents

CO 144/1–74: Labuan Correspondence: Letters and dispatches from and to the Government of Labuan, minutes and memoranda by Secretaries and Under-Secretaries of State and by officials of the Colonial Office, correspondence with other government departments, also matters relating to Sir James Brooke and Eastern Archipelago Company, miscellaneous papers and documents, 1844–1900.

CO 352/6–7: Labuan and Borneo: Register of Correspondence, 1886–1914.

CO 802/1–6: Revenue and Expenditure of the State of Sarawak, 1900–50; Sarawak: Annual Reports, 1925–50.

B. Foreign Office Documents

FO 12: Vols. 19–21, 'Commission of Inquiry, Sir James Brooke', 1853–4; 'Correspondence and Memoranda as to James Brooke's proposals respecting Sarawak', 1852–69; Vol. 52, 'Cession of Territory (Baram) by the Sultan of Brunei to the Rajah of Sarawak', 1878–81.

FO 93: Vol. 16 (1–3): Cession of Labuan, 1846 (1); Treaty with Brunei, May 1847 (2); Agreement with Brunei, November 1856 (3).

Rhodes House Library (RHL), Oxford

A. Private Papers

The following is the list of personal papers (private correspondence, official letters, typescript memoranda, memoirs and recollections, photographs, etc.) of individuals consulted in this study. A double asterisk denotes 'Restricted', i.e. special permission is required before the papers can be consulted.

T. Stirling Boyd	MSS Pac. s. 86
F. F. Boult	MSS Pac. r. 9**
Mrs M. E. Bowyer [Dr J. H. Bowyer]	MSS Ind. Ocn. s. 315
Basil Brooke Papers	MSS Pac. s. 90

Brooke Family Papers	MSS Pac. s. 83
Sir Charles Vyner Brooke	MSS Ind. Ocn. s. 118
	MSS Ind. Ocn. s. 119
	MSS Ind. Ocn. s. 58
	MSS Pac. s. 62
	MSS Ind. Ocn. s. 74, 1
Harry R. A. Day	MSS Ind. Ocn. s. 229C
C. E. A. Ermen	MSS Pac. s. 63
Reginald William Large	MSS Pac. s. 97**
C. D. Lowe	MSS Ind. Ocn. s. 148
Anthony John N. Richards	MSS Ind. Ocn. s. 213
	MSS Ind. Ocn. s. 234
Walter Francis de Vere Skrine	MSS Ind. Ocn. s. 143
R. N. Turner	MSS Brit. Emp. s. 454
A. C. Vivian	MSS Brit. Emp. s. 345
Arthur Bartlett Ward	MSS Pac. s. 80
Sir Alexander N. A. Waddell	MSS Pac. s. 105

B. Other Documents

Fabian Colonial Bureau	MSS Brit. Emp. s. 365
Borneo Collections	916.18. s. 2 and 3

United Society for the Propagation of the Gospel (USPG) Archives, London

'D' Series, 2 vols., 1850–1938. Copies of Letters Received, Borneo. Also reports from Anglican (SPG) missionaries to their London headquarters. Photocopies of typescripts are also available at Rhodes Library, Oxford.

Liverpool Record Office (LRO), Liverpool

Papers of the 14th Earl of Derby

920 DER (14) 44/2: Disputes between Sir James Brooke and the Eastern Archipelago Company, 11 June 1852. Two versions, viz., Colonial Office (11 pp.) and Foreign Office (4 pp.).

Papers of the 15th Earl of Derby

920 DER (15) 15/2: Sarawak: Proposal for Cession to Great Britain. Lord Stanley (Prime Minister) to the Cabinet, 24 November 1866, with reference to Foreign Office correspondence (24 November 1866) on this issue.

920 DER (15) 30/1/5: Memorandum relative to the Proposals made by Rajah [Charles] Brooke for the annexation of Brunei to the British Dominions.

West Sussex Record Office (WSRO), Chichester

Add MSS 22,427/41: Miscellaneous Correspondence concerning Sarawak and Rajah [James] Brooke, 1846–67.

38. Regarding Spenser St John's schemes for developing Sarawak.
41 and 49. Regarding the Sarawak Sugar Company Limited.

Add MSS 22,431: Correspondence between John Brooke Brooke and James Brooke to Lord John Russell relating to the 'Mukah Incident of 1861'. Complaints of the interference of George Warren Edwardes, Governor of Labuan, against Sarawak's interest at Mukah. See also Letter dated 2 and 6 March 1862 by James Brooke to [?] giving a description and history of events in Sarawak. From the contents, the likely addressee is Earl Russell, Foreign Secretary.

Add MSS 22,434: Firman of the Sultan and Wazeers of Brunei to the people of Mukah ordering to submit to the Rajah of Sarawak, 29 April 1861. Translation from the Malay (Jawi script).

Add MSS 22,435: 'Memorandum' by J. Brooke, 21 December 1861. Relating to the cession of Sarawak.

Add MSS 22,438: 'Memorandum for Lord Clarendon' by J. Brooke, February 1858. Relating to the cession of Sarawak.

Add MSS 22,442: Memorandum on Colonel Orfeur Cavenagh's report on Sarawak, 20 November 1862.

Add MSS 22,451: Introduction to Anthropology by Waitz. Translation from the German [?] by J. Frederick Collingwood, Part II, Section III, p. 366. Handwritten. Regarding James Brooke's treatment of natives.

Add MSS 22,453: 'Paper as to the Formation of Company for developing the resources of Borneo', by Edward E. Kay, 4 March 1864.

Add MSS 22,454: Deed of Settlement of the Sarawak Sugar Company Limited.

Add MSS 22,455: 'Report on Sarawak', unsigned, n.d. From the contents, the author was probably John Abel Smith, principal supporter of James Brooke's efforts in securing Britain's recognition of Sarawak; and, the date probably 'late 1866 or early 1867'.

Devon Record Office (DRO), Exeter

139M/PPP17: Report to Cabinet from Consul Ricketts on Sarawak, [1 February] 1865.

British Library (BL): Department of Western Manuscripts, London

Add MSS 38993: Minutes and Letters relating to Sarawak, 1863–6.

Guildhall Library (GHL), London

MSS 16,209: Guardian Assurance Company Limited reports, including Shell Oil Company operations in Sarawak, 1900–4.

MSS 27,179: Index of Minute Books, 1856–1952. 'The Borneo Company Limited'.

Geological Society of London, London

'Geological Map of Sarawak', by H. Williams, 1846.

Singapore

National Archives and Oral History Department, Singapore

A 000005/06(2): Interview with Ling Lee Hua, 4 January 1980. Relating to his father's (1920s and 1930s) and his own business connections with Sarawak (1950s).

Additional Manuscripts

Cleary, Mark C., 'Changing Patterns of Trade in North-west Borneo, *c.*1860–1930', MS, n.d.

Cook, J. to A. H. M. Kirk-Greene, Oxford University Development Records Project, MS, 3 September 1983.

Cook, J. Interview with, Dundee, Scotland, Transcript, May 1993.

Horton, A. V. M., '"A Pauper with a Valuable Property for Sale": The British–Borneo Petroleum Syndicate and the Search for Oil in Brunei, 1906–1932', MS, n.d.

Ong Yen Jin, Correspondence of 25 October and 25 November 1994.

Ooi Keat Gin, 'The Sarawak Rice Crisis of 1919–1921: Rajah Vyner and the Brooke Rice Self-sufficiency Policy', Paper presented at the First Conference of the European Association for South-East Asian Studies (EUROSEAS) 'Keys to South-East Asia', Leiden, The Netherlands, 29 June–1 July 1995.

———, 'Rentap, Bantin and Asun: Iban "Rebels" or Iban "Nationalists" of Sarawak, 1841–1941', Paper presented at 'Pergerakan Sosial Dalam Sejarah (Social Movements in History)' Seminar of the History Section, School of Humanities, Universiti Sains Malaysia, Malaysia, 23 March 1996.

Published Official Records

Sarawak

The following materials were published by the Government Printing Office, unless stated otherwise.

A. Orders and Laws

Boyd, T. Stirling (comp.), *The Laws of Sarawak 1927–1935 ('The Red Book')*, London: Bradbury & Wilkinson, 1936.

Index to State Orders, Kuching, 1933.

Orders Issued by HH The Rajah of Sarawak or with His Sanction, Part I, Singapore, 1923.

Orders Which Have Not Since Been Cancelled, Issued by HH The Rajah of Sarawak or with His Sanction, from 1863 to 1890, Inclusive, Vols. I–X, Kuching, 1891–1916.

The Penal Code, 1934, Kuching, 1934.

Richards, A. J. N. (comp.), *Dayak Adat Law in the First Division: Adat Bidayuh*, Kuching, 1964.

———, *Dayak Adat Law in the Second Division*, Kuching, 1963.
———, *Sarawak Land Law and Adat*, Kuching, 1961.
Sarawak Government Orders, 1860–1891, 1 vol.
State Orders Enacted during the Year 1936, Kuching, 1937; also issued for the years 1937 to 1941 inclusive.
State Orders ('Green Book' 1933) Issued by His Highness The Rajah of Sarawak or with His Sanction, Kuching, 1933.
Supreme Court of Sarawak: Reports of Divisions, Kuching, 1928. Three more volumes were published in 1936, 1939, and 1946.

B. Reports

Agriculture Department Annual Report for 1948, Kuching, 1949.
Annual Report by the Sarawak Government Concerning Prepared Opium in the Sarawak Territory for the Calendar Year 1939, Kuching, 1940.
Bridges, W. F. N., *Rubber Regulation in Sarawak: Interim Report, 6 January 1937*, Kuching: Kuching Press, 1937.
Clark, C. D. Le Gros, *1935 Blue Report*, Kuching, 1935.
Estimates of Revenue and Expenditure, 1934, Kuching, 1933; also issued for 1935, 1937–42.
Freeman, J. D., *Report on the Iban of Sarawak*, 2 vols., Kuching, 1955.
Goodall, G. M., *Report on Swamp Padi and Other Foodstuff in First Division of the Department of Agriculture for the Years 1928–29*, Kuching, 1929.
Haile, N. S., *The Geology and Mineral Resources of the Starp and Sadong Valleys, West Sarawak, 'Including the Klingkang Range Coal'*, Geological Survey Department, British Territories in Borneo, Memoir 1, Kuching, 1954.
Hepburn, B. A. St J. (comp.), *The Handbook of Sarawak: Comprising Historical, Statistical and General Information Obtained from Official and Other Reliable Records*, Singapore: Malaya Publishing House for the Government of Sarawak, 1949.
Jones, L. W., *Sarawak: Report on the Census of Population Taken on 15th June 1960*, Kuching, 1962.
The Laws of Sarawak, rev. edn., Kuching, 1947.
Newman, C. L., *Report on Padi in Sarawak 1938*, Kuching, 1938.
Noakes, J. L., *Sarawak and Brunei: A Report on the 1947 Population Census*, Kuching, 1950.
Porter, A. F., *Land Administration in Sarawak*, Kuching, 1967.
Rainfall Statistics of the British Borneo Territories (Sarawak–Brunei–North Borneo), 1896–1957, compiled by the Department of Civil Aviation and Metereological Services, British Borneo Territories, September 1961.
Report of the Land Committee, 1962, Kuching, 1963.
Robertson, James R. M., *Report on the Coal Field of Silantik Borneo*, Sarawak: Government Press, 1877.
Roe, F. W. (comp.), *The Natural Resources of Sarawak*, 2nd rev. edn. Kuching, 1952.
Rubber Regulation during 1936, Kuching, 1937.
Rubber Regulation during 1937, Kuching, 1938.

Sarawak Administration Report (SAR), Kuching, 1927, 1928–38 inclusive.

Sarawak Annual Report of the Government Monopolies for 1930, Kuching, 1931.

Sarawak: Annual Report of the Labour Department, 1952, Kuching, 1953.

Sarawak Civil Service List 1925, Kuching, 1925; also issued in 1926–30, 1932, 1934, 1937–39.

Ward, A. B. and White, D. C. (comps.), *Outlines of Sarawak History under the Brooke Rajahs, 1839–1946*, Kuching, 1956.

Wilford, G. E., *The Geology and Mineral Resources of Brunei and Adjacent Parts of Sarawak with Descriptions of Seria and Miri Oilfields*, Geological Survey Department, British Territories in Borneo, Memoir 10, Brunei: Brunei Press Limited, 1961.

Wolfenden, E. B., *Bau Mining District, West Sarawak, Malaysia, Part 1: Bau*, Geological Survey Borneo Region, Malaysia, Bulletin 7, Kuching, 1965.

C. Other Government Publications

'Annual Reports of the Singapore Chinese Protectorate, 1887–1914', in *Singapore Government Annual Reports*, Singapore: Government Printing Office, 1887–1914.

General Council, 1867–1927, Kuching, 1927 [?].

Sarawak as a Field for Planters: Improved and Enlarged, 1879, Sarawak: Sarawak Gazette Office, n.d.

Sarawak as a Field for Planters: Improved and Enlarged, 1886, Sarawak: Sarawak Gazette Office, n.d.

Sarawak Government Almanac, Kuching: National Printing Department, 1993. An annual publication.

Sarawak Gazette, 1870– .

Sarawak Government Gazette, 1908– .

United Kingdom

A. Parliamentary Papers

Command Papers are in brackets and Sessional Papers in square brackets.

1850 Vol. XXXIII (434) Sir James Brooke.

Vol. LV (238) Borneo Piracy; (122) Borneo Piracy; [1197] Borneo Piracy; [1265] Borneo Piracy.

1851 Vol. XXXVI [1374] Borneo, Robert Burns; [1375] Borneo, Robert Burns.

Vol. LVI, Pt. I [1930] 'Piracies in the East Indies ...'; [1351] Borneo Piracy; (53) Farquhar's Operations; (378) *Nemesis* Operations.

1852 Vol. XXXI [1462] Borneo, Robert Burns; [1538] Borneo Piracy; [1536] Borneo, Robert Burns.

1852–3 Vol. LXI (770) Instructions for Commission of Inquiry; (717)

Brooke; (317) Brooke's Dismissal from Governorship of Labuan; (281) Brooke; [1612] Brooke; [1599] Borneo Piracy and Others.

1854–5 Vol. XXIX [1976] Reports of Commission of Brooke Inquiry.

B. Parliamentary Debates (Series iii)

Vol. 112, Cols. 1300–26	'Alleged Piracy off Borneo'.
Vol. 117, Cols. 3–6	'Sir James Brooke—Borneo'.
Vol. 118, Cols. 436–504	'Borneo—Sir James Brooke'.
Vol. 119, Cols. 1257–61	'Brooke—Sir James Brooke'.
Vol. 125, Cols. 723–6	'Sir James Brooke—Piracy in Borneo'.
Vol. 126, Cols. 909–10	'The Borneo Pirates'.

C. Reports

Dames, T. W. G., *Report to the Government of Sarawak on Soil Research in the Economic Development of Sarawak*, FAO Report No. 1512, Rome, 1962.

Freeman, J. D., *Iban Agriculture: A Report on the Shifting Cultivation of Hill Rice by the Iban of Sarawak*, London: HMSO, 1955.

Geddes, W. R., *The Land Dayaks of Sarawak: A Report on a Social Economic Survey of the Land Dayaks of Sarawak Presented to the Colonial Social Science Research Council*, London: HMSO, 1954.

Leach, Edmund, *Social Science Research in Sarawak*, London: HMSO, 1950.

Morris, H. S., *Report on a Melanau Sago Producing Community in Sarawak*, London: HMSO, 1953.

Roe, F. W., *British Territories in Borneo: Report of the Geological Survey Department for the Year 1951*, London: HMSO, 1952.

———, *The Mineral Resources of Sarawak*, British Borneo Geological Survey Annual Report, London: HMSO, 1949.

Sarawak Annual Report 1947, London: HMSO, 1948; also issued annually for the years 1948–63 inclusive.

Books

Adas, Michael, *The Burma Delta: Economic Development and Social Change on an Asian Rice Frontier, 1852–1941*, Madison: University of Wisconsin Press, 1974.

Allen, G. C. and Donnithorne, Audrey G., *Western Enterprise in Indonesia and Malaya: A Study in Economic Development*, London: George Allen & Unwin, 1962.

Arasaratnam, S., *Indians in Malaysia and Singapore*, Kuala Lumpur: Oxford University Press, 1970.

Baring-Gould, S. and Bampfylde, C. A., *A History of Sarawak under Its Two White Rajahs, 1839–1908*, London: Henry Sotheran, 1909.

Bassett, D. K., *British Attitudes to Indigenous States in South-East Asia in the Nineteenth Century*, University of Hull, Centre for South-East Asian Studies Occasional Paper No. 1, Hull, 1980.

Batty-Smith, W. De B. P. and Watterson, W. N., *Sarawak: The Issues of 1871 and 1875 Plating Studies and Postal History*, Irthlingborough; Woolnough Bookbinding, 1990.

Beccari, Odoardo, *Wanderings in the Great Forests of Borneo*, London: Archibald Constable, 1904; reprinted Singapore: Oxford University Press, 1986.

Belcher, Edward, *Narrative of the Voyage of HMS* Samarang, *during the Years 1843–46*, London: Reeve, Benham & Reeve, 1848.

Bennett, George, *Kenya: A Political History—The Colonial Period*, London: Oxford University Press, 1963.

Black, Ian, *A Gambling Style of Government: The Establishment of the Chartered Company's Rule in Sabah, 1878–1915*, Kuala Lumpur: Oxford University Press, 1983.

The Borneo Question, or the Evidence Produced at Singapore before the Commissioners Charged with the Enquiry into the Facts Relating to Sir James Brooke KCB Esq., Compiled from the Singapore Free Press and Other Sources, Singapore: Alfred Simonides, 1854.

Boyle, Frederick, *Adventures among the Dyaks of Borneo*, London: Hurst & Blackett, 1865.

Brooke, Anthony, *The Facts about Sarawak: A Documented Account of the Cession to Britain in 1946*, Bombay, 1947; reprinted Singapore: Summer Times, 1983.

Brooke, Charles, *Queries: Past, Present and Future*, London: The Planet, 1907.

———, *Ten Years in Sarawak*, 2 vols., London: Tinsley, 1866; reprinted Singapore: Oxford University Press, 1990.

Brooke, James, *A Letter from Borneo; with Notices of the Country and Its Inhabitants, Addressed to James Gardner, Esq.*, London: L. & G. Seeley, 1842.

———, *A Vindication of His Character and Proceedings in Reply to the Statements Privately Printed and Circulated by Joseph Hume, Esq. MP, Addressed to Henry Drummond, Esq. MP*, London: Ridgway, 1853.

Brooke, Margaret, *Good Morning and Good Night*, London: Constable, 1934.

———, *My Life in Sarawak*, London: Methuen, 1913.

Brooke, Sylvia, *Sylvia of Sarawak: An Autobiography*, London: Hutchinson & Co., 1936.

———, *The Three White Rajas*, London: Cassell, 1939.

Brown, D. E., *Brunei: The Structure and History of a Bornean Malay Sultanate*, Bandar Seri Begawan: Brunei Museum, 1970.

Browne, F. G., *Forest Trees of Sarawak and Brunei and Their Products*, Kuching: Government Printing Office, 1955.

Bunyon, Charles John, *Memoirs of Francis Thomas McDougall, Sometime*

Bishop of Labuan and Sarawak and of Harriete His Wife, London: Longmans Green, 1889.

Burkill, Issac Henry, *A Dictionary of the Economic Products of the Malay Peninsula*, 2 vols., London: Crown Agents for Colonies, 1935; reprinted Kuala Lumpur: Governments of Malaysia and Singapore by the Ministry of Agriculture and Co-operatives, 1966.

Campbell, Persia Crawford, *Chinese Coolie Emigration to Countries within the British Empire*, London: D. S. King, 1923; reprinted New York: Negro Universities Press, 1969.

Cartwright, Frank T., *Tuan Hoover of Borneo*, New York: Abingdon Press, 1938.

Cavenagh, Orfeur, *Report upon the Settlement of Sarawak*, Calcutta: J. Kingham, 1863.

Chai Hon-Chan, *The Development of British Malaya, 1896–1909*, Kuala Lumpur: Oxford University Press, 1964.

Chamerovzow, L. A., *Borneo Facts versus Borneo Fallacies: An Inquiry into the Alleged Piracies of the Dyaks of Serebas and Sakarran*, London: Charles Gilpin, 1851.

Chater, W. J., *Sarawak Long Ago*, Kuching: Borneo Literature Bureau, 1969.

Cheng Siok-Hwa, *The Rice Industry of Burma, 1852–1940*, Kuala Lumpur: University of Malaya Press, 1968.

Chew, Daniel, *Chinese Pioneers of the Sarawak Frontier, 1841–1941*, Singapore: Oxford University Press, 1990.

Chin, John M., *The Sarawak Chinese*, Kuala Lumpur: Oxford University Press, 1981.

Christie, Jan W., *Ironworking in Sarawak*, University of Hull, Centre for South-East Asian Studies Occasional Paper No. 15, Hull, 1988.

Cleary, Mark and Eaton, Peter, *Borneo: Change and Development*, Singapore: Oxford University Press, 1992.

Cooper, A. M., *Men of Sarawak*, Kuala Lumpur: Oxford University Press, 1968.

Crawfurd, John, *A Descriptive Dictionary of the Indian Islands and Adjacent Countries*, London: Bradbury & Evans, 1856.

——, *History of the Indian Archipelago*, 3 vols., Edinburgh: Constable, 1820.

Crisswell, Colin N., *Rajah Charles Brooke: Monarch of All He Surveyed*, Kuala Lumpur: Oxford University Press, 1978.

Digby, K. H., *Lawyer in the Wilderness*, Cornell University Southeast Asia Program Data Paper No. 114, Ithaca: Cornell University Press, 1980.

Dunn, F. L., *Rain-forest Collectors and Traders: A Study of Resource Utilization in Modern and Ancient Malaya*, Monographs of MBRAS No. 5, Kuala Lumpur: MBRAS, 1975.

Earl, George Windsor, *The Eastern Seas; or Voyages and Adventures in the Indian Archipelago, in 1832–33–34*, London: William Hallen, 1837.

Edwards, Leonard and Stevens, Peter W., *Short Histories of the Lawas and Kanowit Districts*, Kuching: Borneo Literature Bureau, 1971.

Emerson, Rupert, *Malaysia: A Study in Direct and Indirect Rule*, London: Macmillan, 1937; reprinted Kuala Lumpur: University of Malaya Press, 1964.

Foggo, George, *Adventures of Sir James Brooke, KCB, Rajah of Sarawak 'Sovereign de facto of Borneo Proper',...*, London: Effingham Wilson, 1853.

Forest, Thomas, *A Voyage to New Guinea and the Moluccas from Balambangan Including an Account of Magindano, Soloo and Other Islands*, London: G. Scott, 1779; reprinted Kuala Lumpur: Oxford University Press, 1969.

Forrester-Wood, W. R., *The Stamps and Postal History of Sarawak*, Redhill: Commercial Lithographic Co. Ltd., 1957.

Furness, William Henry, *The Home Life of Borneo Headhunters, Its Festivals and Folklore*, Philadelphia: Lippincott, 1902; reprinted New York: AMS, 1979.

Griffiths, Percival, *A History of the Inchcape Group*, London: Inchcape, 1977.

Gullick, J. M., *Indigenous Political Systems of Western Malaya*, London: Athlone Press, 1958.

Haddon, Alfred C., *Headhunters, Black, White and Brown*, London: Methuen, 1901.

Hahn, Emily, *James Brooke of Sarawak: A Biography of Sir James Brooke*, London: Arthur Barker, 1953.

Harper, G. C., *The Discovery and Development of the Seria Oilfield*, Brunei: Brunei Museum, 1975.

Harrisson, Tom, *World Within: A Borneo Story*, London: Cresset, 1959.

——— (ed.), *The Peoples of Sarawak*, Kuching: Government Printing Press, 1959.

———, *The Malays of South-west Sarawak before Malaysia*, London: Macmillan, 1970.

Helms, Ludvig Verner, *Pioneering in the Far East, and Journeys to California in 1849 and to the White Sea in 1878*, London: W. H. Allen, 1882.

Hose, Charles, *The Field-Book of a Jungle Wallah: Being a Description of Shore, River and Forest Life in Sarawak*, London: H. F. & C. Witherby, 1929; reprinted Singapore: Oxford University Press, 1985.

———, *Fifty Years of Romance and Research; or a Jungle Wallah at Large*, London: Hutchinson, 1927.

———, *Natural Man: A Record from Borneo*, London: Macmillan, 1926; reprinted Singapore: Oxford University Press, 1988.

Hose, Charles and McDougall, William, *The Pagan Tribes of Borneo*, 2 vols., London: Macmillan, 1912; reprinted Singapore: Oxford University Press, 1993.

Hsu, Immanuel C. Y., *The Rise of Modern China*, 4th edn., New York: Oxford University Press, 1990.

Hume, Joseph, *A Letter to the Right Honourable the Earl of Malmesbury, Secretary of State for Foreign Affairs, etc. etc., Relative to the Proceedings of Sir James Brooke, KCB, etc. etc. etc., in Borneo*, London, 1853.

Ingleson, John, *Expanding the Empire: James Brooke and the Sarawak Lobby*, Perth: Centre for South and Southeast Asian Studies, University of Western Australia, 1980.

Ireland, Alleyne, *The Far Eastern Tropics: Studies in the Administration of Tropical Dependencies*, London: Archibald Constable, 1905.

Irwin, Graham, *Nineteenth-century Borneo: A Study in Diplomatic Rivalry*, The Hague: Martinus Nijhoff, 1955; reprinted Singapore: Donald Moore, 1965.

Jackson, James C., *Chinese in the West Borneo Goldfields: A Study in Cultural Geography*, University of Hull Occasional Papers in Geography No. 15, Hull, 1970.

———, *Planters and Speculators: Chinese and European Agricultural Enterprise in Malaya, 1786–1921*, Kuala Lumpur: University of Malaya Press, 1968.

———, *Sarawak: A Geographical Survey of a Developing State*, London: University of London Press, 1968.

Jacob, Gertrude L., *The Raja of Sarawak: An Account of Sir James Brooke, KCB, LLD, Given Chiefly through Letters and Journals*, 2 vols., London: Macmillan, 1876.

Jones, Geoffrey, *The State and the Emergence of the British Oil Industry*, London: Macmillan, 1986.

Kennedy, Dane, *Islands of White: Settler Society and Culture in Kenya and Southern Rhodesia*, Durham: Duke University Press, 1987.

Kennedy, J., *A History of Malaya*, 2nd edn., London: Macmillan, 1970.

Keppel, Henry, *The Expedition to Borneo of HMS* Dido *for the Suppression of Piracy: With Extracts from the Journal of James Brooke Esq.*, 2 vols., London: Chapman & Hall, 1846; reprinted Singapore: Oxford University Press, 1991.

———, *A Sailor's Life under Four Sovereigns*, 3 vols., London: Macmillan, 1899.

———, *A Visit to the Indian Archipelago in HM Ship* Maeander *with Portions of the Private Journal of Sir James Brooke, KCB*, 2 vols., London: Bentley, 1853.

Khoo Kay Kim, *The Western Malay States, 1850–1873: The Effects of Commercial Development on Malay Politics*, Kuala Lumpur: Oxford University Press, 1972.

Leakey, L. S. B., *Kenya: Contrasts and Problems*, London: Methuen, 1936.

Lee Yong Leng, *Population and Settlement in Sarawak*, Singapore: Donald Moore, 1970.

Lenin, V. I., *Imperialism: The Highest Stage of Capitalism*, rev. trans., London: Martin Lawrence, 1933.

Leys, Norman, *A Last Chance in Kenya*, London: Hogarth, 1931.

Lim Teck Ghee, *Peasants and Their Agricultural Economy in Colonial Malaya, 1874–1941*, Kuala Lumpur: Oxford University Press, 1977.

Lindblad, J. Thomas, *Between Dayak and Dutch: The Economic History of South-East Kalimantan, 1880–1942*, Dordrecht: Foris Publications, 1988.

Lindsay, Hugh H., *The Eastern Archipelago Company and Sir James Brooke*, London, 1853.

Lockard, Craig Alan, *From Kampung to City: A Social History of Kuching, Malaysia, 1820–1970*, Ohio University Monographs in International Studies, Southeast Asia Series, No. 75, Athens, 1987.

Lo Hsiang Lin, *A Historical Survey of the Lan Fang Presidential System in Western Borneo by Lo Fang-Pai and Other Overseas Chinese*, Hong Kong: Chinese Cultural Institute, 1960.

Loh Fook Seng, Philip, *The Malay States, 1877–1895: Political Change and Social Policy*, Kuala Lumpur: Oxford University Press, 1969.

Longhurst, Henry, *The Borneo Story: The History of the First 100 Years of Trading in the Far East by The Borneo Company Limited*, London: Newman Neame, 1956.

Low, Hugh, *Sarawak: Its Inhabitants and Productions, Being Notes during a Residence in that Country with His Excellency Mr Brooke*, London: Frank Cass, 1848; new impression, 1968.

MacDonald, Malcolm, *Borneo People*, New York: Knopf, 1958.

McDougall, Harriette, *Letters from Sarawak*, reprint edn., London: Wheldon & Wesley, 1924.

———, *Sketches of Our Life at Sarawak*, London: Society for Promoting Christian Knowledge, 1882; reprinted Singapore: Oxford University Press, 1992.

McFadyean, Andrew (ed.), *The History of Rubber Regulation 1934–1943*, London: George Allen & Unwin, 1944.

MacKenzie, Compton, *Realms of Silver: One Hundred Years of Banking in the East*, London: Routledge & Kegan Paul, 1954.

MacPhee, Marshall A., *Kenya*, London: Ernest Benn, 1968.

Marryat, Frank S., *Borneo and the Indian Archipelago with Drawings of Costume and Scenery*, London: Longman, Brown, Green & Longmans, 1848.

Maxwell, W. G. and Gibson, W. S., *Treaties and Engagements Affecting the Malay States and Borneo*, London: Truscott, 1924.

Mills, L. A., *British Malaya, 1824–1867*, Kuala Lumpur: Oxford University Press, 1966.

Moor, J. H. (ed.), *Notices of the Indian Archipelago, and Adjacent Countries*, London: Frank Cass, 1837; reprinted 1968.

Morris, H. S., *The Oya Melanau*, Kuching: Malaysian Historical Society (Sarawak Branch), 1991.

Morrison, Hedda, *Life in a Longhouse*, Kuching: Borneo Literature Bureau, 1962.

———, *Sarawak*, Singapore: Federal Publications, 1957.

Mullen, Vernon, *The Story of Sarawak*, 2nd edn., Kuala Lumpur: Oxford University Press in association with Borneo Literature Bureau, 1967.

Mundy, Rodney, *Narrative of Events in Borneo and Celebes, down to the Occupation of Labuan: From the Journals of James Brooke Esq.*, 2 vols., London: John Murray, 1848.

Nzula, A. T.; Potekhin, I. I.; and Zusmanovich, A. Z., *Forced Labour in Colonial Africa*, London: Zed Press, 1979

Oil in Sarawak 1910–1960, Miri: Sarawak Shell Oilfields Ltd., n.d.

Ong Boon Lin, *Ong Tiang Swee of Sarawak*, Kuching: Lee Ming Press, 1990.

Ooi Keat Gin, *The Japanese Period in Sarawak, 1941–1945*, University of Hull, Centre for South-East Asian Studies, Monograph Series (forthcoming).

———, *World beyond the Rivers: Education in Sarawak from Brooke Rule to Colonial Office Administration, 1841–1963*, University of Hull, Centre for South-East Asian Studies, Monograph Series (in press).

Our Sarawak, Kuching: Persatuan Kesusasteraan Sarawak, 1983.

Owen, Roger and Sutcliffe, Bob (eds.), *Studies in the Theory of Imperialism*, London: Longman, 1972.

Payne, Robert, *The White Rajahs of Sarawak*, London: Robert Hale, 1960.

Pollard, Elizabeth, *Kuching: Past and Present*, Kuching: Borneo Literature Bureau, 1972.

Posewitz, Theodor, *Borneo: Its Geology and Mineral Resources*, London: Edward Stanford, 1892.

Pringle, Robert, *Rajahs and Rebels: The Ibans of Sarawak under Brooke Rule, 1841–1941*, London: Macmillan, 1970.

Purcell, Victor, *The Chinese in Malaya*, Kuala Lumpur: Oxford University Press, 1967.

———, *The Chinese in South-East Asia*, London: Oxford University Press, 1965.

Raffles, Thomas Stamford, *The History of Java*, 2 vols., London: Black, Parbury & Allen, 1817.

Rawlins, Joan, *Sarawak, 1839–1963*, London: Macmillan, 1965.

Reece, R. H. W., *The Name of Brooke: The End of White Rajah Rule in Sarawak*, Kuala Lumpur: Oxford University Press, 1982.

Richards, A. J. N. (ed.), *The Sea Dyaks and Other Races of Sarawak: Contributions to the Sarawak Gazette between 1888 and 1930*, Kuching: Borneo Literature Bureau, 1963.

Rooney, John, *Khabar Gembira (The Good News): A History of the Catholic Church in East Malaysia and Brunei (1880–1976)*, London: Burns & Oates, 1981.

Roth, Henry Ling, *The Natives of Sarawak and British North Borneo*, 2 vols., London: Truslove & Hanson, 1896.

Runciman, Steven, *The White Rajahs: A History of Sarawak from 1841 to 1946*, Cambridge: Cambridge University Press, 1960.

Rutter, Owen, *The Pirate Wind: Tales of the Sea-Robbers of Malaya*, London: Hutchinson, 1930.

——— (ed.), *Rajah Brooke and Baroness Burdett Coutts: Consisting of the Letters from Sir James Brooke, First White Rajah of Sarawak, to Miss Angela (afterwards Baroness) Burdett Coutts*, London: Hutchinson, 1935.

Sadka, Emily, *The Protected Malay States, 1874–1895*, Kuala Lumpur: University of Malaya Press, 1968.

St John, Horace, *The Indian Archipelago: Its History and Present State*, 2 vols., London: Longman, Brown, Green & Longmans, 1853.

St John, Spenser, *Life in the Forests of the Far East*, 2 vols., London: Smith, Elder & Co., 1862; reprinted Kuala Lumpur: Oxford University Press, 1974.

———, *The Life of Sir James Brooke: Rajah of Sarawak; from His Personal Papers and Correspondence*, Edinburgh and London: William Blackwood & Sons, 1879.

———, *Rajah Brooke: The Englishman as Ruler of an Eastern State*, London: Fisher Unwin, 1899.

Sandin, Benedict, *The Sea Dayaks of Borneo before White Rajah Rule*, London: Macmillan, 1967.

Sarawak Shell Berhad, *The Miri Story: The Founding Years of the Malaysian Oil Industry in Sarawak*, Lutong, 1978.

Seagrave, Sterling, *Dragon Lady: The Life and Legend of the Last Empress of China*, London: Macmillan, 1992.

Sharp, Arthur Frederick, *The Wings of the Morning*, London: Greaves, 1954.

Shineberg, Dorothy, *They Came for Sandalwood*, Melbourne: Melbourne University Press, 1967.

Silcock, T. H., *The Commonwealth Economy in Southeast Asia*, London: Cambridge University Press, 1959.

Skinner, G. William, *Chinese Society in Thailand: An Analytical History*, Ithaca: Cornell University Press, 1957.

Song Ong Siang, *One Hundred Years History of the Chinese in Singapore*, London: John Murray, 1923; reprinted Singapore: University of Malaya Press, 1967.

Tarling, Nicholas, *Britain, the Brookes and Brunei*, Kuala Lumpur: Oxford University Press, 1971.

———, *The Burthen, the Risk, and the Glory: A Biography of Sir James Brooke*, Kuala Lumpur: Oxford University Press, 1982.

———, *Piracy and Politics in the Malay World: A Study of British Imperialism in Nineteenth Century Southeast Asia*, reprint edn., Singapore: Donald Moore, 1963.

Templer, John C. (ed.), *The Private Letters of Sir James Brooke, KCB, Rajah of Sarawak, Narrating the Events of His Life, from 1838 to the Present Time*, 3 vols., London: Bentley, 1853.

Thio, Eunice, *British Policy in the Malay Peninsula, 1880–1910. Vol. I, The Southern and Central States*, Singapore: University of Malaya Press, 1969.

T'ien Ju-K'ang, *The Chinese of Sarawak: A Study of Social Structure*, Monograph on Social Anthropology No. 12, London: Department of Anthropology, London School of Economics and Political Science, 1953.

Tregonning, K. G., *Home Port Singapore: A History of Straits Steamship Company Limited*, Singapore: Oxford University Press for Straits Steamship Company Limited, 1967.

———, *Under Chartered Company Rule (North Borneo 1881–1946)*, Singapore: University of Malaya Press, 1958.

Turnbull, C. M., *The Straits Settlements, 1826–1867*, London: Athlone Press, 1972.

Wagner, Ulla, *Colonialism and Iban Warfare*, Stockholm: Obe-Tryck Sthlm, 1972.

Wallace, Alfred Russel, *The Malay Archipelago: The Land of the Orang-Utan, and the Bird of Paradise*, New York: Harper & Brothers, 1869; reprinted Singapore: Oxford University Press, 1986.

Wang Gungwu, *A Short History of the Nanyang Chinese*, Singapore: Donald Moore, 1959.

——— (ed.), *Malaysia: A Survey*, New York: Frederick Praeger, 1964.

Ward, A. B., *Rajah's Servant*, Cornell University Southeast Asia Program Data Paper No. 61, Ithaca: Cornell University Press, 1966.

Warren, James Francis, *The Sulu Zone, 1768–1898: The Dynamics of External Trade, Slavery and Ethnicity in the Transformation of a Southeast Asian Maritime State*, Singapore: Singapore University Press, 1981.

Wickberg, Edgar, *The Chinese in Philippine Life, 1850–1898*, New Haven: Yale University Press, 1965.

Willmott, Donald E., *The Chinese of Semarang*, Ithaca: Cornell University Press, 1960.

Wise, Henry (comp.), *A Selection from Papers Relating to Borneo and the Proceedings of James Brooke, Esq., Now Agent for the British Government in Borneo*, printed for the use of the government offices, London, 1844–6.

W. N., *Borneo*, London: Effingham Wilson, 1853.

Wong Lin Ken, *The Malayan Tin Industry to 1914*, Association for Asian Studies Monograph No. XIV, Tucson, 1965.

Articles

Ahmad Zaidell bin Haji Tahir, Haji, 'Recollections of an Ex-Government Officer: Part I', *SG*, 31 January 1972, pp. 6–8; and 'Part II', *SG*, 29 February 1972, pp. 31–3.

Amarjit Kaur, 'The Babbling Brookes: Economic Change in Sarawak 1841–1941', *MAS*, 29, 1 (January 1995): 65–109.

———, 'Transport and the Sarawak Economy, 1841–1983', *BRB*, 25 (1993): 76–100.

Anderson, J. A. R., 'The Structure and Development of the Peat Swamps of Sarawak and Brunei', *JTG*, 18 (1964): 7–16.

Banks, E., 'The Natives of Sarawak', *JMBRAS*, 18, 2 (August 1940): 49–54.

Baran, Paul A. and Sweezy, Paul M., 'Notes on the Theory of Imperialism', *MR*, 17 (1966): 15–31.

Blythe, W. L., 'Historical Sketch of Chinese Labour in Malaya', *JMBRAS*, 20, 1 (1947): 64–114.

Braddell, R., 'A Note on Sambas and Borneo', *JMBRAS*, 22, 4 (1949): 1–12.

———, 'Poli in Borneo', *SMJ*, 5, 1 (1949): 5–9.

Brooke, Charles, 'The Journal of Charles Brooke, September 1866–July 1868', Appendix in Charles Brooke, *Ten Years in Sarawak*, London: Tinsley, 1866; reprinted Singapore: Oxford University Press, 1990, Vol. II, pp. 345–74.

Brooke, James, 'Proposed Exploring Expedition to the Asiatic Archipelago', *JRGS*, 8 (1838): 443–8.

Browne, F. G., 'The Kerangas Land of Sarawak', *MF*, 15, 2 (1952): 61–73.

Bruggemann, Father, 'The History of the Catholic Church in the Rejang, 1882–1966', *Sarawak Teacher*, Special History Issue, 2 (1966): 15–21.

Burns, Robert, 'The Kayans of North-west Borneo', *JIAEA*, 3 (1849): 140–52.

Cain, P. J. and Hopkins, A. G., 'The Political Economy of British Expansion Overseas, 1750–1914', *EHR*, 38, 4 (1980): 463–90.

Chang Pat Foh, 'Bau Chinese Rebellion 1857', *SG*, April 1986, pp. 34–44

———, 'The History of Gold Mining in Bau, Sarawak', *SG*, September 1992, pp. 32–44.

———, 'Major Events in the History of Bau', *SG*, April 1987, pp. 25–43.

Chater, W. J., 'Chinese Labourers and How They Came to Sarawak', *ST*, 21 February 1964.

———, 'Pieces from the Brooke Past—III: The First Sarawak Chamber of Commerce', *SG*, 31 July 1964, pp. 164–5.

Chiang Liu, 'Chinese Pioneers, AD 1900: The New Foochow Settlement', *SMJ*, 6, 6 (December 1955): 536–48.

Chin, Lucas, 'Impact of Trade Ceramic Objects on Some Aspects of Local Culture', *SMJ*, 25, 46 (July–December 1977): 67–9.

Chin, S. C., 'Shifting Cultivation—A Need for Greater Understanding', *SMJ*, 25, 46 (July–December 1977): 107–28.

'The Chinese in Borneo', *CR*, 7 (1878–9): 1–11.

Christie, Jan Wisseman, 'On Po-ni: The Santubong Sites of Sarawak', *SMJ*, 34, 55 (December 1985): 77–87.

Cochrane, T. G., 'Empire Oil: The Progress of Sarawak', *JRSA*, 72, 3723 (28 March 1924): 308–19.

Cramb, R. A., 'The Commercialization of Iban Agriculture', in R. A. Cramb and R. H. W. Reece (eds.), *Development in Sarawak: Historical and Contemporary Perspectives*, Monash Paper on Southeast Asia No. 17, Centre of Southeast Asia Studies, Melbourne: Monash University, 1988, pp. 105–34.

Crisswell, Colin N., 'Some Historical Aspects of Local and Sovereign Rights in Nineteenth-century Brunei', *JOS*, 10, 1 (1972): 51–61.

Crocker, W. M., 'Notes on Sarawak and Northern Borneo', *JRGS*, 3, 4 (1881): 193–208.

Dalton, G., 'Pepper Growing in Upper Sarawak', *SMJ*, 1, 2 (February 1912): 53–61.

Denison, N., 'Notes on the Land Dyaks of Sarawak Proper', *SG*, 10 October 1876, pp. 5–8; *SG*, 13 November 1876, pp. 6–8; *SG*, 14 December 1876, pp. 5–8; *SG*, 16 January 1877, pp. 4–8.

Dunsmore, J. R., 'A Review of Agricultural Research in Sarawak', *SMJ*, 16, 32–3 (July–December 1968): 309–39.

Durrans, Brian, 'Introduction', in Charles Hose, *Natural Man: A Record from Borneo*, London: Macmillan, 1926; reprinted Singapore: Oxford University Press, 1988, pp. vii–xv.

Eaton, P., 'A History of Bau District', *SG*, 31 May 1967, pp. 126–9.

Everett, A. Hart, 'Notes on the Distribution of the Useful Minerals of Sarawak', *JSBRAS*, 1 (July 1878): 13–30.

Galbraith, J. S., 'The "Turbulent Frontier" as a Factor in British Imperialism', *CSSH*, 2 (1959–60): 150–68.

Gallagher, John and Robinson, Ronald, 'The Imperialism of Free Trade', *EHR*, 4 (1953): 1–15.

Gardner, Estelle, 'Footnote to Sarawak, 1859', *SMJ*, 11, 21–2 (July–December 1963): 32–59.

Geikie, J. Somerville, 'A List of Sarawak Minerals', *SMJ*, 1, 1 (February 1911): 194–201.

———, 'The Occurrence of Gold in Upper Sarawak', Part I, *SG*, 1 December 1908, pp. 297–9; Part II, *SG*, 2 December 1909, pp. 6–7; Part III, *SG*, 16 January 1909, pp. 20–2.

Goldman, Richard H., 'The Beginnings of Commercial Development in the Baram and Marudi Following the Cession of 1881', *SG*, 31 March 1968, pp. 54–60.

Hamid Bugo, 'Economic Development since Independence: Performance and Prospects', in R. A. Cramb and R. H. W. Reece (eds.), *Development in Sarawak: Historical and Contemporary Perspectives*, Monash Paper on Southeast Asia No. 17, Centre of Southeast Asia Studies, Melbourne: Monash University, 1988, pp. 49–56.

Harper, G. C., 'The Miri Field, 1910–1972', *SMJ*, 20, 40–1 (January–December 1972): 21–30.

Harrisson, Tom, 'Ceramics Penetrating Central Borneo', *SMJ*, 6, 6 (1955): 549–60.

———, 'The Kelabits and Muruts', in Tom Harrisson (ed.), *The Peoples of Sarawak*, Kuching: Government Printing Press, 1959, pp. 57–71.

———, 'Robert Burns—The First Ethnologist and Explorer of Interior Sarawak', *SMJ*, 5, 3 (November 1951): 463–94.

———, 'Trade Porcelain and Stoneware in Southeast Asia (including Borneo)', *SMJ*, 10, 17–18 (July–December 1963): 222–6.

Harrisson, Tom and O'Connor, Stanley, 'The Prehistoric Iron Industry in the Sarawak River Delta: Evidence by Association', *SMJ*, 16, 32–3 (1968): 1–54.

Hatta Solhee, 'The Rice Self-sufficiency Policy: Its Implementation in Sarawak', in R. A. Cramb and R. H. W. Reece (eds.), *Development in Sarawak: Historical and Contemporary Perspectives*, Monash Paper on

Southeast Asia No. 17, Centre of Southeast Asia Studies, Melbourne: Monash University, 1988, pp. 69–103.

Heidhues, Mary Somers, 'Chinese Organizations in West Borneo and Bangka: Kongsis and Hui', in David Ownby and Mary Somers Heidhues (eds.), *'Secret Societies' Reconsidered*, New York and London: M. E. Shrape, 1993, pp. 68–88.

Hewitt, John, 'Notes on Kuching Rainfall', *SG*, 2 February 1906, pp. 27–31.

Hipkins, James R., 'The History of the Chinese in Borneo', *SMJ*, 19, 38–9 (July–December 1971): 109–53.

Horton, A. V. M., 'James Hatton Hall (1866–1945): Planter, Merchant, Soldier', *JMBRAS*, 68, 1 (June 1995): 139–47.

———, 'Raja Brooke's Coal Mining Concessions in Brunei', *JMBRAS*, 59, 1 (1986): 49–73.

Hose, Charles, 'The Metamorphosis of Miri', *BM*, 2, 2 (June 1927): 41–6.

Jackson, James C., 'Smallholding Cultivation of Cash Crops', in Wang Gungwu (ed.), *Malaysia: A Survey*, New York: Frederick Praeger, 1964, pp. 246–73.

Kaboy, Tuton, 'The Murder of Steele and Fox: Two Versions', *SMJ*, 12, 25–6 (July–December 1965): 207–14.

Kaboy, Tuton and Moore, Eine, 'Ceramics and Their Uses among the Coastal Melanau', *SMJ*, 15, 30–1 (1967): 10–29.

Kay, K. E. H., 'The Economy of the Peoples Living in the Basin of the Batang Sadong', *SG*, 7 September 1949, pp. 221–3.

King, Frank H. H., 'Notes on the History of Currency in Sarawak', *JOS*, 2, 2 (July 1955): 316–23.

King, Victor T. and Naimah Talib, 'Robert Burns (d. 1851): Explorer of North-West Borneo', in Victor T. King (ed.), *Explorers of South-East Asia: Six Lives*, Kuala Lumpur: Oxford University Press, 1995, pp. 158–93.

Lau, James and Hon, Victor, 'History of Mining in Sarawak', *JMHSSB*, 2 (March 1976): 17–31.

Lawrence, A. E., 'Stories of the First Brunei Conquests on the Sarawak Coast', *SMJ*, 1, 1 (February 1911): 121–4.

Lee, Y. L., 'The Development of Resources in British Borneo and Its Impact on Settlement', *SMJ*, 11, 19–20 (July–December 1962): 563–89.

Leigh, Michael, 'The Spread of Foochow Commercial Power before the New Economic Policy', in R. A. Cramb and R. H. W. Reece (eds.), *Development in Sarawak: Historical and Contemporary Perspectives*, Monash Paper on Southeast Asia No. 17, Centre of Southeast Asia Studies, Melbourne: Monash University, 1988, pp. 179–90.

Lin Wen Tsung, 'The First Decade of New Foochow Colony in Sarawak', *Sarawak Teacher*, Special History Edition, 2, 2 (1966): 13–14 and 28.

Lockard, C. A., 'Charles Brooke and the Foundations of the Modern Chinese Community in Sarawak, 1863–1917', *SMJ*, 19, 38–9 (1971): 77–107.

———, 'Leadership and Power within the Chinese Community of Sarawak: A Historical Survey', *JSEAS*, 2, 2 (September 1971): 195–217.

———, 'The 1857 Chinese Rebellion in Sarawak: A Reappraisal', *JSEAS*, 9, 1 (March 1978): 85–98.

Logan, J. R., 'Borneo', *JIAEA*, 2 (1848): 495–7.

———, 'Manufacture of Pearl Sago in Singapore by Chinese', *JIAEA*, 3 (1849): 303–7.

———, 'Notices of Chinese Intercourse with Borneo Proper prior to the Establishment of Singapore in 1819', *JIAEA*, 2 (1848): 611–15 and 498–512.

———, 'Traces of the Origin of the Malay Kingdom of Borneo with Notices of Its Condition When First Discovered by Europeans, and at Later Periods', *JIAEA*, 2 (1848): 513–27.

———, 'The Trade in Sago', *JIAEA*, 3 (1849): 307–11

Loh Chee Yin, 'Pieces from the Brooke Past—XVII: Matang Coffee Estate', *SG*, 30 September 1965, pp. 279–83.

Low, Hugh, 'Selesilah (Book of Descent) of the Rajahs of Brunei', *JSBRAS*, 5 (1880): 1–35.

Lucas, N. A., 'The Production of Gold in Sarawak', *SG*, 1 February 1949, pp. 30–2.

McCormick, R. B. S., 'Coins in Sarawak's History', *Sarawak Teacher*, Special History Edition, 2, 2 (1966): 1–3.

Maugham, W. Somerset, 'The Yellow Streak', in *The Complete Short Stories of W. Somerset Maugham*, London: Heinemann, 1951, Vol. I, pp. 456–80.

Mead, J. P., 'Forest Reservation in Sarawak', *SG*, 1 December 1919, pp. 307–9.

Morris, H. S., 'The Coastal Melanau', in Victor T. King (ed.), *Essays on Borneo Societies*, Hull Monographs on South-East Asia 7, Oxford: Oxford University Press for University of Hull, 1978, pp. 37–58.

———, 'How an Old Sarawak Society was Undermined', *SG*, March 1982, pp. 51–7.

Morris, R. H., 'Our Economic Future', *SG*, 7 October 1949, pp. 259–60.

Morrisson, H., 'Brunei and the Seria Oilfields', *NC* (April 1951): 498–501.

Moy-Thomas, A. H., 'Economic Development under the Second Rajah (1870–1917)', *SMJ*, 10, 17–18 (July–December 1961): 50–8.

Newman, C. L., 'An Agricultural Policy for Sarawak', *SG*, 1 May 1941, pp. 81–2.

Nicholl, Robert, 'Brunei and Camphor', *BMJ*, 4, 3 (1979): 52–74.

Ong Kee Hui, 'Sago Production in Sarawak', *SG*, 1 November 1948, pp. 212–15.

Ooi Keat Gin, 'Chinese Vernacular Education in Sarawak during Brooke Rule, 1841–1946', *MAS*, 28, 3 (July 1994): 503–31.

———, 'Domestic Servants Par Excellence: The Black and White Amahs of Malaya and Singapore with Special Reference to Penang', *JMBRAS*, 65, 2 (December 1992): 69–84.

———, 'Education in Sarawak during the Period of Colonial Administration, 1946–1963', *JMBRAS*, 63, 2 (December 1990): 35–68.

———, 'Mission Education in Sarawak during the Period of Brooke Rule, 1841–1946', *SMJ*, 62, 63 (December 1991): 283–373.

———, 'Sarawak Malay Attitudes towards Education during the Brooke Period, 1841–1946', *JSEAS*, 21, 2 (September 1990): 340–59.

Outram, Richard, 'The Chinese', in Tom Harrisson (ed.), *The Peoples of Sarawak*, Kuching: Government Printing Press, 1959, pp. 115–28.

Oxley, Thomas, 'Gutta Percha', *JIAEA*, 1 (1847): 25–9.

Parnell, E., 'The Tribute Paid in Former Days to the Sultan of Brunei by the Then Dependent Provinces of Sarawak', *SMJ*, 1, 1 (February 1911): 125–30.

Pole-Evans, R. J., 'The Supreme Council, Sarawak', *SMJ*, 7, 7 (June 1956): 98–108.

Poore, M. E. D., 'Vegetation and Flora', in Wang Gungwu (ed.), *Malaysia: A Survey*, New York: Frederick Praeger, 1964, pp. 44–54.

Pridmore, F., 'Sarawak Currency', *SMJ*, 7, 7 (June 1950): 111–21.

Pringle, Robert, 'Asun's "Rebellion": The Political Growing Pains of a Tribal Society in Brooke Sarawak, 1929–1940', *SMJ*, 16, 32–3 (July–December 1968): 346–76.

———, 'The Brookes of Sarawak: Reformers In Spite of Themselves', *SMJ*, 19, 38–9 (1971): 53–76.

———, 'The Murder of Fox and Steele: Masahor's Version', *SMJ*, 12, 25–6 (July–December 1965): 215–27.

Reece, R. H. W., 'Economic Development under the Brookes', in R. A. Cramb and R. H. W. Reece (eds.), *Development in Sarawak: Historical and Contemporary Perspectives*, Monash Paper on Southeast Asia No. 17, Centre of Southeast Asia Studies, Melbourne: Monash University, 1988, pp. 21–34.

———, 'Political Pioneers', in *Our Sarawak*, Kuching: Persatuan Kesusasteraan Sarawak, 1983, pp. 5–35.

Reinhardt, Jon M., 'Administrative Policy and Practice in Sarawak: Continuity and Change under the Brookes', *JAS*, 29, 4 (August 1970): 851–62.

'The Saga of Slim', *Salam* (Sarawak Shell Berhad Newsletter), 19 February 1955, p. 3.

St John, Spenser, 'Piracy in the Indian Archipelago', *JIAEA*, 3 (1849): 251–60.

Satem, Judith, 'The Changing Nature of Sarawak's Export Trade from 1841 to the Present', *SG*, 31 July 1970, pp. 137–9.

Saunders, Graham, 'The Bau Chinese Attack on Kuching, February 1857: A Different Perspective', *SMJ*, 62, 63 (December 1991): 375–96.

———, 'James Brooke and Asian Government', *BMJ*, 3, 1 (1973): 105–17.

Scrivenor, John B., 'Notes on the Geology of Sarawak', *JMBRAS*, 5, 2 (November 1927): 288–94.

Sinclair, Keith, 'Hobson and Lenin in Johore: Colonial Office Policy towards British Concessionaires and Investors, 1878–1907', *MAS*, 1, 4 (1967): 335–52.

Smythies, B. E., 'History of Forestry in Sarawak', *SG*, 30 September 1961, pp. 167–74.

———, '"To-morrow to Fresh Woods and Pastures New"—A Policy for Shifting Cultivation', *SG*, 7 October 1949, pp. 251–5.

Sorrenson, M. P. K., 'Land Policy in Kenya, 1895–1945', in J. Harlow, E. M. Chilver, and A. Smith (eds.), *History of East Africa,* Vol. II, London: Oxford University Press, 1965, Appendix I, pp. 672–89.

Spurway, B. J. C., 'Shifting Cultivation in Sarawak', *SG*, 1 April 1937, pp. 81–2.

Tarling, Nicholas, 'Brooke Rule in Sarawak and Its Principles', *JMBRAS*, 65, 1 (1992): 15–26.

Treacher, W. H., 'British Borneo: Sketches of Brunai, Sarawak, Labuan and North Borneo', *JSBRAS*, 20 (1889): 13–74; 21 (June 1890): 19–121.

Tremeer, R. E., 'The Early History of Rubber Planting in Sarawak, 1880–1910', *SG*, 31 March 1964, pp. 50–2.

Wall, J. R. D., 'Topography–Soil Relationships in Lowland Sarawak', *JTG*, 18 (1964): 192–9.

Wang Gungwu, 'The Nanhai Trade: A Study of the Early History of Chinese Trade in the South China Sea', *JMBRAS*, 31, 2 (June 1958): 1–135.

Wang Tai Peng, 'The Word Kongsi: A Note', *JMBRAS*, 3, 1 (1979): 102–5.

Ward, Barbara E., 'A Hakka Kongsi in Borneo', *JOS*, 1, 2 (July 1954): 358–70.

Wilford, G. E., 'The Bau Gold Field', *SG*, 30 April 1962, pp. 77–9.

Wong Lin Ken, 'The Trade of Singapore', *JMBRAS*, 33, 4 (December 1960): 5–315.

Theses

Austin, Robert F., 'Land Policy and Social Change: The British Presence in Sarawak', MA thesis, University of Michigan, 1974.

Cotter, Conrad, 'A Guide to the Sarawak Gazette, 1870–1965', Ph.D. thesis, Cornell University, 1966.

———, 'Some Aspects of the Administrative Development of Sarawak', MPA thesis, Cornell University, 1955.

Diu Mee Kuok, 'The Diffusion of Foochow Settlement in the Sibu-Binatang Area, Central Sarawak, 1901–1970', MA thesis, University of Hawaii, 1972.

Doering, Otto C. III, 'The Institutionalization of Personal Rule in Sarawak', M.Sc.Econ. thesis, London School of Economics, 1965.

Horton, A. V. M., 'The Development of Brunei during the British Residential Era 1906–1959: A Sultanate Regenerated', Ph.D. thesis, University of Hull, 1985.

Kedit, Peter Mulok, 'Iban Bejalai', Ph.D. thesis, University of Sydney, 1987.

Lockard, Craig, 'Chinese Immigration and Society in Sarawak, 1868–1917', MA thesis, University of Hawaii, 1967.

———, 'The Southeast Asian Town in Historical Perspective: A Social History of Kuching, Malaysia, 1820–1970', Ph.D. thesis, University of Wisconsin, 1973.

Sutlive, Vinson H., 'From Longhouse to Pasar: Urbanization in Sarawak, East Malaysia', Ph.D. thesis, University of Pittsburgh, 1972.

Wang Tai Peng, 'The Chinese Republic in West Borneo from the Latter Part of the 18th Century to the Middle of the 19th Century', MA thesis, Australian National University, 1977.

Newspapers and Periodicals

Crown Colonist

Mirage: A Quarterly Magazine (of Sarawak Oilfields Limited)

Morning Post

Sarawak Mining Bulletin

Sarawak Tribune (ST)

Singapore Free Press

Singapore Straits Times

The Times (London)

Bibliographies and Guides to Sources

Challis, Joyce (comp.), *Annotated Bibliography of Economic and Social Material in Sabah (North Borneo) and Sarawak: Part I—Government Publications*, Research Bibliography Series No. 4, Singapore: Economic Research Centre, University of Singapore, 1969.

Cotter, Conrad Patrick, *Bibliography of English Language Sources on Human Ecology, Eastern Malaysia and Brunei*, 2 vols., Honolulu: Asian Studies Department, University of Hawaii, 1965.

Frewer, Louis B., *Manuscript Collection (Excluding Africana) in Rhodes House Library, Oxford*, Oxford: Bodleian Library, 1970.

Harrisson, Tom, 'Historical and Related Sources for Sarawak', in K. G. Tregonning (ed.), *Malaysian Historical Sources*, Singapore: University of Singapore Press, 1962, pp. 105–12.

Leigh, Michael B., *Checklist of Holdings on Borneo in the Cornell University Libraries*, Cornell University Southeast Asia Program Data Paper No. 62, Ithaca: Cornell University Press, 1966.

Pearson, J. D. (comp.), *A Guide to Manuscripts and Documents in the British Isles Relating to South and South East Asia*, Vol. I (London) and Vol. II (British Isles excluding London), London and New York: Mansell Publishing Limited, 1989.

Report on Correspondence and Papers of the Brooke Family of Sarawak Including Papers of Charles T. C. Grant (1831–91), Laird of Kilgraston, c. 1830–1977, Oxford University Colonial Records Project, London: Royal Commission on Historical Manuscripts, 1978.

Report on Further Family Correspondence and Papers of the Brooke Family of Sarawak, 1941–1981, Oxford University Colonial Records Project, London: Royal Commission on Historical Manuscripts, 1982.

Report on the Papers of T. Stirling Boyd (1886–1973), Chief Justice of Sarawak, Oxford University Colonial Records Project, London: Royal Commission on Historical Manuscripts, 1976.

Turnbull, C. M., 'Bibliography of Writings in English on British Malaya, 1786–1867', in L. A. Mills, *British Malaya, 1824–1867*, Kuala Lumpur: Oxford University Press, 1966, pp. 287–361.

Wainwright, M. D. and Matthews, Noel (comps.), *A Guide to Western Manuscripts and Documents in the British Isles Relating to South and South East Asia*, London: Oxford University Press, 1965.

Index

SOUTH-EAST ASIAN HISTORICAL MONOGRAPHS

Of Free Trade and Native Interests